New to This Edition

① A new section of the book, "Contemporary Issues Facing Social Workers," provides six chapters that support instructors introducing students to some issues, challenges, and rewards they might expect to experience if they enter the profession of social work. (Chs. 10-15)

② A new chapter, "Spirituality in a Secular Profession," surfaces a contemporary issue often downplayed in social work education. It introduces some of the issues experienced by students, social workers, and clients who often have strong religious or spiritual beliefs, yet are obligated in a secular profession to not impose their beliefs on others. Should spiritual and religious cultural competence be required of social workers? (Ch. 10)

③ Chapter 11 has been updated to examine the challenge faced in balancing "Social Work's Dual Focus on Solving and Preventing Problems."

④ A new chapter addressing a highly controversial political issue, "Social Work Practice with Immigrants, Refugees, and Unaccompanied Minors," that is impacting a substantial segment of the U.S. population. The chapter is a springboard for class discussion regarding the impact of immigration policies ranging from individuals and families to social policy considerations. (Ch. 14)

⑤ A completely revised chapter focusing on "Social Work Practice with Older Adults," the most rapidly growing vulnerable population group in the U.S. (Ch. 19)

⑥ A new chapter. Two leading Native American educators have prepared a chapter entitled "Social Work Practice with Indigenous Peoples and Tribal Communities." (Ch. 23)

⑦ A completely revised chapter on "Social Work Practice with African Americans." (Ch. 25)

⑧ Extensive editing throughout the book to provide many chapters that are realistic in length for a one class session assignment and basis for discussion.

Social Work

"Give me your tired, your poor, your huddled masses yearning to breathe free."
—Lazarus, 1883

TWELFTH EDITION

Social Work
A Profession of Many Faces

BRADFORD W. SHEAFOR ARMANDO T. MORALES
Colorado State University *Deceased*

MALCOLM E. SCOTT
Colorado State University

Allyn & Bacon

Boston   New York   San Francisco
Mexico City   Montreal   Toronto   London   Madrid   Munich   Paris
Hong Kong   Singapore   Tokyo   Cape Town   Sydney

Senior Acquisitions Editor: Patricia Quinlin
Series Editorial Assistant: Carly Czech
Marketing Manager: Wendy Albert
Production Supervisor: Beth Houston
Editorial Production Service: Elm Street Publishing Services
Manufacturing Buyer: JoAnne Sweeney
Electronic Composition: Elm Street Publishing Services
Photo Researcher: Jessica Riu
Cover Administrator: Kristina Mose-Libon

Copyright © 2010 Pearson Education, Inc., publishing as Allyn & Bacon, 75 Arlington Street, Suite 300, Boston, MA 02116

All rights reserved. Manufactured in the United States of America. No part of the material protected by this copyright notice may be reproduced or utilized in any form or by any means, electronic or mechanical, including photocopying, recording, or by any information storage and retrieval system, without written permission from the copyright owner.

To obtain permission(s) to use material from this work, please submit a written request to Pearson Higher Education, Rights and Contracts Department, 501 Boylston Street, Suite 900, Boston, MA 02116, or fax your request to 617-671-3447.

Credits appear on page 560, which constitutes an extension of the copyright page.

Library of Congress Cataloging-in-Publication Data

Sheafor, Bradford W.
 Social work : a profession of many faces / Bradford W. Sheafor, Armando T. Morales.—12th ed.
   p. cm.
 Morales' name appears first on 11th ed.
 ISBN 978-0-205-63683-9
 1. Social service—United States. 2. Social work education—United States. 3. Social service—Vocational guidance—United States. 4. Social work with minorities—United States. I. Morales, Armando. II. Title.
HV91.M67 2010
361.973—dc22

2009000344

10 9 8 7 6 5 4 3 2 1   RRD-VA   13 12 11 10 09

Allyn & Bacon
is an imprint of

www.pearsonhighered.com

ISBN-10:   0-205-63683-7
ISBN-13: 978-0-205-63683-9

Dedication

We dedicate this edition of *Social Work: A Profession of Many Faces* to the late **Armando T. Morales.** Dr. Morales, a friend and coauthor for the first eleven editions of this book, died of complications from cancer on March 12, 2008 after an eight year battle with this dreaded disease. As young educators, Armando and Brad Sheafor began collaborating on this textbook in 1972 and maintained their initial vision of an introductory textbook that would focus on the features that make social work a single profession and provide new social workers with an appreciation of the unique experiences of the several vulnerable populations social workers are committed to serve. Beginning with the last edition, Malcolm Scott joined Armando and Brad as a third author, bringing the perspective of a young African American social work educator to the book.

Armando Morales was a truly exceptional human being. In the Los Angeles area, Armando was a well-known activist promoting social justice for the Latino community. Growing up in East Los Angeles, Dr. Morales experienced the discrimination of a racist society and personal acts of cultural insensitivity. For example, with Spanish as his first language and the cultural bias imbedded in IQ exams, he was treated as a student with limited academic ability. When tested later while in the military, his IQ scores jumped a full 100 points. His first book, *Ando Sangrando: I Am Bleeding,* traced the injustices experienced by Mexican Americans as they settled in what is now the United States and provided a roadmap for ending (or at least reducing) such injustices. With a BA degree from California State University, Los Angeles, and his MSW and Ph.D. degrees from the University of Southern California, Dr. Morales practiced social work in the Los Angeles County Department of Mental Health and became director of UCLA's Spanish-Speaking Psychosocial Clinic. He later served as director of the clinical social work department at UCLA's Neuropsychiatric Institute and Hospital, earning UCLA's highest academic rank, "Professor of Great Distinction in Psychiatry and Behavioral Sciences." An expert in juvenile gang behavior, Dr. Morales served in an advisory position to the Los Angeles mayor, spoke widely on community and police relations, provided expert testimony in high-profile court cases, and was interviewed several times by National Public Radio regarding related issues. A member of the national NASW Board of Directors, Dr. Morales was concerned not only with the many faces of the people of his community but also the social work profession. Armando's passion for social justice, skilled advocacy, highly developed clinical skills, intelligent scholarship, and personal charm will all be missed.

Contents

Preface xxi

part one
A Social Worker Makes a Difference — 2

chapter 1   A Child Welfare Case: The Social Worker in Action — 5

PREFATORY COMMENT 5
Demetria's First Case 5
CONCLUDING COMMENT 11

part two
Social Work in U.S. Society — 12

chapter 2   Social Welfare: A Response to Human Need — 15

PREFATORY COMMENT 15
Social Welfare Programs 16
The Evolution of Social Welfare 17
Social Welfare in the Early 2000s 21
The Successes and Failures of Human Service Programs 26
CONCLUDING COMMENT 28
KEY WORDS AND CONCEPTS 29
SUGGESTED INFORMATION SOURCES 29
ENDNOTES 29

x Contents

chapter 3 Social Work: A Comprehensive Helping Profession ... 31

PREFATORY COMMENT 31
The Central Themes Underpinning Social Work 32
The Mission of Social Work 36
Defining Social Work 37
Social Work Practice Approaches 40
Social Workers: Their Many Faces 43
CONCLUDING COMMENT 48
KEY WORDS AND CONCEPTS 50
SUGGESTED INFORMATION SOURCES 50
ENDNOTES 50

chapter 4 The Emergence of Social Work as a Profession ... 53

PREFATORY COMMENT 53
Social Work as a Profession: A Historical Perspective 55
Social Work Confronts a Disaster: Evidence of a Maturing Profession 67
CONCLUDING COMMENT 69
KEY WORDS AND CONCEPTS 70
SUGGESTED INFORMATION SOURCES 70
ENDNOTES 70

part three
Social Work Career Options ... 72

chapter 5 Entry to the Social Work Profession ... 75

PREFATORY COMMENT 75
Issues in Social Work Preparation and Employment 76
Options for Human Service Practice 79

Levels of Professional Social Work
    Practice   84
CONCLUDING COMMENT   91
KEY WORDS AND CONCEPTS   92
SUGGESTED INFORMATION SOURCES   92
ENDNOTES   93

chapter 6   **Fields of Social Work Practice**   95

PREFATORY COMMENT   95
Aging   96
Alcohol and Substance Abuse   97
Child Welfare   98
Community/Neighborhood Work   101
Corrections/Criminal Justice   102
Disabilities (Physical and Mental)   103
Family Services   104
Income Maintenance   105
Medical and Health Care   106
Mental Health and Illness   107
Occupational or Industrial Social Work   108
Schools   109
Youth Services   110
CONCLUDING COMMENT   110
KEY WORDS AND CONCEPTS   112
SUGGESTED INFORMATION SOURCES   112
ENDNOTES   112

chapter 7   **Settings for Social Work Practice**   115

PREFATORY COMMENT   115
Characteristics of Practice Settings   115
Issues Affecting Agency-Based Practice   119
Issues in Private Practice   126
CONCLUDING COMMENT   129
KEY WORDS AND CONCEPTS   130
SUGGESTED INFORMATION SOURCES   130
ENDNOTES   130

chapter 8   Values and Ethics in Social Work   133

PREFATORY COMMENT   133
The Nature of Values   134
The Place of Values in Social Work   135
Social Values in U.S. Society   136
Values Held by Social Workers   138
Areas of Practice Addressed by the NASW Code of Ethics   140
Illustrations of Values and Ethics Operating in Social Work Practice   142
CONCLUDING COMMENT   145
KEY WORDS AND CONCEPTS   147
SUGGESTED INFORMATION SOURCES   147
ENDNOTES   147

chapter 9   Identifying the Knowledge and Skills Required for Social Work Practice   149

PREFATORY COMMENT   149
The Universal Social Work Competencies   150
Frequently Utilized Social Work Competencies   151
Competencies Occasionally Needed by Social Workers   154
Low Utilization Competencies for Most Social Workers   157
CONCLUDING COMMENT   158
KEY WORDS AND CONCEPTS   159
SUGGESTED INFORMATION SOURCES   159
ENDNOTES   159

part four
Contemporary Issues Facing Social Work and Social Workers   160

chapter 10   Spirituality in a Secular Profession   163

PREFATORY COMMENT   163
Historical Context of Spirituality in the Human Services   164
Social Work Education and Spirituality/Religion   166

Religion and Spirituality in Cultural
    Competence   168
Spirituality and Religion in Professional
    Practice   168

CONCLUDING COMMENT   172

KEY WORDS AND CONCEPTS   172

SUGGESTED INFORMATION
    SOURCES   172

ENDNOTES   173

chapter 11 Social Work's Dual Focus on Solving and Preventing Problems   175

PREFATORY COMMENT   175
The Social Worker's Role in Problem
    Solving   175
The Social Worker's Role in Problem
    Prevention   177
Balancing Problem Solving with Problem
    Prevention   182

CONCLUDING COMMENT   183

KEY WORDS AND CONCEPTS   184

SUGGESTED INFORMATION SOURCES   184

ENDNOTES   184

chapter 12 Social Work's Role in Addressing Terrorism   187

PREFATORY COMMENT   187
Examples of Terrorism   188
Terrorism and Terrorist Gangs   190
Social Workers and Work with Gangs   194
Types of Gangs   195
Micro Social Work Practice with Gangs   197
Macro Intervention with Domestic
    Terrorist Gangs   198

CONCLUDING COMMENT   198

KEY WORDS AND CONCEPTS   199

SUGGESTED INFORMATION SOURCES   200

ENDNOTES   200

chapter 13 Social Work with U.S. Casualties of the Middle East Wars — 203

PREFATORY COMMENT   203
Social Work with Soldiers and Veterans   204
Social Work with the Families of Soldiers and Veterans   206
Social Programs for Soldiers and Veterans   206
Social Work Practice during Reintegration Efforts   207
Special Considerations Regarding Today's Victims of War   211
Social Work and the Prevention of War   214
CONCLUDING COMMENT   216
KEY WORDS AND CONCEPTS   216
SUGGESTED INFORMATION SOURCES   216
ENDNOTES   216

chapter 14 Social Work Practice with Immigrants, Refugees, and Unaccompanied Minors — 219

PREFATORY COMMENT   219
Immigration Gateways   221
Social Work with Immigrants, Refugees, and Unaccompanied Minors   222
Immigrants and Refugees: Areas of Concern for Social Work Practitioners   225
Unaccompanied Minors: Areas of Concern for Social Workers   226
A Case Vignette   229
CONCLUDING COMMENT   231
KEY WORDS AND CONCEPTS   231
SUGGESTED INFORMATION SOURCES   232
ENDNOTES   232

chapter 15 Social Work Becoming a Global Profession — 235

PREFATORY COMMENT   235
World Population Changes: Creating a Global Demand for Social Work in the Future   237
Social Welfare Programs: A Varied Response to Human Need   239

Contents xv

    A Global Approach to Social Work 242
    Employment in International Social Work 246
    CONCLUDING COMMENT 248
    KEY WORDS AND CONCEPTS 248
    SUGGESTED INFORMATION RESOURCES 248
    ENDNOTES 249

part five
Social Work Practice with Vulnerable Populations 250

chapter 16 Social Work Practice with Women 255

    PREFATORY COMMENT 255
    Current Demographics 256
    Health and Mental Health Risk Factors 259
    Ecosystems Model 260
    Intervention Strategies 273
    Emerging Issues and Trends 280
    CONCLUDING COMMENT 281
    KEY WORDS AND CONCEPTS 281
    SUGGESTED INFORMATION SOURCES 281
    ENDNOTES 282

chapter 17 Social Work Practice with Lesbian, Gay, and Bisexual People 289

    PREFATORY COMMENT 289
    Understanding the GLB Population 290
    Ecosystems Framework 294
    Macro Practice with Lesbian, Gay, and Bisexual People 302
    Micro Practice with Lesbian, Gay, and Bisexual People 304
    Emerging Issues and Trends 311
    CONCLUDING COMMENT 316
    KEY WORDS AND CONCEPTS 317
    SUGGESTED INFORMATION SOURCES 317
    ENDNOTES 318

chapter 18 Social Work Practice with Children and Youth — 323

PREFATORY COMMENT   323
Current Demographics   324
The Ecosystems Model   330
Macro Considerations   336
CONCLUDING COMMENT   337
KEY WORDS AND CONCEPTS   338
SUGGESTED INFORMATION SOURCES   338
ENDNOTES   338

chapter 19 Social Work Practice with Older Adults — 341

PREFATORY COMMENT   341
Demographic Factors Affecting Human Services for Older Adults   342
Ecosystems Model Analysis   346
Intervention Strategies with Older People   351
Trends in Gerontological Social Work   356
CONCLUDING COMMENT   357
KEY WORDS AND CONCEPTS   358
SUGGESTED INFORMATION SOURCES   358
ENDNOTES   358

chapter 20 Social Work Practice with People with Disabilities — 361

PREFATORY COMMENT   361
Defining Disability   363
Disability and the Minority Model   371
Societal Responses to Disability   372
The Ecosystems Model and People with Disabilities   375
Emerging Issues for Social Work Practice with People with Disabilities   380

CONCLUDING COMMENT 381
KEY WORDS AND CONCEPTS 381
SUGGESTED INFORMATION SOURCES 381
ENDNOTES 382

chapter 21 Social Work Practice with Muslims in the United States 385

PREFATORY COMMENT 385
A Preliminary Understanding of Islam 386
The Demographics of Muslims in the United States 389
Muslim Families 391
Common Cultural Values in Islamic Discourse 392
Structural Factors in the Social Environment 396
Historical Factors 400
Implications for Micro and Macro Practice 401

CONCLUDING COMMENT 405
KEY WORDS AND CONCEPTS 405
SUGGESTED INFORMATION SOURCES 405
ENDNOTES 406

chapter 22 Social Work Practice with Asian Americans 413

PREFATORY COMMENT 413
Selected Characteristics of the Asian American Population 414
Health and Mental Health Risk Factors 415
Ethnic Group Stressors 416
Service Systems 417
Micro Practice Perspectives 419
Ecosystems Model Framework 421
Macro Practice Perspectives 430
Emerging Issues 432

CONCLUDING COMMENT 433
KEY WORDS AND CONCEPTS 433
SUGGESTED INFORMATION SOURCES 434
ENDNOTES 434

chapter 23 Social Work Practice with Indigenous Peoples and Tribal Communities 437

PREFATORY COMMENT 437
Current Demographics 439
Key Social Issues 439
The Ecosystems Framework 447
Social Work with Native People: Case Examples 454
CONCLUDING COMMENT 456
KEY WORDS AND CONCEPTS 457
SUGGESTED INFORMATION SOURCES 457
ENDNOTES 458

chapter 24 Social Work Practice with Mexican Americans 461

PREFATORY COMMENT 461
Demographic Profile 462
Ecosystems Model 463
Micro Social Work Practice with Mexican Americans 470
Macro Social Work Practice with Mexican Americans 474
CONCLUDING COMMENT 476
KEY WORDS AND CONCEPTS 477
SUGGESTED INFORMATION SOURCES 478
ENDNOTES 478

chapter 25 Social Work Practice with African Americans 481

PREFATORY COMMENT 481
Current Population Demographics 483
Selected Social Issues 484
The Ecological Systems Model and African Americans: A Social Worker's Perspective 490
Social Work Practice with African Americans: A Case Example 495
Competent Social Work Practice with African American Clients 498
Emerging Considerations for Work with African Americans 499

CONCLUDING COMMENT 500
KEY WORDS AND CONCEPTS 501
SUGGESTED INFORMATION SOURCES 501
ENDNOTES 502

chapter 26 Social Work Practice with Puerto Ricans — 505

PREFATORY COMMENT 505
Current Demographics 506
Health and Mental Health Risk Factors 509
General Data on Health Care and Puerto Ricans 514
Beliefs and Practices That Influence Puerto Ricans' Health 515
Ecosystems Perspective 516
Intervention Strategies 522
CONCLUDING COMMENT 523
KEY WORDS AND CONCEPTS 523
SUGGESTED INFORMATION SOURCES 523
ENDNOTES 524

part six
Social Workers in Action — 526

chapter 27 Social Workers in Action: School Homicide and the Death Penalty — 529

PREFATORY COMMENT 529
Planning Social Work Interventions 531
Mobilizing the Agency and Staff for Action 532
Preparing to Serve the Families and School 534
Mobilizing Related Mental Health Disciplines 535
Addressing Community Needs: Indirect and Prevention Tasks 536
The Case Continues 538
The Psychosocial Evaluation 542
The Report Is Challenged by the People 549
The Death Penalty Trial for Rita Gomez 550
A Social Worker's Work Is Never Finished 551

CONCLUDING COMMENT 558
KEY WORDS AND CONCEPTS 559
SUGGESTED INFORMATION SOURCES 559
ENDNOTES 559

Photo Credits 560
Name Index 561
Subject Index 563

Preface

The title of this book, *Social Work: A Profession of Many Faces,* reflects the several themes that have guided the book's development. The words "A Profession" focus our attention on social work and the common features that characterize this profession, and only then do we examine the different ways social work practice plays out in serving the many different people who become the clients of social workers. When we first started writing this textbook, the available texts focused primarily on the differences among the various social work practice settings or practice approaches. A title for those books might have been something like "The Many Faces of Social Work: How They Differ," emphasizing divergence rather than similarity. As you will discover when reading the following pages, we focus on the unifying features that make social work a single profession—albeit one that appears in quite varied forms.

What, then, are the threads that tie together the differing forms of social work practice? Its very name, social work, suggests two features that are present in all expressions of this profession. The term *social* emphasizes that the practice is concerned with enhancing the interactions among individuals and groups of people, as well as between people and the broader institutions of the society. The term *work* distinguishes a career of helping people from other important, but unpaid, volunteer activity. This book's title, too, captures a third critical element of social work—the evolution of social work from work that is just a job to work that is "professional," meaning that social workers are required to draw on the best available knowledge to address complex issues and then skillfully and ethically provide services to people in need of assistance. Finally, by describing social work as a profession of "many faces," our intent is to (1) identify the multiple ways in which this profession conducts its work in delivering human services; (2) reflect the varied population groups that social workers are most likely to serve; and (3) highlight the strength social work has gained by embracing people reflecting racial, cultural, and social diversity as members of the profession.

What makes social work a unique profession? One important feature is that social workers simultaneously use two approaches to helping people: helping individuals, families, and groups deal with a problem or issue in their lives and, at the same time, attempting to change aspects of the society that create or contribute to people's problems. For example, social workers are on the frontlines of delivering services and developing programs that respond to such human needs as homelessness, poverty, family breakup, mental illness, physical and mental disabilities, alcohol and substance abuse, domestic violence, and many other social problems. In addition, social workers are regularly engaged in more long-range activities aimed at keeping those problems from occurring in the first place. This might be done by helping people become contributing members of their neighborhood, school, church, synagogue, mosque, or other community groups in an effort to make larger social institutions more responsive to the needs of all people. Indeed, social work is an umbrella term that covers a diverse set of practice activities.

The clients of social workers might be anyone, ranging from individuals to families to corporations and even to whole communities. Another thread central to the fabric of social work, however, is an emphasis on achieving social justice and giving priority to the most *vulnerable* members of the society, i.e., those most likely to experience a problem in their social interactions due to age, gender, race or ethnicity, sexual orientation, or other characteristics. Thus, social workers tend to focus their efforts more on the poor than the rich, on the ill and disabled over the healthy, on those who experience discrimination over those who have the privilege of enjoying the full opportunities offered by the society.

Social workers, themselves, reflect many different faces. The authors of this text, for example, reflect some of the many faces of social workers. Brad Sheafor is of white non-Hispanic origin, growing up in the Midwest and practicing social work through community change efforts and social work education in the Rocky Mountain region. He is a professor in the School of Social Work at Colorado State University. Prior to his death in 2008, Armando Morales, who was of Mexican American descent, spent most of his life living on the West Coast and practicing as a clinical social worker and educator. He was a professor in the School of Medicine at the University of California at Los Angeles (UCLA). Malcolm Scott is of African American heritage and grew up in the Deep South. His practice experience has been in corrections and child welfare, and he now is an assistant professor in the School of Social Work at Colorado State University. We believe that our diversity has enriched the quality of our work—just as diversity among social workers has enriched the profession.

To assist our readers in critically analyzing the contents of this book, we believe it is important to confess to some biases we hold that no doubt affect the manner in which we present our description of social work. We are not apologizing for these biases, only admitting to them.

- *We are proud to be social workers.* We believe that the social work profession brings an important perspective to the human services by simultaneously performing the role of providing direct services to people in need and, at the same time, advocating for social change. We also believe that the basic values and ethical guidelines that social workers hold in common represent a sound approach to protecting the interests of clients while maximizing the well-being of all people.
- *We recognize that the United States has made progress in creating social programs that respond to the needs of vulnerable people, but we also believe that much more is needed.* According to the U.S. Census Bureau, for example, during the thirty-year period from 1976 to 2006, the poverty rate for individuals worsened from 11.8 percent to 12.3 percent.[1] On the positive side, for older people (who have become a political force) the poverty rate improved from 15.0 percent to 9.4 percent. On the negative side, the percent of older African Americans (22.7 percent) and Hispanics (19.4 percent) living below the poverty

level did not improve proportionally. Further, for families headed by single mothers, the poverty rate only improved from 33.0 percent to 28.3 percent.[2] Also, we have seen phenomenal improvements in the treatment of illnesses and diseases, yet many of these benefits that accrue from living in U.S. society are simply too expensive for many of our citizens. In addition, we have improved our mental health and family counseling services to levels not available elsewhere in the world, but we have not found ways to provide them in culturally sensitive ways to attract persons of minority background or older people. In other areas of special concern to social workers (e.g., corrections, child protection, immigration, prevention of substance abuse), we regret that the United States has made very little progress.

▶ *We believe that trends in the United States favoring those who already have resources, rather than to those in need of resources, are heading us in the wrong direction.* To illustrate what we view as moving in the wrong direction, consider the distribution of wealth in the United States. Although the overall economy improved substantially in the past three decades, we have made little progress in low-income people earning enough to achieve a decent quality of life. In 1976, for example, the income (in money) of the poorest 20 percent of the people was only 4.3 percent of the total income, while the richest 20 percent had 43.7 percent of that total. Thirty years later, the proportion of the U.S. income held by the lowest 20 percent had declined to 3.4 percent and the richest 20 percent of the people had increased their share to 50.5 percent.[3] The poor are getting poorer, and the rich are getting richer! Another example is found in the area of educational advancement, where the average earning power of a person with a college education is substantially more than that of a person with a high school education (i.e., $56,788 per year compared with $31,071 per year).[4] Yet, the 2007 U.S. Census Bureau population survey found that, if a job requires more than a high school education, 58.4 percent of the white population would be eligible as compared with only 46.2 percent of the black population and 32.0 percent of the Hispanic population. Further, if a job requires a bachelor's degree or higher, 31.8 percent of the white population is qualified, compared with only 18.5 percent of the African Americans and 12.7 percent of the Hispanics.[5] For a variety of reasons, the distribution of our educational resources substantially disadvantages the black and Hispanic members in this society, where education is the prerequisite for the better paying jobs. Our bias is that, when persistent patterns reveal that whole classes of people are disadvantaged, we must conclude that policies and practices that are part of the structure of the society contribute to those problems and should be changed. Throughout this book you will find that the focus of much social work practice occurs at the intersection of race, ethnicity, family structure, and educational attainment.

▶ *We are pleased that social work has evolved as an established profession that has the capacity to address both individual and societal social issues.* Social work has successfully expanded its knowledge base, increasingly engages in evidence-based practice, and, through licensing, plays a role in policing its membership to help protect vulnerable clients from the errors and misrepresentations of those who are ill-prepared, incompetent, or unethical in providing these important services. Our observations are that social work is increasingly attracting a competent group of social workers to the profession. In addition, we are proud that social work has become a recognized profession throughout the world, adding to the ability to apply social work knowledge and skills to issues of global importance.

Although our view of social work and social issues is shaped by the biases confessed above, please be aware that we have attempted to present an analysis of social work that is best described as "mainline social work." We have avoided both the radical and conservative orientations found among social workers, have rooted our information in the best data we could locate, and, we believe, reveal the current state-of-the-art for social work.

A Note to Our Readers

In reading this book, it may be useful to be clear about two guiding principles that have shaped how we present the material. First, as social work educators, we know from experience that most students who study social work are action oriented—they want to know how what they learn applies to helping people achieve a better quality of life. Thus as we have presented conceptual or descriptive material, we have included case examples in an effort to provide a basis for understanding its relevance. We begin with a short introductory chapter that features a beginning-level social worker on her first case. This case serves as a reference point for materials in the beginning chapters of the book. We conclude the book with a comprehensive case illustrating social workers providing services at an advanced level of practice. Second, we believe that a text that is intended to introduce students to social work must address the underpinnings of the profession and, thus, must include a certain amount of historical and theoretical information. To avoid a single chapter on the history of social work that is likely to become a "sleep aid" for students, we have disbursed this important, but maybe not "edge-of-your-seat," information throughout the appropriate chapters.

The four parts of the book between the cases follow a pattern of unfolding our description of social work. Part Two begins with the identification of a selected few large social issues (e.g., poverty, discrimination, industrialization, urbanization, technological advancements) that have created the need for human services beyond what can be provided by families and friends and, thus, has created the need for a profession such as social work. We then trace the emergence of social work and its eventual maturity as a profession. Part Three examines the career patterns and options available to social workers in the different fields of practice and practice settings, as well as the values and ethics that guide social workers and an overview of the knowledge and skills that are required for social work practice. Next, in Part Four, we selected six contemporary topics that we believe will be high on the agendas of social workers in the coming decade. We have designed these as short chapters that will stimulate discussion on such topics as spirituality in a secular profession, maintaining a dual focus on solving and preventing problems, social work's potential contributions to dealing with terrorism, serving the needs of people who experience casualties from the Middle East wars, assisting people who confront the complex issues related to immigration, and appreciating the differing expressions of social work throughout the world. Finally, in Part Five, we turn our attention to some of the most vulnerable population groups in the United States and either have written ourselves or have commissioned other experts to write chapters highlighting key issues that affect eleven of the most vulnerable groups—along with providing guidelines for social workers when serving them. We view these chapters as a starting point for social workers in building their cultural competence.

A Note to Instructors

We want to be sure that those who teach from this book are aware of the *Instructor's Manual and Test Bank* that accompanies it. In the manual, each chapter gives a synopsis of the most important content; lists key concepts and terms that the student should master; offers sample exercises for teaching the materials; and provides sample discussion, essay, and multiple-choice questions. A computerized version of the test bank is available from Allyn and Bacon or from your Allyn and Bacon campus representative. In addition, there is a new **media supplement** for students. *MyHelpingKit* is an electronic supplement that offers book-specific Learning Objectives, Chapter Summaries, Flashcards, and Practice Tests as a well as Cases, Video Clips, and Interactive Activities to aid student learning and comprehension. *MyHelpingKit* also includes an Interactice Historical Timeline and interviews with practicing social workers.Also, please visit our web site (www.ablongman.com/sheafor12e) for other useful information.

We want to thank the reviewers of this twelfth edition for their kind remarks and helpful suggestions: Adele Crudden, *Mississippi State University;* Daniel Liechty, *Illinois State University;* Jocelyn S. Martin, *Austin Peay State University;* and Salome Raheim, *University of Iowa.*

Finally, thanks to our families for sacrificing some of our precious time together so that the activity of preparing this edition could be included in our already busy lives—especially Nadine, Cynthia, and Barbara. Their love, support, and encouragement through the years provided meaning to our work and enhanced the quality of our lives.

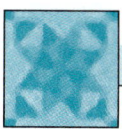

Useful Web Sites for Social Workers

PROFESSIONAL ORGANIZATIONS

Association of Social Work Boards (information on licensing requirements in all states and schedule of licensing examinations) http://aswb.org

Canadian Association of Social Workers (CASW programs, Code of Ethics) http://www.casw-acts.ca

Council on Social Work Education (lists of accredited BSW and MSW programs, publications) http://www.cswe.org

International Federation of Social Workers (IFSW position papers, Code of Ethics) http://www.ifsw.org

National Association of Social Workers (NASW activities, Code of Ethics, and publications) http://www.naswdc.org

SEARCH ENGINES FOR SOCIAL WORK–RELATED TOPICS

Google Scholar (search for peer-reviewed papers, theses, books, abstracts from many academic disciplines) http://scholar.google.com

Government Printing Office Access (link to policy databases including federal budget, economic indicators, federal register, legislative reports, presidential papers, judicial decisions) http://www.gpoaccess.gov/index.html

Healthfinder (guide to health-related information) www.healthfinder.gov

Information for Practice (news and new scholarship from around the world) http://www.nyu.edu/socialwork/ip

Library of Congress (search for all books with U.S. copyrights) http://catalog.loc.gov

Social Work Access Network (links to relevant information sources, social work chatroom, message board, etc.) http://cosw.sc.edu/swan

Statistical Information (centralized data source from most government agencies) http://www.fedstats.gov

Welfare Information Network (clearinghouse for information, policy analysis, and technical assistance related to welfare, workforce development, and other human and community services) www.financeprojectinfo.org

ENDNOTES

1. Carmen DeNavas-Walt, Bernadette D. Proctor, and Jessica Smith, U.S. Census Bureau, Current Population Reports, P60-233, *Income, Poverty, and Health Insurance Coverage in the United States: 2006,* U.S. Government Printing Office, Washington, DC, 2007. Table 3, p. 44. http://www.census.gov/prod/2007pubs/p60-233.pdf.
2. Ibid. Tables B-2 and B-3, pp. 50 and 56.
3. Ibid. Table A-3, p. 38.
4. *U.S. Census Bureau,* "One-Third of Young Women Have Bachelor's Degrees." http://www.census.gov/Press-Release/www/releases/archives/education/011196.html.
5. *U.S. Census Bureau,* "Educational Attainment in the United States: 2007." Table 1. http://www.census.gov/population/www/socdemo/education/cps2007.html.

Social Work

part one

A Social Worker Makes a Difference

If the world were a perfect place, it would provide for everyone warm and safe housing, an adequate supply of nutritious food, challenging jobs, good health care, and love and caring from friends and family. It would be a world with minimal stress, crime, and suffering. All people would find their lives satisfying and fulfilling. Social work exists because the world is less than perfect. Social workers serve people and the institutions of society as they confront this imperfection.

The social worker is not satisfied with this imperfect world that sends too many children to bed hungry at night, has effectively declared too many older people useless, restricts too many people who are physically disabled from productive living, allows too many women and children to be physically and sexually abused, deprives too many members of minority groups of the full opportunity to share in the benefits of this affluent society, has too many single parents trying to raise children in substandard housing without enough money for proper nutrition and food, and deprives too many people who are emotionally and intellectually impaired of satisfying lives because they behave or learn differently from the majority in the society. In fact, when even one person suffers from loneliness, hunger, discrimination, poor housing, domestic violence, or emotional upset, there is a need for social work.

Although social work practice is built on a strong base of *knowledge*—knowledge about the people or social institutions being served, knowledge of the most appropriate practice approach(es) in a specific situation—social workers and other helping professionals use knowledge as the underpinning for *doing*. As opposed to many academic disciplines that develop and synthesize information to expand knowledge, social workers are primarily concerned with applying knowledge to serve clients. This book begins with a case example of a social worker in action. The case depicts the work of a beginning-level social worker employed in a child welfare agency. As the information provided in Parts Two, Three, and Four of this book will indicate, the observable work of the social worker is underpinned by a considerable history and an extensively developed set of knowledge, values, and skills that prepare social workers to address the needs of their clients.

chapter 1

A Child Welfare Case: The Social Worker in Action

Prefatory Comment

Social workers are action oriented. They do things to help people make changes that will improve their lives. Sometimes those changes are related to how a person thinks or behaves, sometimes it involves other people in clients' lives, and at still other times it involves influencing organizations and communities to develop new ways of functioning.

This chapter is designed to help people studying social work observe a few of the underlying factors that make it possible for professional social workers to effectively serve their clients by observing the work performed by a social worker. In the following case, we can observe the activities of a social worker, Demetria, dealing with a case of suspected child abuse or neglect. A case of a beginning-level social worker might just as well be located in a probation office, nursing home, residential center, mental health center, homeless shelter, or one of many other settings. However, child welfare is one of the most common starting places for a new social worker. A contrast to this case is the work of Bob Pla, an advanced social worker, found in the last chapter of this book.

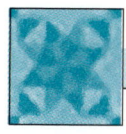

Demetria's First Case

The school year was well under way as the somewhat cooler fall air was beginning to turn the once deep-green leaves of the oak trees to a vibrant red. As was the case most mornings for Demetria, a social worker in the county's child welfare division, hot tea and French doughnuts made for a refreshing start to the usually full day of client visits, child protection investigations, reviewing of case files, and the necessary paperwork. One particular case, however, had been consistently in her thoughts. Just before 5:00 P.M. the previous day, a call had come from a local public school teacher to the office intake worker concerning the possibility that one of the teacher's students was experiencing child abuse or neglect. The office administrator assigned the investigative responsibilities to Demetria, who subsequently made an appointment to meet with school officials and the 12-year-old child who was allegedly the victim of the abuse.

Demetria was a bit on edge when preparing for this neglect or abuse investigation as it was her first "solo" case assignment as a full-time social worker. She would have been anxious if the case had been referred by anyone, but she was particularly so because it was from a *mandated reporter* [a person required by law to report suspicions of child abuse, such as a teacher, doctor, social worker, or nurse]. Demetria had only recently completed her Bachelor of Social Work (BSW) degree and was fortunate to have been hired on at the agency where she had completed her field placement during her senior year. Having now completed her agency orientation and training as a child welfare social worker, she was hopefully prepared for this case assignment—or at least that is what her supervisor had said. Nevertheless, it was pretty scary to have been given so much responsibility for the well-being of a child. It was one thing to talk about working with a child abuse accusation in the classroom, and even working with clients under the careful monitoring of a field instructor during her internship, but quite another to be dealing with a case on her own.

When Demetria arrived at the school the next day, she first spoke with the teacher and school officials about their specific concerns. The school officials reported that Joseph Miles, a 12-year-old Caucasian male, had enrolled in their school just a few months prior. They were concerned that Joseph was having some adjustment issues; he had been late to school numerous times (if he showed up at all) and had been reported of smelling of alcohol by several of his peers. When Joseph did show up for school, he appeared restless and angry, often was dirty and had offensive body odor, and frequently was ridiculed by other students for his apparent lack of personal hygiene.

On the day the telephone call was made to the child welfare office, Joseph had shown up for school that unusually cold fall morning without a jacket and in short sleeves, which allowed some unexplained bruising to be visible on his arms. In addition, he smelled of alcohol and was acting erratically. When questioned by his teacher about the bruising and why he did not have a coat in the cool weather, he only shrugged his shoulders and said nothing. Out of concern for the child's safety, school officials decided to call child welfare to express their concerns over the apparent lack of parental supervision and the possibility that he had been a victim of family violence. Previous attempts by the school to contact the parents had not gone well, and there was no working number for making telephone contact with the household.

After hearing the specific concerns of the school officials, Demetria decided to meet with Joseph, as there was reason to suspect child abuse and neglect. The school principal brought Joseph to the school's counseling room to meet with Demetria. As Joseph sat down in the chair, Demetria also observed the bruises on his arms and his tattered clothing, and she noted that Joseph appeared well underweight for a child his age and height. After a little small talk about his favorite games, subjects in school, and foods (they called this "building rapport" and "initiating client engagement" in school), Demetria shifted the conversation to more personal questions of how things were at home and where his mother and father were. Joseph shut down and stopped talking, only shrugging his shoulders without saying a word. Clearly, the new discussion was making Joseph somewhat uncomfortable. Demetria, not to be shaken by this behavior, asked Joseph if his mother and father would be at home today, as she wanted to stop by for a short visit and speak to them about some concerns that both she and the school staff were having about his missing school so often. Joseph said his mother would be home, but he did not know where his father was, that his father had not been home in several weeks. "He just up and left us here," Joseph stated strongly in a clearly agitated voice. Demetria thanked Joseph for talking with her and sharing his favorite things to do, as some had also been her favorites as well, and indicated to the principal that Joseph could return to class.

Demetria took several minutes to write down a few notes and thanked the school officials for their call and concern, mentioning that she would follow up on the matter with an investigation and a home visit. After returning to the office and meeting with her supervisor about the interviews with Joseph and the school officials, Demetria made a trip to Joseph's home.

As she entered Joseph's neighborhood, Demetria noticed how rundown and dilapidated the mobile homes were in this somewhat older mobile home park; the yards were not well maintained, and trash and graffiti littered the streets and vacant homes. When Demetria arrived at the address, after some difficulty because the numbers were not clearly visible at the residence, she found a woman sitting on the steps of the small wooden porch at the front entrance of the home.

Demetria approached the home and said "hello" and then indicated that she was looking for Ms. Miles. "Hello," the lady on the porch said, "I'm Mrs. Miles." Demetria then explained that she was a social worker with the Division of Child Welfare and would like to speak with her about her son, Joseph. Hesitantly, Mrs. Miles invited her inside.

Demetria noticed that the mobile home was without electricity and barely looked lived in, except for the hot plate on the kitchen counter and a small college dorm-size refrigerator with the cord draped over the front. The house had an apparent roach problem as several scurried across the counter as Mrs. Miles tried to put a few dishes in the sink before offering Demetria something to drink. While Mrs. Miles was fixing a pot of tea on the hot plate, Demetria surveyed as much as she could from the well-used sofa where she sat. She noticed a long orange extension cord running out the window and over to the neighboring mobile home connecting the hot plate and a small space heater in the front room. She also observed that there were no visible signs of a supply of food in the house.

Demetria explained the reason for her visit and began with some basic questions about the family's situation. Mrs. Miles explained that she and Mr. Miles had fallen on hard times, and both she and her husband were currently out of work. They had recently moved to the area in hopes of finding jobs; Mr. Miles had worked on a few odd jobs in construction but had not been called for several months. She had been working part-time cleaning homes and offices through a temporary employment agency, but she fell ill several months prior with a severe case of the flu and lost her job assignments with the agency. The medical bills had mounted, and, although Medicaid covered most of her expenses, the family's lack of income had made meeting basic needs very difficult.

Mr. Miles had left about two weeks earlier to find work in a larger metropolitan area, and Mrs. Miles had not heard from him since, due in part to their lack of a telephone and lack of transportation. She was not sure when exactly he would be returning, though he had never been gone that long without at least some mail correspondence. Nevertheless, she was hopeful that she would be receiving a letter and maybe a check from him very soon—in fact, she had been sitting on the porch awaiting the day's mail delivery.

Mrs. Miles admitted that their struggles were taking an emotional toll on her and that sometimes she did not even want to get out of bed in the morning to make Joseph's lunch and get him ready for school, so often he would not go at all. Since they were new to the area, she knew very little about the community and where to find resources, and neither she nor her husband had family they could turn to for assistance. Demetria also asked about the bruising on Joseph's arms. Mrs. Miles explained that Joseph had become very distant since they moved to the area and was not talking to her very much. He seemed to be increasingly angry and frustrated and had started hanging out with older teenagers from the neighborhood, teenagers she suspected were involved in a gang and, maybe, that was where he got the bruises. She had caught Joseph sneaking back into the house after 1:00 A.M. several times since his father had gone away, and she smelled alcohol on him a couple of times.

As she told the story, Mrs. Miles' eyes filled with water several times as she struggled to hold back tears. "I am at the end of my rope. I don't know what will happen now," she said, her voice shaking in fear and uncertainty. "I need help, but where do I turn?" she asked Demetria. "My only child doesn't talk to me, my husband is away, and my family and I are in disarray," she said with much agitation and disappointment in her voice.

Demetria attempted to be supportive and assured Mrs. Miles that she would work to help her access the services she might need to obtain support for the family. Demetria had grown up in the area, just over the bridge in a neighboring community, and had been very active as a young leader in her community and surrounding area. She also had many dealings with churches, civic organizations, and local social service agencies because she had been very active as a young college student working as a tutor and as a Big Sister volunteer. Demetria knew the resources in the community pretty well.

Demetria returned to the office and met with her supervisor to discuss the Miles's family situation. They identified which community resources would best help the family meet their basic needs of food, clothing, electricity, etc., and what referrals Demetria might make to help Mrs. Miles get the emergency assistance needed by this family in crisis.

Where to begin? Demetria prepared an assessment of the family's presenting issues and needs and drafted a case plan for discussion at the upcoming staff meeting called to review current and new cases. During the staffing, administrators and caseworkers would have an opportunity to share expertise, knowledge, and insights about how to best approach a presenting case situation. Often, this sharing process allows for cases to be discussed at greater depth, which leads to a more comprehensive and competent assessment of the situation and how the agency might better serve clients. Demetria worried that people might think she wasn't very well prepared for her job but decided the client's well-being was more important than maintaining her own comfort level.

The action plan was both thoughtful and comprehensive. After all, this was her first case, and Demetria wanted to be as prepared as possible when presenting her plan to the more seasoned staff members and administrators. When the meeting focus turned to Demetria's case, her skills as a BSW-level professional social worker were clearly evident. She shared background information about the Miles family and highlighted some key points from her initial assessment. Her supervisor complimented her on effectively developing her case plan from a generalist and systems perspective, which Demetria had learned as a BSW student.

The members of the staff team agreed with Demetria that child neglect was present and that the undetermined source of Joseph's bruising needed to be addressed as the child's safety was of immediate concern. Demetria's investigation had not sufficiently documented evidence to open an active case of child abuse at this time, but the investigation was clearly a conduit through which the family's condition of poverty and other struggles had been exposed. In addition, Joseph's difficulties with adjustment, his possible drinking problem, truancy, and gang participation, were all areas of concern. Thus, there were points of focus at a number of levels—individual, family, group, school, and community—that should be addressed in Demetria's work with this family in need.

After the staffing, Demetria called the director of the energy assistance program to see about getting the electricity turned on at the residence. The director assured her that they could get the family's lights turned on before the close of the business day. Demetria was concerned that the family also needed some basic food items and that their lack of transportation and money would make shopping for food problematic. Because there was no telephone, Demetria made a trip back to the Miles's home but first stopped by the local food bank and picked up some basic food items that the family could use. Demetria helped Mrs. Miles complete eligibility forms for subsidized rent and energy assistance and attempted to get the family qualified for the food stamp program. Because of the family's financial problems, Demetria connected them to a child health program that would help with any medical needs that Joseph might have and through which Joseph could obtain a thorough medical checkup.

Last, Demetria wanted to help Joseph deal with his adjustment issues and confront his possible involvement in gang activities and underage drinking. She thought that the Big Brother program in the local community was an excellent way for Joseph to build positive relationships with his peers; the local Boys and Girls Club building had just been renovated and had an indoor pool, basketball court, pool tables, table tennis, and a variety of other activities. In fact, a former classmate of Demetria's was conducting a teen group that focused on development issues, sex education, substance abuse, anger management, and self-esteem building. What a fitting opportunity for Joseph to deal with his adjustment and anger issues and to meet some new people, as well. Demetria knew that getting Joseph to go to the group meeting might be a challenge, but she also knew that he would have a lot to contribute to the other group members and would learn from them. At an age where peer relationships are becoming especially important to young people, this might become a healthy alternative to gang participation for Joseph.

A few weeks later, Demetria and her supervisor sat down to review this case. Working from her generalist perspective, Demetria had understood that this wasn't just a problem about Joseph. It was also the absence of Joseph's dad from the family and the issues he faced at school, both of which contributed to his need to belong and his ill-advised decision to seek that sense of belonging through association with a gang. It also had to do with a family that faced a financial crisis and didn't know how to access the existing resources in the community. Demetria had been able to assist in all of these areas. Her generalist approach to this case, however, left her aware of the lack of resources to help both Mr. and Mrs. Miles with their employment problems. Demetria's supervisor suggested that this issue might be a good discussion topic at an upcoming meeting of the local chapter of the National Association of Social Workers. If the problem was widespread, perhaps an action plan could be developed to create a more adequate job counseling service in the community.

Looking back, Demetria felt pleased with her decision to major in social work and attend an accredited social work education program that provided her with the professional recognition, knowledge, and skills she needed to be reasonably effective in working with her first case. What's more, she knew she would get better with experience. She felt she was off to a good start in her chosen profession.

Concluding Comment

In the above case, we have the opportunity to observe a new social worker dealing with her first case as a full-time child welfare worker. Demetria was apprehensive at first (and who wouldn't be?), but ultimately she was successful in helping address both the short- and long-term issues that were negatively affecting Joseph and his family. What made it possible for the Miles family to receive this assistance? The answer is "many factors," including the creation of a set of human services in the community that allowed people with professional expertise, like Demetria, to deliver helpful programs; the knowledge and skill possessed by this new social worker; and many other elements that underpin social work practice. A box at the conclusion of each of the next few chapters highlights some of the factors that contributed to Demetria's ability to make a difference in the life of this family.

part two

Social Work in U.S. Society

Social work emerged during the twentieth century as a central helping profession in U.S. society. Its development paralleled a seeming roller coaster of public interest in human welfare and social services. At times, particularly during the 1960s, the political climate placed considerable emphasis on improving human welfare, and the popularity of social work soared. At other times, this emphasis yielded to a conservative orientation more concerned with economic prosperity for a few than with meeting the basic needs of all. In such times, the appeal of social work to many young people declined as they sought employment in jobs where there was greater financial opportunity. Clearly, social work is closely tied to the political and economic philosophy that dominates at any time.

Although the supply of social workers may increase or decline from time to time, it is likely that there will always be a strong demand for this profession. Certain fundamental needs of the members of a society must be met if it is to survive, and any successful political philosophy must provide for these needs, even if at a very minimal level. There may be disagreement over how these needs should be met, but there must be some mechanism for providing those services. In relation to needs regarding social functioning, social workers are established as the central providers.

Providing needed human services and contributing to improvement of the quality of life for all people are personally rewarding experiences. Each social worker can enjoy the satisfaction of knowing that he or she makes a small but important contribution to the well-being of society. Yet, social work is not easy work. It can be as emotionally draining as it is rewarding. It can be as frustrating as it is satisfying. The prerequisite to developing the knowledge, values, and skills necessary for competent social work practice must be a basic commitment to social betterment and a willingness to invest oneself in facilitating change.

To understand the current status of social work in the United States, one must first understand the nation's changing social philosophy. Chapter 2 examines the efforts and issues that U.S. society confronts as it responds to the needs of its members. A summary of some of the important events and philosophies that have shaped the current social programs and the society's methods of delivering human services is presented. In addition, some of the continuing issues regarding the provision of human services are highlighted because, as it will later become evident, they affect the tools that social workers have available to serve their clients.

Within the framework of an evolving social welfare institution, a profession concerned with helping people interact more effectively with the world around them, and simultaneously to change that world to make it more supportive of human welfare, has emerged. An overview of that profession, social work, is the substance of Chapter 3. While the central focus of social work is seemingly obscured when one looks at the many different expressions of social work in the wide range of human service organizations and the varied practice activities in which social workers engage, its central feature—attending to the quality of people's social functioning—makes it an important profession in fulfilling society's commitment to the welfare of its people.

Building on the concept of social work as a comprehensive helping profession concerned with enhancing social functioning, Chapter 4 charts its evolution as a profession from well-meaning volunteers to a recognized and credentialed helping profession.

chapter 2

Social Welfare: A Response to Human Need

Prefatory Comment

The Preamble to the Constitution of the United States asserts that this nation was formed to "insure domestic tranquility, provide for the common defense, promote the general welfare, and secure the blessings of liberty to ourselves and our posterity...." In the months and years since the terrorist attacks on September 11, 2001, our tranquility has surely been broken, the commitment to providing common defense has been translated into preemptive strikes against Iraq, and many of the blessings of liberty have been compromised in the name of homeland security. In this context, the main focus of social work, promoting the general welfare (or well-being of the people) has been difficult to achieve. Indeed, people's perceptions of what constitutes well-being have changed, and the country's willingness to share its resources is increasingly characterized by self-interest and a response to special interests, rather than a promotion of the welfare of all of its members. The altruism that once flourished in the United States has diminished.

Human needs periodically change. Sometimes there is gradual change that occurs incrementally over time, and at other times dramatic change occurs quickly, such as in response to a local disaster or the terrorist attacks on September 11, 2001. It is within the context of these changing needs through the decades that new programs and services were developed and several new professions, including social work, emerged to assume responsibility for helping to "promote the general welfare" of the nation's people.

Although each person has his or her unique constellation of needs, some needs are common to all people. Logically, efforts should be made to address the most basic needs and then, if there is sufficient commitment and resources, to deal with those of lesser priority. Abraham Maslow suggests the following priorities, or *hierarchy of human needs,* beginning with the most basic:[1]

- *Physiological survival needs:* nourishment, rest, and warmth
- *Safety needs:* preservation of life and sense of security
- *Belongingness needs:* to be a part of a group and to love and be loved
- *Esteem needs:* approval, respect, acceptance, and appreciation from others
- *Self-actualization needs:* opportunity to fulfill one's potential

A society must decide which of these needs it will attempt to serve and which needs individuals and families should be expected to meet themselves. The more basic the need, the more likely it is that society will make some provision for meeting that need.

Although individual philosophies vary regarding how much responsibility the society should take for responding to human needs, two basic philosophies dominate thinking in the United States and shape political debate. A *conservative* philosophy argues for placing primary responsibility for maintaining the well-being of people with the individual and family, depends on the market system to drive the economy, and tends toward a protectionist national view of issues. In contrast, a *liberal* position favors a more substantial role for government and other social structures in meeting basic needs and in the use of social programs to redistribute income and at least partially influence the economy, and it expects the government to actively address global issues. Thus, the political climate at any time will affect the degree to which the society will take responsibility for the welfare of its members and embrace social programs to maximize the well-being of its citizens. When a more conservative orientation is dominant, the society is most likely to assume responsibility for only the most basic needs (e.g., physiological survival and safety). Social programs would typically be limited to activities such as food programs, provision for the homeless, and intervention in cases of child abuse. If a more liberal orientation dominates, the society would be viewed as needing to also address belongingness, esteem, and/or self-actualization needs. Thus there would likely be support for additional social programs such as family counseling, mental health, services to persons with disabilities, and even for programs aimed at changing social structures to try to prevent social problems from emerging.

Social Welfare Programs

Society's organized efforts to meet some human needs are labeled *social welfare*. The term *social*, when applied to humans, addresses the interactions of individuals or groups with other people, groups, organizations, or communities. The term *welfare* implies concern for the well-being of people. Social welfare programs, then, are developed to help people function more satisfactorily in their interactions with others and thus to lead more fulfilling lives. A useful definition of *social welfare* is the translation of society's dominant social philosophies into social policies, to be carried out by a system of human services agencies and delivered by human services professionals, in order to meet the socially related needs of individuals, families and other households, groups, and/or communities through programs offering social provisions, personal services, and/or social action.

In its early years, the United States was largely rural, and the economy was based on family farms and local trade. Except in the cases of widows and orphans or persons experiencing major physical disabilities or mental illnesses, the social programs were typically of limited scope. With the transition to an industrial society in the 1800s, the family, and particularly the extended family, could not meet many of the needs of its members. Family members often had to move to distant locations to find jobs, making the mutual support one might expect from family members less available. Also, the work depended more on the specialized skills in the use of machines than on an individual's manual labor, and those without suitable skills or intelligence became expendable. Life was further complicated by competition for jobs, with large numbers of skilled immigrants also seeking to enter the labor market. In this environment, social welfare programs began to expand because many individuals and families could no longer be self-sufficient.

More recently, the economy has become more global and increasingly tied to electronic technology, which again is altering the structure of the society. Families are no longer required to work as a unit to survive, although the general well-being of their members often depends on multiple breadwinners. In addition, individuals can work somewhat in isolation (often in a home office) and thus their opportunity for regular social interaction with colleagues is lessened. Further, a few people who are highly skilled in the use of technology can complete work that once required many laborers (for example, through mechanized farming or robotics), leading to job displacement—especially for those experiencing educational, emotional, or mental disabilities or one of the several forms of discrimination. These and other trends that have disenfranchised segments of the population have moved social welfare programs from a relatively minor role in U.S. society to an increasingly central place.

The Evolution of Social Welfare

An index of a nation's continued commitment to its people is its investment in social programs. These programs are the mechanisms by which public concerns are translated into assistance for people. They are expressed in laws and other policies that represent the society's plans to provide for an identified need. In the United States, social welfare programs have been subject to ever-changing philosophies, and consequently support for these programs has increased and decreased at various periods. Knowledge of the evolution of social welfare provides an important context for understanding the work of social workers today.

Colonial Times to the Great Depression

Picture life in the rural United States in the 1700s, when land was plowed and families worked to tame the wilderness. Although there were many trials and tribulations in that agricultural society, the person with average intelligence and a willingness to work hard could usually succeed. Given an open frontier and liberal government policies for staking a claim to fertile land, an individual could readily acquire property and produce at least the necessities of life. Each member had sharply defined roles that contributed to the family's welfare, people survived, and, in time, usually prospered. All members (i.e., grandparents, children, and other relatives) performed the required work and, perhaps as important, were needed. Even the person who was mentally or physically disabled could find meaningful ways to contribute. The "American Dream" became a reality for most (unless one was of African, Asian, Mexican, or Native American background) in this simple agrarian society.

The family was not usually completely independent and self-supporting. For mutual protection, social interaction, and opportunity to trade the goods they produced, families would band together into loosely knit communities. Trade centers eventually emerged as small towns; a market economy evolved; and merchants opened stores, bought and sold products, and extended credit to people until their products were ready for market. Efforts to meet human needs in this environment can best be characterized as *mutual aid*. When special problems arose, neighbors and the community responded. The barn that burned was quickly rebuilt, widows and orphans were cared for, and the sick were tended to. People shared what they had with needy friends and neighbors, knowing that the favor would be returned some day. In this preindustrial society, the quality of life depended on the "grace of God and hard work." Society rarely needed to respond to unmet human needs, but, when it did, churches and synagogues usually provided that service.

Conditions began to change in the mid-1800s and early 1900s when industrialization and urbanization created rapid and dramatic changes in both the family and the market system. People congregated in cities where there were jobs, the individual breadwinner rather than the family unit became the key to survival, and interactions with others were increasingly characterized by impersonality. Those from the vulnerable population groups (e.g., immigrants, the aged, minorities, women, persons with disabilities), in particular, experienced reduced opportunity for employment or, if employed, access to meaningful and personally rewarding jobs. Not only were social problems increased, but, with the changed roles of the family and market system, society had to create new ways to respond to human needs.

Early social welfare programs were heavily influenced by the *Puritan ethic,* which argued that only those people with a moral defect required assistance. According to Puritan reasoning, those who failed did so because they suffered from a moral weakness and were viewed as sinful. It is not uncommon even today for clients to feel that their troubles represent God's means of punishing them for some sin or act of immoral behavior. Following the same philosophy, grudging taxpayers often resent contributing to human services when they believe the client is morally at fault for needing assistance. This view, however, does not take into consideration the structural factors in the society that contribute to or even may cause an individual's problems.

The United States was not settled by wealthy people. When social needs were addressed by this developing society, small voluntary organizations were formed to provide services. If voluntary organizations did not meet needs, town meetings were held and actions taken to provide assistance, thus creating the first public social services. Any assistance was considered charity, not a right. Requests for help were either supported or rejected, depending on the judgments made by the townsfolk.

The philosophy derived from the *French Enlightenment* of the eighteenth century contradicted the Puritan view. It argued that people are inherently good and that need for assistance is not related to morality. People needing help were judged as deserving of assistance depending on the causes of their problems.

The *worthy poor* were viewed as good people who required help because they were afflicted with an ailment or were women and children left destitute by the death or desertion of the breadwinning husband and father. The *unworthy poor* were thought to have flaws of character. That one's plight may have been caused by others, by chance, or even by structural conditions in the society was only beginning to be recognized.

There were, of course, those who held a sympathetic view of persons in need and attempted to reform the punitive and uncaring approaches to providing services. One of the first great social reformers, Dorothea Dix, chronicled the deplorable conditions in prisons and almshouses (also referred to as "poor farms") and sought to establish government responsibility for meeting human needs. Her effective lobbying contributed to the passage of a bill in the U.S. Congress to grant federal land to states to help them finance care for the mentally ill. The veto of that bill in 1854 by President Franklin Pierce established a precedent that was to dominate thinking about society's responsibility for social welfare for the next three-quarters of a century—that the federal government should play no part in providing human services. As late as 1930, President Herbert Hoover relied on the precedent established by the Pierce Veto. When he approved an appropriation of $45 million to feed livestock in Arkansas during a drought while opposing an additional $25 million to feed the farmers who raised that livestock.[2]

Other social reformers, too, began to advocate for programs to meet needs—mostly through voluntary associations such as the Charity Organization Societies, Settlement Houses, the Mental Hygiene Movement, and programs to assist former slaves to integrate into the dominant society. When the federal government refused to engage in providing human services, the states sporadically offered services, with several states creating state charity boards or public welfare departments. However, not until the Great Depression of the 1930s led to severe economic crisis and the ensuing New Deal programs of President Franklin D. Roosevelt was it recognized that private philanthropy, even in combination with limited state and local government support, could not adequately address the major human needs.

This picture of life in the United States is based largely on the experience of the white European immigrant. But what if one were African American, Mexican American, or Native American? Certainly life was different for these segments of the population. Consider, for example, the experience of African Americans in the 1800s. Families brought to this nation as slaves often had little control over their lives or their ability to function as a family unit. In slave families, males were often demeaned and females sexually abused, and family members were frequently sold as property to other slave owners. Even after emancipation, few social programs were available to meet even basic needs as the former slaves either remained as sharecroppers in the South or struggled to meet their basic needs in the discriminatory society in the North.

Similarly, the movement of people from Mexico into the Southwest United States in the mid-eighteenth and nineteenth centuries was characterized by discrimination and hardship. The United States had purchased and acquired by military force nearly one million square miles of Mexican territory. The Mexicans, who subsequently became Mexican Americans because of U.S. birth, were subjected to extensive acts of brutality at the hands of the Texas Rangers and lynchings by Anglo Americans who resented their competition for farming, grazing, and water rights.[3]

Native Americans, too, lived a different experience. As the westward movement progressed, the original Americans increasingly had their cultural identity eroded through treaties (often to be broken later) and government policies that dramatically changed the Native Americans' way of life. Policies during this period were intended to accomplish *extermination* of the Native Americans through war, lack of disease control, provision of alcohol, and slavery; lead to *expulsion* from their land; *excluded* them from their tribal life by sending young people to "Indian schools"; and *assimilated* them into the larger society by destroying tribal collective action.

These three racial/ethnic groups clearly did not participate in the "American Dream," although their labor played a significant role in the growing economic prosperity of the nation.

The Great Depression to the 21st Century

The Great Depression was also the great equalizer. People who had previously been successful suddenly required help. These were able-bodied people of European descent who needed assistance. Could they be blamed for their condition, or did other factors contribute to their troubles? In this case, it was the deterioration of the worldwide economy that forced many people into poverty. U.S. society began to recognize that indeed there were structural factors in modern society responsible for many social problems. With the Pierce Veto now defunct, the government began an unprecedented period of expansion in social welfare that became inclusive of many more people.

World War II rallied the United States to a common cause and helped people recognize their interdependence. Each person was counted on to contribute to the common good during wartime conditions, and the nation could ill afford to create "throwaway" people by failing to provide for their basic needs. By the 1960s, economic recovery was complete, and a brief period of prosperity and responsiveness to human needs followed. The Kennedy and Johnson administrations fostered the War on Poverty and Great Society programs, and the Human Rights Revolution was in its heyday. These activities focused public concern on the poor, minorities, women, the aged, people who were mentally and physically disabled, and other population groups that had previously been largely ignored. Legislation protecting civil rights and creating massive social programs was passed; court decisions validated the new legislation, and a vast array of new social programs emerged.

The bloom on social programs began to fade in the middle of the 1970s, and public apathy replaced public concern. Under the Carter administration, a deteriorating economy was accompanied by a growing political conservatism, and the continued commitment to human services was placed in direct competition with military buildup and the maintenance of U.S. superpower status. By the 1980s, the time was ripe for conservatives to attempt to dismantle the social programs that had developed over the past two decades. President Ronald Reagan's effort to limit the federal government's social programs echoed the political rhetoric based on the distrust of government that characterized the conservative philosophy, mixed with punitive, moralistic views regarding the recipients of human services that revealed vestiges of the Puritan philosophy. The Reagan administration had only moderate influence over expenditures for "mandated" social programs such as Social Security but was able to decrease by almost 15 percent the expenditures on "discretionary" social programs.

The Reagan administration attempted not only to cut federal expenditures but also to shift responsibility to state and local governments or, where possible, to the private sector of the human services. However, the combination of a more liberal Congress and a series of Supreme Court decisions that protected most of the gains made in human services and civil rights during the prior two decades partially blunted the radical changes that President Reagan promised. In the 1990s, implementation of President Clinton's moderate social agenda of health and welfare reform was diminished somewhat by a very conservative Congress, leaving little opportunity to roll back the decreased support for human services. Health care reform failed completely, and welfare reform was characterized by stringent employment-training requirements and a maximum of financial aid for five years, elimination of any benefits for noncitizens, the shift of more responsibility to state governments, and the reduction of benefits for out-of-wedlock children. According to the Urban Institute, the outcome of this reform after eight years was mixed with the number of financial assistance recipients declining and, as one indicator, the overall well-being of poor children remaining unchanged.[4]

Social Welfare in the Early 2000s

Our historical review of social programs indicates that, in the early stages of U.S. society's development, the expectation was that the individual would take care of himself or herself or, if not, that the families would ensure that their members' needs were met. Laws placed primary responsibility on the family unit for caring for its members, and, to a larger extent than in many societies, these laws have protected the sanctity of the family's decisions about how to achieve this goal. If this expectation could have been fulfilled, there may not have been the need for a social welfare institution, or perhaps society would reluctantly intervene only in cases where family members were being damaged (e.g., child abuse or neglect, domestic violence, elder maltreatment).

U.S. society evolved, however, in a way that the family became unable to meet many social needs, and voluntary social services provided by religious or voluntary human services agencies began to expand. Today, these contributions amount to only a small portion (3.2 percent) of the total expenditures on human resources, yet they are particularly important because they are relatively flexible funds that can be used to respond to changing needs. Although some of these important human services continue to be offered under the auspices of religious organizations, most are now related to secular nonprofit human service organizations, such as those typically associated with the United Way or those that raise their own funds to supplement client fees. As revealed in Table 2.1, these private nonprofit organizations are more likely to contribute their resources to educational programs rather than to health or human services programs, and they simply do not have the funds to support income maintenance programs, except for emergency food, clothing, and shelter.

Table 2.1

Government and Private Sector Allocations to Health, Education, and Social Welfare (in billions of dollars)

	Federal Government 2007	State/Local Government 2005	Private/ Nonprofit 2006	Total
Health, hospitals, Medicare	$ 642.1B	$ 170.2B	$ 20.2B	$ 832.5B
Elementary, secondary, and higher education and job training	70.2	689.4	33.8	793.4
Human services (e.g., social services, criminal justice, housing, and food and nutrition assistance)	115.3	76.4	24.4	216.1
Income security (cash assistance, other public welfare except Social Security)	271.8	362.0	0	633.8
Total	$ 1,099.4B	$ 1,298.0B	$ 78.4B	$ 2,675.8B
% Total Expenditures	44.4%	52.4%	3.2%	100.0%

Sources: Federal Government. Office of Budget Management. Fiscal Year 2009 Budget. Table 3.2. Outlays by Function and Subfunction: 1962-2009. http://www.whitehouse.gov/omb/budget/fy2009/pdf/hist.pdf; State & Local Government. U.S. Census Bureau. Summary of State & Local Government Finances by Level of Government: 2005. http://www.census.gov/govs/estimate/0500ussl_1.html; Private/Nonprofit. *GivingUSA 2007: The Annual Report on Philanthropy for the Year 2006, 52nd Annual Issue.* GivingUSA Foundation. http:givingusa.org/downloads, p. 27.

Local and state governments were the next line of defense. Today, city, county, and state governments supply 52.4 percent of the funds that underwrite the health, education, and social welfare programs in the United States. These government units focus largely on education at all levels (see Table 2.1), but they also provide significant support in other human resource areas.

Finally, the federal government provides a large portion of all human resource funding. The massive social programs that evolved have made it evident that voluntary and local government resources are insufficient to provide for people's most basic needs. Although controversy continues over the extent of participation and the role of the federal government in providing human resources, today more than $1,099 billion is invested annually in health, income security, and other programs. The rationale for this extensive involvement of the federal government is that many human problems are created by national and international factors such as enormous national debt, chronic unemployment, pervasive discrimination, inflation, the international trade deficit, and even the volatile price of goods and services on the worldwide market. Local areas have little, if any, influence over these factors, and it is necessary to create national programs to equalize the burden of responding to the needs of the victims of these largely uncontrollable events.

The federal government outlays for *discretionary programs* (i.e., those where the president and Congress have some choice regarding the allocation of federal funds) are an indicator of public priorities. Discretionary expenditures have changed substantially since the initiation of the Afghanistan and Iraq wars, shifting the emphasis from enhancing the quality of life in the United States to supporting the war effort. At the end of the Clinton Administration in 1999, and prior to the initiation of those wars, the National Defense allocation was $275 billion, or 48.2 percent of the discretionary program outlays. The budget for 2009 estimates the Defense budget will be $670 billion, or 55.4 percent of the total.[5] Many other areas of government support are, therefore, not growing in proportion to defense, including education, health, housing, and income security programs.

An outcome of the varied patterns of funding for human services has resulted in a patchwork of programs, and it is often difficult for potential clients to navigate through the collection of services. Social workers perform an important role in helping people find their way through the maze of human services. The de-emphasis on federal programs in the areas of health and income security should not detract from appreciation of the programs provided at the state and local levels of government or from voluntary contributions from individuals, foundations, and businesses. As Table 2.1 indicates, almost $2.5 trillion are spent each year on health, education, income security, and other human services. That amounts to more than $8,144 for each of the 303 million people in the United States in 2008. The United States in many respects is a generous nation.

Purpose and Goals for Social Programs

Social programs are created to accomplish three general purposes. First, most are designed for the *remediation* of a social problem. When a sufficient number of people experience difficulty in a particular aspect of social functioning, social programs are created to provide services intended to correct that problem—or at least to help the clients deal with it more effectively. Remediation programs include services such as income support for the poor, counseling for the mentally ill, and job training for the displaced worker. Remediation has historically been the central form of human service.

A second general purpose of human services has evolved more recently—the *enhancement* of social functioning. In this form of social program, the emphasis is on the growth and development of clients in a particular area of functioning without a "problem" having necessarily been identified. Well-baby clinics, parent-effectiveness training, and various youth recreation programs are all examples of social programs designed for personal enhancement.

Finally, the purpose of some social programs is the *prevention* of social problems. As opposed to treating symptoms, prevention programs attempt to identify the basic causes of difficulties in social functioning and seek to stimulate changes that will keep problems from ever developing. Prevention programs, for example, might include helping parents learn appropriate ways to discipline children or conducting community education to make the public aware of the negative impact racism, sexism, or poverty has on the growth and development of children.

Social programs have been created to serve at least four specific goals. The goal of some social programs is to facilitate the *socialization* of people to the accepted norms and behaviors of society. Such programs are designed to help people develop the knowledge and skills to become full participating and contributing members of society and include, for example, such programs as scouting, Boys Clubs and Girls Clubs, and YMCA or YWCA activities. Another goal of social programs is to assist in *social integration*, where people are helped to become more successful in interacting with the world around them. Counseling, therapy, and rehabilitation programs, for example, attempt to achieve this goal. A third goal of social programs is, at times, to provide *social control* by removing people from situations when they might place themselves or others at risk, or when they require some period of isolation from their usual surroundings in order to address problems. Examples of these programs are found in mental hospitals and correctional facilities. Finally, some programs are intended to achieve *social change,* that is, to express the conscience of society by stimulating changes that will enhance the overall quality of life. For example, public education to encourage the practice of safe sex to reduce the risk of AIDS and the solicitation of employers to hire persons who are developmentally disabled are activities that help to bring about social changes that benefit the society.

Social Program Conceptions

The design of social programs also reflects differing perceptions about who should be served and when services should be given. The most basic programs are based on a *safety net approach* and are planned as a way for society to assist people when other social institutions have failed to resolve specific problems. An alternative conception of social programs, the *social utilities approach,* views human services as society's frontline in addressing common human needs.

The Safety Net Approach. This conception views human services as a safety net that saves people who have not had their needs met by their primary resources such as the family or employment/economic systems. This approach begins with the presumption that a predefined problem exists—for example, a family's income is too low, a person's behavior is deviant, a child is at risk. Services are then provided to address the problems, and, when a satisfactory level of problem reduction is achieved, the services are terminated. One negative aspect of such programs is that, to be eligible for a safety net program, a client must also take on the stigma of having failed in some aspect of social functioning. Further, at times clients must be terminated from service because they have reached a predefined level of functioning, even though the service providers may recognize that the clients would benefit from additional assistance.

Safety net programs are thought of as *residual* because they are designed to deal with the residue of human problems—that is, those problems that are left after all other processes of helping are exhausted. Programs based on this approach are also *selective* in the sense that they are designed to serve a specific population experiencing a specific need. Finally, safety net programs are *time-limited* in the sense that services are terminated when a problem is solved (or at least reduced), a predetermined level of functioning is achieved, or a time limit for service reached.

The Social Utilities Approach. The social utilities conception of human services views social programs as one of society's primary social institutions for meeting needs. Like public utilities for water and electricity, these social utilities are available to all people who wish to make use of them. They do not assume that the person who receives services is at fault or has necessarily failed if he or she requires services. Rather, this concept recognizes that society creates conditions where all people can benefit from social programs, whether the program is designed to help people solve problems or enhance already adequate functioning.

Social utility programs are *universal* in the sense that they do not have strict eligibility requirements. Such programs are also based on an *institutional* conception of human services that considers social programs a regular or institutionalized way of meeting human needs. They do not assume that the individual, family, or any other social institution has failed if, for example, parents place a child in day care, if a young person joins a scouting program, or if a senior citizen takes advantage of a senior center's lunch program.

Human Services Program Categories

It is also useful to recognize that social programs can be divided into three distinct categories: social provisions, personal services, and social action. In a developed nation, all of these program categories are required.

Social Provisions. This category of social programs is designed to meet the most fundamental needs of the population, and such programs are typically viewed as part of the safety net. *Social provisions* are the tangible resources given to persons in need, either as cash or as direct benefits, such as food, clothing, or housing.

Social provisions are the most costly programs in outlay of actual dollars. As social programs have evolved, governmental agencies have assumed the primary responsibility for providing these services, and the private sector has taken the role of providing backup for those people who slip through the mesh of the public safety net. Such major social provision programs as Temporary Assistance to Needy Families (TANF), Supplemental Security Income (SSI), food stamps, low-rent public housing, and many others are provided under governmental auspices. Meals and lodging for transients and the homeless, emergency food programs, financial aid in response to crisis situations, shelters for battered wives, and many other social provision programs, however, are offered by voluntary social agencies.

Personal Services. The personal services category of programs includes both problem-solving and enhancement programs. Unlike social provisions, *personal services* are intangible services that help people resolve issues in their social functioning. Examples of personal service programs are marriage and family counseling, child protection services, client advocacy, family therapy, care for the disabled, job training, family planning and abortion counseling, foster care programs, human service brokering and referral activities, and many other programs aimed at helping clients strengthen their social functioning.

Social Action. When one works with people, it quickly becomes evident that it is often insufficient just to help a person or group cope with an unjust world. Efforts must be made to create a more just and supportive environment. For example, it is not enough to help a woman understand and cope with discrimination in the workplace. Although these activities may be important for her ability to keep her job, they do not resolve the basic problem, and they place the burden of change and adjustment on the victim. *Social action* programs help change conditions that create difficulties in social functioning. They require specialized knowledge and skill to effect change in organizations and communities. These efforts involve fact finding, analysis of community needs, research and interpretation of data, and other efforts to inform and mobilize the public to action in order to achieve change.

The Successes and Failures of Human Service Programs

It is not possible to fully assess the array of human service programs in the United States in this overview chapter. The poverty rate is perhaps the most revealing single indicator of quality of life because severely limited income is clearly associated with many social problems that affect people's well-being, including health, disabilities, mental health, nutrition, housing conditions, and so on.

To what extent, then, have there been improvements in the rates of poverty* in the United States in recent years? Beginning with the end of the War on Poverty (approximately in the year 1970) and ending near the conclusion of G. W. Bush's final term, with the exception of older people, the black population, and to some degree households headed by single mothers, we find little change in poverty rates (see Table 2.2). Several consistent patterns stand out in these data, however, that will be developed further in this book. First, children under age 18 are highly vulnerable to poverty. Poverty has been substantially reduced for older people but has increased for children and youth. Second, the white non-Hispanic population has experienced less poverty than any other racial or ethnic group. Third, the poverty rate for married couples is considerably less than for households headed by single parents, and if the single parent is a female the rate more than doubles than if the single parent is a male. Finally, poverty is highest in the central cities of urban areas and in rural areas. The escape of the wealthy to the suburbs is evident in these data. The picture is more complex on closer examination. A cross tabulation of these data for children under age 18, for example, reveals that young males experience less poverty than young females, white children are less likely to live in poverty than are children of color, children living with married parents are much better off than those living with a single parent, and children residing in the suburbs are much less likely to

---

*The experience of poverty is much more than living on a limited income, yet income is used as the single indicator of the degree of deprivation an individual or family experiences. The poverty threshold is adjusted annually by the federal government to reflect the minimum amount of money required by families of different sizes to be able to afford nutritious food, obtain adequate housing, sufficiently clothe family members for work and school, and provide needed health care. The poverty threshold in 2007, for example, was approximately $10,787 for a single-person household, $14,291 for a single parent with one child, and $19,157 for the typical two-parent family with two children. As a reference point, the median income for all families in 2007 was $44,389. Poverty thresholds for households of various sizes can be found at http://www.census.gov/hhes/www/poverty/threshld/thresh07.html.

Table 2.2

Percent of Individuals Below the Poverty Level by Age, Race and Ethnicity, Family Relationship, and Location of Residence: 1970 to 2006

	2006	2000	1990	1980	1970
Total Population	12.3 %	11.3 %	13.5 %	13.0 %	12.6 %
Children under age 18	17.6	16.2	20.6	18.3	15.1
Adults ages 18–64	10.8	9.6	10.7	10.1	9.0
Older adults ages 65 and over	9.4	9.9	12.2	15.7	24.6
White, non-Hispanic	8.2	7.4	8.8	9.1	7.3 (1973)*
Asian & Pacific Islander	10.3	9.9	12.2	**	**
Black	24.3	22.5	31.9	32.5	33.6
Hispanic	20.6	21.5	28.1	25.7	21.9 (1973)*
Married Couple	4.9	4.7	5.7	6.2	ND
Male householder (no wife present)	13.3	11.3	12.0	11.0	ND
Female householder (no husband)	28.3	25.4	33.4	32.7	32.5
Central city	16.1	16.3	19.0	17.2	14.2
Not central city (suburbs)	9.1	7.8	8.7	8.2	7.1
Nonmetropolitan area (rural)	15.2	13.4	16.3	15.4	16.9

* Classification revised in 1973.
** Data first reported in 1987.

Source: DeNavas-Walt, Carmen, Bernadette D. Proctor, and Jessica Smith. U.S. Census Bureau, Population Reports, P60-233, *Income, Poverty, and Health Insurance Coverage in the United States: 2006*, Washington, D.C.: U.S. Government Printing Office, 2007. Tables B1, B2, and B3.

experience poverty than other children. In short, these data suggest that the person at greatest risk for experiencing poverty would be a young female of color, living with a single mother in the central city of an urban area or in rural America.

These consistent patterns do not happen by chance. The data in Table 2.2 represent the culmination of laws, policies, norms, and cultural patterns that characterize life in the United States. Factors such as racism (and the opposite side of that coin, "white privilege"), sexism, and the other "isms" that separate people in this society play out in the rates of poverty and other social indicators (see Part Five of this book). Social workers are committed to helping individuals and families whose lives reflect these conditions. Although some individuals and families may have contributed to making their own situations more difficult, social workers are also committed to examining these patterns and their causes in order to bring about changes in the cultural patterns and structures that will help to prevent such unfair and disproportionate opportunities that limit people from achieving a high quality, fulfilling, and satisfying life.

Concluding Comment

The United States was formed with a goal of joining people to promote, among other things, the general welfare of all citizens. At times that goal has taken a back seat to individual and corporate interests, but at other times, when national leadership has had support for strengthening its social programs, the nation has come closer to realizing that objective. All people, however, do not equally experience that goal. If the United States is to remain strong and minimize the likelihood of attacks from internal or external terrorists—or by foreign powers—it must find ways to share the benefits of civilization with its own and other citizens.

More effective provision of social programs will require skilled professionals to help clients achieve more desirable levels of social functioning. Social workers are one of the groups of professional helpers who are central to the efforts to improve the general well-being of people. By examining Box 2.1, we can observe how the social programs that have evolved in the United States underpin the practice of a child welfare worker, Demetria, as she carried out the work in the case situation described in Chapter 1.

Box 2.1

Social Welfare Programs Accessed by Demetria

In dealing with the case of Joseph Miles in Chapter 1, the social worker, Demetria, was able to make a difference in the lives of the Miles family because a number of social welfare programs were available in the community. As described in this chapter, the case involved at least three of the basic needs described by Maslow: *physiological survival needs* (the family's financial problems led to concern about adequate food and heat), *safety needs* (Joseph's bruising, whether from family violence or gang activity), and *belongingness needs* (Joseph's isolation from family and peers). Given the report that these fundamental needs may not have been met—or perhaps that the problems were caused—by Joseph's family, the society stepped in to protect a vulnerable child who may have been in danger by giving the authority and responsibility to the child welfare division to investigate.

There was no indication in the way Demetria investigated that she was influenced by the *Puritan ethic,* which would lead her to make moral judgments about why the family needed help, or even the *French Enlightenment* philosophy, which would judge the Miles family worthy or unworthy for the reasons they were poor. Rather, because a child was at risk—and indeed the whole family was at risk—several *safety net programs* were called into play. The child protection service represented by Demetria falls into the *personal services* category of social programs, while Medicaid and food stamps help the family secure *social provisions.* All of these programs were provided by a *government* or *public agency,* the county Social Welfare Department, of which the Child Welfare Division was one unit. The referral of Joseph to the teen group at the Boys and Girls Club (a *private, nonprofit agency*) was another *personal service* activity, aimed at *socialization* to more acceptable norms of behavior for a 12-year-old boy. This counseling program was open to any child in the community, with or without a defined "problem," and thus would be viewed as a *social utility program.* Finally, the recommendation by Demetria's supervisor to place the lack of resources to address employment problems on the agenda of the next local National Association of Social Workers meeting for discussion could, if the problem is determined to be widespread, lead to *social action* to correct that problem. Without these programs, Demetria would have been of limited help to this family.

KEY WORDS AND CONCEPTS

Hierarchy of needs
Social welfare
Mutual aid philosophy
Puritan ethic
Social program goals (i.e., socialization, social integration, social control, and social action)

Social program conceptions (i.e., safety net, social utilities)
French Enlightenment philosophy
Human service program categories (i.e., social provisions, personal services, social action)

SUGGESTED INFORMATION SOURCES

Day, Phyllis J. *A New History of Social Welfare*, 5th Edition. Boston: Allyn and Bacon, 2006.
Ehrenreich, Barbara. *Nickel and Dimed: On (Not) Getting By in America*. New York: Henry Holt, 2001.
Herrick, John M., and Paul H. Stuart, eds. *Encyclopedia of Social Welfare History in North America*. Thousand Oaks, CA: Sage Publications, 2004.
Katz, Michael B. *The Price of Citizenship: Redefining the American Welfare State*. New York: Metropolitan Books, 2001.
Trattner, Walter I. *From Poor Law to Welfare State*, 6th Edition. New York: Free Press, 1999.

ENDNOTES

1. Abraham H. Maslow, *Motivation and Personality* (New York: Harper & Row, 1970), pp. 25–28.
2. Harold L. Wilensky and Charles N. Lebeaux, *Industrial Society and Social Welfare* (New York: Free Press, 1965), p. 42.
3. Armando Morales, *Ando Sangrando (I Am Bleeding): A Study of Mexican American-Police Conflict* (La Puente, CA: Perspectiva Publications, 1972), p. 11.
4. Olivia A. Golden, *Assessing the New Federalism: Eight Years Later* (Washington, D.C.: The Urban Institute, 2005), p. 18.
5. U.S. Office of Budget, *Budget of the United States Government: Fiscal Year 2009*. Historical Table 8.7.

chapter 3

Social Work: A Comprehensive Helping Profession

Prefatory Comment

The human services have become a central part of the fabric of U.S. society. Founded on the commitment to promote the general welfare of its people, society has gradually assumed increasing responsibility for ensuring that people have access to assistance in meeting their basic needs. This assistance takes the form of various social programs that are delivered by people who possess a variety of helping skills. The ability to help others is highly valued in all societies, whether provided to family and friends or others in one's community. In highly developed societies, including the United States, much of this helping has become so complex that human services programs require highly trained professionals. It is within this context that social work was born.

What is perhaps the most basic form of helping has been termed *natural helping*. Before reaching a social worker or other professional helpers, clients often have been counseled or assisted in some way by family, friends, neighbors, or volunteers. Natural helping is based on a mutual relationship among equals, and the helper draws heavily on intuition and life experience to guide the helping process. The complexity of many social issues and the extensive knowledge and skill required to effectively provide some human services today exceed what natural helpers can typically accomplish. This has resulted in the emergence of several occupations, known as human services professions, that deliver more complicated services to people in need.

Professional helping is different from natural helping in that it is a disciplined approach focused on the needs of the client, and it requires specific knowledge, values, and skills to guide the helping activity. Both natural and professional helping are valid means of assisting people in resolving issues related to their social functioning. In fact, many helping professionals first became interested in these careers because they were successful natural helpers and found the experience rewarding. Social workers often work closely with natural helping networks (i.e., both family members and friends) during the change process and as a source of support after professional service is terminated. However, natural helpers are not a substitute for competent professional help in addressing serious problems or gaining access to needed services.

Social work is the most comprehensive of human service occupations and, through time, has become recognized as the profession that centers its attention on helping people improve their social functioning. In simplest terms, social workers help people strengthen their interaction with various aspects of their world—their children, parents, spouse or other loved one, family, friends, coworkers, or even organizations and whole communities. Social work is also committed to changing factors in the society that diminish the quality of life for all people, but especially for those persons who are most vulnerable to social problems.

Social work's mission of serving both people and the social environment is ambitious. To fulfill that mission, social workers must possess a broad range of knowledge about the functioning of people and social institutions, as well as have a variety of skills for facilitating change in how individuals, organizations, and other social structures operate. This comprehensive mission has made social work an often misunderstood profession. Like the fable of the blind men examining the elephant with each believing that the whole elephant is like the leg, trunk, or ear that he examined, too often people observe one example of social work and conclude that it represents the whole of professional activity. To appreciate the full scope of this profession, it is useful to examine its most fundamental characteristics—the themes that characterize social work.

The Central Themes Underpinning Social Work

Five themes capture the character of social work. No one theme is unique to this profession, but in combination they provide a foundation on which to build understanding of social workers and their practice.

A Commitment to Social Betterment

Belief in the fundamental importance of improving the quality of social interaction for all people, that is, *social betterment,* is a central value of the social worker. The social work profession has taken the position that all people should have the opportunity for assistance in meeting their social needs.

Social work has maintained an idealism about the ability and responsibility of this society to provide opportunities and resources that allow each person to lead a full and rewarding life. It has been particularly concerned with the underdog—the most vulnerable people in the society. This idealism must not be confused with naivete. Social workers are often the most knowledgeable people in the community about the plight of the poor, the abused, the lonely, and others who for a variety of reasons are out of the mainstream of society or experiencing social problems. When social workers express their desire for changes that contribute to the social betterment of people, it is often viewed as a threat by those who want to protect the status quo.

A Goal to Enhance Social Functioning

Social workers take the position that social betterment involves more than addressing problems—it also involves assisting those who want to improve some aspect of their lives, even though it may not be considered "a problem." Social work, then, is concerned with helping people enhance their *social functioning,* that is, the manner in which they interact with people and social institutions.

Social workers help people and social institutions change in relation to a rapidly changing world. The technology explosion, information explosion, population explosion, and even the threat of nuclear explosion dramatically affect people's lives. Those who can readily adapt to these changes—and are not limited by discrimination because of race; cultural background; gender; age; or physical, emotional, or intellectual abilities—seldom use the services of social workers. Others who have become victims of this too rapidly changing world and its unstable social institutions, however, are likely to require professional help in dealing with this change.

An Action Orientation

Social work is a profession of doers. Social workers are not satisfied just to examine social issues. Rather, they take action to prevent problems from developing, attack problematic situations that can be changed, and help people deal with troublesome situations that cannot be changed. To do this, social workers provide services that include such activities as individual counseling, family and group therapy, linking people to the network of services in a community, fund raising, and even social action. Indeed, social work is an applied science.

An Appreciation for Human Diversity

To deal effectively with the wide range of change to which social work is committed, it has become a profession characterized by *diversity*—diversity of clientele, diversity of knowledge and skills, and diversity of services provided. In addition, social workers themselves come in all shapes, colors, ages, and descriptions.

Social workers view diversity as positive. They consider human difference desirable and appreciate the richness that can be offered to a society through the culture, language, and traditions of various ethnic, racial, and cultural groups. They value the unique perspectives of persons of different gender, sexual orientation, or age groups, and they recognize and develop the strengths of persons who have been disadvantaged. What's more, social workers view their own diversity as an enriching quality that has created a dynamic profession that can respond to human needs in an ever-changing world.

A Versatile Practice Perspective

The wide range of human conditions with which social workers deal, the variety of settings in which they are employed, the extensive scope of services they provide, and the diverse populations they serve make it unrealistic to expect that a single practice approach could adequately support social work. Rather, the social worker must have a comprehensive repertoire of knowledge and techniques that can be used to meet the unique needs of individual clients and client groups.

The versatile social worker, then, must have a solid foundation of knowledge about the behavior of people and social institutions in order to understand clients' situations. He or she also needs to understand that differing beliefs may affect the way people will interpret and react to those situations. And, finally, the social worker must have mastered a number of helping techniques from which he or she can imaginatively select to help individuals, families, groups, organizations, and communities improve their social functioning.

How do these themes affect social work practice? The following case example* is just one of many situations where a social worker might help a client:

> Karoline Truesdale, a school social worker, interviewed Kathy and Jim Swan in anticipation of the Swans' oldest son, Danny, beginning school in the fall. The Swans responded to Ms. Truesdale's invitation to the parents of all prospective kindergartners to talk over any concerns they might have about their children's schooling. When making the appointment, Kathy Swan indicated that her son Danny was near the cut-off age for entering school and may not be ready yet for kindergarten. When questioned further, Kathy expressed considerable ambivalence indicating that having him in school would help to relieve other burdens at home but may be too much for Danny.

Karoline's notes from the interview contained the following information:

> Kathy Swan is 20 years old and about to deliver her third child. She indicates that they did not need another mouth to feed at this time, but "accidents happen" and she will attempt to cope with this additional child when the baby is born (although she already appears physically and emotionally depleted). Jim is 21 years old and holds a temporary job earning minimum wage. He moved the family to the city because "money in agriculture has gone to hell" and a maintenance job was available at a manufacturing plant here. However, he was laid off after three months when the plant's workforce was reduced. Jim is angry that he moved the family for this job, yet the company felt no obligation to keep him on. He stated that "people in the country don't treat others like that." He is also worried that his temporary job will last only a few more weeks and commented that Kathy "spends money on those kids like it was going out of style." Jim said in no uncertain terms that he did not want and they could not afford another baby, but Kathy had refused to even consider an abortion.
>
> The children are quite active, and Danny pays little attention to Kathy's constant requests that he calm down. When Jim attempts to control Danny, Kathy accuses him of being too physical in his discipline. When questioned about this, Jim reported that his dad "beat me plenty and that sure got results." Kathy complains that Jim does not appreciate the difficulty of being home with the children all of the time, and she objects to the increasing amount of time he is away in the evenings. Jim replied rather pointedly that "it is not much fun being at home anymore." Tension between Kathy and Jim was evident.
>
> When questioned about their social contacts since moving to the city, both Kathy and Jim reported that it had been hard to make friends. They knew "everyone in town"

---

*Sonia Nornes and Bradford W. Sheafor originally developed this case material for the Fort Collins (Colorado) Family Support Alliance.

before they moved, but it is different now. With his changing employment, Jim has not made any real friends at work, and Kathy feels isolated at home since Jim takes the car to work each day, and the bus is her only means of transportation. She did indicate that one neighbor has been friendly, and they have met two couples they liked at church.

When asked specifically about Danny, Kathy reported that he has been ill frequently with colds and chronic ear infections. She hesitantly described his behavior as troublesome and hoped the school's structure would help him. Kathy described a Sunday school teacher who called him hyperactive and suggested that she not take him to Sunday school anymore. Kathy wondered if there was some kind of treatment that would help Danny and allowed that she was "about at the end of her rope with that child."

It was clear to Karoline that both Kathy and Jim wanted Danny to begin school. But was Danny ready for school—and would the school be ready for Danny? Would Danny's entering school be best for him? Would it resolve the family's problems? Are there other things that could be done to help this family and, perhaps, prevent other problems from emerging?

Within the strict definition of her job, Karoline could assist the Swans in reaching a decision about school attendance and complete her service to this family. With her "social betterment" concern, however, resolution of only the question about Danny's entering school would not be sufficient. As a social worker, Karoline would hope to help the Swan family address some of the more basic issues they face in order to improve the overall quality of their lives.

Social workers are not experts on all problems clients may experience. Karoline's experience, for example, would not prepare her to make judgments about Danny's health and the possible relationship between his chronic colds and ear infections and his behavior problems. She might refer the Swans to a low-cost medical clinic where a diagnosis of Danny's health problems can be made. She is, however, an expert in "social functioning" and can help Jim and Kathy Swan work on their parenting skills, strengthen the quality of their communication, assist them in developing social relationships in the community, and, perhaps, help Jim obtain job training and stable employment. Karoline's "action orientation" would not allow her to procrastinate. She would be anxious to engage this family in assessing the issues it faces and would support Kathy and Jim as they take action to resolve them.

The Swan family represents at least one form of "human diversity." They are a rural family attempting to adapt to an urban environment. Karoline knows that it will take time and probably some help to make this adjustment. She will explore strengths that may have been derived from their rural background. Perhaps Jim's skills in gardening and machinery repair would prove to be an asset in some lines of employment. Also, their rural friendliness may prove beneficial in establishing new social relationships, and they might be helped to build friendships through their church or neighborhood, or to use other resources where they can find informal sources of support (i.e., natural helping).

Service to the Swan family will require considerable practice "versatility." Karoline will need to assist the family in problem solving around whether or not to send Danny to school. She will hopefully engage them in more in-depth family counseling. She might invite them to join a parents' group she leads to discuss child-rearing practices, link them with medical and psychological testing services for Danny, and help Mr. Swan obtain job training. If Danny does attend school next year, Karoline might work closely with his teacher and Mrs. Swan to monitor Danny's progress and address any problems in his social functioning that may arise. If he does not attend school, an alternative program might be found where he can develop the socialization skills required in the classroom. Clearly, a wide range of practice activities would be needed, and Karoline must be versatile in her practice to apply them.

The Mission of Social Work

While social work practice requires considerable variation in activity, at a more abstract level the profession has consistently maintained that its fundamental *mission* is directly serving people in need and, at the same time, making social institutions more responsive to people. Although this unique mission has been steadfastly held for more than a century, it has been difficult to develop public understanding of its uniqueness among the helping professions. One way to understand this profession is to examine its three primary purposes: caring, counseling, and changing.

Caring

At times the best knowledge social workers can muster is inadequate to prevent or resolve the many problems encountered by the disabled, elderly, terminally ill, and other persons with limited capacity for social functioning. Social workers recognize that certain conditions in life cannot be corrected. Yet the victims of these conditions deserve not only humane but high-quality care.

Caring that makes people comfortable and helps them cope with their limitations is frequently the most valuable service a social worker can provide. Sometimes caring takes the form of arranging for meals to be delivered or for income to be supplemented, and ensuring that adequate housing is provided. At other times, the person and/or family may require help to better adjust to an unchangeable situation like a disability or terminal illness. There is also an important leadership role for social work in helping communities create the necessary services to provide such care. The fundamental intention of caring for those in need is a central purpose of social work practice.

Counseling

Another thrust of social work practice has been to provide treatment for individuals and families experiencing problems in social functioning. Depending on client needs, direct services ranging from psychosocial therapy to behavioral modification, reality therapy, crisis intervention, and various group and family therapy approaches are used by social workers.[1] These approaches do not automatically cure social problems in the same way a physician might prescribe a medication to cure an infection. In fact, most social workers would argue that at best they can only help clients find a way to resolve their issues. The contribution the social worker makes is the ability to engage the client in actively working toward change, to accurately assess the individual and societal factors that have created the need for change, to select appropriate techniques for a given client and situation, and to use these techniques effectively in conjunction with the clients to accomplish the desired results.

Changing the Society

Social change is the third primary purpose of social work. Social workers are committed to reforming existing laws, procedures, and attitudes until they are more responsive to human needs. Many pioneer social workers were reformers who worked to improve conditions in slums, hospitals, and poorhouses. Today, social workers actively influence social legislation in an effort to create new social programs or to change factors that contribute to damaging social conditions such as racism, sexism, and poverty.

Social workers also seek to change negative public attitudes about the more vulnerable members of society by providing public education and facilitating the empowerment of the affected members of the population to advocate for their own interests. Social workers, then, bring about change in the society by representing the interests of their clientele and/or helping clients persuade decision makers at the local, state, or national levels to respond to human needs.

The mission of social work is captured in the following three-part statement. Social work's mission includes:

▶ Caring for those who must live with an unchangeable social problem
▶ Counseling people addressing their social problems by helping them change and/or attempt to change the condition that causes the problem
▶ Changing conditions in the society that make some people more vulnerable to social problems

This mission, however, does not in itself clearly distinguish social work from other helping-oriented occupations. To gain further clarity, one must examine definitions of social work.

Defining Social Work

Unfortunately, social work has been hard to define. Different dictionary definitions treat social work as a set of skills, a job title, or even an activity that might be performed by volunteers. None treat this as a profession with extensive academic and practice experience required for the work. These definitions typically fail to distinguish social workers from others who engage in similar activities. Therefore, it is informative to examine how social workers define themselves.

Three concerted efforts have been made by the social work profession to arrive at a clear definition of social work. The first occurred in the 1920s when the American Association of Social Workers convened a series of meetings of key agency executives in Milford, Pennsylvania. These representatives from a range of practice settings identified several factors that appeared to be common to all social work practice, but they could not agree on a concise definition of social work. However, the Milford Conference encouraged further efforts at articulating a definition of social work when it concluded that social work's common features were more substantial than the differences.[2]

The 1950s brought a second surge of interest in developing a clear conception of social work. The merger of several specialized social work practice organizations and the more generic American Association of Social Workers into the National Association of Social Workers (NASW) was completed in 1955. For a time, a spirit of unity dominated the social work profession, and the effort to find a definition of social work that would reflect the commonality in diverse practice activities began in earnest. A critical step was the publication of the "Working Definition of Social Work Practice" in 1958. Although not yet providing a comprehensive definition of social work, the document established an important basis for subsequent definitions by identifying three common goals of social work practice:[3]

1. To assist individuals and groups to identify and resolve or minimize problems arising out of disequilibrium between themselves and their environment.
2. To identify potential areas of disequilibrium between individuals or groups and the environment in order to prevent the occurrence of disequilibrium.
3. To seek out, identify, and strengthen the maximum potential of individuals, groups, and communities.

Thus, the "Working Definition" established that social workers are concerned with curative or treatment goals, as well as emphasizing the importance of social change or prevention. In addition, the definition recognized the focus of social work on the interactions between people and their environments and the responsibility of social workers to provide services to people as individuals, as parts of various groups, and as members of communities.

Third, in the 1970s and 1980s, NASW published three special issues of its major journal, *Social Work*, that generated substantial debate and discussion about the nature of social work.[4] This activity enhanced understanding of the central features that characterize social work but did not lead to a definitive description of this profession.

Although NASW has never formally adopted a definition of social work, a one-sentence definition developed by one of its committees has gained widespread acceptance.

> Social work is the professional activity of helping individuals, groups, or communities enhance or restore their capacity for social functioning and creating societal conditions favorable to that goal.[5]

This statement provides a clear and concise "dictionary definition" of the profession. It draws important boundaries around social work. First, social work is considered professional activity. Professional activity requires a particular body of knowledge, values, and skills, as well as a discrete purpose that guides one's practice activities. When practice is judged professional, community sanction to perform these tasks is assumed to be present, and the profession, in turn, is expected to be accountable to the public for the quality of services provided.

Second, this definition captures a uniqueness of social work. It makes clear that social workers serve a range of client systems that include individuals, families or other household units, groups, organizations, neighborhoods, communities, and even larger units of society. For social work, the identification of one's client is tricky because a client or target of practice activity may range from an individual to a state or nation. The unique activities of the social worker are directed toward helping all of those systems interact more effectively and therefore require professional education as preparation.

Finally, the last part of the definition concerns social work's *dual focus on person and environment*. Social workers help people enhance or restore their capacity for social functioning. At the same time, they work to change societal conditions that may help or hinder people from improving their social functioning. Herein lies another uniqueness of social work. Whereas some professions focus on change in the person and others on changing the environment, social work's attention is directed to the connections between person and environment.

When working with clients, social workers must take into consideration both the characteristics of the person and the impinging forces from the environment. In contrast, the physician is primarily prepared to treat physical aspects of the individual, and the attorney is largely concerned with the operation of the legal system in the larger environment (although both the physician and attorney should give secondary attention to other, related systems). Social work recognizes that each person brings to the helping situation a set of behaviors, needs, and beliefs that are the result of his or her unique experiences from birth. Yet it also recognizes that whatever is brought to the situation must be related to the world as that person confronts it. By focusing on transactions between the person and his or her environment, social interaction can be improved.

Figure 3.1 depicts this unique focus of social work. Social workers operate at the boundary between people and their environment. They are not prepared to deal with all boundary matters. Rather, they address those matters that are judged problematic or have been selected as a way to contribute to the enhancement of social functioning. In sum, social workers temporarily enter the lives of their clients to help them improve their transactions with important elements of their environment. To further understand social work, it is instructive to examine the approaches social workers use when assisting their clients or advocating for social change.

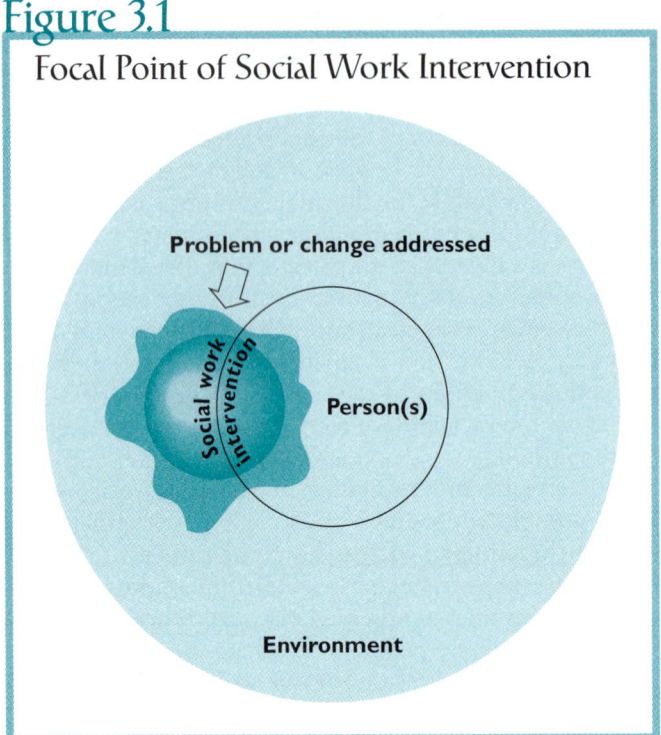

Figure 3.1
Focal Point of Social Work Intervention

Social Work Practice Approaches

Arriving at a practice approach that is sufficiently flexible and encompassing to relate to this complex profession has proven difficult. In fact, social work might be characterized as a profession in search of a practice approach. That search began with the development of several distinct practice methods.

Traditional Practice Methods

The first practice method to develop, *social casework,* was described in the 1917 classic social work book, *Social Diagnosis.*[6] In this book, Mary Richmond focused on the requirements for effective practice with individuals and families, regardless of the type of problem presented. The book filled an important void in social work by introducing a literature describing social work practice. The principles of social casework identified by Richmond were enthusiastically adopted by social workers, and the profession moved its primary focus to work with individuals and families. The popularity of Freudian psychology in the 1920s and 1930s also directed social work toward considering the individual primarily responsible for his or her condition, rather than viewing problems in the structure of society as also contributing to people's issues. Abbott noted that Richmond later expressed concern over this trend to overemphasize the person side of the person-environment mission of social work:

> The good social worker, says Miss Richmond, doesn't go on helping people out of a ditch. Pretty soon she begins to find out what ought to be done to get rid of the ditch.[7]

Social workers concerned with providing services to groups took longer to develop a set of guiding principles, partially because those social workers disagreed among themselves as to whether they should identify professionally with the emerging field of social work. This disagreement was resolved in the 1930s in favor of identifying with social work, and thus a second distinct method, *social group work*, evolved.

The third practice method to develop was *community organization*. With many social agencies and social programs being created in each community, their coordination and the evaluation of their effectiveness became important and, to meet that need, another distinct practice area emerged. Community organization became the practice method primarily concerned with coordinating the distribution of resources and building linkages among existing services.

In addition to using one of these three primary practice methods in their work, many social workers found themselves responsible for administering social agencies and conducting research on the effectiveness of social programs. By the late 1940s, *administration* and *research* had evolved as practice methods in social work. Viewed as secondary methods, they were seen as a supplement to a person's ability as a caseworker, group worker, or community organizer.

Multimethod Practice Approach

Concurrent with the development of these five distinct practice approaches was the growing commitment to unifying social work as a single profession with a well-established practice method. A major study of social work and social work education, the Hollis–Taylor Report, was concluded in 1951. It recommended that, because the breadth of social work practice required social workers to intervene at more than one level of the client system, social work education should prepare students with a beginning level of competence in each of the five practice methods.[8]

The multimethod practice approach proved a good fit with the varied demands for social work practice but failed to yield the unifying practice theme the profession needed. Practitioners typically identified with a dominant method and used the others sparingly.

Generalist Practice Approach

Supported by concepts drawn from social systems theory, the generalist approach to practice began to emerge in the late 1960s. As Balinsky stated, "The complexity of human problems necessitates a broadly oriented practitioner with a versatile repertoire of methods and skills capable of interacting in any one of a number of systems."[9]

The generalist model provided versatility and met the requirement for a flexible approach to social work practice demanded by the complexity and interrelatedness of human problems.

Generalist practice contains two fundamental components. First, it provides a perspective from which the social worker views the practice situation. Social systems theory helps the social worker to maintain a focus on the interaction between systems—that is, the person–environment transactions—and to continually look for ways to intervene in more than one relevant system. Second, rather than attempting to make the client's situation fit the methodological orientation of the social worker, the situation is viewed as determining the practice approach to be used. Thus, the social worker is required to have a broad knowledge and skills and to have the ability to appropriately select from those basic competencies to meet the needs of clients.

Although many social workers contend that the generalist approach has been part of social work practice since its inception, only recently have there been analysis and explication of this practice approach. With the accreditation requirement that both baccalaureate- and master's-level social workers be prepared as generalist practitioners, there has been a resurgence of activity aimed at clarifying the nature of generalist practice in recent years. In their article titled "Milford Redefined: A Model of Initial and Advanced Generalist Social Work," Schatz, Jenkins, and Sheafor delineate the key elements of generalist social work at both the initial and advanced generalist levels.[10]

This model recognizes that there is a *generic foundation* for all social work, whether generalist or specialist, that includes such factors as knowledge about the social work profession, social work values, the purpose of social work, ethnic/diversity sensitivity, basic communication skills, understanding of human relationships, and others.

The *generalist perspective,* according to this model, (1) is informed by sociobehavioral and ecosystems knowledge; (2) incorporates ideologies that include democracy, humanism, and empowerment; (3) requires a worker to be theoretically and methodologically open when approaching a practice situation; (4) is client centered and problem focused; (5) includes both direct and indirect interventions; and (6) is research-based.

At the *initial generalist* level of practice, the social worker builds on the generic foundation and, using the generalist perspective, must at least be capable of (1) engaging effectively in interpersonal helping, (2) managing change processes, (3) selecting and utilizing multilevel intervention modes, (4) intervening in multiple-sized systems as determined by the practice situation, (5) performing varied practice roles, (6) assessing and examining one's own practice, and (7) functioning successfully within an agency.

The *advanced generalist* social worker engages in more difficult practice tasks and, therefore, operates from an expanded knowledge base about individuals, groups, organizations, and communities that is developed in master's degree programs. The advanced generalist must also develop increased skills to intervene in direct service provision with individuals, families, and groups at one end of the multiple-level practice spectrum and, at the other end, address more complex indirect practice situations such as supervision, administration, program evaluation, and policy development. Finally, the advanced generalist is expected to approach social work practice from an eclectic, but disciplined and systematic, stance and to simultaneously engage in both research and practice evaluation.

Specialist Practice Approaches

In contrast to the generalist, a number of specialized practice approaches have emerged. *Specialist* social work practice is characterized by the application of selected knowledge and skills to a narrowed area of practice based on practice setting, population served, social problems addressed, and/or practice intervention mode used. In other words, this practice approach begins with a preference about the knowledge and skill required for practice in that specialized area and serves clients whose needs fit into those more narrow, but in-depth, worker competencies.

While education for initial generalist practice is offered in baccalaureate programs or the early part of master's-level programs, specialist education has increasingly become the emphasis of the latter part of a master's degree. Master's social work education programs sometimes offer the advanced generalist as their area of concentration but more typically build their curricula on one or more specialty areas. Although individual schools of social work usually focus on only a limited number of specialties, the following illustrates the range of specializations a school might offer.

- *Fields of Practice:* for example, services to families, children, and youth; services to the elderly; health; mental health; developmental disabilities; education; business and industry; neighborhood and community development; income maintenance; employment.
- *Problem Areas:* for example, crime and delinquency; substance abuse; developmental disabilities; family violence; mental illness; neighborhood deterioration; poverty; racism; sexism.
- *Populations-at-Risk:* for example, children and youth; the aged; women; single parents; ethnic populations; persons in poverty; migrants; gay and lesbian persons; the chronically mentally ill.
- *Intervention Methods or Roles:* for example, specific practice approaches with individuals, families, and groups; consultation; community organization; social planning; administration; case management; social policy formulation; research.
- *Practice Contexts and Perspectives:* for example, industry; hospitals; schools; rural or urban areas.

Today social work embraces both generalist and specialist approaches to practice. The generalist viewpoint supports the commonality that unites social work into one profession; the specialist approach helps to delineate unique areas for in-depth social work practice.

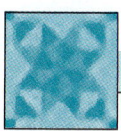

Social Workers: Their Many Faces

How has the emergence of a profession concerned with helping people change conditions that affect their social functioning played out? First, a fairly specific career pattern has emerged, and, second, a substantial number of people have selected social work as a career.

Career Patterns of Social Workers

Varying career patterns have evolved as the practice of social work has changed over time. The early social workers were volunteers or paid staff who required no specific training or educational program to qualify for the work. When formal education programs were instituted at the turn of the twentieth century, they were training programs located in the larger social agencies. In fact, it was not until 1939 that accreditation standards required that all recognized social work education must be offered in institutions of higher education. There was also controversy over whether appropriate social work education could be offered at the baccalaureate level as well as at the more professionally respectable master's level. The reorganization of social work into one professional association (the National Association of Social Workers, or NASW) and one professional education association (the Council on Social Work Education, or CSWE) in the 1950s yielded a single education-level profession. At that time, only the master's degree from an accredited school of social work was considered "legitimate" social work preparation. Today, the Master of Social Work (MSW) degree still is considered the "terminal practice degree" in social work, but other professional practice levels are now recognized. In 2006, 173 of the 181 accredited programs reported their graduation statistics indicating that 17,209 persons received the MSW degree, making it the dominant qualification for social work practice.[11]

It was not until 1970 that the NASW recognized baccalaureate-level (BSW) social workers as fully professional social workers. The Council on Social Work Education subsequently created accreditation standards, and, by 2006, 433 of the 458 accredited schools throughout the United States reported graduating 12,845 persons with the BSW (at times this may be a BA or a BS degree).[12] Another career level had indeed been established.

Increasingly, social workers are also completing doctoral degrees in social work, either the Doctor of Social Work (DSW) or the Doctor of Philosophy (Ph.D.). In 2006, for example, 293 persons completed a doctorate in social work from the sixty-one reporting schools in the United States.[13] In addition, a number of other social workers also complete doctorates in related disciplines. Most doctoral-level social workers are employed in teaching or research positions, but doctoral programs aimed at preparing people for direct social work are beginning to emerge. Doctoral programs, however, are not subject to accreditation by CSWE and are not recognized as professional practice preparation in social work. Thus, the MSW continues to be viewed as the terminal practice degree.

By 1981, NASW found it necessary to develop a classification system that would help to clarify the various entry points to social work and define the educational and practice requirements at each level. This system sorts out the career levels into four categories: *basic professional* (BSW), *specialized professional* (new MSW), *independent professional* (MSW plus at least two years experience), and *advanced professional* (doctorate or special practice proficiency).[14] NASW's classification scheme has several benefits. First, it identifies and clarifies the practice levels existing in social work and, in general terms, spells out the competencies that both clients and employers can expect from workers at each level. Second, it describes a continuum of social work practice with several entry points based on education and experience. Finally, it suggests a basis for job classification that can increasingly distinguish among the various levels of social work competence and assist agencies in selecting appropriately prepared social workers to fill their positions.

A Snapshot of Today's Social Workers and Their Work

Who are the people who have elected a career in social work? It is difficult to determine accurately the characteristics of today's social workers because a single source based on an agreed upon definition of social work does not exist. NASW reports a membership of approximately 150,000, but given that more than 500,000 social workers graduated from CSWE accredited programs in the past 30 years, it is clear that only a fraction of the qualified social workers have elected to join NASW.[15] All social workers are not required to be licensed, but approximately 310,000[16] hold a state license to practice social work. Based on positions classified by employers as social work jobs, the Bureau of Labor Statistics (BLS) estimates there are approximately 595,000 social workers in the United States. Finally, the most current population survey in which people self-classify their occupation estimates that there are 670,000 to 730,000 social workers.[17] Each estimate is flawed, but it is likely that the BLS estimate is the most accurate representation of the number of practicing social workers in the United States today.

The most current and complete data set regarding social workers and their practice activities was conducted by the NASW Center for Workforce Studies. The 2004 study included a random sample of 10,650 licensed social workers from 48 states and the District of Columbia with a 49.4 percent response rate. Thus it can be considered a good representation of licensed social workers. The social workers reporting in this study were 81 percent female and 86 percent non-Hispanic white persons.[18] One limitation is that a number of states have not embraced the basic social worker (BSW) in their licensing, and many baccalaureate social workers are not licensed—thus only 12 percent of the sample practices at that level.

The data in Table 3.1 indicate that mental health, as a social worker's primary practice area, is almost twice as likely as any other focus of practice. Also, although more than 80 percent of the social workers are employed in some form of organization or agency, the largest single practice setting was private practice. This represents a substantial change over the past few decades in the ability of social workers to attract clients to their independent entrepreneurial practice. Increasingly, social workers must be able to manage their own small business, as well as administer large social agencies. The primary work, or function, social workers perform in these jobs is working directly with clients as individuals or in families and groups.

Table 3.1

Characteristics of Licensed Social Workers: Practice Areas, Employment Settings, and Job Functions

Social Worker Characteristic	Percentage
Primary Practice Area	
Mental Health	37
Children/families/adolescents	19
Medical health	13
Aging	9
Schools	8
Developmental disabilities	3
Addictions	3
Primary Employment Setting	
Private practice (solo or group)	18
Social service agency	15
Behavioral health clinic	9
Hospital/medical center	9
School (preschool through grade 12)	9
Nursing home/residential group care facility	5
Case management agency	2
Courts/justice system	2
Primary Job Function (20 hours or more per week)	
Direct/clinical practice	61
Administration/management	20
Supervision	7
Planning/community organization/social policy	7
Consultation	6
Teaching/training	6

Source: Tracy Whitaker, Toby Weismiller, and Elizabeth Clark, *Assuring the Sufficiency of a Frontline Workforce: A National Study of Licensed Social Workers, Executive Summary* (Washington, D.C.: NASW Center for Workforce Studies, 2006), pp. 15–19.

Who are the clients of social workers? Table 3.2 indicates that social workers must be prepared to work with clients from all age groups—from young children to older adults. Even if a social worker works primarily with one age group, he or she inevitably works with family members and others across the age spectrum. The need for social workers to become culturally competent in working with all racial/ethnic groups is

Table 3.2

Characteristics of Social Workers' Clients

Client Characteristic	Percentage	
Client Age	51% or more of workload	Any part of workload
Children	15	62
Adolescents	15	78
Adults	39	90
Older adults	25	78
Client Race/Ethnicity		
Non-Hispanic white	59	99
Black/African American	10	85
Hispanic/Latino	5	77
Asian/Pacific Islander	1	49
Native American/Alaska Native	1	30
Client Condition	**Client issue**	
Psychosocial stressors	76	
Medical conditions (acute and chronic)	48	
Co-occurring conditions	42	
Mental illness	39	
Affective conditions	33	
Substance abuse	27	
Physical disabilities	19	
Developmental disabilities	10	

Source: Tracy Whitaker, Toby Weismiller, and Elizabeth Clark, *Assuring the Sufficiency of a Frontline Workforce: A National Study of Licensed Social Workers, Executive Summary* (Washington, D.C.: NASW Center for Workforce Studies, 2006), pp. 15–19.

evident from the data indicating that, although social workers may work primarily with persons of one background, they end up doing some work with persons from all groups. Finally, social workers deal with a wide variety of client conditions. More than two-thirds deal with clients experiencing psychosocial stressors as these are interrelated with other problems, but many social workers also deal with social issues related to medical conditions, mental illness, and many other conditions.

A 2004 member salary survey conducted by NASW helps to provide a picture of the earning power of social workers. The median annual income for social workers in that membership sample was $51,900 for full-time social workers during the calendar year 2003.[19] Previous membership studies indicated that social workers begin at a lower salary level upon completing the professional degree and then reach the median salary at around 15 years of experience. Prior data also indicate that the typical person with a BSW degree earns about $1,000 per month less than the person with an MSW degree, and a person with a doctorate earns about $1,000 per month more than the MSW graduate.[20]

These salary levels are not sufficient in themselves to draw top-quality professionals to this demanding work. While social work wages are considered "high" by the Bureau of Labor Statistics (i.e., in the second highest quartile of earnings for all occupations),[21] social work salaries are relatively low for positions requiring professional preparation. Other rewards from the work must therefore be considered more important than earning power to maintain a competent labor force of social workers. In a substantial analysis of the labor market for social workers, Michael Barth concludes that social workers' "taste" for providing their services is exceptionally strong. Barth indicates that, from an economist's perspective, a strong taste for a profession implies that the worker would seek that work even if it conveys greater risk of low pay and despite the potential of the worker to earn greater pay elsewhere.[22] In short, social workers appear to be more attracted to the opportunity to make a difference in the lives of people than to select a profession that will result in high earning power.

Concluding Comment

Since its inception more than a century ago, social work has emerged as a comprehensive helping profession. From the beginning, social workers sought that elusive common denominator that would depict this profession as clearly as possible and help social work form into a cohesive entity. The characteristic of working simultaneously with both people and their environments to improve social functioning has consistently served as social work's primary mission and thus differentiates social work from the other helping professions. In addition to helping people deal with their environments, social workers also consider it their mission to bring about social change in order to prevent problems or to make social institutions more responsive to the needs of people—especially the most vulnerable members of the society. With this person and environment focus, social workers provide a combination of caring, counseling, and changing activities that help people improve the quality of their lives and, therefore, help the society accomplish its goal of promoting the general welfare. In Box 3.1, the practice activities of Demetria (see Chapter 1), illustrate how her social work orientation plays out in her work with the Miles family.

Data in Table 3.1 indicate that social workers today are employed in a wide range of practice areas, from mental health to addictions; work mostly within the context of some form of agency or organization; and mostly work directly with clients to address social issues. Table 3.2 also reinforces social work's claim to be especially concerned with the persons in society who are most vulnerable to social problems. They work with people of all ages and races or ethnic groups, and they address a wide range of client conditions.

Social work has evolved a career ladder that recognizes professionals at four levels: basic, specialized, independent, and advanced. This classification scheme recognizes that at each of the four levels somewhat different job activities occur. The two entry levels (i.e., basic and specialized professional levels) require that the worker complete the requisite educational preparation represented in the accreditation standards of the Council on Social Work Education. At the latter two levels, additional practice experience and expertise and/or advanced education warrant the recognition.

Box 3.1

Demetria's Social Work Orientation

The case in Chapter 1 revealed a social worker's approach to investigating and beginning service when addressing a possible child abuse or neglect complaint. Demetria, the social worker, had just completed her social work degree, and the report from the school related to Joseph Miles was her first "solo" case. Of course, she had the backup of her supervisor, but nevertheless she was understandably apprehensive about being able to do a good job. Clearly the demands for knowledge and skill were beyond that expected of a *natural helper* or *volunteer*. Complex human issues such as this require a well-equipped *professional helper*, in this case, a professional social worker.

Demetria's work clearly demonstrated a commitment to *social betterment* as she carried her assessment beyond the minimum required to establish or reject the suspected child abuse. She sought to understand and address the multiple issues that were combining to affect Joseph; was *versatile* in her practice approach by addressing individual, family, and community issues; and did something about what she found (an *action orientation*). Because none of the issues in this case were unchangeable, the work did not fall into the *caring* aspect of social work's mission. Most of the effort involved the *counseling* and *changing* functions that social workers address. Fitting Demetria's work into the NASW *definition of social work*, the paraphrasing might read "Demetria's practice was the professional activity of helping Joseph and the Miles family restore their capacity for social functioning and creating a more supportive societal resource for those needing employment assistance."

In the NASW classification of levels of professional social work practice, Demetria was a *basic social worker*, having just completed her BSW preparation, and her supervisor was probably an *independent* or *advanced social worker* according to that classification system. Demetria's practice approach was that of an *initial generalist*. She did not try to fit Joseph and his mom into a specialized method or practice approach. Instead, she started by identifying their issues and drawing on multiple approaches to resolve those issues, such as individual counseling (for Joseph and his mother); involvement in a peer group (for Joseph); referral to other needed resources in the community; and a consideration of social action to improve the community resources.

KEY WORDS AND CONCEPTS

Natural and professional helping
Social betterment
Social functioning
Human diversity
Caring/Counseling/Changing
"Working Definition" of social work
"NASW Definition" of social work
Dual focus on person and environment
Generalist social work practice
Specialist social work practice
Traditional practice methods
NASW classification of practice levels (basic, specialized, independent, advanced)

SUGGESTED INFORMATION SOURCES

Canadian Association of Social Workers, http://www.casw-acts.ca.
Corey, Mariane Schneider, and Gerald Corey. *Becoming a Helper,* 4th ed. Pacific Grove, CA: Brooks/Cole, 2003.
LeCroy, Craig W. *The Call to Social Work: Life Stories.* Washington, D.C.: NASW Press, 2002.
National Association of Social Workers, http://www.naswdc.org.
Payne, Malcolm. *What Is Professional Social Work,* 2nd ed. Chicago, IL: Lyceum Books, 2006.

ENDNOTES

1. For a brief description of a number of practice approaches, see Bradford W. Sheafor and Charles R. Horejsi, *Techniques and Guidelines for Social Work Practice,* 7th ed. (Boston: Allyn & Bacon, 2006), Chapter 6.
2. American Association of Social Workers, *Social Casework: Generic and Specific: A Report of the Milford Conference* (New York: National Association of Social Workers, 1974), p. 11. (Original work published in 1929.)
3. Harriet M. Bartlett, "Towards Clarification and Improvement of Social Work Practice," *Social Work* 3 (April 1958): 5–7.
4. See *Social Work* 19 (September 1974), *Social Work* 22 (September 1977), and *Social Work* 26 (January 1981).
5. National Association of Social Workers, *Standards for Social Service Manpower* (Washington, D.C.: NASW, 1973), pp. 4–5.
6. Mary E. Richmond, *Social Diagnosis* (New York: Russell Sage Foundation, 1917).
7. Edith Abbott, "The Social Caseworker and the Enforcement of Industrial Legislation," in *Proceedings of the National Conference on Social Work, 1918* (Chicago: Rogers and Hall, 1919), p. 313.
8. Ernest V. Hollis and Alice L. Taylor, *Social Work Education in the United States* (New York: Columbia University Press, 1951).
9. Rosalie Balinsky, "Generic Practice in Graduate Social Work Curricula: A Study of Educators' Experiences and Attitudes," *Journal of Education for Social Work* 18 (Fall 1982): 47.
10. Mona S. Schatz, Lowell E. Jenkins, and Bradford W. Sheafor, "Milford Redefined: A Model of Initial and Advanced Generalist Social Work," *Journal of Social Work Education* 26 (Fall 1990): 217–231.
11. Council on Social Work Education, *Statistics on Social Work Education in the United States: 2006* (Alexandria, VA: Council on Social Work Education, 2007), pp. 4, 16.

12. Ibid., pp. 4, 12.
13. Ibid., pp. 4, 17.
14. *NASW Standards for the Classification of Social Work Practice*, Policy Statement 4 (Silver Spring, MD: National Association of Social Workers, 1981), p. 9.
15. Bradford W. Sheafor, "Three Decades of Baccalaureate Social Work: A Grade Card on How the Professionalization of the BSW has Played Out," *Journal of Baccalaureate Social Work* 6 (Spring 2001): 32.
16. Tracy Whitaker, Toby Weismiller, and Elizabeth Clark, *Assuring the Sufficiency of a Frontline Workforce: A National Study of Licensed Social Workers, Executive Summary* (Washington, D.C.: NASW Center for Workforce Studies, 2006), p. 9.
17. Bureau of Labor Statistics, "Occupational Employment and Wages, November 2007." http://www.bls.gov/opub/mlr/2007/11/art5full.pdf.
18. Whitaker, op. cit., p. 9.
19. "Survey Data Show Earnings Increased," *NASW News* 49 (October 2004): 1.
20. Practice Research Network Report 1–1, *Social Work Income* (Washington, D.C.: National Association of Social Workers, 2000).
21. U.S. Bureau of Labor Statistics, "May 2004 National Occupational Employment and Wage Estimates." http://www.bls.gov/oes/2004/may/oes_21Co.htm.
22. Michael C. Barth, "Social Work Labor Market: A First Look," *Social Work* 48 (January 2003): 9–19.

Social work pioneer Jane Addams visits with young women at Chicago's Hull House in the early 1900s.

chapter 4

The Emergence of Social Work as a Profession

> **Prefatory Comment**
>
> The growth and development of social work were not planned events. The profession evolved from the humanitarian response to human suffering in the late 1800s that led to the creation of a workforce to address social problems and later to the profession of social work. The title of this book, *Social Work: A Profession of Many Faces*, highlights the importance social work has given to becoming a fully recognized profession. This chapter examines social work's emergence in the United States, with emphasis on how the desire to become a profession has shaped its actions. It begins with a review of the nature of professions, particularly the helping professions, and traces the emergence of social work during the past century.

A field of sociological inquiry is devoted to the definition and description of the nature of professions. One of the central figures in this field, Wilbert Moore, concluded that "to have one's occupational status accepted as professional or to have one's occupational conduct judged as professional is highly regarded in all post industrial societies and in at least the modernizing sectors of others."[1] Professions are highly regarded, in part, because they have been granted authority to perform essential services that ensure survival and help people enhance the quality of their lives. The benefit of being considered professional has drawn many occupational groups to claim professional status. The term has sometimes been used to describe persons who are paid for activities that others might perform for recreation or pleasure or is at times applied when a person becomes highly specialized in an area of competence, for example, a real "pro" at finding bargains on the Internet. In this book, however, the term *profession* is used in its more traditional sense of identifying a set of carefully prepared and highly qualified persons who assist people in dealing with complex matters in their lives.

Three elements help to explain the unique characteristics of the occupations that are considered to be professions. First, professionals must be free of constraints that might limit their ability to select what they consider to be the best way to assist people in situations to resolve problems or improve the quality of their lives. The maintenance of this *professional autonomy* has been most successful in the "private professions" that typically contract directly with their clients (e.g., medicine, dentistry),

53

although increasingly constraints imposed by managed care companies are eroding this flexibility. In agency-based or "public professions" such as social work and teaching, organizations employ the professionals and then contract with the clients to provide the needed services. In these situations, it is recognized that the organization's rules and regulations will inevitably limit the autonomy of the professionals to exercise their independent judgment.

Second, society has granted *professional authority* to a few people who have acquired the necessary knowledge and skills to provide the needed services in a given area of professional practice. Society grants this authority because it has, in effect, determined that it is inefficient, if not impossible, for every person to acquire all the knowledge and skill needed to meet complex human needs. Thus, these professionals are given the exclusive right to make judgments and give advice to their clients in their specific service areas. In granting this professional authority, society, in essence, gives up the right to judge these professionals except in extreme cases of incompetent or unethical practice. Society depends on the members of that profession to determine the requisite entrance preparation and to be sure those who are practicing as members of that profession do so competently.

Third, when the right to judge practice is relinquished by granting professional authority, the public becomes vulnerable and rightfully expects the professions to protect them from abuses that may accrue from the professional monopoly. Hughes indicates that the motto of the professions must be *credat emptor* ("buyer trust"), as opposed to the motto of the marketplace, *caveat emptor* ("buyer beware").[2] For example, where the layperson would rarely question the prescription given by a physician, that same person might be very cautious when buying a used car and might have it thoroughly tested by an independent mechanic before making a purchase. To maintain this buyer trust, the professions must be accountable to the public that has granted them the sanction to perform these services. To establish and maintain this *professional responsibility,* professions develop codes that identify the expected ethical behavior of practitioners and establish mechanisms for policing their membership regarding unethical or incompetent practice.

In a sense, the professions and society struck a deal. In exchange for responsible service in sensitive areas of life, the professions were granted exclusive authority, that is, a *professional monopoly,* to offer these services.

How does an occupation achieve recognition as a profession? There is no precise dividing line between occupations and the professions. It is most useful to think of a continuum of occupations, from those that have few characteristics associated with the professions to those that have many such attributes. Ronald Pavalko summarizes the attributes necessary to achieve recognition as a profession.[3]

▶ The profession must possess a body of theory and intellectual understanding about the people to be served, the condition to be addressed, and the intervention approaches to be used.

▶ The services provided by the profession must relate to a need that is highly valued and for which the society is willing to take responsibility if that need is not met by other social institutions. These services are concerned with aspects of people's lives that require specialized knowledge and skill to address highly sensitive issues, such

as their health, spirituality, learning, or their interpersonal and sometimes intimate interactions with others.
- ▸ The work to be done is not routine and cannot be reduced to tightly prescribed steps or procedures; thus, the professional must have the autonomy to use individual discretion about how the work is performed.
- ▸ The professional must complete an extensive education in which both the general knowledge for informed citizenship is required and the specialized knowledge and skill needed to perform the work are transmitted from the experienced professional to the novice.
- ▸ The profession maintains its focus on service to the clients, as opposed to responding primarily to the worker's self-interest.
- ▸ The professionals are drawn to the work by a sense of commitment, a "calling," or a "taste" for the work to be accomplished.
- ▸ The professionals perceive the profession as a community of persons with common interests and goals with which they identify.
- ▸ The profession creates and promotes adherence to a code of ethical behavior that informs the members of appropriate worker–client relationships and is used to determine if members have abused the privilege of membership in that profession.

The following process, typically followed by professions when developing the requisite attributes, has been identified by Harold Wilensky:

1. A substantial number of people become engaged on a full-time basis in providing the needed services.
2. Training schools or educational programs are established to prepare new practitioners with the advanced knowledge required for the work to be done.
3. A professional organization is formed to promote the interests of the members of that profession.
4. The professional organization engages in political activities to gain protection of the monopoly of the profession in its area through licensing or other forms of regulation of the profession.
5. The professional organization develops a code of ethical behavior to guide the professional's interactions with clients, other professionals, and the general public.[4]

The pattern identified by Wilensky accurately describes the process of social work's evolution as a profession. As professional organizations emerge, a conflict of interest becomes evident. The purely altruistic expectation of professions begins to be compromised because the professional associations operate primarily to promote the self-interest of the professionals, with the interests of clients or patients too often becoming secondary.

Social Work as a Profession: A Historical Perspective

Social work did not evolve in a vacuum. A series of events affected its development and will continue to shape social work in the future. Some of those events are represented by major factors in the history of the United States such as settlement patterns, wars, international conditions, economic fluctuations, the philosophy of elected political leaders, and others. These events influenced decisions about the extent to which this society would respond to its members' social needs and, subsequently, to the social programs that would be supported.

Table 4.1 identifies some of the important events that affected the evolution of U.S. society's approach to the human services and shows selected mileposts in the development of social work. In columns 1 and 2, the table lists dates and events that identify a historical event that may be familiar to the reader, such as the U.S. Civil War or the Great Depression. Column 3 identifies important events that shaped social programs (e.g., the Pierce Veto), and column 4 lists some critical events in the development of the social work profession—for example, publication of *Social Diagnosis* in 1917.

From Volunteers to an Occupation (Prior to 1915)

The roots of social work may be found in the extensive volunteer movement during the formative years of the United States. In the colonial period, for example, it was assumed that individuals and families would care for themselves, but if further difficulties existed, one could depend on *mutual aid*. Friends, neighbors, or other representatives of the community could be counted on to help out when needed. Volunteer activities involved interaction with the poor, the ill, and those experiencing other social problems. As social agencies began to develop, they soon learned how to train volunteers in constructive ways to relate to clients and improved their ability to be helpful.

Developing out of this background came social work as an occupation. The first paid social work–type positions in the country were jobs in the Special Relief Department of the United States Sanitary (i.e., public health) Commission. Beginning as a voluntary agency and then receiving public support as the Civil War progressed, the Special Relief Department and its agents served Union soldiers and their families experiencing social and health problems due to the war. Wartime needs temporarily opened the door to providing social services, and the outstanding performance of these workers helped pave the way for other positions in social work. Several women involved in the war effort performed important leadership roles in the development of human services. For example, Dorothea Dix (Superintendent of Nurses in the U.S. Sanitary Commission) previously had provided leadership in an attempt to secure federal government support for mental hospitals; Clara Barton later founded the American Red Cross; Josephine Shaw Lowell helped start the Charity Organization Society in New York City and also headed the Consumers' League, which worked to protect shopgirls from exploitation; Sojourner Truth gave leadership to the National Freedman's Relief Association; and Harriet Tubman, a central figure in the Underground Railroad, subsequently established a home for elderly African Americans. Following the war, the Special Relief Department was closed.

A short time later, paid social work also appeared when the Massachusetts Board of Charities was established. Founded under the leadership of Samuel Gridley Howe, an advocate for persons who are physically and mentally disabled, this agency coordinated services in almshouses, hospitals, and other institutions of the state. Although its powers were limited to inspection and advice, the Board gained wide acceptance. The concept of boards overseeing state services spread to other states in the 1870s and became the forerunners to today's state departments of human services.

Table 4.1

Timetable of Selected Events in Social Welfare and Social Work History

Approximate Date	U.S. History Event	Social Welfare Event	Social Work Event
Founding of United States	Agriculture-based society	Family responsibility	
	Open frontier	Mutual aid	
	Slavery prevalent	Puritan ethic	
	Open immigration	Town meetings	
		Orphan homes and first charitable societies	
		Poorhouses	
1776	Declaration of Independence Revolutionary War	Growth of voluntary social agencies	
	Act for the Gradual Abolition of Slavery (Pennsylvania)	Society for Alleviating the Miseries of Public Prisons	
	Era of merchant philanthropy		
1789	George Washington inaugurated		
1800	United States prohibits importation of slaves	Elizabeth Seton founds Sisters of Charity	
	War of 1812	Mass. General Hospital	
		Child labor laws	
		Gallaudet School for Deaf	
	Anti-Slavery Movement	Society for the Prevention of Pauperism	
	Chinese immigration began	NY House of Refuge (for juveniles)	Dorothea Dix begins crusade for improved conditions in "insane asylums"
1850	Emergence of industrial society	Pierce Veto	
		Children's Aid Societies	
	Rise of cities and urbanization	Orphan Trains	
1860	U.S. Civil War	YMCA movement	
		Freedman's aid societies	U.S. Sanitary Commission
		Mass. Board of Charities	(first paid social workers)

(Continued)

Table 4.1

(Continued)

Approximate Date	U.S. History Event	Social Welfare Event	Social Work Event
1877	Reconstruction Era	Buffalo Charity Aid Society	Friendly visitors
		Hull House founded	Settlement workers
			National Conference on Charities and Correction
1898	Spanish-American War	First Juvenile Court	NY School of Philanthropy
1910		White House Conference on Children	Medical social work
		U.S. Children's Bureau	Psychiatric social work
		Community Chest (federated fund raising)	School social work
1915	Progressive Era		Flexner, "Is Social Work a Profession?"
			Richmond, *Social Diagnosis*
			National Social Workers Exchange
		NAACP	
		National Urban League	Association of Training Schools for Prof. SW
1920	Women's Suffrage (19th Amendment)	County and state relief agencies	American Association of Social Workers
			American Association of Schools of Social Work
1929	Stock Market Crash The Great Depression	Civilian Conservation Corps (CCC)	
1935		Social Security Act Works Progress Administration (WPA)	
1941	United States enters World War II	U.S.O. organized National Social Welfare Assembly	American Association of Group Workers
			National Association of Schools of Social Administration
	End of WW II		
1945	Postwar recovery period	U.S. Department of Health, Education, and Welfare	Association for the Study of Community Organization

Table 4.1
(Continued)

Approximate Date	U.S. History Event	Social Welfare Event	Social Work Event
			Social Work Research Group
1952			Council on Social Work Education (merger of AASSW and NASSW)
1955	Korean Conflict Civil Rights Movement		National Association of Social Workers (merger of six professional specialization groups and Am. Assn. of Social Workers)
	Women's Movement	Indian Health Service	Greenwood, "Attributes of a Profession" NASW
			"Working Definition of Social Work Practice"
1960		Juvenile Delinquency Act	
	Kennedy administration	Herrington, *The Other America*	NASW "Code of Ethics" Academy of Certified Social Workers (ACSW)
		Equal Pay Act	
		Community Mental Health Act	
1963	Johnson administration Vietnam War	Food Stamp Act	
	Black Power Movement	Civil Rights Act of 1964	
		Economic Opportunity Act	
		Older American Act	
		Indian Civil Rights Act	
1965	Welfare Rights Movement Martin Luther King, Jr., assassination	Immigration Act of 1965	
		Medicare Act	
1968		Medicaid	
	Nixon administration Gay Liberation Movement		

(Continued)

Table 4.1
(Continued)

Approximate Date	U.S. History Event	Social Welfare Event	Social Work Event
		Supplemental Security Income (SSI) approved	
1970			NASW recognition of baccalaureate social worker as professional
1972		Child Abuse Prevention & Treatment Act	
1974	Ford administration	Education of All Handicapped Children Act	NASW "Conceptual Frameworks" series
			CSWE begins BSW accreditation process (generalist emphasis)
			CSWE approves advanced standing for BSWs
			Expansion of doctoral social work education (GADE)
	Carter administration	Social Security Block Grant Act (decentralize some programs to states)	
	AIDS epidemic		
1978		Indian Child Welfare Act	Association of Social Work (licensing) Boards
	Reagan administration	Privatization of human services expanded	
1982		Tax Equity and Fiscal Responsibility Act of 1982 (cutbacks in human service provisions by federal government)	
	Equal Rights Amendment (ratification fails)		
1988	George H. W. Bush administration		
1990			Academy of Certified Baccalaureate Social Workers (ACBSW)

Table 4.1
(Continued)

Approximate Date	U.S. History Event	Social Welfare Event	Social Work Event
	Persian Gulf War	Americans with Disabilities Act	Social workers licensed in all states, D.C., and some territories
1993	Clinton administration	Individuals with Disabilities Education Act	
1996	Oklahoma City federal building bombing	Health care reform fails	ACBSW discontinued "Code of Ethics" revised
	Columbine High School massacre	Family and Medical Leave Act	
		Personal Responsibility and Work Opportunity Reconciliation Act	
2001	George W. Bush administration		ACSW examination discontinued
	September 11 terrorist attacks		
	Invasion of Afghanistan		
	War on Iraq initiated		
2004			NASW Workforce Center Social Work Congress Wingspread Conference on Social Work Unity Social Work Reinvestment Act introduced
2009	Obama administration		

The Massachusetts Board of Charities also introduced social research into human service delivery. An 1893 report, for example, identified the causes of poverty as "first, physical degradation and inferiority; second, moral perversity; third, mental incapacity; fourth, accidents and infirmities; fifth, unjust and unwise laws, and the customs of society."[5] Although the approach was perhaps more moralistic than would be found in social work today, the report reflected the understanding that both personal and societal factors contribute to poverty.

Another significant development leading to the emergence of social work was the establishment of the Charity Organization Society (COS) of Buffalo, New York, in 1877. Modeled after an organization in London, charity organization societies sprang up in a number of communities with the dual purposes of finding means to help the poor and preventing the poor from taking advantage of the numerous uncoordinated social agencies that provided financial assistance. Leaders in social work from the COS movement included Mary Richmond, who helped identify a theory of practice in her books *Friendly Visiting Among the Poor* (1899) and *Social Diagnosis* (1917); Edward T. Devine, a founder of the New York School of Philanthropy in 1898; and Porter Lee, who was instrumental in founding the American Association of Schools of Social Work in 1919.

Another important development that contributed to the emergence of social work was the Settlement House Movement initiated in 1886. Patterning settlement houses after London's Toynbee Hall, settlements were established in New York and Chicago. Within fifteen years, about one hundred settlement houses were operating in the United States. The settlements helped the poor learn skills required for urban living and simultaneously provided leadership in political action efforts to improve the social environment. Robert Bremner sums up the impact of the settlement movement:

> Where others thought of the people of the slums as miserable wretches deserving either pity or correction, settlement residents knew them as much entitled to respect as any other members of the community. Numerous young men and women who lived and worked in the settlements during the 1890s carried this attitude with them into later careers in social work, business, government service, and the arts.[6]

The residents of Chicago's Hull House are a good example. Its founder, Jane Addams, won the Nobel Peace Prize in 1931; Julia Lathrop became the first director of the U.S. Children's Bureau and was succeeded by other Hull House alumnae Katherine Lenroot and Grace Abbott, thus contributing to the protection of children and youth for several decades.

The efforts to integrate the African American population into the mainstream of U.S. society following the Civil War also contributed to the development of social work. George Haynes, the first African American graduate of the New York School of Philanthropy, for example, helped found the National Urban League, while Mary McLeod Bethune, who gave leadership to the education of African American women, was a founder of the National Council of Negro Women and was influential in making New Deal policies more equitable for the African American population.

Social work expanded into another setting in the early 1900s when Richard Cabot and Ida Cannon opened a social work program at the Massachusetts General Hospital. There social workers provided services for patients experiencing health-related social problems and simultaneously worked to strengthen the services of related health and welfare agencies throughout the community. Roy Lubove identifies the significance of this development for the professionalization of social work:

> The enlistment of medical social workers marked an important stage in the development of professional social work. (An occupation) limited to the charity organization and child welfare societies provided too narrow a base for professional development, associated as it was with problems of relief and economic dependency. Medical social work added an entirely new institutional setting in which to explore the implications of casework theory and practice.[7]

Medical social workers became interested in professional education as a means of moving beyond social work's "warm heart" image and into a more disciplined understanding of psychological or social conditions as the base of patient distress. In 1912, the hospital's one-year training program in medical social work was established in the Boston School of Social Work.

Through these years, social work jobs were also springing up in other practice areas such as mental hygiene (mental health), prisons, employment and labor relations, and schools. Beginning in 1873, an organization designed to draw together members of this diverse occupation was formed, the National Conference on Charities. Later renamed the National Conference on Charities and Correction, this organization brought volunteer and professional staff members of social agencies together to exchange ideas about the provision of services, discuss social problems, and study the characteristics of effective practice. By the time World War I began, social work was an established occupation clearly distinguishable from the many volunteer groups and other occupations concerned with the well-being of members of U.S. society.

Professional Emergence (1915–1950)

With social work firmly established as an occupation, attention then turned to its development as a profession. At the 1915 meeting of the National Conference on Charities and Correction, Abraham Flexner addressed the subject, "Is Social Work a Profession?" Dr. Flexner, an authority on graduate education, had previously done a penetrating study that led to major changes in medical education. The organizers of this session of the National Conference apparently hoped Flexner would assure them that social work was, or was about to become, a full-fledged profession. However, that was not in the cards. Flexner spelled out six criteria that an occupation must meet to be considered a profession:

1. Professions are essentially intellectual operations with large individual responsibility.
2. They derive their raw material from science and learning.
3. This material is worked up to a practical and clear-cut end.
4. Professions possess an educationally communicable technique.
5. They tend to self-organization.
6. They become increasingly altruistic in motivation.[8]

Based on these criteria, Flexner concluded that social work had not yet made it into the professional elite. Following Flexner's admonition to "go forth and build thyself a profession," social workers busily attended to these functions over the next thirty-five years.

One effort was to develop a code of ethics. In 1921 Mary Richmond indicated that, "we need a code; something to abide by, or else we will have low social standing."[9] One code, the "Experimental Draft of a Code of Ethics for Social Case Workers," was discussed at the 1923 meeting of the National Conference on Social Welfare. Although this proposed code was never acted on, it represented a beginning effort at formulating a statement of professional ethics.

Probably the greatest amount of effort was devoted to self-organization. The National Social Workers Exchange opened in 1917 to provide vocational counseling and job placement for social workers and later became actively involved in the identification and definition of professional standards. In 1921 its functions were taken over by the broader American Association of Social Workers, which made significant efforts to develop a comprehensive professional association. This effort was later weakened by the attempts of some specialized practice areas to develop their own professional organizations. A chronology of the development of these specialized groups follows:[10]

- 1918 American Association of Hospital Social Workers
- 1919 National Association of Visiting Teachers
- 1926 American Association of Psychiatric Social Workers
- 1936 American Association for the Study of Group Work
- 1946 Association for the Study of Community Organization
- 1949 Social Work Research Group

At this point, it was not clear whether social work was one or many professions.

Another development during this period concerned the required preparation to enter the social work profession. Social work education had begun as agency-based training, but a concerted effort was made during this period to transfer it to colleges and universities, where other professions had located their professional education. In 1919 the Association of Training Schools for Professional Social Workers was established with seventeen charter members—both agency and university affiliated schools. The purpose of that organization was to develop standards for all social work education. By 1927 considerable progress toward that purpose had been made, and the Association of Training Schools reorganized into the American Association of Schools of Social Work (AASSW). Although education programs had been offered in agencies, as well as at both undergraduate and graduate levels in colleges and universities, the AASSW determined that by 1939 only university-affiliated programs with two-year graduate programs would be recognized as professional social work education.

That action led to a revolt by schools whose undergraduate programs prepared professionals to meet the staffing needs of the social agencies in their states. A second professional education organization was formed in 1942, the National Association of Schools of Social Administration, made up largely of public universities in the Midwest that offered baccalaureate-level and one-year graduate-level professional education programs. Ernest Harper, a leader in that organization, described this development as "a protest movement against unrealistic and premature insistence upon graduate training and overemphasis upon professional casework as the major social work technique."[11]

With leadership from governmental and voluntary practice agencies, the two organizations were later merged (1952) into the Council on Social Work Education (CSWE) following the landmark Hollis–Taylor study of social work education.[12] The outcome of that decision favored the two-year master's program as the minimum educational requirement for full professional status. Undergraduate social work education temporarily faded from the scene.

Another important area of concern that was given only limited attention during this period was strengthening the knowledge and skill base of social work practice. Richmond's rich contribution, *Social Diagnosis,* was the first effort to formalize a communicable body of techniques applicable to the diverse settings in which social caseworkers were found.[13] Momentum from this thrust, however, was lost as social work slipped into the grasp of the popular psychoanalytic approach. Nathan Cohen comments, "The search for a method occurred just at the time the impact of psychoanalysis was being felt. Did social work, in its haste for professional stature, reach out for a ready-made methodology for treating sick people, thus closing itself off from the influence of developments in the other sciences?"[14] This question must be answered in the affirmative. By adopting the helping methodology that was currently in vogue, social work embraced firmly, but perhaps inappropriately, the private model of professionalism.

Consolidating the Gains (1950–1970)

The move to consolidate the accrediting bodies for the schools of social work into the CSWE set an important precedent for the field and was part of a movement to treat social work as a single and unified profession. In 1950 the several specialized associations and the American Association of Social Workers agreed to form the Temporary Inter-Association Council of Social Work Membership Organizations (TIAC). The purpose behind the formation of TIAC was to bring these specialized groups into one central professional association. After considerable efforts by the specialties to maintain their identities, TIAC proposed a merger of the several groups in 1952. By 1955 this was accomplished, and the National Association of Social Workers (NASW) was formed.

NASW membership rose from 28,000 to 45,000 between 1961 and 1965, largely because of the formation of the Academy of Certified Social Workers (ACSW), which required both NASW membership and a two-year period of supervised experience. Many job descriptions were revised to require membership in the Academy, forcing social workers to join the NASW and obtain certification.

The late 1950s were a time of great introspection, and the professional journal *Social Work* was filled with articles such as "The Nature of Social Work,"[15] "How Social Will Social Work Be?,"[16] and "A Changing Profession in a Changing World."[17] Perhaps the most significant work was Ernest Greenwood's classic article, "Attributes of a Profession," in 1957.[18] Greenwood identified five critical attributes of professions that, depending on the degree to which they have been accomplished, determine the level of professionalism for any occupational group:

1. A systematic body of theory
2. Professional authority
3. Sanction of the community
4. A regulative code of ethics
5. A professional culture

He related the development of social work to each of these five criteria and concluded that social work was now a profession. He observed:

> When we hold up social work against the model of the professions presented above, it does not take long to decide whether to classify it within the professional or nonprofessional occupations. Social work is already a profession; it has too many points of congruence with the model to be classifiable otherwise.[19]

To the credit of social workers, they were as stimulated by Greenwood's declaration that they had become a profession as they were by Flexner's conclusion that they were not yet in the select circle. In 1958 the NASW published the "Working Definition of Social Work Practice," a valuable beginning to the difficult task of identifying professional boundaries.[20] This was followed by Gordon's excellent critique, which helped strengthen and clarify some parts of the working definition, particularly in relation to knowledge, values, and practice methodology.[21] In 1960, the NASW adopted a Code of Ethics to serve as a guide for ethical professional practice,[22] thus completing the steps to become a fully recognized profession.

Turning Away from the Elitist Professional Model (1970–Present)

From the turn of the twentieth century to the late 1960s, social work displayed a pattern typical of an emerging profession. It created a single association to guide professional growth and development; adopted a code of ethical professional behavior; provided for graduate-level university-based professional schools and acquired recognition to accredit those educational programs; successfully obtained licensing for social work practice in some states; conducted public education campaigns to educate the public about social work; achieved recognition for social work among the helping professions; and moved in the direction of other professions by increasing specialization and limiting access to the profession. Indeed, social work was on its way to carving its niche among the helping professions.

However, social work did not vigorously pursue the path that would lead to even greater professional status. Perhaps influenced by a renewed spirit of concern emanating from the Civil Rights, Welfare Rights, and Women's Rights movements, the development of social work as a profession during the 1970s and 1980s was marked by ambivalence over following the more traditional format of the established professions.

First, there was a resurgence of social change activity on the part of social workers. A legacy from Lyndon Johnson's Great Society programs was federal support, in the form of jobs and other resources, toward efforts to eliminate social problems and alleviate human suffering. Social work was already committed to those goals, and social workers were prepared to move away from their clinical orientation and onto the front lines of social action.

For social workers bent on achieving higher professional status, activist social workers were sometimes unpopular. Their somewhat controversial activities created an unwelcome public image of social workers as militant activists on the front lines of social change. This change in the balance of activities performed by social workers, however, helped to bring social work back to its roots and reestablish the "change" orientation in its purposes of caring, counseling, and changing the society. The more liberal political climate that supported social work activism was short lived. Federal support for programs encouraging social change dwindled and was nearly nonexistent under the Reagan and George H. W. Bush administrations.

Next, in 1970, NASW made a dramatic move by revising its membership requirements to give full membership privileges to anyone who had completed a baccalaureate degree in social work from an undergraduate program approved by CSWE. In opposition to the pattern of professions becoming more exclusive, social work opened its membership to more people by determining that professional qualifications could be gained through professional education at the undergraduate level. However, social work has been uneasy about operating as a multilevel profession, and, although the NASW classification system is clear about the "basic social worker" being viewed as professional, the social worker at this level has never been fully embraced by many MSW social workers. Some advocates for the baccalaureate social worker contend that NASW did not devote sufficient attention to this practice level and that its program priorities in the 1980s "centered too much on licensing, vendor payments, private practice and other issues that were not sufficiently relevant to the baccalaureate worker."[23] NASW's creation of the Academy of Certified Baccalaureate Social Workers in the early 1990s represented movement away from that overemphasis on the interests of master's level social workers, but the discontinuance of that certification in 1996 was a retreat from that position.

With NASW's formal recognition of baccalaureate social work as fully professional, in 1974 the Council on Social Work Education began accrediting baccalaureate social work education (BSW) programs. Initially, 135 schools met the undergraduate accreditation requirements, and by 2008 that number had increased to 464 schools in the United States and Puerto Rico, with another 16 schools in candidacy for accreditation. With 190 MSW programs and an additional 19 in candidacy status, social work has developed a substantial place in higher education.[24]

In 2007 and 2008 a surge of interest in strengthening social work as a single, somewhat unified profession developed. Underpinning this effort was the creation of the Center for Workforce Studies by NASW in 2004, where data are collected to document the work of social workers. These data suggest that a large portion of today's social workers, especially males, are age fifty or older and that the profession faces the likelihood of many of its members "aging out" in the next decade. Also, it is estimated that forty to fifty different organizations had been formed around various interests in social work practice and education, with no unified voice of the profession articulating the needs and concerns of social workers. In response, NASW and CSWE jointly facilitated a "Social Work Congress," where many of these organizations were represented and that called for greater unity within the profession. Subsequently, representatives of several of these organizations met at the Wingspread conference facility in Wisconsin to begin mapping ways to strengthen unity—through mergers of organizations or greater collaboration among existing professional associations. Finally, with the sponsorship of two social workers who were U.S. senators, along with a companion bill in the House of Representatives, the Social Work Reinvestment Act containing several provisions that would strengthen social work and social work services, was introduced in the federal legislature in 2008.

Social Work Confronts a Disaster: Evidence of a Maturing Profession

In the mid-1950s, Marion K. Sanders published a highly critical article on the social work profession titled "Social Work: A Profession Chasing Its Tail." Although some of his criticism was no doubt accurate, Sanders essentially cast social work as an ill-defined occupation that had compromised too much of its original concern for the vulnerable members of society to achieve professional status. Illustrating the intangible nature of social work practice and the poor definition of the profession at that time, Sanders created the following story to illustrate his point.

> The day after the bomb fell, the doctor was out binding up radiation burns. The minister prayed and set up a soup kitchen in the ruined chapel. The policeman herded stray children to the rubble heap where the teacher had improvised a classroom. And the social worker wrote a report: since two had survived, they held a conference on Interpersonal Relationships in a Time of Intensified Anxiety States.
>
> Of course the bomb hasn't fallen. And the social workers have not yet abdicated all the hard and daring tasks to the other benevolent callings. But it could happen. Despite their shortcomings, the doctors, teachers, and reverend clergy at least know what is expected of them.... In contrast the social workers—though specialists in good deeds—seem to have lost track of what particular good needs doing by them.[25]

Contrast Sanders' depiction of social work in the 1950s with the reports of the activities social workers performed when terrorists crashed airplanes into several critical locations in the United States. On September 11, 2001, social workers were immediately on the front lines—in New York; Washington, D.C.; and elsewhere. A few representative stories confirm that today social workers are prepared to effectively apply their knowledge and skills in a time of crisis.

- Already in place was an agreement with the American Red Cross that the National Association of Social Workers (NASW) would facilitate the delivery of mental health services to victims of disaster, rescue workers, military personnel, and their families. NASW, through its national and chapter offices, immediately coordinated efforts to make social work services available, and more than 1,000 social workers were contacted to provide services through this mechanism.
- In New York City, the NASW Chapter's eighty-five-member Disaster/Trauma Working Group immediately made itself available to provide a variety of mental health and other services.[26]
- Ilia Rivera-Sanchez was on the scene at the Pentagon by 6:00 P.M. the afternoon of the attacks, comforting and counseling firefighters and military personnel engaged in the rescue work. She later worked at the morgue offering counseling to those bringing in the bodies recovered from the Pentagon.[27]
- Social workers at Bellevue Hospital in New York City operated two support centers—one for staff members who were working around the clock with victims and another for families of victims. They also prepared lists of missing persons, handled emotional telephone calls from people searching for missing family members, coordinated with other human services agencies, provided clothing for persons unable to reach their homes, and so on.[28]
- In airports, train stations, and bus stations around the world, social workers provided services to people whose travel was interrupted by the attacks. Housing was often needed, funds for meals were provided, alternate transportation arrangements had to be made, and loved ones were contacted regarding the whereabouts of stranded travelers. Social workers were there to assist.

Indeed, social work has matured in its capacity to contribute to the society and was prepared to respond to this emergency, and the society recognized and made use of the competencies of many social workers.

Concluding Comment

In the past century, social work has developed in a manner that meets the criteria for professions. Consensus about its unique purpose among the professions has been reached, and social work has achieved sanction as the appropriate profession to help people resolve problems in their interaction with their environments. Social workers have been granted the professional authority to provide the necessary helping services for people in need and have taken their authority to provide these professional services seriously. The National Association of Social Workers and the Council on Social Work Education have worked through the decades to clarify social work's knowledge, value, and skill base. Social work has developed educational programs that prepare new people to enter this profession and has established a process for accrediting the programs that meet qualitative educational standards at both the baccalaureate and master's levels. Social work has also adopted and regularly updated a Code of Ethics and has established procedures for dealing with violations of that code, which allows the profession to carry out its professional responsibility to protect clients and the general public from abuses that might arise from the monopoly it has achieved.

We can observe the subtle but important influence that professional recognition, educational preparation, and practical training have had on Demetria (see Box 4.1) as she carries out her investigation and initiates services in the suspected child abuse case found in Chapter 1.

Box 4.1

Demetria's Functioning as a Professional Social Worker

Demetria's work with the Miles family (see Chapter 1) illustrates professional social work activity. What made her work "professional"? First, Demetria had the recognized educational preparation (a BSW degree from an accredited social work education program) for a beginning social worker. It appears that, at least partially because of that status, she was granted adequate professional autonomy to exercise her professional judgment about the case; she had sufficient professional authority, which allowed Mrs. Miles to trust her with quite a bit of information about family problems; and Demetria reflected professional responsibility in the discrete way she handled client information and her willingness to extend beyond the minimum job expectations to initiate discussion of needed social change.

Second, if one ticks through the criteria for being a professional, Demetria and her work exemplify a number of ways social work practice is professional. For example, she was prepared from her social work education with enough knowledge about people and programs to be able to immediately work constructively in this case; the child welfare services she provided were highly valued by the society, as the protection of children is one of the most strongly supported human services; Demetria functioned in a highly ethical manner throughout the interactions around this case, and so on. These factors, largely unseen by Joseph and Mrs. Miles, were instrumental in the agency hiring Demetria in the first place, the school personnel working with her to identify Joseph's issues, Mrs. Miles' openness to Demetria's offer to help, and Demetria's competence in carrying out the work. This preparation for social work practice and the sanction from the community facilitated Demetria's ability to quickly establish rapport and successfully begin the helping process.

KEY WORDS AND CONCEPTS

Profession
Attributes of professions
Professional autonomy, authority, and responsibility
Public vs. private professions

State boards of charities
Charity organization societies
Settlement houses
Council on Social Work Education
National Association of Social Workers

SUGGESTED INFORMATION SOURCES

Greenwood, Ernest. "Attributes of a Profession," *Social Work* 2 (July 1957): 45–55.
Leighninger, Leslie. *Social Work: Search for Identity*. Westport, CT: Greenwood, 1987.
———. *Creating a New Profession: The Beginnings of Social Work Education*. Alexandria, VA: Council on Social Work Education, 2000.
Lubove, Roy. *The Professional Altruist*. Cambridge, MA: Harvard University Press, 1989.

ENDNOTES

1. Wilbert E. Moore, *The Professions: Roles and Rules* (New York: Russell Sage Foundation, 1970), p. 3.
2. Everett C. Hughes, "Professions," *Daedalus* (Fall 1963): 657.
3. Ronald M. Pavalko, *Sociology of Occupations and Professions*, 2nd ed. (Itasca, IL: F. E. Peacock, 1988), pp. 19–29.
4. Harold Wilensky, "The Professionalization of Everyone?" *American Journal of Sociology* 70 (September 1964): 137–158.
5. Cited in Ralph E. Pumphrey and Muriel W. Pumphrey, eds., *The Heritage of American Social Work* (New York: Columbia University Press, 1961), p. 12.
6. Robert H. Bremner, *From the Depths* (New York: New York University Press, 1956), 66.
7. Roy Lubove, *The Professional Altruist* (Cambridge, MA: Harvard University Press, 1965), 32.
8. Abraham Flexner, "Is Social Work a Profession?" in *Proceedings of the National Conference on Charities and Correction, 1915* (Chicago: National Conference on Charities and Correction, 1916): 576–590.
9. Pumphrey and Pumphrey, *Heritage*, p. 310.
10. John C. Kidneigh, "History of American Social Work," in Harry L. Lurie, ed., *Encyclopedia of Social Work*, 15th ed. (New York: National Association of Social Workers, 1965), pp. 13–14.
11. Herbert Bisno, "The Place of Undergraduate Curriculum in Social Work Education," in Werner W. Boehm, ed., *A Report of the Curriculum Study* Vol. II (New York: Council on Social Work Education, 1959), p. 8.
12. Ernest V. Hollis and Alice L. Taylor, *Social Work Education in the United States* (New York: Columbia University Press, 1951).
13. Mary E. Richmond, *Social Diagnosis* (New York: Russell Sage Foundation, 1917).
14. Nathan E. Cohen, *Social Work in the American Tradition* (New York: Holt, Rinehart, & Winston, 1958), pp. 120–121.

15. Werner W. Boehm, "The Nature of Social Work," *Social Work* 3 (April 1958): 10–18.
16. Herbert Bisno, "How Social Will Social Work Be?" *Social Work* 1 (April 1956): 12–18.
17. Nathan E. Cohen, "A Changing Profession in a Changing World," *Social Work* 1 (October 1956): 12–19.
18. Ernest Greenwood, "Attributes of a Profession," *Social Work* 2 (July 1957): 45–55.
19. Ibid., p. 54.
20. Harriet M. Bartlett, "Towards Clarification and Improvement of Social Work Practice," *Social Work* 3 (April 1958): 5–7.
21. William E. Gordon, "Critique of the Working Definition," *Social Work* 7 (October 1962): 3–13; "Knowledge and Values: Their Distinction and Relationship in Clarifying Social Work Practice," *Social Work* 10 (July 1965): 32–39.
22. National Association of Social Workers, *Code of Ethics* (Washington, D.C.: The Association, 1960).
23. Bradford W. Sheafor and Barbara W. Shank, *Undergraduate Social Work Education: A Survivor in a Changing Profession* (Austin: University of Texas School of Social Work, 1986), Social Work Education Monograph Series 3, p. 25.
24. "Archive of COA Decisions, February 2008." http://www.cswe.org.
25. Marion K. Sanders, "Social Work: A Profession Chasing Its Tail," *Harper's* Monthly 214 (March 1957): 56.
26. John V. O'Neill, "Social Workers Heed Call After Attacks," *NASW News* 46 (November 2001), p. 8.
27. Ibid., p. 1.
28. Ibid., p. 8.

part three

Social Work Career Options

The payoff in social work is in the services rendered to clients and the improvements made to problematic social conditions affecting the quality of life for people. After all, these are the primary motivations for entering this profession. Nevertheless, if one is to be satisfied in his or her work, that social worker must find a niche in the profession where the work is fulfilling. Although one can change directions during the course of a social work career, it is helpful to make at least preliminary decisions about level of education one will need, type of client issues to be addressed (i.e., field of practice), kind of organization in which to work (i.e., practice setting), providing services compatible with one's basic values, and identifying the specific knowledge and skills to begin acquiring. The five chapters in this part of *Social Work: A Profession of Many Faces* introduce the elements included in these career choices.

Each social worker must make certain decisions that will affect his or her career path. One important decision concerns one's level of educational preparation. Chapter 5 summarizes a considerable amount of data about social workers at different educational levels and highlights the employment opportunities at each. In essence, the baccalaureate-level social worker works primarily in direct services with clients and is more likely than master's-level social workers to serve either children and youth or older adults. The master's-level social worker may also hold administrative and supervisory positions, and those in direct service positions are most likely to address medical, mental health, and school-related issues with the adult population. Some doctoral-level social workers can be found in complex administrative and direct practice jobs, but the majority is concentrated in research and teaching positions.

A second decision concerns the practice area one chooses to enter. Chapter 6 surveys thirteen unique fields in which social workers apply their trade. Despite the differences in these fields of practice, a basic pattern emerges of the social workers helping people address their issues and interact more effectively with the world around them.

A social worker must decide if he or she is to work in a human service organization or engage in private practice. Chapter 7 examines those organizations where most social workers are employed. Factors affecting agency structure and functioning are discussed. Private practice presents a different set of problems than are experienced by those social workers employed in human service organizations, and these differences are examined.

Chapter 8 examines the basic values that have shaped social work's approach to practice. Examples of these values are beliefs that all people are worthy of being treated with respect, that people should be helped to have meaningful interactions with others, that people should be guided toward becoming independent and taking responsibility for themselves, and that society has a responsibility for helping people lead fulfilling lives. In addition, we examine the ethical guidelines imbedded in the NASW Code of Ethics that guide social workers in the way they conduct their work on a day-to-day basis.

Finally, Chapter 9 describes the basic knowledge and skills required of social workers. Based on research about the tasks social workers perform, this chapter then identifies what a social worker needs to know and be able to do in order to carry out those tasks. Although this is not an exhaustive list of competencies, it suggests the content that one would expect to find in a social work education program and the activities social workers will be expected to perform in working with clients.

chapter 5

Entry to the Social Work Profession

Prefatory Comment

Selecting a career is one of the most important decisions a person must make. Whether that decision is to become a homemaker, physician, salesperson, teacher, chemist, or social worker, it should be based on a thorough understanding of the physical, emotional, and intellectual demands of the field and a close look at one's own suitability for that type of work. Whatever the choice, it will dictate how a person spends a major part of each day. It will also spill over into other aspects of life, including lifestyle, general satisfaction with self, and quality of life.

The decision to enter a particular profession does not lock a person into that occupation for a lifetime, but it does represent a substantial commitment of time, energy, and resources to prepare for professional practice and to obtain the requisite credentials. If it is a good career choice, one's job can be an exhilarating and stimulating experience. However, if there is a poor fit between a person and his or her chosen occupation, work can be frustrating and unrewarding. Further, the complexity of human situations requiring professional assistance and the growing knowledge about effective helping, obligate the professional to a career of continued learning and skill development. Unless a person is willing to make such a commitment, a professional career should not be pursued.

For the person considering the social work profession, it is useful to have a clear perception of the career opportunities this profession affords. Social work has evolved a four-level career ladder that has two entry points (i.e., the basic and specialized social worker) and two additional levels based on more advanced experience and education. This chapter describes the educational preparation and practice experience required for each practice level and identifies factors that shaped the evolution of social work practice at those levels.

Making a career choice is difficult because of the wide range of careers to choose from but, more importantly, because of the problems an outsider experiences in gaining an adequate and accurate understanding of a career. Too often, only after a person has made substantial commitments in time, energy, and money or has cut off other opportunities by taking steps to enter a career does he or she find that it is not what was expected or wanted. Another difficulty lies in having a clear perception of one's own needs, interests, and abilities. Personal introspection, occupational preference testing, guidance counseling, and experience in activities related to the career are all resources for making this choice.

The person contemplating a career in social work must consider a number of factors. It is evident that social work is extremely broad in scope—ranging from social action to individual therapy—with a knowledge base that is far from stable or well developed. Thus, explicit guidelines for social work practice do not exist, leaving the social worker with the responsibility for exercising a great deal of individual judgment. Furthermore, the skills demanded of the social worker vary widely and require a flexible, creative, and introspective person to practice them. The pressures of a social work job create a degree of stress because the outcome of the work is critically important to the clients. In addition, social workers are regularly criticized by both clients and the general public, frequently in regard to programs over which they have little policy-making influence. If a person can tolerate the ambiguity, responsibility, pressures, and criticism that are a part of social work; if the values, skills, and interests required of social workers are compatible; and if it is rewarding to work constructively to help people improve their level of social functioning, social work offers a very satisfying career.

Issues in Social Work Preparation and Employment

Membership in any profession requires that its members acquire specified qualifications. The very act of defining professional membership inherently excludes some persons who operate with similar knowledge and values but lack the identified qualifications. In social work, for example, completion of the education and practice experience specified by the National Association of Social Workers (NASW) in its membership qualifications is necessary to gain professional recognition. However, social workers are cognizant that many other helping people with different educations and experiences also make important contributions to the delivery of human services. For the person entering social work, it is important to be aware of several issues that relate to professional qualifications.

Education and Accreditation

The social work profession requires that a person must have a formal social work education; that is, either a baccalaureate degree with a major in social work (BSW) or a master's degree in social work (MSW) from an accredited social work education program, as a minimum for professional recognition. The *accreditation* process is administered by the Council on Social Work Education (CSWE) and has become a significant factor in social work because the graduate of the accredited program is assumed to be prepared to enter practice ready to apply the appropriate knowledge, values, and skills in the service of clients. For all practical purposes, education is the gatekeeper of the profession. This does not mean that all graduates are equally prepared to enter practice, that some people who do not have all the required social work courses are unable to perform some tasks expected of the social worker, or even that all schools offer the same opportunity for learning the essentials of social work. Rather, accreditation attests to the fact that the public can have confidence that graduates are at least minimally prepared for beginning-level social work practice because they have completed an instructional program that is soundly designed and taught by competent faculty.

Professional Certification

The National Association of Social Workers provides confirmation to clientele and employing human services agencies that some social workers have demonstrated the requisite knowledge and competence to engage in practice, that is, *professional certification*. Where accreditation is testimony to the quality of an educational program, certification is the profession's testimony regarding the individual's knowledge, values, and skills.

Following it's formation in 1955, the NASW created two professional certification programs that were based on the social worker's practice level. In 1960, the Academy of Certified Social Workers (ACSW) was created. The ACSW was the profession's nationally accepted mechanism for designating those social workers who were qualified at the "independent social worker" level and was often a requirement for social work jobs. It required the MSW degree, two years' post–master's experience, a sufficient score on a national exam, and favorable evaluation of the worker's competence by peers. With exam-based licensing of social workers implemented in every state, the exam portion of the ACSW became redundant and in 2005 was discontinued as a requirement for membership in the Academy. In 1990, NASW also created the Academy of Certified Baccalaureate Social Workers (ACBSW), but this credential did not catch on as a job credential and was discontinued in 1996.

In addition to the ACSW, for many years NASW also maintained two professional recognition programs for advanced social workers engaged in clinical practice: the Qualified Clinical Social Worker (QCSW) and the Diplomate in Clinical Social Work (DCSW). More recently, the demand to recognize qualified social workers in specialty areas has led NASW to create credentialing programs in several practice areas. At the MSW level are the Certified School Social Work Specialist; Certified Social Worker in Health Care; Certified Clinical Alcohol, Tobacco, and Other Drugs Social Worker; Certified Advanced Social Work Case Manager; Certified Advanced Children, Youth, and Family Social Worker; Advanced Social Worker in Gerontology; and Clinical Social Worker in Gerontology certificate programs. At the BSW level are the Certified Social Work Case Manager; Certified Children, Youth, and Family Social Worker; and the Social Worker in Gerontology certificates. All of these certificates require NASW membership, graduation from a CSWE-accredited educational program, practice experience after graduation, and adherence to the NASW Code of Ethics. Usually a state license to practice social work or a passing score on the appropriate social work exam offered by the Association of Social Work (licensing) Boards is required, as well as a favorable evaluation by the worker's supervisor and a professional colleague. These credentials are designed to serve as indicators of competency by the profession of social work to clients and employers, as well as to the insurance companies that offer reimbursement for social workers' services.

Licensing or State Regulation of Social Work Practice

The social work profession has shaped its educational programs through accreditation requirements and, through NASW, has sought to identify its competent and experienced practitioners by creating its certification programs. However, over the past two decades, perhaps the most dominant issue on NASW's agenda has been to encourage the licensing of social workers throughout the United States. As described by the Association of Social Work Boards, *licensing* is:

> ...a process by which an agency of state government or other jurisdiction acting upon legislative mandate grants permission to individuals to engage in the practice of a particular profession or vocation and prohibits all others from legally doing so. By ensuring a level of safe practice, the licensure process protects the general public. Those who are licensed are permitted by the state to use a specific title and perform activities because they have demonstrated to the state's satisfaction that they have reached an acceptable level of practice.[1]

The intent of licensing is to have state governments identify those social workers who are properly prepared through professional education and experience to provide client services. Both consumers of service (particularly in private practice settings) and health insurance companies that reimburse for the cost of social work services have looked to licensing as a desirable way to determine a social worker's practice competence.

As opposed to the uniform national requirements for professional certification used by NASW, each state controls whether there will be licensing of social workers, the levels of practice it will license, and the requirements to be licensed. Thus there is substantial variability among the states. After many years of effort by NASW and the Canadian Association of Social Workers to achieve legal regulation of social work, all fifty states, the District of Columbia, Puerto Rico, the U.S. Virgin Islands, and ten Canadian provinces license (register or certify) social workers. Approximately two-thirds of the states provide for licensing or registration of social workers at the basic level, and most have more than one level requiring the MSW as the educational preparation.[2] The Association of Social Work Boards serves as the coordinating agency for the state boards and offers testing at the following levels:

- **Basic:** BSW degree on graduation
- **Intermediate:** MSW with no post-degree experience
- **Advanced Generalist:** MSW with two years' post-master's supervised experience
- **Clinical:** MSW with two years' post-master's direct clinical social work experience

The individual states then determine whether they want to use these test results for licensing of social workers and whether they want to grant *reciprocity* (i.e., accept the licenses of social workers from other states) when social workers move from state to state.

Professional Standards

A profession is expected by society to protect the public from those members who abuse the professional monopoly. To conduct this self-policing, professions must establish standards and develop procedures for evaluating complaints and imposing negative sanctions if a member engages in incompetent or unethical practice. State licensing, too, performs this client protection function by withdrawing the legal right to practice as a social worker if such violations occur.

NASW establishs appropriate standards of conduct through its Code of Ethics and maintains a process to ensure the public that recognized professional social workers meet those standards. The Code spells out in some detail the social worker's ethical responsibilities to clients, colleagues, practice settings, other professionals, the profession of social work, and the broader society.[3] When a social worker becomes a member of NASW, he or she must profess willingness to practice within the guidelines prescribed by the Code of Ethics, and the Code, in turn, becomes the baseline for evaluating the professional behavior of social workers.

The process established for reviewing complaints begins with the local chapter of NASW when an individual or organization lodges a formal complaint about the practice of a social worker. A committee of the chapter will then conduct an investigation of the complaint and make a determination that the complaint is or is not substantiated. Either party has the right to appeal to the NASW National Committee on Inquiry, which reviews the charges and makes a final judgment. If the Committee on Inquiry concludes that ethical standards have been violated, a plan to correct the behavior through training or treatment may be developed, or the individual's membership in NASW may be suspended. The sanctions remain in effect until the terms established by the Committee on Inquiry are satisfied.

Options for Human Service Practice

Addressing complex human needs requires providers equipped with a variety of knowledge and skills. The human services, therefore, are made up of many people—from volunteers to highly trained professionals—who provide many different forms of helping. The person considering a career in a helping profession should carefully compare social work with other human service providers to determine if serving as a social worker would be the most satisfying way to spend one's work life.

Volunteers

One cannot fully examine the human services without recognizing the important role played by volunteers. For many people who have other vocations, one way to be involved with human services is to volunteer. The willingness to give of oneself, without monetary reward, in order to help others is expressed in the activity of millions of people who give their time, energy, and talents to make this a better world. It was from efforts to prepare volunteers to provide more effective human services that social work became an occupation and, later, a significant helping profession.

Today, social workers work closely with volunteers in many agencies. Their jobs often include the recruitment, selection, training, and supervision of volunteers. The qualifications of volunteers vary from activity to activity. At times professionals volunteer their services beyond their jobs in their own agencies. These volunteer activities may use their professional abilities but may also require skills unrelated to professional training. Like any other good citizen, the social worker has an obligation to donate his or her talents to improve social conditions.

Nonprofessional Service Providers

Not all human service practice requires the competencies of a social worker or someone with related professional skills. These providers have been referred to in the literature as *indigenous workers*. They may be clients, former clients, or others who have rapport with low-income or other client groups based on having similar experiences to the client population. At times indigenous workers can build relationships with clients when professionals have difficulty establishing rapport. Their life experience and knowledge of the individuals or groups being served are the most important qualifications.

Another important source of nonprofessional personnel for human service agencies are *graduates of community colleges*. These Associate of Arts (AA) degree programs vary considerably from school to school but focus on preparing for very specific human service jobs with titles such as mental health technician, community service aide, case aide, or social work technician. The AA degree programs usually include the study of human growth and behavior, social problems, the social service delivery system, personal values and self-awareness, and basic communication skills. These programs may provide field experiences so students have an opportunity to apply knowledge acquired in the classroom. The tasks the AA graduate can be expected to perform are typically very concrete and supervised by experienced workers.

Other Baccalaureate-Level Disciplines

Several disciplines offer majors in colleges and universities that are closely related to social work. Completing these degrees can serve as helpful preparation for some human service jobs and can also be good preparation for a subsequent degree in social work. However, these programs of study should not be confused with social work degree programs that, if accredited, carry professional recognition.

Social Science Disciplines. Social work has traditionally had a close relationship with the social science disciplines for two reasons. First, social work has drawn on basic knowledge from the disciplines of psychology, sociology, anthropology, economics, and political science, while developing its theoretical base for understanding the individual, family, group, organization, community, and the impact of culture on all of these. Second, in higher education, social work has had close administrative ties with these disciplines at the baccalaureate level. It is not uncommon to find a baccalaureate-level social work education program housed in a department that includes one or more social science disciplines.

Most positions for social scientists involve research or teaching in a college or university, and, thus, a Ph.D. is necessary to be competitive in the job market. With the exception of specialized areas of clinical psychology and the small branch of applied sociology, social scientists do not typically engage in the provision of human services. Their purpose is to develop and test theories that will increase understanding of the people or places they study, but they do not intend to intervene to help people or social institutions change.

Related Helping Professions. When making a career choice within the human services, a person should examine a range of helping professions that might fit his or her individual talents and interests. The more established professions are medicine, law, nursing, teaching, and psychology. Other helping professions, such as physical therapy, music therapy, occupational therapy, marriage and family therapy, urban planning, and school counseling, also offer challenging and rewarding careers.

Each of these is an established profession, and there are accredited educational programs a person must complete to be recognized as a member of that profession. Like social work, these professions identify standards for competent and ethical practice and take responsibility for policing the membership for compliance with these standards. The clientele of these professions, then, have some protection from the possible misuse of professional authority. Employment opportunities in these professions vary considerably, but most jobs are defined as requiring professional education for entry.

It is instructive to compare estimates of the demand for social workers with that of other helping professions. Table 5.1 provides a comparison of selected helping professions based on the projections of the U.S. Bureau of Labor Statistics (BLS). The BLS estimates of annual growth indicate that social work is already one of the largest professions and is expected to be a moderately fast-growing occupation. Table 5.1 also reveals that the average annual earnings of social workers is on the low end of the helping professions. For comparison purposes, the table identifies the expected terminal professional degree for each discipline.

Emerging Human Service Occupations. During the 1970s a new occupational group began to emerge, known generally as *human services* or *human development.* The human services occupations differ from the helping professions we have reviewed because they intend to be nonprofessional. Most people giving leadership to these occupations are professionally trained in other disciplines and have been largely involved in corrections and mental health services—although they branch into every aspect of the social services.

The development of the human services field was stimulated by dissatisfaction with the service delivery system. Fundamental to the philosophy behind this field are two viewpoints.[4] First, the human services have been fragmented into problem areas

Table 5.1

Estimated Employment, Earnings, and Training Requirements for Related Professions: 2006–2016

Profession	Total Employment 2006	Estimated Employment 2016	Est. Annual Growth (%)*	Annual Job Openings (Attrition and Job Growth)	Estimated Annual Earnings 2004	Expected Professional Degree
Registered Nurse	2,505,000	3,092,000	2.35	100,100	$62,480	Assoc. or Bachelor's
Elem./Middle School Teacher	2,214,000	2,496,000	1.27	76,600	50,040	Bachelor's + License
Social Worker	595,000	727,000	2.22	25,800	47,170	Bachelor's or Master's
Special Ed. Teacher	459,000	530,000	1.55	17,300	51,230	Bachelor's + License
School Counselor	260,000	292,000	1.26	8,400	51,690	Bachelor's or Master's
Clinical/Counseling/School Psychologist	152,000	176,000	1.58	5,100	68,150	Master's or Ph.D.
Rehabilitation Counselor	141,000	173,000	2.30	6,000	33,350	Bachelor's or Master's
Mental Health Counselor	100,000	137,000	3.00	5,000	39,450	Bachelor's or Master's

(Continued)

Profession	Total Employment 2006	Estimated Employment 2016	Est. Annual Growth (%)*	Annual Job Openings (Attrition and Job Growth)	Estimated Annual Earnings 2004	Expected Professional Degree
Occupational Therapist	99,000	122,000	2.31	3,700	$ 65,540	Master's
Marriage/Family Therapist	25,000	32,000	2.98	1,200	45,310	Master's

*Annual Growth Rate: Bureau of Labor Statistics projections are based on the assumption of an average growth rate of 0.80 between 2006 and 2016. Social work, for example, is in the highest projected growth category with a 2.22 per year projected growth.

- (Employment Projections) U.S. Bureau of Labor Statistics. http://www.bls.gov.emp/cmptabapp.htm.
- (Mean Wage Estimates) U. S. Bureau of Labor Statistics. http://data.bls.gov/oes/search.jsp.
- (Expected Professional Degree) U. S. Bureau of Labor Statistics. http://www.bls.gov/oco/home.htm.

(e.g., child welfare, corrections, mental health) that create barriers to good service because many clients experience complex problems and must deal with multiple agencies, programs, and service providers. Second, the integration of services into "umbrella agencies" and the creation of a broad discipline that can provide a wide range of services is preferable to the more focused professional orientation.

Social workers would agree that the fragmented methods of delivering social services often make it difficult for clients to locate help. However, the profession does not regard service integration as a solution (division lines can exist just as rigidly within one large agency as in several smaller ones) and believes that the professional model, with all its limitations, continues to be the most valid means of identifying the people who are prepared with the knowledge, values, and skills to respond to specific human needs. Social work would argue that clients are better served through greater efforts at *interdisciplinary practice*, rather than the emergence of new human service disciplines that have no clear service focus or practice approach, no established standards for ethical conduct, no professional responsibility for quality control, and no standardized educational preparation subject to professional accreditation.

Levels of Professional Social Work Practice

Social work's evolution as a profession has been uneven, and the career paths one might follow as a social worker can be confusing. Figure 5.1 portrays the various career options available to the professional social worker. It recognizes that, before a person decides to begin the educational preparation required to become a professional social worker, he or she will typically have had some positive experiences that have motivated this decision. This future social worker will typically have been a good natural helper or volunteer, the client of a social worker who received useful services, or perhaps a human services provider who did not have professional preparation. If he or she has not already completed a bachelor's degree, the most likely place to begin would be in a BSW program. However, if this is a person who has a degree in another discipline, a second entry point is available—an MSW program.

To make appropriate career development decisions, it is useful for the potential social worker to understand what is expected of a social worker at each of the four practice levels and how that practice level has emerged historically. The following materials, based on NASW's classification system,[5] briefly describe each level, identify the qualifications, and trace the manner in which its central characteristics have emerged.

The Basic Professional

Description: Practice as a basic social worker requires professional practice skills, theoretical knowledge, and values not normally obtainable in day-to-day experience but that are obtainable through formal social work education. This knowledge is distinguished from experiential learning by being based on conceptual and theoretical

Figure 5.1
Career Options for the Professional Social Worker

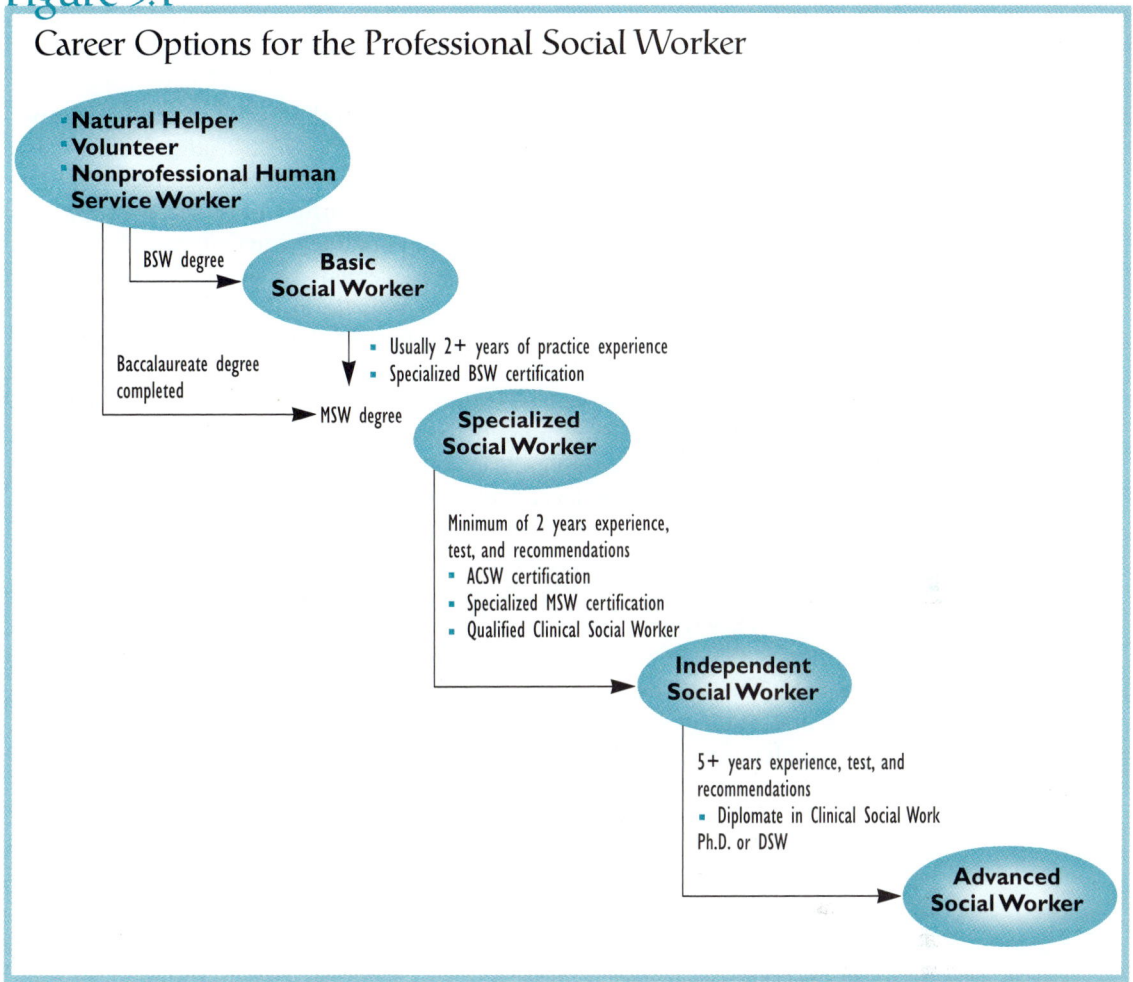

knowledge of personal and social interaction and by training in the disciplined use of self in relationship with clients.

Qualifications: Requires a baccalaureate degree from a social work program accredited by the Council on Social Work Education.

Characteristics: Practice at this first level has been formally recognized as professional only since 1970, when the NASW first admitted to full membership persons with a degree from a social work program approved by the Council on Social Work Education. This recognition substantially increased the quantity and quality of undergraduate social work programs.

A few schools offered baccalaureate-level social work courses as early as the 1920s.[6] However, the thrust of social work was toward graduate education. In 1932 the American Association of Schools of Social Work (AASSW) declared that, to be recognized as professional, a social worker must graduate from a four-year college and complete at least one year of graduate education. In 1937 this requirement was revised to establish two years of graduate education as the minimum level for professional practice.

In response to the AASSW policy, in 1942 several schools created a competing organization, the National Association of Schools of Social Administration (NASSA), for the purpose of having undergraduate programs recognized as professional preparation. After several years of conflict over the legitimacy of undergraduate professional education, thirteen organizations interested in the resolution of this issue and in the overall enhancement of social work education formed the National Council on Social Work Education. In 1952 these organizations morphed into the single accrediting body for social work education: the Council on Social Work Education (CSWE).

The CSWE offered membership to both undergraduate and graduate schools and undertook a thirteen-volume curriculum study of social work education at both levels. One volume of this study recommended establishment of professional social work education at the undergraduate level with a continuum developed from undergraduate to graduate programs.[7] This recommendation was initially rejected by the CSWE. During most of the 1960s, undergraduate programs operated under CSWE guidelines that might best be described as a traditional liberal arts education oriented toward social welfare.[8] They were usually taught in departments of psychology or sociology, offered no more than three or four social work courses, and sometimes had no social workers as faculty. These programs were not professional education, and neither employers nor graduate social work education programs gave credit for this background or preference in admissions to applicants who had completed this major.

Disenchantment of students, employers, and professional social workers with undergraduate education contributed to the establishment of a joint CSWE–NASW Ad Hoc Committee on Manpower Issues in 1968. The Committee's recommendations contributed to concurrent actions in 1970 by NASW members to grant full membership to graduates of approved undergraduate programs and by the CSWE to establish standards for approval of these programs. The first standards adopted were essentially structural: they contributed to the visibility of social work programs, required that social workers be included in faculty, and demanded specification of educational objectives.[9] CSWE "approval" was granted to 220 schools by 1973 but was at best a limited and informal type of accreditation. Specification of curriculum content was slower to develop because a workable division between baccalaureate- and master's-level education had not yet evolved.

In 1973 CSWE took the second step to complete formal accreditation: it adopted much more substantial standards for baccalaureate degree programs, placing the primary focus on preparation for professional social work practice. Some previously "approved" programs could not meet the new standards, but most were able to secure the necessary resources to upgrade their programs and achieve accredited status. In 1984 another significant step to upgrade the quality of baccalaureate social work education was taken when the CSWE operationalized a new set of accreditation standards and a much more substantive Curriculum Policy Statement. Rigorous application of the accreditation standards did not deter colleges and universities of all sizes in all states from building and maintaining undergraduate social work education programs. As of 2006, 458 colleges and universities had BSW programs that were fully accredited and enrolled more than 27,000 junior- and senior-level students.[10]

With NASW recognition came the gradual acceptance of baccalaureate-level social work, both by employers as preparation for practice and by the graduate programs as preparation for advanced education. Increasingly, jobs were defined to recognize the competence and abilities of social workers who had completed this type of educational program, and salary and work assignments were differentiated from those without this preparation. Furthermore, in 1972 CSWE granted approval for graduate schools to accept up to one year's credit for special groups of students. Today, approximately 85 percent of the graduate programs offer some form of *advanced standing* to graduates of accredited programs that typically amount to waiving one to two terms of graduate work.[11]

Clearly, the developments since the 1970s enhance the conclusion that the social worker who has completed an accredited undergraduate social work program should be prepared with the competencies for that level of professional practice. Perhaps the most valid test of the acceptance of baccalaureate or basic social workers is whether they find employment as social workers. One study of 5,228 graduates of BSW programs found that 71.4 percent found their first job in social work, and 86.8 percent of these graduates secured employment within six months after graduation. Over time, 84.3 percent of the BSW graduates were employed as social workers. These data suggest that the human service agencies found baccalaureate-level social workers attractive, especially in direct service positions, in which 90.2 percent were employed in their first social work job.[12]

The basic social worker is now well established in the United States as the first level of professional practice. The demand for social workers is increasing, and agencies readily employ these graduates. A niche has developed for BSW graduates that involves working largely with children and youth, with the aged, in the traditional nonprofit social service agencies and residential centers, and primarily on the front lines of social work practice providing services directly to clients.

The Specialized Professional

Description: Practice at this level requires the specific and demonstrated mastery of therapeutic techniques in at least one knowledge and skill method, as well as general knowledge of human personality as influenced by social factors. Specialized practice also requires the disciplined use of self in treatment relationships with individuals or groups, or a broad conceptual knowledge of research, administration, or planning methods and social problems.

Qualifications: Requires a master's degree (MSW) from a social work program accredited by the CSWE.

Characteristics: Prior to the reemergence of baccalaureate-level social work education and the basic social worker, the generally accepted level of preparation for social work practice was that of the specialized social worker. It is expected that the MSW social worker will have sufficient competence to function effectively in at least one area of specialized practice.

Historically, master's-level social work education began much like the more sophisticated in-service training programs of today. The first formal education program, known as the New York School of Philanthropy (now the Columbia University School of Social Work), was a six-week course offered under the auspices of the New York Charity Organization Society in 1898. The early curricula of the evolving schools incorporated preparation for a range of services, from individual helping approaches to economic and reform theory. They included a heavy investment in internships or field experiences as tools for learning practice skills and tended to be organized around practice settings, such as hospital social work and school social work. The MSW programs' greatest emphasis was on preparation for the services offered by private social agencies, and they tended to neglect the growing demand for social workers in the public social services.

By the 1940s the two-year MSW had become the minimum requirement for professional practice. The two-year programs were typically organized around what was known as the "Basic Eight," in reference to what at that time were considered the eight primary divisions of social work practice: public welfare, social casework, social group work, community organization, medical information, social research, psychiatry, and social welfare administration. By 1965 the schools had largely abandoned programs structured on the basis of practice setting and instead organized curricula around the practice methods of casework, group work, community organization, administration, and research.

Two factors have significantly influenced social work education at the master's level in the past quarter-century. First, the emergence of baccalaureate-level social work forced a reorientation of master's education; it was necessary to adapt to the student who entered the MSW program with a substantial social work education already completed. For this student, provision was made for advanced standing in the graduate-level program that typically has meant waiving out of up to one year of graduate work, usually with a few summer courses designed to help students for different BSW programs balance out differences between their programs and the initial year of the school's MSW program.

Second, the Council on Social Work Education's Standards for Accreditation and Curriculum Policy Statement allowed individual schools increased flexibility in determining curriculum content. As the typical two-year MSW program evolved, it offered a general orientation to social work practice during the first year and then provided more specialized content based on population served, social problem addressed, practice intervention approach, or client group served during the second year. Prior to that development, students attending MSW programs could expect pretty much the same basic curriculum regardless of which school they attended. Today, because of the breadth of social work practice, the accreditation standards require that during the introductory or "foundation" part of the program the student must be prepared to practice from a generalist perspective. Thus, the first year of master's-level social work education is relatively similar from school to school. However, after that base is developed, the final year (or its equivalent) prepares the student for a specific area of concentration, and at this level the schools differ widely. The dominant specializations increasingly have been related to the clinical aspects of social work practice. In the 2006 academic year, for example, the concentrations MSW students chose were mental health (18.6 percent), child welfare (14.3 percent), family services (12.8 percent), school social work (7.2 percent), and health and aging (both 7.0 percent) as their specialized practice areas.[13]

For the 2006 academic year, 24,910 full-time and 14,656 part-time students were enrolled in the 173 reporting master's-level programs. About two-thirds of the applicants were accepted for admission, and about 40 percent actually enrolled—often because students apply to several schools and end up enrolling in only one. The reporting master's programs graduated 17,207 new MSWs that year.[14]

As opposed to the basic social worker, this specialized worker is expected to possess advanced knowledge and skill in specific areas of social work practice. The worker at this level has been awarded the highest professional social work practice degree (i.e., the terminal professional degree).* Yet, he or she is not yet expected to work independently, that is, outside the structure and supervision provided in a human services agency.

The Independent Professional

Description: The independent practice level is based on appropriate specialized training beyond the MSW plus continued professional development under supervision that is sufficient to ensure dependable, regular use of professional skills in independent private practice. A minimum of two years of post-master's experience is required to demonstrate this direct practice, administration, or training competence.

Qualifications: Requires an accredited MSW and at least two years of post-master's experience under appropriate professional supervision.

Characteristics: The independent social worker is expected to have acquired and integrated the knowledge, values, and skills of social work in at least one practice area. From this experience, he or she should be able to develop sufficient expertise in that field to function independently and skillfully in sensitive situations and should be prepared to practice outside the auspices of a social agency. Furthermore, the independent social worker should be able to provide leadership in at least one practice arena and to supervise and consult with other social workers.

---

*Advanced degrees such as the DSW or the Ph.D. are not subject to accreditation standards established by the profession and are not considered to be professional practice degrees. Most doctorates in social work are academic degrees intended to prepare students for positions in teaching and research rather than in the more typical practice methods.

One indicator of reaching the independent professional level is membership in the *Academy of Certified Social Workers* (ACSW). The ACSW was established in 1960 to establish a more favorable public image, to obtain societal sanction, and to increase confidence and understanding in social work. Requirements for becoming a member of the Academy include maintaining membership in NASW, having a minimum of two years of full-time practice experience, and providing reference letters from professional peers.

As Figure 5.1 indicates, NASW has also developed a credential to recognize the social worker with additional clinical practice experience who has demonstrated knowledge and competence above that expected of the new master's-level worker, that is, the *Qualified Clinical Social Worker* (QCSW) credential. As an additional means of recognizing practice areas where the worker has increased capability, NASW has developed additional areas where specialized certification is possible—school social work; case management; health care; children, youth, and families; gerontology; and alcohol, tobacco, and other drug abuse. Although many social workers employed in human services agencies have attained greater skill and experience than required at the "specialized" social worker level, those engaged in private practice are expected by the profession to have attained this "independent" practice level. The assumption is that the social worker at this level is prepared to function independent of the monitoring typically provided by other staff members in a human services agency. Therefore, credentials become an important means of verifying that the worker is prepared to perform high-quality and ethical services without the need for additional professional oversight.

The Advanced Professional

Description: Practice at the advanced level is that which carries major social and organizational responsibility for professional development, analysis, research, or policy implementation, or is achieved by personal professional growth demonstrated through advanced conceptual contributions to professional knowledge.

Qualifications: This level requires proficiency in a special theoretical, practice, administration, or policy area, or the ability to conduct advanced research studies in social welfare; this is usually demonstrated through a doctoral degree in social work or another discipline—in addition to the MSW.

Characteristics: This classification is reserved for the most highly experienced practitioners as well as for social workers who have obtained a doctorate in social work or a related field. In contrast to many professions, relatively few social workers seek or achieve the advanced professional level.

For direct service or clinical practitioners who aspire to the advanced level, NASW has developed the *Diplomate in Clinical Social Work* (DCSW). To be recognized as a diplomate in clinical social work, a person must have completed an accredited MSW program, possess an advanced or clinical state license, have a minimum of five years of post-master's clinical experience, perform satisfactorily on an advanced-level examination, and receive a favorable comprehensive supervisory evaluation.

Doctoral education represents the second route to the advanced social work level. The curricula for doctoral degrees (DSW or Ph.D.) in social work do not reflect a uniform pattern. Most programs devote their efforts to preparing the researcher and teacher, but increasingly there has been some focus on preparation for the advanced practitioner. Because the doctorate is not viewed as an entry practice degree for the social work profession and it is not accredited by the profession, the doctoral programs receive their sanction only from their universities. Therefore, the schools have considerable flexibility to determine the focus of their curricula and thus have developed unique identities. By 2006, sixty-nine doctoral programs in social work were available throughout the United States, enrolling 1,637 full-time and 917 part-time students, yet only 293 doctoral degrees in social work were awarded.[15] These numbers do not, however, reflect the total number of social workers completing doctoral degrees because some complete doctoral work in related fields such as sociology, psychology, public health, higher education, and public administration.

Concluding Comment

Through the years of its emergence, social work has gradually evolved four distinct practice levels. The National Association of Social Workers has codified these levels into a classification system with expectations for the practitioner at each level defined and education and experience qualifications specified. This classification system encompasses two problems in terminology—both created by the acceptance of the concept of an advanced generalist social worker. First, the MSW graduate prepared as an advanced generalist is qualified under the classification system as a "Specialized Social Worker." Can one be a specialized generalist? Also, an advanced generalist social worker is not the same as an Advanced Social Worker in NASW's classification system. Persons new to social work should be aware of this confusing terminology.

Nevertheless, the NASW classification of social work practice levels is a useful tool for both social agencies wanting to match workers with job demands and for persons considering a career in social work. For the latter, the selection of a particular practice level as a career goal requires that one assess his or her desire to provide the particular types of service and then consider the necessary preparation and the ability to arrange one's personal life to acquire the requisite professional education. In social work, in contrast to some of the other helping professions, one can change directions after entering the profession. A person might enter social work in a particular field of practice, such as providing services to the aged or developmentally disabled, and later transfer the skills used in that job to employment in mental health or corrections. Box 5.1, for example, depicts several factors our social worker, Demetria (see Chapter 1) may have considered as she thought about what her BSW degree represented and what options she might have in the future. Or the direct service worker (usually with a master's degree) might transfer into a job involving agency administration or move away from agency-based practice and into private practice.

Box 5.1

Demetria's Career in Social Work

Demetria, the social worker investigating the report received from Joseph's school of possible child abuse or neglect (Chapter 1), was employed in her first social work job after completing her BSW degree. What did it mean for her future that she had completed the degree, had joined the National Association of Social Workers (NASW), and was now considered a professional social worker?

First, to achieve professional recognition, Demetria's educational program must have met the *accreditation standards* established by the Council on Social Work Education. Her school, then, had required courses and field experiences that included the content specified in national curriculum requirements and were taught by faculty members meeting national standards, making her education comparable to the education students would receive at other accredited schools. Already receiving professional supervision, Demetria was likely to be in the process of applying for the *Basic Social Worker license* in her state (if her state was one that offered a license at this level) and would soon start preparing for the examination she would need to pass to become a licensed social worker. To become an NASW member, Demetria signed a pledge to uphold the *Code of Ethics* and would be deepening her knowledge of the meaning of those guidelines to ethical practice as she periodically examines them to inform her practice decisions.

Second, Demetria was just beginning her career as a social worker. She knew that one positive feature of this profession was that the social work career ladder provided the opportunity for a social worker to make changes in the work he or she does in the future. For now it would take all Demetria could manage to perform her entry-level social work job in an effective manner, but later she might want to change to work with older people, in corrections, or in some other field of practice. For some changes, such as a move to more clinical work or agency administration, she would need an MSW degree and would transition to the next practice level, the *specialized professional*.

KEY WORDS AND CONCEPTS

Accreditation (of educational programs)
Professional certification
Licensing (state regulation of practice)
Indigenous workers
Advanced standing

Basic social worker
Specialized social worker
Independent social worker
Advanced social worker

SUGGESTED INFORMATION SOURCES

Gibelman, Margaret, and Phillip H. Schervish. *Who We Are: A Second Look*. Washington, D.C.: NASW Press, 1996.

National Association of Social Workers. "NASW Credentials Specialty Certification." http://www.naswdc.org.

Randal, Amanda Duffy, and Donna DeAngelis. "Licensing," in Terry Mizrahi, ed., *Encyclopedia of Social Work*, 20th ed. New York: Oxford University Press, 2008.

Whitaker, Tracy, Toby Weismiller, and Elizabeth Clark. *Assuring the Sufficiency of a Frontline Workforce: A National Study of Licensed Social Workers.* Washington, DC: National Association of Social Workers. http://workforce.socialworkers.org/studies/natstudy.asp.

ENDNOTES

1. Robert R. Wohlgemuth and Thomas Samph, *Summary Report: Content Validity Study in Support of the Licensure Examination Program of the American Association of State Social Work Boards* (Oak Park, IL: The Association, 1983), p. 2.
2. Association of Social Work Boards, "Social Work Laws and Regulations: Online Comparison Guide." http://www.aswb.org.
3. National Association of Social Workers, "Code of Ethics." May be downloaded from http://www.socialworkers.org/pubs/code/code.asp.
4. Joseph Mehr, *Human Services: Concepts and Intervention Strategies,* 8th ed. (Boston: Allyn & Bacon, 2001), pp. 11–20.
5. National Association of Social Workers, *NASW Standards for the Classification of Social Work Practice* (Washington, D.C.: The Association, 1981).
6. A comprehensive analysis of the evolution of baccalaureate-level social work can be found in Bradford W. Sheafor and Barbara W. Shank, *Undergraduate Social Work Education: A Survivor in a Changing Profession* (Austin: University of Texas at Austin School of Social Work, 1986).
7. Herbert Bisno, *The Place of Undergraduate Curriculum in Social Work Education, Social Work Curriculum Study* Vol. 2 (New York: Council on Social Work Education, 1959).
8. Council on Social Work Education, *Social Welfare Content in Undergraduate Education* (New York: The Council, 1962), pp. 3–4.
9. Council on Social Work Education, *Undergraduate Programs in Social Work* (New York: The Council, 1971).
10. Council on Social Work Education, *2006 Statistics on Social Work Education: A Summary* (Alexandria, VA: CSWE, 2007) pp. 4, 10, 12.
11. Council on Social Work Education, *Summary of Information on Master of Social Work Programs: 2001–02.* (Alexandria, VA: Council on Social Work Education, 2002).
12. Bradford W. Sheafor, "Three Decades of Baccalaureate Social Work: A Grade Card on How the Professionalization of the BSW Has Played Out." *Journal of Baccalaureate Social Work* 6 (Spring 2001): 25–43.
13. Council on Social Work Education, *Statistics,* op. cit., pp. 4, 15.
14. Ibid., pp. 4, 14.
15. Ibid., pp. 4, 18.

chapter 6

Fields of Social Work Practice

Prefatory Comment

One factor that makes social work different from many other professions is the opportunity to help people deal with a wide range of human problems without needing to obtain specialized professional credentials for each area of practice. During his or her lifetime, for example, one social worker might organize and lead self-help groups in a hospital, deal with cases of abuse and neglect, develop release plans for persons in a correctional facility, plan demonstrations protesting social injustices, arrange for foster homes and adoptions for children, secure nursing home placements for older people, supervise new social workers, and serve as director of a human service agency. Regardless of the type of work performed, the social worker always has the same fundamental purpose—to draw on basic knowledge, values, and skills in order to help achieve desired change to improve the quality of life for the persons involved.

Although there are similarities in the tasks performed by social workers regardless of the nature of the services provided, there are also unique aspects of their practice with each population group. For example, services to a single mother differ from services to a frail older adult, the needs of an adult with a disability differ from those of a person about to be released from a correctional facility, and the assistance required by a pregnant teenager differs from that needed by a teenager engaged in gang activity. Each of these fields of practice typically uses some specialized language, emphasizes specific helping approaches and techniques, or may be affected by different laws or social programs. Therefore, what a social worker does and needs to know will vary to some extent from field to field.

The human services system is indeed complex, and the layperson cannot be expected to negotiate this system alone. As the profession with the primary responsibility for helping people to gain access to the services in a community, the social worker must not only know what services are available but must also be prepared to interpret them to their clients and help these clients gain access to the resources they need. To reduce the client's sense of "getting the runaround" in securing services, and perhaps reduce the chance of the client becoming discouraged and not getting the needed help, the social worker must be sure that the referral is to an appropriate resource. In addition, the professional, at times, may need to provide a variety of supports, such as encouragement, telephone numbers, names of individuals to contact, or even transportation to facilitate the client's getting to the correct resources. Thus, the social worker must not only work within a single practice field but should also be prepared to help clients negotiate services among practice fields.

This chapter identifies some of the features of the primary fields of social work practice. *Field of social work practice* is a phrase used to describe a group of practice settings that deal with similar client problems. Each field may include a number of different agencies or other organized ways of providing services. For example, in any community, the social agencies concerned with crime and delinquency might include a juvenile court, a residential center or halfway house, a community corrections agency, a probation office for adult offenders, and/or a correctional facility where offenders are incarcerated. All of these agencies work with people who have come to the attention of the legal system and would be considered part of the practice field of corrections. Although the fields discussed in the remainder of this chapter do not exhaust the full range where social workers might practice, those identified suggest the great variety of settings in which social workers provide services.

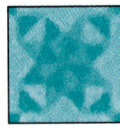

Aging

Sara May is a social worker with the Senior Center, a community recreation program offering programs geared to the needs and interests of the community's older citizens. The center's hot lunch program draws many older people daily, and Sara interacts informally with the "Lunch Crowd" as a means of building relationships and encouraging the participants to ask her for advice and counseling, if needed. Today Mrs. Jackson, a widow in her early 80s, asked if she could visit with Sara for a few minutes after lunch to talk over a difficult decision she needed to think through. Quickly Mrs. Jackson summarized her issues. It was getting much more difficult for her to manage living alone, and she was considering moving to a retirement center or possibly moving to another state to be near her daughter. The following are some questions Sara anticipated Mrs. Jackson should be helped to consider: If she stayed in this community, could she afford to live in an independent living center? What could she do with her long-time companion, her dog Sidney? Mrs. Jackson had lived in the community most of her life and in her home for 25 years. How difficult would it be to make friends somewhere else? What implications might there be for her daughter's family if she moved to be near them?

In 2006, nearly 38 million people in the United States were age 65 and over, making up 12.6 percent of the total population. This part of the population is expected to double over the next thirty years, partially as a result of the large number of baby boomers (those born between 1946 and 1965) reaching this age level and partially as a result of better health care that is increasing life expectancy. Of particular significance is the fact that the group aged 85 and older is expanding substantially and is becoming much more ethnically diverse. At age 85, the population is already 70 percent female, and, as age increases, the percentage of women living alone increases even more.[1]

The aging population is served by a substantial number of social workers. Sometimes the services are provided directly to the older persons and at other times through their families. Most of the direct work with older people is provided by "basic" social workers, with the "specialized" and "independent" workers more likely to work with families around the health and mental health problems of their older parents. Progress has been made in reducing the poverty rate for older people, although in 2006 a total of nearly 3.4 million older people (9.4 percent) had incomes at or below the poverty line.[2] Thanks to Medicare coverage, 99.3 percent of older people have health insurance, minimizing some of their financial worries over health care,[3] and assistance with expensive prescriptions makes the economic position of older people less precarious. This population group is projected to be the fastest growing of all age groups at least into the mid-2000s and is a substantially expanding area of specialization for social workers.

A number of programs are available to help older people remain in their own homes as long as doing so is a safe and satisfying experience. Social workers help older people make links to community programs that bring health care, meals, and homemaker services into their homes; provide transportation services; and offer daycare or recreation programs. Increasingly, when older people are faced with a terminal illness, social workers help them deal with their impending death through counseling or referral to a hospice program.

For approximately 4 percent of the older population, some form of long-term care in a nursing home or other group living facility becomes a necessity. Social workers frequently help the individual and/or family select the facility and make moving arrangements; some are even staff members of the facility.

While much attention in a long-term care facility is directed toward meeting the basic physical and medical needs of the residents, social workers in these facilities contribute to the quality of life for residents by helping them maintain contact with their families and friends when possible, develop meaningful relationships with other people within the facility, and engage in a variety of activities within the facility. They also facilitate access to other social services when needed and help residents secure arrangements that protect their personal rights and ensure quality care while living in the long-term care facility.

Alcohol and Substance Abuse

Andrew Richards is a social worker in an outpatient drug and alcohol center. Each Tuesday evening Andrew facilitates a group of parents who have a high school-age child experiencing a drug and/or alcohol problem. The topic of discussion tonight concerns peer influence and ways that parents might help their child deal with peers who pressure them to use drugs or alcohol. One parent argues for a get-tough, "just say no" stance, another believes getting the child to therapy is the only solution, and still another contends that giving a child room to make mistakes is the only way the child can learn to make mature judgments. Andrew knows his skills in group work will help him be sure that everyone has a chance to share his or her views and have the pros and cons of each position carefully considered. Ultimately, each parent must decide how he or she will address this matter.

Although some social workers are employed in agencies that exclusively treat drug and alcohol problems, social workers in virtually every type of human services agency deal with problems that are associated with this social problem. It is estimated that each individual experiencing a drug or alcohol problem affects at least four other persons in some negative, unhealthy, or destructive manner.[4] The social implications of alcohol and substance abuse are significant since they are highly correlated with murders, suicides, accidents, health problems, and domestic violence.

Using current scientific understanding of these problems, Lawson and Lawson have identified three primary factors that should be considered in treating and preventing alcoholism and substance abuse. First, they recognize that physiological factors such as physical addiction, disease or physical disorders, medical problems, inherited risk, and/or mental disorders with physiological causes may contribute to the problem. Second, they identify several sociological factors, such as ethnic and cultural differences, family background, education, employment, and peer relationships, as also related to alcoholism and substance abuse. Finally, they note that psychological factors, including social skills, emotional level, self-image, attitude toward life, defense mechanisms, mental obsessions, judgment, and decision-making skills, can be contributors to this disease.[5] Growing understanding of these associated and interrelated factors has provided the helping professions with an opportunity to apply their knowledge and skills to helping clients prevent and resolve their problems. Social work plays a particularly important role, as the addictions inevitably have a significant effect on family, friends, coworkers, and others who are in contact with the person experiencing the addiction. Both the person and the environment must be helped to change when this disease is treated.

Child Welfare

Megan Messer, a social worker with the County Division of Child Welfare, has a difficult recommendation to make to the judge. Her job is to evaluate the conditions in the Benjamin Bradford home to determine whether Kate, the Bradford's new baby, is getting proper care. Neighbors reported that the house is always dirty, food and unwashed clothing are left around, and the baby can be heard crying at almost any time of the day or night. When Megan called Mr. Bradford to schedule an interview, he told her it was none of her damn business and to butt out of his life. Megan had to be very persistent to get an appointment scheduled. She wasn't looking forward to the interview.

The U.S. society has entrusted the family with full responsibility for the care and nurturing of children. Law and custom mandate that other social institutions must not interfere with the rights and responsibilities of the family to care for its children. Historically, it has been assumed that parents would make choices that were in the best interest of both themselves and their children. For example, if parents thought it more important for children to contribute to the family's income by working in a factory or helping with farm work than attending school or having time for play, that decision was honored. That authority, however, left children vulnerable. Legislation permitting other social institutions (e.g., child protective services, police, and courts) to intervene in family situations that were potentially harmful to children was reluctantly adopted. Today, children and youth continue to be somewhat hidden within families with only limited protection when abusive situations are present.

In most situations, social workers seek to work with both the parents and the children by providing support services in order to keep children in their own homes. These services might involve one-to-one counseling with a parent, child–parent counseling to resolve a particular problem, or family counseling to resolve issues affecting some aspect of the family's functioning. Family members may also participate in group counseling with other parents of children experiencing similar problems where a social worker guides the group to address issues relevant to their problems. Finally, the social worker may assist the families to use outside resources such as day care and homemaker services. The following services are typically provided by social workers employed in child welfare.

Protective Services

More than 825,000 cases of child maltreatment occur in the United States each year. Of these cases, 56 percent are classified as neglect, 21 percent are related to physical abuse, 11 percent involve sexual abuse, 8 percent are psychological or emotional abuse, and the remainder are unclassified or related to other forms of abuse or neglect.[6] *Abuse*, whether it is physical, sexual, or emotional, is an active mistreatment or exploitation of the child. *Neglect* is a more passive mistreatment but can be just as damaging. It can take the form of inadequate food and shelter, unwholesome conditions, failure to have the child attend school, or inadequate provision of medical care.

The social worker, as an agent of society, seeks to protect the child without infringing on the rights of the parents. When a referral is received, the social worker must determine if the child is in immediate danger, assess the ability of the parents to resolve the problem, and make a judgment about the risks of working with the family while keeping the child in the home. If the child is removed from the home (with approval of the courts), the social worker continues to work with the family in an effort to eliminate the difficulties that led to the referral. This process may involve individual, family, or group counseling; the provision of support services; or education of family members in the areas of their incompetence.

Foster Care

At times children may need to be removed from their own homes, but it is not possible, or desirable, to permanently sever their relationship with their natural parents. In these cases, temporary (and sometimes long-term) foster care is required, and the social worker must work with the parents, the child, and the courts to obtain a decision to remove a child from his or her own home and make a foster home placement. The process involves a careful assessment and a plan whereby the child can return home if conditions improve. Although both federal and state laws discourage removing children from their families, a total of 513,000 children were living in foster care in 2005.[7]

The social worker is also responsible for developing a pool of good quality foster homes. He or she must recruit, select, train, and monitor those families that are entrusted with the care of foster children. The placement of a child in a foster home often creates severe stress on the child, the natural parents, and the foster parents. Considerable practice skill by the social worker is required if he or she is to help resolve these problems.

Residential Care

At times the appropriate placement for a child is a residential care facility, that is, a group home or residential treatment center. These facilities are most likely to be chosen when the child exhibits antisocial behavior or requires intensive treatment to change behaviors that may create problems for him- or herself or for others.

In these situations, one role of the social worker is to select an appropriate residential care facility, which involves working with the child, the family, and, often, the courts. In addition, other social workers are usually staff members of such a facility, providing care and treatment for the children who are placed there. They are especially involved in helping maintain positive contact between the child and the family and in making plans for the child to return home when appropriate. The fact that these residential care facilities require licensing creates another role for the social worker—evaluating facilities for the purpose of licensing.

Adoption and Services to Unmarried Parents

Child welfare work also involves assisting expectant mothers, often unmarried, address the difficult decision of whether to keep the baby or place the child for adoption. Nearly 36 percent of all children born in the United States in 2004 were born to unmarried parents, a factor that substantially increases the likelihood that the child will grow up in a household with income below the poverty line.[8] A few of the factors to be considered in this decision include the mother's plans for the future, such as attending school or securing employment and child care, the attitudes of the mother's family about the pregnancy, the feelings of the father's and the mother's relationship with him, and where the mother will live while pregnant and after the baby arrives. Social workers use both individual and group counseling to help women consider the implications of their decisions. They also, at times, offer counseling to unmarried fathers to help them deal with this situation.

If the decision is made to place the child for adoption, the social worker must screen and select adoptive parents carefully. Matching parents and children is a task that requires considerable knowledge and skill. To gain the best information possible on which to base these decisions, the social worker might conduct group orientation meetings and develop social histories of the prospective adoptive parents. Detailed information on the child's background and even special interests of the natural mother for the child's future (religious affiliation, for example) become part of the basis for final adoptive placement. It continues to be difficult to secure satisfactory adoptive homes for older children or those who experience a physical or mental disability. An important function of the social worker is to recruit parents for these hard-to-place children.

Community/Neighborhood Work

Luis Garcia is a social worker at a storefront neighborhood center in a large city. His job is to help residents rectify substandard housing conditions in the area. Tonight Mr. Garcia is helping a group from the neighborhood plan a strategy for pressuring some of the landlords to improve the quality of housing and to demand that the city increase traffic safety in the neighborhood.

From their beginning, social workers have clearly seen the need both to coordinate the multiple human services that exist in a community and to stimulate change in communities to make them more responsive to the needs of people or change patterns of operation that have negative effects on people. When social workers provide neighborhood or community services, three approaches characterize this work: community organization, community planning, and community development.

Community Organization

The primary job of some social workers is to work within the network of human services to increase their effectiveness in meeting human needs. This activity involves collecting and analyzing data related to the delivery of services, matching that information with data on population distribution, securing funds to maintain and enhance the quality of services, coordinating the efforts of existing agencies, and educating the general public about these services. The principal agencies in which social workers are employed to do this type of work are community planning councils, United Way agencies, and other federations of agencies under the auspices of religious groups, such as the Jewish Welfare Federation.

Community Planning

Social workers sometimes have the specialized training to join physical, economic, and health planners in creating long-range plans for communities. This work requires the ability to apply planning technology, with the special contribution of the social worker to analyze the needs for human services as towns, cities, or regions undergo change. These contributions might mean anticipating the demands that result from, for example, creating a new ski area in rural Colorado or helping an urban neighborhood plan for changes in the demand for human services when a factory shuts down, leaving the community with an eroding tax base.

Community or Neighborhood Development

Social work joins a number of disciplines in giving assistance to people in communities as they seek to improve conditions. This approach is based on a self-help philosophy that encourages members of the community to mobilize their resources in order to study their problems and seek solutions. In rural areas, the social worker contributes to this "grass roots" approach by guiding those involved toward a process that maximizes the participation of many concerned citizens. The social worker or other professional also serves as a resource for obtaining technical consultation in areas where there is not expertise among the community members. In urban areas this process, sometimes known as an "asphalt roots" approach, is used to help neighborhoods or special population groups (such as the poor, minorities, or older people) work together to improve the quality of their lives.

Corrections/Criminal Justice

Jean Drobek, a social worker employed as a juvenile probation officer, is preparing her testimony for a court hearing regarding one of her clients, Miranda Herman. Following an intense argument with her mother over her increasingly frequent use of "recreational drugs" when hanging out with her friends, Miranda impulsively decided to run away. She stole a neighbor's automobile and wrecked it when entering a nearby highway. Luckily no other vehicles were involved, and Miranda sustained no serious injuries. Since Miranda had not been using drugs when the accident occurred, she was assigned community service and placed on probation. At the start of probation, Miranda frequently failed to show up for community service assignments, although more recently she and her mother had actively participated in counseling with Ms. Drobek and were just beginning to deal with their conflicts. Should Ms. Drobek recommend that probation be continued until more progress is made?

Another important expression of social work practice occurs in the area of corrections and criminal justice. Correctional social workers are employed in courts, parole and probation offices, and correctional facilities. Social workers often find corrections a perplexing field of practice because the structure of services is usually based on punishment and taking custody of the lives of offenders, which conflicts with many social work values and principles. Yet, because the problems experienced by persons who come to the attention of professionals in this field are basically those of social functioning, the social worker has a valuable contribution to make.

The corrections field embraces offenders from all aspects of society—youth and adults, males and females, rich and poor, members of dominant population groups and minorities, and even well-known celebrities. In correctional settings, the poor, especially minorities, are very much overrepresented. The social worker's involvement with the criminal justice system can begin at the time of arrest and terminate at the person's release. Some social workers serve as, or work with, juvenile officers in diversionary programs, where they provide crisis intervention or referral services at the time of arrest. These programs divert people from the criminal justice system and into more appropriate community services. Social workers also prepare social histories and make psychosocial assessments of individuals charged with crimes as part of the data a judge uses in making decisions about a case. If the person is placed on probation, a social worker might be the probation officer providing individual, family, or group counseling and helping the convicted person make changes in behavior that will satisfy the terms of probation and hopefully prevent additional problems from developing.

Social workers are also found in correctional facilities. In these facilities, they provide counseling and serve as a link to the outside world, which encompasses the family, potential employers, and the community service network that will provide support to that person at the time of release. If parole is granted, a social worker might serve as the parole officer or work in a halfway house where the person may live prior to a completely independent re-entry to the community.

Disabilities (Physical and Mental)

K. G. Murder is executive director of the Council on Disabled Persons. This council identifies and seeks solutions to problems experienced by persons with disabling conditions, including mental retardation; physical deformity; or hearing, visual, or speech impairments. As executive director, Mr. Murder provides leadership to the citizen board as it develops programs to meet the needs of its clientele. Tonight the board will work on designing a plan for evacuating handicapped persons throughout the community should there be a disaster that requires removing people from their homes or residential care settings.

Assisting persons with physical, mental, and developmental disabilities is a field of practice in which basic social workers are most likely to be the primary service providers. Yet helping people deal with disabling conditions affects most fields of social work. Social workers are concerned with such disabling conditions as mental retardation, visual and hearing impairment, communication disability, learning disability, and cerebral palsy, which affect not only the person's physical and intellectual functioning but also interaction with others, that is, social functioning. The special role of social work is to help these persons and their families learn to live as successfully as possible in a society structured for the more fully functioning individual.

The U.S. Centers for Disease Control and Prevention estimates that, in 2007, 36 million people (12 percent of the population) experienced one or more chronic conditions that limited their activities. About 4 million people experienced such a severe condition that they needed help with daily living activities such as eating, dressing, or bathing. Another 9 million people could not do household chores or shopping without help. Health-related conditions prevented another 6 percent of the adult working-age population from employment, and another 3 percent were limited in the kind of work they could perform. Further, 6 percent of the school-age children were receiving special education services. Indeed, a substantial part of the U.S. population experiences some form of disability, and these disabilities are experienced to a greater extent among people who have the least education and the lowest income.[9] In addition to the physical disabilities, many more people experience mental or emotional conditions (or both) that are disabling.

The term *developmental disability* has evolved to include a broad range of disabling conditions that affect the physical, social, and intellectual development of a person. The Developmental Disabilities Assistance and Bill of Rights Act (Public Law 95-602) includes the following definition of a developmental disability:

> . . . a severe chronic disability of a person which: a) is attributable to a mental or physical impairment or combination of mental or physical impairments; b) is manifested before

the person attains age 22; c) is likely to continue indefinitely; d) results in substantial functional limitations in three or more of the following areas of major life activity, including self-care, receptive/expressive language, learning, mobility, self-direction, capacity for independent living, and economic self-sufficiency; and e) reflects the person's need for a combination and sequence of special, interdisciplinary, or generic care, treatment, or other services which are individually planned and coordinated.[10]

While the definition of a disabled person contained in PL 95-602 does not include all people who are physically and intellectually disabled, it does encompass a large share of the most seriously disabled. In an effort to enhance the quality of life for all people, social workers serve clients who experience both mild and severe disabilities. To accomplish this goal, social workers help people find suitable living arrangements (either with their families or in community facilities), assist in the alleviation of problems associated with the disability, contribute to public education efforts about the causes and society's responses to these disabilities, and help individuals gain access to needed services.

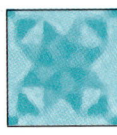

Family Services

Nadine Harrison is a specialized social worker and an expert in family casework. She has just begun working with the Machin family to help each member change his or her patterns of interacting with other family members to reduce conflict and make each a more productive member of the family. Ms. Harrison has asked that all family members come to the family counseling session and will encourage each to identify the behaviors of others that make him or her feel unsupported by the family. Then they will collectively look for ways to prevent or modify those behaviors, as well as identify ways to reinforce improved behaviors. Ms. Harrison hopes that all members of the Machin family arrive on time as there is much to be done in the next hour.

Social workers at all levels are likely to be involved in helping families address issues in their social functioning. Changing marital arrangements, child-rearing practices, and patterns of employment in the United States have placed considerable strain on the nuclear family. A growing number of single-parent families, reconstituted families (often involving her children, his children, and their children), duo-breadwinner families, and gay/lesbian households, for example, have dramatically affected previously established family patterns. Social workers have a key role in helping society address these changes and in assisting individual families and households to adapt to these newer conditions or resolve problems associated with them.

Three broad service areas capture the bulk of family services provided by social workers. First, much of the activity involves providing various forms of counseling or therapy to families. Patterns of interaction may develop that are dysfunctional for the individual members; membership may change through marriage or death, requiring new ways of relating to each other; or one member experiencing a severe social or emotional problem may create strain among the family members. Family life is often difficult and taxing for members, and issues sometimes cannot be resolved without professional help. Thus social workers working with troubled families must be skilled at providing family casework, family therapy, and other forms of family services.

Second, as opposed to working to solve family problems, social workers also work proactively to strengthen families through activities that fall under the label of *family life education.* This social work practice activity recognizes that all families face certain kinds of stress and seeks to prevent family breakdown by educating family members to cope with anticipated problems. It teaches about interpersonal, family, and sex relationships to help people to have more satisfactory and fulfilling lives.

Finally, social workers have long been sensitive to the fact that both an unwanted child and his or her parents often experience problems. Adequately carrying out the responsibilities of raising a child is difficult under the best of circumstances, and an unwanted pregnancy makes it even more difficult. Thus, helping families plan the number, spacing, and timing of the births of children to fit with the family's capacities improves the quality of life for all family members.

Income Maintenance

> Dorothy Simmons, a social worker in the local public human services agency, has an appointment with Mrs. Sang Woo. She knows from a telephone call arranging the appointment that Mrs. Woo is terribly worried about her future and that of her two small children. Her husband was killed two months ago in a robbery at the neighborhood market where he worked. In addition, Mrs. Woo found that, after paying funeral expenses, little money was left for raising the children. She hopes that Ms. Simmons can help her find a way to secure the financial resources to get by temporarily and to obtain job training and daycare so that she can support the family in the long run.

Once income maintenance was a primary practice activity engaged in by social workers, but today relatively few professionally prepared workers are employed in income maintenance positions. However, social workers in many fields of practice regularly deal with clients for whom financial matters are a primary factor in the situations they bring for help. Therefore, the social worker's knowledge of the various programs that can be accessed for financial assistance is a valuable resource for their clients.

On an emergency or short-term basis, there are usually many local agencies that provide support in the form of used clothing outlets, food banks and food kitchens, shelters for homeless individuals and families, emergency child care facilities, transportation vouchers, subsidized housing, and other resources where the poor can obtain social provisions for meeting basic needs. These resources are so unique to local areas that few people have a good understanding of what resources are available. Knowledge of these resources and how to gain access to them is therefore a special responsibility of the social worker.

In addition to locally developed services, a number of government-sponsored programs exist to meet basic needs or provide a minimum level of support in order to prevent more serious health or income problems from developing. Among the income maintenance programs are "safety net" programs that require that the recipients experience serious social or economic problems before the resource can become available to them. Examples of these programs are *Food Stamps, Temporary Assistance for Needy Families (TANF), Social Security Income (SSI),* and *Medicaid*. In addition, several social insurance programs anticipate the needs of special populations that have been designed in the "social utilities" philosophy and are available as a right for the designated client situations without the stigma of demeaning eligibility tests. These programs include *Old Age Survivors, Disability, and Health Insurance (OASDHI); Medicare; Unemployment Insurance;* and *Worker's Compensation Insurance.* Social workers practicing in most settings need to be familiar with these programs and skilled at helping clients access them.

Medical and Health Care

Ahmed Al Awam is a social worker employed in a large community hospital. For the past two years, he was assigned to the emergency room (ER), assisting individuals and families as they dealt with or adapted to the traumatic situations that brought them to the ER. Mr. Al Awam's crisis intervention skills were of primary importance in this work. Now, he has moved to the rehabilitation unit, where he is engaged in much more long-term work with patients who have experienced a substantial disabling injury. Today he is having his first session with Ted Barker, a bricklayer who sustained an injury in a construction accident that resulted in the amputation of his right arm. Mr. Barker is understandably depressed as he recognizes that he will undergo a substantial change in his life. He will no longer be able to practice his trade, and therefore he has lost his source of income to support his family, his social group of fellow bricklayers will no longer be part of his life, and he believes his wife will no longer view him as the "man" she once did. Mr. Al Awam and Mr. Barker have many issues to address.

Medical social work was initiated in the early 1900s, with social workers playing a peripheral role to physicians and nurses in health and medical settings. With increased understanding that illnesses can be caused or exacerbated by social factors, social workers gained a more central role in providing medical and health care. Today, social work in hospitals, outpatient clinics, and other health-related organizations is one of the largest practice fields for both basic and specialist/independent social workers.

A primary place for social work practice in this field is in hospitals. In these settings, for example, social workers address social and psychological factors that are either contributing causes of medical ailments or are side effects of a medical condition that must be dealt with to facilitate recovery and prevent excessive dependence on others. Social workers help to link patients experiencing changed levels of functioning due to a medical problem with their environments by providing individual, group, and family counseling; serving as patient advocates; and working with self-help groups of patients experiencing similar medical or social problems. Social workers also might be engaged in counseling terminally ill patients and their families.

In addition, social workers are involved in other health and medical care facilities besides hospitals. They work in public health clinics and private physicians' offices providing counseling and referral services to people who have sought medical treatment related to family planning, prenatal care, child growth and development, venereal disease, and physical disability, for example. They have also taken an active role in health maintenance and disease prevention programs in local communities. With the skyrocketing costs of medical care, it is even more important that these efforts be continued by the social work profession.

Mental Health and Illness

Kirsten Laurali is a social worker in the adolescent unit of a large psychiatric hospital. Although she counsels some patients individually, this afternoon she will meet with a group of adolescent girls who are expected to be released from the hospital in a few weeks. Ms. Laurali plans to facilitate the girls in expressing any concerns they feel about leaving the security of the hospital and to discuss any family, school, and peer interaction problems they anticipate experiencing when returning to home and school. She will also help to connect them and their parents with a local mental health clinic where they can receive ongoing support after their hospitalization has ended.

It has long been recognized that one's mental health and capacity for healthy social functioning are highly correlated. A person who is depressed, hyperactive, hallucinating, or experiencing any of the other symptoms of mental illness is likely at some time to become the client of the social worker. It is estimated that 15 percent of the general population experience some form of emotional disturbance at any one time, creating a high demand for social workers, who are twice as prevalent as psychologists and psychiatrists in the mental health field. In the field of mental health and illness, the specialized social worker (with an MSW degree as preparation) is the usual practice level—although social workers in other settings, at all practice levels, regularly work with clients for whom emotional illness is at least a contributing factor to their problems.

Social workers in mental health settings work with people experiencing these difficulties by treating those who have the potential to improve the quality of their lives. They help them learn to cope with problems in their social functioning and, at the same time, work to change factors in their environment to promote better mental health or eliminate social conditions that have a negative effect on their functioning.

There are three practice settings where social workers are most likely to engage in psychiatric social work: outpatient mental health clinics, inpatient psychiatric hospitals, and private practice. In an outpatient clinic, social workers provide clinical or therapeutic services to individuals and families or to small groups of clients. They may also consult or work with a variety of organizations, such as group homes or the mass media, in an effort to create an environment that is conducive to the healthy growth and development of all people. When employed in a psychiatric hospital, social workers may provide a variety of treatment activities to the patients themselves, but they also serve as a liaison to the patient's outside world and help family or friends maintain contact while the person is hospitalized. The social worker might also assess the impact of family, friends, an employer, school, and so forth on the client's situation and offer assistance in helping these significant others change in ways that will benefit the client. When patients are ready to return home, social workers help to arrange appropriate living situations, ranging from housing accommodations (if needed) to ongoing service from a community mental health center. Finally, the social worker in private practice is most likely to focus on treatment for individuals and families, although small group intervention approaches may be used on occasion.

Occupational or Industrial Social Work

Working for a large manufacturing firm was a new experience for Doug Perry, an experienced clinical social worker. The CEO of the company was concerned that the employees increasingly are experiencing social problems such as marital conflict, alcohol dependence, and issues related to their children that interfere with their ability to perform their work in the company's plant. Mr. Perry's first assignment was to prepare a plan to increase worker productivity by reducing these social problems. Next week a report is due to the Board of Directors, and Mr. Perry is outlining a plan that includes (1) establishing a case-finding and referral service on the premises, staffed by social workers; (2) outsourcing the most serious cases to community agencies and private practitioners; and (3) strengthening prevention efforts by creating a company foundation with sufficient funding to support research into the factors contributing to these problems.

Social work has been practiced in business and industrial settings since the late 1800s. Social workers have been employed both by management and labor unions to offer services and provide consultation through employee assistance programs. In recent years, with businesses increasingly realizing that worker productivity is closely related to the workers' general satisfaction with the quality of their lives, an investment in helping employees resolve problems in social functioning is seen as simply good business. This perspective has created a small but growing field of practice known as occupational or industrial social work. With more than 154.5 million people in the civilian labor force in 2008,[11] the workplace is an opportune setting in which to identify social problems and provide needed services. Often, early intervention at the location of one's employment can prevent more serious problems from developing later.

Shank and Jorve identify three models of social work practice in business and industry: the employee service model, the consumer service model, and the corporate social responsibility model.[12] An explanation of each follows.

The *employee service model* of occupational social work focuses on activities that provide direct service to the employees of a business or industry. The social worker using this model might develop and implement employee assistance programs and various supervisory training programs. In addition, the social worker might provide counseling to individuals or families in relation to marital, family, substance abuse, aging, health, and retirement problems, and offer referral to other community agencies or self-help groups. Typical problems the social worker might also address would be the identification of job-related factors such as boredom or stress, an employee's desire to find resources to upgrade his or her job skills, or the need for preretirement planning.

The occupational social worker following the *consumer service model* might serve as the company's representative to various consumer groups and focus on identifying consumer needs and methods of meeting them. Typically found in banks, public utilities, and government agencies, these social workers help to provide a liaison between consumer groups and social service agencies, develop outreach programs, and provide counseling to customers to meet unique needs.

The third model of practice, the *corporate social responsibility model,* places the social worker in the role of assisting corporations and businesses to make a commitment to the social and economic well-being of the communities in which they are located. The social workers consult with management on their policies concerning human resources, their donations to nonprofit organizations, and social legislation they may wish to support. In addition, social workers may administer health and welfare benefit programs for employees; represent the company in research and community development activities; and provide linkage between social service, social policy, and corporate interests.

Schools

> The death of a loved one seems to be epidemic in Cesar Chavez Elementary School this year, and Bruni Baez, the school social worker, is aware that five children in the fifth and sixth grades have experienced the deaths of grandparents or siblings in the few months since the school year began. For all of these children, performance in the classroom has deteriorated, and they show little interest in extracurricular activities. With the support of their teachers, Mrs. Baez has arranged for a 30-minute group session once each week in which these children can work on their grief and loss issues. Each week they will talk about a different issue, such as normal grief reactions, healthy and unhealthy coping patterns, the effect of grief on social relationships, understanding physical and mental reactions to grief, talking about the person who died, and so on. She wonders which of these topics might be best for the first session with the students.

Just as places of employment are important locations for identifying and addressing problems of social functioning for the employed population, schools are an important place to serve children and youth. It is known that individual and family problems directly affect a child's ability to learn, and school social workers are employed to help parents, teachers, and children address these complex issues.

The traditional approach of social workers in schools has been to counsel the child and confer with the family. They have depended on the cooperation of teachers to make referrals when problems are evident and have had varying degrees of effectiveness, depending on the willingness of teachers and school systems to use them as a resource. Problems of truancy, suspected child abuse, inadequate nutrition, substance abuse, parental neglect, and inappropriate behavior are often referred to the social worker.

Social workers serve as a link between school, family, and community. Some activities that school social workers typically perform include offering counseling to children, their families, and teachers related to factors that affect the child's performance at school; serving as an advocate for children with school administrators and community agencies when specialized services are needed; organizing parent and community groups to strengthen school and community relationships; and coordinating teams that draw on different disciplines' expertise and parents' interests to assess a child and develop a plan to assist a child's development.

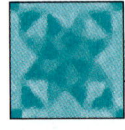

Youth Services

Diversion programs have become a hot item in human services agencies designed to work with youth. At the Michael Jordan Recreation Center, Bob Jackson draws on his social work skills to involve members of several neighborhood gangs in activities at the center. He knows that the traditional approach of attempting to engage these youths in competitive sports has not been successful, and he is seeking new forms of activities that might capture the interest of these gang members and help divert them from the more harmful activities in which they are now engaged. Mr. Jackson had decided to create an advisory board of former gang members and is preparing for a focus group session in which he hopes to draw out information that will assist in his planning.

Very early in U.S. history a number of human service programs were developed to provide educational and recreational opportunities for people of all social classes. These services were aimed at character building among youth, with organizations such as the YMCA, YWCA, Boys and Girls Clubs, and various scouting groups developing. Later, with the growth of settlement houses, programs were broadened to serve other age groups. Although other disciplines also provide staff for these organizations, this field of practice continues to be a small but important area of social work.

These services seek to enhance the growth and development of all interested participants, from the poor to the well-to-do. Through the use of such activities as crafts, sports, camping, friendship groups, drama, music, informal counseling, and other forms of group participation, the members are guided toward personal development. The role of the social worker might be to administer these agencies, to lead the group process, or to provide individual counseling.

Concluding Comment

For the person considering a career in social work, it is important to have an understanding of the many different fields of practice open to the social worker. It is evident that the attention social workers give to helping people and their environments interact more favorably makes an important contribution to resolving social problems or enhancing social functioning in many areas.

The most current data about social work practitioners indicate there are some practice areas where substantial numbers of both basic and specialist/independent social workers are employed, and this includes such areas as work with children and youth, families, and health care. BSW-level workers are much more likely than their MSW counterparts to be engaged in providing services to the aged and working in the disabilities area, while the primary practice area for the MSWs, by a substantial margin, is mental health.

A clear picture of client needs addressed by social workers emerges from data presented in this chapter. Helping clients resolve problems in family functioning stands well above all others. A second and often interrelated tier of issues are those of client functioning that have been affected by mental illness or retardation, character disorders or behavior problems, health-related matters, anxiety or depression, difficulties in interpersonal relations, and problems associated with alcohol and substance abuse.

The knowledge and skills acquired when obtaining a baccalaureate or master's degree in social work are intended to prepare one to engage in social work practice in any of these practice fields. The social work practice performed by Demetria (Chapter 1) is located in the field of child welfare practice, i.e., working with children and youth. However, the discussion presented in Box 6.1 also highlights the fact that a practicing social worker must be knowledgeable about the work performed in other fields to serve clients effectively, should he or she someday transition to a different field. The ability to transfer these competencies from field to field gives the social worker considerable flexibility in selecting where he or she will work and what type of client issues will be the focus of practice. This job flexibility has long been an attractive feature of social work.

Box 6.1

Demetria's Field of Practice

In the case presented in Chapter 1, the primary field of practice for our social worker, Demetria, was *child welfare*. In this case she was employed by a county human services department, although child welfare work is performed in virtually any type of agency setting—public, private nonprofit, private for-profit, and even in private practice. Demetria's work was related to one of several child welfare programs, *protective services,* with the mission of protecting children and youth from various forms of abuse and maltreatment.

In this field of practice, Demetria might also have had responsibility for placing a child with severe emotional or behavioral problems in a *residential care* facility, placing children who can benefit from a different home environment in a *foster care* home, or arranging for the legal *adoption* of children who cannot reside with their natural parents for a variety of reasons but who do not have such serious problems that they cannot become part of another family permanently.

Demetria's work in this case touched other fields of practice where social workers might be employed. The case was initiated from a school in which there might have been a *school social worker,* her colleague in the Boys and Girls Club was employed in a *youth services* agency, and the root of the Miles family's issues appeared to be related to unemployment and the subsequent financial problems that would be addressed by social workers in the field of *income maintenance*. Should the issues experienced by Joseph diminish and Mr. Miles return home, a helpful referral might be to a *family services* agency where in-depth counseling could occur to help this family get its life back in order. In short, although Demetria was employed in child welfare, she needed knowledge of the work that occurs in several other fields of social work practice to do her job adequately.

KEY WORDS AND CONCEPTS

Field of social work practice
Developmental disability

Occupational or industrial social work

SUGGESTED INFORMATION SOURCES

Literally hundreds of books and articles are published each year on the various fields of practice described in this chapter. The four books listed below are recommended as resources for beginning the process of acquiring additional information about the various fields of social work practice.

Mizrahi, Terry, and Larry E. Davis, eds. *Encyclopedia of Social Work*, 20th ed. Washington, D.C.: NASW Press and Oxford University Press, 2008. The four-volume *Encyclopedia of Social Work* is a valuable resource for investigating most topics relevant to social workers. The author(s) of each chapter is selected by the *Encyclopedia's* editorial board as a highly respected expert on the subject matter. Each author provides a "state-of-the-art" summary of the topic and a bibliography of the seminal literature on that subject. Its availability as an electronic document makes searching for specific topics efficient.

Gibelman, Margaret. *What Social Workers Do*, 2nd ed. Washington, D.C.: NASW Press, 2004. This book is packed with short chapters describing more than fifty different examples of social work practice. Each contains a short case vignette that helps the reader gain insight into what the social worker does while serving clients.

Grobman, Linda May, ed. *Days in the Lives of Social Workers*. Harrisburg, PA: White Hat Communications, 1996. Forty-one practitioners tell their stories about what they do in a typical day as a social worker. The sections are organized around fields of practice (for example, health care, school social work, mental health, and so on) with several examples of social work in each field.

LeCroy, Craig Winston. *The Call to Social Work: Life Stories*. Thousand Oaks, CA: Sage, 2002. Thirty-four social workers share the experiences that led them to select social work as a career, and in the process they provide insight into why they selected a particular field of practice.

Ritter, Jessica A., Havaevalu F. O. Vakalahi, and Mary Kiernan-Stern. *101 Careers in Social Work*. New York: Springer, 2009. Helpful for exploration of the many career possibilities in social work.

ENDNOTES

1. U.S. Census Bureau, "National Population Estimates: Characteristics." http://www.census.gov/popest/national/asrh/NC-EST2007-sa.html.
2. U.S. Census Bureau, "Historical Poverty Tables, Table 3": Poverty Status of People, by Age, Race, and Hispanic Origin: 1959 to 2006." http://www.census.gov/hhes/www/poverty/histpov/hstpov3.html.
3. U.S. Department of Commerce News, "More People Have Health Insurance, Census Bureau Reports." http://www.census.gov/Press-Release/www/2001/cb01-162.html.
4. Ronald E. Herrington, George R. Jacobson, and David G. Benzer, eds., *Alcohol and Drug Abuse Handbook* (St. Louis: Warren H. Green, 1987), p. xiii.
5. Gary W. Lawson and Ann W. Lawson, *Alcoholism and Substance Abuse in Special Populations* (Rockville, MD: Aspen Publishers, 1989), pp. 5–7.

6. U.S. Department of Health and Human Services, *Trends in the Well-Being of Children and Youth, 2001*. Washington, D.C.: U.S. Government Printing Office, 2001, p. 143.
7. Child Trends Data Bank, "Foster Care." http://www.childtrendsdatabank.org/indicators/12FosterCare.cfm.
8. Federal Interagency Forum on Child and Family Statistics, *America's Children in Brief: Key National Indicators of Well-Being, 2007*. http://www.childstats.gov/americaschildren06/pop.asp.
9. *Summary of Health Statistics for the U.S. Population: National Health Interview Survey, 20037*. National Center for Health Statistics, Series 10, Number 238. http://www.cdc.gov/nchs/data/series/sr_10/sr10_238.pdf.
10. Robert L. Schalock, *Services for Developmentally Disabled Adults* (Baltimore: University Park Press, 1982), p. 12.
11. U.S. Bureau of Labor Statistics, "Civilian Labor Force and Unemployment." http://data.bls.gov/cgi-bin/surveymost?bls.
12. Barbara W. Shank and Beth K. Jorve, "Industrial Social Work: A New Arena for the BSW." Paper presented at the National Symposium of Social Workers, Washington, D.C., 1983, p. 14.

chapter 7

Settings for Social Work Practice

Prefatory Comment

Our society's commitment to the welfare of its members is played out through an extensive array of social programs that are delivered by several different helping professions—including social work. For people to gain access to these programs and the professionals who deliver them, there must be some form of organizational structure that serves as a vehicle for delivering the services. Usually that is a formal organization that operates under the auspices of a federal, state, or local government; a nonprofit community agency; or a for-profit organization operated as a business. The latter setting includes social workers who are private practitioners; that is, they create their own business in the same manner as the private physician or attorney who maintains an office where clients receive the services.

These differing practice settings influence the nature of client problems a social worker addresses, the clients served, the amount of paperwork required, the salary earned, and many other factors that affect one's work activity and job satisfaction. This chapter examines the advantages and disadvantages for both social workers and their clients in the different practice settings.

Throughout its history, social work has been primarily an agency-based profession. Like teaching, nursing, and the clergy, social work practice emerged primarily within organizations, and today, as in the past, most social workers are employed in some form of human service organization. In recent years there has been a shift in the employment patterns of social workers into the for-profit sector. Nevertheless, today the nonprofit sector employs the largest percentage of today's social workers (37 percent), followed closely by the government sector (34 percent), with the remaining 29 percent employed in the business or for-profit sector.[1]

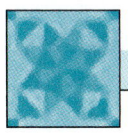

Characteristics of Practice Settings

When social programs are created, a decision must be made about whether the program will be delivered under the auspices of a human service organization or by an independent practitioner. When programs are provided by human service organizations, the agencies establish the necessary policies and supply the administrative structure to make the program available to recipients. Clients then contract with that agency for the needed service, and the agency employs staff to deliver the program. The organization is responsible for determining who is eligible for service and how that service will be performed, for screening and selecting its staff, for assigning the work to various staff members, for monitoring the quality of the work, and for securing funds to pay the costs of providing the service.

When the service is delivered by a social worker in private practice, the client contracts directly with the social worker or the private practice group with which the worker is associated. The client then pays directly for the service or draws on insurance, Medicare, or other funds to pay for the service. Licensing helps the clients or companies paying for this service determine if the practitioner is qualified to perform this service.

Government Sector Settings

Government organizations are established and funded by the general public with the intent to provide services that preserve and protect the well-being of people in the community. These agencies must operate within the provisions of the laws under which they were established. The largest government sector social programs are created by lawmakers in Washington, D.C., or a state capital. These policy makers are usually geographically distant from the clients and service providers alike and, too often, are unfamiliar with the day-to-day issues that arise when these laws are implemented by local agencies. For this reason, social workers often find their practice in government agencies frustrating. There is inherent inflexibility in these settings because laws are difficult to change, budgeting and auditing systems are highly structured, and cumbersome civil service or personnel systems are mandated. Further, these organizations are subject to political manipulation, and financial support and program development can be significantly influenced by a changing political climate. Except through substantial political action efforts, those who must carry out these programs have limited opportunity to influence their structure and funding.

On the positive side, although sometimes client fees are required, public agencies are financed largely by taxes, and the regular flow of tax money offers some stability to the programs. Legislative bodies are authorized to levy taxes so human needs can be met, and, in times of economic difficulty when voluntary contributions may be reduced, legislators have the power to tax and, therefore, maintain the services.

It should be recognized that government sector agencies provide services that are likely to meet the most basic human needs such as food, clothing, and shelter. It simply has not been possible to adequately respond to the fundamental needs of the poor, homeless, disabled, aged, and others through voluntary and for-profit human services.

Nonprofit (Voluntary) Sector Settings

Out of the history of providing assistance for persons needing help, a number of *mutual aid organizations* have been created to facilitate members of a group providing services for other members of that group. Churches and labor unions, for example, support some human service programs for their members, yet they rarely employ professional staff.

Some religious groups have created *sectarian* or *faith-based programs* for the general public that are sometimes staffed by social workers. A substantial number of human services, from counseling to social provisions, are provided to members by synagogues and various denomination groups. Other religious groups believe it is part of their mission to serve all persons in need, whether members of their faith or not, and they have a long history of providing services for the benefit of the general public. These *nonsectarian programs* include the sponsorship of hospitals, group homes, retirement centers, and family counseling agencies.

Labor unions represent another mutual aid setting where social workers might be found. Unions historically have been successful in organizing workers who are underpaid and undervalued by management and advocating for their rights. Today, the labor union setting presents an exceptional opportunity to intervene with people at the place they work and therefore improve the likelihood of resolving problems before they reach a crisis level. Social workers in these settings typically help union members with such work-related problems as finding child care, dealing with family problems related to work schedules, and addressing stress created by changed family roles when both spouses are employed.

A second type of practice setting in the voluntary sector of human services is the *private nonprofit agency*. Private agencies traditionally have depended on voluntary individual and corporate support for their operation. Their sources of funds have included gifts and bequests, membership dues, fees for service, and participation in federated campaigns such as a United Way or a Jewish Welfare Federation. More recently, however, private agencies have begun receiving a substantial share of their funding through contracts with government agencies to provide specific services, conduct research and demonstration projects, or to support their programs through block grants or revenue sharing. Government agencies have increasingly found this a desirable arrangement because it has allowed them to bypass much of the rigidity of the large bureaucratic organizations in favor of the more flexible private agency structures.

Although there has been an intermingling of taxes and donated funds in the budgets of these private agencies, they are classified as part of the voluntary sector because they operate with policies established by a governing board made up of community volunteers. In their governance, then, nonprofits differ dramatically from government agencies that have elected officials responsible for making basic policy decisions. In most instances, these agencies have the advantage of being small and primarily concerned with the provision of local services. Thus, the board members are able to become directly exposed to the agency and are usually more prepared to respond to changing conditions and needs for services in a local community.

The term *nonprofit* indicates that if the agency should end a year with any funds remaining, those resources are allocated to enhance the agency's operation and not paid to staff, board, or any other parties. Because no one profits financially from the operation of the agency and it serves the public good, the Internal Revenue Service has created a process to approve agencies [Section 501(c)(3) of the Internal Revenue Code] as nonprofit organizations. With this designation, persons who donate funds to support the agency can deduct the contribution from their income taxes. In this way, the government is underwriting the voluntary sector human services.

Business Sector Settings

The most rapidly growing setting for social work practice is the for-profit or business sector. This category of practice includes both private practice and employment in large organizations that exist to earn a profit for their owners. The term *private practice* is used to indicate a practice situation where a contract for the provision of service is made directly between the worker and the clients. Usually this term is applied in reference to social workers who provide clinical services, but sometimes private practice involves nonclinical activities such as consulting, conducting workshops or training programs, or contracting to perform research or other professional service for a fee.

With direct client–worker contracts, the practitioners have considerable autonomy in determining how the practice situation will be addressed and what intervention approaches will be used. However, without the monitoring of services that human services agencies provide, clients are more vulnerable to incompetent or unethical practitioners. It is fundamentally for client information and protection that all 50 states license or certify social workers, as well as for NASW's development of the several specialized credentials.

For some social workers, private practice is an attractive alternative to agency-based practice. Usually there is less paperwork to manage, more flexibility in scheduling, and, often, the elimination of unnecessary supervision. In addition, private practice is among the highest-paying settings for social workers. The downside of private practice is that it is a small business and, like many small businesses, is difficult to sustain. A practice must attract a sufficient number of clients who can pay the fees to support the ongoing operating costs (e.g., space, utilities, clerical staff) and also provide a wage for the social worker. For this reason, many social workers engage in private practice on a part-time basis and maintain their primary employment in a human services agency.

Another entrepreneurial setting for social work is in *for-profit organizations*. There has been a transformation in the funding of human service programs. From the 1930s through the 1970s, legislative bodies allocated substantial funds for government agencies to provide services directly to clients. Therefore, a relatively large public sector developed. Later, that pattern shifted to purchase-of-service agreements, with nonprofit agencies rather than governmental agencies providing many of these services. A second, and perhaps even more dramatic, shift known as *privatization* is now occurring where governmental agencies invest in the purchase of service from for-profit organizations that are owned and operated as any other business. In fact, many are owned and operated by large corporations.

Several fields of practice have rapidly increased their reliance on these businesses to provide human services. For example, in child welfare, proprietary firms are used extensively as vendors for services for residential treatment, institutional care, and group homes. To a lesser degree, public agencies rely on contracts with for-profit organizations to provide daycare, day treatment services, nursing home care, correctional facilities, and health care.

Social work professionals are uneasy about the growing amount of for-profit practice. The trend toward the privatization of human services threatens to replace the profession's service orientation with the profit motive. Privatization risks making the bottom line the amount of return to the shareholder, rather than the quality of service to the client. When the shareholder is also the service provider, additional ethical issues arise that can erode public trust in the professions.

One development that has affected all social workers in the business sector, whether in private practice or employed by for-profit organizations, is the evolution of *managed care*—or perhaps more accurately, managed costs. Stimulated by the escalating cost of health and mental health services, a variety of plans have been developed to provide health care consumers with needed services at controlled costs. On the positive side, these plans require greater accountability for the quality of services offered, which ultimately should enhance the services clients receive. However, many decisions about the nature and extent of services provided are shifted from the professionals and clients to the managers of the insurance companies. These are not typically people with the qualifications to determine an individual's need for professional services. In relation to mental health services, Stroul, Pires, Armstrong, and Meyers analyzed the effects of managed care and concluded that under managed care programs children and adolescents have had greater access to outpatient services but reduced access to inpatient hospital care—particularly youths with serious emotional disorders or those who are uninsured. In addition, they note that services have become briefer, more problem-oriented, and more focused on behavioral health disorders.[2] The social worker's role with managed care also includes advocating for clients who are not receiving authorization for needed services from these health insurance companies.

Social workers have a central role to play in all three sectors of the human services—government, voluntary, and business. The ability of these professionals to perform their function depends at least partially on their ability to work effectively within a human services organization or manage a private practice. Understanding several issues typically experienced in each of these settings can help future social workers anticipate difficulties they may face and be prepared to deal with them head on.

Issues Affecting Agency-Based Practice

When considering a social work job, potential employing agencies should be examined in relation to their relative compatibility with professional values and standards and the autonomy workers have to exercise their professional judgment in performing the job tasks. Also, the manner in which a human service organization deals with the following issues will affect the work of its professional staff.

Accommodating Horizontal and Vertical Influences

Social workers employed in most human service organizations, as well as those in private practice, often find they cannot successfully work in isolation from other agencies. At the local level, social workers often lead efforts to coordinate the services provided to clients by several social agencies in that community. This coordination sometimes requires that interagency networks, or *horizontal affiliations,* are developed among the agencies. The form of these horizontal networks may range from informal discussions among agency representatives regarding human service programs to the formal creation of human resources planning organizations that study the local service network, encouraging efforts to fill gaps in the services, and facilitating cooperation among the agencies. Decisions made through these horizontal affiliations will influence the choices the social worker can make in serving his or her clients.

Social agencies and social workers are also influenced by *vertical affiliations,* that is, those organizations external to the community that have the authority at least partially to shape the services or operating procedures of a local agency. Voluntary agencies, for example, might affiliate with a national organization, which can give the agency name recognition, provide the community with some assurance that at least minimum standards acceptable in that practice field are being met, make staff development opportunities available through national meetings, and sometimes help secure financial resources. At the same time, these agencies give up some local autonomy as they are committed to operate within the guidelines of the national organization. Vertical affiliation with the American Red Cross, Child Welfare League of America, YWCA or YMCA, and the Family Service Association of America are typical examples of such affiliations. Further, many local voluntary agencies must meet state licensing requirements or other state standards if they are vendors of services to public agencies. This also limits their discretion.

Public agencies typically have more formal vertical relationships. A local governmental agency may be implementing programs that have been created and partially funded at the federal level, further defined and partially funded at the state level, and finally modified and also funded by county government. Thus, a county human services department, for example, is constrained by requirements imposed by federal, state, and county governments. Although these vertical affiliations add to the complexity of tailoring service programs to local needs, they have the advantage of fostering greater equality in the services provided to people throughout a region and the nation. In addition, vertical affiliation creates a larger geographic area for securing funds to support the services, making it possible to more adequately meet needs in a local or regional area that lacks its own resources.

Balancing Efficiency and Effectiveness

A fundamental goal of all human service agencies, whether they are public or private, is to use the scarce resources available to provide the most and best service possible. To achieve this goal, agencies must operate both efficiently and effectively. An agency that leans too far in favoring one over the other ultimately creates problems for the staff members employed in that agency.

Efficiency represents the efforts of the agency to achieve the maximum output of services with a minimum input of resources. The goal of efficiency places the emphasis on the quantity of services provided and often attracts most of the attention of lawmakers, governing boards, and local media. Yet, quantity must be related to quality if an agency is to find a balance that represents the maximum level of service. The qualitative aspects of service are represented in an agency's *effectiveness*, or the degree to which the agency achieves its goals.

The governance of most social agencies has been dominated, in both the public and voluntary sectors, by people who have experience in business and industrial enterprises. They often bring a strong bias toward efficiency, and, although some degree of effectiveness in producing goods was necessary for their success, low cost-per-unit production was clearly their most valued goal. That orientation is especially evident in managed care and the for-profit human service organizations. Thus, the social worker considering agency employment should carefully examine the agency's effectiveness orientation lest the quality of his or her work be seriously compromised in favor of overemphasis on efficiency.

How can efficiency be attained in human service organizations? One management tool used successfully in business and industry and transferred to the human services is bureaucratic structure. Bureaucracy worked to build automobiles and appliances at a fraction of the cost of handmade products. Weber created the clearest statement of bureaucratic theory. His "ideal-type" description of the characteristics of a bureaucratic organization was intended to reflect the fundamental elements of a bureaucracy. The following is a synthesis of Weber's extensive work on this topic.[3]

1. *Division of Labor.* Each person in the organization has a clearly defined and specialized assignment in the organization.
2. *Hierarchy.* Specific lines of authority exist in which every person is not only responsible for his or her own assignments but is also responsible for the performance of subordinates.
3. *Consistent System of Rules.* Every task in the organization is governed by an explicit set of rules that specify the standards of performance and the relationships among tasks.
4. *Spirit of Impersonality.* Work is to be performed without favoritism or prejudice entering official decisions.
5. *Employment Constitutes a Career.* Persons are employed on the basis of qualifications required by the organization, with rewards provided to encourage loyalty and to offer opportunity for a career in that organization.

With some modifications, when applied to the assembly line that produces automobiles in Detroit or toasters in New Jersey, bureaucratic principles led to a high degree of organizational efficiency. This model yielded good results when the product was made from standardized parts. In fact, the greater the standardization, the more effective the bureaucratic organization becomes. A person could quickly be trained to perform a very specific function, for example, installing a fuel pump as an automobile passes on the assembly line. With a line supervisor to provide quality control and enforce the rules established for efficiency (the worker cannot be taking a break when the engine arrives for a fuel pump), the company usually produced a good-quality product. Under this system, there could be no allowance for the worker's personal problems, nor could the boss play favorites. Bureaucratic theory assumes that the rewards of job security, salary increases, and retirement benefits are sufficient to keep the successful employee satisfied with the organization—although some of these companies have recently reneged on providing these promised benefits.

When these principles are applied to human services agencies, social workers and other professionals often find that bureaucratization has both positive and negative consequences. Indeed, the application of bureaucratic principles can ensure equity for both clients and workers, facilitate efficiency in operation, and enhance public support of the organization. Rigid application of bureaucratic principles, however, is in direct conflict with the very nature of professions. As opposed to manufacturing products, in human services the parts being worked with are people who are constantly changing, and the product (attaining maximum client well-being) differs to some degree in each situation. It is simply not realistic to provide narrow technical training, to create highly specialized assignments, or to establish an inflexible system of rules that a staff must follow without adjusting for the uniqueness of the client or practice situation.

Accommodating the Professional Model in Bureaucratic Organizations

When the professional model is compared with the bureaucratic model of conducting work, inherent conflicts emerge that are likely to result in some level of tension for professionals employed in bureaucratic organizations. Scott suggests the following conflicts almost always exist between these two models:[4]

- *Resistance to bureaucratic rules.* When a division of labor exists, each person provides only a narrowly defined part of the work. Procedures are then established to coordinate the activities among workers, and these procedures often make it difficult for professionals to individualize services and respond to the unique needs of each client.
- *Rejection of bureaucratic standards.* Standards of client eligibility for services and procedures that determine the extent of the services a worker can provide are designed to respond to the "typical client." In reality, clients represent great variability, and professionals in bureaucratic agencies often feel frustrated in their ability to fulfill their obligation to provide the best services possible to their clients.
- *Objection to bureaucratic supervision.* In bureaucratic organizations, authority is assigned to a position (e.g., a supervisor or foreman) who is primarily charged with responsibility to monitor the work of the line workers for compliance with agency rules and regulations. Conversely, professional authority is generated from practice competence as judged by one's peers. Professionals, then, object to assigned supervision where the supervisor may or may not possess sufficient practice competence to consult about the worker's practice.
- *Conditional loyalty to the organization.* Employees in bureaucratic organizations are trained in the specific job tasks needed by that organization and their success is judged by movement up the organizational ladder, that is, from line

worker, to supervisor, to foreman, and so on. Thus, the workers usually have few skills that can be transferred to another organization and are therefore somewhat locked in to their companies. Professionals, however, tend to be primarily committed to careers in their professions and are prepared with competencies that are transferable from one organization to another, making it relatively easy to change their work environment.

How does a professional social worker address these areas of incompatibility? Clearly, an employee is obligated to work within the legitimate requirements of his or her employer, and a social worker cannot ethically ignore the rules and regulations of the agency. However, it is not sufficient to be merely a passive employee who unquestioningly accepts and carries out the rules and regulations of the agency. Client services can be compromised if social workers do not actively work to promote agency flexibility in service provision and, when warranted, be willing to challenge the agency's methods of operating. At times, this may mean taking some risks that may affect one's evaluations, pay increases, or even employment in the agency. Thus the successful agency-based social worker must be smart about organizational change efforts.

Many times constricting agency rules and regulations do not need to be changed. Creative interpretations that stretch the rules to fit client needs are often possible and frequently can be applied with the full support of one's supervisor. Some regulations, however, may not lend themselves to this flexibility, and it may be necessary to attempt to initiate a process to change these rules. Change, especially in large public agencies, takes considerable time and effort. With skill, patience, and perseverance, such change can be accomplished and the professional obligation of the worker to provide the best services possible fulfilled. If this effort fails, however, the worker must either learn to live with the existing regulations or make the decision to seek employment elsewhere.

Assuming that satisfactory conditions exist in an agency for performing social work practice, it becomes important for the worker to discover ways to be responsible to the agency and at the same time maximize the ability to provide services to clients. Pruger suggests four helpful tactics that a worker might employ.[5] First, it is important to understand the agency's (or supervisor's) legitimate authority. Within the guidelines of responsible behavior, one should discover the limits of the discretion a worker has in providing services to clients. Second, because organizations often present demands (e.g., paperwork, staff meetings) that divert the worker's time and energy from the work of providing services, the worker should be cautious about overcommitting to these activities that are of secondary importance. Third, the worker should develop supplemental competencies that are needed by the agency. Professional work involves more than carrying out the routine job duties. It involves making a commitment to expand one's contributions by learning, for example, new practice techniques, skills in grant writing, knowledge of computer applications in practice, or methods of interpreting the agency and its services to the public. Finally, the worker should not yield unnecessarily to agency requirements established for administrative convenience. For instance, it may be convenient to have clients come to the worker's office to receive services so that back-to-back interviews can be scheduled and the worker's time used efficiently. However, for some clients, the requirement of arranging transportation, leaving work, or the unfamiliarity with the agency may discourage them from keeping the appointment. In such a case, a home visit by the worker may be far more successful. Although challenging unproductive regulations may not help the social worker win popularity contests, this action can be a valuable contribution to the organization's effectiveness.

Another contribution that a social worker can make to an employing agency is to prepare to move into a supervisory role or assume an executive or high-level administrative position in the agency. Making such a transition is difficult. As compared to direct service practitioners, the social workers who are administrators are much more involved in activities such as making staff assignments and conducting evaluations of their work, representing the agency and helping to build the service delivery system in the community, engaging in program development, and carrying out various tasks (e.g., budget development, expense approval, staff coordination) that help to maintain the organization's daily operations.

Finally, a worker should be prepared to engage in teamwork and interprofessional practice. Agency practice typically draws together volunteers, persons from varying professions, and other staff members in an effort to respond to human needs. In theory the unique roles and capacities of each discipline appear clear and workers need only coordinate their efforts. In reality, however, there is considerable blurring of lines between the various helping disciplines. Turf problems inevitably emerge that, if not resolved, can jeopardize good client service. Thus, interprofessional collaboration and teamwork are essential.

Human service agencies continue to seek means of improving interprofessional cooperation through various administrative structures, team approaches to case situations, the development of protocols that spell out the functions to be performed by each discipline, and the use of case managers charged with coordinating the services an individual or family might require. Social workers, with their mission to facilitate the interface of clients with their environments, have a particularly important leadership role to perform in facilitating interprofessional collaboration.

Determining the Centrality of Social Work

One final factor to consider when selecting a place of employment is the centrality of social work to the mission of that particular setting. The status of social work in an agency influences the manner in which a social worker spends much of his or her time and affects the opportunity of clients to have the full benefit of the perspective that social work brings to the helping situation. When the policies and procedures of the organization are designed to maximize social work services, social workers can most effectively serve their clientele. However, in a practice setting where another discipline is dominant, social workers often spend considerable effort educating others about the contributions social work can make to the agency's clientele.

In some practice settings, social work is the *primary (or host) discipline*. The primary services provided call for social work expertise, most key jobs require social work training, and social workers hold the major administrative jobs. In practice fields such as child welfare, family services, and income maintenance, social work has traditionally been the primary discipline. In these settings, other disciplines may be involved to provide specialized expertise or consultation, but the services are organized to maximize the contributions of the social worker.

In other practice settings, the social worker is an *equal partner* along with members of one or more other disciplines. The services are organized to maximize interdisciplinary cooperation, and a member of any of the disciplines might provide administrative leadership to the agency. The fields of aging, mental health and retardation, and community and neighborhood services are examples of practice fields that are shared by several disciplines.

In still other settings, social work might provide supporting services to another profession. As the *secondary discipline* in these agencies, social work is, in one sense, a guest of the primary discipline. The agency is organized to allow the primary discipline to work as effectively as possible, and the needs of social work or other professions receive lower priority. The role of the social worker in a medical setting illustrates social work as a secondary discipline. Hospitals, a setting for medical practice, are geared to the needs of the physician. Social services are provided at the physician's referral and are organized so they do not compete with the schedule and work of the medical profession. A similar role would be assumed by the social worker in corrections, schools, and industrial settings.

Advantages of Agency-Based Practice

Given the complexities of agency practice, why does social work continue to function as an agency-based profession? Why not adopt the private practice model of other successful professions?

First, services offered through an agency are more visible and, therefore, more accessible to all persons in need. The existence of agencies in a community over time and the attendant publicity about their operations typically make both their programs and their locations familiar to members of the community. As opposed to nonagency practice, which caters to those who can pay the cost of services, public and private human service agencies are more likely to have as clients the most vulnerable members of society. For the social worker committed to serving the part of the population most vulnerable to serious social problems, agency practice provides the preferable setting.

Second, agencies survive because they have received the sanction, or approval, of the community for the services they provide. Clients approach the helping situation with trust in the services they will receive because of the agency's responsibility to ensure that quality services are delivered. In private practice situations, the client must place full trust in the individual practitioner to perform high-quality practice.

Third, clients have the benefit of an extra layer of protection against possible misuse of professional authority in social agencies. Clients in any setting are protected by both the professional ethics of the workers and, in many cases, the legal regulation or licensing of that practice. In agencies, however, they are also protected by the agency's selection of staff and ongoing monitoring of the quality of services.

Fourth, human service agencies tend to have a broad scope and often employ persons from several different professions, which provides clients with ready access to the competencies of multiple professions and gives the worker the opportunity for interdisciplinary practice activities. In addition, as opposed to the more limited service focus found in private practice, agencies typically offer a broad range of services, from direct practice to social action. Thus, they provide the social worker with the stimulation of engaging in a range of different practice activities and make it possible to change the focus of one's practice area or move into supervisory or management positions without changing employers.

Fifth, most agencies offer staff development opportunities that stimulate professional growth among workers. Characteristically, social agencies employ a large enough number of staff members that workers do not feel isolated and, in fact, typically carry out programs that contribute to the continued professional growth and development of other staff members. The rapidly changing knowledge and skill base of the helping professions makes continuing professional development important to the services the clients receive and adds to the intellectual stimulation of the staff.

Last, agencies have the ability to raise funds from the community, whether from taxes or voluntary contributions, and to offer a stable salary to employees. Agencies do not face as great a risk of a fluctuating income as is experienced by persons in private practice settings.

Issues in Private Practice

The principal alternative to agency-based practice for the social worker is private practice, which is the fastest growing sector of social work today. Why is private practice gaining such popularity among social workers? From the vantage point of the social worker, private practice is attractive partially because of the greater opportunity for financial gain but also for the freedom to exercise professional autonomy in how one conducts social work practice. The bureaucratic constraints of many human service agencies have placed restrictions on practice activities that compromise the ability of social workers to fully use their professional competencies for the benefit of clients. Thus, some social workers have actively sought a different practice setting that would not constrain their work.

Although private practice avoids many of the limitations that accrue from practice within a bureaucratic structure, it also places greater responsibility on the social worker to follow the ethical guidelines of the profession. There is no professional monitoring of private practice, although complaints can be filed with a state licensing board or the local NASW chapter.

The Organization of Private Practice

What does a social worker do in private practice? In his study of clinically oriented private practice, Wallace found that the average for these social workers was "63 percent of private practice time in individual treatment, 19 percent devoted to work with marital couples, 8 percent to group therapy, 7 percent to family treatment, and 2 percent to joint interviews with clients other than married couples."[6] For the delivery of these clinical services, three organizational approaches are used.

In the first approach, the social worker engages in multidisciplinary practice. In this arrangement, the social worker participates with members of other disciplines (for example, psychiatry and psychology) to provide a *group practice* that can meet a broad range of client needs. The social worker is an equal partner with the other disciplines and, in fact, is often a co-owner of the business.

In the second form of private practice, the social worker provides a *supportive practice* for a member of another profession. For example, some physicians are hiring social workers to help patients deal with social problems related to specific illnesses. The social worker might also provide more general services in the physician's office such as educating expectant parents about child development, counseling families that need help with child-rearing practices, or referring people to appropriate community resources for help with other problems.

In the third form, social workers are the *sole owners* of their private practice. Sole ownership involves securing office space, hiring staff, advertising services, making contacts to acquire referrals, overseeing the determination and collection of fees, and doing everything related to the management of a small business. Like any other business, private practice is a "sink or swim" proposition with no guarantee of income equivalent to expenses. The main problems for full-time private practitioners are generating sufficient referrals to be able to keep the business solvent, handling the business details including securing payment from third-party vendors, obtaining competent consultation, minimizing the inherent isolation, arranging for backup in managing crisis situations, and protecting practitioners against their vulnerable position if there should be malpractice charges.

It is estimated that 17.5 percent of all social workers are primarily engaged in private practice, yet many agency social workers also maintain a small part-time private practice. Kelley and Alexander identify four groups of social workers who elect to engage in part-time private practice:[7]

1. Agency practitioners who welcome the independence and additional income
2. Social workers in supervisory or administrative positions in agencies who wish to maintain client contact and clinical skills
3. Educators who wish to have sufficient practice activity to remain current with a practice to effectively teach clinical courses
4. Social workers who are parents of young children and need to control their hours of work

Some social workers in private practice provide indirect services such as consultation. Consultation might be provided to another social worker or to a member of another helping profession concerning the handling of a case. For example, a social worker might consult with a lawyer about a divorce or child custody case or might be involved in working with a social agency, such as helping a nursing home with staff–patient relations, administrative procedures, or program development.

Concerns Related to Private Practice

The private practice approach has not been without controversy in the profession, and three issues have emerged concerning this practice mode.

First, private clients do not have an agency monitoring system to provide protection against incompetence or abuses of the professional monopoly. Therefore, social work has been careful to specify more extensive education and experience as minimum preparation for the private practitioner than for the agency-based practitioner.

Second, because many private practitioners work on a part-time basis, some agencies are concerned that private practice will detract from agency practice and may not do justice to his or her agency responsibilities because of the amount of time and energy that may go into maintaining a private practice. On the other side of this issue, it is argued that private practice offers different professional stimulation than is found in agency practice and also provides a supplemental income to agency salaries that keeps workers satisfied with their agency employment.

Finally, some critics have accused private practitioners of diverting social work from its mission of serving the most vulnerable members of society, thus failing to perform the social action responsibilities that are central to social work's mission of facilitating both person and environment change. Teare and Sheafor confirmed this accusation but additionally found that most other direct service practitioners also failed to engage in social change activities.[8]

Advantages of Private Practice

There are also arguments in favor of social work's movement toward private practice. First, in most human service agencies, clients have little opportunity to exercise individual choice in regard to which professionals will provide services. Clients typically cannot select their individual social workers nor can they fire them if unsatisfied with the services received. Clients exercise considerably more control in a private setting.

Second, from the social worker's perspective, agency rules and regulations place constraints on the worker's ability to conduct practice in the manner he or she believes would be most effective. Professional autonomy is inherently compromised. For example, agency-based social workers typically cannot choose their clients; are not completely free to determine the length and type of service to be given; and are almost always supervised, at times by one who interferes with the professional judgment of the worker.

Third, agency salaries tend to be lower than those of the private practitioner. As opposed to the market-driven income of the private practitioner that is, at least theoretically, based on competence, agency salaries are based to a greater degree on seniority and position within the agency.

Last, few agencies avoid the pitfalls that plague most bureaucratic organizations, in which workers find that a disproportionate share of their time is devoted to meetings and paperwork. The less elaborate mechanisms required for accountability in private practice free the worker from much of the less people-oriented activity found in agency practice.

Concluding Comment

Social work practice has permeated U.S. society to the extent that it occurs in every sector of society: government, voluntary, and business. Although the roots of social work are in agency-based practice, social work now is offered through both for-profit and private practice modes.

Most social workers continue to be employed in agency settings; thus, they must be able to work effectively within agency structures if they are to maximize their ability to serve clients. Understanding the principles on which agencies are organized and the problems social workers commonly experience in matching their professional orientation with agency requirements is, therefore, important for providing quality services. Box 7.1 identifies some of the factors related to work in a government sector agency that influenced the work of the child welfare worker, Demetria, in Chapter 1.

An increasing number of social workers have entered private practice to avoid some of the problems experienced by the agency-based practitioner and, at the same time, to increase potential income. However, private practice is certainly not trouble-free. Social work is concerned about important issues related to private practice: adequate preparation for the responsibilities of independent practice, the move away from the social work mission of focusing services on the poor and other vulnerable population groups, and client protection for this relatively new method of service delivery.

Box 7.1

The Influence of Setting on Demetria's Practice

In the case that is the substance of Chapter 1, Demetria is employed in the child welfare division of a county social welfare department where social work would be considered the *primary discipline*. From this information, we know that she works in a *local government setting*. Thus the programs are established through legislation and funded through taxes. At least for the child protection services, it would be likely that fees for the services performed would not be charged to the clients. Even in an agency with *sliding scale fees* based on income, the Miles family would no doubt be well below the threshold for fees.

In a *government or public* agency such as this department, it is often difficult for staff to effectively lobby for a change in the services should they become aware of ways the services could be improved. The *bureaucratic structure* evident in the case (e.g., presence of a supervisor, intake worker, and office administrator) indicates that Demetria would

(Continued)

Box 7.1 (Continued)

need to carefully work up the chain of command, perhaps even to the county commission or legislature, if she was to affect major change in agency functioning. Her colleague in the Boys and Girls Club, a *voluntary nonprofit agency,* however, would have a much less cumbersome structure if she wanted to promote change.

The concept of *horizontal and vertical influences* is evident in Demetria's work. Her activity was affected by the other agencies and resources in the community (i.e., *horizontal influences*). The actions of the local school; the counseling group at the Boys and Girls Club; the limited employment counseling/finding services; and the immediate access to Medicaid, food stamps, and other social programs all supported her work with this family. However, the policies and procedures, as well as the amount of funding available to the Division of Child Welfare, are likely to be affected by *vertical influencers,* i.e., a combination of actions of county commissioners, state legislature/governor/social welfare boards, and even by federal legislation and the executive branch of the government that administers these programs—the U.S. Department of Health and Human Services.

KEY WORDS AND CONCEPTS

Government sector
Nonprofit or voluntary sector
Business (for-profit and private practice) sector
Mutual aid organization
Privatization

Horizontal/vertical influences
Efficiency vs. effectiveness
Bureaucratic vs. professional model
Social work as primary discipline, equal partner, secondary discipline

SUGGESTED INFORMATION SOURCES

Kamerman, Sheila, and Alfred J. Kahn, eds. *Privatization and the Welfare State.* Princeton, NJ: Princeton University Press, 1989.

Mosley, Jennifer E., David Storz, Ram A. Cnaan, Kelly McNally Koney, and Sandra A. Lopez. "Contexts/Settings," in Terry Mizrahi and Larry E. Davis (eds.). *Encyclopedia of Social Work*, 20th ed. Washington D.C.: National Association of Social Workers and Oxford University Press, 2008.

National Association of Social Workers. "Clinical Social Workers in Practice: A Reference Guide" (brochure). Washington, D.C.: NASW, 2004.

ENDNOTES

1. Tracy Whitaker, Toby Weismiller, and Elizabeth Clark, *Assuring the Sufficiency of a Frontline Workforce: A National Study of Licensed Social Workers, Executive Summary* (Washington, D.C.: NASW Center for Workforce Studies, 2006).
2. B. A. Stroul, S. A. Pires, M. I. Armstrong, and J. C. Meyers, "The Impact of Managed Care on Mental Health Services for Children and Their Families." *The Future of Children* 8 (Summer–Fall 1998): pp. 119–133.

3. Peter M. Blau and Marshall W. Meyer, *Bureaucracy in Modern Society,* 2nd ed. (New York: Random House, 1973), pp. 18–23.
4. W. Richard Scott, "Professionals in Bureaucracies—Areas of Conflict," in Howard M. Vollmer and Donald L. Mills, eds., *Professionalization* (Englewood Cliffs, NJ: Prentice-Hall, 1966), pp. 264–275.
5. Robert Pruger, "The Good Bureaucrat," *Social Work* 18 (July 1973): 26–27.
6. Marquis Earl Wallace, "Private Practice: A Nationwide Study," *Social Work* 27 (May 1983): 265.
7. Patricia Kelly and Paul Alexander, "Part-time Private Practice: Practical and Ethical Considerations," *Social Work* 30 (May–June 1985): 254.
8. Robert J. Teare and Bradford W. Sheafor, *Practice-Sensitive Social Work Education: An Empirical Analysis of Social Work Practice and Practitioners* (Alexandria, VA: Council on Social Work Education, 1995), p. 117.

chapter 8

Values and Ethics in Social Work

Prefatory Comment

At the heart of social work are its values. Values assist the social worker and the social work profession in setting goals related to both clients and society. Of course, like any other population group, every social worker does not have identical values. Yet, there are some common themes in social work that suggest that social workers hold some fundamental beliefs in common. As opposed to many other groups of people, for example, social workers tend to believe that society has the responsibility to assist people in meeting their needs, people should be included in making decisions that affect their lives, positive change in people's lives can be attained through professional help, and so on. This chapter examines these and other values that are central to social work's belief system.

The most concrete expression of social work's ethical guidelines is embodied in the NASW Code of Ethics. This code helps social workers to make the inevitable moral choices that arise in their daily practice. If unethical practice is suspected, the Code also becomes the criteria by which the social worker's ethical behavior is evaluated.

From formulating social programs to helping clients, values affect social work practice. Social programs created to "promote the general welfare" of the people are influenced by the values held by legislators, board members, or owners of for-profit organizations who created or maintain those programs. Beliefs about who should be responsible for meeting human needs, what role government or private charity should play, and how much of the nation's wealth should be invested in meeting people's social needs are just three examples of values that have shaped human services programs.

Also, values affect the manner in which human service organizations operate. Values, at least partially, determine the answers to important questions: Should potential clients be encouraged or discouraged from asking for help? Should clients be required to pay for services? To what extent should an agency attempt to make services readily accessible to clients and assure that the surroundings are comfortable and pleasant? Should a social worker be allowed to terminate services before a client's insurance benefits are exhausted when the agency needs the funds to meet its financial obligations? Should services be terminated just because the client can no longer pay yet continues to need help? In short, the dominant values of an agency can have a direct impact on social work practice.

The values of a social worker's clients, too, affect practice. If a client feels stigmatized, demeaned, or embarrassed to ask for assistance, the client's ability to productively use the service is affected. If the client is unnecessarily demanding of a worker's time and attention or resents being required to use social services (i.e., an involuntary client), that, too, affects the way a social worker assists the client. Further, much of practice involves helping clients identify, clarify, and resolve value issues that are almost always present in human interactions.

As members of a profession that has based many of its practice approaches and principles on certain beliefs about people and how they can best be served, social workers must be cognizant of the profession's values. Further, because social work must protect the public from potential abuses of the professional monopoly, it has adopted a code of ethical practice that prescribes certain professional behaviors related to interactions with clients, colleagues, employers, and the community. Each social worker must be prepared to adhere to the NASW Code of Ethics.

Finally, the social worker must be clear about how the profession's values and ethical standards interact with his or her own belief system. Therefore, understanding one's own values becomes critical for the social worker. Most of us do not typically contemplate our values unless they somehow create problems for us as we address the issues we confront in life. This chapter, however, asks the reader to consider the nature of values, their place in promoting people's welfare through shaping social programs, the values and ethics of social workers, and, finally, the fit between social work's values and one's own. Understanding the central place of values and ethics in social work is another important factor in making a career choice or preparing to enter the social work profession.

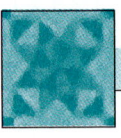

The Nature of Values

Unlike knowledge, which explains what is, values express what ought to be. Rokeach more precisely defines a *value* as "a type of belief, centrally located in one's total belief system, about how one ought or ought not to behave, or about some end-state of existence worth or not worth attaining."[1] This definition helps to clarify the two central functions our values perform. The first function, for example, how we should or should not behave, reflects our *instrumental values*. These values provide the moral or ethical guidelines that help determine how we conduct our lives and, as social workers, how we perform our work. The second function performed by our values, known as *terminal values,* reflects the bottom line of what we want to accomplish. Ensuring a safe environment for all people, a sufficient distribution of the world's wealth to eliminate hunger, ensuring strong families that nurture the development of children, and achieving social justice within the society are just a few examples of terminal values.

Values are much more than emotional reactions to situations or doing what feels right. Values are the fundamental criteria that lead us to thoughtful decisions. It is important to recognize, however, that people do not always behave in a manner consistent with their values. Values guide decisions but do not dictate choices.

People can and do make decisions contrary to their values. Such decisions might be made when other factors are given priority ("I know that I shouldn't have done that, but when will I ever get another chance to make that kind of money?"), the person acts on emotion ("I was just so angry, I hit her without thinking"), or when one fails to adequately think through and understand the value issues in a situation ("It just didn't occur to me that my quitting school would make my parents think that they had failed").

Each person values a variety of things in life. Differences in the strength with which one holds any particular value and the priority a particular value will have among the whole constellation of that person's values, that is, the person's *value system*, is a part of what makes individuals unique. For example, for many people, the most important value is feeling secure in their relationships with loved ones. For some, generating income is the driving force in their lives. For others, giving service dominates their value system.

Dealing with values is particularly difficult for several reasons. First, values are such a central part of our thought processes that we often are not consciously aware of them and therefore are unable to identify their influence on our decisions. The social worker should constantly be alert to values in practice situations as these values may subtly influence the thoughts, feelings, attitudes, and behaviors of both the client and the social worker.

Second, a person may be forced to choose among values that are in conflict with one another. Who can avoid wrestling with a *value conflict* when confronted by a person on the street asking for money to buy something to eat? We may value responding to people in need, but we may equally value encouraging people to use the organized system for receiving financial assistance that does not put the person into the degrading position of panhandling.

Third, addressing values in the abstract may be quite different from applying them in a real-life situation. The social worker must recognize, for example, that clients may not act on the basis of value choices selected in a counseling session when they are confronted with the actual people and conditions where this value must be operationalized.

Finally, values are problematic because they change over time. Various events, experiences, and even new information can lead clients to adapt their system of values to more closely fit their current situation. A person whose job is eliminated, for instance, may be much more supportive of a universal health insurance program than when he or she was employed and receiving health insurance benefits from the employer.

The Place of Values in Social Work

Helping people to be clear about their individual values, that is, *values clarification*, and facilitating their understanding of how the particular set of values they hold influences their goals and decisions is an important aspect of social work practice. At times, clients also must be assisted in recognizing and understanding the values of others. Taking into consideration the values of family members, friends, employers, teachers, or others in that person's environment may be prerequisite to making appropriate and workable decisions. The matter becomes more complicated when social work practice involves more than one person, as it is likely that each will potentially have a somewhat different value system. In that case, the social worker may need to help resolve issues that stem from differences in values.

Further, the social worker must be concerned with his or her own values and control for their inappropriate intrusion into practice situations. Value choices that may be viable personally for the social worker may not coincide with the needs, wants, priorities, or realities the client experiences. Ultimately, the client must live with the decisions that are made, and those decisions should be consistent with his or her own value system—not the value system of the social worker. Learning to suspend one's own values (i.e., *value suspension*) to keep the focus of helping on the client or client group is an important, yet difficult, task for every social worker.

With social work practice focused at the interface between person and environment, the social worker must simultaneously address several sets of values. It is no wonder that social work has perhaps devoted more attention to values than has any other helping profession. Yet it has not developed a sufficiently clear and adequately tested statement of its core values to offer a definitive description of its central beliefs. At best, there is only rather general agreement that some values are fundamental to social work practice.

Social Values in U.S. Society

Values differ from *needs*. The latter refers to people's basic biological or psychological urges, while values reflect what people hope to get out of life and how this should be accomplished. The choice of which needs a society will attempt to meet depends on what it values. The most predominant feature of Western values is the central place of the individual; that is, the society exists to help individuals lead satisfying and productive lives. These values have their roots in at least four different sources, all of which are concerned with the responsibilities of the individual toward self and society and/or the society's responsibility to the individual.[2] These sources include:

1. Judaism and Christianity with their doctrine of the inherent worth of humans and their responsibilities for their neighbors
2. The democratic ideals that emphasize the equality of all people and a person's right to "life, liberty, and the pursuit of happiness"
3. The Puritan ethic, which says that character is everything, circumstances nothing; that the moral person is the one who works and is independent; and that pleasure is sinful
4. The tenets of Social Darwinism, which emphasize that the fittest survive and the weak perish in a natural evolutionary process that produces the strong individual and society

It is evident that much of the disagreement in the United States over the provision of human services results from value conflicts inherent in the U.S. public's value system. Brill and Levine point out: "Even the casual reader will see that a dichotomy exists within this value system. We hold that all men are equal, but he who does not work is less equal....We hold that the individual life has worth, but that only the fit should survive. We believe that we are responsible for each other, but those who depend on others for their living are of lesser worth."[3]

In carrying out the society's values to respond to human needs, the social worker becomes an intermediary between people in need and society's value judgments about what needs are to be met. As one saying puts it, the social worker stands "between the demanding recipient and the grudging donor." Therefore, the social worker must be particularly skilled at mediating between these divergent views.

What constellation of values is held by the U.S. population? In this nation of people with widely diverse backgrounds and interests, it is not surprising that there is considerable variation in belief systems. The answer to the question "Am I my brother's (or sister's) keeper?" is not a categorical "yes" or "no." Protecting a woman's "right to choose" in regard to abortion in one person's value system, for example, is viewed as a "license to kill" in another's. Determining the preferred values held by the U.S. public is the basis for considerable political debate, but rarely a clear consensus on such issues exists.

Kahle's study of the social values held by Americans suggests that value preferences differ substantially for different segments of the population.[4] The study asked respondents to indicate which of eight fundamental social values was the most important for a person to achieve in life.* The data reveal that the more vulnerable groups consistently hold two values, security and being respected, at much higher levels than the general population. Perhaps that is not surprising. If one is poor, has a limited education, is a minority group member, or is old, he or she is likely to worry about having basic health insurance, sufficient income, and safety. It is also likely that he or she is regularly disregarded by others or will suffer various forms of discrimination. Under these conditions, one values highly what he or she does not have—security and respect. From the vantage point of social work, these data reinforce the view that it is important to support the development of social programs that increase people's security and to deliver those programs in a manner that treats the recipients with dignity. With those two basic social values achieved, people are then ready to address other areas of need that can enhance their lives.

---

*The eight social values, in order of numbers of times it was selected as most important, were (1) having *self-respect* (feeling good about oneself and what has been accomplished in life); (2) attaining a *sense of security* (feeling safe and comfortable about the future); (3) having *warm personal relationships* (maintaining satisfying interpersonal relations with friends and family); (4) *feeling successful* in life's undertakings; (5) being *respected by others;* (6) *feeling fulfilled* by the quality of life experiences; (7) experiencing *a sense of belonging* to valued groups of people; and (8) finding *fun, enjoyment, and excitement* in life's activities.

Social workers and other professionals must be particularly alert to what the client values because those values are not likely to be held with the same strength by the professionals themselves. The data from the Kahle study indicate that attaining such basic values as security and being respected by others were not of high priority to professionals. After all, they really don't need to worry about those basics. Professionals are highly educated, usually have secure jobs with relatively high income and can feel pretty safe about their futures. Their value preferences are related to items such as achieving self-respect, having a sense of accomplishment, and experiencing fulfillment.[5] It takes discipline and commitment to avoid the trap of seeing the world only through one's own eyes and actively seeking to understand and appreciate the value preferences of others.

Values Held by Social Workers

To avoid imposing personal values on the client or making inappropriate judgments about a client's values, the social worker must have a clear understanding of his or her own personal values. In addition, the social worker must be fully aware of, and guided by, the fundamental values of the social work profession.

What, then, are the values commonly held by social workers? When developing its classification scheme for different levels of practice, the National Association of Social Workers identified ten basic social work values.[6] These statements express the basic values that underpin the profession of social work.

1. *Commitment to the primary importance of the individual in society.* Social work accepts the position that the individual is the center of practice and that every person is of inherent worth because of his or her humanness. The social worker need not approve of what a person does but must treat that person as a valued member of society. Commitment to the centrality of the individual has also led social workers to recognize that each person is unique and that practice activities must be tailored for that person's or group's uniqueness. Such individualization permits the worker to determine where and how to intervene in each helping situation, while at the same time communicating respect for the people being served.

2. *Commitment to social change to meet socially recognized needs.* Giving primacy to the individual does not minimize the commitment of the social worker to achieve societal change. Rather, it suggests that the social worker recognizes that the outcome of change activities in the larger society must ultimately benefit individuals. Social workers, then, are committed to the belief that the society has a responsibility to provide resources and services to help people avoid such problems as hunger, insufficient education, discrimination, illness without care, and inadequate housing.

3. *Commitment to social justice and the economic, physical, and mental well-being of all in society.* Social workers believe that social justice will be achieved if each person has the opportunity to develop his or her unique potential and, therefore, make his or her maximum contribution to society. Thus, social workers believe that each person should have the right to participate in molding the social institutions and engage in the decision-making processes in U.S. society so that programs, policies, and procedures are responsive to the needs and conditions of all. Of course, when resources are limited, choices must be made. Not every person can have all needs met. When social workers are making choices, the values they hold emphasize the importance of responding to the needs of the most vulnerable members of the society. Typically, these vulnerable people are children, the aged, minority group members, persons who are disabled, women, and others who have been victims of institutionalized discrimination.

4. *Respect and appreciation for individual and group differences.* Social workers recognize that there are common needs, goals, aspirations, and wants that are held by all people. In some ways, we are all alike. However, social workers also recognize that, in other ways, each individual's life experience and capacities make him or her unique. Where some may fear differences or resist working with people who are not like themselves, social workers value and respect uniqueness. They believe that the quality of life is enriched by different cultural patterns, different beliefs, and different forms of activity. In contrast to efforts to assimilate persons who are in some way different from the general population, social workers value a pluralistic society that can accommodate a range of beliefs, behaviors, languages, and customs.

5. *Commitment to developing clients' ability to help themselves.* Social workers do not view people as static or unchanging, nor is anyone assumed to be unable to engage in activities that may produce a more satisfying and rewarding life. Rather, social workers view people as adaptable. Although there are conditions that some people face that cannot be changed, the people themselves or the world around them can be helped to adapt to these conditions. Within the individual's or group's capacities, the social worker places high value on helping people take responsibility for their own decisions and actions.

6. *Willingness to transmit knowledge and skills to others.* A significant part of guiding the change process involves helping clients understand the situation they experience from both a personal perspective and the perspectives of others, as well as helping them develop the skills to resolve their problems. Effective helping avoids making clients dependent on helpers and prepares them to address other issues that arise in their lives. Thus, it is important that social workers assist clients in identifying strengths that can be mobilized for solving immediate problems and to help clients learn how to use these strengths in solving problems that may arise in the future.

7. *Willingness to keep personal feelings and needs separate from professional relationships.* It is important for the social worker to recognize that the focus of practice must be maintained on the client—not on the social worker. However, because social workers care about the people they work with, it is easy to become overidentified with clients' lives or even to develop personal relationships with them. If that happens, the client loses the benefit of an objective helper, and the quality of the helping process is diminished because the relationship has changed from professional to personal.

8. *Respect for the confidentiality of relationship with clients.* Although it is rare that the social worker can guarantee "absolute confidentiality," social workers value achieving the maximum possible protection of information received in working with

clients. The very nature of a helping relationship suggests that there is sensitive information that must be shared between the person being helped and the helper. In each case, some information typically passes between client and worker that could potentially be emotionally or economically damaging if it is inappropriately revealed to other parties. Also, unless the client can trust the worker to protect this information, he or she is unlikely to reveal this important information, thus limiting the social worker's ability to be of help.

9. *Willingness to persist in efforts on behalf of clients despite frustration.* Situations that require social work intervention typically do not develop quickly and usually cannot be resolved readily. Recognizing the frustration that they experience when change is slow to occur, social workers have come to value tenacity in addressing both individual problems and advocating to address issues that affect groups of people, organizations, communities, and society in general. Social workers must be persistent.

10. *Commitment to a high standard of personal and professional conduct.* The final value on the NASW list directs the worker to use the highest ethical standards in his or her practice. It suggests that the worker must conduct professional activities in a manner that protects the interests of the public, the agency, the clients, and the social worker. This value has been operationalized in the form of the *NASW Code of Ethics,* which is perhaps the single most unifying element among social workers.

Shortly after its founding, the NASW began to formulate a code of ethics that could serve the needs of this profession. First adopted in 1960 as several broad statements to guide ethical practice, the *Code of Ethics* has undergone several major revisions and now is an elaborate document used not only as a practice guide but also as a statement on which to assess allegations against social workers of ethical misconduct.

With a clearly explicated code of ethics in place, NASW members can be clear about expectations for competent and ethical practice, and the profession has a standard against which to assess any complaints that the public trust has been violated. To join NASW, the social worker must sign a statement agreeing to abide by the ethical standards contained in the Code and to participate in the adjudication process if a complaint is made. By renewing one's membership each year, he or she reaffirms the commitment to adhere to NASW's ethical code. NASW has created an elaborate procedure for hearing grievances at the local level with appeal to the national level possible for all parties to the complaint. A member found to have violated the Code of Ethics can be asked to take corrective actions, may be listed on a published report of code violators, or may have his or her NASW membership revoked.

Areas of Practice Addressed by the NASW Code of Ethics

The *NASW Code of Ethics* has evolved from its 1960 format of fourteen general statements to its current format that consumes twenty-seven pages of ethical prescriptions. Mastering the specifics of the Code and interpreting its provisions in actual practice situations is an ongoing challenge for all social workers. This process

begins by recognizing the general areas of practice activity that the Code addresses.*
The following statements summarize the main sections of NASW's Code of Ethics.

1. Standards related to the social worker's ethical responsibilities to clients. This section of the Code of Ethics is concerned with such factors and principles as the following: the worker's primary responsibility is to the client; respect for client self-determination; securing client's informed consent; the worker's competence to provide needed services; the worker's cultural competence; avoiding conflict of interest; respecting clients' rights to privacy and confidentiality; the prohibition of sexual involvement, sexual harassment, inappropriate physical contact, and abusive or derogatory language; special considerations when clients lack decision-making capacity; avoiding the interruption of services; and the planned termination of services.

2. The social worker's ethical responsibilities to colleagues. Section 2 is concerned with the social workers' responsibility to treat colleagues with respect; concern for maintaining confidentiality among professionals; appropriate collaboration and teamwork; proper handling of disputes and disagreements; developing appropriate consultation relationships; proper referral of clients to colleagues; the prohibition of sexual harassment and sexual involvement with one's supervisees or students; and the requirement for responsible action in relation to a colleague who is impaired, incompetent, or unethical in his or her practice.

3. The social worker's ethical responsibilities in practice settings. This section of the Code of Ethics relates to services performed that only indirectly relate to clients. The items addressed include the competence required for providing supervision, consultation, education, and training; responsible evaluation of the performance of other workers; maintaining proper client records and billing properly; carefully evaluating client needs before accepting transfers; assuring an appropriate working environment and providing ongoing education and training in human services agencies; demonstrating commitment to agency employees; and guidelines for acting responsibly in labor disputes.

4. The social worker's ethical responsibilities as a professional. Section 4 includes items related to the social worker accepting employment and job assignments when he or she may not be competent to perform that work; prohibition from practicing, condoning, or participating in any form of discrimination; engaging in private conduct that compromises the ability to fulfill professional responsibilities; restriction from engaging in dishonesty, fraud, and deception; the responsibility to address one's own problems if impaired; the requirement to be clear in public statements regarding whether acting as a professional or a private citizen; prohibiting uninvited solicitations for business; and properly acknowledging any contributions to one's written or other work made by others.

---

*The full text of the NASW Code of Ethics can be obtained in both English and Spanish from the National Association of Social Workers, 750 First Street, NE, Washington, DC 20002-4241, or it can be downloaded from NASW's web site (http://www.socialworkers.org/pubs/code/code.asp). The Canadian Code of Ethics (which contains similar provisions) can be downloaded by members of the Canadian Association of Social Workers at (http://www.casw-acts.ca/practice/code3_e.html).

5. **The social worker's ethical responsibilities to the social work profession.** The Code of Ethics is also concerned with issues related to the social worker promoting high standards for social work and contributing time and energy to the profession's growth and development, as well as addressing items related to social workers continuously monitoring and evaluating social policies, programs, and their own practice interventions.

6. **The social worker's ethical responsibilities to the broader society.** In its final section, the Code of Ethics charges social workers with promoting the general welfare of the society and seeking to ensure social justice for all people, participating in public debate to shape social policies and institutions, providing services in public emergencies, and actively engaging in social and political action.

The Code of Ethics helps to satisfy social work's obligation to be responsible in performing its duties as a recognized profession. It provides guidance to social workers as they make ethical decisions in their day-to-day practice; spells out expected behaviors in areas where ethical compromises may arise; and provides clarity to the general public, employers, and other professionals who may feel that a social worker has violated the principles of ethical practice and wish to have NASW and/or the courts determine if a social worker has violated the public trust granted to professions.

Illustrations of Values and Ethics Operating in Social Work Practice

For most social workers, theoretical or abstract discussion of values and ethical dilemmas is not a daily event. It is usually when these issues are experienced while working with clients that they take on full significance—and they do indeed occur while working with clients. Hokenstad, for example, estimates that "half of professional decision making requires ethical rather than scientific judgment."[7] Thus, examining one's values in the context of a case example helps to translate the value-related issues that regularly arise in practice from the abstract value statements to their more concrete application.

RAGAN ADAMS' VALUE DILEMMA

The interview began as most begin. The school social worker, Ragan Adams, had initiated an interview with the Warring family as a follow-up to a conference she had conducted with the Warring's oldest daughter, Sally Kay. In the conference with Sally Kay regarding her sudden change from being a model student to one who was frequently absent from school, with a sudden burst of tears Sally Kay revealed that she was pretty sure she was pregnant and was afraid to tell her parents. She was sure it would hurt her mother deeply, and she was physically afraid of how her father might react.

Sally Kay indicated that her parents are deeply religious and decidedly "pro-life" in their philosophy about abortion. She felt trapped in the situation as she believed that she was in no way ready to raise a child, knew her parents would not condone her having an abortion, and thought adoption was not a good option because she would need to carry the baby to term and that would ruin her future and bring shame to the family.

When questioned, she indicted that "Yes, she had considered suicide as a way out" but had abandoned that thought because "it would only make things worse." She needed help in figuring out what to do and asked Ms. Adams for help.

Ms. Adams knew that an unintended pregnancy could destabilize a family, especially if the pregnant family member is an unmarried teenager. Also, Sally Kay's fear of possible violence by her father hinted that there could have been violence in the home previously. It would be important to plan helping in a way that would be supportive of Sally Kay's revealing her situation to her parents while minimizing the chances of the father's becoming violent with Sally Kay or others, and then turn the attention to making a decision that would be with Sally Kay for the rest of her life and that, hopefully, the parents would support.

Before taking any action, Ragan Adams needed to do a little soul-searching herself. What were her beliefs about these options, and could she suspend them to allow the family to make the best choice for itself? Might her own values intrude and affect her actions as a social worker? As an agent of the school, was she free to support whatever choice Sally Kay might make? What if the choice should be to help Sally Kay have an abortion, and Sally Kay's parents complain to the principal that Ms. Adams had influenced Sally Kay to make that choice against their will? Who is the client, and to what extent should client self-determination prevail?

Ms. Adams concluded that the safest place for the family interview would be at the school. After introducing herself to the parents, she indicated that she had called the meeting to talk over issues that were interfering with Sally Kay's success in school. As she and Sally Kay had planned and practiced before the interview began, Ms. Adams invited Sally Kay to share her thoughts on the matter. When Sally Kay indicated that she was pregnant, the father went "ballistic," wanting to know "who the hell was the father" and why had Sally Kay let him take advantage of her. The mother burst into tears, mumbling that she had failed as a mother and surely God was punishing them for something she had done wrong. Sally Kay hid her face in her hands and silently sobbed. It was clear that many different emotions and values would have to be reconciled when working with this family.

Where the above case centers around values held by both the clients and the worker, the subset of values related to the conduct of one's professional practice represents the ethical principles that should guide the social worker. Most ethical decisions, unfortunately, are not clear and require the social worker to make choices when, sometimes, none of the alternatives are desirable. The worker must weigh one choice against others and make a decision about which option is best or, too often, which is least harmful. Further, ethical issues sometimes appear relatively easy to resolve in the abstract but are much more difficult in real-life situations. Consider the following case example.

TERRI PERRY'S ETHICAL DECISION

Terri was a good student and was pleased to have discovered social work as a career option. She had always wanted a career helping people, and her friends regularly sought her out in the dormitory to ask advice about problems in relationships with parents, broken love affairs, difficulty in finding a direction in college, and getting through the freshman plague—roommate problems. Her social work professors had described these qualities as those of a good natural helper, and now she is preparing to move her talents to another level, professional helping.

To Terri, the culmination of her social work education was to be her field placement in the county probation office. There she would be able to combine her natural helping skills and the knowledge from her social work classes into her own professional helping style to start down the track of being a social worker. When the placement was planned with the school's field instruction coordinator, Terri had interviewed with the chief probation officer, Mr. DeMiranda, and Ms. Sills, the social worker who was to be her field instructor. She especially liked Ms. Sills, who indicated that she planned to regularly observe Terri working with clients, either directly or through recording, and to meet with her weekly to plan and critique her work so that Terri might improve her competence as a social worker.

At the end of the first month in placement, Terri concluded that the experience had lived up to her expectations—unlike the reports from some of her classmates in other placements. Then it happened! Mr. DeMiranda began to take a special interest in her—too special, she thought. At first he casually brushed against her at the water fountain (it might have been an accident), and then he asked her to sit next to him in a staff meeting where he pressed his leg against hers under the table (maybe he thought her leg was the table leg), making her very nervous. Terri tried to avoid Mr. DeMiranda after that and no longer looked forward to going to her placement.

Terri had learned that avoiding problems did not resolve them. What should she do? Perhaps she should not do anything. What would happen to her field placement if she makes waves? And what if she is just imagining that Mr. DeMiranda is making advances? What would happen to Mr. DeMiranda and his family? What if it is true and yet she has no "proof"? What would happen to her career as a social worker? "Maybe it is wise to just let this one go by," she thought. "After all, I'm just a student."

On the other hand, Terri pondered the implications of letting this pass. What if this happens to others who are in positions where Mr. DeMiranda possesses power over them, for example other interns, staff members, and even probationers? They are just as vulnerable, or perhaps even more vulnerable. If no one speaks up, won't this behavior continue? What policy does the Probation Office have regarding sexual harassment? Will the Department of Social Work at my university stand behind me? What guidance might I find from the NASW Code of Ethics?

The ethical dilemma experienced by Terri Perry, the social worker in the above case, is only one of many a social worker might encounter. The following list gives some examples of the range of decisions a social worker must address that have ethical implications. Fortunately, the Code of Ethics provides the worker with some guidance on each of them, but sometimes, if the worker follows one code guideline, another may be violated.

▶ What should a social worker do if a client announces the decision to return to an abusive spouse when the worker fears for the client's safety?
▶ Is it ethical for a social worker to attempt to provide specialized therapeutic services for which he or she is not trained if the worker doubts the competence of the only credentialed person with that expertise in the area?
▶ Should a social worker accept a personal gift from a client beyond the fee the client pays for the professional service? What about in lieu of a fee for professional service?

- Should a social worker report a colleague to NASW or the state licensing board if that colleague reveals that he or she has developed a sexual relationship with one of his or her clients?
- What should a social worker do if a grand jury requests a client's file that contains case notes that may be damaging to the client?
- Is a social worker obligated to do anything if he or she believes a colleague has developed a substance abuse problem?
- What should be done if a client asks a social worker in a probation setting to overlook (and not mention in the case record) a violation of a condition of parole—promising not to repeat the activity?
- Is it okay for a social worker not to record information given by a client in confidence in the case file when the agency's administrative procedures require recording all pertinent information to the case? What about if state law requires reporting that information to a central registry or a protective services agency?
- If the administrator in a nursing home directs the social work staff to transfer out of the agency all patients who do not have insurance or other benefits because the nursing home is experiencing financial difficulty, should the social workers abide by this directive?
- Is it ethical for a social worker who develops a successful helping technique to obtain a patent and market the technique for a profit to other social workers?
- Is a social worker obligated to engage in social and political action when his or her job description does not specify such activity?

Concluding Comment

One cannot understand social work without being sensitive to values. Values represent a highly individual and personal view that must be constantly examined during practice. The social worker must be aware of the value system of the client or client group and the values held by society that impinge upon the client. These values, however, are not held equally by all people, and client groups can be expected to vary in the intensity with which they hold particular values. Certainly it would be unrealistic to expect, or even desire, that the helping process occur in a value-free environment. Yet the social worker must attempt to avoid imposing personal beliefs inappropriately on the client or client groups. To practice social work, one must be prepared to accept and understand people who hold values that are different from their own.

The social worker also must be guided by the values and ethics of the social work profession. These beliefs are not held exclusively by social workers. Some overlap with the values of other professions, and there is indication that professionals hold distinctly different values from the general population.[8] Social work's constellation of core values, however, is unique. Roberts, for example, has identified five areas where the values of physicians and those of social workers are quite different, including attitudes about such factors as saving life versus quality of life, the professional's control versus patient autonomy in establishing treatment plans, and so on.[9] Further, Abbott's research identified areas of difference in the values held by social workers, physicians, nurses, teachers, psychologists, and business people. Of these groups, psychologists were most like social workers in their beliefs.[10] A difficulty in addressing values is that they are not usually explicitly stated and must be inferred from people's behaviors. In Box 8.1, some of the values and ethical considerations we can infer from Demetria's work with the Miles family (see Chapter 1) are enumerated.

In many ways, values or beliefs about how things ought to be or how people ought to behave are the cornerstone of social work. Even when the knowledge available to guide practice is limited, the social worker who falls back on the values of the profession cannot go far wrong in guiding the helping process. When the worker is value-sensitive and effectively supplies the competencies of social work practice, clients receive the quality of services they should expect from a professional.

Box 8.1

Values and Ethical Considerations in Demetria's Practice

Although Demetria's values are not directly expressed in the Miles family case (Chapter 1), some values are evident in her actions. It is clear that Demetria valued creating a safe and supportive family environment for Joseph and thus elected to help the family address its issues so that Joseph would not need to be removed from the home and could get help in dealing with his problems with alcohol and gang involvement. Demetria seems to be aware that Mrs. Miles, like other vulnerable people, places a priority on attaining *security* before she could be open to addressing other issues in her life. Thus, attaining food and electricity became a first order of business. Demetria also appeared to recognize that people in vulnerable situations place high priority on *being respected* and politely accepted the offer of a cup of tea (although she couldn't be sure the cup was very clean) and made herself comfortable on the worn couch that might house more of the roaches she had observed in the kitchen.

At least two of the basic social work values were evident in Demetria's performance. One was her *commitment to the primary importance of the individual*. She took Joseph seriously and honored his reluctance to provide her with much information about some of his behaviors by not prying or threatening. She also allowed Mrs. Miles to spill her heart about the issues she faced without judging her as a bad mom or an incapable parent. This would be termed an *instrumental value*, or a value that guided Demetria's actions in her relationship with Mrs. Miles. In her concern about the adequacy of employment counseling for this family, Demetria reflected the basic social work value of *commitment to social change to meet socially recognized needs*. This is a *terminal value* that leads to actions regarding an outcome, better employment services, that she wanted to accomplish.

Demetria seemed not to experience any significant ethical issues in this case. One example of her practice that was in line with the *Code of Ethics* was her commitment to client *self-determination*. She pointed Joseph and Mrs. Miles to certain resources (i.e., the counseling group at the Boys and Girls Club for Joseph and the application for food stamps for Mrs. Miles), but ultimately the decision was left to them to use or not use those resources. Demetria also reflected the Code's commitment to *collegial interaction* as she risked criticism when presenting her case plan for consultation at an agency staffing meeting.

KEY WORDS AND CONCEPTS

Values
Ethics
Value conflict
Value system

U.S. society's values
Social workers' values
NASW Code of Ethics
Value suspension

SUGGESTED INFORMATION SOURCES

Gambill, Eileen, ed. *Social Work Ethics.* Burlington, VT: Ashgate, 2009.

Hultman, Ken, and Bill Gellerman. *Balancing Individual and Organizational Values: Walking the Tightrope to Success.* San Francisco: Jossey-Bass/Pfeiffer, 2002.

Reamer, Frederic G. *Ethical Standards in Social Work: A Review of the NASW Code of Ethics.* Washington, D.C.: NASW Press, 2006.

Reamer, Frederic G. *Social Work Values and Ethics,* 3rd ed. New York: Columbia University Press, 2006.

Rothman, Julie C. *From the Front Lines: Student Cases in Social Work Ethics.* Boston: Allyn & Bacon, 2005.

ENDNOTES

1. Milton Rokeach, *Beliefs, Values, and Attitudes: A Theory of Organization and Change* (San Francisco: Jossey-Bass, 1968), p. 124.
2. Naomi I. Brill and Joanne Levine, *Working with People: The Helping Process,* 7th ed. (Boston: Allyn & Bacon, 2002), p. 29.
3. Ibid., p. 12.
4. Lynn R. Kahle and Susan Groff Timmer, "A Theory and a Method for Studying Values," in Lynn R. Kahle, ed., *Social Values and Social Change: Adaptation to Life in America* (New York: Praeger Publishers, 1983), pp. 47–108.
5. Ibid., p. 110.
6. National Association of Social Workers, *NASW Standards for the Classification of Social Work Practice* (Silver Spring, MD: The Association, September 1981), p. 18.
7. M. C. Hokenstad, "Teaching Practitioners Ethical Judgment," *NASW News* 32 (October 1987): 4.
8. William C. Horner and Les B. Whitebeck, "Personal versus Professional Values in Social Work: A Methodological Note," *Journal of Social Service Research* 14 (Issue 1/2 1991): 21–43.
9. Cleora S. Roberts, "Conflicting Professional Values in Social Work and Medicine," *Health and Social Work* 13 (August 1989): 211–218.
10. Ann A. Abbott, *Professional Choices: Values at Work* (Silver Spring, MD: National Association of Social Workers, 1988), pp. 74–75.

chapter 9

Identifying the Knowledge and Skills Required for Social Work Practice

> **Prefatory Comment**
>
> Equipped with adequate social programs to meet client needs, sanction to perform professional services, a suitable agency or private practice environment, and professional values and ethical guidelines, the social worker is prepared to deliver services. Little of this background for practice is usually recognized or even of interest to clients, although the absence of any one of these factors would minimize the social worker's ability to be helpful. Instead, the clients' primary concern is with the social worker and the social worker's competence in delivering services to meet their needs or influencing social policies and programs to address their issues. An important part of learning about social work, then, is to be familiar with the basic knowledge and skills needed for social work practice.

The perception of what knowledge and skill a social worker needs varies considerably depending on the vantage point of the person identifying the areas of practice competence. Although there are some basics required of all social workers, the knowledge and skills required of the direct-service, beginning-level social worker in a child welfare setting (see Chapter 1), for example, will differ from that required of an advanced-level agency administrator (see Chapter 27). Once the basics are mastered, the career track (or tracks) one follows as a social worker will dictate additional areas of knowledge and skill that will increasingly build the social worker's practice competence.

What do social workers need to know and be able to do in order to fulfill the expectations of their clients? In the preceding chapters, social work is described as a profession with an exceptionally broad charge, i.e., serving individuals, groups of people, and even working with community issues and influencing broad social policies. The techniques and skills required, as well as the knowledge that underpins the selection of skills and techniques (also called the art and science of social work[1]) are also quite varied. At most, a single chapter in this book can only provide a broad outline of the competencies a social worker must possess. It does, however, provide a map of the competencies one can expect to develop in a social work education program.

149

A sample of tasks performed by 7,000 social workers from throughout the Unites States perhaps best reflects the knowledge and skills required of social workers from the range of activities involved in social work practice.[2] Using statistical procedures (i.e., cluster and factor analysis), more than 130 tasks potentially performed by social workers were grouped into eighteen sets of activities and a mean score for the frequency with which those activities were performed computed. A subsequent and parallel study of 5,000 master's-level social workers confirmed the accuracy of the eighteen clusters as discrete sets of social work activities.[3] In the following pages, the clusters are presented in the order of those most universally performed by social workers (i.e., the most basic knowledge and skills for social work) and then those increasingly related to more specialized aspects of social work practice. Students in both BSW and MSW programs should expect to master the knowledge and skills required for those near the top of the list, and those items further down the list will most likely be performed by those social workers with more specialized practice.

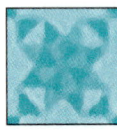

The Universal Social Work Competencies

Two clusters of tasks, interpersonal helping and professional competence development, were consistently performed by most social workers. They represent the clearest indication of a common set of work activities that help to bind social workers into a single profession.

Interpersonal Helping

To perform this set of activities, the social worker must be prepared to use basic helping skills (e.g., interviewing, questioning, counseling) to assist individuals and/or families in understanding the problems they experience in social functioning and in helping them to examine possible options for resolving those problems. In carrying out these activities, the worker actively involves individuals and families in discussions designed to explore options for solving problems. The worker encourages people to express their points of view and share their feelings. Throughout this process, the worker attempts to communicate an understanding of other people's points of view and establish a relationship of trust with them. Some of the competencies needed to carry out these interpersonal helping tasks are:*

1. Self-awareness and the ability to use self in facilitating change
2. Knowledge of the psychology of giving and receiving help
3. Ability to establish professional helping relationships
4. Understanding differing ethnic and cultural patterns, as well as the capacity to engage in ethnic-, gender-, and age-sensitive practice[4]

---

*More complete explanations of each competency identified in this chapter may be found in the 7th through 11th editions of this text, *Social Work: A Profession of Many Faces*.

5. Knowledge and application of the Code of Ethics as a guide to ethical practice[5]
6. General understanding of individual and family behavior patterns
7. Skill in client information gathering
8. Ability to analyze client information and identify both the strengths and problems evident in a practice situation
9. Capacity to counsel, problem solve, and/or engage in conflict resolution with clients
10. Possession of expertise in guiding the change process

Professional Competence Development

To maintain high-quality practice, the social worker in every position must carefully monitor his or her own work and continually work to improve his or her job performance. To accomplish these goals, the social worker must regularly engage in activities that strengthen one's own practice effectiveness and expand one's professional competence. The key tasks involve periodically taking stock of one's performance by evaluating actions and decisions made when serving clients. Other tasks involve attendance at workshops, seminars, or professional meetings, as well as reading professional journals and searching for online information to inform practice. Professional competence development also applies to one's contribution to the enhancement of other professionals' learning by sharing knowledge and skills developed through such activities as presenting at professional meetings, writing for professional journals, or contributing to online sources of practice information. More specifically, professional competence development requires the social worker to possess the knowledge and skills to:

1. Become introspective and critically evaluate one's own practice
2. Make use of consultation
3. Consume and extend social work's professional knowledge

Frequently Utilized Social Work Competencies

Six additional clusters of activity were regularly performed by most social workers. The knowledge and skills to perform these tasks, however, are sufficiently important for all social workers to master.

Case Planning and Maintenance

This cluster of practice activities requires the social worker to be competent to perform ongoing case planning, coordinate any additional services the client requires, monitor and evaluate case progress, obtain case consultation when appropriate, and complete required paperwork for case records. Most of the work in this cluster is considered *direct service* activity, i.e., work that is conducted on a face-to-face basis with one's clients. To perform these activities, the social worker should be prepared with the following:

1. Expertise in service planning and monitoring
2. Ability to carry out the employing agency's programs and operating procedures
3. Knowledge of client background factors
4. Skill in interagency coordination
5. Ability to engage in case advocacy

Individual and Family Treatment

A set of tasks frequently performed by social workers in direct service positions involves providing social treatment to individuals and families. This treatment requires that the social workers select and use clearly defined formal treatment approaches to help individuals and/or families improve their social functioning or resolve their social problems. In addition to the basic interpersonal helping skills (described previously), the worker must also possess:

1. Sufficient knowledge of human development to make in-depth psychosocial assessments
2. Understanding of variations in family (and other households) functioning
3. Skill in the selection and application of the most appropriate and effective individual and/or family treatment modalities from among the many intervention approaches available to social workers

Delivery System Knowledge Development

As the profession most likely to help clients connect with the services offered throughout a community, the social worker should develop thorough knowledge of the various regulations, policies, and procedures that affect social programs. Thus the social worker must develop the skills necessary to gather information about the network of services and service resources within the social worker's geographic area. To develop this knowledge, the worker might visit agencies, attend interagency meetings, and monitor agency web sites to become acquainted with and keep up to date with changes in the services provided. This cluster of work is an *indirect service* in which the worker develops important background information for serving clients, but this gathering of information does not usually occur in the presence of the client or relate only to a single client or group of clients. To develop this knowledge, the social worker should have:

1. An ability to maintain up-to-date knowledge of a variety of human services programs
2. Skills in building interagency coordination and linkage

Staff Information Exchange

As an agency-based profession, social workers must also be thoroughly versed in the programs and operating procedures of their own agencies. In addition, a worker must be prepared to contribute to the effective operation of that organization by working to resolve problems in agency functioning and contributing to decisions that strengthen the agency and its services. The knowledge and skills required of the social worker to perform these tasks include:

1. An ability to prepare and understand written and oral presentations regarding agency programs
2. The capacity to facilitate staff members in making decisions and resolving problems
3. An ability to facilitate interdisciplinary collaboration

Risk Assessment and Transition Services

All direct service providers have to make judgments about the urgency for services and the consequences of not providing services. Based on that assessment, they determine the type of services needed, facilitate the transition of clients from one service to another, and/or decide on the appropriateness of terminating the helping process. To perform these tasks, the worker must have the competence to assess a case situation to determine its difficulty (i.e., risk, urgency, or need) and engage clients either in making use of services or preparing them for transition or termination of services. This work often involves obtaining the client's perception of the reasons services are required; learning the viewpoints of significant people in the client's life; and, if working as part of an interdisciplinary team, securing information others have collected. To conduct this activity, the social worker must have:

1. An ability to apply general systems and/or ecosystems theory when assessing factors affecting a practice situation (See, for example, the Ecosystems Model used as the organizational format for Part Five of this book, the vulnerable populations section.)
2. Skill in engaging clients in examining problems in social functioning
3. Competence in utilizing appropriate social work assessment techniques and arriving at accurate diagnoses of client issues
4. Skill in the use of crisis intervention
5. Ability to facilitate client transitions between services and/or to terminate service

Staff Supervision

Supervision of agency personnel, students, and volunteers often becomes part of the social worker's workload. To provide this supervision, one must be prepared to guide the day-to-day work of staff members by orienting them to the organization and its requirements, assigning work and teaching them to perform their jobs, and monitoring and assessing their performance. The social worker performing staff supervision must possess:

1. Knowledge of the literature regarding the supervisory process
2. Capacity to facilitate the work of supervisees
3. Ability to conduct worker evaluation and guide worker professional development

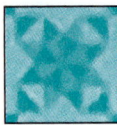

Competencies Occasionally Needed by Social Workers

The following eight task clusters of social work practice activity are occasionally performed by most social workers and more regularly required in one or more specific practice areas or with specialized job assignments. To some degree, all social workers need at least basic knowledge about these activities, and some need to have mastered both the knowledge and skills to perform them.

Group Work

Many social workers use small groups as an environment for teaching clients basic skills for performing daily living tasks, communicating information to enhance social functioning, or for facilitating problem resolution or therapeutic change. The group process is used to teach individuals how groups work and how to act as a group member. In its more specialized application, group work is used by advanced social workers as a treatment method or when teaching or engaging staff in program-changing activities. To be competent in this area, the social worker should possess:

1. Knowledge of group structure and functioning
2. Capacity to perform the staff role of leading and guiding a group
3. Ability to engage in group therapy

Dispute Resolution

Disagreements and disputes inevitably arise in human service agencies. For example, at times clients are unhappy with the services provided, staff members may disagree with each other regarding some aspect of agency functioning, or staff members may believe that the agency (their employer) or a supervisor has treated them unfairly. Such disputes must be resolved if the agency is to devote maximum attention to client services. The social worker should be prepared to help address such issues and, therefore, should possess the following competencies:

1. Understanding of agency procedures and its decision-making structure
2. Skill in advocacy, negotiation, and mediation

Service Connection

As brokers for the human services who link clients with community resources, social workers must be prepared to employ techniques that help clients to connect with established services and take action to eliminate barriers that prevent them from receiving those services. Service connection tasks overlap with some of those used in case planning and maintenance (discussed previously), but they differ to the extent that the worker engaging in service connection helps the client make the desired connection with a community service and then drops out of the picture. Competencies that are particularly important in this cluster of activity are the following:

1. Maintaining an ongoing critical assessment of the battery of social programs in the community and region
2. Ability to make an accurate intake assessment of a client's needs and to skillfully refer clients to appropriate resources
3. Expertise in advocating for clients within one's agency or with other human service programs

Program Development

Social workers who hold administrative or management positions often carry responsibility for either modifying existing programs or creating new ones. They must have the competence to document and interpret the need for additional human service programs, develop working relationships with relevant resources for program support (e.g., boards, funding sources, legislative bodies), oversee implementation of new programs, and evaluate the success of these programs. These social workers must be able to convert program goals and objectives into specific plans, develop budgets and staffing plans, "sell" the program(s) to funding sources and other decision makers, and compile data for evaluation purposes. To conduct these activities, the social worker must possess:

1. Skill in community and organizational data collection and analysis
2. Ability to design and implement social programs
3. Capacity, including coalition building, grant application preparation, and public education, to obtain agency and/or community support for new or revised programs

Instruction

Most social workers engage in a certain amount of teaching. Much of their teaching is in informal work with clients to help them learn skills for addressing the issues they face in life. However, many social workers also engage in formal instructional activities in which a planned curriculum is delivered to groups of clients, agency staff members or volunteers, students, or community groups. To provide instruction effectively, the social worker must be prepared to plan, arrange, conduct, and evaluate educational programs. To successfully perform teaching or instruction activities, the social worker should have the following competencies:

1. Capacity to develop curriculum for instruction or training programs
2. Skill in planning workshops, seminars, or classroom sessions
3. Ability to engage students, trainees, or groups of clients in learning activities
4. Capacity to assess and evaluate the success (or failure) of instructional activities

Staff Deployment

Human service agencies are labor intensive; that is, they work with relatively few tangible products, and most of their resources are invested in people. Thus, the knowledge and skill to effectively assign or deploy personnel in a way that makes efficient use of staff time and ensures that appropriate personnel are available to serve clients is important. The tasks involved in staff deployment include recruiting and selecting staff, arranging staffing patterns and workload assignments, monitoring staff productivity, and overseeing compliance with organizational policies. To carry out these tasks, the worker must possess:

1. Capacity to match personnel with job assignments
2. Ability to create a clear organizational structure for conducting the work of the agency and a fair means of assigning the workload
3. Skill in developing instruments that evaluate worker performance

Protective Services

Some social workers are employed to specifically offer protective services, especially for the very young and the very old, when there is suspected physical, mental, or economic abuses. To provide those services, the social worker is required to collect and analyze data to be used in assessing at-risk clients and presenting information to appropriate authorities if clients are judged to be in danger or of having their basic rights violated. As part of this process, the worker may be expected to start legal proceedings and testify or participate in court hearings involving custody, competence, outplacement, or institutionalization. Specialized knowledge and skill to perform these activities include:

1. Capacity to identify at-risk factors such as physical and emotional maltreatment
2. Knowledge of the law and legal processes concerning protective services
3. Knowledge of local resources to be contacted if clients are in danger
4. Ability to deal with conflictual situations

Organizational Maintenance

To keep our human services agencies functioning as places where clients can receive the assistance they need and where social workers can use their skills effectively, skilled management is required. Thus, performing activities that maintain those organizations as viable places for providing services sometimes becomes a primary function of the social worker. These social workers require the knowledge and skills to secure, allocate, and oversee the utilization of resources (e.g., staff, funds, supplies, space), as well as representing the agency in the community and marketing its services to the public. Most agencies are a public trust (both public and private nonprofit agencies) and it is particularly important that the administrators are skilled at financial management. These social workers should obtain the competence to:

1. Understand the operation of basic business systems and the requirements for oversight of agency resources

2. Create and manage systems of agency information flow
3. Market the agency's services so that both potential clients and potential funders are aware of the agency and the services it provides

Low Utilization Competencies for Most Social Workers

Two more sets of activities are an important part of social work practice but primarily are performed by social workers in very specialized positions. Both have been important aspects of social work in its historical development but appear to have slipped out of the mainstream in recent years.

Research and Policy Development

If social workers are to fulfill their mission of assisting communities to improve social conditions or contribute to improved social conditions through influencing laws or regulations at the state or federal levels, they must be skilled at collecting data about those social conditions and assisting policy makers as they apply that knowledge to various social policies and programs. In short, the social worker in these highly specialized positions must be prepared to collect, analyze, and publish data; present technical information to the general public, legislators, or other decision makers responsible for changes in human services programs or community conditions; and/or interact with community groups. To do this, the social worker must possess:

1. The ability to develop and implement program and needs assessment research
2. Skill in social policy analysis and influencing decisions of policy makers
3. Competence in public education and advocacy

Tangible Service Provision

The limited tangible service provision activity of social workers is largely provided by beginning-level direct services workers. This activity focuses on meeting the basic needs of the poor and at-risk members of the society as they cope with issues of subsistence and survival in everyday life. The tasks include teaching such basic skills as budgeting, money management, food preparation, and homemaking; helping clients find jobs and housing; and putting clients in touch with people who can help them address legal and other issues. The knowledge and skills required for this activity include:

1. Knowledge of local resources that provide clients with social provisions such as shelter, food, clothing, money, and employment
2. Ability to develop positive helping relationships with clients who are often feeling defeated and unmotivated
3. Competence in teaching clients to use resources effectively

Concluding Comment

For a profession with the broad mission of helping people interact more effectively with their environments, it is not surprising that the identification of common features that bind social work practitioners into one profession has proved difficult. It is only at the somewhat general level of defining its mission that social workers have gradually moved toward consensus. This perception is further strengthened by the empirical data underpinning this discussion of competencies. The data from the national task analysis of social work practice makes it evident that there is much knowledge and many skills that are common to all of social work—certainly enough to conclude that social work should be considered a single profession. It is also evident that there are many specialized areas of social work practice that require supplemental knowledge and skills if one is to effectively perform the duties of the social worker.

In the preceding pages, we identified competencies social workers are expected to possess—and the list does not exhaust what social workers need to know and be able to do. By examining Demetria's work with the Miles family in Chapter 1, the new social worker can obtain an overview of at least a few of the competencies displayed by Demetria (see Box 9.1).

Box 9.1

Some Competencies Displayed by Demetria

As evidenced by Demetria's work with the Miles family (see Chapter 1), social work practice requires even the beginning worker to possess considerable knowledge and many skills. Demetria's BSW program had provided her with many of the basic competencies needed to begin her work in child welfare, and she will no doubt develop them further through her practice experience and by attending relevant professional conferences and workshops in the future. Demetria's primary job function was that of a direct practitioner, i.e., working directly with Joseph and Mrs. Miles, although she benefited from the indirect practice insights of her supervisor.

Examples of Demetria's competencies in the most universal cluster of social work practice tasks, the *interpersonal helping cluster,* were evident in her ability to develop professional helping relationships. In her beginning contacts with both Joseph and Mrs. Miles, Demetria did not rush the conversation and allowed time to chat, not for fear of getting to the point and possibly facing conflict, but rather to establish some mutual connections that would yield sufficient rapport to move ahead in addressing the tough issues. Demetria was also competent in client information gathering. Through a relatively sparse amount of interviewing, she was able to accumulate a substantial amount of information about this family, which assisted her in understanding the family dynamics and, perhaps, the root causes of the issues Joseph was experiencing.

Among the frequently used clusters of competencies, Demetria was especially effective in the *case planning and maintenance* tasks. She formalized her *service planning* tasks by presenting her plan to the staff team for consultation and, in the process of conducting

> her investigation into the case, demonstrated the ability to carry out the employing agency's programs and operating procedures. Demetria also demonstrated good *delivery system knowledge.* She had an adequate degree of up-to-date knowledge of a variety of human services programs and used that knowledge to help the Miles family find the resources to begin addressing their issues. Finally, Demetria was engaged in providing a *risk assessment.* The school had reported the possibility that child abuse and/or neglect had occurred, and Demetria's job was first to determine the degree to which this child was at risk and then to attempt to help resolve the issues that were detrimental to the child's well-being. In the process, she engaged the clients in examining their problems in social functioning and demonstrated skill in utilizing social work assessment techniques.

KEY WORDS AND CONCEPTS

Competence
Skill
Knowledge

Primary job function
Direct practice
Indirect practice

SUGGESTED INFORMATION SOURCES

Sheafor, Bradford W., and Charles R. Horejsi. *Techniques and Guidelines for Social Work Practice,* 8th ed. Boston: Allyn & Bacon, 2008.

Teare, Robert J., and Bradford W. Sheafor. *Practice-Sensitive Social Work Education: An Empirical Analysis of Social Work Practice and Practitioners.* Alexandria, VA: Council on Social Work Education, 1995.

ENDNOTES

1. Bradford W. Sheafor and Charles R. Horejsi, *Techniques and Guidelines for Social Work Practice,* 8th ed. (Boston: Allyn & Bacon, 2008). See especially Chapter 3, "Merging the Person's Art with the Profession's Science."
2. Robert J. Teare and Bradford W. Sheafor, *Practice-Sensitive Social Work Education: An Empirical Analysis of Social Work Practice and Practitioners* (Alexandria, VA: Council on Social Work Education, 1995).
3. National Association of Social Workers, "Task Frequency and Importance Mean Ratings," Unpublished material from ACSW Blueprint Committee (Washington, D.C.: NASW, no date).
4. National Association of Social Workers, *Indicators for the Achievement of the NASW Standards for Cultural Competence in Social Work Practice* (Washington, D.C.: NASW, 2007). Also found at http://www.socialworkers.org/practice/standards/NASWCulturalStandards.pdf.
5. National Association of Social Workers, *NASW Code of Ethics* (Washington, D.C.: NASW, 1996, revised 1999). Also found at http://www.naswdc.org/pubs/code/code.asp.

part four

Contemporary Issues Facing Social Work and Social Workers

The motivation that attracts most people to social work is the desire to make a difference in the quality of life for others. It truly is an altruistic profession. When a person decides to commit to the required years and costs to obtain the necessary education, to accept the relatively low potential earning power, and to deal with the inevitable stress associated with helping others reduce the pain that comes from problems in social functioning, the person must know that there is at least the emotional reward of the satisfaction that comes from helping clients.

How successful are social workers? Unfortunately, a means of determining the success rate of social workers has not yet been developed. After all, how could we determine what would be a success? A complete cure for a person with a persistent mental illness would be unlikely, but incremental progress might be a realistic indicator of success. Achieving stable employment, even if at minimum wage, might be a success for the primary breadwinner of a family, yet that would be insufficient to remove the need for financial assistance or move the family out of poverty. Is that success? Yes and no. Is the success that might be achieved in helping a client work through a crisis situation equivalent to the difficulty of helping a family change its pattern of harmful child-rearing practices? In short, entering social work must involve an act of faith that one will be able to make a difference in the lives of at least some clients—or in strengthening social policies and programs that affect the larger population.

Throughout this book, many of the issues social workers face today are identified, but what about tomorrow? It is informative for the new social worker to consider some of the issues that social workers are now beginning to address as a means of assessing what challenges and opportunities might be in the future of social work. Although many issues might have been selected, the six chapters in this part of *Many Faces* represent a sample of issues that range from individual client focus to the emergence of social work as a global profession. The relatively short chapters are intended to identify the issues and stimulate thinking about social work's future related to the matter.

Chapter 10, for example, considers the role of spirituality in social work practice. Although many social programs evolved out of religious and spiritual commitments—and many social workers have been motivated to enter this profession from a religious orientation—social work has emerged as a secular profession. Social workers attempt to

part four Contemporary Issues Facing Social Work and Social Workers

help clients address complex social issues by addressing the whole person (i.e., social, physical, intellectual, emotional, economic, and cultural dimensions). Can they ignore the client's spiritual considerations and still address the whole person?

In Chapter 11, a long-standing issue that is still prevalent in social work is captured in the question "Is it useful for social workers to devote most of their effort to helping people address their problems without making an effort to prevent those problems for occurring in the first place?" The potential to engage in social change activities that reduce or eliminate the sources of difficulty for many clients (e.g., discrimination, family violence, inadequate housing and income), and therefore prevent client problems from developing or becoming more pronounced, will continue to be an issue for social workers.

Terrorism takes many forms, but when it is created by domestic or international gangs, it becomes a powerful tool for manipulating human behavior. In Chapter 12, "Social Work's Role in Addressing Terrorism," an old problem (i.e., terrorist activities performed by U.S. gangs) is explored as new forms of domestic gangs have emerged. The chapter also draws a parallel to international terrorist activities perpetrated by extremist groups in the Middle East, such as al-Qaeda, suggesting that much of our understanding of gang domestic behavior and programs could be transferred to the international scene.

The impact of wars, specifically the recent wars in the Middle East, will have an influence on social workers, not only in veteran service agencies but also in mental health, physical rehabilitation centers, hospitals, and practically every type of human services agency that will have contact with the surviving veterans and their family members. Chapter 13, "Social Work with U.S. Casualties of the Middle East Wars," identifies issues created by wars that social workers will need to be prepared to address.

Chapter 14, "Social Work Practice with Immigrants, Refugees, and Unaccompanied Minors," is concerned with a highly political and controversial issue that generates strong emotion on both sides of the U.S. immigration debate. What issues arise in practice for the social workers who serve both legal and undocumented immigrants, refugees, and unaccompanied minors? What happens to families and children when immigrants are harassed, jailed while documentation is investigated, or deported to their home countries? This chapter is concerned with factors that are important for social workers to consider related to immigration issues in the United States.

Finally, although this book is primarily concerned with how social work is practiced in the United States, Chapter 15 reports on social work's movement toward becoming a global profession. With its emphasis on working with people regarding issues related to their interactions with the world around them (i.e., their social environment), the context of practice is an important dynamic in the helping process. Thus, the context varies from country to country, and the future of social work will involve sorting out that which is common to all of social work from that which is unique to each country.

chapter 10

Spirituality in a Secular Profession

> **Prefatory Comment**
>
> In recent years, increasing attention has been given to the role of spirituality and religion in social work. This contemporary dialogue is value-laden and complex. However, the reality that issues of religion and spirituality in social work are here to stay is not in debate. What is debated, however, is whether modern social work curricula should educate and train the professional social worker to handle the intersection of a secular profession in a world with spiritual and religious underpinnings.
>
> To keep pace with the ever-evolving social work profession, it is useful to further the conversation among students, educators, and practitioners about the relevance of this issue for social workers. This chapter addresses religion and spirituality from a historical perspective, as well as the implications spirituality has on today's professional practice. The authors believe these issues have a place in the classroom, if for no other reason than to better equip social work professionals to serve their clients with an expanded level of cultural awareness.

Religion and spirituality are terms often used interchangeably, but that is misleading. To understand the context of this chapter in relation to these two terms, it is critical to define religion and spirituality. For the purposes of this chapter's discussions, *religion*, as articulated by Edward Canda,[1] is "the patterning of spiritual beliefs and practices into social institutions, with community support and traditions maintained over time." Canda further indicates that *spirituality* "relates to the person's search for a sense of meaning and morally fulfilling relationships between oneself, other people, the encompassing universe, and the ontological [metaphysical] ground of existence, whether a person understands this in terms that are theistic, atheistic, non-theistic, or any combination of these."[2] Religion, then, is a term rooted in a narrower cultural and formalized base, with particular experiences, rituals, and value beliefs established by particular religious institutions and governed by their covenants. Spirituality, however, is a much more broad-based concept that may or may not be constrained by a specified religion or denominational affiliation or association.[3] Regardless of which concept one embraces, or neither, the two terms are important realities in the contemporary cultural value composition in the United States and should be recognized and validated as components of human diversity.

Gallup and Lindsay report that an overwhelming majority of U.S. citizens (between 92 percent and 97 percent) believe there is a God or a higher power. In addition, they assert that some 87 percent of American citizens value religion highly and feel it is an important component of their lives.[4] These numbers, perhaps, explain why there is a recent surge in research on the relationship of religion and spirituality in social work practice and increased consideration of its inclusion in curricula in professional schools. Much like the cultural competence discussions that focus on race and ethnicity, sexual orientation, disability, women's issues, socioeconomic diversity, and others, religion and spirituality are poised to take a place among these considerations. To serve clients as effectively as possible, it is increasingly recognized that greater understanding of the impact of spirituality and religion in the practice arena, in social work curricula, and in agency settings must be encouraged and supported.

It is important that we address these issues as the population continues to grow and become more diverse. Our efforts should be to equip practitioners with the knowledge and skills necessary to serve individuals and groups who have varying spiritual and religious cultural beliefs. The tendency to focus on the large organized religions in the United States marginalizes those who fall outside these affiliations. Christianity clearly is the largest organized religion with 160 million members in the United States (76 percent), and those with nonreligious or secular beliefs are a distant second at 13.2 percent.[5] However, Judaism, Islam, Buddhism, Agnostic, Hinduism, Unitarian Universalist, and Wiccan/Pagan/Druid religions are also part of the religious culture of America, not to mention Spiritualists and Native American spiritual traditions and practices.

Clearly, there is heterogeneity among U.S. citizens and their religious, secular, and spiritual beliefs, but the challenge for social workers is that few could become experts in all of them. Rather, the challenge, as formidable as it may be, is to establish ways of honoring and respecting clients' values and beliefs and discovering how these beliefs influence their lives and might serve them in improving their social functioning and well-being.

Spirituality also appears to have a role in the motivations of the persons providing the help. When asked, social work students often assert that they were brought up to be concerned for the welfare of their neighbor. Another common response from students is that their altruistic motives (i.e., placing the needs of others before one's own) are firmly centered in their spiritual or religious beliefs. Whichever the case, persons who enter helping professions tend to find value and personal satisfaction in helping persons in need—and for many that motivation is rooted in spiritual beliefs.

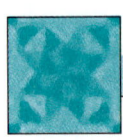

Historical Context of Spirituality in the Human Services

Religion and traditional spiritual practices have had significant influence in the establishment of human services in the United States. From early sectarian and Christian human services to contemporary faith-based church and governmental programs, spiritual values and beliefs, as well as religious doctrines, have played a significant role in the past and current landscape of American social welfare services. According to the *Encyclopedia of Social Work*, the social work profession in North America developed with a strong influence from religious ideologies of service (especially Christianity and Judaism) and humanistic spiritual views.[6] Examples include the Charity Organization Society, the Settlement House Movement, and Jewish Communal Services. Slogans from "it takes a village to raise a child" (African proverb) to "the poor shall not be forgotten" often reverberate in contemporary speeches referencing the struggles of the poor and today's troubled youth.

Perhaps the drifting that has occurred from these historical religious and spiritual foundations through the years has been more in word rhetoric than in the shifting of fundamental values and beliefs guiding the responsibility of the individual to those less fortunate. Canda and Furman, in their book *Spiritual Diversity in Social Work Practice*, assert that spirituality is at the heart of helping.[7] Although there has been a resurgence of discussions on religion and spirituality in the aftermath of terrorist attacks and natural and man-made disasters, many people have increasingly reflected on the meaning of their lives. In historical context, many in the social work profession have been at the center of efforts to care for and help direct society toward becoming more responsive to those suffering from the effects of poverty and disease. How, then, could a profession so guided by religious and spiritual duty evolve to a place that, until recently, seldom mentioned or discussed its historic foundations of religion and spirituality? Perhaps the evolution of social work as a secular profession is to blame. Thus, central to our discussion is the contemporary intersection of a secular profession and its responsibility to both acknowledge and support the reality that many of social work's clients are grounded and guided by their religious and spiritual beliefs, as are many social workers.

The central question, then, becomes "how much personal belief is not professional?" This question rings loudly among social workers of religious and nonreligious affiliations. For example, social workers in the early 1960s, according to Zilboorg, viewed religious and spiritual practices as "an atavism left over (i.e., a throwback) from primitive magic and animism."[8] Such assertions, as simplistic as they were concerning the personal and cultural relevance to the individual, helped to "push or pull" the social work profession away from its historical religious and spiritual roots.

Frank Loewenberg further asserts that many social workers, regardless of their personal religious and spiritual beliefs, do not feel religion and spirituality has any relevance or place in professional practice. "Just as they are committed to the principle of the separation of church and state in government, so have they accepted the principle of separating the sacred and the profane in their own lives."[9] The assertion here is not that the whole of social work endorses such beliefs concerning the role of religion and spirituality in their personal lives and the lives of their clients, but it does echo the diversity of values and beliefs among social work professionals and how such positions have run counter to the profession's historical roots. Loewenberg offers, for further clarity, the following useful typology of social worker's religious beliefs:

> Type 1: These social workers have no formal religious affiliations. They include a wide range of social workers who identify themselves as atheists, agnostics, or humanists.
> Type 2: These social workers have maintained an affiliation with a religious group and accept, more or less, the obligations and rituals of that group, but they do not see any relevance of their religious beliefs for social work practice.
> Type 3: These social workers are affiliated with a religious group and their entire life, including their professional practice, is guided by the tenets of that group.[10]

The influence on the social worker's professional practice found in these varying belief types might be depicted in a graphical representation resembling that of a bell-curve. At one extreme are the Type 1 believers and, at the other, Type 3. For example, a Type 3 social worker who identifies with some fundamentalist religions would find unconscionable the option of abortion under any circumstance and might refuse to counsel a pregnant teenage mother toward this option (personal value conflict). As such, it is not inconceivable then, to have social workers who would adopt a position at the other extreme given this case situation and advocate for abortion with the same client. Given this scenario, what consideration should be given to the clients' religious or spiritual values and beliefs? And in what ways should the culturally aware social worker approach this and similar case situations where religion, spirituality, and culture so boldly intersect?

Social Work Education and Spirituality/Religion

The National Association of Social Workers (NASW) in its Code of Ethics espouses the need for social work practitioners to be sensitive to clients' needs and self-efficacy and to be culturally competent in the delivery of services to clients in need who may have differing values and beliefs from their own.[11] Often in the literature, the focus has primarily been directed toward issues of racism, sexism, classism, heterosexism, and "ableism," all of which present formidable and daunting challenges in their own right to the social work profession in its efforts to assist clients with issues of individual, group, and social functioning. However, one area that has largely been overlooked, or at least underemphasized, is the influence spirituality can have in the helping and healing process. Except in religion-based universities, schools of social work rarely offer courses on spirituality, and only sporadically do professors address the issue in the classroom.

If clients and social workers hold in high regard their personal spiritual and religious values and beliefs, have their worldviews influenced by these beliefs, and make key life decisions directed by these spiritual and religious value positions, should there be place in social work curricula and research for such dialogue? Many social workers and social work educators would conclude, "There certainly should be." However, others would surely reply, "Certainly not." The current literature reflects a growing presence of articles and research with spirituality and religion as their focus. Many contemporary medical and psychology journals, and those more specific to social work (e.g., *Journal of Social Work Education, Social Work,* and *Health and Social Work*), are finding places for articles specifically addressing religion and spirituality. Also, at national meetings and conferences held by social workers, the issues of religion and spirituality have found their place at roundtable discussions and formal presentations. Increasingly, more attention is being given to these issues and to their relevance in the classroom and practice settings. Williams and Smolak, in their article "Integrating Faith Matters in Social Work Education," assert that schools of social work rarely address matters of faith, but that religion and spirituality are significant factors that warrant attention and influence nearly all areas of practice. They further assert that if the profession is to respond competently and sensitively, much less effectively, to clients' multiple layers of culture, we cannot continue to overlook relevant religious and spiritual factors.[12]

In addition to the ideological and philosophical positions of social work professionals engaged in practice and education, what of the value of students' perspectives on spirituality and religion in the social work classroom? Graff, in her exploratory study, found that, among 324 undergraduate social work students from seven Council on Social Work Education (CSWE)-accredited schools, just over 80 percent identified themselves as practicing Christians. In addition, she found that the vast majority desired more social work courses that included content reflecting religious and spiritual diversity, and the overwhelming majority expressed a desire to have content on how to effectively deal with these issues.[13]

Developing understanding of spirituality and religion is troublesome as it relies heavily on individual experiences and interpretation. Both arguments for and against the inclusion of these social and cultural realities in social work education have merit, but the debate continues to polarize social work professionals. Williams and Smolak identify topics that should be considered in the classroom. For example, consider the following benefits identified by proponents of introducing spirituality in the classroom: the value of spirituality as part of culturally competent practice, effective communication with people of faith, the practice of social work in religious settings, and the unnecessary limitations on professional practice imposed by a purely secular view. Those who argue that it is not appropriate to address spirituality in a secular profession contend that the inclusion of faith matters in the social work classroom could compromise the following: the view that social work is a scientific, empirically based profession; the need to maintain clear lines of separation between church and state; opening the door to proselytizing; and contributing to sectarian conflict.[14]

While spirituality and religion, and their inclusion in social work curricula, continue to be a contentious issue among social work professionals, most recent evidence from the literature indicates that the profession's longstanding commitment to creating a social work workforce that is knowledgeable of clients' values may potentially be compromised by the lack of attention to religion and spirituality. The evidence further points to attempts by educators to offer instruction in the form of electives or a more comprehensive approach by the integration of religious and spiritual content in core curriculum courses. Williams and Smolak recommend a more holistic approach that would combine both, rather than either/or, as a plausible strategy. A more comprehensive approach, they argue, would maximize student learning and prove most effective toward adequately preparing future social work practitioners to serve clients with various levels of religious and spiritual beliefs.[15]

Religion and Spirituality in Cultural Competence

The presence of spirituality and religion among U.S. citizens is well documented. Among most developed nations, the United States is one of the most religious, with several studies indicating that some 90 percent of Americans say they believe in God or some higher power. Not so pronounced, however, is the influence these religious beliefs and spiritual practices have on individuals' decision-making. Though most Americans self-identify as "believers," there is substantial variation in the degree and level of individuals' religious and spiritual practices and, ultimately, the impact on their daily lives.

However, social work continues to hold in high regard the responsibility of its workforce to practice with a level and degree of cultural competence and skill. Appreciation of human diversity is embedded in the profession's commitment to helping individuals realize their fullest potential, as set forth in social work's professional code of conduct and the duties, roles, and responsibilities performed by social workers. To this end, as it relates to spirituality and religion, the profession must also include the preparations of new social work practitioners in these areas. It is vital that social workers better understand these influences on clients' actions and how best to access and support religious and spiritual resources to achieve improved client outcomes.

Spirituality and Religion in Professional Practice

The intersection of spirituality and religion in social work has until recent decades been a hidden phenomenon or, at best, a seldom discussed reality. Perhaps, for reasons of discomfort and/or anxiety, the nature and impact of spirituality, religion, and faith seemed out of bounds as a legitimate topic for practice consideration and social work education. However, as history will attest, with the passing of time, change often occurs. Likewise, many professions that serve individuals, families, groups, and communities find themselves confronted with peoples' spiritual and religious cultural values and beliefs.

Bullis asserts that "social work and spirituality are natural allies in personal and social healing." Social work is beginning to seriously consider the inclusion of religious and spiritual influences on the helping and healing process. The resurgence of religion and spirituality in the popular culture and among professional fields of practice (i.e., social work, medicine, psychology, and nursing) suggests that spirituality must be considered when addressing the personal and social challenges people face.[16] For example, one can only wonder how a more inclusive and genuine affirmation of Native peoples' spiritual beliefs and respect for "mother nature" might have affected the nation's current environmental troubles. How might the culture of the United States be different if it had adopted a more cooperative economic approach (interdependence) rather than one more aligned with the notions of rugged individualism (independence)? Spirituality and religion bring to light a perspective that moves beyond the merely concrete and catapults the mind and body into a more subjective dimension of thinking and being. It is to this place that many people are turning to recapture a part of them that they had forgotten existed.

In his book, *Spirituality in Social Work Practice*, Bullis presents four primary rationales for addressing spirituality in clinical practice:

▸ Social work is historically and philosophically connected to spirituality; philosophically, both social work and spirituality promote common interests and self-respect, and social work and spirituality are natural allies.
▸ Social work and spirituality have much to learn from each other. Spirituality offers social work experiences and insights on personal and community levels that promote social and personal transformations.
▸ Knowledge of spirituality helps social workers construct spiritual cosmologies and spiritual anthropologies. Cosmologies are graphic depictions of a person's worldview. A spiritual cosmology is necessary to examine the spiritual sensitivity of the client or the social worker. Likewise, spiritual anthropology is necessary for any examination of healing—whether it be personal or community.
▸ There is no reason why social workers and spiritual leaders cannot collaborate. The historical estrangement notwithstanding, social work and spiritual professionals have no ethical or philosophic barriers to such collaboration.[17]

In essence, a more inclusive view of spirituality in social work practice adds yet another lens to the view of self for the social worker, the client, and the social environment. To lack such a key perspective, may marginalize the impact a practitioner could potentially have in the helping relationship at all levels of social work practice. The seemingly immense gulf that exists philosophically between social work and issues of religion and spirituality can be minimized. Derezotes, for example, asserts that social work practitioners need practical methods that can be used cross-culturally and across the vastness of religious and spiritual diversity among differing populations and cultures. What is now needed, he further asserts, are theoretical foundations and research-based methodologies that serve the spiritual and religious dimensions of practice.[18]

The science of social work alone may not be sufficient to address the multiple dimensions of the individual—mind, body, and soul conceptions. Hodge argues that social work oppresses Evangelical Christians by its sanctions and legitimizes discrimination against Evangelicals and other people of faith.[19] Many people of faith, particularly those viewed as radicals, hold hard-line positions on issues of homosexuality, lesbianism, abortion, and gay marriage, and they can find strong levels of intolerance from and for a profession that engenders such a strong secular orientation. As the Code of Ethics asserts, social workers should strive to eradicate all forms of discrimination, including racial, gender, age, and religious indifference.

What would a philosophical conception geared more toward the mutually beneficial coexistence of religious and spiritual differences require of social work and social work professionals? Would a more spiritually centered practice orientation be appropriate in the different fields of practice and with different client groups? Consider the following chapter titles from Derezotes' book: Spiritually Oriented Practice with Children, Youth, and Families; Spiritually Oriented Practice with Adult and Aging Clients; Spiritually Oriented Practice in Mental-Health Settings; Spiritually Oriented Practice in Criminal Justice Settings; and Spiritually Oriented Practice in Public Social Service Settings.[20] When examining how spirituality and religion might influence these different expressions of social work, many thoughts, feelings, emotions, and perhaps personal judgments are likely to surface. It is meaningful for social workers and social work students to take some time to personally reflect on why these conceptions might generate such reactions within themselves. Perhaps it is the mind's attempt to struggle with the mingling of a secular professional orientation with the spiritual and religious values and beliefs of social workers and their clients. In social work practice, it stands to reason that the conflict between secular expectations and spiritual feelings and emotions might cause discomfort for the social work practitioner who has not thoughtfully considered these matters.

A CASE VIGNETTE: CHRISTIAN'S SPIRITUAL CHALLENGE

Christian Thomas, a 23-year-old social work intern at the Big Valley Medical Center, found his mind wandering as he headed to work on the light rail into downtown. He was very excited about his field placement at the Medical Center as he hoped for a career in medical social work. He wondered what new and exciting challenges his internship would present during his semester at the hospital.

Christian, the only child of Bill and Kate Thomas, was the joy of his parents' lives. For them, Christian was their "miracle baby" and a precious gift from God they both cherished deeply. As fundamental Christians, Bill and Kate found that their faith and spiritual commitment was strengthened through the five-year struggle to have a child. Both parents felt God had smiled on them—they even named him Christian when their child was born—because their effort to have a child had presented them with the opportunity for spiritual growth.

A dedicated young fundamentalist Christian himself, Christian was committed to his religious beliefs and felt that through these precepts he could offer hope to those with whom he connected. Christian found comfort in his faith and the uncompromising positions regarding the "sins" of abortion, fornication (premarital sex), pornography, and homosexuality that his long-time pastor, John Mitchell, had preached about. Christian had absorbed the teachings of his beloved pastor for many years and had strong convictions regarding the importance of morality in his life and the choices he should make to remain faithful to the principles his parents and others had taught him.

Having arrived at the hospital somewhat early, Christian decided to walk around the hospital before reporting to his MSW field instructor for today's assignments. As he made his way near the emergency room entrance, he heard the blaring siren of an emergency transport vehicle. His heart raced, and his legs gained momentum as he was curious to know what the emergency was all about. Christian followed the emergency medical technicians

(EMTs) into the emergency room. A 45-year-old Caucasian male named Isaac Peterson was in cardiac distress and was barely conscious. The medical team scrambled to stabilize his racing heart before he was in full cardiac arrest. "Phillip, call Phillip," Isaac mumbled through the oxygen mask. The nurse assured him they would contact his family. Isaac fell unconscious and stopped speaking. Christian said a little prayer as they rushed Isaac into emergency surgery. The attending physician asked the nurse to page a social worker to notify the family. "Tell them the situation is life threatening and very serious," she instructed.

Christian's field instructor, Karen, entered the nursing station and asked for an update on the situation with the patient. Christian relayed what he had heard and that the doctor would like the next of kin notified immediately. He continued to inform her that Isaac was only conscious for a short moment after he arrived and then was out, but he mentioned the name "Phillip" several times before he passed out. Karen asked Christian if he felt he could handle assisting with this case. Eager to get more responsibility, Christian jumped at the opportunity to serve as the medical social worker on this case.

Christian contacted the parents and informed them of their son's situation. They lived only about 15 minutes away and said they would be down to the hospital right away. Christian really wanted to be prepared when they arrived. He spoke with his field instructor and shared the progress with her. Karen complimented Christian on his follow-up effort and encouraged him to come and ask any questions he felt necessary. When Mr. and Mrs. Peterson arrived, they both seemed very worried about their son. "Is he alright?" they asked. Christian asked the Petersons to be seated. He told them that Isaac had gone into cardiac arrest and was in emergency surgery, but the doctor would be out to speak with them about his condition as soon as he was out of surgery. Christian asked if he could get them anything while they waited for the doctor. "No, nothing," they both replied in concert. "I will come by a little later to see how you are doing," Christian responded.

Nearly two hours later, Christian was sitting with the parents, but no one was talking. A surgeon dressed in scrubs appeared and reported "Mr. and Mrs. Peterson, Isaac is out of surgery and in the Intensive Care Unit (ICU). His situation is still touch-and-go, and he is in a coma. There has been some damage to the heart muscle, and he is facing a long recovery, if he pulls through the next 72 hours. I will keep you updated on his progress." They both thanked the doctor for his efforts in caring for their son. "Can we see him?" the mother asked. "Yes," the doctor replied, "but I have restricted visitation to immediate family, and you can only stay about five minutes each hour." They understood and agreed to comply with the doctor's wishes.

Christian stood and watched as Isaac's parents walked away with the doctor to see their son. At that moment, in rushed a tall, lean, African-American man, nearly out of breath, asking at the nurses' station about Isaac. Christian introduced himself as the medical social worker and asked how he could help. "My name is Phillip, and I got a call that Isaac was rushed into emergency surgery. How is he?" the man asked. Christian remembered that Isaac was asking for Phillip before he fell unconscious. "How do you know Isaac? Are you a family friend or coworker?" Christian asked politely. "No," Phillip replied strongly, "Isaac is my partner. We have been together for 15 years." At that moment, Christian realized that Isaac and Phillip were in a same-sex relationship and that the two gay men had been a couple for some time.

Mr. and Mrs. Peterson returned to the waiting area. Their eyes locked with Phillip's eyes. Christian felt a huge tension in the room. The parents began to grumble to each other, though not audibly. They turned toward the nurses' station without a word and started to walk away. "Can I see Isaac now?" Phillip pleaded. "He's not family," Mr. Peterson declared. "Only immediate family can visit."

What was Christian to do? Clearly, Isaac had stated before he became unconscious that he wished to have Phillip present. It was also obvious there was tension between Phillip and Isaac's parents, and the parents made it clear they did not want Phillip present. Should Christian advocate for Phillip to be admitted to the ICU as a family member? Should he consult with his field instructor for guidance? Should he call Pastor Mitchell for consultation? How should Christian resolve his own secular–spiritual dilemma, given the conflict of his personal spiritual beliefs versus the patient's clear request?

Concluding Comment

Religion and spirituality are complex personal and cultural issues. The challenge to appropriately consider these powerful forces is particularly great in an increasingly secular society. Indeed, the intersection of religion and spirituality with secularism in American society is real. Social work, as a secular profession, must come to grips with this intersection. As a profession, social work historically has been committed to social, political, and economic justice; the elimination of poverty and discrimination; and social betterment (i.e., the increased social functioning of individuals, groups, and communities that make up the human family). All of these beliefs are compatible with most religious doctrines. To this end, social workers must not only consider the implications of religion and spirituality in the lives of their clients but also must identify and confront personal spiritual and religious beliefs and value orientations that run counter to the overall goals and aspirations of the profession.

KEY WORDS AND CONCEPTS

Spirituality
Religion
Spiritually oriented social work practice
Spiritual diversity in social work

Spirituality in social work curriculum
Integrating spirituality, faith, and social justice in social work practice

SUGGESTED INFORMATION SOURCES

Tirrito, Terry, and Toni Cascio, eds. *Religious Organizations in Community Services: A Social Work Perspective.* New York: Springer Publishing, 2003.

Lee, Daniel, and Robert O'Gorman, eds. *Social Work and Divinity.* Binghamton, NY: Haworth Press, 2005.

Graff, Dorothy L., "A Study of Baccalaureate Social Work Students' Beliefs about the Inclusion of Religious and Spiritual Content in Social Work." *Journal of Social Work Education* 43 (2007): 243–256.

ENDNOTES

1. Edward Canda, "Spirituality in Social Work," in *Encyclopedia of Social Work, Supplement* (Silver Spring, MD: National Association of Social Workers, 1997), pp. 299–309.
2. Ibid.
3. Michael A. Dover, Barbara Hunter, Randall Joseph, Ruth Paris, Ellen R. DeVoe, Toba Schwaber Kerson, Edward R. Canda, and Susan J. Lambert "Human Needs," in Terry Mizrahi and Larry E. Davis, eds., *Encyclopedia of Social Work* (New York: Oxford University Press, 2008).
4. George Gallup and Michael Lindsay, *Surveying the Religious Landscape: Trends in U.S. Beliefs* (Harrisburg, PA: Morehouse Publishing, 1999), pp. 7–41.
5. Adherents.com, *Top Ten Religions in the United States, 2001.* http:// www.urbandharma.org/udharma5/toprelig.html.
6. Canda, op. cit., 1997.
7. Edward Canda and Leola Furman, *Spiritual Diversity in Social Work Practice: The Heart of Helping* (New York: The Free Press, 1999), pp. xv and 1–5.
8. Gregory Zilboorg, *Psychoanalysis and Religion* (London: Farrar Strauss Giroux, 1962), p. 227.
9. Frank, M. Loewenberg, *Religion and Social Work Practice in Contemporary American Society* (New York: Columbia University Press, 1988).
10. Ibid., pp. 3–58.
11. National Association of Social Workers, *Code of Ethics*, 2008. http:// www.socialworkers.org/pubs/code/code.asp.
12. Mark Williams and Alex Smolak, "Integrating Faith Matters in Social Work Education," *Journal of Religion and Spirituality in Social Work* 26 (2007): 25.
13. Dorothy L. Graff, "A Study of Baccalaureate Social Work Students' Beliefs about the Inclusion of Religious and Spiritual Content in Social Work," *Journal of Social Work Education* 43 (2007): 243–256.
14. Williams and Smolak, op. cit.
15. Williams and Smolak, op. cit.
16. Ronald K. Bullis, *Spirituality in Social Work Practice* (Philadelphia: Taylor & Francis, 1996).
17. Ibid., p. 7.
18. David S. Derezotes, *Spiritually Oriented Social Work Practice* (Boston: Allyn & Bacon, 2006).
19. David R. Hodge, "Does Social Work Oppress Evangelical Christians? A New Class Analysis of Society and Social Work," *Social Work* 47: 401–414.
20. Derezotes, op. cit.

c h a p t e r 11

Social Work's Dual Focus on Solving and Preventing Problems

Prefatory Comment

If social work was to define itself as only a problem-solving profession, that definition would incorporate most of the work that social workers do. However, that somewhat narrow perception of social work would lead to an inaccurate understanding of this profession. First, that view would not differentiate social workers from other human service occupations, such as counseling and family therapy, which are focused almost entirely on helping people resolve problems in their lives. Second, important as it is to help people solve problems, continuing to address problems without attempting to deal with their root causes of those problems is a limited approach that holds little promise of eventually eliminating those issues. Third, when addressing only an individual's problems, there is an implied assumption that the problem is entirely caused by some fault of the person and the issue will be resolved only when that person changes. It fact, it is most likely that the issue is also at least partially caused or influenced by factors in the person's family, community, or the society at large, and those factors, too, need to change.

Social works' claim of simultaneously addressing person and environment indicates that at its very foundation is concern for both helping those who experience social problems to resolve those issues and also seeking to identify and address "upstream" issues that cause or exacerbate the issues for their clients. In short, they must attend to both solving and preventing problems.

The Social Worker's Role in Problem Solving

The perception of social work presented in this book suggests that the social worker's mission is to assist at the boundary between people and their environments. NASW's Workforce Study, for example, provides documentation that 64 percent of the BSWs and 70 percent of the MSW social workers devote the majority of their time and energy to direct services that involve helping clients reduce or resolve individual or family problems.[1] It is clear that most social workers begin working at the person side of the boundary and get involved in the environment by responding to needs of individual clients.

When working to help clients solve the problems they confront, the social worker uses a complex practice framework that he or she develops and continuously builds as part of becoming a social worker. Perhaps the clearest statement that can be made about the approach social workers use is that there is not a social work approach that fits all practice situations. Depending on the nature of the client issues, the practice models supported by one's employing agency, the specialized knowledge and skill of the individual social worker, the cultural background of the client, and many other factors, the intervention approaches will vary. The term *eclectic* is used to describe the tendency of social workers to select their interventions from a broad repertoire of possible approaches.

One can develop a sense of the possible variation in a social worker's practice framework by recognizing there are several levels to a worker's intervention approach. At the most general level, the worker must select a practice perspective—or develop a practice framework that involves multiple perspectives. A *perspective* determines how the worker will approach understanding and assessing a client's issues. It is the lens, or combination of lenses, the worker brings to understanding the client and his, her, or their problems. One perspective commonly used by social workers is based on theories known as a *systems perspective*. There are several refinements of system theory a social worker might adopt (e.g., general system theory, social system theory, ecosystems theory), but all are based on the view that any client system contains several components (i.e., subsystems) and, at the same time, is influenced by interactions with larger systems. This guides the social worker in viewing the client (e.g., the individual, couple, family, or group) as having important characteristics to assess but recognizing that the client is affected by interactions with larger systems that should also be explored to fully understand the client and the practice situation. Another perspective a social worker might use is *a strengths perspective*, where the emphasis is on what the client can do rather than emphasis on the client's deficiencies or limitations. A *feminist perspective,* which might be used by either a male or female social worker, gives attention to the experiences of women from the viewpoint of the gender roles and the traditional devaluing of women in U.S. society. This perspective reinforces characteristics of compassion, caring, sharing, and openness that are thought to be commonly possessed by women. One more example is an *ethnic-sensitive perspective.* This perspective directs the social worker to give careful attention to clients' ethnic, cultural, religious, and other background characteristics that influence their self-perception and also shape the perceptions of them by others.

A second level of choice affecting the social worker's practice framework involves selecting a generalist or specialist approach to client services. The *generalist* social worker approaches practice by being prepared to work with both the client and the client's environment. Thus, that worker must be skilled at working at multiple levels (e.g., with individuals, families, groups, the community), addressing a variety of client issues, and serving clients of differing backgrounds. The social worker who elects to practice as a specialist, however, chooses to work with a more narrow range of clients and client situations but offers services in more depth. A specialist social worker, for example, might be particularly skilled in working with older women in relation to mental health issues—or with teenagers who have been placed on probation.

Depending on the perspective a social worker adopts, if he or she is operating as a generalist or specialist, and the type of agency or client issues being addressed, the worker then will begin to accumulate a set of practice intervention approaches that can be used to serve clients. It is important to recognize that the social worker does not begin his or her career having mastered a large number of approaches. Rather, one keeps adding to the repertoire of interventions for working with clients or client groups as part of ongoing professional development. It is beyond the scope of this book to elaborate on the available practice approaches for direct practice with clients. However, as examples, Sheafor and Horejsi[2] provide thumbnail sketches of some of the intervention approaches most frequently used by direct service social workers.*

It is evident that the social worker seeking to help clients solve the problems or address the issues they bring for assistance must possess substantial knowledge and skills. Most social workers would agree, however, that if client problems could be prevented or reduced, the world would be a better place, and they would be happy to find a diminished demand for their services. Although this is unlikely to occur anytime in the foreseeable future, most social workers remain optimistic that progress can be made in preventing client issues.

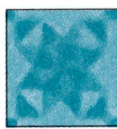

The Social Worker's Role in Problem Prevention

The effort of social workers to modify environments to reduce or eliminate social, economic, mental health, and other conditions that may cause or contribute to human problems is known as *primary prevention*. The social worker believes that, if humans created the systems that lead to inequitable distribution of wealth, discrimination, and similar factors that make some parts of the population more vulnerable to social problems than others, humans can make changes in those action systems that will minimize or correct these problems. Thus social workers consider prevention to be a part of their mission.

Not all client issues that social workers address can be prevented from occurring. Some issues can be treated in a manner that keeps them from getting worse (sometimes referred to as *secondary prevention*)—for example, helping a child with an emotional disturbance find ways to become less disruptive in the classroom. At other times, clients are helped by social workers to deal with conditions that cannot

---

*Practice based on psychodynamic theory, behavioral theory, cognitive-behavioral theory, person-centered theory, or exchange theory. Often practice is based on the following models: interactional, structural, crisis intervention, task-centered, psychoeducational, addiction, self-help, solution-focused, family therapy, and so on.

be changed. This *tertiary prevention* might relate to serving the family of an Iraq War veteran adjusting to an amputation or assisting a person in hospice care to face impending death with a sense of calm and fulfillment. The service provided in these situations involves helping the client accept the condition, adapt to its existence, and adjust to a different way of functioning and viewing the situation.

The social issues appropriate for primary prevention approaches did not evolve quickly—and cannot be resolved quickly. Public attitudes, behaviors, and social policies take considerable time and effort to change. The saying "social change requires the time-sense of a geologist" perhaps overstates the difficulty, but indeed social change takes someone who can remain hopeful in the face of discouragingly small incremental changes. The following are some examples of efforts to prevent social problems from occurring or getting worse.

Prevention Initiated When Serving Individuals

At times, when working with individuals, social workers become aware that the issues a single individual brings to them is also the same problem experienced by many other clients. It is not unreasonable, then, to suspect that the problem may not only be the fault of the individual but also the fault of the society. In addition to helping an individual client deal with the problem, the social worker should begin to look for and address the basic cause of that problem. The use of the class action legal suit is an example of this form of prevention.

One well-documented class action case is that of a social worker engaging with the legal profession to address a social problem that affected many children. In this California case, a social worker, John Serrano, was concerned that the state's school financing system, which was based on neighborhood property taxes, inherently discriminated against children from poor neighborhoods because their schools had less funding. Recognizing that one's level of education and that person's eventual earning power were linked, Serrano and the Western Center on Law and Poverty filed a class action suit that became the *Serrano vs. Priest* case. A *class action* is a legal procedure for resolving issues affecting many people. Those persons appearing before the court represent the unnamed members of the class of people in the proceeding, thereby avoiding multiple case-by-case actions.

The California Supreme Court eventually upheld Serrano's position by a 6 to 1 vote. The court's policy consideration focused on the pervasive influence of education on an individual's development and earning capacity within modern society, as well as on education's essential role in the maintenance of a free enterprise democracy. No court had previously placed education within the framework of interests meriting strict equal-protection scrutiny, and this decision represented the first time any type of governmental service had been held to involve these fundamental rights.[3] Considering the *Serrano* case, one might extend the precedent to include the human services, health, corrections, and mental health services as areas that represent a set of circumstances as unique and compelling as education. Class action social work is clearly a tool for changing policies and helping to prevent fundamental social problems.

Prevention Related to a Community Issue

A substantial social problem in the United States has been the emergence of youth violence and the high homicide rate among gang members. When addressed as a political issue, conservative politicians have argued that crime prevention is best addressed by increasing penalties for crimes as a deterrent to individuals considering the commission of a crime or by incarceration as a means of keeping potential offenders "off the streets." The result has been a burgeoning corrections system that is largely unable to attend to little more than holding prisoners until their sentences are completed.

From the centrist and more liberal sides of the political spectrum, support has been directed to efforts to prevent or reduce youth crime and gang violence. Such prevention programs typically involve strategies that include public education about the seriousness and ramification of violence, understanding contributing factors to violence and gang activity, services to deter violence among high-risk group members, and the need for social policies that would lead to improvement of economic, health, and mental health services for vulnerable population groups.

Several model programs have demonstrated that prevention programs can make a difference. Some of these programs have been based on an education model. The *Boston Youth Program,* for example, was instituted in four high schools and included a curriculum to address anger and violence.[4] The ten-session curriculum provided (1) information on adolescent violence and homicide; (2) discussion of anger as a normal, potentially constructive emotion; (3) knowledge for developing alternatives to fighting; (4) role-playing and videotapes to help recognize positive behaviors; and (5) training related to fostering nonviolent values. Subsequent evaluation of the control group (those with no exposure to the curriculum) and the experimental group (those experiencing the curriculum) revealed a significant, positive change of attitude in the experimental group. Another education-based program, *Peer Dynamics*, was designed to reduce the incidence of risk-taking behaviors associated with juvenile delinquency and substance abuse among public school students in Nebraska.[5] This program engaged students in group interaction activities designed to improve self-esteem and increase communication skills. A follow-up evaluation indicated that, in comparison to other students, program participants showed a noticeable drop in discipline referrals. Finally, a Los Angeles program called the *Paramount Plan* was designed as a "gang-prevention" program directed at fifth- and sixth-graders.[6] The program included neighborhood parent meetings and a fifteen-week anti-gang curriculum taught in the schools. Prior to initiation of the program, 50 percent of the students were "undecided" about joining gangs, and, after the program was completed, 90 percent indicated they would not become a gang member.

Another approach to prevention of juvenile and gang issues involves a combination of court- and community-based programs. In Baltimore, *Strike II* was developed as a court-based program linking juvenile justice with mental health care.[7] Its "clients" were court-adjudicated first-time offenders for violent crimes, assault, robbery, arson, and breaking and entering. In addition to the traditional probation supervision, Strike II participants worked with a multidisciplinary team of paralegal staff, counselors, social workers, and psychiatrists and were involved in programs including recreation, education, job readiness, and ongoing counseling and medical care as needed. The recidivism rate for Strike II clients was 7 percent, compared with 35 percent statewide and 65 percent for those leaving correctional institutions. A different effort aimed at prevention of high-risk gang activity was the *Community Youth Gang Services Corporation* in Los Angeles.[8] Counselors worked with about one-fourth of the L.A. gangs and were able to develop a peace treaty with a substantial reduction in gang-related gang activities during the period of the peace agreement. Such plans are short term, they "buy time" for all concerned, but if the community then does not respond with needed resources (e.g., employment opportunities, job training, physical and mental health services, educational opportunities), prevention will not be accomplished.

Social workers in hospitals, particularly those working in emergency rooms, are in the "trenches" for dealing with casualties related to gang and other juvenile violence. Wounded youth are in reality a "captive audience," which creates an excellent intervention opportunity. Many hospitals have developed teams to address suspected child abuse and neglect—often known as SCAN teams. These are typically multidisciplinary teams composed of physicians, social workers, nurses, and other hospital personnel. By adding an additional social worker who is a gang or youth specialist to the team and has primary treatment-coordinating responsibility with the victim and his or her family, the underlying causes of the violent act can more readily be identified and the needed community resources can be accessed. When a person is seriously injured, often one's psychological defenses are down, and the openness of the victim and family members to engage in treatment and other means of changing the situation is increased, at least for a time. Should the injury result in the death of the victim, the social worker on the SCAN team might then work with the juvenile's parents and siblings to engage in grief counseling, avoiding acts of retribution, finding ways to avoid similar assaultive behavior, and providing assistance with applying for victim's assistance and Social Security benefits.

Prevention at the National and International Levels

Prevention efforts may also reach the national and international levels. In these situations, social workers may not only serve in the capacity of promoting the prevention efforts but also assuring that they are not over-enforced to the point that innocent people become victims of the prevention program. A case related to actions taken following the 9/11 terrorist attacks provides an example of a social worker helping a U.S. citizen deal with overzealous enforcement of border security measures included in the Homeland Security Act of 2002. In this legislation, the Department of Homeland Security was charged to:

1. Prevent terrorist attacks within the United States
2. Reduce the vulnerability of the United States to terrorism
3. Minimize the damage and assist in the recovery from terrorist attacks that occur within the United States

Strategies implemented by the Department of Homeland Security (DHS) involved the questioning and interrogation of persons who *might* be suspected of being possible terrorists, even though they may not have committed an illegal act. DHS authorities interpreted their mandate as including the detention for an indefinite period of time of U.S.-born American citizens, without legal due process and without representation by an attorney, if they matched an established profile.[9] Such actions have been interpreted as violations of the U.S. Constitution's Fourth Amendment (unreasonable search and seizure), Sixth Amendment (right to a speedy trial), Seventh Amendment (right to a trial by jury), and Fourteenth Amendment (equal protection under the law).

A case in point is that of Mrs. Kani Hadi, an American of Arab descent whose experience as a victim of overzealous enforcement by Homeland Security officers.

> Mrs. Hadi was born, raised, and college educated in the United States, and her husband, Muhammed, of Muslim Arab descent, was also born in the United States. While her husband attended a conference related to his business, Mrs. Hadi took her children on a trip to visit the Canadian side of Niagara Falls. When being processed through customs upon their return to Los Angeles, a DHS agent began an interrogation of Mrs. Hadi, especially regarding her motive in making four trips to Saudi Arabia (to visit her aging grandparents) in the last ten years. Her digital camera was confiscated, and pictures of Niagara Falls and the large electric generators on the U.S. side of the Falls (taken for her son's science fair project) led to the confiscation of her passport and the accusation that it was forged. Her cell phone, too, was confiscated (prohibiting her from calling her husband) to track her local and international calls.
>
> An Air Canada flight attendant recognized Mrs. Hadi and her children from the flight from Canada and connected her with a social worker from the Travelers Aid Society (TAS) office in Los Angeles International Airport. TAS is a national nonprofit organization and is part of a network of social service agencies responding to persons facing a crisis during their travels. Sue Kang, the social worker in the TAS office, listened while an emotionally upset Mrs. Hadi recounted her story, left a message for Mr. Hadi (who was still away at his business conference) to contact the TAS office, and returned with Mrs. Hadi to the Homeland Security offices. When the legality of the officer's actions was challenged by Ms. Kang, only then did the officer clarify that original birth certificates for Mrs. Hadi and her children would be required if she was to have her possessions returned. The social worker then drove Mrs. Hadi home, dropped the children with a family member, and they returned to the airport and presented the birth certificates to the DHS officer. He returned Mrs. Hadi's passports and other papers, but the cell phone remained confiscated while the DHS examined all of her international calls.

In Mrs. Hadi's case, the social worker, who was serving as a direct services practitioner working initially to resolve an individual's troubles, was confronting excessive efforts to prevent terrorism. Here the social worker served as part of the checks and balances to help assure that prevention efforts are not interpreted as unrestricted license to ignore a person's constitutional rights. In fulfilling social work's mission to change an unjust environment, we might hope that Sue Kang (perhaps along with Mrs. Hadi) would publicly challenge the DHS officer's behavior, inform her Congressperson of this behavior, and perhaps even provide testimony to a legislative committee urging more appropriate guidelines for implementing the Homeland Security Act.

Balancing Problem Solving with Problem Prevention

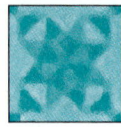

To what extent do social workers balance their attention to the person and the environment? The Teare and Sheafor study of the activities of social workers (see Chapter 9) points to an imbalance between direct practice and prevention activities. Using factor analysis as a statistical tool to examine the relationships among the task clusters, it was determined that the 7,000 social workers in that sample most frequently engaged in activities relative to providing services directly to specific clients (mean score of 25.51), next they performed activities that related to working within the context of one's employing organization (mean score of 14.29), followed by work related to increasing their professional competence (mean score of 9.42), and finally working toward change in the environment (e.g., prevention), such as advocating for change in the human services delivery system or changing community attitudes and policies (mean score of 6.78).[10] Clearly emphasis in the practice of the typical social worker is slanted heavily in the direction of client services. In short, social workers devote considerably more of their effort to problem solving with clients than to efforts to prevent those problems in the first place.

When Teare and Sheafor reported to professional audiences that their study (see Chapter 9) revealed that social workers spend only about 11 percent of their effort on items that might be considered primary prevention, the consistent response was "that may be true because my job description insists that I direct my attention to individual clients, not social change." However, these audience members consistently reported that they engaged in social change efforts on their own time through participation in local NASW chapter activities, volunteering with local social action groups, and even testifying before legislative committees. Indeed, these social workers observed the need for social change as they worked with their clients and took action in arenas that were open to them.[11]

A social worker working in an agency serving homeless youth offers a clear example of translating understanding of individual problems into prevention efforts. In this case, the social worker worked primarily with kids on the streets, young people who, for a variety of reasons, had dropped out of school, left their families, and taken up a life involving drugs, prostitution, and petty crime to support themselves. Each young person had unique needs and problems, and the issues they faced were complex—one size didn't fit all. Yet, some patterns began to become evident. Usually a youth's home life had been chaotic, succeeding in school had been difficult, developing close friends had not been successful, the use of alcohol and/or drugs had seemed a way to lessen the pain and loneliness, and so on. Usually a crisis such as a fight with parents or siblings, suspension from school, or a brush with the law led to running to the streets. The young person's well-being was at risk, and survival was a daily issue.

One particular group of youth was especially of concern to this social worker—young men who, when attempting to understand their sexual orientation, came to grips with the fact they were part of the approximately 2.5 percent to 4.0 percent of the young men in the United States who are gay. Rejection by family and friends, ostracism at school, and deterioration of the youths' self-esteem contributed to actions that led to eventually abandoning home and family (or sometimes being thrown out) and attempting to survive on the streets. The social worker's effort was to help each of these young men to deal with their homelessness by at least temporarily finding food and shelter, encouraging them to consider job training programs or develop plans to complete high school and possibly go on to college, and providing basic counseling to identify strategies to resolve family issues and return home. This approach was moderately successful with some clients, but each time one left this social worker's service, another seemed to appear.

In this case, the social worker began to consider what might be done "upstream" to prevent such serious problems for these young men. For these young men, rejection typically centered in three parts of their social environment—at home, at church, and at school. Because many had not publicly "come out," addressing this on a case-by-case basis was not viable, as individuals identified as gay faced a higher risk of ostracism, taunting, and even the physical violence of hate crimes. Running to the streets helped avoid some of the risk of abuse—at least from persons in the youth's immediate environment—but too often considerable damage to his well-being had already occurred. This social worker considered several strategies to at least partially prevent the social, physical, and emotional damage to young gay men. As a start, the decision was made to become involved in the local organization of families of gay and lesbian young people, i.e., Parents, Families, and Friends of Lesbians and Gays (PFLAG).[12] Working within that context, the social worker thought it would be possible to contribute to public education efforts to help people throughout the community learn more about the causes and challenges that exist for young people who identify with a gay or lesbian sexual orientation. The social worker recognized that educating the public may contribute to a long-term improvement of conditions for these youth, but something more immediate was needed to keep the problems from being experienced so acutely by the youth in the high schools. Might there be a way to mobilize groups of students, both gay and straight, to create an understanding and supportive atmosphere in the schools—and perhaps offer some protection from verbal or physical abuse in the hallways? To begin, the worker concluded that joining with school social workers through the NASW chapter might be a good starting place because they typically have early contact with students who eventually face these problems.

Concluding Comment

In a developed country such as the United States, caring for vulnerable populations cannot be accomplished only by family, neighbors, and others who want to make life better for persons in need. A formalized battery of human services has been developed to make needed services available in an efficient and effective manner. Strides are being made to equip social workers and other human services providers with the knowledge and skills to effectively address the problems of individuals, families, and groups of people, yet the escalating costs and relative shortage of well-prepared professionals threaten to make them impotent in addressing the complex human problems brought by clients to human services providers.

> Although it is important to help individuals and families minimize or eliminate the effects of these problems on their lives, it is essential to also attempt to prevent the problems from having such an impact in the first place. When social workers approach their work with a prevention mindset, as well as a problem-solving mindset, they have an opportunity to stem the flow of direct service needs. Indeed, as illustrated in this chapter, several prevention-oriented programs have demonstrated success in reducing the incidence of client problems.
>
> If social workers are to fulfill their mission of addressing both person and environment through solving and preventing problems, they must continuously address the balance between the two approaches. On the agenda for social workers in the future must be an examination of the currently heavy emphasis on direct client services and the drift away from efforts at prevention. If social workers should lose this element of their mission altogether, the field would quickly become indistinguishable from several other helping professions.

KEY WORDS AND CONCEPTS

Prevention
Primary/Secondary/Tertiary Prevention
At-risk population
Class action social work
Gang homicide psychosocial prevention model

SUGGESTED INFORMATION SOURCES

Loeb, Paul Rogat, ed. *The Impossible Will Take a Little While: A Citizen's Guide to Hope in a Time of Fear.* New York: Basic Books, 2004.

Sheafor, Bradford W., and Charles R. Horejsi. *Techniques and Guidelines for Social Work Practice*, 8th ed. Boston: Allyn & Bacon, 2008.

ENDNOTES

1. National Association of Social Workers, *Assuring the Sufficiency of a Frontline Workforce: A National Study of Licensed Social Workers Executive Summary* (Washington, D.C.: NASW Center for Workforce Studies, 2006).
2. Bradford W. Sheafor and Charles R. Horejsi, *Techniques and Guidelines for Social Work Practice*, 8th ed. (Boston: Allyn & Bacon, 2008), particularly see Chapter 6.
3. Robert B. Keiter, "California Educational Financing System Violates Equal Protection," *Clearinghouse Review* 5 (October 1971): 287–299.
4. The Boston Youth Program, cited in *Report of the Secretary's Task Force on Black and Minority Health*, Vol. 5, U.S. Department of Health and Human Services, January 1986, pp. 43–44.
5. C. Cooper, "Peer Dynamics, Final Evaluation Report, 1979–1980," Nebraska State Commission on Drugs (Lincoln: Nebraska State Department of Health, 1980).

6. "Early Gang Intervention," Transfer of Knowledge Workshop, California Youth Authority, Office of Criminal Justice Planning, 1985, pp. 11–12.
7. "Strike II," Hopkins Adolescent Program, Johns Hopkins Hospital, Park Building, Baltimore, MD, 1986.
8. Armando T. Morales, "The Role of Social Work in Prevention," in Armando T. Morales, Bradford W. Sheafor, and Malcolm E. Scott, *Social Work: A Profession of Many Faces*, 11th ed. (Boston: Allyn & Bacon, 2007), p. 189.
9. Phil Hirschkorn, "U.S. Can Hold 'Dirty Bomb' Suspect." http://archives.cnn.com/2002/LAW/12/04/padilla.ruling/index.html.
10. Robert J. Teare and Bradford W. Sheafor. *Practice-Sensitive Social Work Education: An Empirical Analysis of Social Work Practice and Practitioners* (Alexandria, VA: Council on Social Work Education, 1995).
11. Personal reflections of Bradford W. Sheafor.
12. Parents, Families, and Friends of Lesbians and Gays. http://www.pflag.org/Vision_Mission_and_Strategic_Goals.mission.0.html.

chapter 12

Social Work's Role in Addressing Terrorism

Prefatory Comment

The twentieth century could have been characterized as the "Age of Anxiety," given the overwhelming episodes of deliberate human carnage that caused anxiety for millions of people in the United States and around the world. To name a few of these events, for example, there were two world wars, Hitler's genocide of six million Jews, World War II ending with the atomic bomb, and the Korean and Vietnam wars. The Cold War that followed World War II, between nuclear superpowers Russia and the United States, did not detract from this anxiety.

Now in the twenty-first century, with the wars in Afghanistan and Iraq, America's experience following the 9/11 terrorist attacks in New York City, Washington, D.C., and Pennsylvania, that killed 3,200 citizens, and countless terrorist attacks around the world, this era could be called the "Age of Fear." Many now feel they might become victims of terrorism. Following 9/11, Congress and President Bush established the Department of Homeland Security to focus the full resources of the American government on the safety of the American people. But what do we actually know about domestic terrorists *in* the United States and those originating in the Middle East, such as Osama bin Laden and the terrorist group al-Qaeda, who claimed responsibility for the terrorist attacks of 9/11? In reality, these groups are terrorist *gangs* that have contributed to the deaths of thousands of Americans, leading to social disorganization, economic hardship, psychological trauma, grief, and family dysfunction.

Human consequences that result from terrorism are in social work's practice arena. Many social workers deal daily with people suffering the effects of social, psychological, economic, and political oppression and dehumanization, some of whom eventually become either victims or perpetrators of violence. Indeed, social workers are often in a position to articulate the relationship of micro to macro psychosocial forces to violence and to contribute recommendations for positive change.

Examples of Terrorism

Anyone who has experienced intense fear understands the feeling of terror. Terrorism captures those feelings and translates them into intimidation. Webster defined a *terrorist* as a person, usually the member of a group, who uses or advocates terrorism; a person who terrorizes or frightens others.[1] Intimidation by terrorists can be observed in the actions of such large entities as national governments and international terrorist gangs and in smaller entities such as local juvenile gangs and even individuals engaging in behaviors that terrorize the public.

International Terrorism by Militant Groups

Perhaps the primary reason terrorism is an issue in the United States today is the fear of additional attacks such as those perpetrated on the World Trade Center and the Pentagon on September 11, 2001. Al-Qaeda, the international terrorist gang led by Osama bin Laden that claims responsibility for the 9/11 attacks, maintains membership cells throughout the world and periodically reinforces the public's fears thorough releases of threatening videotapes and formal statements. Efforts to track down international terrorists such as bin Laden as a proactive means of avoiding terrorist attacks became, in part, the rationale for U.S. invasions of Afghanistan and Iraq. Enormous expense in human lives, financial resources, and U.S. prestige throughout the world has resulted from these actions. The costs for national defense and homeland security measures have diverted resources that might have been spent on improving education, reducing poverty, assisting developing countries, and other factors that would improve the human condition at home and abroad.

National Terrorism by the U.S. Government

There can be occasions in which a formal government can subject its citizens to terrorism to achieve a desired social control outcome. For example, a controversial case in which federal law enforcement intervention exposed U.S. civilians to terrorism involves the burning of the Branch Davidian compound in Waco, Texas, in 1993, under the authority and direction of U.S. Attorney General Janet Reno. Charging the Branch Davidians with child abuse, sexual abuse and misconduct, and stockpiling weapons, a deadly standoff between the Branch Davidians and the Bureau of Alcohol, Tobacco, and Firearms (ATF), who were attempting to serve weapons warrants, resulted in the deaths of four ATF agents and six of the Branch Davidians. What followed was a fifty-one-day siege led by the FBI, which ended in a fierce fire that destroyed the compound. Among the dead were the Branch Davidians' leader, David Koresh, and approximately eighty of his followers, including forty-one women and children.[2]

Domestic Terrorism by Individuals

Another example of the application of terrorism is represented by Timothy McVeigh, a onetime member of the Ku Klux Klan and a highly decorated veteran of the Gulf War who became disillusioned about how the U.S. military treated Iraqis and its own troops with the use of chemicals. He was also outraged by the lethal actions taken by federal law enforcement at Waco, Texas, in 1993. McVeigh claimed that he waited patiently for two years for justice for the victims of Waco, which never came. He therefore chose to bomb the Murrah federal building in Oklahoma City on April 19, 1995, which was the second anniversary of the siege in Waco. He stated in his letters: "Foremost the bombing was a retaliatory strike; a counterattack for the cumulative raids and subsequent violence and damage that federal agents had participated in over the preceding years, including, but not limited to Waco."[3] McVeigh and three associates bombed the federal building, killing 168 people, including 19 children; 642 people were injured. Was McVeigh simply another disturbed war veteran trained to kill, who acted out his pathology upon U.S. citizens (many federal employees) and in the process modeled the behavior of his government? Did he represent a domestic militant terrorist group that was still active? McVeigh tells us that the reason for his heinous act was retaliation. In turn, the government retaliated against McVeigh and executed him on May 16, 2001.[4]

Domestic Terrorism by Juvenile Gangs

A more familiar form of terrorism has been present in the United States for more than 150 years. Many young people, because of their psychosocial stage of development and their need to be in groups, to conform, and at times to dress in provocative clothing and hairstyles, often maintain their identity by engaging in acts of violence and intimidation against other gangs or the community at large. Gang researchers frequently use five criteria to define such gangs: (1) formal organizational structure, (2) identifiable leadership, (3) identification with a territory, (4) recurrent interaction, and (5) engaging in serious or violent behavior.[5] Typical crime-related activities of gangs include assault with a deadly weapon, robbery, homicide or attempted homicide, sale or possession of narcotics, shooting at a house or vehicle, arson, and vehicle grand theft.[6]

A different example of a radical juvenile gang displaying terrorist characteristics was the "Trench Coat Mafia," a white suburban terrorist gang in Littleton, Colorado, which killed 13 students and a teacher at Columbine High School in 1999. Where gangs had previously been thought to be a lower-class, inner-city phenomenon, this suburban gang has made it clear that gang-related terrorism can pervade all communities.

Whether in the inner city, city, or suburbia, it is difficult to determine who is actually a violent threat to the community. Yet, racial profiling appears to dominate reactions to gang activity. Today, because of 9/11, many "Arab-looking" males of all ages are under suspicion and experience greater surveillance by citizens and law enforcement officers alike. Middle-class youth, particularly non-Hispanic white youths, are often given the benefit of the doubt by police and are not interrogated or arrested. For example, following the Oklahoma City bombing, which prior to 9/11 was the greatest single act of domestic terrorism in the history of the United States, young adult non-Hispanic white males were not under suspicion as possible future bombers, nor were associates of the McVeigh group. Inner-city, city, and suburban lower- or middle-class African American, Asian, and Hispanic youth, however, are overly suspected of being gang members and considered a genuine threat to society and, hence, are often arrested as a preventive tactic. This controversial practice is known as *racial profiling*; that is, that "criminal suspects" meet the arrest profile of certain offenders.

Terrorism and Terrorist Gangs

A definition of a terrorist gang that is not biased against any ethnic or racial group, age level, social economic class, or location of terrorist crime yet captures the essence of its violent, deadly behavior follows:

> A ***terrorist gang*** is a peer group in which members participate in unlawful terrorist activities and violence against persons or property to intimidate or coerce a government, the civilian population, or any segment thereof, in furtherance of domestic or international political or social objectives. Such violent behavior may be harmful to themselves (e.g., suicide bombings, crashing vehicles or planes into structures, suicide by gang) and others (killing of civilians and/or military personnel) in society.

Every member of a terrorist gang does not embrace the purposes of the gang in the same way. Most gang members begin and end their gang activity in their youth, but some continue gang identification and behavior into adulthood. The *Gang Behavior Career Continuum* (see Figure 12.1), identifies seven levels of involvement in the aspects of gang behavior and participation and demonstrates the parallels between domestic and international gangs. Note that female gang members are not included because 95 percent of U.S. gang members are males. Female gang members are even less represented in terrorist gangs and their motivations are less understood.

The "Non-Gang" Level In the United States, at the least involved level, referred to as "non-gang," are found the largest numbers of youth, up to 70 to 80 percent in some inner-city areas, who have engaged in some aspects of the gang culture prevalent in their community. They have accepted some of the gang music (e.g., gangsta rap), clothing, walk, talk, hairdo, tattoos, and even knowledge and skills in writing and understanding graffiti (i.e., *tagging*). But they have no arrests or juvenile court convictions for offenses related to gang involvement. As an international comparison, for example, Afghanistani and Palestinian preadolescents and young adolescents who cast stones at American troops or Israeli army tanks and are not apprehended might fit into this category. They are imitating the behavior of older youth and young adults who are protesting against "the enemy."

Figure 12.1
Gang Behavior Career Continuum: U.S. Gangs and International Gangs

U.S. GANGS

Gang Terrorism Begins Here

Non-Gang	Pre-Gang	Wannabe	Soft-Core	Moderate Core	Hard-Core	Super-Hard-Core
Exhibits some gang culture traits, no contacts with police, no arrests or *convictions*.	Some gang culture and contacts with police. No convictions.	Unpredictable, few police contacts to major *convictions*.	Few contacts, arrests, and *convictions* for minor gang crimes, on probation, in school.	Arrests and *convictions* for violent gang crime, institutionalized at local and state level, on probation/parole, rarely in school, unemployed. Will take risks for "hood."	Arrests and *convictions* for attempted and/or homicide, long-term placement in juvenile or adult state prison, no school or job. Shot caller. Will kill or die for gang.	Adult court *convictions* for one or more homicides, long-term prison or death row, poor school and work history. Shot caller in and out of prison. Will kill or die for gang.

INTERNATIONAL GANGS

Gang Terrorism Begins Here

Non-Gang	Pre-Gang	Wannabe	Soft-Core	Moderate Core	Hard-Core	Super-Hard-Core
Plays at "war," casts stones at U.S. military; imitates violent behavior of older children.	First contacts with U.S. military. Curfew violations and associating with known activists.	Idolizes al-Qaeda, takes risks without authorization, unreliable, not al-Qaeda talent. Not recruited.	Detained for stealing ammo or rifle from U.S. soldier; caught with gasoline and empty bottles.	Recruited into al-Qaeda, indoctrinated to al-Qaeda perspective of religion. Caught with Molotov cocktails.	Trained to fight and make bombs. Assists in bomb attacks, leaves homeland for terrorist assignments "somewhere." Learning to be a "shot caller." Wants to be a martyr.	Has been leader in bombing attacks. Supervising several al-Qaeda cells, has direct contact with top shot callers, including bin Laden. Willing to die for cause and become a martyr.

This *Gang Behavior Career Continuum* for U.S. gangs was developed by Armando T. Morales, UCLA Neuropsychiatric Institute and Hospital, School of Medicine, Los Angeles, California, in May, 1990. The *Gang Behavior Career Continuum* for International gangs was developed in 2002. Terrorist gang behavior for both U.S. and international gangs begins at the moderate-core level.

The "Pre-Gang" Level At the "pre-gang" level, these youths have also absorbed some of the gang culture previously mentioned, but now they are beginning to have some contact with police and have experienced a few arrests and have been taken to the police station for being with more sophisticated gang members. But no petitions (charges) are filed in juvenile court. In Afghanistan or Palestine, these youngsters might be having their first formal contacts and warnings by U.S. or Israeli authorities for suspicious behavior, curfew violations, or associating with known "troublemakers."

The "Wannabes" Level The "Wannabes" (want-to-bes) are in the next level on the gang career continuum. These youths at times are quite disturbed and unpredictable and very much want to be in the gang. But they are not respected by legitimate gang members, nor are they wanted in the gang because they lack the consistency, dedication, and loyalty expected of "good" gang members. Wannabes have been known to abandon their pursuit of the gang when they experience their first incarceration or first real fight with rival gang members. Some are manipulated by the gang to "prove themselves" by asking them to carry out an assigned gang assault or homicide. Afghanistan adolescent Wannabes might be those youngsters who look up to and want to be part of al-Qaeda, for example, but who have not yet been formally accepted due to their inexperience, lack of intelligence, impulsivity, or unreliability. U.S. gangs, as is the case with al-Qaeda, are looking for "good" soldier material to help carry out their goals.

The "Soft-Core" Level The soft-core level includes the young U.S. gang member with his first minor gang-related arrest for group drinking or drugs, or perhaps a gang-related "joy ride" (auto theft), or misdemeanor gang assault requiring an arrest, probation investigation, juvenile court appearance, and a sustained petition (conviction). The soft-core gang member is now placed on probation and continues going to school. A budding Afghan teenage terrorist at this level might have his or her first detention by authorities for having attempted to steal a military rifle from an American soldier or being caught with an unlit gasoline "Molotov cocktail" near a U.S. Army base camp. Individuals and gangs in the first four levels of the gang behavior career continuum are rarely involved in serious violent behavior, as is the case with most gangs, and hence could not be considered terrorist gangs.

The "Moderate-Core" Level The moderate-core U.S. gang member is a lot more experienced, a little older, and rarely attends school. By now he has had two or three convictions in juvenile court for gang-related violent offenses and has tasted incarceration at least two or three times in youth detention or correctional facilities. His multiple tattoos not only advertise his local gang but also represent an affiliation with statewide gangs. He is also beginning to have contact with ex-convicts who are the "shot callers" (give orders) for the gang. While institutionalized, the moderate-core gang member is further indoctrinated into the values, norms, and expectations of gang culture.

Similarly, a bright, talented, older Afghan adolescent or young adult at this level might feel honored that he is being recruited into al-Qaeda and will be receiving a modest salary that will keep his family from starving. He will be indoctrinated with the al-Qaeda perspective of Muslim religion and will learn about the importance of bringing *jihad* (holy war) to Christian Western nations.[7] Instead of being incarcerated, he will have to leave his home for intensive training in guerilla warfare by al-Qaeda. Rather than boasting his membership in al-Qaeda through tattoos, gang colors, and a shaved head like many American gang members, the new recruit will learn how to make himself inconspicuous. He will have a more formidable "code of silence" than U.S. gang members. He will assume a low profile as he is prepared for a terrorist assignment "somewhere" in the Middle East, South or North America, or elsewhere in the world. Gang members at the moderate-, hard-, and super-hard-core level *are* participating in violent behavior causing harm to others and therefore would be considered members of terrorist gangs.

The "Hard-Core" Level   The hard-core gang member not only has been incarcerated in juvenile facilities but also now has convictions in adult court for gang-related offenses, including attempted homicide and homicide. Some hard-core gang members had their first experience at being sentenced to state prison as adults even though they might have been only 16 or 17 years old when they committed their first serious crime. Usually the hard-core members are a little older (18 to 25) and are among the local leaders of the gang, have impressive respect and "juice" (power) in the gang, and often are "shot callers" (give orders). Hard-core gang members not only have injured others in battle but also wear their "war medals" (knife and bullet wound scars) proudly.

An al-Qaeda member at this level has been taught how to prepare bombs and other tools of mass destruction (biological and chemical warfare) and has assisted in some smaller terrorist bombing activities involving a handful of victims somewhere in the Middle East. By now, those closest to him (family, wife, or girlfriend) have no knowledge of his al-Qaeda involvement or where he lives. He occasionally might write to them to let them know he is "fine" and will see them soon. Subsequent strong emotional messages may indicate that he has been assigned to a suicide bombing mission.

The Super-Hard-Core Level   Finally, the most violent terrorist level of the gang career continuum is the "super-hard-core" gang member. In the United States, they have adult court convictions for gang-related terrorist offenses, such as one or more homicides, "three strikes," or witness and victim intimidation including the killing of potential witnesses. Some have even killed police officers or prison guards. They continue to have close ties with local gangs and are well established in the prison gang hierarchy. Following parole, some may attempt to serve a liaison function under orders from prison gang members to conduct "business" (e.g., drugs, extortion, executions) in the community of the local gang. They are not only respected by the local gang but also feared because they might be in a position to carry out contracted "green light" hits (executions) locally or even order "hits" on gang members not complying with their wishes, such as not paying "taxes" (protection money) to the prison gang. Some of the super-hard-core terrorists are serving sentences of ten to twenty years or life without the possibility of parole, and a few are on death row for multiple gang-related homicides.

An international gang terrorist at this level would be someone like Imam Samudra, age 35, an alleged al-Qaeda member. He admitted that he was the organizer and leader of the October 12, 2002, bombing that killed 191 people at a Bali entertainment facility. The victims were mostly foreign tourists, and among the dead were seven Americans. Samudra claimed that he received training in making bombs in Afghanistan when he was about 25 years of age.[8] Also, Osama bin Laden, alleged leader of al-Qaeda, certainly would fit in this category as an ultimate "shot caller."

Social Workers and Work with Gangs

The National Youth Gang Survey of 2,629 responding agencies reported that 53 percent of the agencies worked with gangs that were active in their jurisdiction. Respondents in large cities claimed the highest level of gang activities, 74 percent, followed by suburban areas (57 percent), small cities (34 percent), and rural counties (25 percent). Based on this response, the researchers concluded that up to 4,824 cities were experiencing gang problems and that there may be as many as 31,000 gangs, with a total membership of 846,000 in the United States alone.[9] Thus social workers in virtually every part of the United States are likely to deal with clients who are gang members, victims of gang behaviors, or terrorized by potential gang activities.

For social workers, addressing gang behavior before it reaches the terrorism level can be a powerful tool in preventing the more violent acts perpetrated by the more hard-core gang members. Answers to the question "Why do people join gangs that seek to terrorize other human beings?" help to inform social work practice. The answer is not simple, as there are several theoretical perspectives explaining why people identify with gangs in the first place.

One theory views gang membership as a natural progression from, and the consequence of, a youth's search for excitement in a frustrating and limiting environment. This theory argues that the motivation to identify with a gang is usually a result of a general breakdown of social controls and is characterized by persons with few social ties, such as immigrants, the mentally ill, and the destitute, and by a corresponding lack of parental control over the young.[10]

A second theory of factors causing youth to join gangs is that gang members tend to be males who usually were reared in female-dominated households, and consequently, in adolescence, the gang "provides the first real opportunity to learn essential aspects of the male role in the context of peers facing similar problems of sex role identification."[11]

A third perspective is that the gang is the collective solution by young, lower-class males to a situation of stress wherein opportunities for the attainment of wealth and status through legitimate channels are blocked through classism and racism in the society. In response, the gang develops a subculture or *contra-culture*. The gang, then, can best be explained as a reaction to social conditions in which lower-class youths are placed by the dominant society.[12]

A fourth perspective is that gangs exist because adolescents are in a state of suspension between childhood and adulthood; hence, they spend most of their time with peers and are anxious about both their gender identity and their acceptance by the peer group (gang). They conform to the norms of the gang because not to do so would threaten their status.[13] This "anxious about their identity" theory might not apply to Afghanistan young men in international terrorist gangs such as al-Qaeda. Rather, they are anxious about being able to provide food and other resources to their families.

All of the above theories have merit and are applicable in many instances, as gangs tend to be very heterogeneous and complex and cannot be explained by any *one* theory. What they all have in common is a group contagion, cohesion, loyalty, dedication, and a deep feeling of the Three Musketeers saying: "One for all, and all for one."

A fifth theoretical perspective, proposed by Armando Morales and based on a study of East Los Angeles *Latino* gang and non-gang probation juvenile camp graduates, is that gang members, significantly more than non-gang members, come from families exhibiting more family breakdown, greater poverty, poorer housing, more alcoholism, more drug addiction, more major chronic illness, and with more family members involved with law enforcement and correctional agencies.[14] In the face of these overwhelming problems, the youngster turns to the gang as a *surrogate family*. Here, the gang member receives affection, understanding, recognition, loyalty, and emotional and physical protection. Many terrorist gang members will voluntarily die or kill rival gang members for their gang, turf, political mission, or neighborhood. When this occurs, membership then becomes maladaptive.

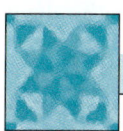

Types of Gangs

In addition to understanding why people participate in gangs, it is also useful for social workers to understand the type of gang to which a gang member belongs. Today we find at least four types of gangs in the United States: the *criminal*, the *conflict*, the *retreatist*, and the *cult/occult gang*.

The *criminal gang* has as its primary goal material gain through criminal activities. Success is obtained through the theft of property from premises or persons, extortion, fencing, and obtaining and selling illegal substances such as drugs.

The *conflict gang* is very turf oriented and will engage in violent battle with individuals or rival groups that invade their neighborhood or commit acts they consider insulting or degrading. Respect from other gang members is highly valued and defended.

The predominant feature of the *retreatist gang* is the pursuit of getting "loaded" or "high" on alcohol, marijuana, heroin, acid, cocaine, meth, or other drugs. Retreatism is characterized by a breakdown in relationships with other persons. The drug user has a need to become affiliated with other retreatist users to secure access to a steady supply of drugs. What distinguishes the criminal gang involved in drugs from the retreatist gang is that the former is primarily involved for financial profit. The retreatist gang's involvement with drugs is primarily for consumption.

The fourth type of adolescent delinquent group, the *cult/occult gang*, is the most recently identified form of gang.[15] The word *cult*, as used here, pertains to a system of worshiping the devil or evil. *Occult* means something hidden or secret, or a belief in mysterious or supernatural powers. Not all cult/occult devil or evil worship groups are involved in criminal activity or ritualistic crime. The Ku Klux Klan, for example, may be seen as a cult group, and some KKK chapters, in spite of their hate rhetoric, are law abiding, whereas other chapters have committed criminal acts. The majority of occult groups are composed of adults, although some juvenile groups are becoming interested in satanic and black magic practices and are using them for their own gratification of sadistic, sexual, and antisocial impulses. They are not turf-oriented like conflict gangs but are typically found in middle-class locations. For example, a neo-Nazi subtype of white cult/occult gang groups are the Skinheads, whose racist, anti-Semitic, homophobic "gay bashing," and other violent behavior has appeared in the South, Midwest, and West Coast. Their group structure and behavior comply with the gang pattern, including use of colors, tattoos, common dress and hairstyle, name, drug use, and criminal behavior (usually "hate" crimes). The majority of Skinheads come from middle-class and working-class white families.[16] The gothic-cultural Trench Coat Mafia, the terrorist gang that perpetrated the Columbine High School killings in Colorado, could have fit in with the Skinhead neo-Nazi cult gang.

As an international terrorist group, al-Qaeda conforms to the requirements of the criminal gang as it is involved in receiving financial benefits from the drug trade in Afghanistan to help finance its terrorist activities. The group in power at that time, the Taliban, helped finance several international terrorist groups and their leaders. Clearly al-Qaeda represents a conflict, turf-oriented gang at a macro level as its international terrorist acts are acts of retaliation intended to discourage all U.S. military occupation and presence in Arab nations. Al-Qaeda views U.S. presence in Arab nations as an act of imperialism with a specific interest in their extensive oil resources. Additionally, bin Laden is perceived as having a cult-like following concerning his personal violent interpretations of the Quran, a thirteenth-century Arab bible or doctrine, regarded as the eternal words of God himself by at least 1.3 million Muslims around the world. Many moderate interpreters of the Quran condemned the attacks on 9/11 and other terrorist acts resulting in the killing of civilians. As indicated in Chapter 21 of this book, these moderates believe that these atrocities are antithetical to the teaching of the Quran.[17] The charismatic bin Laden, however, interprets the Quran as providing him the spiritual authority to participate in *"jihad"* (holy war) against those he considers enemies of Islam.

Micro Social Work Practice with Gangs

Is there a difference between a U.S. gang member who dies in gang conflict protecting his "hood" and an Afghanistan youth terrorist who is shot to death while hurling a Molotov cocktail at a U.S. Army tank? Gang behavior does not appear in a vacuum and is in many ways related to the violent cultural condition of society, marital and family vulnerabilities exacerbating the individual's psychosocial condition, and finally the individual's biological and psychological endowment. With some exceptions, interventions to minimize gang behavior in the United States should be comparable to efforts to minimize international gang participation. Because social workers are most likely to have access to persons experiencing domestic gang or terrorist activity, the remainder of this chapter will focus on gang-related social work practice in the United States. Nevertheless, it is suspected that many of the lessons learned from working with domestic gangs are transferable to work with international gangs.

A significant amount of controversy exists about attempting to link biological factors to violence. At best it can be said that some biological factors, such as genetic conditions, hormonal imbalances, brain diseases, and chemistry dysfunctions, may predispose some individuals toward violence.[18] Nevertheless, many traditional forms of social work intervention are thought to be effective in helping individuals have their needs met in ways other than through participation in gangs. For example, the efforts of school social workers to engage teachers and parents in supporting a child's academic development helps the child find school more rewarding and satisfying. Hospital social workers are often among the first to interact with victims or family members of victims experiencing gang violence. They provide services involving acquisition of tangible resources, as well as counseling about the terrorizing event that helps to minimize psychological damage and lower the likelihood of escalating the situation into one of retaliatory violence. In mental health centers, residential treatment facilities, probation departments, and many other human services agencies, it is not uncommon for social workers to help gang members or the victims of gang violence address issues resulting from gang activities.

What about the role of the family? Is it in any way contributing to the gang problem, and why are parents finding it more likely that sons, rather than daughters, become gang members? For example, the high percentage in the U.S. of working single mothers and the number of families with two parents working with children under the age of 6 years makes it more difficult for parents to be home nurturing and supervising their children. A national poll of children ages 12 to 14 living in twenty-five cities revealed that 60 percent of sampled respondents reported that they wanted to spend more time with their parents.[19] As in many areas of social concern, social programs are created to help fill this gap, but the problem persists. In addition, family counseling, family therapy, and other social work services to families can help to minimize family breakdown. Social programs such as Boys and Girls Clubs, Partners, and various recreation programs are examples of how social workers can assist youth in identifying with positive adult role models, as opposed to the role models represented by gang members.

Macro Intervention with Domestic Terrorist Gangs

One macro preventive intervention approach for this U.S. gang population involves the creation and provision of community mental health programs for children. These are designed to assist in the early elementary school detection of problem behavior symptoms such as attention deficit disorder (ADD), attention deficit hyperactivity disorder (ADHD), fetal alcohol syndrome (FAS), "crack cocaine babies," and childhood conduct disorder and depression. The creation of such community-based programs makes services to these young people possible.

An example of a specific community program is one developed by social workers Spergel and Grossman in Chicago called "The Little Village Project." This community approach to the prevention and control of gang violence was based upon the following six key interrelated intervention strategies:[20]

1. *Community mobilization* (involvement of local residents, agencies, police, and youth)
2. *Opportunities provision* (jobs, special education, and training programs)
3. *Social intervention* (outreach to gang youths in the streets)
4. *Suppression* (controlling the gang in order to suppress its criminal behavior)
5. *Organizational change and development* (agency collaboration to reduce crime)
6. *Targeting* (multidiscipline team targets specific to youths and gangs)

The results of this macro, social work, community organization, gang-intervention program was positive. An analysis of 125 targeted youth over a three-year period indicated that 98 percent had contact with community youth workers, and 95 percent received some kind of informal counseling or support from project staff. Facilitating this contact through the community-based program was the first step in helping these youth address some of the issues that made gang involvement attractive to them.

Concluding Comment

Today, 94 percent of U.S. urban and suburban areas with 100,000 people or more (177 of 189 areas) report that they have youth gangs.[21] For the past twenty to thirty years, Americans have shown a callousness and indifference to the thousands of predominantly African American, Hispanic, and Asian American inner-city gang killings occurring each year nationally but received a shocking "wake-up call" when the white neo-Nazi Trench Coat Mafia gang massacred thirteen people (twelve students, one teacher) at Columbine High in affluent white suburbia. The suicide of these two perpetrators, who were also the gang's leaders, "cooled off" the violence potential of the remaining twelve to fifteen Trench Coat Mafia gang members.

The George W. Bush administration received support from both Republican and Democratic elected officials and the general public for spending billions of dollars for a war with Iraq. A total of 124 U.S. soldiers were killed from the beginning of the war in March 2003 to May 2003, when President Bush declared "mission accomplished." Having lost 124 lives out of 300,000 military personnel in Iraq represents a death rate of 41.3 per 100,000. The annual death rate for 500 gang members in a population of 100,000 Los Angeles gang members represents a rate of 500 per 100,000. In other words, our soldiers were nearly thirteen times safer on the battlefields of Iraq in the initial stages of the war than gang members walking the streets of Los Angeles. Yet in the five years since President Bush announced the "end of the Iraq war" in May 2003, more than 4,000 additional U.S. soldiers were killed by Iraqi insurgents.[22] One strategy to address domestic and international terrorism would be to change environments that encourage and support gang behavior. As then–Secretary of State Colin Powell stated at the World Trade Forum in February 2002, "...terrorism really flourishes in areas of poverty, despair, and hopelessness where people see no future." Powell was speaking about the Middle East, but it certainly is relevant to U.S. gang terrorism where strong social programs could help prevent domestic terrorism.

Another approach might be for the National Association of Social Workers, with its Washington, D.C., influence, to begin a political process by appealing to politicians, the Mexican American Legal Defense and Education Fund, the National Association for the Advancement of Colored People, the American Civil Liberties Union, and other civil rights attorneys concerning this important issue. Our profession is strategically in position to designate this effort as one of its highest priorities. Leadership for such social policy development would reestablish social work's commitment to special populations in dire psychosocial need on a macro public policy level. We cannot afford to lose another 10,000 to 20,000 young Americans to gang terrorism in the coming five to ten years.

KEY WORDS AND CONCEPTS

Conflict gangs
Retreatist gangs
Criminal gangs
Cult/occult gangs
Neo-Nazi gangs
al-Qaeda
Domestic and international gang terrorism

SUGGESTED INFORMATION SOURCES

Li, Xiaoming, Bonita Stanton, Robert Pack, Carole Harris, Lesley Cottell, and James Burns. "Risk and Protective Factors Associated with Gang Involvement among Urban African American Adolescents," *Youth and Society* 34, No. 2 (December 2002).

Morales, Armando T. "Urban, Suburban, and International Terrorist Gangs," in Armando T. Morales and Bradford W. Sheafor, *Social Work: A Profession of Many Faces*, 10th ed. Boston: Allyn & Bacon, 2004.

Patterns of Global Terrorism. U.S. Department of State, Publication #10940, Office of the Coordinator of Terrorism, May 2002.

"Terrorism in the United States 1999." Federal Bureau of Investigation, U.S. Department of Justice. Washington, D.C., U.S. Government Printing Office, 1999.

ENDNOTES

1. *Webster's Encyclopedic Unabridged Dictionary of the English Language* (San Diego, CA: Thunder Bay Press, 2001), p. 1960.
2. Michelle Mittelstadt, "Lawyers at Odds Over Reno's Testimony on Waco Siege. http://www.amarillo.com/stories/032900/usn_LA0719.001.shtml.
3. "The McVeigh Letters: Why I Bombed Oklahoma," http://www.papillonsartpalace.com/timothy.htm (p. 2).
4. Ibid., p. 3.
5. James C. Howell, "Youth gangs," *Fact Sheet* #12 (Washington, D.C.: U.S. Department of Justice, Office of Juvenile Justice and Delinquency Prevention, December, 1997).
6. Penal Code Section 186.22, Participation in a criminal street gang, *West's California Juvenile and Court Rules 1993* (St. Paul, MN: West Publishing Co., 1993).
7. Associated Press, "Suspected al-Qaeda Appointee Is Revealed," *Los Angeles Times* (November 24, 2002): A44.
8. Richard C. Paddock, "Indonesia Seizes Alleged Planner of Bali Bombing," *Los Angeles Times* (Friday, November 22, 2002): A3.
9. J. Moore and C. P. Terret, "Highlights of the 1996 National Youth Gang Survey," *Fact Sheet* #86 (Washington, D.C.: U.S. Department of Justice, Office of Juvenile Justice and Delinquency Prevention, November 1998).
10. Frederick M. Thrasher, *The Gang: A Study of 1313 Gangs in Chicago* (Chicago: University of Chicago Press, 1963), pp. 31–35.
11. W. B. Miller, "Lower Class Culture as a Generating Milieu of Gang Delinquency," *Journal of Social Issues* 14 (1958): 5–19.
12. See A. K. Cohen, *Delinquent Boys: The Culture of the Gang* (Glencoe, IL: Free Press, 1955); and R. A. Cloward and L. E. Ohlin, *Delinquency and Opportunity* (New York: Free Press, 1960).
13. D. Matza, *Delinquency and Drift* (New York: Wiley, 1964).
14. A. Morales, "A Study of Recidivism of Mexican American Junior Forestry Camp Graduates," unpublished master's thesis (School of Social Work, University of Southern California, 1963).
15. *Report on Youth Gang Violence in California*, The Attorney General's Youth Gang Task Force, June 1981, p. 8.
16. Irving A. Spergel, "Youth Gangs: Continuity and Change," in *Crime and Justice* (Chicago: University of Chicago Press, 1990), p. 613.

17. K. L. Woodward, "In the Beginning There Were the Holy Books," *Newsweek* (February 11, 2002): 50–57.
18. "Ounces of Prevention: Toward an Understanding of the Causses of Violence," *1982 Final Report to the People of California,* Commission on Crime Control and Violence Prevention, State of California, pp. 81–82.
19. C. Wallis, "The Kids Are Alright," *Time* (July 5, 1999): 56–58.
20. I. Spergel and S. F. Grossman, "The Little Village Project: A Community Approach to the Gang Problem," *Social Work* 42, No. 5 (September 1997): 456–470.
21. M. W. Klein, "The Gang's All Here, There and Everywhere," *USC Trojan Family Magazine* 26 (1) (1997), p. 14.
22. Iraq Coalition Casualty Count, 2008. http://icasualties.org/oif.

chapter 13

Social Work with U.S. Casualties of the Middle East Wars*

> **Prefatory Comment**
>
> Since the beginning of World War II, the United States has been at war nearly 45 percent of the time. In terms of human sacrifice, 379,000 soldiers have been killed in action and another 970,000 severely injured and maimed.[1] These data do not include the uncounted millions of civilian casualties in countries where the fighting occurred. For example, icasualties.org estimates that, in the Iraq War during 2007, nearly 52 Iraqi security forces and civilians were killed every day.[2] And the devastation doesn't end with the death or injury of a soldier. In the Iraq War, many soldiers survived but experienced severe wounds. Meeting the needs of warfare survivors—those who were injured as well as surviving family members—will present a unique challenge for social workers for decades to come.
>
> Social workers in hospitals and veterans' outreach centers play a central role in the recovery process—for both survivors and their loved ones. Social workers in military hospitals help patients and their families maintain communication. They arrange for transitions to other forms of care that might be necessary for rehabilitation or for the development of new job skills. They also address psychological injuries. Social workers in other human service agencies, too, have a role in the aftermath of war. They play a critical role in helping survivors and their families overcome or cope with the often unrecognized long-term consequences of war.

Working with survivors of war is not new for social workers. The first paid social workers in the United States were appointed to help with issues experienced by soldiers and their families in the 1860s, during the Civil War (see Chapter 4). Trattner notes that, "Like all wars, the 'War Between the States' created enormous relief problems, not only for wounded and disabled soldiers but for bereaved families who lost their male breadwinners during the conflict."[3] Social workers continued to provide these important services not only during the seven wars subsequent to the Civil War but also during the intervening years when physical and emotional scars persisted.

---

*This chapter was prepared by Joanne E. Clancy, Clinical Social Worker with the Trauma Recovery Team, Veterans Affairs Medical Center, Houston, Texas, and Bradford W. Sheafor, Professor of Social Work, Colorado State University.

Today and in the foreseeable future, social workers will attend to survivors of wars. Some will serve as social workers in the military. Others will be civilians employed by the Veterans' Administration and other veterans' organizations. Social workers employed in schools, hospitals, courts and prisons, mental health centers, child welfare agencies, drug and alcohol rehabilitation centers, nursing homes, and other practice settings will also serve survivors or families affected by war. Because survivors of warfare access services in many different settings, all social workers should develop skills in grief counseling and management of trauma survivors' complex needs.

As in other areas of the human services, social workers are the professionals most likely to make referrals. They must not only know the general resources available to clients but must also be informed about services specifically designed for veterans and their families. If needed services are not available, social workers must advocate for their creation. Social workers, unlike individuals in the general population, are in a position to observe the far-reaching aftermath of war as it affects members of society for years after the hostilities have ceased. It is from this vantage point that social workers have special insights to contribute regarding the importance of preventing wars.

Social Work with Soldiers and Veterans

The recent wars in Afghanistan and Iraq are the most sustained combat efforts initiated by the United States since the Vietnam War. This new generation of combat veterans requires the focused energies of many service providers (physicians, nurses, psychologists, occupational and physical therapists, and social workers) as the veterans strive to reintegrate into society. The social work profession has a unique opportunity to take the lead in this stabilization and recovery process because the systemic manner through which social workers approach problems, coupled with their ability to provide multiple levels of service in a variety of settings, maximizes their ability to affect the lives of both veterans and their families.

People die in wars—both in battle and increasingly by suicide. An even greater number survive but sustain serious, life-changing injuries on the battlefield. During World War II, one out of every three wounded soldiers died. In Vietnam, one out of four wounded soldiers died. Soldiers serving in Iraq have even better odds of surviving; only one out of every eight wounded soldiers die.[4] Despite this "good news," many surviving soldiers return home with catastrophic injuries that disfigure and emotionally scar them for life. Advances in the field medicine may save their lives but, as one former medic quite eloquently stated: "I'm not sure we did them any favors. These men and women were young, healthy people in the prime of life. They went home with missing arms, legs, and eyes. A lot of them have psychological problems as well. Even the lucky ones, the ones who have people to help and support them, face decades of physical and emotional pain, discrimination, and the challenge of learning to live a life very different from the one they planned. Yeah, I'm not sure we did them any favors."

Adjustment to the traumatic loss of one's physical integrity, especially when functional ability is seriously compromised, is a long and painful process. Simple tasks once taken for granted become impossible or require Herculean effort to accomplish. Depending on the nature and severity of the loss, the affected individual may require months or years of physical therapy to regain even a fraction of his or her former independence. Dramatic changes in body image, coupled with others' reactions to the veteran's altered physical appearance, further complicate the recovery process. One young soldier, a quadriplegic, stated, "I want to commit suicide, but I can't move my arms or legs. No one will help me do it. My mother keeps telling me things will get better if I just have patience. I'm 21 years old... how can things ever get better? I was an athlete. I planned to become a physical therapist. I wanted to get married and start a family someday. Who would want me now? I am completely helpless until someone cleans me up and sits me in my motorized chair. All my dreams are gone. What's the point?"*

Sustained exposure to potentially life-threatening experiences escalates the risk for psychological problems. This is especially true in a war zone where death and serious injury are not only feared but also expected. In a study targeting the effects of combat on the mental health of soldiers in Afghanistan and Iraq,[5] researchers discovered a strong correlation between combat experiences (being shot at, handling dead bodies, witnessing the death of a peer, killing enemy combatants) and the prevalence of posttraumatic stress disorder (PTSD). The presence of PTSD increased proportionately with the number of battles in which soldiers engaged during their deployment. Mental illnesses most commonly identified among study participants include acute stress disorder, posttraumatic stress disorder, generalized anxiety disorder, major depression, traumatic brain injury (TBI), and substance abuse. An even more recent study conducted by the U.S. Army Surgeon General's Office[6] indicated that 15 to 20 percent of all soldiers fighting in Iraq and Afghanistan experienced PTSD, and that rate increased to 30 percent for those serving their third tour of duty. In addition, the number of Army suicides hit a record in 2007, and two in ten soldiers reported that their marriages were in trouble.

Despite the high incidence of mental distress among combat troops, few soldiers express interest in pursuing mental health treatment. This holds true even when the soldiers are presented with opportunities to visit "wellness tents" in the field, participate in debriefings post-deployment, or meet with mental health professionals in more formal settings. Researchers in one study[7] determined that only 38 to 45 percent of soldiers who met criteria for a mental disorder were interested in receiving help. Even more startling, only 23 to 40 percent of those expressing a desire for assistance actually sought help post-discharge. The stigma of mental illness (i.e., "I am weak, crazy, not normal") and the fear that seeking mental health care will adversely affect future career opportunities were primary factors in their decision-making process. Thus

---

*All stories told by soldiers and veterans throughout this chapter were reported to social workers in veterans' centers and hospitals.

mental health conditions often become interpreted as "adjustment issues" so that seeking help does not become a negative experience for the soldier.

Social Work with the Families of Soldiers and Veterans

Combat survivors struggle to escape traumatic memories that assault them through intrusive thoughts and nightmares. At the same time, their loved ones struggle to understand what happened to the individual they sent to war. The person who returns is altered in ways that cannot always be seen or explained. One soldier's mother poignantly stated, "I sent my son to war. The person they sent back is not my son... it is a shell that looks like my son. He is angry and distant. My heart is breaking because nothing I say or do can recapture what he, and we, have lost."

When soldiers receive orders for deployment into a combat zone, a kaleidoscope of emotional reactions emerge from both the soldier and from his or her family members: denial, "this isn't really happening... is it?"; fear, "what if he or she is seriously injured, crippled, or killed in combat?"; anger, "I never really thought he or she would be sent to war"; confusion, "what will become of our family before, during, and after my loved one's deployment into a war zone?" The emotional impact of impending deployment is magnified by the reality that war inevitably results in death and sacrifice.

The free-floating sea of emotional reactions within and between family members can wreak havoc on a family's ability to prepare for, endure, and recover from the deployment experience. Individuals process and cope with emotional distress in ways uniquely their own. Age, gender, and past experiences influence each family member's willingness and ability to openly challenge and move through their collective emotional experience. During this critical time in the family's life cycle, forging a united front is crucial to the healthy adjustment of all involved. Without adequate guidance and support, many of these "at-risk" families will become "collateral casualties" of war.

Social Programs for Soldiers and Veterans

In the event of the death of a soldier, family members not only must deal with the death of a loved one, but most families will also be poorer. Initially, government programs help to offset expenses and the wages of the soldier who died, but these resources are designed to decline over time, thus challenging social workers to help the families develop alternate sources of income. Further, many families require emotional assistance as they cope with grief and loss. Social workers in hospice agencies and mental health centers regularly provide valuable counseling to parents, siblings, spouses, and children of soldiers killed while performing military duty.

Social workers also encounter soldiers returning from a war zone who experience problems meeting basic social needs. If the individual is a professional soldier who has not yet fulfilled his or her commitment to military service, reassignment to a new duty station often occurs. This forestalls any immediate concerns about housing and income. If, however, the individual has fulfilled his or her military obligation, an additional challenge of separation from service and transition to civilian life ensues. The presence or absence of extended family support during this time of transition is a primary variable in determining post-discharge outcomes. If family support is not present, homelessness may become an issue. The National Alliance to End Homelessness, for example, reports that, although veterans make-up 11 percent of the population, one-fourth of all homeless people in the United States are veterans.[8]

The financial issue is more complex for reservists and National Guard personnel mobilized to an active duty status. Although job security is guaranteed, many of these individuals incur significant financial reversals while on active duty. The military cannot, and does not, match the salaries these individuals receive from their civilian employers. This disparity in income often generates far-reaching consequences for these individuals and the family members they leave behind. In one instance, a young mother of three stated, "What does the military expect us to do? My husband made over $100,000 a year as a computer analyst. I am a housewife. How am I supposed to pay the mortgage and keep our household running on what the Army is paying him? We will probably have to file bankruptcy. So much for supporting those willing to serve their country!"

Social Work Practice during Reintegration Efforts

Outreach and Resource Mobilization

Although several disciplines work with active duty military personnel and veterans, social workers are best qualified to address their subsequent emotional and social needs. Historically what sets the social work profession apart from other disciplines is the willingness to meet individuals "where they are," emotionally and geographically. Social workers display great flexibility in their willingness to engage in outreach efforts designed to identify and engage elusive populations. This willingness to aggressively pursue populations most at risk "where they work, live, and play" allows social workers to intervene early on, before the problems escalate.

Social workers assigned to active duty military positions, and those working civilian contracts for the Department of Defense or other divisions of the federal government, play a critical role in outreach efforts. Their presence at military bases, in the field, and at veterans' outreach centers and hospitals across the country provide opportunities to identify the needs of soldiers and veterans at each stage of the deployment process. The following case study highlights the role social work plays in promoting a healthy transition for soldiers and their family members.

> Mr. X. is a 22-year-old, married Marine sergeant recently discharged from the military after a tour of duty in Iraq. He was discharged approximately two months before the social worker's initial contact with him at a local veterans' outreach center. The social worker assigned to his case identified a number of problem areas. The veteran had

limited income and needed temporary financial assistance. He was interested in securing employment and returning to school but had no idea how to access vocational services. He and his spouse were experiencing a variety of marital problems they had not been able to resolve on their own. Both partners had little understanding of the emotional problems this soldier was experiencing.

The social worker immediately set forth to identify and mobilize available resources. The veteran and his wife received referrals to community-based agencies for financial services. A referral to the vocational counseling department at the local veterans' hospital was initiated to assess his readiness for training and job placement services. The social worker also initiated a referral to the hospital's PTSD program so the veteran and his spouse could receive assistance coping with the veteran's psychiatric problems. The couple also received a list of Internet referrals where they could download information pertinent to issues encountered by veterans of Middle Eastern wars.[9]

The social worker met with this couple weekly at the outreach center for several months. She provided emotional support and monitored their progress accessing identified resources. When the couple expressed frustration due to snags in the referral process to several agencies, the social worker assumed an advocacy role. Several months later when the veteran returned for follow-up services at the veterans' hospital, he was asked what had been most helpful during the initial months following his military discharge. The veteran replied, "The Vet Center social worker. We felt lost, alone, and confused. Our social worker was very kind. She guided us through a maze of resources we would never have figured out on our own. She seemed to really care about what happened to us and gave us hope that, in time, things would get better. I don't know where we would be if this caring professional had not stepped up to bat for us."

Education and Skill Building

The transition from soldier to civilian, especially after serving in a war zone, is challenging. If physical and/or mental disabilities factor into the equation, the adjustment process becomes even more complicated. Through individual, group, and family sessions, social work professionals provide knowledge about specific conditions, identifying existing treatment options and introducing coping skills so those affected can more readily navigate the challenges at hand. The simple act of "naming the problem" brings relief and provides direction. As one veteran so aptly stated, "Now that I know what the problem is, I can begin identifying ways to attack it."

Skill building is another critical piece of the recovery process. The majority of combat veterans are young, and they possess a limited range of coping skills. Exposure to a variety of problem-solving techniques, offered through educational classes and skill-building sessions, provides them with a "toolbox for recovery." These tools, once acquired and reinforced, empower individuals to assume the lead in creating their own solutions. The social worker's role during this process is to impart knowledge and guide individuals through role-play sessions designed to enhance their effectiveness in skills application. The case of a young female amputee clearly illustrates this point.

Ms. P. is a 23-year-old female soldier severely wounded during a terrorist attack in Iraq. She was standing guard when a jeep carrying explosives crashed into a building near her position. She lost both legs below the knees. Emotionally devastated by her loss, this young veteran had no idea how to cope with the drastic life changes brought about by her amputations. Her family was equally at a loss. The social worker assigned to her case provided information about typical reactions experienced by amputees and their family members. He invited them to attend a support group with other amputees and their families. This provided opportunities for mutual support and the exchange of ideas and information. He also invited the family to attend a series of classes that focused on independent living skills. During these classes, the veteran developed strategies to assertively communicate her needs. Role-plays where family members assumed the role of amputee helped sensitize them to the challenges faced by their loved one on a daily basis. The veteran and her family also received instruction on the variety of prosthetic devices she would need to normalize her life. Stress management and play therapy classes introduced healthy alternatives for coping with distress inherent after traumatic losses.

When asked to describe this educational experience Ms. P. replied, "My first reaction... this is a big waste of time. I didn't see how going to classes would help me or my family deal with the fact I have no legs. I attended grudgingly at first to humor the social worker. Then, as the weeks went by, I realized things were getting better. We were learning new ways to get things done that really worked. I learned to communicate with my family more productively, and they stopped being afraid to tell me how they really felt. We have even learned to laugh together when the going gets tough. Meeting with other amputees and their family members was also helpful. We learned a lot from each other and made some new friends, too. I never realized how important these classes would be to my recovery. I hope all the other veterans coming back with injuries like mine have a chance to participate in this kind of program. The classes made me realize I still have a life to live, but it is up to me to get out there and live it."

Supportive Interventions

Taking a human life or witnessing the traumatic death of another human being produces far-reaching consequences for even the most psychologically sound individual. Although loss is a normal part of the life cycle, most humans never encounter the type of traumatic losses identified above. During the heat of battle, most soldiers report feeling numb. One young soldier described his experience by saying, "I was on autopilot. I saw people dying all around me, and all I could focus on was staying alive. I had to kill several enemy soldiers and didn't think much of it at the time."

The psychological impact of one's actions in combat may take days, weeks, even months to surface. Another young veteran reported the following experience: "I was a helicopter door gunner in Iraq. My job was to kill enemy soldiers on the ground. One day we came across a band of rebels, and they started shooting at our helicopter. I returned fire, knowing I would kill at least some of them. After the battle, we landed to do a body count. Among the dead were a young woman and her baby. As we flew back to base camp, it felt like I was dying inside, one piece at a time. Things have never been the same since that day."

Survivors of combat trauma face three significant challenges as they strive to recover from traumatic losses incurred on the battlefield. First, taking human life, even in the name of self-preservation, transforms them into "old souls." An *old soul* is a young person who has seen the darkest side of him- or herself. Although all humans have the capacity to kill when confronted with life-and-death situations, few of us ever cross this line. Thinking you can kill someone, and knowing you have, are very different experiences.

Second, the taking of a human life generates tremendous conflict between one's beliefs and values, and actions taken during the heat of battle. One young soldier participating in a PTSD program expressed the following thoughts. "I grew up in the church. I learned that harming others was a mortal sin. I remember one day, when my unit was preparing for battle, a preacher stopped by our tent to pray with us. He asked God to protect us and keep us safe. Then he told us to go out there and kill those bastards. His comment really confused me. He sanctioned behavior that is in direct conflict with what I spent the first 18 years of my life believing. It really messed me up. Now I question if God even exists. I also worry about my soul... if there is a God, am I doomed to hell because of what I did in Iraq?"

Finally, returning combat soldiers often experience profound guilt. This guilt stems not only from taking human lives but also for surviving when others do not. One young man, traveling in a convoy, described the following experience. "My buddies and I were driving supplies between two base camps. My truck was scheduled to take the lead, but the other driver begged me to let him go first. He was new in the country and wanted to prove himself. I said yes against my own better judgment. We were on a narrow road with a steep ravine on one side. The truck in front of me hit a mine. All I could do is watch in horror as the truck plunged over the cliff. Bodies flew everywhere. I stopped my truck and we scrambled down the cliff to rescue survivors. There weren't any.... We ended up collecting dead bodies instead. If I had refused to let the new guy lead the way, this wouldn't have happened. It's a hell of a burden to carry around each day."

Social workers provide the bulk of mental health services to individuals seeking assistance from veterans' outreach centers, hospitals, and mental health trauma programs. The focus of treatment is empowering veterans to identify, process, and move beyond their traumatic experiences. Social workers conducting individual and group therapy sessions encourage trauma survivors to "remember and let go" of traumatic memories, since forgetting is not a realistic option. Multifamily group therapy adds yet another dimension to the recovery process. Allowing veterans and family members to share their common experiences provides hope and encouragement that life can, and will, go on. A final case study illustrates the social worker's role as change agent when addressing veterans' mental health concerns.

> Mr. M. is a 25-year-old, married combat veteran who served two tours of duty in Iraq. During the second tour, his unit encountered a group of insurgents, which resulted in intense hand-to-hand combat. Several of his buddies were killed during the attack. Mr. M. sustained only minor injuries. Unfortunately, his traumatic experience continued to haunt him after discharge. He reported a great deal of inner conflict about having killed several enemy soldiers during the battle. He also felt guilty for surviving when many of his peers did not. During his first session with a social worker in an outpatient trauma program, he shared the following information: "I have been a wreck since I got back from Iraq. I have nightmares about killing and being killed. I think about the war all the time

and have to avoid watching the news or I get all stressed out. I am irritable a lot of the time and don't want to be around anyone. Life just doesn't seem worth living anymore."

The social worker's first intervention involved consultation with the clinic psychiatrist. The psychiatrist prescribed medication to help alleviate Mr. M.'s symptoms. Next, Mr. M. was enrolled in both individual and group therapy. The goal of individual therapy was to provide a milieu where the veteran could discuss the most painful aspects of his combat experience. The social worker identified a number of techniques to aid him in redirecting painful thoughts when they occurred. Mr. M. was also assisted in challenging self-defeating thoughts about his survival and reframing his feelings about killing enemy soldiers in the line of duty.

During group therapy sessions, the focus was helping Mr. M. realize he is not alone in his struggle. Opportunities to process thoughts and feelings with other veterans experiencing similar reactions helped him develop a new appreciation of his own situation. It also provided exposure to others' coping strategies, some of which he adopted with great success. During one session, he remarked that things at home were not going very well between him and his spouse. This resulted in a referral to a multifamily group. In this context, Mr. M. and his wife learned how to join forces so they could combat symptoms of the veteran's PTSD instead of fighting with one another.

After three months of treatment, the veteran and his wife met with the treatment team to discuss his progress and identify ongoing issues for work. Both expressed great relief that things were beginning to improve. Mr. M. was less irritable and anxious. His nightmares were less frequent and intense. He noted a return of optimism about the future. His wife reported that participating in the multifamily group was the best possible thing that could have happened. She felt supported and validated both by the social work leader and other members of the group. She stated, "Attending family group made me realize we are not in this alone. I heard our story coming out of the mouths of other veterans and their wives. Some of them have been in treatment longer than we have. Their testimonies gave us hope that things can and will get better if we just hang in there. I don't know what might have happened if we hadn't come in for help. We still have a long way to go, but at least we are moving in the right direction!"

Special Considerations Regarding Today's Victims of War

It is clear that social workers have an important role to play in assisting individuals who are survivors of war and their families. There is, however, special knowledge and unique insights required of social workers as they serve these individuals.

Quality of Care for Veterans

For a period of time in 2007, the news was filled with stories reporting substandard treatment provided to Afghanistan and Iraq war veterans at the nation's premiere medical facility, Walter Reed Army Hospital in Washington, D.C. This firestorm was partially initiated by the resignation of a social worker on the Walter Reed Army Medical Center staff, Joe Wilson, who was frustrated with the failure of the hospital's administrators to address the deplorable conditions experienced by wounded soldiers at Walter Reed. The situation was pushed into the public spotlight by an article published in the *Washington Post* on February 18, 2007, that eventually resulted in the replacement of the hospital commander, the Army Surgeon General, and the Secretary of the Army and the creation of a presidential-level task force headed by former senator Bob Dole and former Health and Human Services Secretary Donna Shalala. Another social worker, Kristin Day, then–acting national director of Social Work Service at the Department of Veterans Affairs (VA), actively supported the Commission's recommendations, calling for better coordination between the Department of Defense and the VA, creation of a comprehensive recovery plan to provide the right care at the right time for hospitalized soldiers and veterans, a restructuring of the disability determination and compensation systems, additional efforts to prevent and treat PTSD and TBI, and a stronger role in treating families.[10]

If these changes are eventually accomplished, they will be too late for many veterans. A 2008 investigation of the Army's care of returning soldiers by *Time* magazine focused on the subsequent death of Sergeant Gerald Cassidy, who had suffered a traumatic head injury in Iraq. The report summarizes:

> Soldiers fall through the cracks in every war. But the death of Sergeant Gerald (GJ) Cassidy, a cheerful 31-year-old husband and father of two, highlights the tragic and persistent shortcomings of Army medicine. The same Army that spends $160 billion on tomorrow's fighting machines is shortchanging the shell-shocked troops coming home from war in need of healing. Cassidy was promised world-class health care. But he didn't get the simple help—quick treatment, pain-management classes, knowledge of his whereabouts or even a roommate—that could have saved his life.[11]

Serving an All-Volunteer Force

Previous generations of soldiers resulted from a combination of draftees and enlistees. Present-day soldiers are members of an all-volunteer force who have elected to spend at least part of their careers in the military. This difference affects the characteristics of who is in the military and how they respond when they face physical or mental injuries, presenting special challenges for the social workers who serve them. For example, more than 50 percent of soldiers serving in Afghanistan and Iraq are between the ages of 20 and 29. Although early intervention and outreach efforts are much improved since the Vietnam War, youth often deters returning soldiers from accepting available support. Young veterans tend to minimize symptoms and avoid seeking professional help. When problems are psychiatric in nature, these problems are even more difficult to identify, and young soldiers are more reluctant to engage in treatment.

Further, more than 50 percent of service members are married, and about 11 percent of marriages are to other service members. This generates serious concerns when married couples are simultaneously deployed to high-risk areas, especially when minor children are involved. Complex issues facing couples in this situation include the constant worry that one's partner will be injured or killed, child care during the parents' deployment, the impact of separation from parental figures on offspring at critical points during the developmental process, and reestablishing family ties once members reunite. Of even greater concern are the consequences for children when one or both parents die in combat.

Finally, the ability to choose whether or not one engages in military service affects post-discharge adjustment, especially for individuals deployed to a war zone. When an individual is free to choose whether or not to join the military, it creates a sense of self-determination (i.e., "This is something I elected to do, and going to war may or may not be part of the package"). When one is conscripted, it generates a sense of powerlessness and anger, especially when bad things happen (i.e., "I had no choice... the government ruined my life").

Women in the Military and Associated Gender Issues

During previous wars, female soldiers were forbidden to participate in direct combat. Present-day women can and do select military occupation specializations (MOS) that place them on frontlines of the battlefield. As a result, female combat veterans face the same physical and mental health risks as their male counterparts. This role transition creates far-reaching consequences in regard to treatment. Patients currently treated by veterans' hospitals are predominately male. When females do seek treatment, the primary focus, until now, has been military sexual trauma and health-related issues. The influx of females joining the military is changing the face of post-military intervention. As female veterans become a larger percentage of those seeking care, clinicians must create and implement programming designed to meet the unique needs of this population.

The Need for Cultural Competence When Serving Returning Troops

America has made great strides in addressing racial discrimination since the 1960s, when African American soldiers who had been drafted into the military often felt they were fighting to free the South Vietnamese people from oppression but continued to experience oppression themselves at home. Today, ethnic minorities make up a portion of military personnel that is very close to the minority distribution in the United States. As of September 30, 2004, combined deployment lists from the Afghanistan and Iraq wars report the following racial analysis of troops: 70 percent white, 15 percent African American, 9.5 percent Hispanic, and 5 percent other or unknown. These figures do not include soldiers deployed within the United States.[12]

Despite these gains in addressing racial discrimination, prejudice is still very much present in certain segments of U.S. society. Professionals working with returning veterans of color must be careful to avoid assumptions based on race or ethnicity. It is imperative to remember that strategies applied to the dominant culture with great success might fail miserably with minority groups. Cultural and racial sensitivity affords clinicians the opportunity to learn from their patients what is most and least helpful during the reintegration process.

The Affects of Guerrilla Warfare and Acts of Terrorism

As opposed to the more traditional forms of battlefield warfare, in Iraq and Afghanistan the greatest sources of danger are guerrilla warfare and terrorist acts, not direct combat.[13] In an urban war, threats are ambiguous. Anyone, anywhere, might be the enemy. This lack of an "identified enemy" places soldiers in a constant state of alert. During the Iraq War, the ratio of seriously wounded to those killed in action was the highest in U.S. history.[14] Ninety-four percent of soldiers in Iraq reported exposure to hostile small arms fire, 86 percent reported knowing someone who was seriously injured or killed, and 68 percent reported seeing dead or seriously injured Americans. The majority of these losses were the result of random acts of violence. One young Iraq veteran relayed his feelings by saying, "I never felt safe over there. I was a truck driver, not a combat soldier, but every time I got in my vehicle, I worried about being ambushed or hitting a mine. I saw too many of my friends die that way. . . . I always worried I might be next."

Social Work and the Prevention of War

Social workers directly serve the survivors of war and, drawing upon the person-in-environment perspective, further contend it is important to address the broader issues that are the causes and consequences of war. Identifying the cause of war is a complex issue. Surely one factor is the grossly unequal distribution of wealth and resources throughout the world when a few rich and developed countries (and especially the United States) possess a significant part of the world's wealth and use a substantial proportion of the earth's natural resources (e.g., oil, timber, minerals), allowing their people to enjoy a substantially higher quality of life than exists elsewhere. It is not surprising that others who experience the social consequences of such poverty (i.e., poor housing, inadequate diet, poor health, limited transportation, etc.) are willing to go to war to correct this inequality. Another factor contributing to wars is growing religious fanaticism, both in the United States and throughout the world, in which one extremist religion attempts to force its religious beliefs onto others. This condition polarizes people and leaves little room for compromise, often preempting efforts to address other human concerns. Finally, excessive emphasis on "nationalism" and "patriotism," although laudable in spirit, too often leads to a false sense of superiority and unwillingness to compromise national desires for the greater good of the world's people.

The cost of war in terms of both human and economic resources is enormous. The loss of life and the maiming of human beings not only have a substantial emotional impact on those affected but also have a significant economic drain on the nation. Resources that might have been devoted to resolving the social, health, and economic issues discussed elsewhere in this book are diverted to maintaining a military presence throughout the world, protecting homeland security, and absorbing the direct costs of active battle. For example, the change in U.S. expenditures reflects the diversion of resources from 2000 (before the Afghanistan and Iraq wars) to the estimated fiscal year (FY) 2009 budget (see Table 13.1).[15]

Clearly, the cost of war has shifted resources away from meeting the needs of vulnerable U.S. citizens. The spiraling national debt resulting from this action must be paid off by future generations—with financial interest. In their book, *The Three Trillion Dollar War: The True Cost of the Iraq Conflict,* noted economists Joseph Stiglitz and Linda Bilmes project that only a fraction of the cost is represented in the federal budget. Most of the costs are funded offline through increasing the public debt and that many costs related to lifetime health care, maintaining a military presence in Afghanistan and Iraq, combat pay, death benefits, Social Security, disability and medical care, and other hidden costs were not made public by the George W. Bush Administration.[16]

In its policy statement on "Peace and Social Justice,"[17] the National Association of Social Workers takes a stand on three issues related to war:

- Although we have recently gone through a new military buildup and actions against terrorist groups and the countries that harbor them, the United States needs to emphasize economic support rather than Western dominance. ...Whenever possible, the United States must foster cooperation in its foreign policy rather than unilateral military action. A long-range goal should be the reduction of military spending and diversion of the subsequent savings to social needs.
- Even in the face of overt terrorist attacks on the United States, it is still vital that we work in creative ways with other nations and international organizations to reduce violence against innocent civilians.
- The United States needs to continue using qualified professional social workers to serve the armed forces and military dependents to ensure that a high priority is given to human values and social welfare needs in those settings.

Table 13.1

Change in Actual U.S. Expenditures for National Defense (2000 to 2007) Compared with Expenditures for Domestic Social Programs

	2000	2007	Increase
National defense	$294.4 billion	$549.2 billion	86.6%
Training/employment/social services	15.3 billion	20.0 billion	30.7%
Income security	41.4 billion	56.4 billion	36.2%

Note: The Bush Administration budget for 2009 further increased defense spending to $670.7B, reduced training/employment/social services to $19.7B, and increased income security to $58.4B.

Concluding Comment

War has far-reaching consequences for combat soldiers, their family members, and society as a whole. Without timely and effective intervention, soldiers returning from Afghanistan and Iraq are at risk for a lifetime of maladjustment and misery. Social work professionals—acting as teachers, guides, and advocates—can significantly reduce this risk. Strategic placement of social workers during all stages of the recovery process will enhance soldiers' potential to move beyond their combat experiences. Although social workers cannot stop wars, prevent deaths during combat, or undo physical and/or psychiatric injuries incurred during war, they can empower survivors to live happier, more productive lives. Further, they can use their advocacy skills to help prevent wars and improve the quality of life for all people throughout the world.

KEY WORDS AND CONCEPTS

Role of social work during reintegration efforts
Collateral casualties
Social implications of war for returning veterans
Consequences of deployment for families
Old souls
Women in the military
Cultural competence in social work practice with soldiers

SUGGESTED INFORMATION SOURCES

Farber-Silk, Lisa H. *Giving My Heart: Love in a Military Family.* Ann Arbor, MI: Modern History Press, 2008.
Riverbend. *Baghdad Burning: Girl Blog from Iraq.* New York: Feminist Press at the City University of New York, 2005.
Roberts, Cheryl A. *Coping with Post-Traumatic Stress Disorder: A Guide for Families.* Jefferson, NC: McFarland, 2003.
Sheeler, Jim. *Final Salute: A Story of Unfinished Lives.* New York: Penguin Press, 2008.
Tripp, Elise Forbes. *Surviving Iraq: Soldiers' Stories.* Northampton, MA: Olive Branch Press, 2008.

ENDNOTES

1. Ross Doutkat, Abigail Cutler, and Terrence Henry, "Casualties of War," *Atlantic* 29 (March 2004): 50.
2. "Iraq Coalition Casualty Count," icasualties.org. Retrieved January 6, 2008, from http://icasualties.org/oif.
3. Walter I. Trattner, *From Poor Law to Welfare State: A History of Social Welfare in America,* 6th ed. (New York: Free Press, 1999), p. 77.
4. Nancy Gibbs, "The Lucky Ones," *Time Magazine* 165 (March 21, 2005): 36.
5. C. Hoge, C. Castro, S. Messer, D. McGurk, D. Cotting, and R. Koffman, "Combat Duty in Iraq and Afghanistan, Mental Health Problems, and Barriers to Care," *New England Journal of Medicine* 351 (2004): 13–22.

6. Gregg Zoroya, "A Fifth of Soldiers at PTSD Risk: Rate Rises with Tours, Army Says," *USA Today* (March 7, 2008): 11A.
7. Hoge, et al., op. cit.
8. Kimberly Hefling, "Veterans Make Up Quarter of Homeless," *The Coloradoan* (November 8, 2007): A11.
9. The National Center for Posttraumatic Stress Disorder, www.ncptsd.org, identifies multiple links to Internet sites offering education materials, support networks, and benefits and resource information. For detailed information, refer to the following: National Center for PTSD and Walter Reed Army Medical Center, *Iraq War Clinician Guide,* 2nd ed. (Washington, DC: Department of Veterans Affairs, June 2004) and *VHA Office of Public Health and Environmental Hazards Analysis of VA Health Care Utilization among Southwest Asian War Veterans Combined: Operation Iraqi Freedom/Operation Enduring Freedom* (Washington, DC: Department of Veteran's Affairs, March 2005).
10. Paul R. Pace, "Reforming Care for Afflicted Soldiers," *NASW News* (October 2007): 4.
11. Mark Thompson, "Death at the Army's Hands," *Time* (February 25, 2008), 40–42.
12. Han Kang, Director of Epidemiology Services, Department of Veterans Affairs, e-mail communiqué on May 9, 2005.
13. "The Unique Circumstances and Mental Health Impact of the Wars in Afghanistan and Iraq: A National Center for PTSD Fact Sheet." Retrieved May 3, 2005, from http://www.ncptsd.va.gov.
14. T. Ricks, "Where Does Iraq Stand Among U.S. Wars? Total Casualties Compare to Spanish-American, Mexican, and 1812 Conflicts," *The Washington Post* (May 31, 2004): A16.
15. *The U.S. Budget for Fiscal Year 2009: Historical Tables,* "Table 8.7—Outlays for Discretionary Programs: 1962–2009." (Washington, DC: Office of Management and Budget, 2008): 154–155.
16. Joseph Stiglitz and Linda Bilmes, *The Three Trillion Dollar War: The True Cost of the Iraq Conflict* (New York: W. W. Norton, 2008).
17. National Association of Social Workers, *Social Work Speaks: National Association of Social Workers Policy Statements, 2003–2006,* 6th ed. (Washington, DC: NASW Press, 2003): 267–269.

chapter 14

Social Work Practice with Immigrants, Refugees, and Unaccompanied Minors*

Prefatory Comment

One of the most perplexing current issues for social workers, and for many Americans, revolves around immigration. A nation built on welcoming new inhabitants to its shores, the Unites States has been enriched by the many different faces of its citizens. However, life for new immigrants has not been without tension. Settled by people largely from England, immigrants from Ireland, Italy, and other European countries typically experienced resistance as they introduced new ways of doing things into U.S. culture. Nevertheless, they were eventually absorbed into the culture.

For persons of color, the experience was different. People from Africa were brought as slaves, and the Chinese and other Asian nationals came primarily as manual labor, as well as those from Mexico and other Latin American countries who came largely as agricultural workers, yet all experienced difficulty integrating into U.S. society. Their labor was needed to build the United States' successful economy, and thus immigration laws and their enforcement were relatively lax.

Today the number of immigrants, both legal and undocumented, is rapidly expanding. In some areas, particularly on both coasts and the southern U.S. border, the proportion of immigrants to established citizens is changing political, social, and economic structures. The dominant population in these and other areas is resisting this change and calling for strict enforcement of laws excluding undocumented immigrants, adopting more stringent immigration laws, deporting undocumented persons who are in the country, and building a massive fence along the U.S.–Mexico border to discourage people from countries south of the United States from entering without U.S. approval. Racial and cultural tensions have elevated, creating problems for many children and families, thus creating a new set of issues for social workers serving these families.

---

*This chapter was prepared by Dr. Maria Elena Puig, associate professor of social work, Colorado State University.

> *Good fences make good neighbors: Why do they make*
> *good neighbors? Before I built a wall I'd ask to know*
> *What was I walling in or walling out?*
> *And to whom I was like to give offence.*
> ("Mending Wall" by Robert Frost, 1914)

The United States' current population is estimated to be more than 303 million people, including more than 37.9 million immigrants of which 11 million to 12 million are guesstimated to be undocumented.[1] Known as a safe haven for immigrants, refugees, and other displaced persons, the United States has had a long and proud immigration history. From its earliest inception, this country was founded on the principles of liberty, justice, and freedom—values that pull immigrants to our shores and beliefs that create a basis for diversity that has enriched this nation and challenged all who call this country home.

Fast forward a few hundred years, and now the United States is building a fence between the U.S.–Mexico border, or the Great Wall of Mexico, consisting of more than 2,000 miles of fencing to ensure our security and reduce the number of undocumented immigrants who cross the border. What would Robert Frost say about this fence; who are we "walling in or walling out," and why?[2] Even more disturbing is the number of U.S. citizens who favor such a move, even though the Department of Homeland Security estimates that building such a fence would cost taxpayers "... $851 million for a standard 10-foot prison chain link fence topped with razor wire and another $362 million if the fence was electrified."[3] What happened to cause such a sweeping change in our country's regard for immigrants? One needs only to examine our history to recognize that, traditionally, the United States has had mixed feelings and reactions toward immigrants, particularly if they were people of color or too culturally and religiously "different" from the majority population.[4]

Evidence of this change concerning immigration and immigrants was apparent as early as the 1830s to 1854, with the anti-Catholic crusade against Irish immigrants. Later, similar nativist and xenophobic feelings pushed Congress to enact anti-immigrant legislation with the passage of the Anti-Chinese Act of 1882. This act stopped most immigration and naturalization of Chinese immigrants. By the late nineteenth and early twentieth centuries, immigration to the United States from parts of Europe declined, but immigrants from Eastern Europe still arrived on our shores. Once again, the United States restricted immigration with the passage of the Immigration Act of 1921, which barred entry to anyone who was illiterate in any language. The "literacy test," as this act became known, was enacted to reduce immigration because of the economic troubles the United States and Europe were experiencing and as a result of this country's isolationism and nationalism during World War I.[5]

A few years later, the Immigration Act of 1924 was ratified, establishing a national *origins quota* for all countries. The national origins quota was based on the 1920 census, which limited the number of visas to the United States for all nations on an annual 3 percent immigration cap. The cap was rooted in the number of previous immigrants and their descendants who were already living in this country.

It was not until the end of World War II that the United States began to admit large numbers of immigrants and refugees. This was made possible after the 1951 Protocol Relating to the Status of Refugees established the Office of the United Nations High Commissioner on Refugees to deal with the resettlement of refugees and residual refugees from World War II. The passage of the 1953 Refugee Relief Act subsequently allowed 209,000 refugees, primarily expelled ethnic Germans and "escapees" from East Germany to enter the United States.[6]

By the 1960s, a congressional act, which later became the Cuban Refugee Act of 1962, created a pathway for Cubans fleeing the Castro regime to enter the United States as refugees. Immigration from the Western Hemisphere also was facilitated with the passage of the Immigration and Naturalization Act of 1965, which helped to bring in skilled workers and relatives of U.S. residents. By the end of the Vietnam conflict, the Indochinese Refugee Act of 1977 provided a way for admitting and resettling refugees and asylees who had fled Cambodia and Vietnam.[7] From the 1960s and continuing through the present, immigration from Mexico has been constant and ever increasing. Currently, legal immigrants to the United States come primarily from Mexico, the leading sending country (37%), followed by India (16%), and refugee sending countries including Vietnam and the former Soviet Union (22%).[8]

As a result of increased immigration from Mexico, Latin America, and Asia, current anti-immigrant sentiments have risen as more and more people express concerns over the influx and impact new immigrants are having on our cities' infrastructures. As legal and undocumented immigrants move into rural communities, the suburbs, and urban cities, new immigration patterns are changing the composition and appearance of America. According to Singer, Hardwick, and Bretell,[9] the foreign-born population of the United States increased by 57.4 percent in the 1990s, causing some western and southeastern states to more than double their foreign-born population. Included in these are Colorado, Nevada, Georgia, and North Carolina, states that previously had not been gateways for immigration. It is in these states that more often than not anti-immigrant sentiments are rising due to population shifts, creating competition for jobs and perceptions that immigrants "are taking our jobs." Another problem fueling the anti-immigrant reaction is that, as communities change, so does the fabric of America. Americans are concerned about the trend toward *downward assimilation* by new immigrants, which often leads to undesirable social outcomes such as joining youth gangs, substance abuse, and a general reluctance to learn and accept American cultural norms and patterns.[10]

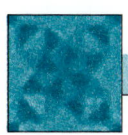

Immigration Gateways

Immigration gateways have long existed in this country.[11] These entry points, or "gateways," have been geographically located in certain regions and cities in the United States. In the early 1900s, cities like Buffalo and Cleveland were immigration magnets but now are considered former gateways because they no longer attract immigrants. On the other hand, Chicago and New York are considered to be continuous gateways because they have always attracted immigrants. Los Angeles and Miami, deemed post–World War II gateways because immigration to these cities grew quite rapidly during the past 50 years, continue to have a steady immigration flow. From time to time, these cities experience unexpected influxes of refugees, such as the Mariel boatlift during the 1980s, which brought more than 125,000 Cubans and Haitians to South Florida.[12] Emerging gateways are cities like Atlanta; Dallas; and Washington, D.C., which have encountered economic growth and more recently have started to attract more and more immigrants. Similarly, Seattle and the Twin Cities are presently viewed as re-emerging gateways because they too are seeing an increase in the immigrant population. Raleigh-Durham, on the other hand, is a pre-emerging gateway as a result of the growth in agricultural and related jobs, which have drawn thousands of new immigrants into the area. Immigration into re-emerging and pre-emerging gateways is coming primarily from Mexico and Asia, bringing people who are more likely to live in the suburbs, speak little English, are generally poorer than the native born population, and are unlikely to attain U.S. citizenships.[13] As immigrants move into these cities, they also participate in what Schaefer[14] calls *chain immigration,* or the process by which one immigrant, once he or she arrives in this country, sponsors several other immigrants and who, in turn, then sponsor other immigrants.

Compounding the immigration problem is the boost in *domestic migration,* where native-born people cross state borders and resettle in new communities that are simultaneously experiencing foreign migration augmentation. Arizona, Colorado, Georgia, Nevada, North Carolina, Oregon, and Texas have seen increases in domestic migration, or migration by U.S.-born people, in part because of greater economic opportunities, relatively lower costs of living, weather and recreational opportunities, and because some of these states are regarded as "retirement havens." These states now have been labeled "domestic migration magnets" because of the reasons listed above.[15]

As new immigrants and domestic migrants settle in these communities, a phenomenon known as "barbell economies" occurs. According to Frey,[16] *barbell economies* are those in which domestic migrants are highly educated and somewhat affluent, and the newly arrived immigrants are not. These differences, Frey believes, will keep the two groups apart, will segregate them from each other, and may increase the tensions and anti-immigrant feelings proliferating in this country.

Social Work with Immigrants, Refugees, and Unaccompanied Minors

Many professional social workers practice in communities abounding with legal and undocumented immigrants, refugees, and unaccompanied minors. For most social workers, this will be a challenge, as unfamiliarity with immigration laws and policies limits one's abilities as a practitioner. However, as with any new undertaking, it is important to learn, understand, and become familiar with the needs, strengths, and challenges immigrant clients bring to social work practice. It is also vital that all social workers uphold the value that these are human beings who need help, support, and guidance, regardless of their immigration status or how they entered this country. The culturally competent practitioner also knows that a client's immigration status determines his or her eligibility for many social services.

Immigrants

An *immigrant* is any person who voluntarily leaves his or her country of origin, usually in search of better economic and living conditions. Legal immigrants are granted entry to the United States and generally are eligible for services (depending on date of entry into this country and other requirements). Legal immigrants can also be called a*liens*. A *resident alien* is a foreign-born person who entered the U.S. and who has a legal right to be in this country, has valid documents, and is given a "green card." After having his/her immigration status adjusted, the individual becomes a permanent resident.[17]

An *undocumented immigrant* or *undocumented alien* is a person who does not have the legal right to be in this country. These individuals are *deportable,* or people the United States can send back to their home countries. An undocumented person has either entered the country illegally or stayed beyond the date for which he or she was originally given entry. Undocumented immigrants are barred from most federal and state means-tested public assistance, pursuant to the *Personal Responsibility and Work Opportunity Reconciliation Act of 1996 (PRWORA)*. This act also blocks legal immigrants who entered the United States after the date of enactment of this law from most federal means-tested programs for five years, provides states with broad legal authority to set public benefits eligibility rules, and requires Immigration and Naturalization Services (INS) to verify a person's immigration status in order to receive most federally funded public benefits.[18]

Undocumented immigrants are ineligible for Social Security benefits, under the Illegal Immigration Reform and Immigrant Responsibility Act of 1996 (IIRIRA). They are also required to provide proof of citizenship for federal public benefits and higher education assistance. However, this act does exempt undocumented immigrants who are victims of domestic violence from denial of public assistance, and it exempts nonprofit organizations from verifying a person's immigration status of public benefits.[19]

Refugees

A *refugee* is any individual who flees his or her country due to human rights violations. A refugee, according to the 1951 Convention Relating to the Status of Refugees, is anyone outside his or her country who is unable or unwilling to return to that country due to a well-founded fear of persecution because of race, religion, nationality, political opinion, or membership in a particular social group. Children who enter the United States with a parent who is admitted as a refugee are also granted refugee status due to the parent–child relationship. The same principle is applied to husbands and wives.

The number of refugees the United States admits each year is determined in consultation between the current administration and the U.S. State Department. Worldwide, there are an estimated 15 million refugees; the United States typically admits between 50,000 to 75,000 of these refugees each year.[20] According to the U.S. Department of State Bureau of Populations, Refugees, and Migration, the number of refugees who arrived in the United States for fiscal years 2004 through 2006 was 41,150. The largest number was from Somalia (10,357), followed by Russia (6,003), Cuba (3,143), and Vietnam (3,039). It should be noted that Cubans often self-identify as *exiles* rather than refugees.[21]

The Refugee Act of 1980 officially defined the term refugee, established a comprehensive program for domestic resettlement of refugees, allowed people classified as refugees to gain permanent residency after living in the United States one year and for asylees one year after asylum was granted, and removed refugees from worldwide limits on immigration. Services for refugees are often funded and administered by the Office of Refugee Resettlement (ORR) in the United States and through local agencies with which ORR subcontracts.

Asylees and Parolees

There are also political situations worldwide that push individuals to seek entry into the United States as either asylees or parolees. The two terms, however, are not mutually inclusive. An *asylee* is someone who is living outside of the United States and who is in the process of applying to enter this country. Generally, asylees are seeking political asylum or protection from prosecution in their home countries and, as a result, want to legally come to this country. The United States admitted 26,113 asylees during fiscal years 2004 through 2006, the largest number of whom came from China (5,568), followed by Haiti (3,001), and Colombia (2,964).[22] Once admitted, asylees become refugees. A *parolee* is a person who enters the United States for humanitarian reasons and is pending an immigration hearing for final determination of his or her status.

Unaccompanied Minors

Finally, u*naccompanied minors* are children under the legal age of 18 who come into the United States without a parent or legal guardian who is able to provide care and physical custody of that child.[23] Sometimes these children are referred to as "separated children," which includes all children who may have been disconnected from their parents, whether or not they were accompanied by another adult upon entering the United States.[24] Unaccompanied or separated children enter the immigration system for similar reasons as adults: they are fleeing wars or other internal conflicts in their homelands, they are escaping poverty or abusive situations, or they may just be coming in search of their parents or other family members.

Historically, the majority of unaccompanied minors enter this country through planned resettlement efforts.[25] As a humanitarian and developed nation, the United States has been at the forefront of such organized resettlements. Starting with World War II, this country helped resettle British children in the 1940s, during the Battle of Brittan. In the 1960s, in a joint and coordinated effort between the U.S. State Department and the Catholic Archdiocese of Miami, the evacuation and resettlement of more than 14,000 Cuban children took place after the Bay of Pigs Invasion. This effort became known as "Operation Peter Pan or Pedro Pan." It was also the first time that federal foster care funds were used for such a resettlement effort, a fact with which most social workers and child welfare practitioners are unfamiliar.[26]

In 1975, after the end of the Vietnam conflict, more than 2,500 Vietnamese children were brought to the United States during "Operation Babylift."[27]

Today, the Office of Refugee Resettlement estimates that each year between 7,000 and 9,000 unaccompanied minors enter this country, primarily from Central American countries like El Salvador, Guatemala, and Honduras.[28] Like past unaccompanied children, these children are coming to this country fleeing civil wars and related hardships in their home countries.

Although not an exhaustive list, this summary encompasses the most common immigrant populations social workers may encounter in practice.

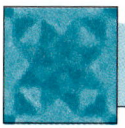

Immigrants and Refugees: Areas of Concern for Social Work Practitioners

As vulnerable populations, immigrants and refugees share many problems for which social workers are the first-line service providers. Some of the most common problems these populations experience include migration stress, grief, culture shock, acculturation strain, trauma, posttraumatic stress disorder (PTSD) and secondary stress, alienation and loneliness, depression, anxiety, guilt, intergenerational family conflicts, language acquisition, economic displacement, racism, discrimination, and oppression.

It goes without saying, however, that these are not the only problems immigrants and refugees encounter. Nor should the practitioner ever construe that they all go through such predicaments. Social work practice with immigrants and refugees requires a high degree of cultural competence that enables the practitioner to assess clients' individual needs and adeptly evaluate, intervene, and mediate the micro, mezzo, and macro systems interventions needed with these at-risk populations. For example, the most commonly observed mental health problems of immigrants and refugees include grief, alienation, loneliness, depression, anxiety, guilt, PTSD, and substance abuse.[29] Social workers providing services to immigrants and refugees will need to keep in mind that:

1. Grief is a natural emotion people experience, but immigrants and refugees may feel it even more intensely because of the multiple losses they have encountered. They have left behind family members and friends, along with everything they have ever known or worked for. Many, if not most, also know that they may not be able to return to their homelands, experience homesickness, and often idealize their previous life. Refugees, in particular, may experience anger, distrust, and confusion, repeatedly questioning whether they made the right decision to flee. Often, because they have fled oppressive government regimes that viewed mental health as a tool for "reforming" political dissidents, refugees may not understand our concept of mental health as a service that anyone should access when needed.[30] It is only when the person begins to put his or her life back in order through gainful employment, making new friends, and re-establishing himself or herself in the new country that these feeling can be reduced and kept at bay.[31]

2. Guilt is another setback plaguing refugees and immigrants. They can feel guilty over what they did or did not do to survive and to get to this country while questioning what else they could and should have done for others. Immigrants often experience

guilt because of their financial inability to provide for their family members back home, a usual reason and expectation for migrating in the first place.[32]

3. Alienation and loneliness often go hand in hand. The major reason why refugees and immigrants have these feelings is because they know they have left behind lifelong friends and family, many of whom were part of a close and tested support system. Upon arrival, most do not speak English nor understand the culture and corresponding social norms. It is akin to being a stranger in a strange land. Combine these feelings with negative experiences stemming from racism and discrimination, and many immigrants and refugees are more likely to need mental health services.

4. Immigrants experience anxiety and depression, in part, because of the constant fear of being apprehended, detained, and deported. Panic attacks and the development of phobias are not uncommon among this group.[33] Likewise, refugees face these symptoms but for different reasons. Any trauma they may have experienced in the past, such as incarceration and torture, may bring on an anxiety attack and exacerbate depression-related symptoms.[34]

5. Depression, by far, is the most frequently diagnosed mental health problem among these groups. It often includes many of the above-mentioned risk factors and can manifest itself in a variety of symptoms. Depression also can be expressed in somatic terms, where the client complains about physical troubles such as lack of sleep or appetite to describe psychological symptoms. Other somatic complaints can include headaches, allergies, and sexual dysfunction.[35]

Unaccompanied Minors: Areas of Concern for Social Workers

Unaccompanied minors are at high risk of needing mental health services because of the precarious nature in which they come to this country. Because "migration is regarded as one of the most obvious instances of complete disorganization in the individual's role system,"[36] it is understandable that it can create tremendous stress and changes for these children.

One problem often faced by unaccompanied minors is *adultification* or *parentification,* where children assume responsibilities and experience role reversals that do not correspond to their developmental or physical age. Puig, for example, found that Cuban children who had come as unaccompanied minors during the Mariel boatlift had significantly experienced adultification.[37]

Other problems unaccompanied minors confront are quite similar to those faced by adult immigrants and refugees. Although children, they still remember "home," the place where they lived with their families and friends. This attachment to the past offers them a sense of security and self-identity that will need to be re-created in the new country. Unaccompanied children, just like adults, also experience loss, grief, anxiety, and loneliness. Many are bereaving their old "self" and life as they knew it. Fear and anxiety about "what's going to happen" is real, as is the loneliness and anxiety that comes from not knowing whether they will ever be reunited with their parents. Alvarez discusses how "relational impasses" occur when children are separated from their parents for long periods and experience feelings of abandonment, exclusion, a clash in expectations, and the sense of becoming strangers to one another.[38]

Social workers may also need to explore how the migration or transit took place. How did this child come to this country? What did the travel experience involve? Did the children understand why they came by themselves? What were the reasons given by their parents for sending them all alone? The possible trauma elicited by this experience must be resolved. Otherwise, the shock and strain of the event will linger and haunt the unaccompanied child. Looking back at his experience of being an unaccompanied child, a Cuban refugee said, "I am a Cuban who is an orphan, even though my parents are still living." Although it had been more than 40 years since he came to the United States as an unaccompanied minor, he was never able to reconcile why his parents sent him all alone.

Unaccompanied children also suffer from *acculturative stress,* particularly if they came at a very young age, as they quickly assimilate and integrate the dominant culture, values, norms, and language. In many ways this is positive, as their "Americanization" facilitates their integration and acceptance by the host society. On the other hand, unaccompanied children feel a responsibility to retain their culture of origin and the language as a way to maintain a connection with their parents and everything they knew and valued before.

Developmentally, it is important for social workers to understand that age is a key factor when working with these children. As a buffer, age can temper what the children understand about the process and reasons for their departure. It can, therefore, be a protective factor. However, it can also be a risk factor, as younger children need the security, love, and attention parents provide. Practitioners must ensure that these basic familial needs are appropriately provided by other caring adults with whom the child can bond and trust.

With more and more unaccompanied children coming to this country, an added and complex dilemma is now facing social work practitioners. As a result of the passage of the Homeland Security Act of 2002, Congress transferred the care and custody of unaccompanied minors from INS to ORR. Part of the dilemma comes from the fact that, even though one could argue these children are "dependent," U.S. immigration laws have not incorporated the "best interest" principle into immigration laws. The "*best interest principle*" in family law has generally required that family court judges balance the following factors: 1) the parent's interest in family integrity, 2) the state's interest in protecting the child, and 3) the child's interest in safety and a stable family environment. Generally, the best interest principle is used when there is a finding in juvenile or family court that a child has been abused or neglected. Otherwise, the assumption is that parents act in the child's best interest.[39]

When an unaccompanied child is apprehended by the authorities, possibly Immigration and Customs Enforcement (ICE), the U.S. Coast Guard, or other government entities, they are placed in a detention facility. Once Homeland Security verifies the age of the child (a minor, under the legal age of 18) and confirms the child's unaccompanied status, it has three to five days to refer the child to ORR custody. Homeland Security also has the legal right to release the child, within the first 72 hours of custody, if it finds a family member or sponsor for the child. If the child withdraws his or her application for admission to the United States, Homeland

Security also can contact the consulate of that child's country of origin to make arrangements for the child's return.[40]

Once in ORR custody, unaccompanied minors are placed in licensed facilities that are operated by agencies with which the government has contracted for social services. These can be group homes, foster homes, or secure detention facilities, if the unaccompanied minor is also involved in the juvenile justice system. Typically, foster care placements are made through social agencies such as the Lutheran Immigrant and Refugee Services and the U.S. Conference of Catholic Bishops.[41] Social workers in these agencies (or in other settings such as child welfare or juvenile justice agencies) need to advocate for these children and utilize exitisintg legal relief to prevent their removal and deportation. The two most common types of legal relief used for unaccompanied minors are to file for asylum or for Special Immigrant Juvenile Status (SIJS) to obtain lawful permanent residency.[42]

Filing for asylum can be done through an affirmative or a defensive application. An *affirmative asylum application* can be filed when a child entered the United States legally or when the child entered illegally but was not apprehended by INS or the border patrol. A *defensive application* is filed when the unaccompanied minor entered without documentation and was caught at the border or within U.S. territory. Most unaccompanied minors, however, end up needing to file a defensive application because they were caught by INS when entering this country illegally. As a result of the passage of the Immigration Act of 1990, undocumented children can obtain legal permanent residency through a Special Immigrant Juvenile Status, or SIJS.[43] Under the conditions of this act, an unaccompanied minor who is undocumented must demonstrate that:

1. He or she has been declared dependent by a U.S. juvenile court; or

2. Has been placed under the custody of a state department or agency by a U.S. juvenile court (if in federal custody, the child must obtain the consent of the Secretary of Homeland Security through the local ICE office before a juvenile court can take jurisdiction); or

3. Has been deemed eligible by a juvenile court for long-term foster care due to abuse, neglect, or abandonment; or

4. It has been determined through judicial or administrative proceedings that it would not be in the child's best interest to be returned to his or her home country or to his or her parents' home country.[44]

Once a juvenile court judge affirms any of the above-mentioned findings, the child can then petition INS for a Special Immigrant Juvenile Status (SIJS) and for adjustment of status to lawful permanent residency. Some unaccompanied minors also seek legal relief by petitioning INS through the T-Visa program, which is part of the Victims of Trafficking and Violence Protection Act of 2000 (Public Law 106-386). The trafficking of children involves the transportation of a child across borders for the purpose of exploitation, usually forced labor, or for sexual activity. Researchers have described it as a contemporary version of slavery.[45]

Social workers attempting to help unaccompanied minors should always seek legal representation for these children, as they have a statutory right to counsel pursuant to Section 292 of the Immigration and Nationality Act. Unfortunately, the law does not provide these children with government-funded legal counsel (Section 292 of the INA, p. 1362). The only other way for these children to have legal representation is by *pro bono* legal assistance, which is difficult to secure. The inability of most unaccompanied children to have appropriate legal representation has made legislators and policy makers aware of the sensitivity of this issue. Social work practitioners should establish linkages with their state's American Bar Association so that they can help these children have adequate representation in the courts. If all else fails, social workers should also go to court and ask that a judge appoint a *Guardian ad Litem* for these children, as it is their legal duty to advocate for the child's best interest in court.

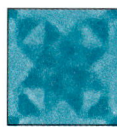

A Case Vignette

The following case illustrates a typical situation facing immigrant families that enter this country illegally. It reflects personal and familial issues for which many immigrant families may need help. Imagine that you are a social worker assigned this case, and consider how you might collaborate with government agencies that have legal and administrative jurisdiction for these cases.

Facts about the Case

Julian and Rosario Chavez (35 and 30 years of age, respectively), came to the United States five years ago with their daughter, Lily, now age 8. The family crossed the U.S.–Mexico border near Del Rio, Texas, and were able to find refuge with family members who had settled in the area years earlier. Once in the United States, Julian and Rosario remained among the many other Mexican families in the community and began working at a local agricultural processing plant. With forged documents, and no one really asking too many questions about their legal status, the Chavez family was able to work and save some money. Eventually, they were even able to move into a rented home of their own, get a small car, and lead a quiet and happy life. Lily, when they first arrived, was taken care of by the "adopted" grandmother, while Julian and Rosario worked. When she turned 5, Lily was placed at a local day care center where she continued to speak Spanish and learn English.

Four years after arriving in the United States, Julian and Rosario decided to move to Colorado, as one of Julian's friends had found a job at a meat packing plant making twice as much as they had made in Texas. By then both Julian and Rosario felt safe and somewhat complacent about being in this country illegally. Many of their friends and family members were in the same situation, also having come without "papers," and they knew that as long as they didn't violate any laws that brought them to the attention of the local authorities, they were out of harm's way.

Moving to Colorado was an exciting experience for the family, as they had heard wonderful stories about the state and the growing Mexican population in this community. After settling in a mid-sized, working class community, the Chavez family felt at home. The community had several Mexican-owned businesses and restaurants. There was also a large Latino community that provided them with social support and plenty of cultural activities. Most important for both parents was that Lily be able to attend a good school because they wanted their only child to have an education. A caring and compassionate Catholic church fulfilled their religious and spiritual needs. In their minds, all was well.

One week before the Christmas holidays, ICE conducted an unannounced raid at the meat packing plant and took into custody every man and woman who had a Latino last name and physically looked Mexican. No distinction was made whether the people apprehended were legally or illegally in this country. In a single moment, everything drastically changed for Julian and Rosario. All they could think about was Lily and what would happen to her while they were in detention. Unable to contact Lily at her school, their worst fears came to fruition—Lily was turned over to the Department of Children Services when school personnel were not able to locate her parents.

Presenting Problems

As a social worker for the Department of Children Services, you have been assigned Lilly Chavez's case. Currently, she is in shelter care, awaiting a hearing in juvenile court, as the department is in the process of filing a dependency petition on Lily. All you know about her is what school personnel have told you and what Lily herself has disclosed. By now, everyone is aware that there was an immigration raid at the meat packing plant, and Lily has indicated that's where her parents worked. The department believes Lily's parents have been detained by ICE. As the social worker, what would you do?

"Working" the Case

The first issue to recognize is that, as undocumented immigrants, the Chavez family has limited, if any, recourses available. INS will detain both parents for entering the country illegally, falsifying their personal and work identification, and for believing they will be a flight risk if released back into the community. However, they are still entitled to legal representation and due process before a federal immigration judge. It will be necessary for you to contact Legal Services to see if there are any immigration attorneys willing to take the case *pro bono*. Lily will also need legal representation by an immigration attorney, since the majority of child welfare and family lawyers have limited, if any, immigration expertise. If Legal Services cannot help, you will need to work with the state's Bar Association as an advocate for the family and ask their help in securing appropriate legal representation. The parents' situation is one that more than likely will result in their deportation. In the meantime, however, you should find a member of the Chavez family willing to take Lily so that she can be released in their custody and removed from shelter care. However, it is in Lily's best interest to remain under supervision of Children Services, particularly in light of the pending immigration court action.

Once Lily is safe and in the temporary custody of a family member, your next move is to determine what Lily's parents want for her. If they are to be deported, do they want Lily to go with them? Or, do they want Lily to remain in this country, even if they cannot stay? This must be ascertained before you can proceed. If Lily's parents want her to remain in the United States and this is something that Lily wants for herself, too, you need to make sure that an immigration attorney works hand in hand with you.

You should do everything possible to have Lily adjudicated dependent, under the principles of "best interest," as it is in her interest to remain in this country. Second, ask the juvenile court judge to appoint an attorney as *Guardian ad Litem* for Lily. Using legal findings in juvenile court, the immigration attorney can then file for *asylum* for Lily, through an *affirmative application*. This means that Lily entered the United States illegally but was not apprehended by INS or any other government agency during or after her entry. The immigration attorney can also petition INS for legal permanent residency for Lily through a *Special Immigrant Juvenile Status*. The basis for such a petition is founded on her adjudication as dependent in juvenile court, the fact that she is currently in the care and custody of a family member and under the Department of Children Services' supervision, and that it is in her best interest to remain in this country. Concurrently, as the social worker, you will assess Lily to determine what other ancillary services she may need such as mental health counseling, life skills training, and group counseling for acculturation stress, educational services, and other services to help her cope and adjust to the situation.

As Lily's social worker, you will need to monitor her parents' situation with INS, as this will be a lengthy and protracted process. Lily, too, will need much care and attention, as she remains in legal "limbo" until her immigration status is determined. If at any time her parents change their minds and want the whole family to return to Mexico (which could always happen), the immigration attorneys for the parents and Lily will have to proceed accordingly. If the parents and Lily are deported, according to current immigration laws and INS policies, they will never be able to legally enter the United States.

The Case Conclusion

Two years after the ICE raid and the detention of Lily's parents, they now have been deported back to Mexico. During this time, Lily continued to live with her aunt and uncle, attained permanent residency, and could travel to Mexico to visit her parents two to three times a year. By the time Lily turns 18, she will be able to apply for U.S. citizenship. Once she is an adult and has U.S. citizenship, Lily can begin to explore the possibilities of sponsoring her parents, particularly if there are new immigration laws in effect that could facilitate the process.

Concluding Comment

This chapter illustrates the need for all social work practitioners to learn and become knowledgeable about U.S. immigration laws and policies. U.S. Census demographers project that almost every state in this country will be affected by immigration. As the immigrant population in the United States grows, as well as the refugee and undocumented minor population, so will the need for the social work profession to have competent practitioners who know how to address immigration issues. If these projections are correct, immigration will not only change the fabric of America but the framework of social work practice, too.

KEY WORDS AND CONCEPTS

"Great Wall of Mexico"
Origins quota
Chain immigration
Immigration gateways
Immigrants

Refugees
Asylees and parolees
Unaccompanied minors
Adultification and Parentification
"Best interest" principle

SUGGESTED INFORMATIONAL SOURCES

Delgado, M., K. Jones, and M. Rohani. *Social Work Practice with Refugee and Immigrant Youth in the United States.* Boston: Allyn & Bacon, 2005.

Potocky-Tripodi, M. *Best Practice for Social Work with Refugees and Immigrants.* New York: Columbia University Press, 2002.

Segal, U. A. *A Framework for Immigration: Asians in the United States.* New York: Columbia University Press, 2002.

Von Drehle, D. "The Great Wall of America," *Time* 171(26) (2008): 28–35.

ENDNOTES

1. Center for Immigration Studies, 2008 http://www.cis.org/immigrants_profile_2007.
2. Robert Frost, "Mending Walls," *North of Boston* (Gloucestershire, England: 1914).
3. Global Security, 2008. http://www.globalsecurity.org/security/systems/mexico-wall.htm.
4. R. Takaki, *A Different Mirror: A History of Multicultural America* (New York: Little, Brown and Company, 1993).
5. R. T. Schaefer, *Racial and Ethnic Groups,* 11th ed. (Upper Saddle River, NJ: Prentice Hall, 2008).
6. The Migration Policy Institute (2005). Immigration Facts. www.migration policy.org/pubs/FS12_immig_US_2005.pdf.
7. Ibid.
8. Center for Immigration Studies. http://www.cis.org/articles/2001/back1101.html.
9. A. Singer, S. W. Hardwick, and C. B. Bretell, *Twenty-First Century Gateways: Immigrant Incorporation in Suburban America* (Washington, DC: Brookings Institute Press, 2008).
10. A. Portes and R. G. Rumbaut, *Legacies: The Story of the Immigrant Second Generation* (Berkeley, CA: University of California Press, 2001).
11. Singer et al., op. cit.
12. M. E. Puig, "Organizations and Community Intervention Skills with Hispanic Americans," in R. Fong and S. Furuto, eds., *Culturally Competent Practice: Skill Interventions, and Evaluations* (Boston: Allyn & Bacon, 2002), pp. 269–284.
13. Singer et al., op. cit.
14. Schaefer, op. cit.
15. W. Frey, *U.S. Census Shows Different Paths for Domestic and Foreign-born Migrants* (Ann Arbor, MI: University of Michigan, Population Reference Bureau, 2008).
16. Ibid.
17. Glossary of Immigration Terms (April, 2008). http://info.dhns.state.nc.us/olm/manuals/dma/fcm/chg/ MA333ofl.pdf.
18. Ibid.
19. Ibid.
20. United States Conference of Catholic Bishops, "Migration and Refugee Services," 2008. http://www.usccb.org/mrs/reshome.shtml.
21. Puig, op. cit.
22. Grantmakers Concerned with Immigrants & Refugees, GCIR, http://www.gcir.org/immigration/facts/refugees.html.
23. UNHCR, "Unaccompanied Minors Refugee Claimants." http://www.ccrweb.ca/uam.html.
24. S. Schmidt, *Separated Refugee Children in the United States: Challenges and Opportunities* (St. Paul, MN: *Bridging Refugee Youth and Children's Services, 2004).*

25. O. Byrne, *Unaccompanied Children in the United States* (New York: VERA Institute of Justice, 2008).
26. M. E. Puig, "The Adultification of Refugee Children: Implications for Cross-Cultural Social Work Practice" in J. B. Torres and F. G. Rivera, eds., *Latino/Hispanic Liaisons and Visions for Human Behavior in the Social Environment* (New York: The Haworth Press, 2001), pp. 85–95.
27. D. J. Steinbock, "The Admission of Unaccompanied Children into the United States," *Yale Law and Policy Review* 7 (1989): 137–200.
28. Vera Institute. http:vera.org/publication_pdf/478_884.pdf.
29. P. M. Arrendondo-Dowd, "Personal Loss and Grief as a Result of Immigration," *Personnel and Guidance Journal* 59 (1981): 376–378; L. A. Rebhun, "Substance Use Among Immigrants to the United States" in S. Loue, ed., *Handbook of Immigrant Health* (New York: Plenum, 1998), pp. 493–520.
30. B. Brodsky, "Mental Health Attitudes and Practices of Soviet Jewish Immigrants," *Health and Social Work* 13 (1988): 130–136.
31. Arrendondo-Dowd, op. cit.
32. Y. S. Ben-Porath, "The Psychological Adjustment," in J. Westermeyer, C. L. Williams, and A. N. Nguyen, eds., *Mental Health Services for Refugees* (Washington, D.C.: U.S. Government Printing Office, 1991), pp. 1–23.
33. K. J. Aroian, "A Model of Psychological Adaptation to Migration and Resettlement," *Issues in Mental Health Nursing* 14 (1993): 379–397.
34. R. E. Garcia-Peltoniemi, "Clinical Manifestation of Psychopathology," in J. Westermeyer, C. L. Williams, and A. N. Nguyen, eds., *Mental Health Services for Refugees* (Washington, D.C.: U.S. Government Printing Office, 1991), pp. 24–41.
35. Ibid.; J. Barudy, "A Programme of Mental Health for Political Refugees: Dealing with the Invisible Pain of Political Exile," *Social Science and Medicine* 28 (1989): 715–727.
36. R. Bar-Yosef, "Desocialization and Resocialization: The Adjustment Process of Immigrants," in E. Krausz, ed., *Studies of Israel Society: Migration, Ethnicity, and Community* (New Brunswick, NJ: Transaction Books, 1980), pp. 85–95.
37. Puig, "Adultification," op. cit.
38. M. Alvarez, "The Experience of Migration: A Relational Approach in Therapy," *Journal of Feminist Therapy* 11 (1999): 1–29.
39. J. K. Dalrymple, "Seeking Asylum Alone: Using the Best Interests of the Child Principle to Protect Unaccompanied Minors," *Boston College Third World Law Journal* 26 (2006): 131–168.
40. C. C. Haddal, *Unaccompanied Alien Children: Policies and Issues* (Washington, DC: Congressional Research Service. RL33896, 2007).
41. Ibid.
42. D. A. Corneal, "On the Way to Grandmother's House: Is U.S. Immigration Policy More Dangerous than the Big Bad Wolf for Unaccompanied Juvenile Aliens?" *Pennsylvania State Law Review* 109 (2004): 609–656.
43. J. Bhabha and S. Schmidt, *Seeking Asylum Alone: Unaccompanied and Separated Children and Refugee Protection in the U.S.* (Cambridge, MA: Harvard University Press, 2006).
44. Immigration and Nationality Act, U.S. Code 8, Public Law No. 82–414. http://topics.law.cornell.edu/wex/immigration.
45. E. M. Gozdziak and M. MacDonnell, "Closing the Gaps: The Need to Improve Identification and Services to Child Victims of Trafficking," *Human Organization* 66 (2007): 171–184.

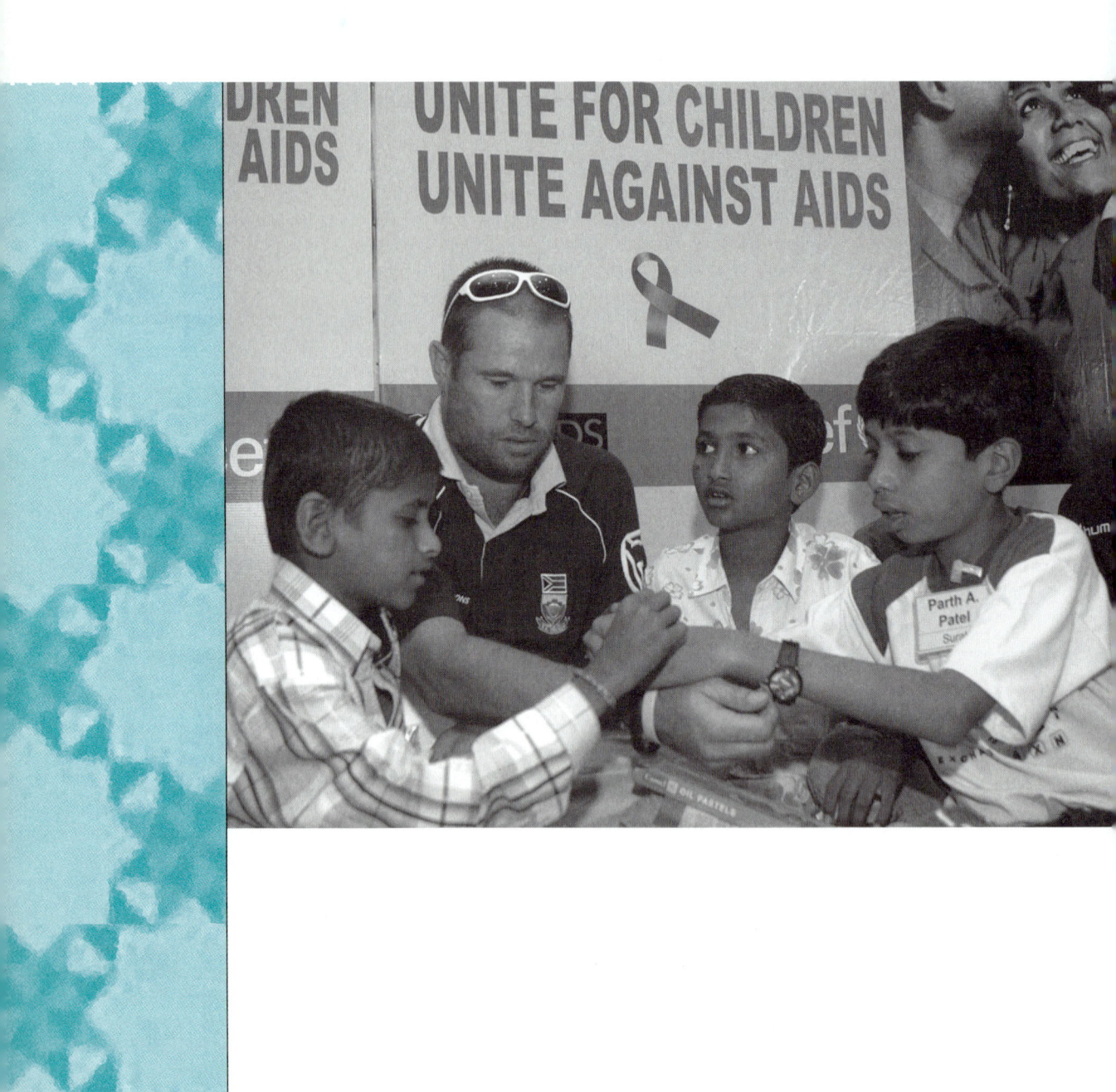

chapter 15

Social Work Becoming a Global Profession

> **Prefatory Comment**
>
> People everywhere need assistance in addressing social issues that affect their lives, as well as help in resolving or reducing specific social problems that individuals from time to time confront. Thus, the need for social work, as the profession dedicated to both serving people and improving social conditions, is global.
>
> Other sections of this book focus on the ways in which social work evolved in the United States. Lest the reader assume that the functioning of social workers in the United States is the only model for this profession, this chapter is concerned with similarities and differences in the expressions of social work throughout the world. In addition, it reflects the growing globalization of social work and the evolving efforts to address international social issues.

With increasing speed, people throughout the world are becoming interdependent. Concerning the environment, for example, global warming (thought to be caused largely by industrial and auto emissions in developed countries) alters the rainfall and growing seasons for crops worldwide and threatens to melt the icebergs and flood coastal cities. In relation to the economy, the extreme poverty experienced by persons in underdeveloped countries often forces them to work for relatively little pay and accept deplorable working conditions, thus reducing the cost of products in developed countries but also contributing to outsourcing of manufacturing and services and the loss of employment in the developed countries. Or the failure to curb an epidemic (e.g., HIV/AIDS, bird flu) in one area of the world causes that health problem to spread throughout the world. Indeed, people are more interdependent than at any other time in history.

Directly affecting the work of social workers are such international issues as refugees and immigration, international adoptions, engagement in wars (e.g., Afghanistan, Iraq), epidemics of diseases, terrorist threats, natural disasters, and so on. International tension increases when some segments of the population conclude that others experience a substantially better quality of life. Although quality of life is influenced by many factors, wealth (or lack of wealth) is often considered a broad indicator of human well-being and a signal for the need of human services. Information accumulated by the World Bank indicates that the gap in wealth between the richest one-fifth of the world's population and the poorest one-fifth is increasing at the rate of approximately 3 percent each year.[1] More specifically, the bottom 20 percent of the population has an average per capita income with a buying power of approximately $326 per year. For the lowest 44 percent of the world's population, the buying power increases to $786 per year. Contrast that with the average income in the thirty-three highest income nations (plus Hong Kong), where the average per capita income is $26,000 per year. The stark difference in income between the lowest almost one-half of the population and the highest one-fifth suggests a substantial difference in many quality-of-life factors. Of the 6.7 billion people worldwide, it is estimated that the following numbers of people experience the identified poverty-related conditions.[2]

▸ 790 million people lack adequate nutrition
▸ 880 million people lack access to basic medical care
▸ 1 billion people lack safe drinking water
▸ 1 billion people lack adequate shelter
▸ 1 billion people are illiterate
▸ 2 billion people lack access to electricity
▸ 2.4 billion people lack adequate sanitation

Clearly, many people are suffering in a world that currently has the resources to improve the well-being of millions of people. For social workers with a global perspective, addressing these conditions multiplies their concerns regarding the prevalence of social injustices in the United States.

Most social workers would accept that some of the wealth in the United States should be reallocated to reduce poverty throughout the world. Some would argue that these funds could come through more efficient use of tax funds by the various levels of government; others believe that corporate taxes or taxes on the wealthy could be increased; and still others contend that even the cost of current wars, if redistributed to the poor of the world, could improve the lives of millions of people and reduce the likelihood of wars and terrorist activities. To use the cost of wars as an example, consider the following data.[3]

6,700,000,000	Estimated world population
$60,000,000,000	Initial Bush administration estimate of the cost of Iraq War, 2003
$600,000,000,000	Pentagon estimate of the cost of first five years of Iraq War, 2008
$2,000,000,000,000	Congressional Budget Office estimate of long-term total expenditures on Iraq War, 2008

The reallocation of the Iraq War funds would provide nearly $9 to every person in the world, reallocation of the Pentagon five-year estimate of actual expenditures would add $90 to each person's income, and the long-term estimate by the Congressional Budget Office would yield $290 per person. Compared to the $786 average income of the lowest 44 percent of the world's population, the funds devoted by the Unites States to the Iraq War could make a substantial difference in the quality life for many people throughout the world.

World Population Changes: Creating a Global Demand for Social Work in the Future

The projections for future population changes suggest additional issues social workers should be particularly prepared to address. It is estimated that, as of 2008, the world's population was more than 6.7 billion people, which is double the population as recently as 1965.[4] It had taken all of human history until 1804 to reach 1 billion people, and the earth easily supported this population. Now, even with vastly increased agricultural productivity, it is recognized that the world's food supply cannot indefinitely support a growing population. Nor can the air support increasing pollution, or the oceans produce a sufficient supply of fish, or the rivers provide the needed drinking water for the people and animals, and so on. As Figure 15.1 indicates, this growth and the ensuing demands on the earth and its people will continue through at least the next fifty years.

There is encouraging news in the fact that, worldwide, the fertility rates are decreasing. Where in 1970 the annual rate of population growth was 2 percent, that figure has now dropped to about 1.25 percent, and by 2050 it is expected to be down to less than 0.5 percent. Although the growth trend looks favorable, the sheer number of people being added places great demand on the earth and its people to accommodate

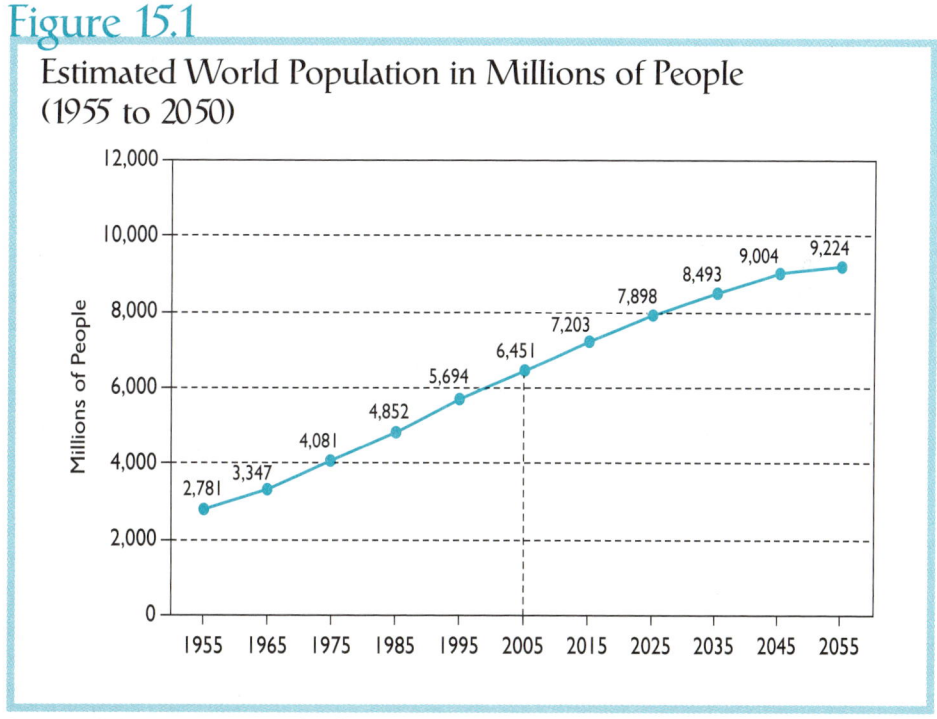

Figure 15.1

Estimated World Population in Millions of People (1955 to 2050)

Source: U.S. Census Bureau, "Total Midyear Population for the World: 1950–2050." http://www.census.gov/ipc/www/worldpopinfo.html.

the increased population. To place this growth in perspective, consider the following: the Census Bureau estimates that in one month in 2005 there were 10.8 million births, 4.7 million deaths, and an overall population increase of 6.2 million people (approximately the number of people living in the state of Massachusetts.[5] Population experts predict that the earth's carrying capacity for people is in the 7.7 billion to 12 billion range.[6] Within a relatively few years (i.e., by 2023), we will reach the lower limit of this estimate, and the projection for 2050 is above 9.4 billion people, well toward the middle of the estimated capacity of the earth to support its population. Virtually every country in the world will be challenged to find the means to purify the air, manage the forests, secure an adequate supply of water, protect the land to sustain necessary food production, provide required energy resources (e.g., for heat, light, and transportation), and—of special interest to social workers—develop social structures to allow the people to achieve quality lives and live peacefully in an overcrowded world.

The problems associated with this growth are more than sheer increases in the number of people. The demographics, too, are shifting, which will require changes in many of our social institutions. Projections by the United Nations indicate that, in the next one-half century, the percentage of children will decline by 9.5 percent, and the percentage of people age 60 and over will increase by 10.6 percent. Those in the "breadwinner" age group will remain about the same (around 60 percent of the population), supporting both the children and older people. What are the implications for these population changes? This aging of the population will have many social implications. For example, today only 10 percent of the older population is made up of those people who draw most heavily on health and human services, that is, individuals ages 80 and older. That percentage is expected to double by the year 2050 and will include approximately 400 million people worldwide. Also, as the population ages, a greater percentage of the survivors are female, who have a life expectancy much longer than that of males. At age 60, 55 percent of the population is female; at age 80, that portion increases to 65 percent; and by age 100, females make up 83 percent of the population.[7] Unique financial, social, and health issues will confront this growing number of older women.

The United Nations highlights three areas in which the changes in age structure will have an impact.[8]

> Population ageing is profound, having major consequences and implications for human life. In the economic area, population ageing will have an impact on economic growth, savings, investment and consumption, labour markets, pensions, taxation and intergenerational transfers. In the social sphere population ageing affects health and health care, family composition and living arrangements, housing and migration. In the political arena, population ageing can influence voting patterns and representation. (p. xxviii)

Similar patterns of change will occur related to increased urbanization and the issues associated with living in overcrowded conditions, the spread of communicable diseases, the protection of women and children from abuses, opportunities for employment and economic supports for those who cannot be employed, care for mentally disabled persons, and so on.

Such global population stresses call for world communication, collaboration, and planning to address impending problems. Social work has an important role to perform in helping the world address these and related issues, but action is sometimes hampered by the difficulty of speaking with a single professional voice. Hokenstad indicates that, with increasing globalization, "social workers need to think about the equitable sharing of both its benefits and burdens so that the marginal sectors of society are not overlooked" and by advocating "on such matters as development, refugees, health care, human rights, discrimination, children's rights, and peacekeeping."9

Social Welfare Programs: A Varied Response to Human Need

Each country, according to its own culture, resources, and the extent of its human needs, has developed a unique mix of social welfare programs. The structures of those programs affect what services can be provided and, for social workers, the roles they will perform. No two countries have evolved identical human services, although they have borrowed ideas from each other.*

Social Welfare in Preindustrial Nations

Several social welfare philosophies characterize the different approaches to human services throughout the world. For example, in preindustrial or agriculture-based societies, social needs are met primarily by families, churches, the few wealthy persons in the society, and various guilds (e.g., agricultural trade groups and civic organizations). This type of society is typically found among developing countries in Africa, Latin America, Asia, and elsewhere. In these societies, direct human services are most likely to be provided on a natural helping or volunteer basis, and social work practice tends to evolve as a macro social change profession. Thus, in many of these societies, social workers' efforts have been orientated toward *social development,* that is, social, economic, and political change to improve basic human conditions.

The country of Rwanda, located in east-central Africa, provides an example of an underdeveloped country and the manner in which very serious human needs are being addressed. As the most densely populated country in Africa, the people of Rwanda find community and extended family networks of kin and fictive-kin relationships the primary resource for meeting basic human needs. The absence of any substantial governmentally administered social welfare services and programs places this responsibility to provide the basic needs such as clean drinking water, basic health care, education, and the provision of adequate nutrition solidly in the hands of the people. Perhaps, what is more remarkable concerning many of the lay people of Rwanda is the high degree of

---

*A particularly informative source when examining social work in several different countries is M. C. Hokenstad, S. K. Khinduka, and James Midgley, eds., *Profiles in International Social Work* (Washington, D.C.: NASW Press, 1992). Included in this book are descriptions of social work in Chile, Great Britain, Hungary, India, Japan, Hong Kong, Singapore, South Korea, Taiwan, South Africa, Sweden, Uganda, and the United States. A second useful source is Pete Alcock and Gary Craig, eds., *International Social Policy: Welfare Regimes in the Developed World* (New York: Palgrave, 2001).

vigilance in their commitment to unity, self-determination, creativity, and collective work and responsibility for rebuilding their country in the aftermath of the genocide of 1994. In spite of this horrific and tragic past and the slow progress toward any comprehensive social service infrastructure, ordinary citizens (e.g., those with little formal education or training) share the little they have with those with even fewer resources (i.e., the elderly, widows, and orphans specifically). This is testament to the strength and resilience of the people and of their humanity, civic responsibility, and duty. The absence of such humane efforts by everyday people would assuredly result in the needless deaths of thousands. Professionally credentialed social work practitioners are virtually nonexistent in Rwanda, particularly among Rwandan natives, and professional training or education does not exist in any formalized manner. In this and similar social welfare systems, professional social work practitioners generally are working through international nongovernmental organizations (NGOs) or other faith- or community-based nonprofit international groups and organizations that require highly specialized and trained personnel to direct, organize, and coordinate their international aid efforts to provide services in these preindustrial countries.

Social Welfare in Postindustrial Nations

Another philosophy tends to emerge when industrialization begins to occur in a country. When this happens, individual and family mobility is required, urbanization increases, and people are viewed as commodities whose time and talent can be bought and sold. There is reliance on the market system to provide people with needed resources because the extended family may not be present or have the capacity to meet its members' social needs. Thus a set of social programs and persons to deliver these programs evolves. It is in these postindustrial societies that professional levels of social work are most likely to develop.

Epsing-Anderson has developed a typology of three distinct social welfare systems that have emerged in postindustrial societies. Epsing-Anderson's typology is based on the analysis of the degree to which the social welfare system (1) treats people as having a right to services, and not just as commodities used in the production of goods and services; (2) redistributes money and other resources to achieve greater equality and reduce poverty; and (3) maintains a balance between the government and private sectors having responsibility for the well-being of people.[10] Examination of how countries differ on these three points (i.e., comparative social welfare) yields the following distinct variations in postindustrial welfare approaches—or social welfare states.

First, the *corporatist welfare state* is designed to maintain existing social class differences and the distribution of resources by the system. Services are distributed primarily by private or corporate entities, and people are not viewed as having the right to services. This approach to social welfare is at the most conservative side of the continuum of approaches and attempts to maintain the status quo. Examples of countries where this approach is dominant include France, Italy, Spain, and Austria. In these countries, social workers' activities are primarily related to delivering social provisions and resolving marriage and family issues. Social work practice under this system is highly specialized, and most recognized social workers are required to hold a social work credential, usually with training at the vocational level.[11]

Second, the *liberal welfare state* is best represented by the United States, Canada, Great Britain, Australia, India, and Japan—although these countries differ in the degree to which each of Epsing-Anderson's criteria for comparing welfare systems is embraced. These programs typically focus on redistributing income to the low-income population; are designed to reinforce the work ethic and view peoples' labor primarily as an economic commodity; maintain minimum standards of well-being through government programs, yet also subsidize the private for-profit and nonprofit welfare programs; tend to stigmatize people receiving services, thus maintaining social stratification; and only minimally treat people as having a right to services. In these countries, social workers provide a range of services, from direct practice interventions to efforts to facilitate at least incremental change in social structures. Professional social workers in these countries hold a social work credential at the undergraduate or graduate level.[12]

Last, the *social democratic welfare state* provides universal services and contends that the peoples' work should not simply be treated as another commodity. Social programs in countries that have adopted this model (e.g., Norway, Sweden, and the Netherlands) attempt to achieve maximum standards of human well-being through universal health insurance systems and are designed to socialize the costs of family living through governmental transfers such as children's allowances, sharing costs of caring for the aged and handicapped, and guaranteeing full employment to all who can work. In this type of welfare system, relatively few of the service providers hold a social work credential. Those who have credentials are prepared at the vocational or secondary levels, except when offering therapeutic services typically related to child behavior issues and parenting problems.

Of special note are Russia, the Czech Republic, Romania, Bulgaria, and other countries formerly associated with the United Soviet Socialist Republics (USSR). During the existence of the USSR, social work and its democratic orientation to helping people individually or collectively address social injustices was banned, and social work, at least as we know it today, disappeared in these countries. Although these are postindustrial countries, social welfare programs, social work, and social work education have just recently begun to re-emerge.

The Emergence of Social Work Training and Education

It is difficult to mark the beginning of a profession. In the United States, for example, the National Association of Social Workers designated 1998 as the centennial year for the profession, presumably because in 1898 the New York Charity Organization created a six-week training program known as the New York School of Philanthropy. If one holds social work up to all the criteria for professions proposed by Abraham Flexner and other experts on the sociology of professions (see Chapter 4), it is more likely that social work in the United States met the criteria to become a recognized profession somewhere around the late 1920s. Nevertheless, the initiation of education and training programs is usually documented and thus is used here to signal the advent of professions. It is informative, therefore, to note a few of the dates when significant training or education in social work was introduced. The following is a partial list of the approximate starting dates for social work education in countries throughout the world.

1898	United States	1924	South Africa
1899	The Netherlands	1931	Ireland
1903	England	1932	Spain
1908	Germany	1936	India and Egypt
1920	Belgium	1963	Uganda
1921	Sweden	1989	Hungry
1922	Chile	1992	Italy

Social work also varies in different countries in the educational levels recognized as preparation for practice. In some countries, it is *training*, with no particular academic preparation (not even a high school diploma required). In others, high school or specific community college vocational training is the requisite preparation, while in many countries college-level *professional education* is the requirement to enter social work. In a few countries, including the United States, a professional master's degree is the terminal practice degree. Nowhere is a doctoral degree the expected preparation for social work practice.

Barretta-Herman's analysis of social work education throughout the world suggests that the educational programs are relatively consistent in the content they offer.[13] More than two-thirds of the respondents to her survey from 35 different countries indicated that the schools required coursework in the following areas: personal communication, research, social and public policy, community intervention, ethnic or culturally focused content, organizational theory, and biopsychosocial theory. In the social work practice areas, there was again considerable consensus in requiring content regarding work with groups, case work, work with communities, marital and family counseling, and work with social agencies. These data indicate there is relatively high consistency throughout the world regarding the fundamental content required for social work practice.

A Global Approach to Social Work

As recently as the late 1900s, a worldwide perspective on social work was accurately termed *international social work* and was concerned with comparing social work as it existed in the different countries and how the different social welfare conceptions shaped social work practice. As social work has matured, it has become possible to address social work from a *global perspective,* that is, as one profession practicing in different countries. However, in some countries, social work is almost entirely offered through government agencies; in others, it is mostly in the private sector; and in yet others it is balanced between the two. Sometimes it is highly clinical and oriented toward change in the person, and in other countries it is mostly focused on changing the structure of the society and the human services delivery system.

chapter 15 ◆ Social Work Becoming a Global Profession

When social work education is required, there is a common set of knowledge, values, and competencies that unite social work activities into a single worldwide profession. In 2005, Weiss[14] published the results of a study in which she surveyed 781 BSW-level student social workers from ten countries reflecting all three social welfare conceptions defined by Epsing-Anderson (discussed previously) and located in North and South America, Europe, Africa, Australia, and the Middle East. The results of this study pinpoint (statistically significant at the < 0.001 level) three fundamental perspectives that serve as the theoretical and value center of social work:

> The major finding of this study is the substantial similarity in the students' perceptions of the source of poverty, the way to deal with poverty, and the goals of the profession.... The similarities in students' views are indicative of a common understanding of poverty as rooted in social or structural, rather than individual, causes and as requiring state intervention for its alleviation. The similarities also reflect the dual commitment of the profession to social justice, understood as the need for the redistribution of resources for the benefit of those who have been deprived, and to (enhancing) individual well-being. (p. 108)

In a world in which people and countries are highly interdependent, the existence of a global social work profession is a step toward addressing the major issues that shape the quality of life for the peoples of the world. To facilitate the development of and advocacy for positions to address these global issues, to encourage sharing of relevant knowledge and skills for social work practice, and to educate social workers who can strengthen the human services throughout the world, several important steps have been taken.

International Professional Organizations

Two international organizations provide the basic leadership for the globalization of social work. One, the International Federation of Social Workers (IFSW), is structured to work through various national professional membership organizations such as the National Association of Social Workers and the professional trade unions of social workers that exist in some countries. Begun in 1928 following the International Conference on Social Work held in Paris, today organizations from approximately eighty-four countries, representing 470,000 social workers, participate in the IFSW. The activities of IFSW include publication of a newsletter, maintaining a commission that advocates for the protection of human rights throughout the world, the development of a statement of ethical guidelines for social workers, and maintenance of updated policy positions on global social welfare issues.[15]

The second important international social work organization is the International Association of Schools of Social Work (IASSW), which was also formed in 1928. This organization now includes 410 member social work education associations (e.g., Council on Social Work Education) and individual schools from 90 countries. The IASSW is concerned with facilitating the inclusion of international content into social work education programs, providing consultation to the United Nations and the United Nations Children's Fund, and facilitating the transfer of academic credit among schools from different countries. With the IFSW, it publishes the journal *International Social Work*.[16]

Defining Social Work Globally

Arriving at a generally accepted definition to describe social work in the United States proved difficult (see Chapter 3). Finding a definition that embraced the common features of social work throughout the world was even more challenging. However, in 2000 the IFSW adopted a definition of social work that encompassed the many expressions of this profession throughout the world. This definition was a major accomplishment that makes it possible for social work to act as a single profession in addressing global issues, to allow workers to gain employment in other countries, and to create educational programs that transfer from country to country. The strong social justice and humanitarian emphasis of social work is evident in the IFSW definition:[17]

> The social work profession promotes social change, problem solving in human relationships and the empowerment and liberation of people to enhance well-being. Utilising theories of human behaviour and social systems, social work intervenes at the points where people interact with their environments. Principles of human rights and social justice are fundamental to social work.

Although this definition is similar to the NASW definition that characterizes social work in the United States, the strong orientation toward changing the social structures that affect people, as opposed to the U.S. emphasis on individual change, is evident.

Values and Ethics Held by Social Workers Globally

The underlying beliefs about the inherent value of people and the responsibility of societies to create conditions in which people can thrive are perhaps the glue that binds social workers together. These basic principles transcend the particular cultures and social welfare systems in various parts of the world and are the most universal expressions of the common beliefs that characterize social work globally.

The International Federation of Social Workers has devoted considerable effort to developing an international code of ethics. Underpinning the statement of ethical principles is recognition that "Ethical awareness is a necessary part of the professional practice of social workers. Their ability and commitment to act ethically is an essential aspect of the quality of the services offered to those who use social work services."[18] This code addresses three sets of basic principles that characterize social work practice throughout the world:

▶ *Human Rights and Human Dignity.* Social work is based on respect for the inherent worth and dignity of all people and the rights that follow from this. Social workers should uphold and defend each person's physical, psychological, emotional, and spiritual integrity and well-being, including respecting the right to self-determination, promoting the right to participation, treating each person as a whole, and identifying and developing client strengths.

- *Social Justice.* Social workers have a responsibility to promote social justice, in relation to society generally and in relation to the people with whom they work, e.g., challenging negative discrimination, recognizing diversity, distributing resources equitably, challenging unjust policies and practices, and working in solidarity with others to break down barriers to an inclusive society.
- *Professional Conduct.* Social workers should act in accordance with the ethical code or guidelines current in their countries that will provide more nationally relevant guidance to ethical practice. However, several universal guides to conduct are suggested, including, for example, maintaining practice competence, acting with integrity and maintaining appropriate boundaries, giving priority to the interests of clients over personal interests, maintain confidentiality, and so on.

Global Views of Social Issues

One direct result of the similar values held by social workers is that agreement has been reached regarding understanding and developing approaches to resolving social problems that are experienced throughout the world. For example, workers and organizations of social workers are concerned with such worldwide issues as achieving and preserving peace, distributing human and economic resources more equitably, protecting the rights and preventing the exploitation of children and youth, enhancing women's status and safety, facilitating international adoptions, and so on. Evidence of these concerns is found in the issues addressed in the IFSW policy statements that have been adopted to date.*

- Health
- Human Rights
- Older Persons
- Refugees
- Women
- Peace and Social Justice
- Globalization and the Environment
- HIV-AIDS
- Migration
- The Protection of Personal Information
- Conditions in Rural Communities
- Youth
- Displaced Persons
- Indigenous People

The value of these position papers is not only to identify topics for which social workers are in general agreement but also to provide a more influential voice to international organizations such as the United Nations (UN). In that venue, social workers have been actively involved with a number of UN-related agencies, including the United Nations Children's Fund (UNICEF), the UN Development Program, the Department of Policy Coordination and Sustainable Development, the Office of the UN High Commissioner for Refugees, and the World Health Organization.

---

*All position papers are available from the International Federation of Social Workers Secretariat, PO Box 6875, Schwarztorstrasse 22, CH-3001 Berne, Switzerland, in English, French, and Spanish. They are also available at the IFSW web site: http://www.ifsw.org/en/p38000079.html.

Employment in International Social Work

Many of the basic principles imbedded in social work are also important contributors to successful international work. Social workers with considerable international experience identify the following as critical in international work: skills in interdisciplinary collaboration, sensitivity to other cultures, attention to the person in environment, searching to address the whole picture, emphasis on self-sufficiency, comfort in serving as a generalist, and maximizing self-determination.[19]

Four forms of international practice are possible for a social worker. One form is to secure a position in an international organization that advances human services on a worldwide basis. The UN serves as the primary agency to coordinate the efforts of the various countries to overcome oppression, facilitate the delivery of health and welfare services that cross international boundaries, and promote social justice. Social work with UN-related agencies such as UNICEF, the Economic and Social Council, the World Health Organization, and the UN High Commissioner on Refugees are examples of such positions.

Second, the U.S. government, too, has positions concerned with international social welfare issues. The Department of Health and Human Services maintains an international affairs staff to give attention to worldwide human services issues, and its Office of Refugee Resettlement is actively involved in promoting the safety, welfare, and rights of refugees. The International Development Cooperation Agency (USAID) administers foreign aid programs in approximately one hundred countries throughout the world, and the Peace Corps has provided developing countries with the human and technical resources to improve their physical infrastructure (e.g., water, sanitation, roads), health care, and human services.

Third, perhaps the most common form of international employment for social workers is to find a social work job in a government or voluntary agency in another country. These roles typically include service provision, consultation, and teaching or training activities. Particularly for countries that are in the process of developing services to individuals and families, the skills possessed by most U.S. social workers are highly valued. The reverse is true, too, for social workers from developing countries, who often have a strong social development background and bring a helpful expertise not typically found among U.S.-educated social workers.

Last, some international social work positions exist in multinational corporations or the U.S. military, which locate personnel in foreign countries. When families are relocated (or left behind), there are inevitable social adjustments to be made. As in other social work practice in business and industry, social workers provide direct services to help individuals and families to deal with their social problems, assist the company in sharpening its cultural sensitivity, and represent the company as a participant in the local community, making contributions to and interfacing with the human services delivery system.

How does one become prepared for international social work? Certainly, the demands on workers differ depending on the nature of a country's social welfare system and the type of position that the social worker holds. Specific preparation, then, cannot be identified that is essential for all positions. However, a few fundamental areas of preparation are somewhat universal.

First, become informed and stay current regarding international affairs, particularly issues of social and economic justice, human rights, and peace. Careful reading of both the social work literature on international issues and the general news sources is essential.

Second, develop competence in the use of one or more foreign languages. Although English is used for general communication in most parts of the world, it is respectful to others to attempt to speak to clients in their language (however faltering) and, particularly if providing direct services, much subtle meaning in communication is lost if one does not know the language.

Third, it is also essential to develop knowledge of the host county's culture. This is prerequisite to helping to avoid the tendency toward *ethnocentrism* (i.e., to believe that one's own culture is superior) and, therefore, to force his or her way of doing things into the other culture. The concept of "the ugly American" reflects the reputation persons from the United States have developed by reflecting such cultural insensitivity. The study of the others' culture and experience is a first step in increasing awareness and avoiding inadvertent acts of insensitivity, such as not recognizing cultural patterns related to age and gender when addressing family members or becoming frustrated by differing commitments to timeliness and punctuality.

Finally, the unique contribution that a professional social worker brings is his or her professional knowledge and skill. Experience in practicing social work after completing one's professional education is prerequisite for most international social work positions.

Although all the above competencies are necessary for successful international social work practice, one research project identified the basic social work principles of "individualizing the client," "maximizing client empowerment," "maximizing client participation," and "maximizing client self-determination"[20] as the factors most associated with successful Peace Corps and USAID projects. Ghavam's study of 74 projects throughout the world found that "the greater the villagers' role and participation in start-up, assessment, and design phases of the projects resulted in more overall success of the development projects." This study also found that the project director's technical preparation for the position, experience in international work, and adequacy in the culture and language of the area were also associated with the overall success of the projects.[21] In short, good social work practice, plus orientation to the language and culture of the specific country, corresponds with successful international practice. The competent social worker already has a foundation for international practice.

Concluding Comment

As technology advances, the world shrinks. The presence of a worldwide economy makes countries increasingly interdependent. The ability of the media to immediately transmit information around the globe creates an unprecedented awareness of events as they occur in even remote areas of the world. And the availability of the World Wide Web and e-mail allows human services agencies and human services providers to exchange information through a virtually cost-free and instantaneous process. Although some parts of the world have not yet fully experienced the Technological Revolution, in many ways international boundaries have become less significant.

Parallel to the diminishing isolation of individual countries, social work, too, is beginning to blur national distinctions and think of itself as a global profession. Writing for the *NASW News,* Sheryl Fred suggests that global social work might accurately be considered an emerging field of practice:

> Counseling victims of the tsunami disaster. Helping immigrants and refugees in the United States receive the services they need. Empowering tribal communities in India to fight for their land rights. All of these are direct practice examples of the international field of practice in social work, a career path that has long been in practice, but is only recently gaining attention from the social work profession as a whole.[22]

A challenge for the next generation of social workers will be to evolve a concept of social work that will bridge the differing philosophies of society's role in meeting human needs and yet maintain the social worker's unique mission as the profession that addresses individual and family needs and, simultaneously, is concerned with changing the society to reduce or eliminate factors that contribute to people's problems in social functioning.

KEY WORDS AND CONCEPTS

Global social work
International social work definition
International Declaration of Ethical Principles for Social Work
Corporatist welfare state
Liberal welfare state

Social democratic welfare state
International Federation of Social Workers
International Association of Schools of Social Work

SUGGESTED INFORMATION RESOURCES

Brinkerhoff, Derick W., and Jennifer M. Brinkerhoff. *Working for Change: Making a Career in International Public Service.* Bloomfield, CT: Kumarian Press, 2005.

Gray, Mel, John Coates, and Michael Yellow Bird. *Indigenous Social Work Around the World: Towards Culturally Relevant Education and Practice.* Williston, VT: Ashgate, 2008.

International Federation of Social Workers. http://www.ifsw.org.

Robb, Matthew. "International Social Work: Go Global!" *Social Work Today* (January/February) 2005, pp. 15–18.

Ramanathanm, Chathapuram S., and Rosemary J. Link. *Principles and Resources for Social Work Practice in a Global Era.* Belmont, CA: Brooks/Cole-Wadsworth, 1999.

ENDNOTES

1. "Global Poverty: The Gap Between the World's Rich and Poor Is Growing, and the Dying Continues," *Public Affairs Report,* 2001 (Berkeley, CA: Institute of Governmental Studies 42(2)).
2. Ibid.
3. David M. Herszenhorn, "Estimates of Iraq War Cost Were Not Close to Ballpark," *New York Times.* Found at http://www.nytimes.com/2008/03/19/washington/19cost.html?_r=1&oref=slogin.
4. U.S. Census Bureau, "U.S. and World Population Clocks—POPClocks." Found at http://www.census.gov/.
5. U.S. Census Bureau, "World Vital Events Per Time Unit 2008." www.census.gov/ipc/www/idb/worldpopinfo.html.
6. Geoffrey Gilbert, *World Population: A Handbook* (Santa Barbara, CA: ABC-CLIO Press, 2001), pp. 16–17.
7. United Nations, *World Population Aging 1950–2050* (New York: United Nations Population Division, 2001).
8. Ibid.
9. M. C. Hokenstad, cited in Peter Slavin, "Profession Has a Global Role," *NASW News* 47 (March 2002): 1–2.
10. Gøsta Epsing-Anderson, *The Three Worlds of Welfare Capitalism* (Princeton, NJ: Princeton University Press, 1990), pp. 21–29.
11. Matthew Colton, Ferran Casas, Mark Drakeford, Susan Roberts, Evert Scholte, and Margaret Williams, *Stigma and Social Welfare: An International Comparative Study* (Brookfield, VT: Ashgate, 1997), pp. 138–140.
12. Judith Norman and Heather Hintze, "A Sampling of International Practice Knowledge," *International Social Work* 48(5) 2005: 553–567.
13. Angeline Barretta-Herman, *A Re-Analysis of the IASSW World Census 2000;* unpublished manuscript (St. Paul, MN: University of St. Thomas, 2002), pp. 16 and 18.
14. Idit Weiss, "Is There a Global Common Core to Social Work?" *Social Work* 50 (April 2005): 101–110.
15. International Federation of Social Workers, "General Information," http://www.ifsw.org.
16. International Association of Schools of Social Work, "Welcome," http://www.iassw-aiets.org.
17. International Federation of Social Workers, "Ethics in Social Work, Statement of Principles," http://www.ifsw.org/en/p38000324.html.
18. Ibid.
19. Sheryl Fred, "Building an International Field of Practice," *NASW News* 50 (April 2005), p. 4.
20. Bradford W. Sheafor and Charles R. Horejsi, *Techniques and Guidelines for Social Work Practice,* 8th ed. (Boston: Allyn & Bacon, 2008), pp. 66–79.
21. Hamid Reza Ghavam, "Characteristics of External Activators in Third World Village Development." Unpublished Doctoral Dissertation, Colorado State University, Fort Collins, CO, pp. 148–149.
22. Fred, op. cit.

part five

Social Work Practice with Vulnerable Populations

The term "vulnerable populations" is used throughout this book. In this context, vulnerable populations are groups of people who are especially susceptible to experiencing problems in some aspect of social functioning. They are populations at risk because of factors in the environment, imbedded in the social structures and stereotypes about these groups, which increase the probability they will experience social problems. The populations addressed in the following chapters have the same universal needs as all humans, but in addition a higher percentage experience the need for special attention by social workers. These are population groups who are characterized by uniqueness based on race, ethnic origin, gender, age, sexual orientation, a handicapping condition, or other characteristics that make them more vulnerable to problematic social conditions and second-class status in the society.

It is important to recognize that the term *vulnerable populations* is applied to groups of people with a common characteristic, where an increased incidence of social issues is associated with people sharing that characteristic. When applied to individuals, vulnerability is often countered by *resilience*. Many individuals overcome their vulnerability, and, although the conditions making them vulnerable persist, they are not affected by them to the extent that they experience the social issues typically associated with vulnerable populations.

In addition to helping people individually address the issues they confront, the social worker also addresses the forces in American society that keep these groups vulnerable. For example, poverty, poor physical and mental health, premature death, chronic substance abuse, and education deficits are all factors that are symptomatic of vulnerability. Some people would argue that these special population groups are vulnerable because they are biologically or emotionally inferior to the majority—leading to a view labeled "isms," i.e., racism, sexism, classism, ageism, and so on. Social workers reject the "isms" and conclude that, when a group consistently experiences a social condition more severely than others, there is systematic bias built into the society's structure that can, and should, be changed.

In the following chapters, important practice considerations for several special population groups are identified as a means of sensitizing the new social worker to the unique characteristics and experiences of each group. Each of the eleven chapters in Part Five addresses a different special population. Chapters 16 through 20 are concerned with groups that are disadvantaged because of physical characteristics such as gender, age, sexual orientation, and physical disability. Chapters 21 through 26 address populations who experience discrimination and oppression due to race, ethnicity, and culture—including the experiences of the Muslim American community (especially since 9/11), Asian Americans, American Indians and Alaska Natives, Mexican Americans, African Americans, and Puerto Ricans. For populations in which the authors did not have sufficient expertise, nationally recognized experts in working with that population were commissioned to write those chapters. To bring continuity to the chapters, each author was provided with guidelines that suggested including demographic information about that population, analyzing the group's experience in U.S. society through a five-level ecosystems model (see Box P5.1), discussing issues in social work practice when working with this population, and providing case material that would help readers recognize the application of these materials to social work practice.

In working with special population groups, once a sound knowledge base is established through the use of a conceptual tool such as the ecosystems model, the social worker is pointed toward intervening at both micro- and macro-intervention levels—attending to both the person and the environment. Usually a variety of assessment tools to identify biological, psychological, sociological, cultural, and historical factors influencing the client's situation are used to know what is needed and, more important, what should be done. Fitting that information into this ecosystems model helps organize these varying factors affecting the clients, thus assuring there is consideration of both individual characteristics and factors that contribute to one's vulnerability.

One useful tool for social work assessment is the ecosystems model derived from ecological theory[1] and general systems theory.[2] This model provides a structured way to examine system interactions that should be considered regarding a client situation. Figure P5.1 provides a synopsis of this model.

First, at the *individual level*, the focus is on the biopsychological endowment each person possesses, including personality strengths, level of psychosocial development, cognition, perception, problem-solving skills, emotional temperament, habit formation, and communication and language skills. Additionally, it is important to be knowledgeable about the person's attitudes, values, cultural beliefs, lifestyle, skills, and abilities; their view of the world; and how they respond to and cope with physical and psychological stress and problems. This listing represents some of the key factors at the individual level; the list is by no means exhaustive.

Second, at the *family level*, the focus is on the nature of family lifestyle, culture, organization, family division of labor, sex role structure, and interactional dynamics. Within a cultural context, each family is unique. It is therefore

Box P5.1

An Ecosystems Model for Assessing Special Populations

Professions require the disciplined used of values, knowledge, and skills when serving clients. One expression of this discipline is in how one organizes information to make an assessment of the client situation. For social workers, that means drawing together considerable information about the client's past and present and the factors in the world around the client that may affect the situation. The next step is to plan interventions to facilitate change in the client and his or her environment. The intervention phase of the change process will usually require the investment of time and energy from the client and resources from the community. Thus an accurate and thorough assessment, as the essential first step in the process of change, is prerequisite to a successful outcome.

Figure P5.1
Ecosystems Model for Analysis of Psychosocial Factors Affecting Special Populations

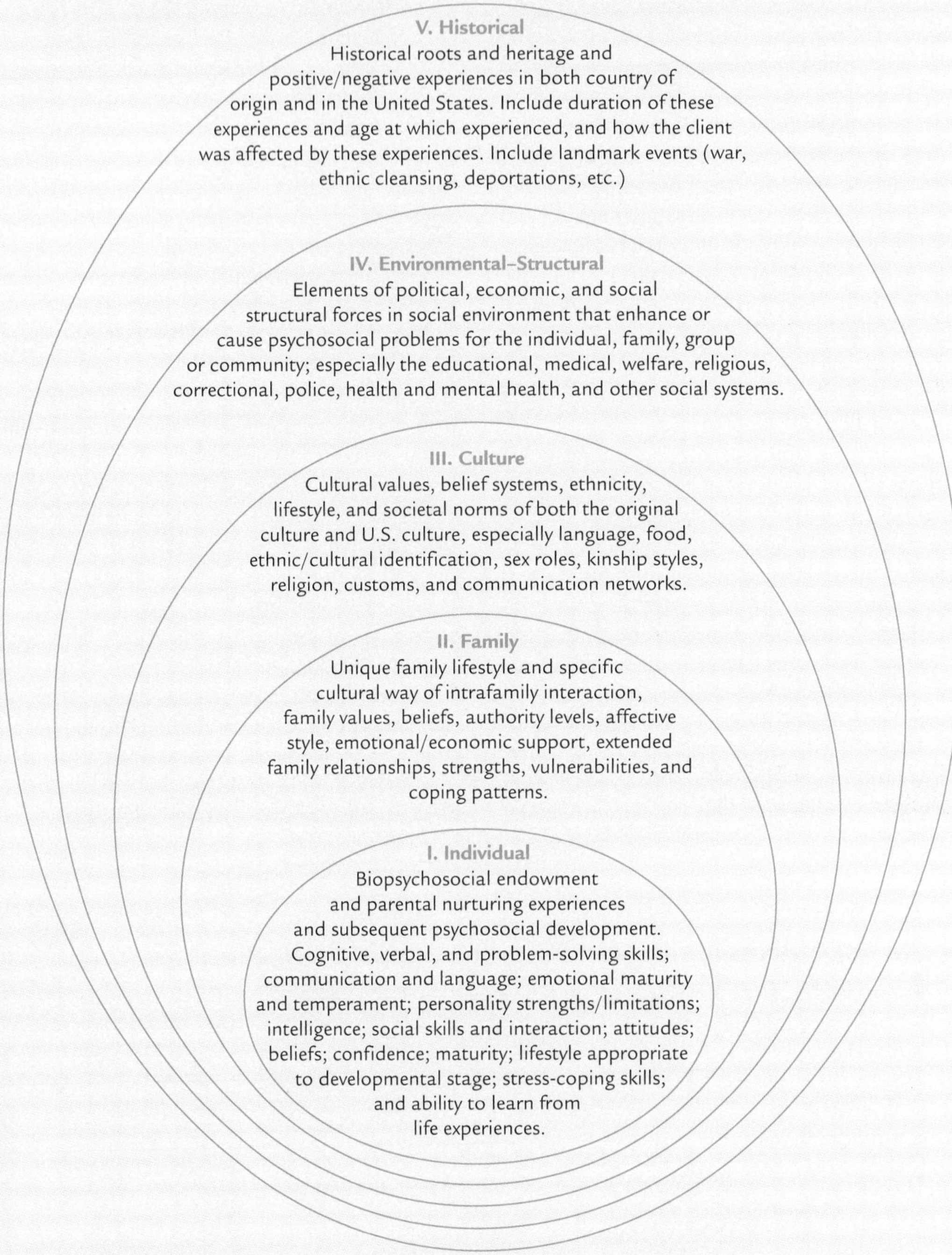

V. Historical
Historical roots and heritage and positive/negative experiences in both country of origin and in the United States. Include duration of these experiences and age at which experienced, and how the client was affected by these experiences. Include landmark events (war, ethnic cleansing, deportations, etc.)

IV. Environmental–Structural
Elements of political, economic, and social structural forces in social environment that enhance or cause psychosocial problems for the individual, family, group or community; especially the educational, medical, welfare, religious, correctional, police, health and mental health, and other social systems.

III. Culture
Cultural values, belief systems, ethnicity, lifestyle, and societal norms of both the original culture and U.S. culture, especially language, food, ethnic/cultural identification, sex roles, kinship styles, religion, customs, and communication networks.

II. Family
Unique family lifestyle and specific cultural way of intrafamily interaction, family values, beliefs, authority levels, affective style, emotional/economic support, extended family relationships, strengths, vulnerabilities, and coping patterns.

I. Individual
Biopsychosocial endowment and parental nurturing experiences and subsequent psychosocial development. Cognitive, verbal, and problem-solving skills; communication and language; emotional maturity and temperament; personality strengths/limitations; intelligence; social skills and interaction; attitudes; beliefs; confidence; maturity; lifestyle appropriate to developmental stage; stress-coping skills; and ability to learn from life experiences.

A special thanks to Professor Lois Miranda and social work faculty and students at the University of Wisconsin, Oshkosh, for assisting in the further refinement of the ecosystems model.

important to know its values, beliefs, emotional support capacity, affective style, tradition, rituals, overall strengths and vulnerabilities of the family, and how it manages internal or external stress. The nature and quality of the spousal relationship and the depth of connectedness to children and extended family are other areas requiring examination.

Third, in all civilizations, cultures have evolved for survival purposes. Each culture develops behavioral responses influenced by the physical environment, and historical and social processes incorporating specific structures such as language, food, kinship styles, religion, communications, norms, beliefs, and values. At the *cultural level* of the ecosystems model, therefore, the focus should be on understanding the cultural values, belief systems, and societal norms of the host culture and, in the case of minorities, their original culture. There may exist a conflict of cultures that may result in mental–emotional impairment due to culture shock. The enhancing and nurturing aspects of the culture(s) should be noted, as well as noxious elements such as sexism, ageism, and racism.

The fourth level of analysis involves *environmental–structural* factors and the positive or negative impact they have on special populations. Environmental–structural theories postulate that many of the problems of vulnerable populations are caused by the economic and social structure of U.S. society. Women, for example, are not poorer as a group than men because of biological or cultural inferiority. Rather, sexism is a U.S. cultural value that is expressed and reinforced through the structure of economic, political, educational, and other social institutions. Ryan states that when U.S. white society looks at the poorly educated minority group of children in the ghetto or *barrio* school, blame is placed on the parents (no books in the home), the child (impulse-ridden, nonverbal), minority culture (no value on education), or their socioeconomic status (i.e., they are socially and economically deprived and don't adequately provide for their children). In pursuing this logic, Ryan adds, no one remembers to ask questions about the collapsing buildings; old, torn textbooks; insensitive teachers; relentless segregation; or callous administrators—in short, the environmental structure imposed upon the person with its accompanying negative consequences.[3] These are important considerations for social workers to introduce into the assessment.

The fifth and final level of the ecosystems model concerns positive and problematic factors in the *historical experience* of the special population members. The historical roots and experiences of female subordination by males, for example, will affect the nature and quality of women's interaction with human services agencies and their representatives. The male social worker may not be aware of his unconscious sexist behavior—the result of decades of conditioning—as he attempts to "help" female clients with their problems. Years of minority group oppression and exploitation, at times including genocide, lynching, and police executions without trial, have left deep scars on minority group members and will affect the way they relate to human services agency representatives. Some elderly whites may recall very positive historical experiences remembering how supportive and encouraging U.S. social institutions have been, only to become depressed and discouraged when abandoned by the government when old. One more example of knowing about the U.S. historical experience is to appreciate the historical experience of immigrants and the countries from which they came.

ENDNOTES

1. Urie Bronfenbrenner, "Toward Experimental Ecology of Human Development," *American Psychologist* 32 (1977): 513–551.
2. Lars Skyttner, *General Systems Theory: Ideas and Applications* (River Edge, NJ: World Scientific, 2001).
3. William Ryan, *Blaming the Victim* (New York: Pantheon Books, 1971), p. 4.

chapter 16

Social Work Practice with Women*

Prefatory Comment

Our examination of vulnerable populations in U.S. society begins with considering issues in social work practice related to women. Although women make up more than one-half of the population, they do not share the benefits and resources of the society with their male counterparts. For example, the median income for married couples with children under 18 was $63,110; for single mothers with children under 18, it was $24,693. Even in the profession of social work, where women make up 81 percent of the licensed workers, when controlled for factors such as age, geographic area, highest degree, employment role and sector, and others, the NASW Workforce Study found an average full-time salary gap between men and women of 14 percent, or more than $7,000 a year.[†] With income being only one indicator of gender bias, it is evident that sexism pervades our society.

When other risk factors for vulnerability are added to the mix, for example women of color, lesbian women, women experiencing disability, etc., the problem is even worse. Further, within male–female relationships, violence is a major issue, especially partner violence, with approximately 1.5 million women being raped or assaulted each year by an intimate partner. This chapter also points out that gender is a determining factor in interactional patterns in families. For example, men who have higher education and employment than women often use this fact as justification for their exerting power and control over wives and children. Correspondingly, women typically have primary responsibility for the unpaid work of childrearing, caretaking, and maintaining the household, thus ensuring their subordinate status within the family. Understanding these and other dynamics is critical to successful social work practice.

---

*This chapter was prepared by Dr. Diane Kravetz, professor of social work, University of Wisconsin, Madison.
†Source: Tracy Whitaker, Toby Weismiller, and Elizabeth Clark, *Assuring the Sufficiency of a Frontline Workforce: A National Study of Licensed Social Workers, Executive Summary* (Washington, D.C.: National Association of Social Workers, 2006), p. 29.

The special needs and concerns of women are relevant for every field of practice, social problem area, and level of intervention. This chapter reviews the political, social, economic, and personal problems of women in the United States; it highlights women's personal strengths and political accomplishments; and it presents the principles and methods of practice that provide the foundation for effective and ethical social work practice with women. In the past four decades, dramatic changes have occurred in women's status and roles. The ecosystems model provides an excellent framework for understanding these changes and the current conditions of women's lives. The model ensures that we fully understand how women's personal issues and problems are inextricably connected to larger social, political, and economic structures and cultural beliefs.

Current Demographics

In 2000, 143.4 million females constituted 51 percent of the population of the United States. White women accounted for 70 percent of the female population; black women, 13 percent; Hispanic women, 12 percent; Asian American/Pacific Islander women, 4 percent; and American Indian/Alaska Native women, 1 percent. The median ages for American Indian/Alaska Native women (29) and Hispanic women (26) were significantly lower than those of Asian American/Pacific Islander (34), black (32), and white (40) women. Just over half (53 percent) of all women ages 15 to 64 were married. A majority of women (61 percent) were in the paid labor force.[1]

Gender differences have largely disappeared at the high school and college levels. Of women 25 years and older in 1998, the large majority of white women (88 percent), black women (78 percent), Asian American/Pacific Islander women (83 percent), and American Indian/Alaska Native women (80 percent) had graduated high school. Only Hispanic women had low rates of completing high school (56 percent). Disparities were more pronounced among women who had graduated college. Asian American/Pacific Islander women had the highest rates (39 percent); white women (25 percent) were also more likely to graduate college than black women (16 percent), Hispanic women (11 percent), and American Indian/Alaska Native women (17 percent).[2] Differences in graduation rates have major implications since median weekly earnings vary significantly by educational level. In 2001, college graduates earned $924 per week, while high school graduates earned $520 and those with less than a high school diploma earned $378.[3]

Gender differences are significant, however, at the advanced degree level, where women received only 28 percent of professional and doctorate degrees in 1996. Of all advanced degrees earned by women in 1996, more than one-third (35 percent) were in education. Women outnumbered men in advanced degrees in literature (72 percent), education (66 percent), foreign language (58 percent), liberal arts (58 percent), and nursing and public health (85 percent). Although their numbers have increased, women continue to receive a relatively small proportion of advanced degrees in business (26 percent), engineering (8 percent), law (21 percent), medicine and dentistry (27 percent), natural science (27 percent), and philosophy (19 percent).[4]

The percentage of women 16 years and older in the labor force has doubled from 30 percent in 1950 to 61 percent in 2000. Labor force participation differs somewhat among black women (64 percent), white women (61 percent), Asian American/Pacific Islander women (59 percent), Hispanic women (57 percent), and American Indian/Alaska Native women (55 percent). The traditional arrangement—married couple, wife not in the paid labor force—accounts for less than one-third (29 percent) of married-couple families with children under 18. Large numbers of mothers with children under 18 were employed, including married mothers (70 percent) and unmarried mothers (79 percent). In 2000, 79 percent of women with children 6 to 17 years of age and 65 percent of women with children under 6 years of age were in the labor force. In 1972, less than 45 percent of children ages 6 to 17 and less than 30 percent of children under age 6 had working mothers.[5]

Even with their advances in education and increased participation in the labor force, women still earn much less than men. In general, women earn about 73 cents for every dollar men earn. In 2000, the median earnings for men who worked full time were $37,339; for women with similar work experience, median earnings were $27,355. In married-couple families, women's employment reflects not only changing social attitudes and their increased access to higher education but also the economic advantage of two incomes. Most high-income households (79 percent) have two or more wage earners, compared with only a small number (7 percent) of low-income households. In 2000, the median income for married-couple families ($59,346) was significantly higher than the median income for a family maintained by a man without a spouse present ($42,129) and more than double the median income for a family maintained by a woman without a spouse present ($28,116). The median income for married couples with children under 18 was $63,110; for single mothers with children under 18, it was $24,693.[6]

In 2000, the large majority of family households (77 percent) continued to be married-couple households. The proportion of married-couple families differed among racial groups, with whites (83 percent) and Asian American/Pacific Islanders (80 percent) having the highest rates, and Hispanics (68 percent), American Indian/Alaskan Natives (65 percent), and blacks (48 percent) having the lowest. Female-householder families represented 17 percent of all families in 2000, whereas they made up 10 percent of all families in 1959.

The most significant change in American families has been in the marital status of the parents with whom children live. Married-couple families with children represented 69 percent of all families with children in 2000, compared with 87 percent in 1970. At the same time, the proportion of single-mother families has more than doubled, increasing from 12 percent of all families in 1970 to 26 percent in 2000, while single-father families have increased from 1 percent to 5 percent. High divorce rates and childbearing outside of marriage are the primary reasons for the rise in female-headed households. White single mothers are more likely to be divorced (50 percent) than never married (30 percent). Black single mothers are more likely to be never married (65 percent) than divorced (17 percent). Hispanic single mothers, who represented 17 percent of single mothers in 2000, were more likely to be never married (44 percent) than divorced (25 percent). The majority (51 percent) of single mothers are white.[7]

Most often, children living with an unmarried parent are living only with their mother (83 percent). Only 9 percent live with their father without their mother being present, with a portion (16 percent) of these fathers cohabiting with an unmarried partner. An additional 8 percent of these children live with their unmarried fathers and mothers. In 1996, many Hispanic (73 percent) and black (54 percent) children and about a third (35 percent) of white children living with their unmarried fathers also lived with their mothers.[8]

One significant factor for the increase in families maintained by women has been the increased birth rate among unmarried women. In 1950, 4 percent of all births involved single women. By 2000, the proportion of births to single women increased to 31 percent. Of these births, 87 percent (1,063,000) were to never-married women, and 13 percent (163,000) were to widowed or divorced women. Among African Americans, births to unmarried women represented 38 percent of births in 1970 and 69 percent in 2000. Among whites, the rates of births to unmarried women increased fourfold between 1970 and 2000, from 6 percent to 27 percent. Rates for American Indian/Alaska Natives increased from 22 percent to 58 percent.

From 1980 to 2000, rates of birth to unmarried Cuban American women increased from 10 percent to 27 percent; Mexican American women, from 20 percent to 41 percent; and Puerto Rican women, from 46 percent to 60 percent. While rates among unmarried Chinese and Japanese American women have ranged between 3 percent and 11 percent, rates increased from 33 percent in 1980 to 50 percent in 2000 among Hawaiian unmarried women. Among teens, 83 percent of births were out-of-wedlock; more than half (54 percent) of out-of-wedlock births were to women who had not graduated from high school.[9]

The increase in female-headed families has also been caused by increasing rates of divorce. For men and women born from 1925 to 1934, only about 15 percent were divorced by age 40. In contrast, for those born from 1945 to 1954, 34 percent were divorced by age 40. By 1996, 40 percent of ever-married white and Hispanic women, 48 percent of black women, and 24 percent of Asian American/Pacific Islander women had divorced from their first marriage. Most separated (64 percent) and divorced (57 percent) women live with their own children under age 18, whereas only about 18 percent of separated and divorced men do.

Highly limited employment options, social norms that assign women primary responsibility for caring for children, and high rates of divorce and out-of-wedlock childbearing are largely responsible for the feminization of poverty. In 1998, black (27 percent), Hispanic (26 percent), and American Indian/Alaska Native (21 percent) women were most likely to be poor, compared with Asian American/Pacific Islander (13 percent) and white (9 percent) women, but most women living in poverty were white (about 7 million).[10] Female-headed families are particularly at risk of poverty, with women of color being most vulnerable. In 2000, for families maintained by single women, the poverty rate was 25 percent, more than double the rate for families maintained by men without a spouse (11 percent) and five times the rate for married-couple families (5 percent). Among families maintained by single mothers, black women (34 percent) and Hispanic women (36 percent) had the highest rates of poverty, while white women (18 percent) and Asian American/Pacific

Islander women (22 percent) had somewhat lower rates. Among families maintained by men without spouses present, black men (16 percent) and Hispanic men (14 percent) had the highest rates of poverty; white (9 percent) and Asian American/Pacific Islander (5 percent) men had the lowest. In every case, the poverty rates for men were substantially lower than those for women of the same race.[11]

With separations and divorce, most women experience drastic declines in their standard of living and income, with their financial problems compounded by inadequate or unpaid child support, divorce settlements that fail to take into account wives' investments in their husbands' careers rather than their own, reductions in welfare programs, and limited employment options. In 1996, 29 percent of separated and 21 percent of divorced women were living in poverty, more than twice the rates of separated (12 percent) and divorced (9 percent) men. A large majority (73 percent) of divorced men had incomes at least twice the poverty level, while just over half (52 percent) of divorced women did.[12] Still, children living with divorced mothers are generally more economically secure than children living with never-married mothers, because divorced women tend to be older, have more education, and have higher incomes.[13] In 1995, about 45 percent of children raised by divorced mothers and 69 percent of children raised by never-married mothers lived in or near poverty.[14]

Women constitute the majority of older Americans. In 2000, women accounted for 59 percent of the population age 65 and over.[15] Significantly more older women than men live alone due to women's greater longevity and the fact that widowed or divorced men are more likely to remarry. Because of their relatively low incomes and greater likelihood of being widowed, older women have higher rates of poverty than do older men. In 2000, among people ages 65 years and over, 12 percent of women were poor compared with 7 percent of men.[16] Many older women lack adequate health care since Medicare does not fully cover, for example, prescription drugs and long-term care, and Medicaid provides additional benefits to only one-half of Medicare recipients who are poor. Older women spend 22 percent to 53 percent of their income on out-of-pocket health care expenses.[17]

Health and Mental Health Risk Factors

Across the life span, women's health and mental health concerns differ from those of men. There are also differences among racial and ethnic groups of women, but these are largely due to economic factors.

Cardiovascular disease is the number one cause of death and disability among American women, with African American women having the highest rates. While the incidence and mortality rates of lung cancer for men have declined, between 1960 and 1990 lung cancer deaths among women have increased by more than 400 percent. Approximately 80 percent of lung cancer cases in women are thought to be attributable to cigarette smoking. Breast cancer is the most frequently diagnosed cancer in women. The incidence is higher for white women than for women in other racial and ethnic groups, but the mortality rate for breast cancer is highest for black women, most likely because, until the mid-1990s, they had lower rates of having a mammogram.[18]

An estimated one-fourth of the 800,000 to 900,000 Americans living with HIV/AIDS are women. Throughout the 1990s, there were significant declines in AIDS-related deaths and in the numbers of new AIDS cases, but these decreases have been much greater for men than for women. Most HIV-infected women are poor and do not have the resources to take advantage of the treatment advances that have led to the dramatic declines in new AIDS cases and AIDS-related deaths. Women account for 30 percent of new HIV infections, which are primarily due to heterosexual sex (75 percent), followed by injection drug use (25 percent). In 1999, African American women made up 63 percent of new AIDS cases among women; white women and Hispanic women each accounted for 18 percent; Asian American/Pacific Islander women and American Indian/Alaska Native women each accounted for less than 1 percent. The majority (58 percent) of new AIDS cases among teenagers were girls.[19]

Large numbers of women are victims of physical, psychological, and sexual abuse. More than half of all working women are sexually harassed on the job, and between 30 percent and 50 percent of female students are harassed at college.[20] More than half (52 percent) of all women have been physically assaulted either as a child or as an adult. One in six women (18 percent) has experienced an attempted or completed rape at some time in their lives. Many of these women (22 percent) were under 12 years old when they were first raped; 32 percent were 12 to 17 years old. Approximately 1.9 million women are physically assaulted, and approximately 302,100 women are forcibly raped each year.

Violence against women is primarily partner violence. Approximately 1.5 million women are raped or physically assaulted each year by an intimate partner. Of women raped or physically assaulted since the age of 18, 76 percent were assaulted by a current or former husband, cohabiting partner, or date; 17 percent were victimized by an acquaintance; and 9 percent were victimized by a relative other than a husband. Only 14 percent were victimized by a stranger. In contrast, men are primarily raped and physically assaulted by strangers (60 percent) and acquaintances (32 percent), not by intimate partners (18 percent). Most of the violence against women (93 percent) and against men (86 percent) is perpetrated by men. Almost one-third of murdered women are killed by an intimate partner, compared with about 4 percent of men. More than 1 million women are stalked each year, and about half of these women are stalked by an intimate partner.[21]

Ecosystems Model

The statistical picture painted above highlights important changes that have taken place in women's lives over the past four decades. It reveals progress as well as serious problems and inequities. The ecosystems model provides a framework for understanding the beliefs, norms, institutional arrangements, and social roles that define and maintain women as a subordinate social group. Each of the five interconnected levels of the ecosystems model (historical, environmental–structural, culture, family, and individual) is discussed below in relation to the role it plays in the social and personal problems of women. Each level helps us understand the persistent and pervasive inequality between the sexes.

Historical Factors

Throughout history, women have been defined as innately and inevitably different from and inferior to men. This androcentric view is supported by socially constructed definitions of women as biologically destined to be dependent, nurturant, and domestic. *Patriarchy* is the term used for the social, economic, and political arrangements that emerge from these cultural assumptions and that give males authority over females and formal power over public policies and practices. Patriarchy is evident in the privileging of male perspectives and needs throughout society.

Historically, women had few legal rights; they were viewed as the property of their fathers or husbands and in need of male protection. Securing women's rights began when the right to vote was extended to women in 1920 through ratification of the Nineteenth Amendment to the Constitution, after fifty-one years of advocacy by feminists in support of women's suffrage.

Until the middle of the twentieth century, social norms viewed paid work as deviant for married women. As a result, most female workers were young, single, and primarily from white working-class, immigrant, and African American families. Some college-educated women chose to remain single in order to pursue careers as teachers, librarians, caseworkers, settlement house workers, and nurses. Also, employment was more common for married African American women and married immigrant women.[22]

A series of changing social conditions made employment socially acceptable and necessary for women, including middle-class, married, white women. These included "labor-saving" devices in the home, recruitment of female labor during the World Wars and expanded employment opportunities post–World War II in "pink-collar" work (clerical work and sales), increased economic need for two-income families, increased educational opportunities for women, a rising divorce rate and increasing numbers of female-headed households, and women's increased control of reproduction. The organized efforts of feminists resulted in new antidiscrimination laws in education and employment; changing views of gender roles; and sweeping changes in women's status and in their roles in public life, work, and in the family.[23]

Environmental–Structural Factors

Women's Legal Rights   Federal legislation and Supreme Court decisions have played a critical role in women's having the opportunity to pursue equality. They have provided the necessary leverage for women's gaining access to and demanding fair treatment in public institutions; changes in public attitudes and behaviors have followed.

Between the early 1960s and the late 1970s, there was substantial progress in advancing women's rights in higher education and in the workforce. For example, Title VII of the 1964 Civil Rights Act prohibited sex discrimination in hiring, firing, promotions, and working conditions. The 1963 Equal Pay Act required equal pay for women and men holding the same jobs. Under pressure from NOW and other women's rights organizations, President Lyndon Johnson signed Executive Order 11375 in 1967, which strengthened Title VII of the Civil Rights Act. This order directed employers who received federal contracts to provide equal employment opportunities for women and to develop affirmative action programs to redress the effects of past discrimination. Other far-reaching legislation included the 1974 Equal Credit Opportunity Act, which allowed married women to obtain credit in their own names, and Title IX of the 1972 Education Amendments Act, which prohibited sex discrimination in education by institutions that received federal funding. Abortions became legalized through the 1973 *Roe v. Wade* decision, although court decisions and legislative policies since then have greatly restricted access to abortion for many women.

More recent legislation benefiting working women includes the Civil Rights Act of 1991, which extended the protection of Title VII to victims of intentional discrimination to allow recovery of damages previously limited to victims of racial discrimination, and the 1993 Family and Medical Leave Act, which granted unpaid time off to care for a sick child or relative without losing one's job. There has also been some degree of reform in the laws and policies governing the treatment of victims of rape, domestic violence, and sexual harassment. For example, in 1980, sexual harassment in the workplace was included as a violation under Title VII of the Civil Rights Act of 1964. The Civil Rights Act of 1991 permitted compensatory and punitive damages for victims of sexual harassment in the workplace, and in 1992 the U.S. Supreme Court ruled that sexual harassment in educational settings was a form of gender inequality and thus was covered by Title IX of the 1972 Educational Amendments Act.

Women in the Labor Force With higher levels of educational attainment, women have increased their presence in the higher status managerial and professional occupations. In 2001, women accounted for 47 percent of those in executive, administrative, and managerial occupations, compared with 34 percent in 1983. In professional occupations, their proportion increased from 47 percent to 52 percent. However, within each group, many more men than women are in the higher paying occupations. Women earn just 67 percent as much as men in the executive, administrative, and managerial occupations and just 73 percent as much as men in the professions. Most women are in lower paying jobs, where they also earn less than men in those same job categories. Women accounted for 45 percent of the sales jobs and earned 62 percent as much as men. They made up 77 percent of workers in administrative support, including clerical, where their earnings were 81 percent of men's. For private household work, which includes child care workers, cleaners, and servants, no earnings comparisons were calculated since very few men (4 percent) work in this area.

Earnings differences between the sexes cannot simply be attributed to differences in degrees and jobs. Women earned less than men at every degree level. With a high school degree or less, women earned about $600 less per month than comparable men. With a bachelor's degree, women earned, on average, $1,400 less per month than men. With an advanced degree, women earned about $2,000 less per month. The fact that men entered higher paying fields only partially accounts for their overall higher earnings. For example, if women with bachelor's degrees had entered the same fields at the same rates as men with bachelor's degrees, the earnings gap would be only slightly reduced, from $1,380 to $1,250.[24]

In schools of social work in 2000, in graduate and joint graduate–baccalaureate programs, 10 percent of the women and 24 percent of the men were at the rank of professor. The median salary of full-time female faculty with a doctorate at the rank of professor was $68,503 for whites and $61,516 for minorities. For comparable male faculty, salaries were $76,435 for whites and $72,000 for minorities. In baccalaureate programs, 9 percent of women and 20 percent of men were professors. The median salaries of white male and female professors with a doctorate were $57,445 and $57,985, respectively. For comparable minority faculty, female salaries were $45,000; male salaries were 54,735.[25]

Cultural Factors

The *gender system* organizes society in terms of gender differences and then values one gender over the other, giving males more power, more prestige, more resources, and more privilege. Cultural ideology serves to "normalize" the ways in which men and women are viewed and valued differently, so that the domination of one gender over the other becomes unquestioned, as does the power of the gender system to define individual behavior, interpersonal relationships, and formal roles. While popular views about women's capacities and proper place in the social hierarchy have been transformed over the past four decades, there is still considerable resistance to the principle of equality between the sexes.

New options and opportunities have opened for women in every arena. For example, in 1981—fifteen years after the founding of the first women's rights organization, the National Organization for Women (NOW)—Sandra Day O'Connor was named as the first woman appointed to the U.S. Supreme Court. Two years later, Sally Ride became the first American woman in space. In 1985, Wilma Mankiller became the first woman elected to lead a major Native American tribe when she was elected principal chief of the Cherokee Nation of Oklahoma. Barbara Harris, an African American, was ordained as the first female bishop in the Episcopal Church in 1989.

Still, evidence of the persistence of traditional, patriarchal beliefs about women's rights and roles is abundantly clear in the antifeminist efforts of the New Right.[26] Their first victory was the defeat of the simple proposition that women should have the same citizenship rights as men. The Equal Rights Amendment (ERA), which read: "Equality of rights under the law shall not be denied or abridged by the United States or by any state on account of sex," remained three states short of the number required for ratification when the deadline for ratification expired on June 30, 1982. To defeat the ERA, opponents promulgated numerous myths about the ERA, including claiming that it would force women into combat. Ironically, one indicator of social change is that, during the Gulf War in 1990–1991, 11 percent of the armed forces on active duty were female, two women were taken as war prisoners, and 15 women died serving their country. By 1994, women were no longer barred from combat in the air and on the sea, and in the Iraq War about 20 percent of the combat support troops are women.[27]

The interconnections of patriarchy with other social inequalities create different systems of subordination for different groups of women. The concept of *triple oppression* is particularly useful in understanding the experiences of many women of color. This concept recognizes "the interplay among class, race, and gender, whose cumulative effects place women of color in a subordinate social and economic position relative to men of color and the majority white population. . . . Their inferior status is reproduced concurrently in the home and in all other social arenas."[28] Within every subgroup of every major racial and ethnic group, female and male experiences differ significantly, with women in each group having problems related to gender inequality within their own group and in society at large. For women of color, issues related to gender must be understood in terms of the overwhelming influence of racism, ethnic prejudice, and class discrimination.

Lesbians are oppressed not only by sexism but also by heterosexism, that is, the belief that heterosexuality is superior to and more natural than homosexuality. As a lifestyle and subculture in which women function relatively independently of men, lesbianism challenges the cultural mandates that women seek personal fulfillment and economic security through heterosexual bonding. By creating hate and fear toward lesbianism, heterosexism maintains gender inequality. Homophobia and fear of being labeled homosexual serve to keep women (and men) within the confines of traditional gender roles. Since the Stonewall riots in New York City in 1969, there has been a proliferation of gay- and lesbian-centered organizations and businesses, the inclusion of sexual orientation in nondiscrimination legislation, increased visibility of gays and lesbians in public life, and broader acceptance of gays and lesbians and their lifestyles. Still, discrimination, stigmatization, violence, and invisibility continue to define the lives of gays and lesbians. Just as there has been organized resistance to the progress that has been made toward gender equality, there has been a backlash against gay rights, including vicious condemnation by the Christian Right and an increase in hate crimes against gays and lesbians.[29]

The Family

As in other social institutions, the gender system is a determining factor in family life. It is in the family where children learn gender role expectations and obligations; it is generally where heterosexuality is taught and enforced. Although there are specific differences based on race and class, gender is the primary basis for determining family roles and responsibilities and for distributing family resources. In the past in most families, men's participation in public life has determined their privileged status in their families. Men's achieving higher levels of education and employment than women provided justification for their exerting power and control over women and children. Correspondingly, women's having primary responsibility for the unpaid work of childrearing, caretaking, and maintaining the household has determined their subordinate status within the family.[30]

However, women's employment has disrupted patriarchal family norms and roles, regardless of class and race. Contributing financially to the household increases women's self-esteem, assertiveness, and independence. At the same time, paid work can be a source of stress. Many husbands resist and resent their wives' increasing autonomy, and, although men's involvement in family life is increasing, the balancing of work and family roles is still primarily an issue only for women.

Despite women's expanded responsibilities as wage earners, they continue to have primary responsibility for household tasks and for meeting the needs of husbands, children, and older relatives. Taking care of young children and providing long-term care for the elderly are stressful and time-consuming and can have damaging consequences for women's paid work, social lives, personal relationships, and mental health. Women assume these family responsibilities with no financial compensation, little recognition, and few public supports. Leaving the labor force at various times in order to care for children and elderly family members places women at a disadvantage in competing for jobs and reduces their earnings and retirement benefits.[31]

With increased education and labor force participation and wider availability of contraception and abortion, women are marrying at a later age, delaying childbearing, and having fewer children. In 1970, the median age at the time of first marriage was 21 years for women and 23 years for men. Now, men and women are marrying in their late 20s (median ages 27 and 25 years, respectively).[32] In 1998, births to women in their 20s and early 30s represented 75 percent of all births. Women 35 to 44 years of age (13 percent) and women 15 to 19 years of age (12 percent) accounted for the remaining births. Almost half of women with a college education gave birth to their first child after age 30.[33] Among women 40 to 44 years old in 2000, Hispanic women had the highest average number of births (2.5). Black women had an average rate of 2.0 births, and white women and Asian American/Pacific Islander women averaged 1.8 births. Among women 40 to 44 years old, 19 percent were childless in 2000, compared with 10 percent of the same age in 1980.[34]

About half of the approximately 5.4 million pregnancies occurring in the United States each year are unintended, and slightly more than half (54 percent) of these unintended pregnancies ended in abortion in 1996. The actual percentage is probably higher, given the underreporting of induced abortions in population surveys. The rate of abortion was highest in 1980, at 29.4 per 1,000 women, and has declined consistently since then. In 1996, the overall induced abortion rate was 22.9 per 1,000 women aged 15 to 44 years. Most abortions (88 percent) are performed in the first twelve weeks of pregnancy; 54 percent occur in the first eight weeks. One-third of women having abortions are 20 to 24 years old, and 48 percent are 25 years old or older; 83 percent are unmarried; 41 percent are white; 61 percent have given birth before. About 14,000 women have abortions each year following rape or incest. It is estimated that, by age 45, 43 percent of women in the United States will have had an abortion.[35]

Lesbian Families Lesbian women have always created families as lesbian couples, with or without children, and as lesbian mothers with children. It has been estimated that gay and lesbian families make up at least 5 percent of all families.[36] On the 2000 U.S. Census, 594,391 households self-identified as same-sex, unmarried partners, of which 49 percent were lesbian couples. Of the lesbian couples, 73 percent were white, 12 percent black, 12 percent Hispanic, 2 percent Asian American/Pacific Islander, and 1 percent American Indian/Alaska Native. Same-sex, unmarried partner households were reported in 99.3 percent of all counties in the United States and accounted for 0.6 percent of all households.

Like many heterosexual women, many lesbians choose to be mothers. In a recent study of black gay, lesbian, bisexual, and transgender people, 40 percent of women, 18 percent of men, and 15 percent of transgender people reported having at least one child.[37] Estimates of the number of lesbian mothers have ranged from 1 to 5 million. Beginning in the 1990s, more lesbians are choosing to adopt or to have children through heterosexual sexual intercourse or artificial insemination. Like other families, lesbian mothers create support networks of men and women to assist them in raising their children. Their extended families of choice, consisting of gays and non-gays, serve the same functions that extended families have traditionally served.[38] Of the research on the psychosocial development of children of gay men and lesbians, "not a single study has found children of gay or lesbian parents to be disadvantaged in any significant respect relative to children of heterosexual parents . . . home environments provided by gay and lesbian parents are as likely as those provided by heterosexual parents to support and enable children's psychosocial growth."[39]

Although there has been some progress, lesbian families continue to be stigmatized and marginalized. Lesbians confront discrimination in employment, housing, education, medical care, and credit with little or no legal protection. Only twelve states and the District of Columbia prohibit sexual orientation discrimination.[40] A majority (62 percent) of the U.S. population has no legislative protection at the state or local level against sexual orientation discrimination in private employment. In most states, lesbian couples are denied the legal and economic benefits and protections extended to married couples, including hospital visitation rights, Social Security spousal benefits, inheritance rights, health insurance coverage, and being able to stay together legally in the United States under immigration provisions for family reunification. In 1996, President Clinton signed the "Defense of Marriage Act," which prohibits federal recognition of same-sex marriages. In addition, 35 states have specific anti–same-sex marriage laws. Only eight states and 83 municipal governments offer domestic partner benefits.[41]

Without the option of marriage in most states, partners of biological parents are seeking joint custody or second-parent adoptive rights. Four states now have laws or regulations prohibiting gays and lesbians from adopting or being foster parents. In twenty-three states and the District of Columbia, the state adoption law permits second-parent or stepparent adoptions by same-sex couples.[42]

With all of these legal and social concerns, lesbians create families that are not much different than others of their race and class in many respects. However, lesbians and their children are likely to be much more open to diversity. Lesbian (and gay) couples tend to have more egalitarian relationships than heterosexual couples. Their approaches to parenting are less likely to promote traditional gender role ideologies in children.[43]

Families of Women of Color For women of color, women's roles and experiences in the family are shaped by the culture of a specific racial or ethnic group as well as by the values, traditions, and social circumstances of the particular subgroup to which they belong. Women of color have always had the primary responsibility for transmitting cultural, spiritual, and family values from one generation to the next and thus have been in the center of the inevitable tensions between preserving cultural identity and accommodation to mainstream American values. Their family life can be profoundly influenced by the effects of prejudice, discrimination, poverty, and, for some, language barriers. Differences in family members' levels of acculturation can add considerable conflict and strain. Extended family households are more prevalent among people of color, partially due to cultural histories and partially due to the necessity of sharing resources with and providing support to new immigrants, the elderly, single mothers and their children, and other family members with financial difficulties.

African American women share many common values and a history of racial oppression in the United States, even though they may represent different subgroups, including those who are U.S.-born descendants of slaves from Africa and those who have emigrated from the Caribbean, Great Britain, Africa, and other countries. African American two-parent families were common during and after slavery until a sharp decline occurred, beginning in the 1960s.[44] By 2000, 48 percent of African American families were headed by married couples, as compared with 56 percent in 1980 and 68 percent in 1970. Social and economic forces have severely limited the number of African American men available for economically and emotionally secure marriages. These forces have included the decline of manufacturing jobs in the cities of the Northeast and Midwest and the accompanying decline in employment opportunities, high rates of unemployment or employment in jobs that offered very low pay and little security, and high rates of male mortality and incarceration.[45] Unmarried mothers had less incentive to marry unemployed men, and married women no longer had economic security as a reason to stay married.

Institutionalized racism has placed extraordinary burdens on many African American women, including poor housing, lack of education opportunities, and poor health care; high rates of unemployment and limited job opportunities; and racial violence. Nonetheless, they have managed to create and maintain strong family and community networks. Because of their long-standing tradition of participation in the paid labor force, African American women are less tied to stereotypic female roles and behaviors and view paid work as compatible with family roles. Of course, their success in the labor force poses the same challenges in terms of balancing multiple roles as it does for other women.[46]

African American families often consist of immediate and extended family members, both kin and non-kin, who have strong bonds and share roles in egalitarian and flexible ways. Single mothers and single grandmothers are most likely to be the heads of households, while the extended family provides support and resources over several households. Grandmothers are held in high esteem and play critical roles, often assisting parents by caring for children and by providing emotional support and financial assistance to all members of the family. The responsibility for caring for children is generally shared by older siblings. When necessary, it is not unusual for children to be adopted informally by extended family members.[47]

African American grandmothers are currently facing a new set of challenges as a result of a growing number of "skipped generation" families in which grandparents are raising grandchildren with no parent in the home. This trend has been linked to increased rates of teen pregnancy, AIDS, mental and physical illnesses and drug abuse among parents, and incarceration of parents. In 1997, African American grandmothers accounted for more than half (54 percent) of "skipped generation" families. White grandmothers constituted the next largest group (28 percent), while Hispanics made up the smallest group (16 percent). Of the grandchildren who lived only with their grandmothers, 63 percent were black. Parenting grandmothers do not expect or plan to mother their grandchildren and have few models or established services to help them deal with the needs of their grandchildren, the parents of their grandchildren, their other adult children, and their own needs as older African American women.[48]

Although Hispanic women may share linguistic, religious, and family traditions, they belong to groups with very different histories in the United States. Many Cuban American women came to the United States as political refugees, beginning in 1959, and are now middle and upper middle class. Cubans who arrived since 1980 are more likely to be economically disadvantaged. Mexican Americans represent many different groups, including, for example, U.S.-born descendants of the original settlers in the Southwest, U.S.-born descendants of Mexicans who migrated to the United States, and documented and undocumented migrant farm workers. Many Mexican American and Puerto Rican women are relatively uneducated and work in low-status, low-paying jobs. Conversely, Mexican American women (16 percent) and Puerto Rican women (20 percent) also hold the higher status and higher paid managerial and professional positions. Of all Hispanic women in the United States, 38 percent are foreign born; most (73 percent) of these women are not U.S. citizens.[49]

The family has traditionally been the center of Hispanic life. *Familismo* refers to the traditional Hispanic view of the family as a source of strength and support. It stresses the importance of family loyalty, mutual assistance, and preserving the family's honor. Familismo refers to relationships within the extended family and includes kin beyond the nuclear family, godparents, and friends who lend emotional and economic support. Within the traditional Hispanic family, *machismo* refers to a man's strong sense of obligation to and responsibility for family and his expectation that he will provide for and protect his family. Men are viewed as the heads of the household and expect to have final authority in family decision making. The complement of machismo is *marianismo,* which emphasizes women's self-sacrifice for the sake of family members. Mothers, and often grandmothers, have responsibility for raising children and maintaining strong families. Marianismo promotes female dependence on men and devotion to husbands and children, and it discourages education and employment for women. Thus, for Hispanic women, preserving their own culture has meant preserving gender roles that are much more restrictive and subservient than those of other women in the United States. The contradiction between economic and educational accomplishment and "proper" conduct for Hispanic women is particularly stressful for women who pursue higher education.

Hispanic women who work outside the home may be isolated by language barriers and in low-status, low-paying jobs with few opportunities for advancement. Their employment is most often viewed by their husbands as an extension of their traditional gender roles, as simply one more way for them to contribute to the well-being of the family. However, with employment, the perspectives and family roles of many Hispanic women have changed. Differences in gender expectations between employed women and their husbands have created considerable stress in Hispanic families. Men's continuing expectations of dominance and control and women's increased independence have contributed to increased incidences of domestic violence and rates of divorce. Divorce itself is seen as a failure to fulfill the appropriate role for women in the Hispanic community and thus as a failure to preserve the family's honor. Divorced women often find themselves blamed and stigmatized by their ex-husbands and by the larger Hispanic community.[50]

Asian American/Pacific Islander women represent ethnic groups that differ by race, language, and culture. Women of Asian ancestry have come to the United States under very different circumstances, with some groups having been in the United States for several generations (e.g., Chinese and Japanese) and others being comparatively recent immigrants (e.g., Hmong and Vietnamese). Although they are often stereotyped as the "model" minority, only some groups of Asian American/Pacific Islander women are highly educated and in high-status occupations. Asian American/Pacific Islander women (41 percent) are more likely than white women (26 percent) to have earned a college degree but also more likely to have less than a ninth-grade education (11 percent compared with 4 percent). A higher proportion of Asian American/Pacific Islander women (19 percent) than white women (15 percent) have incomes higher than $50,000 but also are more likely to be poor (11 percent as compared with 9 percent). Overall, 62 percent of Asian American/Pacific Islander women are foreign born, and more than half (54 percent) of these women are not citizens.[51]

More than one-third (39 percent) of Asian American/Pacific Islander women are in the higher paid managerial and professional occupations.[52] Their upward mobility has been limited, however, by stereotypes of Asian women, by discrimination, and by racism.[53] Other groups of Asian American women who came as refugees or immigrants have limited education, occupational skills, and proficiency in speaking English. Regardless of the number of generations in the United States, many traditional values are upheld, including rigidly defined hierarchical family structures. It is expected that Asian American women will be unassuming, deferential, and subservient to their husbands, to their husbands' fathers, and to their sons, who will become the heads of their families after the father's death. Mothers and daughters are expected to serve as the nurturers and caretakers of the household. Family welfare and status are considered more important than those of the individual. Traditional Asian taboos against taking problems outside the family reinforce traditional gender expectations, since deviating from tradition brings dishonor to the family, not only to the individual woman.

In Asian communities, maintaining large kinship networks is very important, but those networks generally disappear in the United States. Problems are magnified for many refugee women whose families were disrupted through war, refugee camps, and resettlement. Asian American refugees experienced the personal tragedies and traumas of war, including malnutrition, disease, and sexual abuse; the deaths of husbands and children; and the loss of their country, home, family, and friends. With little education, few urban job skills, and poor facility with the English language, many Asian American women rely on their children to negotiate their interactions with U.S. society. The discrepancies between the levels of acculturation between parents and children add additional burdens to women.

Much like Hispanic men, Asian American men consider women's work in small family-run businesses or in other jobs to be an extension of their family obligations. However, women who are working to supplement the family's income are exposed to U.S. values of independence and individualism, which are in stark contrast to traditional Asian values of emotional restraint, social conformity, and altruism; many begin to recognize that their family system is more responsive to the needs of men than the needs of women. Tension in the family increases with women's new sense of independence. Asian American men's loss of power in the family can lead to domestic violence and divorce, especially if they are also suffering from a much reduced socioeconomic status as immigrants or refugees.[54]

American Indian/Alaska Native women represent more than 500 federally recognized tribes, many having different histories, geographic locations, languages, political and economic structures, and kinship systems. It has been estimated that a third live in urban areas, a third live on reservations, and a third move back and forth between the two.[55] Those who live on reservations have particularly high rates of poverty, poor-quality housing, and health problems.

American Indian/Alaska Native societies were cooperative, clan-based systems in which women had considerable authority over political and social life. When the U.S. government assumed control, they imposed capitalism, the nuclear family, and patriarchy. American Indian/Alaska Natives were forcefully removed from their lands, and their children were placed in U.S. government–run schools where native language, dress, and spiritual practices were prohibited. American Indian/Alaska Natives were again relocated from 1945 to 1968 by the Bureau of Indian Affairs from tribal lands into the cities.[56] All of these changes disrupted large, extended kinship networks and women's roles as the transmitters of culture and custom.

Federal policies and practices have contributed to American Indian/Alaska Natives having low rates of graduation from high school, high rates of unemployment, and high rates of drug and alcohol abuse, which have led to high rates of homicide, suicide, and motor vehicle–related injuries and fatalities. Being in the center of family and tribal life, women have suffered the consequences of these social conditions. American Indian/Alaska Native women have the highest mortality rates from alcoholism and illicit drug use of all American women and a higher mortality rate from suicide than the other three minority populations. Their rate of violent victimization is also significantly higher than that found among all other women.[57]

Depending on the tribe, American Indian/Alaska Native women still have considerable influence. Mothers, grandmothers, and other older female members of the tribe are responsible for teaching younger women, passing on tribal traditions and customs. "Grandmother" refers to a number of female elders, not necessarily kin, or medicine women who are considered wise and deserving of great respect. Women are often involved in the day-to-day leadership of their tribes and in political work related to treaty rights and the protection of native resources. The Apache still operate within a matrilineal extended family system in which the grandmother plays a central role, and the family is the center of cultural and political life. In this tribe, wife abuse is practically nonexistent. In other tribes and in out-marriages (where women marry men of other races), family structures are patriarchal, and women face the problems and powerlessness that traditional gender roles present.[58]

The Individual

Because gender is a central determinant of social status and socialization, it influences all of the individual's experiences, including those that contribute to the development of psychological disorders. The influence of conventional gender roles and female socialization can be seen especially clearly in disorders prevalent among women. Two primary examples are eating disorders and depression.

About one in five women will experience an episode of major depression during her lifetime, twice the rate seen in men. Each year, about 13 percent of women have a diagnosable depressive disorder. Suicide is the fourth leading cause of death among women ages 15 to 24 years and the fifth leading cause of death among women ages 25 to 44 years. Depression is almost twice as likely to be reported by female teens than by male teens. Girls are 80 percent to 90 percent more likely than boys to consider suicide or attempt suicide and 50 percent more likely to make an attempt that requires medical attention.[59]

Biological processes and hormonal changes do not explain sex-related differences in rates of depression; they may play a role, however. For example, an increase in depression among girls at the time of puberty is more likely if there are pre-existing risk factors, like rape or sexual abuse.[60] Similarly, postpartum depression is more likely among women struggling to be the ideal mother, wife, and homemaker: self-sacrificing, patient, and always in control. Other risk factors for postpartum depression include being less educated and poor and having less social support, including less support from the baby's father.[61]

For most girls, depression in adolescence is related to their beginning to feel the pressures of conforming to the female gender role. As teens, girls learn the importance of maintaining an attractive physical appearance and are exposed to sexual harassment and dating violence.[62]

Married women are at greater risk for developing depression than are single women. Their primary roles as nurturer, caretaker, and homemaker have low social status and can be socially isolating. Striving to conform to culturally idealized notions of the intensely involved mother can be a source of low self-esteem and anxiety for women who do not have the time, physical ability, social support, or material resources necessary for such intense mothering, which describes the social and economic situations of most women. Stress from combining work and family roles can also lead to depression. Finally, since women tend to be concerned with personal relationships and caretaking, they are likely to be more aware of and affected by the stressful events experienced by family members, coworkers, and friends.[63]

More than 90 percent of people with bulimia nervosa, anorexia nervosa, and binge eating disorder are female. Cultural pressures are related to the prevalence of these disorders. Women are still evaluated based on the extent to which their physical appearance conforms to cultural standards of beauty and femininity; women are still socialized to be dependent on the external approval of others.[64] Eating disorders have also been linked with racism, homophobia, and sexual abuse. Restrictive dieting, bingeing, and purging are common among white women and among women of color.[65]

Low-income women have a high rate of mental health problems, with low-income single mothers particularly at risk. Social and economic stresses contribute to low-income women's heightened risk of distress and disorder. They are more likely to experience crime and violence, the illness or death of children, and the imprisonment of husbands, and they are more likely to suffer from chronic life conditions such as inadequate housing, dangerous neighborhoods, and financial insecurities.[66]

For older women, the stresses of poverty, widowhood, and increased dependency on family members often result in loneliness, isolation, depression, alcoholism, and drug abuse. Also, women are at higher risk of elder abuse than are men.[67]

Racism, ethnic prejudice, discrimination based on race and sex, and racial violence exacerbate the mental health problems of women of color. Many women develop physical and psychiatric disorders because of traumatic experiences as refugees and immigrants. Also, the high levels of stress associated with the process of acculturation may produce a higher prevalence of mental illness and alcohol and drug abuse.[68]

For lesbians, the pervasive homophobia and heterosexism of society can create psychological distress. Lesbians often experience rejection, ridicule, and actual or threatened physical violence. Other stresses include the risk of unwanted exposure and the ongoing process of coming out; discrimination in housing, employment, and child custody; and the lack of legal protection for and social recognition of their partnerships and parental status. These problems contribute to higher rates of depression, alcoholism, and suicide.[69]

Finally, victimization creates profound emotional difficulties for many women. Many victims of sexual harassment, physical assault, rape, stalking, and domestic violence experience high levels of fear and anxiety, shame, social and sexual withdrawal, low self-esteem, and depression. As compared with nonassaulted women, rape survivors are more likely to develop posttraumatic stress disorder and have higher rates of depression, nightmares, physical health problems, and suicide. A history of physical, emotional, and sexual abuse increases the likelihood that women will abuse alcohol and other drugs, which can lead to other serious health problems, including HIV infection.[70]

Intervention Strategies

For every level of intervention, social workers can use the ecosystems model to frame their understanding of how sexism affects the psychosocial problems experienced by women and the social conditions that enhance or restrict their lives. Social workers must analyze and evaluate the personal, social, and economic consequences of gender inequality to determine appropriate goals, targets of change, and interventions with women clients.

To counter the pervasive influence of incomplete, inaccurate, or biased information about women, it is essential that social workers be knowledgeable about current research on gender differences, gender roles, differences in the socialization and life experiences of women and men, and the nature of institutionalized inequality and female oppression. Social workers also need to understand the effects of sexism on their own beliefs, values, expectations, and behavior. They need to identify the range of ways gender bias can influence every phase of the planned change process.

In social work practice, issues related to female socialization and *gender inequality* will be of varying significance, depending on the specific problem or issue. In every situation and for every client, the social worker needs to evaluate (1) the relationships between traditional gender roles and gender inequality and the presenting problem; (2) the ways in which gender bias affects the established knowledge base about that problem and contaminates traditional services and treatments; (3) the relevant theories and research on women, especially those that address explicitly the intersections of gender, intragroup variance among racial and ethnic groups, class, sexual orientation, and other sources of oppression; and (4) the range of methods and approaches that have been developed to deal with the gender-related aspects of the presenting problem and desired outcomes. At best, ignoring the realities and complexities of women's lives, fails to provide clients with the opportunity to reduce their social and economic powerlessness and vulnerability. At worst, social work practice that ignores the social circumstances of women may actually promote female subordination and victimization.

Micro Practice with Women

Social workers use a range of microlevel interventions to help women deal with problems in psychosocial functioning. In the assessment phase, a social worker needs to evaluate women's functioning at home, at work, and in the community in terms of existing gender-role norms and discriminatory practices. Although the immediate target of change is the woman and her family, there must be ongoing recognition of the ways in which a woman's personal problems are shaped by her social, economic, and legal circumstances. Social workers must be realistic about the many ways in which discriminatory employment practices, sex-biased community attitudes, and restrictive family roles create barriers and place limits on women's options for change.

Understanding the full range of factors that shape women's lives, a social worker can extend the range of solutions and life changes to be considered and select interventive strategies that will help clients reach their goals. Social workers should incorporate knowledge concerning female oppression and gender-role socialization in the same manner that they incorporate knowledge concerning all other aspects of clients' problems and situations selectively and sensitively, taking into account the values, needs, concerns, and goals of their clients.

With an awareness that women's lack of social power can generate passivity and dependence, workers should include female empowerment as a central goal. This can be accomplished by sharing resources, power, and responsibility with clients. Interventive strategies consistent with these principles include appropriate self-disclosure by the worker, having the client take an active part in goal-setting and outcome evaluation, making the worker's own values explicit, and emphasizing the client's strengths and assets. Such strategies minimize clients' dependency on the worker, increase the likelihood that clients feel free to reject the values and approaches of the worker, and concretely demonstrate the belief that women are capable of being autonomous and in control of their own lives.

As with all oppressed groups, it is empowering for women to understand the influence of social factors on their personal lives. Social workers can incorporate *gender-role analyses* into their work with women to encourage clients to evaluate the ways in which social roles, norms, and structural realities limit female autonomy and choice. Through this process, women can come to understand how, by internalizing cultural values about women, they sometimes act as co-conspirators in their own oppression.

All-women groups can be used to de-emphasize the authority of the social worker and help members share and understand the experiences that have influenced them as women. Such groups facilitate the respect and trust of women for one another and help them to develop a sense of solidarity with women as a group. Finally, workers can encourage their clients to participate in social action on their own behalf. It is growth-producing for women to engage in social actions designed to change those conditions at work and in their community that most directly have negative effects on their lives.

Being female increases the worker's ability to empathize with clients and to understand and share experiences related to being female in a male-dominated society. In their practice, male social workers must develop ways to ensure that traditional male–female power relationships and interactive strategies do not characterize their work with women clients. They need to recognize that there are limitations in their ability to empathize with women and to serve as role models and that the male worker–female client combination reinforces cultural views that women are dependent on male authority.

In working with groups, workers must be aware of the intersection of gender issues with group dynamics. This includes recognition of the differences between mixed groups and all-female groups in stages of group development, goals and structure, leadership, interpersonal relations, and communication patterns. Workers should be aware of the ways in which groups have been especially useful in work with women with common issues—for example, with substance-abusing women, women with eating disorders, lesbian mothers, unwed teenage mothers, women of color, and low-income women.

Work with families must take into account the social, economic, and political realities that shape family roles and relationships and, conversely, how women's roles and responsibilities in their families support or constrain their participation in public life. In working with families, social workers can provide support and direction to help mothers and their female children become more assertive and self-directed. They can help clients challenge gender-role stereotypes in the family, examine more flexible and nontraditional roles, and equalize power.

In establishing goals, in planning interventive strategies, and in evaluating outcomes, workers and clients must recognize that some changes *will* increase women's self-esteem, feelings of autonomy, and social functioning, but at the same time produce new stresses and conflicts. Presenting a self-image and behaviors that deviate from traditional roles and norms may incur difficulties for women. Some relationships may become more satisfying, but others are likely to become more stressful. Parents, spouses, children, friends, relatives, and coworkers may be ambivalent, if not hostile, toward a woman's desire to make nontraditional changes in her life. Also, because of sexism in education and employment as well as in other social institutions, women may not be able to fully or easily achieve the changes they desire; assessment and evaluation must focus, therefore, on whether women are behaving in a self-directing, autonomous manner and whether their behavior is the result of a conscious understanding of available options and a deliberate weighing of costs and benefits.

Macro Practice with Women

The principles and methods that are incorporated into nonsexist micro practice are also used in nonsexist approaches to macro practice. Empowerment of women and the development of responsive policies and services require that workers emphasize client participation, egalitarian relationships, and collaborative decision making and that they reduce the power and status differences between themselves and their clients.

At the macro level, workers' tasks include assessing the impact of sexism, heterosexism, racism, and poverty on female clients; analyzing the unmet service needs of women and their children; evaluating the presence of bias in the design and delivery of existing services; and developing or modifying programs and services to meet the special needs of women. Neighborhood organizing, community development, and social action provide a range of methods that workers can apply to provide and improve local resources for women. Social planning, program development, and policy analysis engage higher level political processes and public education efforts on behalf of women.

Empowering women includes helping them to gain the power to control their own lives. Community organization skills can be used to help women build and maintain their own groups, organizations, and agencies. Social workers can help women to translate their concerns into specific objectives and goals, to develop their organizational and leadership skills, to increase the resources available to the group, and to identify and evaluate strategies that will help them to reach their goals. Workers' knowledge of funding and resource development can be particularly valuable to such groups.

In community and organizational practice, as in micro practice, there are some circumstances in which a female social worker is likely to be more effective than a male. For example, in the areas of physical abuse, child sexual abuse, and teen pregnancy, a female social worker is likely to be trusted more. Women workers' experience as women, and often as mothers, helps them identify women's needs and concerns and may enhance their credibility. Also, women community organizers, planners, and administrators can work with female client systems without the power-status differential that is inherent when men work with women.

For female social workers, macro practice requires recognition that the workers themselves are likely to be influenced by the sexism pervading both the systems in which they work and those they want to influence. Administration and community organization are viewed as male domains and rely primarily on male models. Further, the policies, programs, and services that are targets of change are most likely controlled and administered by men. Women who enter these domains as workers or who attempt to change them on behalf of their clients often encounter gender-role stereotyping, devaluation, exclusion, suspicion, prejudice, sexual harassment, and discrimination.

Micro Practice with a Battered Woman

The following case illustrates the ways in which women's problems involve social, economic, and legal factors; role socialization; and interpersonal and psychological distress and dysfunction. It demonstrates how micro practice can be used to improve the lives of battered women.

BACKGROUND

Tracy was brought to the shelter for battered women from the emergency room of the local hospital. She had been severely beaten by her husband, who had also threatened to kill her. She had two black eyes, two broken ribs, severely bruised legs and arms, and a broken finger on her left hand. According to Tracy, her husband pulled the phone from the wall when she tried to call the police; it was then that she sustained the black eyes. Fortunately, a cousin came by for an unexpected visit, at which time Tracy's husband fled the house. The cousin drove Tracy and her 3-year-old daughter, Jane, to the hospital. Tracy's husband had taken her purse when he fled from the house. The only possessions Tracy and her daughter had with them were the clothes that they had on.

INITIAL CLIENT CONTACT AND ENGAGEMENT

When she met with the social worker, Tracy expressed much concern about whether this was really the right thing to do. She was angry, confused, and very worried about how she would manage for herself and her child. The worker reassured Tracy that her feelings were common to many of the women when they first came to the shelter. The worker emphasized that the shelter would provide Tracy with safety and security; no decisions about other services or goals would be made until Tracy was ready. The worker's goals were to communicate her caring and her willingness to help; to reduce the fears and anxiety associated with being in this new situation; and to assure Tracy of safety and confidentiality. The worker explained that she would be meeting with Tracy and that Jane would have her own social worker and be part of the children's play group at the shelter.

IDENTIFYING NEEDS AND OBTAINING RESOURCES

At their second meeting later that same day, the worker began to collect information about Tracy's situation and needs for service. Tracy was severely depressed and on antidepressants. Following their session, the worker contacted Tracy's psychiatrist to coordinate services. She also began to work with the county social service department to obtain financial assistance for Tracy's medical and psychiatric care. The worker told Tracy about the range of resources and services available at the shelter and in the community.

PROMOTING CLIENT SELF-DETERMINATION

The worker explained that her role was to help Tracy make decisions about her life, not to make decisions for her. Tracy would need to decide what she wanted to do and what would be in her best interests. The worker emphasized that she would support, encourage, and advocate for Tracy throughout but that it was Tracy's right and responsibility to make her own decisions.

EMPATHY AND EMPOWERMENT

Tracy told the worker that she was very confused, that she trusted the worker, and that she would like the worker to develop a plan for her to leave her husband. The worker reassured Tracy that she appreciated her trust and that she understood her anxiety, but that Tracy would be able to determine her own needs and set her own goals, with the worker's help. Not taking over at this point, although this was the request of the client, began the process of empowering Tracy to take control of her own life.

FACILITATING EMPOWERMENT THROUGH GROUP SUPPORT
The worker encouraged Tracy to join the shelter's counselor-facilitated support group. Here, Tracy was able to see that she was not alone. She saw the ways that other women were able to come to terms with their abuse; she heard from women who had begun to work with lawyers and to find housing; and she began to see some commonalties between her experiences and those of other battered women. The group helped her to feel more optimistic about her own ability to change and to become more assertive. She felt less isolated and received support for her attempts to help other women deal with their issues.

ENHANCING SELF-ESTEEM THROUGH VALIDATION
Tracy particularly liked group discussions about how they had been raised as females and brought up to expect that a happy marriage was a certainty and their most important goal. They described the pressures they felt from family to remain married no matter what. Tracy felt increasingly free to talk and express her own opinions, since she felt support and acceptance from the other members of the group. She became active in helping think through problems and possible alternatives for herself and other group members. The support group provided Tracy with opportunities to share experiences, overcome her social isolation and lack of female friendships, and find hope and strength by seeing the successes of others.

TRANSFORMING FEELINGS INTO ACTION
In their individual sessions, the worker progressed from encouraging Tracy to express her feelings and helping her to clarify emotions to encouraging Tracy to take steps to improve her situation. The worker reassured Tracy that she was not to blame. She was neither the instigator of the abuse nor a willing participant; she was not responsible for her husband's violence. She helped Tracy believe she had the right to be safe and that no one had the right to abuse her.

DEVELOPING CLIENT INSIGHT
The worker also wanted Tracy to recognize that, with new information and options, she was responsible for protecting herself and her child. The worker helped Tracy to understand the dynamics of wife abuse and the ways in which social factors contributed to her abuse. In discussing social factors and common patterns of domestic violence, it was important that the worker not reinforce Tracy's feelings of helplessness. Instead, by understanding these social factors, Tracy could take increased responsibility for the choices she made, thereby gaining a sense of personal power.

PLANNING FOR CHANGE
In considering Tracy's leaving her husband, they discussed her needs for housing, employment, child care, and improved parenting skills, as well as financial aid to cover transportation, medical and psychiatric expenses, and legal assistance. Tracy did decide

to leave her husband, although she was worried about her actual ability to do so. As Tracy set her goals, she and the worker outlined the steps that would be necessary, including Tracy's spending time with workers in other agencies. The worker also introduced Tracy to the legal advocate who worked for the shelter program. She would explain her legal rights, including arrest policies and the legal process of obtaining a restraining order.

Macro Practice on Behalf of Battered Women

Macro social work practice finds the social worker providing services on behalf of people, as opposed to micro practice in which the worker provides a direct service on a face-to-face basis with an identified client. In macro practice, the worker attempts to make organizations, neighborhoods, and communities responsive to the needs of clients. Macro practice may also involve developing or changing policies, regulations, and laws to help people. This can be seen in the following macro case.

DEFINING THE PROBLEM AND NEED

Shelter staff had already established community education programs with business leaders and church groups, and they had recruited volunteers to assist with the twenty-four-hour crisis line. However, several problems were constantly confronting the staff and their clients. All the workers at the shelter were frustrated with the ineffectiveness of restraining orders. Also, they increasingly saw ties between domestic violence and substance abuse, but their programs could not deal with the substance abuse, and the alcohol and drug programs did not address the battering. Finally, they knew that therapists in their community continued to offer battered women marital therapy when it is now widely accepted that it places women in danger to provide relationship counseling or mediation where there has been battering.[71]

DEVELOPING STRATEGIES

The shelter staff decided to meet with workers from the mental health and health, social service, and substance abuse treatment systems to discuss approaches for addressing the psychological, social, medical, and financial needs of women and their children.

The shelter workers also decided to develop a coordinated community response to the problem of domestic violence. They were aware that this is a strategy being applied across the country to improve services and to develop community-wide public awareness campaigns and primary prevention efforts in the schools.[72] "This activity is propelled by an understanding that, in spite of legal advances, unless there is a coordinated community response, batterers will take advantage of the fragmentation, misunderstanding, and bias of the criminal justice system to avoid prosecution and subsequent consequences for their acts of violence, often further isolating, manipulating, and controlling their victims in order to do so."[73] They would involve several key agencies, including battered women's shelters, prosecutors' offices, police and sheriff's departments, programs for men who batter, and other human service agencies.

SYSTEMS ADVOCACY

Staff evaluated what changes in policies they should address at the macro level, advocating on behalf of an entire population rather than advocating only on behalf of individual women.

With workers from other agencies, they reviewed the changes that systems advocacy has accomplished elsewhere. These included waivers to the work requirement for battered women applying for welfare; collaborations between advocates and child welfare agencies to prevent abusers from using children to punish victims for leaving or to coerce them to return; routine screening for domestic violence in medical settings; and provision of immediate advocacy initiated by the advocacy program upon notification by law enforcement, instead of waiting for the victim to initiate contact. They discussed the need for new arrest policy legislation that distinguishes victim's self-defense violence from the primary aggressor assault and battering. They were aware that police are increasingly arresting battered women for allegedly assaulting their partners, which makes battered women much more vulnerable to future abuse.[74]

PLANNING/IMPLEMENTATION/EVALUATION

Over the next months, representatives from each agency will meet together to establish a common philosophy and a set of policies and procedures that will provide individual and systems advocacy as part of a coordinated community response to domestic violence. The group will be responsible for developing strategies to implement policy changes and to obtain feedback from advocates and victims on the impact of these changes.[75]

Emerging Issues and Trends

There have been profound changes in women's rights and status in the United States. Women from many social groups have more freedom to make choices about education, sexuality, marriage, childbearing, parenting, and paid employment. There is less tolerance of violence against women. There is more acceptance of lesbians and lesbian lifestyles. There is increased understanding of the common and unique experiences of different groups of women.[76] Still, we are far from achieving equality for women. Women who are not attached to men are poorer than those who are, and women of color are poorer than white women. Health care is inaccessible and inadequate for many women. Most employed women continue to be in sex-segregated, low-wage jobs. Compared with men, women continue to have less independence and fewer resources.

The profession of social work has a major role to play in the design and implementation of social policies, programs, and services. The feminization of poverty will continue to dominate the focus of social welfare policies and programs. Divorce and out-of-wedlock pregnancies, sex segregation and discrimination in the labor force, and the lack of federal family-support policies will maintain women's disadvantaged status. Our challenge is to find ways to support the needs of employed women and at the same time create alternate approaches to support childrearing and caregiving. By developing strategies for eliminating traditional gender role socialization and inequality, social workers can alter the conditions that contribute to female victimization as well as debilitating health and mental health problems for women.

Concluding Comment

Throughout the 1980s and 1990s, legislation and court decisions on affirmative action, abortion rights, discrimination in education and employment, and welfare narrowed women's rights and options. With the increased strength of the New Right and the backlash against feminism at the beginning of the new millennium, it will be important that social workers join with other groups concerned with social justice to protect the gains of the past.

Most important, social workers need to eliminate gender inequality within the profession as it affects the lives of female clients and workers. In evaluating services and programs, workers need to understand gender, race, class, sexual orientation, age, and disability status as interconnected sources of female subordination, and that meaningful change for women must take into account the multiple systems of domination that operate in women's lives. Social workers must be knowledgeable about the relationships between female subordination, women's problems, and social work services. They must proactively work to eliminate male dominance in schools of social work and in social work agencies and organizations. Until these conditions are met, we cannot presume that we have the theoretical, empirical, and ethical base for our practice with women. To develop meaningful and nonoppressive policies, services, programs, and interventions for women, social workers must work to eliminate stereotyping and discrimination for clients and women social workers as well.

KEYWORDS AND CONCEPTS

Women's legal rights
Gender system
Gender inequality
Gender-role analysis

Lesbians
Triple Oppression
Violence against women
Patriarchy

SUGGESTED INFORMATION SOURCES

Adams, D., ed. *Health Issues for Women of Color: A Cultural Diversity Perspective.* Thousand Oaks, CA: Sage, 1995.

Bricker-Jenkins, M., N. Hooyman, and N. Gottlieb, eds. *Feminist Social Work Practice in Clinical Settings.* Newbury Park, CA: Sage, 1991.

Julia, M. *Constructing Gender: Multicultural Perspectives in Working with Women.* Belmont, CA: Wadsworth, 2000.

Renzetti, C., J. Edleson, and R. Bergen, eds. *Sourcebook on Violence Against Women.* Thousand Oaks, CA: Sage, 2001.

Rosen, R. *The World Split Open: How the Modern Women's Movement Changed America.* New York: Viking Press, 2000.

Straussner, S., and S. Brown, eds. *The Handbook of Addiction Treatment for Women: Theory and Practice.* San Francisco: Jossey-Bass, 2002.

Van Den Bergh, N., ed. *Feminist Practice in the 21st Century.* Washington, D.C.: NASW Press, 1995.

ENDNOTES

1. U.S. Census Bureau, *Women in the United States: March 2000* (PPL-121), Internet release date: March 15, 2001.
2. Henry J. Kaiser Family Foundation estimates based on Urban Institute analyses of the March 1999 Current Population Survey, U.S. Bureau of the Census.
3. U.S. Department of Labor, *Highlights of Women's Earnings in 2001,* Report 960 (Washington, D.C.: U.S. Government Printing Office, May 2002).
4. U.S. Census Bureau, *What's It Worth? Field of Training and Economic Status,* Current Population Reports, Series P70-72 (Washington, D.C.: U.S. Government Printing Office, April 2001).
5. U.S. Department of Labor, *Employment Characteristics of Families in 2001,* Current Population Survey, Internet release date: March 29, 2002; S. S. Dhooper and S. E. Moore, *Social Work Practice with Culturally Diverse People* (Thousand Oaks, CA: Sage, 2001).
6. U.S. Census Bureau, *Money Income in the United States: 2000,* Current Population Reports, Series P60-213 (Washington, D.C.: U.S. Government Printing Office, September 2001).
7. U.S. Census Bureau, *America's Families and Living Arrangements: 2000,* Current Population Reports, Series P20-537 (Washington, D.C.: U.S. Government Printing Office, June 2001); U.S. Census Bureau, *Census Facts for Native American Month (November 1–30, 1997),* Press Release, October 31, 1997.
8. U.S. Census Bureau, *Living Arrangements of Children: 1996,* Current Population Reports, Series P70-74 (Washington, D.C.: U.S. Government Printing Office, April 2001).
9. U.S. Census Bureau, *Fertility of American Women: June 2000,* Current Population Reports, Series P20-543RV (Washington, D.C.: U.S. Government Printing Office, October 2001); National Center for Health Statistics, *Chartbook on Trends in the Health of Americans: Health, United States, 2002* (Washington, D.C.: U.S. Government Printing Office, 2002).
10. D. Misra, ed., *Women's Health Data Book: A Profile of Women's Health in the United States* (Washington, D.C.: Jacobs Institute of Women's Health and The Henry J. Kaiser Family Foundation, 2001).
11. U.S. Census Bureau, *Poverty in the United States: 2001,* Current Population Reports, Series P60-219 (Washington, D.C.: U.S. Government Printing Office, 2002).
12. U.S. Census Bureau, *Number, Timing, and Duration of Marriages and Divorces: 1996,* Current Population Reports, Series P70-80 (Washington, D.C.: U.S. Government Printing Office, February 2002).

13. U.S. Census Bureau, *America's Families and Living Arrangements: 2000,* op. cit.
14. U.S. Census Bureau, *Marital Status and Living Arrangements: March 1995 (Update),* Current Population Reports, Series P20-491 (Washington, D.C.: U.S. Government Printing Office, December 1996).
15. U.S. Census Bureau, Census 2000, Summary File 1, Table 1, Total Population by Age and Sex for the United States: 2000.
16. U.S. Census Bureau, *Women in the United States: March 2000* (PPL-121), Internet release date: March 15, 2001.
17. Misra, op. cit.
18. Misra, op. cit.
19. The Henry J. Kaiser Family Foundation, *Fact Sheet: Women and HIV/AIDS,* May 2001.
20. B. M. Britton, "Sexual Harassment," in S. Ruzek, V. Olesen, and A. Clarke, eds., *Women's Health: Complexities and Differences* (Columbus: Ohio State University Press, 1997), pp. 510–519.
21. U.S. Department of Justice, *Intimate Partner Violence,* Bureau of Justice Statistics, NCJ 178247, (Washington, D.C.: National Institute of Justice, May 2000); U.S. Department of Justice, *Full Report of the Prevalence, Incidence, and Consequences of Violence Against Women: Findings from the National Violence Against Women Survey,* NCJ183781 (Washington, D.C.: National Institute of Justice, November 2000); U.S. Department of Justice, *Extent, Nature, and Consequences of Intimate Partner Violence: Findings from the National Violence Against Women Survey,* NCJ 181867 (Washington, D.C.: National Institute of Justice, July 2000).
22. V. Sapiro, *Women in American Society* (Mountain View, CA: Mayfield Publishing, 1994); M. Zinn and D. Eitzen, *Diversity in Families* (New York: Addison Wesley Longman, 1999).
23. A. Kessler-Harris, *Securing Equity* (New York: Oxford University Press, 2001); R. Rosen, *The World Split Open: How the Modern Women's Movement Changed America* (New York: Viking Press, 2000); Sapiro, op. cit., 1994; Zinn and Eitzen, op. cit.
24. U.S. Census Bureau, *What's It Worth? Field of Training and Economic Status,* op. cit.
25. T. Lennon, *Statistics on Social Work Education in the United States: 2000* (Alexandria, VA: Council on Social Work Education, 2002).
26. S. Faludi, *Backlash: The Undeclared War Against American Women* (New York: Crown, 1991).
27. D. Moniz, "Public Backs Female Troops in Iraq: But Not in Ground Force: (*USA Today,* 5/25/05), http://www.usatoday.com/news/world/iraq/2005-05-25-women-combat_x.htm
28. D. Segura, "Chicanas and Triple Oppression in the Labor Force," in T. Cordova, N. Cantu, G. Cardenas, J. Garcia, and C. Sierra, eds., *Chicana Voices: Intersections of Class, Race, and Gender* (Austin, TX: CMAS Publications, 1990), pp. 47–65.
29. G. Appleby and J. Anastas, *Not Just a Passing Phase: Social Work with Gay, Lesbian, and Bisexual People* (New York: Columbia University Press, 1998); C. Tully, *Lesbians, Gays, & the Empowerment Perspective* (New York: Columbia University Press, 2000).
30. P. Boss and B. Thorne, "Family Sociology and Family Therapy: A Feminist Linkage," in M. McGoldrick, C. Anderson, and F. Walsh, eds., *Women in Families: A Framework for Family Therapy* (New York: W. W. Norton and Company, 1989), pp. 78–96; M. M. Ferree, "Feminism and Family Research," in A. Booth, ed., *Contemporary Families: Looking Forward, Looking Back* (Minneapolis: National Council on Family Relations, 1991), pp. 103–121.

31. N. Chappell, "Aging and Social Care," in R. Binstock and L. George, eds., *Handbook of Aging and the Social Sciences* (San Diego, CA: Academic Press, 1990), pp. 438–454; N. Hooyman and J. Gonyea, *Feminist Perspectives on Family Care* (Thousand Oaks, CA: Sage, 1995); D. Spain and S. Bianchi, *Balancing Act* (New York: Russell Sage Foundation, 1996).
32. U.S. Census Bureau, *America's Families and Living Arrangements: 2000,* op. cit.
33. Misra, op. cit.
34. U.S. Census Bureau, *Fertility of American Women: June 2000,* op. cit.
35. Misra, op. cit.
36. J. Stacey, "Gay and Lesbian Families: Queer Like Us," in M. Mason, A. Skolnick, and S. Sugarman, eds., *All Our Families: New Policies for a New Century* (New York: Oxford University Press, 1998), pp. 117–143.
37. J. Battle, C. Cohen, D. Warren, G. Fergerson, and S. Audam, *Say It Loud: I'm Black and I'm Proud* (Washington, D.C.: The Policy Institute of the National Gay and Lesbian Task Force, March 2002).
38. Appleby and Anastas, op. cit.; C. Patterson, "Children of Lesbian and Gay Parents," *Child Development* 63 (1992): 1025–1042; Tully, op. cit.
39. Patterson, op. cit., p. 1036.
40. Data from the National Gay and Lesbian Task Force. http://www.thetaskforce.org/issues/marriage_and_partnership_recognition.
41. W. van der Meide, *Legislating Equality* (Washington, D.C.: The Policy Institute of the National Gay and Lesbian Task Force, January 2000); data from the National Gay and Lesbian Task Force.
42. Data from the National Gay and Lesbian Task Force.
43. K. Allen and D. Demo, "The Families of Lesbians and Gay Men: A New Frontier in Family Research," *Journal of Marriage and the Family* 57 (February 1995): 111–127; M. Allen and N. Burrell, "Comparing the Impact of Homosexual and Heterosexual Parents on Children," *Journal of Homosexuality* 32 (1996): 19–35; L. Kurdek, "The Allocation of Household Labor in Gay, Lesbian, and Heterosexual Married Couples," *Journal of Social Issues* 49 (1993): 127–139; L. Lott-Whitehead and C. Tully, "The Families of Lesbian Mothers," *Smith College Studies in Social Work* 63 (1993): 265–280; C. Patterson and R. Redding, "Lesbian and Gay Families with Children," *Journal of Social Issues,* 52 (1996): 29–50.
44. W. Devore, "'Whence Came These People?' An Exploration of the Values and Ethics of African American Individuals, Families, and Communities," in R. Fong and S. Furuto, eds., *Culturally Competent Practice: Skills, Interventions, and Evaluations* (Needham Heights, MA: Allyn & Bacon, 2001), pp. 33–46; Zinn and Eitzen, op. cit.
45. Zinn and Eitzen, op. cit.
46. G. Winbush, "African American Women," in M. Julia, *Constructing Gender: Multicultural Perspectives in Working with Women* (Belmont, CA: Wadsworth, 2000), pp. 11–34.
47. S. S. Dhooper and S. E. Moore, "Understanding and Working with African Americans," in S. S. Dhooper and S. E. Moore, *Social Work Practice with Culturally Diverse People* (Thousand Oaks, CA: Sage, 2001) pp. 98–134.
48. U.S. Census Bureau, *Coresident Grandparents and Grandchildren,* Current Population Reports, Series P23-198 (Washington, D.C.: U.S. Government Printing Office, May 1999); D. Burnette, "Grandparents Raising Grandchildren in the Inner City," *Families in Society* (1997): 489–501; P. Gibson, "African American Grandmothers: New Mothers Again," *Affilia: Journal of Women and Social Work* 14 (Fall 1999): 329–343.

49. U.S. Census Bureau, Current Population Survey, March 2000, Ethnic and Hispanic Statistics Branch, Population Division. Internet release date: March 6, 2001.
50. G. Acevedo and J. Morales, "Assessment with Latino/Hispanic Communities and Organizations," in Fong and Furuto, op. cit., pp. 147–162; H. Burgos-Ocasio, "Hispanic Women," in Julia, op. cit., pp. 109–137; L. Negroni-Rodriguez and J. Morales, "Individual and Family Assessment Skills with Latino/Hispanic Americans," in Fong and Furuto, op. cit., pp. 132–146.
51. U.S. Census Bureau, Current Population Survey, March 2000, Racial Statistics Branch, Population Division, Internet release date: June 28, 2001.
52. U.S. Census Bureau, Current Population Survey, March 2000, Racial Statistics Branch, Population Division, Internet release date: June 28, 2001.
53. Dhooper and Moore, op. cit.
54. Y. Song-Kim, "Battered Korean Women in Urban United States," in S. Furuto, R. Biswas, D. Chung, K. Murase, and F. Ross-Sheriff, eds., *Social Work Practice with Asian Americans* (Newbury Park: Sage, 1992), pp. 213–226; Dhooper and Moore, op. cit.; A. Zaharlick, "Southeast Asian-American Women," in Julia, op. cit., pp. 177–204.
55. W. Leigh and M. Jimenez, *Women of Color Data Book* (Washington, D.C.: National Institutes of Health, 2002).
56. Dhooper and Moore, "Understanding and Working with Native Americans," in S. S. Dhooper and S. E. Moore, *Social Work Practice with Culturally Diverse People* (Thousand Oaks, CA: Sage, 2001), pp. 174–211; B. Neal, "Native American Women," in Julia, op. cit., pp. 157–175; W. Leigh and M. Jimenez, *Women of Color Data Book* (Washington, D.C.: National Institutes of Health, 2002).
57. Office of Justice Programs, *Promising Practices and Strategies to Reduce Alcohol and Substance Abuse Among American Indians and Alaska Natives,* An OJP Issues & Practices Report, U.S. Department of Justice (Washington, D.C.: National Institute of Justice, August 2000); Office on Women's Health, *The Health of Minority Women* (U.S. Department of Health and Human Services, May 2000); H. Weaver, "Native Americans and Substance Abuse," in S. Straussner, ed., *Ethnocultural Factors in Substance Abuse Treatment* (New York: Guilford Press, 2001), pp. 77–96.
58. Dhooper and Moore, op. cit.; S. Evans, "Women," in F. Hoxie, ed., *The Encyclopedia of North American Indians* (New York: Houghton Mifflin, 1996), pp. 665–689; T. LaFromboise, J. Berman, and B. Sohi, "American Indian Women," in L. Comas-Diaz and B. Greene, eds., *Women of Color: Integrating Ethnic and Gender Identities in Psychotherapy* (New York: Guilford Press, 1994), pp. 30–71.
59. Misra, op. cit.; *Health, United States, 2001* (National Center for Health Statistics, 2001).
60. S. Nolen-Hoeksema and J. Girgus, "The Emergence of Gender Differences in Depression during Adolescence," *Psychological Bulletin* 115 (1994): 424–443.
61. A. Dunnewold, *Evaluation and Treatment of Postpartum Emotional Disorders*, Practitioners Resource Series (Sarasota, FL: Professional Resource Press, 1997).
62. B. Levy, ed., *Dating Violence: Young Women in Danger* (Seattle: Seal Press, 1991); S. Nolen-Hoeksema, "Sex Differences in Depression During Childhood and Adolescence," in *Sex Differences in Depression* (Stanford, CA: Stanford University Press, 1990), pp. 178–196; J. Stoppard, "Depression in Adolescence: Negotiating Identities in a Girl-Poisoning Culture," in *Understanding Depression: Feminist Social Constructionist Approaches* (New York: Routledge, 2000), pp. 113–136.
63. E. Galinsky and J. Bond, "Work and Family: The Experiences of Mothers and Fathers in the U.S. Workforce," in C. Costello and B. Krimgold, eds., *The American Woman, 1996–97* (New York: W. W. Norton, 1996), pp. 79–103; Nolen-Hoeksema, op. cit.;

S. Nolen-Hoeksema, "Epidemiology and Theories of Gender Differences in Unipolar Depression," in M. Seeman, ed., *Gender and Psychopathology* (Washington, D.C.: American Psychiatric Press, 1995), pp. 63–87; A. Rhodes and P. Goering, "Gender Differences in the Use of Outpatient Mental Health Services," in B. Levin, A. Blanch, and A. Jennings, eds., *Women's Mental Health Services: A Public Health Perspective* (Thousand Oaks, CA: Sage, 1998), pp. 19–33; Stoppard, "Women's Lives and Depression: Marriage and Motherhood," *Understanding Depression: Feminist Social Constructionist Approaches*, 2000, pp. 137–160.

64. S. Bordo, *Unbearable Weight: Feminism, Western Culture, and the Body* (Berkeley, CA: University of California Press, 1993); K. Halmi, "Eating Disorders," in M. Goldman and M. Hatch, eds., *Women and Health* (San Diego: Academic Press, 2000), pp. 1032–1041; S. Raeburn, "Women and Eating Disorders," in S. Straussner and S. Brown, eds., *The Handbook of Addiction Treatment for Women: Theory and Practice* (San Francisco: Josse-Bass, 2002), pp. 127–153.

65. B. Thompson, "'A Way Outa No Way' Eating Problems among African-American, Latina, and White Women," *Gender & Society* 6 (1992): 546–561; Office on Women's Health, *The Health of Minority Women* (Washington, D.C.: U.S. Department of Health and Human Services, May 2000).

66. D. Belle, "Poverty and Women's Mental Health," *American Psychologist* 45 (1990): 385–389; G. Brown and P. Moran, "Single Mothers, Poverty, and Depression," *Psychological Medicine* 27 (1997): 21–33.

67. C. Beck and B. Pearson, "Mental Health of Elderly Women," in J. Garner and S. Mercer, eds., *Women As They Age: Challenge, Opportunity, and Triumph* (New York: Haworth Press, 1989), pp. 175–193; M. Hudson, "Elder Mistreatment: Its Relevance to Older Women," *Journal of American Women's Association* 52 (1997): 142–146, 158; D. Padgett, B. Burns, and L. Grau, "Risk Factors and Resilience: Mental Health Needs and Services Use of Older Women," in Levin, Blanch, and Jennings, op. cit., pp. 390–413; B. Turner and L. Troll, *Women Growing Older: Psychological Perspectives* (Thousand Oaks, CA.: Sage, 1994).

68. D. Adams, ed., *Health Issues for Women of Color: A Cultural Diversity Perspective* (Thousand Oaks, CA: Sage, 1995); E. Cole, O. Espin, and E. Rothblum, eds., *Refugee Women and Their Mental Health: Shattered Societies, Shattered Lives* (New York: Haworth Press, 1992); Comas-Diaz and Greene, op. cit.; S. Straussner and S. Brown, eds., "Addictions Issues for Ethnically Diverse Women" in *The Handbook of Addiction Treatment for Women: Theory and Practice, Part Four* (San Francisco: Jossey-Bass, 2002), pp. 299–374; C. Willie, P. Rieker, B. Kramer, and B. Brown, eds., *Mental Health, Racism, and Sexism* (Pittsburgh: University of Pittsburgh Press, 1995).

69. C. Alexander, ed., *Gay and Lesbian Mental Health: A Sourcebook for Practitioners* (New York: Harrington Park Press, 1996); Appleby and Anastas, op. cit.; Tully, op. cit.; K. Van Wormer, J. Wells, and M. Boes, *Social Work with Lesbians, Gays, and Bisexuals: A Strengths Perspective* (Needham Heights, MA: Allyn & Bacon, 2000).

70. S. Covington and J. Surrey, "The Relational Model of Women's Psychological Development: Implications for Substance Abuse," in S. Wilsnack and R. Wilsnack, eds., *Gender and Alcohol: Individual and Social Perspectives* (New Brunswick, N.J.: Rutgers University Press, 1998); J. Newmann, D. Greenley, J. Sweeney, and G. Van Dien, "Abuse Histories, Severe Mental Illness, and the Cost of Care," in Levin, Blanch, and Jennings, op. cit., pp. 279–308; C. Renzetti, J. Edleson, and R. Bergen, eds., *Sourcebook on Violence Against Women* (Thousand Oaks, CA: Sage, 2001); B. Schell and N. Lanteigne, *Stalking, Harassment, and Murder in the Workplace: Guidelines*

for Protection and Prevention (Westport, CT: Quorum Books, 2000); K. Stout and B. McPhail, *Confronting Sexism & Violence Against Women: A Challenge for Social Work* (New York: Longman, 1998).

71. J. Austin and J. Dankwort, "A Review of Standards for Batterer Intervention Programs," *Violence Against Women Online Resources,* 1997, www.vaw.umn.edu; D. Saunders, "Interventions for Men Who Batter: Do We Know What Works?" *In Session: Psychotherapy in Practice* 2/3 (1996): 81–94.
72. D. Saunders, "Domestic Violence: Legal Issues," in R. Edwards, ed., *Encyclopedia of Social Work,* 19th ed. (Washington, D.C.: NASW Press, 1995), pp. 789–795.
73. R. Thelen, "Advocacy in a Coordinated Community Response: Overview and Highlights of Three Programs," *Violence Against Women Online Resources,* 2000, www.vaw.umn.edu.
74. Ibid.
75. S. Riger, L. Bennett, S. Wasco, P. Schewe, L. Frohmann, J. Camacho, and R. Campbell, *Evaluating Services for Survivors of Domestic Violence and Sexual Assault* (Thousand Oaks, CA: Sage, 2002).
76. This chapter focused primarily on differences among women based on race/ethnicity and sexual orientation. However, a fuller discussion would examine, for example, the unique experiences and needs of women with disabilities, older women, and women of different religions.

Chapter 17

Social Work Practice with Lesbian, Gay, and Bisexual People*

Prefatory Comment

A social work intern came to realize that a significant number of her clients were lesbian or gay youth who had been kicked out of their homes or who had run away from home because of parental reactions to their gayness. As she got to know each individual, she was struck by recurring themes: the individuals' recognition of their sexual orientation; family rejection; hostility of peers and friends; verbal and physical abuse; and the resulting confused, angry, and fearful feelings that increased their self-doubt. Homophobia and discrimination can create problems with self-esteem and self-image for people who do not fit comfortably into the heterosexual majority.

Our intern, like all good social workers, attempted to formulate an assessment and intervention plan based on her knowledge of the clients' life situations. Unfortunately, she was unable to recall any required readings related to this topic, and she did not remember any in-depth discussions about lesbians or gays in her social work classes. She did recollect, however, that once someone in class said that "faggots and dykes" should not be allowed to work with children because what they did was sinful and would have a bad influence on the development of those in their care. The professor did not say much, and the subject was dropped. She thought this seemed consistent with a National Association of Social Workers (NASW) workshop she had attended where the presenter confirmed that there is homophobia among social work students and faculty.[1]

However, this intern knew that the NASW Code of Ethics encouraged her to further the cause of social justice by promoting and defending the rights of persons suffering injustice and oppression. Gays and lesbians certainly met this requirement. She recalled that the Code was translated into NASW policy statements that prescribed the practice behavior of members. In it, social workers are enjoined to view discrimination and prejudice directed against any minority as adverse to the mental and social health of the

---

*This chapter prepared by Dr. George A. Appleby, professor of social work and dean of the School of Health and Human Services, Southern Connecticut State University, and Dr. Jeane W. Anastas, professor of social work, New York University.

affected minority as well as a detriment to society. Furthermore, social workers are urged to work to combat discriminatory employment practices and any other form of discrimination that imposes something less than equal status on bisexual, gay, or lesbian individuals. NASW, she recalled, affirmed the right of all persons to define and express their own sexuality. All persons are to be encouraged to develop their individual potential to the fullest extent possible. Our budding Jane Addams, while highly motivated to act ethically and to give the most effective help, had no idea where to start. After some thought, she decided to ask her supervisor for assistance. Her supervisor had received her master's in social work (MSW) more than a decade ago and knew little herself. She suggested that the intern do a literature review on this topic.

Understanding the GLB Population

An understanding of the lesbian, gay, and bisexual population in the United States must begin with a presentation of the current demographic picture.* There is a significant gap in our knowledge because scholars, like the general public, have been affected by the societal myths and taboos surrounding homosexuality. Thus, they have often avoided the objective analysis of this aspect of human functioning entirely. When the topic has been studied at all, its science has often been limited by moral and social doctrines, seldom debated, about the ways humans ought to behave. Twenty years ago, public discussion of homosexuality was minimal, very little research existed, and available studies were usually limited to the investigation of individuals who sought treatment or attempted to change their sexual orientation; thus, the studies were not helpful in understanding the vast majority of gay, lesbian, and bisexual people who were not in treatment.

Even today, a process of selective attention in the study of gay, lesbian, and bisexual people continues to limit our knowledge. However, while few national studies include information on sexual identity or sexual orientation, the 2000 Census for the first time generated data on same-sex households in which respondents called themselves "unmarried partners."[2] While such data excludes anyone not living with a partner or not describing themselves in those specific terms, it is the first time that the existence of gay and lesbian households has been acknowledged in our national self-enumeration.

Because oppression has resulted in the invisibility of gays and lesbians as a whole until recently, and because it is hard to define and describe an invisible population, much of the data we have about the homosexual population today comes from local surveys and ethnographic studies. Developing representative samples of lesbian, gay, and bisexual populations for research is notoriously difficult.[3] The data we do have suggest, however, that there is greater similarity than difference between gay and straight people.

---

*Transgender issues, while an emerging and very important topic in social work, are not addressed in all parts of this chapter to keep its length manageable.

Defining a Gay, Lesbian, or Bisexual Identity

Because of the myths and lack of knowledge that have surrounded this topic, it is especially important that we discuss who is and who is not lesbian, gay, or bisexual. A young graduate student has a crush on her female professor. She manufactures numerous ways to be near her. Is she a lesbian? An Army captain is discharged from the service for having sexual relations with an enlisted man. Is he gay? Two adolescent boys masturbate one another to orgasm. Are they homosexual? While having sexual intercourse with her husband, a woman frequently fantasizes about having sexual relations with other women. She has never had actual sexual contact with another woman. What is her sexual orientation? Because human sexuality occurs on a spectrum of feelings, thoughts, and behavior, the answers to these questions are not so easy.

Categorization can lead to understanding—or to stereotyping. For example, if a woman is labeled a lesbian, it may be assumed that she will only date women, be involved in many tempestuous short-term relationships, wear pants, play sports, raise dogs, and drive a truck. Likewise, if a person is a gay male, then he may be assumed to be sexually promiscuous, be overly concerned about his body and youth, obsess about fashion and style, frequently flick his wrists, and become a hairdresser or decorator. These are common stereotypes, but in reality attributes such as these are seldom so predictable or clear.

Despite these dangers, the task of understanding any phenomenon starts with naming and defining, and the terminology has been changing. The term *lifestyle* has been confused with the definition of homosexuality. The term is used more appropriately to describe certain forms of lesbian, gay, and bisexual social and cultural expression, not fundamental sexual orientation, but is usually rejected as trivializing a core sense of identity. Also problematic for similar reasons is the term *sexual preference*, once widely used. Same-sex emotional, affectional, and sexual feelings and behavior are not something that is consciously and freely chosen. Thus, the more appropriate terms are *sexual orientation* or *sexual identity*.

The term *homosexual*, once the most common, is now sometimes rejected because it denotes a category first imposed from a medically oriented, heterosexual perspective. *Gay* is now the most commonly used term in contrast to the term *straight*. While *gay* is sometimes used to describe both men and women, many women prefer to call themselves *lesbians*.

Contemporary definitions of being gay, lesbian, or bisexual emphasize affectional and emotional ties as well as sexual behavior. *Lesbian* is thus defined as "a woman who has **primary** emotional and sexual attraction to other women." Similarly, "*gay* most commonly refers to men who **primarily** have emotional and sexual attraction to men." In both cases, however, it is noted that in either case cross-gender sex may sometimes occur as well. The term *bisexual* refers to "a man or woman with sexual and emotional and affectional orientation toward people of both sexes," meaning that neither same- nor opposite-sex orientation is primary, but same-sex feelings and behavior is acknowledged. Therefore, in the health field, it is common to refer to *MSMs*, meaning "men who engage in same-sex behavior but who may not necessarily self-identify as gay."

A sexual orientation or sexual identity as gay, lesbian, or bisexual "involves acknowledging the significance" of same-gender feelings and sexual behavior. What a person does, how he or she defines who he or she is, how others define the person, and the social scripts into which a person fits him- or herself are all influences on sexual orientation and sexual identity.[4]

All of these definitions take into account that self-definition and sexual orientation do not always conform with sexual behavior. The National Opinion Research Center at the University of Chicago reported that approximately 5 percent of the male population and approximately 4 percent of the female population claimed to have had sex with a same-sex partner since the age of 18, while almost 8 percent reported experiencing attraction to persons of their own sex. However, when respondents were asked to self-identify as either heterosexual, homosexual, or bisexual, only about 3 percent of the males and less than 2 percent of the females stated "homosexual." The same study reported a homosexual or bisexual identity of 9.2 percent for men and 2.6 percent for women among residents of the twelve largest American cities.[5] Thus, population estimates differ substantially depending on geography and on whether the questions are related to sexual conduct, enduring attraction, or sexual orientation and identity.

Young people are increasingly using the terms *queer* and *questioning* (for an individual "who may be experiencing lesbian, gay, bisexual, or transgender feelings or urges but has not yet identified his or her sexual orientation or gender identity," known by the acronym LGBTQ). These newer terms reflect the stance that lesbians and gay men will no longer allow the heterosexual majority to name and define them.

Given the complexities of terminology and definitions just described, it is essential to be sensitive to language, culture, and geography. Ask clients or colleagues what they mean when you are uncertain of how they are defining themselves or what aspects of sexual identity or orientation they are talking about. Such a question will be interpreted more often as a demonstration of respect and concern than as ignorance.

Population Characteristics

Lesbians, gays, and bisexuals live in every area of the United States, but they appear to be found in larger numbers in urban areas where there is relative tolerance for diversity. They are represented in all occupations and socioeconomic groups. They are white, African American, Hispanic, Asian, and American Indian. They reflect the same demographic characteristics as found in the general population except that there may be higher levels of education among gays and lesbians than are found in the general population. Although there are limits to our knowledge base, failure to acknowledge the variety of lesbians', gays', and bisexuals' social situations only adds to the marginalization of their lives.

Using census and other data and recognizing the complexities in defining and counting the gay and lesbian population in the United States, the Urban Institute estimates that between about 2 percent and 3 percent of the United States population was gay and lesbian in 2000—that is, between 3.9 million and 5.9 million individuals.[6] This translates to between one in fifty and one in about thirty people. Because there are more gay men than lesbians, between 2.5 percent and 3.8 percent of men in the United States are likely gay and between 1.3 percent and 1.9 percent of women are likely lesbian. If we were to consider the typical size of an individual's network of family, friends, work colleagues, and others, these data suggest that most probably know someone who is lesbian, gay, or bisexual, whether or not they are aware of it.

Whatever the true numbers, it is important to recognize that there are a breadth of living situations and a number of subpopulations within the group, many of which overlap. Any community will have different social networks based on age, class, ethnicity, language, race, sex, and special interests. Among gay and lesbian couples identified in the 2000 Census, more than one-quarter included at least one person who identified as a member of a racial or ethnic minority. Hidalgo warns that class differences and racism do divide lesbian, gay, and bisexual communities.[7] Some observers suggest, however, that there is a greater commitment to democratic structures and an integration of subgroups than is commonly seen in heterosexual communities, which is confirmed by the 2000 Census findings that gay and lesbian couples are more likely to live in neighborhoods with non-white and non-English-speaking people than married, heterosexual couples. This may be true because the individuals who live in these communities may be more accepting of diversity in both sexual orientation and in racial and ethnic diversity, since the need for affiliation is often met in a group of similarly oriented people who share the common experience of oppression.

However, racial and ethnic factors do have an impact on associations. African American and Hispanic gays, for both economic and cultural reasons, often maintain residence with or near their families, unlike many white gays, who establish homes away from relatives, often in one of the larger urban areas. This has an impact on the amount and intensity of association with other gays. Smith suggests that is another factor in determining the level of association of African Americans with the gay community: "Gay whites are people who identify first as being gay and who usually live outside the closet in predominantly white gay communities.... black gays, on the other hand, view our racial heritage as primary and frequently live 'bisexual front lives' within black neighborhoods."[8] While there are no empirical data on the subject, the observation has been made that identification is equally important in other racial and ethnic groups.

Carballo-Dieguez notes that religion and folk beliefs strongly influence the Hispanic culture. Conservative and traditional values are barriers to an openly gay lifestyle.[9] Of the various religions, fundamentalists and Baptists seem most likely to condemn homosexuality, and African Americans, as Mays and Cochran point out, hold membership predominantly in these denominations.[10] Newby would concur with the importance of social structure, values, and religion on the public expression of sexual orientation in the African American community and proposes that this may explain the higher rate of bisexuality and lower percentage of gay exclusivity than is found among whites.[11] Thus, African American and Latino gays are a double minority, often stigmatized by being in both the minority of color and being gay, while lesbians of color are in "triple jeopardy" because of being women as well.

Ecosystems Framework

Social work addresses the interaction between the person and the environment. The goal of practice is to enhance and restore the psychosocial functioning of persons, or to change the oppressive or destructive social conditions that negatively affect the interaction between persons and their environments. The ecosystems model of practice, the framework of this text, consists of five interconnected domains or levels: (1) historical, (2) environmental–structural, (3) cultural, (4) family, and (5) individual. The lives and social conditions of lesbians, gay men, bisexuals, and transgender people (LGBT) are now assessed in relation to each of these domains.

Historical Factors

The ecosystems model is concerned with both positive and noxious factors in the historical experience of members of the population of interest. The history of minority group oppression and exploitation has already been noted. It has taken form in religion, culture, law, and social sanction. The United States, strongly influenced by interpretations of Judaic and Christian moral codes, is one of the most homophobic societies. While change is, in fact, taking place in each of these areas, not one of these social structures could be characterized as nurturing. At best, they are benign.

The Stonewall rebellion in 1969, in which a group of gays and lesbians resisted and protested against police harassment and brutality at a gay bar in New York, is usually regarded as the birth of the modern Gay Liberation Movement. Since that time, lesbian, gay, and bisexual individuals have become increasingly visible in our society. They are fighting for equal protection under our laws and for access to the same benefits afforded heterosexuals, such as civil marriage, domestic partnership, and civil unions.

Religious groups have been in the forefront of opposition to homosexuality. However, not all religions oppose it. Biblical interpretations vary widely, with advocates of both sides quoting scriptures as their defense. Presently, each of the major Judaic and Christian denominations has begun to recognize the spiritual and civil rights needs of their lesbian, gay, and bisexual members but often not without controversy. The Metropolitan Community Church, a nondenominational group founded to minister to homosexuals, has more than one hundred member churches throughout the country.

While some members of the gay community choose to remain invisible in an attempt to isolate themselves from the effects of oppression, others have committed themselves to action and self-realization. Many lesbians and gays recognized the community's potential political clout in the 1960s as they became aware of their size as a minority group and their significance as a voting bloc. This led to the enormous growth of gay political and advocacy organizations on local and national levels since the 1970s and 1980s, continuing to the present time. Currently, lesbian, gay, and bisexual civil rights issues, including partnership and marriage rights, foster-parenting protections, custody rights, and access to all available health care and treatment options, especially in relation to the AIDS epidemic, are being addressed at both the state and local levels. For example, gay activists have helped to bring about a general reassessment of federal ethical guidelines in experimental medical treatment and research in order to bring potentially life-saving treatments to patients sooner than in the past. However, there are still no federal protections for gay rights in housing, employment, or in any other area. As efforts to address numerous legal and policy issues continue under the banner of human rights, the visibility and influence of the lesbian, gay, and bisexual minority will continue to grow.

Environmental–Structural Factors

Heterosexism, homophobia, and "homohatred" or homonegativity are probably the most relevant environmental or structural issues affecting lesbian, gay, and bisexual persons, and this chapter has already described some of the ways in which homophobia has been institutionalized as a barrier in this society. Compounded with sexism and racism, they have generated additional barriers to the healthy development and well-being of lesbian, gay, and bisexual persons.

Heterosexism is defined as the belief that heterosexuality is or should be the only acceptable sexual orientation. Blumenfeld suggests that heterosexism, which is encouraged by fear and hatred, results in prejudice, discrimination, harassment, and acts of violence and hatred.[12] These are the wide-range impacts of giving cultural precedence to heterosexuality.

The impact of environmental–structural factors gives a specific social form to this population. Paul and Weinrich identified three such factors: social invisibility, social diversity, and social and personal differentiation.[13] The great majority of gay, lesbian, and bisexual people are not easily identifiable. There are as many kinds of gays as there are kinds of straights.[14] Finally, the ways in which people adapt to having a gay or lesbian orientation vary according to the relative tolerance or hostility of the immediate social environment.

Social invisibility makes it possible for the general public to be ignorant of diversity as it really exists. One result has been widely held inaccurate stereotypes. An example would be the assumed connection between male heterosexuality and involvement in sports. Garner and Smith reported significantly higher rates of homosexual activity in several samples of athletes than had been previously found.[15] The current passion among some gay men for bodybuilding and athletic club membership also serves to challenge this stereotype.

Gays and lesbians have always been the victims of homicides, gay bashing, and extortion because of religious sanctions and legal discrimination. The social acceptance of homophobia, homohatred, racism, and sexism in our society serves only to exacerbate prejudice. And the incidences of hate, violence, and harassment have increased significantly as a result of the HIV/AIDS epidemic.[16] This oppression has had a significant impact on the health and mental health status of lesbians and gay men. The National Education Association (2005) reported that a third of LGBT students drop out of high school because of harassment, and four out of five of them face daily verbal and physical harassment at school.[17]

Because of these various forms of homonegativity, myths and stereotypes about LGBT people are widespread. Tully (2001) identifies twenty-five commonly held beliefs of this kind, noting how research shows them to be untrue.[18] These include that long-term relationships are uncommon among lesbians and gay men, that most gays and lesbians abuse alcohol and other drugs, that children raised in gay or lesbian families are more likely to be gay or lesbian than those raised in non-gay homes, that it is possible to identify gay or lesbian people by commonly held physical characteristics, that lesbians and gay men are more promiscuous than non-gays, that most pedophiles and child molesters are gay men, and that homosexuality is a mental illness. Institutionalized discrimination unfortunately helps such misconceptions to survive.

Cultural Factors

Popular images often suggest that gay and lesbian people are involved with a specific subculture or lifestyle. As a result, gays and lesbians may be thought to be readily identifiable by styles of dress or behavior, or to be invested only in activities or institutions designated as exclusively gay or lesbian. However, as a stigmatized group, lesbians and gays are in fact an invisible minority, only some of whom choose to make themselves and their interests visible individually and collectively in the gay and lesbian communities and queer subculture.

Access to such gay- or lesbian-identified institutions and organizations is often very important for individuals who have affirmed, are exploring, or are consolidating a gay or lesbian identity. People who live in rural or small communities far removed from these centers of activity may sometimes be disadvantaged in making connections with others like themselves, in developing ways to receive affirmation for significant parts of their lives, or in finding help or support in coping with homophobia.

Contact with the gay community, however, will quickly dispel any notion that gay and lesbian people are similar to each other in appearance or lifestyle beyond the sexual orientation that they share. Diversity within the identifiable lesbian, gay, and bisexual community is as great as among heterosexuals as a group. As in any other social group, these differences can be a source of tension, which may disappoint those looking to "the community" for an ideal way of life to emulate, or for a conflict-free environment as they work on developing their own identities or seek refuge from the discrimination from the community at large. The relationship between the individual and the community can thus be either a mutually enhancing or a conflicted one. Many lesbians and gays, however, draw essential support and affirmation from the culture.

In addition, many gay and lesbian people do not participate in the identifiable gay and lesbian subculture even when it is available to them. Their political, social, and recreational pursuits may not be related to their sexual orientation at all, and their social and emotional supports may come exclusively from friends and family. Sometimes this choice may stem from a wish to remain private or "closeted" (or selectively "out") in their sexual orientation out of fear; at other times it may result from a choice to give other dimensions of their lives and identity priority. Thus, the degree of an individual's involvement with the gay or lesbian community is itself a dimension of diversity among lesbians and gays.

The concept of *biculturality* has recently been used to describe the socialization processes that lesbians and gays undergo.[19] Acceptance of a gay or lesbian identity means adopting new norms and values and being rejected by and/or rejecting old standards. Dating and coupling; definitions of family; celebrations and ritual participation, both secular and religious; and political and social interests are all affected by sexual orientation. For lesbians and gay men of ethnic- and racial-minority backgrounds, the cultural issues are even more complex.

This concept of a homosexual culture is viewed as controversial by some, because intergenerational transmission of this culture and socialization into it does not ordinarily take place in the family of origin, as it does in cultures as defined in other contexts. In fact, gay and lesbian individuals are usually first socialized into majority, heterosexual culture. However, applying the concept of culture to gay and lesbian ways of life highlights the inclusiveness of a lesbian or gay identity, the shared experiences of gay and lesbian people over time and across societies, and the diversity of gays and lesbians on other dimensions such as race, class, and gender. The related notion of biculturality points out that gays and lesbians live to differing degrees in multiple worlds, with the attendant opportunities and stresses of negotiation and boundary maintenance.[20]

Family Factors

Lesbians and gay men have been categorized by society as people without families, uninterested in creating families, and threatening to family life. Despite this perception, the fact is that at least 2 million lesbians and gay men are parents of minor children.[21] Census data from 2000 found that one in five same-sex male couples identified and one in three lesbian couples enumerated had one or more children under 18 living with them, although it is assumed that this is likely an undercount. Large numbers of the gay, lesbian, and bisexual population live in long-term, committed, coupled relationships.[22] Achtenberg notes that discriminatory treatment, misunderstanding, and prejudices often pose social and legal barriers to the recognition and protection of families created by lesbians and gay men.[23]

Many gays and lesbians credit their family of origin as the source of their emotional support and strength as well as their positive belief and value system. Yet for other gays and lesbians, the family is a source of interpersonal tension and conflict, hardly the basis for self-acceptance or a healthy adjustment to a hostile society. Many gays credit their "chosen family"—family of design consisting of lovers and friends—as the buffer that has had the greatest impact on their adaptation.

The gay, lesbian, or bisexual person, his or her parents, and the spouse and their children are all confronted daily with stereotyping and social rejection. The images of homosexuality are all negative: the "sinner," the "drag queen," the "child molester," the "bull dyke." By the time one reaches adulthood, the association (not necessarily conscious) between homosexuality and the stereotype is formed. These dehumanizing stereotypes are perpetuated by the peer group, the mass media, and cultural tradition. The individual may feel pressure to establish distance from homosexuality. Few people, then, are socially prepared to deal with this issue when it arises.

"Passing" is a second consequence of stigma. Anyone who does not fit the stereotype can "pass," while those who meet the stereotyped expectations become visible. An individual may come to recognize his or her special sexual orientation without realistic models of what this means. The reaction may be, "I'm the only person in the world like this," or "I'm not like them, thank God." Parents, other family members, and friends are also likely to avoid or deny disclosure when their loved one does not fit the stereotype. Gay, lesbian, and bisexual youths are reared in heterosexual families, peer groups, and educational institutions. Thus, these youths grow up learning the same stereotypes and negative judgments as their straight peers, threatening the sense of self. Because "passing" is so pervasive, they are deprived of positive role models to prepare them for dealing with their sexual orientation. Sustaining self-esteem and a sense of identity becomes problematic at best.

Rejection is the third consequence of stigma, which produces distancing between those with the stigma and those without. Disclosure can become a critical issue within the family. The gay or lesbian child may lose the sense of authenticity characteristic of family relationships if he or she keeps the secret, or face rejection if he or she seeks understanding and emotional support by disclosing his or her sexual orientation. This potential alienation from the family is one way in which the homosexual minority is different from other minority groups, who generally can count on support within the family in the face of stress from the outside world. This same dynamic will be true with friends and work colleagues. Bell, Weinberg, and Hammersmith note that secrecy brings about a different sort of distancing, offering the example of a gay person who appears outwardly popular and well liked by the group yet feels alienated and isolated.[24]

The development of a subculture, a separate space that allows a sense of community and naturalness, is the fourth consequence of stigma. The subculture may be an opportunity to develop a special kinship with fellow victims of stigma. The stronger the disapproval by the majority culture, the more attractive a subculture is as a source of mutual support.

The final consequence is that of the self-fulfilling prophecy or "secondary deviance." This means that features of the stereotype may be embraced in protest or defiance or for lack of support for more normative styles of life. "Drag," "camp," and "leather" are stereotypic styles reflecting theatrical and humorous responses to society's arbitrary distinctions between masculine and feminine cultures. This poking of fun at gender roles by flouting them is often seen by non-gays as confirmation of their worst stereotypic fears.

Forming Families: Myths and Realities

Numerous studies have been made of children being reared by lesbians to determine what effects on development there may be. Because alternative insemination and access to adoption by gays are relatively new phenomena, the studies to date have generally compared children of divorced lesbian mothers with those of divorced women who are not lesbians. Taken together, the studies have consistently shown that gay men and lesbians who parent do not differ in child-rearing practices or lifestyle from other parents and that the children of lesbian mothers and gay men have no more problems in adjustment or development than do others.[25] There is no evidence of gender-role confusion or higher rates of gay or lesbian orientation among them, as had initially been hypothesized. In fact, there is some evidence that children of lesbians have a greater appreciation for diversity of all kinds and value tolerance more highly than others, having seen firsthand the toll that prejudice like homophobia can take.

The concern that a child who grows up with a homosexual parent will develop a gay orientation appears to be a widely held myth. The assumption that children develop their sexual orientation by emulating their parents is false. Remember that the vast majority of lesbians, gays, and bisexuals were raised by heterosexual parents.[26]

Another myth is that children who grow up with a gay or lesbian parent are at risk of molestation or abuse by either the parent or the parent's friends. However, research on the sexual abuse of children shows that the offenders are, in disproportionate numbers, heterosexual men.[27] It is also a common assumption that children in the custody of a lesbian or gay parent will be harmed by social stigma, but there are no clinical reports or research of stigma or unusual emotional problems in these children.[28] The practitioner must also realize that the coping and adaptational qualities of gay people in families are also tempered by economics, ethnicity, race, and class identity.

Individual Factors

The study of why people become gay or lesbian usually starts with an exhaustive review of biological theories focusing on genetic and hormonal factors and on psychoanalytic and behavioral theories addressing pathology and dysfunction. The conclusions of these studies are seldom supported by the data presented. Thus, the attempt to identify etiological factors has a long history, but with close inspection one must conclude that no specific genetic, intrapsychic, or interpersonal causative factors can be generalized to the lesbian, gay, and bisexual population.[29] However, there is knowledge about individual development that has value for practice intervention. One way to improve our understanding or our definitions of sexual orientation is to correct the myths and inaccuracies surrounding homosexuality. One myth, which represents the popular version of an outmoded psychoanalytic explanation of homosexuality, is that male homosexuality represents a fear or hatred of women. (The reverse is also sometimes said of lesbian women.) This myth has led to ineffective treatment based on the assumption that gay men can be converted to heterosexuality simply by having sexual experiences with women. This simplistic view is contradicted by the large proportion of gay men who have had or continue to have sexual experiences with women but retain a positive gay identity.

Another myth is that gay people are compulsively sexual. The Kinsey Institute's estimates of gay sexual activity are probably overstated. Like straights, most gays spend most of their time doing things other than looking for sex or having it. Since 1981, the HIV/AIDS epidemic has struck a large number of gay and bisexual men. The widespread awareness in the gay community that the virus believed to cause AIDS is transmitted through unprotected sex (i.e., without condoms) has led to significant changes in sexual practices and thus, for some years, a reduction in sexually transmitted disease and the rate of HIV infection among gay men.

Finally, while lesbians and gay men may often be accused of flaunting their sexuality, in fact, most conceal their sexual orientation at least part of the time. Stigma and the consequences of discrimination in many areas of daily living are convincing reasons for concealment.[30] Berger suggests that, because lesbians and gay men are generally indistinguishable from other men and women, public attitudes are formed on the basis of those who are most open about their sexual orientation.[31] "Straight" heterosexuals apply a double standard to same-sex and opposite-sex behavior, in that public displays of affection between a man and a woman are taken for granted while even holding hands in public is considered "flaunting" when it occurs between two women or two men.

Identity Formation Sexual orientation may change over time. A woman who is primarily homosexual in early adulthood may become more heterosexual in later life or vice versa. In his study of older gay men, Berger found that it is not uncommon for a man with an essentially heterosexual orientation in early adulthood to develop predominantly homosexual interests in middle age.[32] These observations lead us to the view that homosexuality is an identity formation process occurring over time. This formulation has much promise for social work assessment and intervention.

Berger proposed a model wherein homosexual identity results when a person completes three tasks that are independent of one another. The first in this process is the sexual encounter, that is, physical contact of a sexual nature with someone of the same sex. Second is the social reaction, that is, the process of labeling the individual by others as homosexual. The last component in this model is the identity task; that is, the individual experiences identity confusion (the discomfort felt between a same-sex experience and a heterosexual self-image) and works to come to terms with this in some way.[33]

Viewing lesbian, gay, or bisexual orientation as the result of an identity-formation process has important implications for social work intervention. First of all, and most important, there is no empirical justification for the belief that homosexuality, in and of itself, is a psychiatric illness or a result of poor psychological adjustment. Practitioners who continue to advocate illness models based on "conversion therapies" are ignorant, irresponsible, or both.[34]

Social Stress and Social Supports Like Berger, other theorists have adopted an interactionist perspective to examine the intricate linkage between social life and personal experience. Human beings cannot escape the influence of social position and social expectation on their development and self-perception. Bradford and Ryan note that "those who are discriminated against or who expect to face discrimination if their 'condition' were to become known are different from those who do not occupy stigmatized or 'deviant' social positions. The connection between living on the margins of society and the impact of this upon daily life and an adequate sense of psychosocial security" is yet to be fully documented. However, we do know that lesbians and gay men always live with this tension.[35]

This stress and lack of support—rather than stresses related to sexual orientation—may result in higher rates of alcoholism among lesbians, gays, and bisexuals. Gay bars are among the few public places where gay men and lesbians can meet to socialize. Drinking can also provide emotional insulation from homophobic or racist attitudes.[36] It is estimated that one-third of lesbians are alcoholics. Gay men and MSMs also have higher rates of alcohol and drug use than straight men do. Legal, health, and social service agencies, often insensitive to lesbian, gay, and bisexual persons, have tended to focus on sexual orientation as the cause of this phenomenon, despite evidence that they do not differ in psychosocial functioning from heterosexuals. Lesbians of color, like their male counterparts, have a higher incidence of alcoholism than straights.[37]

Brooks emphasizes the importance of social support networks for lesbians and gay men. These are relationships with significant others, developed as a result of sharing a history of common experience through which people create environments of caring and support for each other.[38] While recognizing that the importance of supportive interactions among people is not new, Bradford notes that research evidence of social supports helping people in health crises is recent. Maintenance of good health is related to the number of people in a social network.[39] Alcalay adds that the number of contacts, the frequency and intensity of contacts, as well as the presence of family and friends within the network are all related to health.[40] In other words, friends can be "good medicine."

Bradford and Ryan have synthesized the research related to social support and crisis in relation to lesbian health. They conclude that supports encourage preventive behavior, provide needed resources, increase a sense of personal control over one's environment, and reduce the social marginality of one's minority status. Supports are buffers against the distress of traumatic life events. Lesbians, gay men, and bisexuals without sufficient supports are especially vulnerable to commonplace stressors as well as the monumental stress related to minority status.[41] It is within the context of stress, social marginality, and minority status that the impact of a hostile, discriminatory environment should be understood. This approach to understanding developmental issues focuses our attention on life adaptations and thus is consistent with the ecosystems perspective.

Macro Practice with Lesbian, Gay, and Bisexual People

Germain and Gitterman, in their advancement of the ecological model, treated stress as a psychosocial condition "generated by discrepancies between needs and capacities, on the one hand, and environmental qualities on the other. It arises in three interrelated areas of living: life transitions, environmental pressures, and interpersonal processes."[42] The social work interventions related to support, empowerment, psychoeducation, consultation, case advocacy, and self-help seem appropriate for most clients, while case management, individual, group, couple, and family therapy might be the preference of some gay, lesbian, and bisexual clients.

Oppression, power, heterosexism, and homophobia form the macro environmental context in which lesbians and gay men develop and function. These social dynamics are experienced as nonnurturing social behaviors and as barriers to optimal social functioning, such as discrimination, prejudice, bias, and violence and therefore are appropriate environmental or macro social change targets of social work intervention. Social workers should act to expand access, choices, and opportunities for all oppressed people. Community development, organizational change, staff training, coalition building, program and policy development, class advocacy, and social action are appropriate for change that will benefit lesbian, gay, and bisexual people as well.

Social workers should help gay and lesbian activists to organize their communities with the intent of developing educational and political strategies and of forming coalitions of advocacy groups, such as the Human Rights Campaign, and *class action social work* alliances with groups such as the American Civil Liberties Union, Lambda Legal Defense, and the National Gay and Lesbian Task Force. Goals are to advance civil rights legislation, to defeat efforts to limit civil rights, to advocate for programs to eliminate hate crimes and antigay violence, and to enhance education, treatment services, and research related to lesbians, gay men, and bisexuals. The intent is that homosexuals are entitled to the same Fourteenth Amendment equal rights, liberties, and privileges as are other citizens, such as in housing, employment, public accommodation, inheritance and insurance, domestic partnership or marriage, child custody, adoption, foster care, and property rights.

The constitutional rights of privacy free from government regulation or intrusion and equal treatment before the law should be afforded to all lesbians, gay men, and bisexuals. This is basic to U.S. citizenship. Criminalization of homosexual acts is a violation of the right of individual privacy, which has recently drawn action from the U.S. Supreme Court. Criminal statutes proscribing adult homosexual behavior create an environment of oppression arising from fear of prosecution and provide the means of blackmail. These statutes are most reprehensible when linked to enforcement by entrapment. Such laws perpetuate discrimination against homosexuals. Discrimination on the basis of homosexuality violates an individual's right of privacy and denies the person equal protection of the law.[43]

Achtenberg reminds us that to favor lesbian, gay, and bisexual rights or to support an end to discrimination must mean to deplore the ways in which society undermines the formation, preservation, and protection of the lesbian, gay, and bisexual family.[44] Gay rights must also include support for custody and visitation statutes that ensure strict neutrality with regard to the sexual orientation of the parent. Advocacy for adoption and foster parenting laws and administrative practices that are strictly neutral are needed. Joint adoptions by same-sex couples should be permitted when it is in a child's best interests and when the parent–child relationship has been cemented. Laws permitting delegation of personal and health care duties to non-relatives should be created, as well as provision for fair determination of the guardian or conservator for an ill person. The same sentiment should inform the laws of intestate succession. Equity, not sexual orientation or marital status, should become the value undergirding the distribution of work-related and governmental benefits.

The National Gay and Lesbian Task Force (NGLTF) and the Human Rights Campaign (HRC), two leading GLBT civil rights organizations, have refocused their attention to civil marriage, domestic partnerships, and civil unions. Grassroots energy has been redirected to the state level to organize against the federal bill, the Defense of Marriage Act (DOMA), which defines this institution as the exclusive domain of heterosexuals, and to build constituencies in support of gay marriage. The focus of this highly emotional debate is on economic issues, illustrating how same-sex couples are discriminated against by not having access to more than 1,000 benefits, protections, and responsibilities granted only through civil marriage. The NGLTF's analysis, using Connecticut as an example, points out that same-sex couples are denied equal treatment under Social Security policy, federal tax laws, immigration, inheritance, and health care protocols that allow married couples to protect their families, as under the Family and Medical Leave Act. Analysis clarifies that, by allowing same-sex couples to marry, no one is harmed, and couples and their children will access benefits and programs designed by the government to promote family stability and financial security.[45]

A nonjudgmental attitude toward sexual orientation allows social workers to offer optimal support and services, thus empowering lesbian, gay, and bisexual people through all phases of the coming out process and beyond. The outcome of interpersonal intervention, however, is also contingent on the agency's policies and procedures. Social workers must first focus on the level of staff knowledge and commitment before introducing gay-affirming programs. Agency policies and procedures should address the needs of lesbian, gay, and bisexual clients and staff.

Legislation embodying the above principles should be the goal of the social work profession. Passage of such legislation on state or national levels requires building coalitions of like-minded civil rights advocacy groups and extensive public education. Social workers are skilled in problem identification and resolution through organization building and strategy development. These are the needed macro skills if environments are to be supportive of positive gay identity development and to remove the barriers to healthful functioning and psychosocial adaptation.

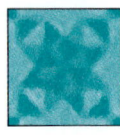

Micro Practice with Lesbian, Gay, and Bisexual People

Failure to consider that a client may be lesbian, gay, or bisexual is the most common mistake made by social workers. Despite stereotypes, most lesbian, gay, and bisexual clients are not visually identifiable as such, and many may not identify themselves as lesbian, gay, or bisexual at first, especially when the problem for which they are seeking assistance may not have much to do with sexual orientation.[46] However, the social worker is unlikely to get a full enough picture of the client's situation to be helpful without keeping an open mind to the possibility of gender identity issues.

Effective work with lesbians and gay men requires what Hall has termed a dual focus: "The practitioner must be able to see the ways in which the client's presenting problem is both affected by and separate from her sexual orientation."[47] Damage to self-esteem resulting from oppression and stigmatization must always be considered, but at the same time the client probably occupies roles, works on developmental tasks, and experiences feelings in which being lesbian, gay, or bisexual is incidental. For example, the teenage prostitutes our intern met through her work at the AIDS service organization must deal with the rejection they experienced from families because they were gay or lesbian. At the same time, these teens have the same developmental needs for the support and approval of adults and peers that others do and would be seeking a way to separate and differentiate themselves from their families even if rejection based on their sexual orientation had not occurred. Thus, a worker counseling any of them might expect to hear both a longing for the love and approval of their parents, despite their rejecting behavior, and a simultaneous longing to be completely free of parental restraint or control.

Whether or not the client seeks help with an issue involving sexual orientation or during the "coming out" process, the worker's feelings, attitudes, and comfort with a lesbian, gay, or bisexual identity or orientation must be examined; they require self-exploration over time.[48] It is the homophobia gay and lesbian individuals may encounter that is likely to be a problem, not the homosexuality itself. Rather than seeking causes or explanations for homosexuality, this perspective leads the social worker to explore and help the client to overcome the obstacles, internalized or external, that may stand in the way of healthy functioning as a lesbian, gay, or bisexual person.

Psychological and psychoanalytic theories have given more attention to male than to female homosexuality over the years.[49] From a contemporary psychoanalytic standpoint, there are many varieties of both heterosexual and homosexual functioning, and homosexual or heterosexual object choices are not viewed in themselves as healthy or unhealthy. Nevertheless, studies suggest that negative attitudes toward homosexuality and homosexual clients persist among some social workers and social work students.[50] Such attitudes create barriers that keep lesbian, gay, and bisexual persons from seeking or receiving effective mental health services in times of need.

When homosexuality was viewed as pathological, it was assumed that some critical experiences early in life produced an outcome, same-gender object choice, which was thought to be immutable without psychological treatment. Not only has it proved very difficult to identify any experiential or developmental "causes" or antecedents of homosexuality with any confidence,[51] but the treatment of homosexuals in psychological distress was usually distorted to mean treatment of the homosexuality itself.[52]

On the one hand, adult developmental theory now tells us that personality and life course are not "cast in stone" in childhood. Additionally, close study of the sexual practices of both heterosexual and homosexual people and attention to the life histories of lesbian, gay, and bisexual people suggest that sexual practices and self-identification may change over time. On the other hand, to self-identified lesbian, gay, or bisexual individuals, the homosexual identity may feel immutable, essential, and core to their sense of themselves as persons. Psychological treatment is thus focused on addressing whatever distress a self-identified lesbian, gay, or bisexual person may be experiencing, rather than on the sexual orientation itself.[53]

Contemporary theory emerging from research and clinical work with lesbians, gays, and bisexuals, then, suggests that the developmental pathways to their sexual identity are numerous. This identity is no longer assumed to be pathological. The task of the worker is to understand and accept these varieties of sexual identity and experience that exist and to assist the lesbian, gay, or bisexual client to deal with any problems that may accompany or simply coexist with his or her particular sexual orientation.

Common Problems

As with other minority groups, oppression that may be visited on gay and lesbian people because of their sexual orientation can be destructive to individual self-esteem and well-being. At early stages of the coming-out process, many people actively resist acknowledging, even to themselves, that they are sexually attracted to or active with others of their own gender. This resistance is often the product of negative attitudes toward homosexuality they themselves have absorbed, as everyone does, from the society as a whole or of negative reactions they fear from significant others such as parents, children, friends, associates, or authority figures such as teachers, coaches, or religious leaders. It is essential that the social work services lesbians, gays, and bisexuals receive be free of the homophobia and heterosexism that would add to or reinforce these fears and attitudes.

CASE EXAMPLE

Lynn, who was 17 and a high school senior, was referred to a social worker for treatment following a brief psychiatric hospitalization. She had been admitted to the hospital after friends of hers, becoming alarmed, reported to her parents that she had ingested a number of pills and was "acting funny." This episode was viewed as a suicidal gesture by both the young woman and her parents. It followed a period of several months during which arguments between the girl and her parents had been growing in frequency and intensity. The arguments were over such issues as Lynn's style of dress, her social activities, her "lack of respect" for her parents, and the fact that she had stopped attending church with the family. Lynn was the youngest of three children and the only one still living at home. Her father owned his own small business and worked long hours; her mother worked as a nurse. Both parents were fundamentalist Christians, and their recreational activities, which were few, were centered on the church. The family lived in a suburban community on the outskirts of a large metropolitan area in the Northeast.

From the beginning of counseling, Lynn announced firmly that she was a lesbian, and she always appeared for her appointments dressed in tight blue jeans, studded leather jacket, and black boots. Her manner appeared angry and "tough," and the image she cultivated was that of the stereotype of the "dyke." Lynn had also told her parents she was a lesbian. Her father was extremely rejecting of homosexuality, which he regarded as sinful; her mother was slightly more sympathetic. Because she had also spoken openly about her sexual orientation in the hospital, Lynn had been referred to a worker who was also a lesbian, although Lynn was not aware of that fact.

Starting with what Lynn had said was important about herself, the worker began exploring Lynn's sexual orientation and what it meant to her. Lynn had begun heterosexual dating at 15 and had enjoyed a relationship with a boy she liked very much. However, as time went on, she realized she experienced her relationship with him as a "good friend" and not as a "boyfriend" like her friends did. About this time, she also became aware of her attraction to other young women. She had her first sexual experience with a woman at 16, which she described as her coming out. After this point, for her "there was no going back."

The worker began exploring what being gay meant to Lynn. It turned out that Lynn knew only two other lesbians, both "tough kids" from her hometown. The worker then asked Lynn if she would be interested in making contact with an organization for lesbian and gay youth in the city. Lynn began to meet a much more varied and congenial group of peers with whom she could begin to talk about the pain of isolation and disapproval she was experiencing at school and at home. She also used the group to talk about her plans for college and her worries about what it would be like to be identified as a lesbian on campus.

As Lynn gained social support from the group and a sense of personal support and acceptance from her social worker in their meetings, her appearance and style of dress began to change somewhat. She also began tentatively to share with her worker some painful feelings she had about being gay, especially her parents' reactions to her and the religious beliefs she still heard from them that regarded her orientation as a sin. Lynn's presentation changed from angry and tough to depressed and vulnerable as she struggled to understand the painful feelings she was dealing with. During this stage, the worker was glad she had not shared information about her own sexual orientation with Lynn, who had never asked about it, thinking that doing so might have made it harder for Lynn to feel comfortable talking about the negative side of her feelings about her own homosexuality.

The more Lynn talked about her experiences in the family, however, the more it became clear that Lynn's parents had been distant from her in other ways for quite some time. It also became clear that her low self-esteem went back to early childhood. Lynn's father was quite rigid in his beliefs and standards and was rarely home because of his work; her mother was alcoholic and thus not reliably available to Lynn. Lynn increasingly expressed interest in understanding things in her family that had been going on long before her sexual orientation became an issue. To deal with these issues and to help prepare Lynn to leave home, Lynn and her parents were referred for family therapy as well.

Lynn continued in counseling until the time came for her to leave for college. Although she continued to suffer some periods of depression, no further suicidal gestures were made, and the conflict at home was somewhat reduced. When she left, Lynn was able to imagine herself meeting others at college who might share both her sexual orientation and some of her other interests as well.

This case illustrates the importance of attending to a range of issues in working with a lesbian, gay, or bisexual client. Clearly, comfort with the client's lesbian identity and understanding the homophobic reactions of others was essential to working with this case. This comfort must encompass both the positive and negative feelings a client will most likely experience in coming out. Second, the typical developmental issues and concerns of the age or stage of development must be considered as well. Here, the anxiety of an impending separation as Lynn "grew up" and went off to school was upsetting to parent and child alike. Third, it was important to be aware of the problems and vulnerabilities of both the individual and the family as they met the challenges of coming out and their life-stage transitions. Finally, the role of social supports and ways to reduce isolation for lesbians and gays—lesbian and gay youth in particular—cannot be overestimated. Lynn's contact with peers provided validation for her sexual orientation and role models for the many ways in which people incorporate and express a gay or lesbian identity.

Working with Couples

Dating and coupling behavior is often what exposes gays and lesbians to their greatest risk from homophobia. It is not simply walking down the street alone but wanting to walk down the street holding a partner's hand that most often produces panic in the individual or fear of abuse from others. Going to a bar or expressing affection to a lover in public may, in fact, even precipitate a gay-bashing attack. With the incidence of such violence on the rise, gay and lesbian relationships are sometimes actually, as well as metaphorically, under assault.

The lack of formal and informal social sanction for the relationship is a source of strain for all gay and lesbian couples. Even if the relationship is one between partners whose lesbian or gay identity has long been established, the lack of validation of the relationship itself can produce a range of reactions, including sorrow and anger, that would otherwise be marked by joy. Holidays, for example, may find the partners separated as they fulfill commitments to families that may not welcome them together. Rituals of courtship and commitment may be lacking entirely or may be limited to the context of the gay community. Family and friends who are prepared to be generally supportive of the individual may react negatively to any steps taken by the couple to make the relationship public or legally sanctioned. Socializing in work or other contexts in which a husband or wife may be automatically included will leave gay and lesbian couples to decide whether to ask for the recognition and inclusion of a partner, or to give up validation of the relationship and the opportunity to be together in order to feel more private or more safe.

In the face of these strains, gay and lesbian couples have invented customs and rituals to sustain themselves and have adapted available supports to their own needs. Small groups of couples or friends may celebrate holidays together as faithfully as many families do. Some churches celebrate the vows of gay and lesbian couples, and some couples have chosen to invent their own spiritual or secular celebrations of commitment. Anniversaries are often carefully observed, although the date chosen is usually that of some significant event signifying involvement other than marriage.

Without the mechanisms of legal marriage (except in Massachusetts, in Canada, and in a few European countries), couples may register as domestic partners where permitted; may enter into joint financial ventures and arrangements, including home ownership; may write wills to benefit one another; and may seek devices such as a durable power of attorney or a living will to give to one another the right to make medical decisions and other legal arrangements on each other's behalf, as married couples can. In the absence of such an instrument as a will, next of kin, who may be estranged, can dispossess a lover of long standing in the event of a death, which can be a significant worry to one or both partners. Laws governing such arrangements and the limits on their use differ from state to state, and people may need assistance in finding information about resources for developing these supports in their own area.

Because these are same-sex couples, sex roles usually do not define the patterns within gay and lesbian couples to the extent they may among mixed-sex couples. In the absence of more common norms, patterns of work-sharing and relating may be more egalitarian, or they may follow some reciprocal pattern invented by the participants. As in all couples, rigid and inflexible roles may come to feel burdensome or stifling to one partner or the other, or both may be unaware of the habits that have developed. As with heterosexual couples, what couples do and what they say they do about roles and work-sharing may not be the same.[54] The role of the social worker, then, is to explore the wishes and feelings of both members of the couple and to help them design whatever arrangement for living seems most comfortable.

While sexuality does not define the lives or adjustment of gay and lesbian people any more than it does for heterosexuals, problems in sexual functioning can affect gay and lesbian relationships. Some of these may relate to social pressures, as partners who must suppress the expression of love and attachment outside the home may have difficulty in expressing tenderness and sexuality spontaneously and comfortably at home as well. Patterns of sexual behavior are often quite different in gay and lesbian couples. On average, lesbian couples often experience low levels of sexual activity after the first few years, and most are monogamous. Although ideologies about monogamy differ among lesbians, an affair often seems to precede the breakup of a relationship. Male gay couples, on average, enjoy higher levels of sexual activity for longer and have often been stably nonmonogamous. For gay couples, sexual behavior within and outside the couple relationship has been changing because of the AIDS epidemic, and the new patterns emerging may call for new adjustments. What is important, of course, is to assist each gay or lesbian couple in achieving open communication, mutually satisfying sexual expression, and acceptable negotiation of any differences that may exist between the partners in the context of their emotional relationship. It is common, however, for the breakup of a couple relationship to precipitate a crisis, when a gay or lesbian person may seek professional help, and the experience of loss of a significant relationship is a piece of personal history for many, if not most, lesbians, gays, and bisexuals.

Working with Lesbian, Gay, and Bisexual Parents

There are some special issues lesbian, gay, and bisexual parents and their children must deal with that the practitioner must be prepared to respond to. Divorced parents and their children often worry that the other biological parent (or even a grandparent) may seek custody, claiming that the custodial parent is unfit simply because of sexual orientation. These fears can have profound effects on how the family represents and conducts itself, both outside and inside the home.

Each lesbian, gay, or bisexual parent must decide how to talk with the children about his or her identity. Children too young to understand much about sex understand clearly about love; a gay or lesbian identity may best be explained in terms of loving other men or women and by differentiating love between adults from the love of an adult for a child. Sex need not be the center of the discussion, any more than it would be if a heterosexual parent were talking about his or her relationship with another parent or lover. In addition, because children identify so strongly with parents, they do need to hear that they will not necessarily grow up to be gay or lesbian just because a parent is gay or lesbian. Most of all, the parent must try to help the child ask any questions or express any fears he or she may have. The meaning of the parent's lesbian, gay, or bisexual identity is not a topic that can be dealt with once and set aside; rather, it must be revisited and reinterpreted as children grow older and their questions change.

In gay and lesbian families with children, the definition of the role of the parent who did not bear or legally adopt the child is usually an issue for the partners. What to call the "other mommy" or the "other daddy" may be a unique challenge, and the lack of language reflects the normlessness that gay and lesbian families face. In other ways, however, the issues of how childcare, housework, and employment responsibilities will be managed and shared may differ little from what heterosexual couples who become parents go through. The issues for blended families in which each partner brings offspring into the relationship may be similar as well. Asking the family about the role of each parent and how each is named and defined will validate both partners and reveal much about how the family has organized and represented itself at home and in the wider world of the extended family, the school, the workplace, and the community at large.[55]

An emerging concern within the child welfare system is the number of LGBT youth in out-of-home care and the problems they are having within it. Some kids are "pushed out" into street life or into the child protection system by parental rejection when they begin to explore or express a non-heterosexual identity. However, LGBT adolescents are often harassed or rejected in congregate care settings, which in some progressive child welfare systems has led to the creation of gay-specialized facilities. However, placement with foster parents who will accept and embrace an emerging gay identity is usually the best option, both to avoid the problems often encountered in group care and to offer positive role models.

Working with Older Lesbians, Gays, and Bisexuals

Lesbians and gays are an invisible minority in general, and older bisexual, gay, and lesbian people may feel invisible both in the gay and lesbian community and among older people. Ageism keeps them marginal to the gay community; homophobia keeps them marginal to elder service agencies and programs. Research has shown that stereotypes of the older lesbian or gay man as isolated, depressed, and unfulfilled are untrue; health, access to needed material resources, and social contacts that reduce loneliness all contribute to life satisfaction among older gays and lesbians, just as they do among the non-gay elderly.[56]

Today's older lesbians, gays, and bisexuals came of age in the pre-Stonewall era, and most had to come to terms with their sexual identity at a time when homophobia was even more widespread and overt than it is today. Professional mental health services were then more likely to be a source of stress than of support to lesbians and gays. Some elders may only have discovered or affirmed their gay or lesbian identity later in life, but they may still carry with them residues of the attitudes that were pervasive in their younger years.

Despite these obstacles, older lesbians and gays of today have much to offer the community. Their life stories are often tales of survival and affirmation that can instruct and inspire their younger counterparts.[57] Life review is often useful to the elderly, whose task is to consolidate a sense of the meaning of their individual lives and to understand them in the context of the historical events that have framed them. Because of the oppression they have confronted and survived, gay and lesbian elders may wish to share their stories with younger gays and lesbians as well as with family and non-gay friends.

The common challenges of aging—retirement, ill health, the death of a lover or close friends—affect older gays and lesbians as well. Although many have strong social support systems, the majority will not have children to turn to when meeting these crises. Those who are sick, who care for a sick or disabled partner, or who are bereaved may find that access to the support services available to other older people in similar circumstances is not so easy for them. How can gay or lesbian partners provide for each other in retirement, illness, or after death? Will the hospital, nursing home, physician, or nurse give the gay or lesbian partner the same consideration and access to the patient a husband or wife would get? Will the widows' or widowers' group or the caregivers' support group accept a gay or lesbian member? Will the gay or lesbian elder feel comfortable in reaching out for the support that is needed?

Emerging Issues and Trends

The future of social work practice with lesbians, gays, and bisexuals will build on the advances in understanding gained in the recent past and highlighted in this chapter. There are some emerging issues and trends we know about today that will take the practice of social work in new directions in the years to come.

Health Disparities

The major U.S. government report on health and health care needs, *Healthy People 2010*, discussed many population groups whose health lags behind others but did not address health disparities for the LGBT population. However, the Gay & Lesbian Medical Association (GLMA) issued its own report on health disparities using government and other data to outline the major issues for gay, lesbian, bisexual and transgender people.[58] Only a few areas will be outlined here, and because HIV/AIDS still affects so many gay men and MSMs, a separate section is devoted below to that topic.

Mental Health

Although homosexuality is no longer regarded as a psychiatric disorder, its history has left traces of distrust among LGBT people and of substandard care on the part of some providers. In fact, some mental health professionals still offer conversion or reparative therapies (designed to change a gay or lesbian's sexual orientation to a straight one) despite that all major mental health organizations have denounced such treatments as ineffective and even harmful.[59] However, effective treatments are now available for such problems as depressive and anxiety disorders, and gay and lesbian people are high utilizers of mental health treatment. In addition, much more needs to be known about the resilience of LGBT people in the face of stigma and discrimination.

Although data are limited, gay men are more likely than straight men to suffer from depression and anxiety disorders.[60] They may also be more likely than other men, and than lesbians, to suffer from an eating disorder. Some studies suggest that depression is also common among lesbians. For example, the National Lesbian Health Care Survey,[61] polling almost 2,000 lesbians, reported that the most common health problem experienced was depression or sadness. Other stress-related illnesses (such as weight problems) were reported by significant percentages. More than half the sample reported that they had been too nervous to cope with ordinary responsibilities sometime during the year. Twenty-one percent had suicidal thoughts, and 18 percent had actually made a suicide attempt. Three-fourths of those surveyed were in counseling. The mental health symptoms reported appear similar to those of other high-stress groups. This study has since been replicated, with similar findings, although other studies suggest that depression rates are no higher among lesbians than among straight women. Being coupled is a protective factor for lesbian women, while being married is a risk factor for heterosexual women. Both lesbians and gay men are at high risk for suicidal ideation and suicide attempts (although not completed suicides).[62]

Mental health problems may be especially common and severe for youth who are gay-, lesbian-, bi-, or trans-identified or who are questioning such an identification. Suicidal thoughts and attempts are alarmingly high among LGBT youth (much higher than among non-gay adolescents), and experiences of victimization contribute to this risk.[63] Because social workers provide the majority of mental health services in the United States, these are all areas in which culturally competent social workers can make a big difference.

Substance Use and Abuse

As noted earlier, lesbians and gay men have high levels of alcoholism and drug abuse, perhaps two to three times the rate as in the general population. However, LGBT face problems with access to gay-affirmative drug and alcohol treatment resources; this problem occurs in a national context in which there is not enough treatment available overall for people with drug and alcohol problems. Two other areas that need attention are treatment options for those with co-occurring mental health and substance abuse problems and prevention approaches that are tailored for use with LGBT people and communities. In addition, rates of tobacco use are higher among gay and bisexual men and among lesbians than among comparable straight men and women, a problem that has not yet been well addressed despite the many well-known health risks associated with smoking. Finally, it should be noted that drug and alcohol problems among LGBT people are associated with other serious health risks, such as HIV/AIDS, other STDs, violence, and cirrhosis and other diseases of the liver.

Cancer

Gay and lesbian people are disproportionately affected by some types of cancer, such as breast cancer (lesbians), cancers associated with the HIV virus, lung cancer, and cancers associated with the human papilloma virus.[64] The higher rates of breast cancer among lesbians is thought to be related to higher rates of general risk factors for the disease including not bearing children, alcohol use, and obesity. Gay and bisexual men are currently at higher risk for non-Hodgkins lymphoma, Hodgkins disease, and anal cancer, the last of which may be due to human papilloma virus (HPV) exposure in anal sex. HIV co-morbidity may be involved in these higher rates of occurrence (and lower survival rates) among these men. In addition, lesbians are less likely than heterosexual women to receive regular gynecological care, which means lower rates of screening for cervical cancer via the pap test and later detection of ovarian cancer. Finally, the elevated rates of cigarette smoking among LGBT people contribute to higher rates of lung cancer.

Violence and Victimization

While there are many forms of violence that affect people's health and well-being, one is hate crime. While the most common form of hate crime is against African Americans, and while many groups can be victims (for example, other racial groups, women, and Jews), "the most socially acceptable" type of hate crime is targeting LGBT people, especially among young people. However, since many states do not include crimes motivated by sexual orientation or gender expression in their definition of a hate crime and hence in their reporting to the federal government, it is likely that current estimates of its occurrence are low. In surveys of gays and lesbians carried out in several localities, 1 to 5 percent of lesbians reported experiencing physical violence based on their sexual identity, while about 25 percent of gay and bisexual men reported a similar experience. When physical assaults against gays and lesbians result in homicide, the specific acts committed tend to be more violent than similar bias crimes against other groups. Among young people, rates are much higher, and many heterosexual youth also experience such harassment in the mistaken belief that they were gay. Much of the verbal and physical abuse of gay, lesbian, and queer youth actually takes place in schools. Obviously, greater efforts at prevention are needed along with better data on these incidents from both criminal justice and health facilities like hospital emergency rooms.

Impact of AIDS

Since the epidemic began, more than a million Americans have developed AIDS; three of five have died. The majority have been gay men. The psychological and social impact on gay men and the gay community has been deep and profound. We are more than 20 years into the HIV/AIDS pandemic, and the myth that lesbians are not living and dying with the disease persists. Unfortunately this perception is held by the general public; the lesbian, gay, and bisexual communities; and many health care providers and researchers, and even educators and activists believe that lesbians are at the lowest or no risk. This false belief is fueled by a narrow focus upon woman-to-woman transmission, limitations of HIV/AIDS surveillance data, the notion that "real" lesbians don't get AIDS, and the failure to recognize differences between "identity" and "behavior."[65]

AIDS is now the leading cause of death among men and women between the ages of 25 and 44 years in the United States. The number of cases is increasing most rapidly among women and among those infected through heterosexual contact. Some 40,000 to 50,000 Americans are infected with HIV yearly. Half are under the age of 25. Worldwide, 8,500 people are infected daily.[66]

After several years of decline in new HIV cases in the gay, bisexual, and transgender communities due to successful safer sex prevention campaigns, the rates are again rising among young gay men and minorities of color. Some common, erroneous beliefs are that AIDS is a chronic disease, reasonably managed by medication, and that HIV infection can be avoided by not having sex with men over 30. In addition, the context of AIDS education has shifted. A politically conservative Christian right wing has forced public policy to focus on abstinence, not evidence-based and targeted safer sex programs (like sero-sorting) and to use faith-based initiatives, which are often anti-gay and may include reparative therapy.

Gay men and lesbians have experienced the death of lovers, friends, and associates in staggering numbers, and, given the numbers of those infected but not yet ill, this experience will no doubt continue until a cure is found. Many have not had the opportunity to process these multiple losses. In addition to the fear of AIDS, which may bring chronic anxiety akin to posttraumatic stress disorder (PTSD), there is a pervasive sense of mourning and depression in the homosexual community, which affects many aspects of life, including sexuality, and a real risk exists of reverting to more negative attitudes about homosexuality, among lesbians, gays, and bisexuals themselves as well as among straights. This backlash has resulted in some bitterness and despair in the gay community, and fear that hard-earned gains and increased acceptance may slip away in the face of AIDS.

For many homosexuals, the stresses of being different in a nonaccepting, nonunderstanding society are intensified by the AIDS health crisis. The irrational fear of AIDS, exacerbated by contradictory information along with the actual threat, has resulted in a population of "worried well."[67] These are persons at risk of AIDS because of past or present sexual activity or intravenous (IV) drug use but without a known exposure to the virus and those who have tested HIV positive but have not developed symptoms. Quadland and Sattles suggest that it is extremely important for mental health and other health professionals to clearly convey the message that homosexuality and sexual behavior did not cause AIDS and not allow society to blame the victims of this tragedy.[68] Without a significant effort to expand affirming mental health services, the emotional needs of lesbians, gays, and bisexuals will continue to be met primarily through organized self-help groups.

In response to the epidemic, lesbians, gays, and bisexuals combined their political energy and skill and assumed leadership of the nation's efforts by organizing local, state, and national self-help efforts, developing services, advocating for patients, lobbying for expanded research and treatment funds, and pressing for protective legislation. Most local AIDS service organizations were founded by gays and continue to be influenced by gays.[69] However, in recent years, there has been concerted effort to move AIDS planning, education, and service into the mainstream of health and welfare programs. This is happening as more health care providers accept their professional responsibility for the epidemic and as the profile of those infected changes from primarily white gay and bisexual men to African American and Latino IV drug users, their sexual partners, and their babies. Presently the fastest growing categories of victims are adolescents and minority women and their children. Because this process of mainstreaming services is quite slow and requires considerable experience, lesbians, gay men, and bisexuals will continue to provide leadership and financial support in this effort.

Lesbian, Gay, and Bisexual Professionals

Many social workers are themselves lesbian, gay, or bisexual, some being openly identified to their colleagues as such, others not. Thus, the professional social worker must consider sexual orientation issues in relation not only to clients and the community but also to professional relationships with students, supervisors, peers, and employers. As the Gay Liberation Movement and the professions come of age, the number of openly lesbian-, gay-, and bisexual-identified professionals is likely to grow.

Whether to "come out" when seeking employment or once on the job is a major dilemma that every lesbian, gay, and bisexual social worker must face. Fear of losing one's job is widespread and a major factor affecting their decisions to remain closeted on their own or a partner's behalf.[70] Although documented instances of such discrimination are scant, except in the military, few states have civil rights legislation explicitly protecting gays and lesbians from discrimination in hiring and other aspects of employment. Despite the provisions of the NASW Code of Ethics, few social work agencies and institutions have antidiscrimination policies of their own that explicitly mention sexual orientation, and most schools of social work also lack such protections. Workers who retain their jobs may experience social or professional isolation, mild harassment, or especially close scrutiny of their performance on the job.[71] For example, a survey of supervisors at one school of social work's field placement agencies suggested that the responses to a social work intern's "coming out" on placement might be quite variable.[72]

Providing training to all staff and support to those working with clients who are lesbian, gay, or bisexual, or who are from families with lesbian, gay, or bisexual members, are ways both to legitimate the issues and to remove pressure from identified lesbian, gay, or bisexual staff to be the resident experts. Such practices are not just affirming for staff; they are therapeutic for clients as well, some of whom may be dealing with issues of sexual orientation themselves.

The profession, through its associations (e.g., NASW, Societies for Clinical Social Work, American Association of Black Social Workers, as well as other ethnic and specialty groups), has begun to respond to minority group pressure by increasing membership education, establishing state-level lesbian and gay caucuses, and supporting civil rights legislation. Many more social agencies, such as child and family services and mental health clinics, have broadened their mission to serve this population. The Council on Social Work Education has added lesbian and gay content to the required human diversity curriculum standards and, with an exception for religious institutions, sanction against those programs that continue to discriminate against lesbian, gay, and bisexual students, staff, and faculty. The profession has responded to similar changes in cultural ideology in the past and will continue to do so in the future.

Concluding Comment

In recent decades, a revolution has taken place in gay people's perception of themselves. The notion of homosexuality as an individual illness has been discredited and replaced with a political and social definition that posits that to be gay is to be a member of an oppressed minority, similar in many ways to racial and ethnic minorities.[73] In response to oppression, lesbians, gays, and bisexuals have organized to reinforce this new self-view and to press for civil rights that are currently denied. The future political agenda of lesbian, gay, and bisexual communities will include macro-level state and national activity around each of the following issues: (1) civil rights (e.g., the repeal of state sodomy laws, passage of antidiscrimination statutes, and legal recognition of relationships); (2) violence and hate crimes (e.g., protection against gay bashing, harassment, and abuse); (3) substance abuse (e.g., increased awareness of, access to, and the development of lesbian- and gay-sensitive drug and alcohol services); (4) health care (e.g., ensuring access to and the quality of gay sensitive services, sexually transmitted disease and AIDS care, reproductive rights, new reproductive technologies such as alternative insemination, and women's health equity); (5) mental health service based on gay-affirmative models; (6) community, family, and social life (e.g., custody, child, and foster care rights); (7) youth services (e.g., education, support services, and legal protections); (8) elder care (e.g., expansion of services to reflect the increase in numbers and the different life histories and expectations of the elders of the future); and (9) equal protection in the workplace, including the right to serve openly in the military without harassment and discrimination.

Same-sex marriage and equal treatment in the military will continue to be the battleground for civil rights activism. Both engage core social institutions where blatant discrimination and breach of a gay or lesbian citizen's privacy and equal protection rights persist. Recently, the State Supreme Court of Hawaii asked for compelling reasons why the state should not permit legal same-sex marriage. Congress, in anticipation of an affirmative decision, passed a "Defense of (heterosexual) Marriage Act" (DOMA) intended to block the state's recognition of same-sex marriages. Many states have followed suit.

Since 2005, however, Massachusetts became the first state to allow same-sex marriages. Vermont and Connecticut have legalized civil unions, while ten states and the District of Columbia offer domestic partnerships. Hawaii, Oregon, and New Jersey have enacted variations of these arrangements. While "domestic partnership" recognition has also been advanced in industry and in some municipalities, these alternatives to marriage can only confer "second-class" rights and privileges in comparison to those awarded with marriage. Because of the Defense of Marriage Act (DOMA), however, even those married in Massachusetts cannot avail themselves of the federal benefits, like spousal Social Security benefits, that marriage usually guarantees.

The "Don't ask, don't tell" military policy is being challenged successfully in the federal courts because of its apparent violation of the Constitution's equal protection and privacy clauses. The legal process is slow, however, and the gains that have been made appear to be made at the margins, for example, more states promulgating administrative policy allowing for gay and lesbian foster parenting and adoptions. These advances are hardly secure in that the "Religious Right" and political conservatives are scapegoating gay men and lesbians as they targeted communists and Jews only decades ago.

Social visibility of lesbian, gay, and bisexual people will become the norm. Social acceptance and integration will be illusory in some sectors of society while a reality in others. Social work professionals are in a position to have an influence on many of the issues facing lesbians, gays, and bisexuals today and in the future: civil rights, access to health and reproductive services, child custody, adoption and foster care, and mental health and substance abuse services, to name but a few. We will all be challenged to use that influence for the good.

KEY WORDS AND CONCEPTS

Gays
Lesbians
Bisexuals
Homophobia

Heterosexism
Oppression
Conversion therapy

SUGGESTED INFORMATION SOURCES

Appleby, G. A., and J. W. Anastas. *Not Just a Passing Phase: Social Work with Lesbian, Gay and Bisexual People*. New York: Columbia University Press, 1998.

Comstock, G. D. *Violence Against Lesbians and Gay Men*. New York: Columbia University Press, 1991.

D'Augelli, A. R., and C. J. Patterson, eds. *Lesbian, Gay, and Bisexual Identities over the Lifespan*. New York: Oxford University Press, 1995.

Edwards, R. L., ed. *Encyclopedia of Social Work*, 19th ed. Washington, D.C.: NASW Press, 1995: featuring the following articles: Berger, R. M., and J. J. Kelly, "Gay Men: Overview," pp. 1064–1074; Hunter, J., and R. Schaecher, "Gay and Lesbian Adolescents," pp. 1055–1063; Gochros, J. S., "Bisexuality," pp. 299–304; Laird, J., "Lesbians: Parenting," pp. 1604–1615; Morales, J., "Gay Men: Parenting," pp. 1085–1094; Shernoff, M., "Gay Men: Direct Practice," pp. 1075–1084; Tully, C. T., "Lesbians: Overview," pp. 1591–1596; Woodman, N. J., "Lesbians: Direct Practice," pp. 1597–1603.

Garnets, L. D., and D. C. Kimmel, eds. *Psychological Perspectives on Lesbian and Gay Male Experiences*. New York: Columbia University Press, 1993.

Gay and Lesbian Medical Association (GLMA). *Healthy People 2010: A Companion Document for Lesbian, Gay, Bisexual and Transgender Health*. San Francisco, CA: Author, 2001. Available at http://www.glma.org.

Geller, T., ed. *Bisexuality: Theory and Research*. New York: Haworth Press, 1991.

Gonsiorek, J. C., and J. D. Weinrich, eds. *Homosexuality: Research Implications for Public Policy*. Newbury Park, CA: Sage, 1991.

Herek, G. M., and K. T. Berrill, eds. *Hate Crimes: Confronting Violence against Lesbians and Gay Men*. Newbury Park, CA: Sage, 1992.

McWhirter, D. P., and A. M. Mattison. *The Male Couple: How Relationships Develop*. New York: Prentice-Hall, 1984.

National Association of Social Workers. "Lesbian, Gay, and Bisexual Issues," *Social Work Speaks: NASW Policy Statements*, 4th ed. Washington, D.C.: NASW Press, 1997.

Nava, M., and R. Dawidoff. *Created Equal: Why Gay Rights Matter to America.* New York: St. Martin's Press, 1994.

Slater, S. *The Lesbian Family Life Cycle.* New York: Free Press, 1995.

Sullivan, A. *Virtually Normal: An Argument about Homosexuality.* New York: Alfred A. Knopf, 1995.

Vaid, U. *Virtually Equal: The Mainstreaming of Gay and Lesbian Liberation.* New York: Anchor Books, 1995.

ENDNOTES

1. A. P. Weiner, "Racist, Sexist, and Homophobic Attitudes among Undergraduate Social Work Students and the Effects on Assessments of Client Vignettes," unpublished doctoral dissertation (New Brunswick, NJ: Rutgers University, 1989); see also G. Appleby, "Hearing: Gay Bashing and Harassment," unpublished conference proceedings (San Francisco: NASW Annual Program Meeting, 1989).
2. J. Ost and G. J. Gates, *The Gay & Lesbian Atlas* (Washington, D.C.: The Urban Institute Press, 2004).
3. J. Martin and W. Meezan, *Research Methods with LGBT People* (Binghamton, NY: Harrington Park Press, 2003).
4. G. A. Appleby and J. W. Anastas, *Not Just a Passing Phase: Social Work with Gay, Lesbian, and Bisexual People* (New York: Columbia University Press, 1998), p. 57.
5. A. P. Bell and M. S. Weinberg, *Homosexualities: A Study of Diversity among Men and Women* (New York: Simon & Schuster, 1978).
6. Ost and Gates, 2004, p. 49.
7. H. Hidalgo, "Third World," in H. Hidalgo, T. Peterson, and N. J. Woodman, eds., *Lesbian and Gay Issues: A Resource Manual for Social Workers* (Silver Spring, MD: National Association of Social Workers, 1985), pp. 14–16.
8. M. C. Smith, "By the Year 2000," in J. Beam, ed., *In the Life: A Black Gay Anthology* (Boston: Alyson Press, 1986), p. 226.
9. A. Carballo-Dieguez, "Hispanic Culture, Gay Male Culture, and AIDS: Counseling Implications," *Journal of Counseling and Development* 68 (September–October 1989): 26–30.
10. V. M. Mays and S. D. Cochran, "Black Gay and Bisexual Men Coping with More than Just a Disease," *Focus* 4 (January 1988): 1–3.
11. J. H. Newby, "The Effects of Cultural Beliefs and Values on AIDS Prevention and Treatment in the Black Community," a paper presented at the Annual Program Meeting of the National Association of Social Workers, San Francisco, October 1989.
12. W. J. Blumenfeld, *How We All Pay the Price* (Boston: Beacon Press, 1992).
13. W. Paul and J. D. Weinrich, "Whom and What We Study: Definition and Scope of Sexual Orientation," in *Homosexuality: Social, Psychological, and Biological Issues* (Beverly Hills, CA: Sage, 1982), pp. 26–27.
14. A. P. Bell, M. S. Weinberg, and S. K Hammersmith, *Sexual Preference: It's Development in Men and Women* (Bloomington: Indiana University Press, 1981).
15. B. Garner and R. W. Smith, "Are There Really Any Gay Male Athletes? An Empirical Survey," *Journal of Sex Research* 13 (1977): 22–34.
16. Jeramy Townsley, Health Risks of Gay Youth, IUPUI, 2001, GLSEN, July 11, 2005, http://www.glsen.org.
17. Gay, Lesbian, Straight Education Network (GLSEN), July 11, 2005, http://www.glsen.org.

18. C. T. Tully, "Gay and Lesbian Person," in A. Gitterman, ed., *Handbook of Social Work Practice with Vulnerable and Resilient Population.* (New York: Columbia University Press, 2001).
19. C. A. Lukes and H. Land, "Biculturality and Homosexuality," *Social Work* 35 (1990): 155–161.
20. Ibid.
21. N. Hunter and N. Polikoff, "Custody Rights of Lesbian Mothers: Legal Theory and Litigation Strategy," *Buffalo Law Review* 25 (1976): 691–733.
22. M. Mendola, *A New Look at Gay Couples* (New York: Crown, 1980); see also D. McWhirter and A. Mattison, *The Male Couple: How Relationships Develop* (Englewood Cliffs, NJ: Prentice Hall, 1984).
23. R. Achtenberg, "Preserving and Protecting the Families of Lesbians and Gay Men," in M. Shernoff and W. Scott, *The Sourcebook on Lesbian/Gay Health Care* (Washington, D.C.: The National Lesbian/Gay Health Foundation, 1988); see also S. K. Hammersmith, "A Sociological Approach to Counseling Homosexual Clients and Their Families," in E. Coleman, ed., *Integrated Identity for Gay Men and Lesbians: Psychotherapeutic Approaches for Emotional Well-Being* (New York: Harrington Park Press, 1988), pp. 174–179.
24. Bell, Weinberg, and Hammersmith, op. cit.
25. M. Kirkpatrick, K. Smith, and R. Roy, "Lesbian Mothers and Their Children: A Comparative Study," *American Journal of Orthopsychiatry* 51 (1981): 545–551; see also B. Miller, "Gay Fathers and Their Children," *The Family Coordinator* 28 (1979): 544–552; F. Bozett, "Gay Fathers: Evaluation of the Gay Father Identity," *American Journal of Psychiatry* 51 (March 1978): 173–179; R. Green, "Thirty-five Children Raised by Homosexual or Transsexual Parents," *American Journal of Psychiatry* (1978): 135; B. Hoeffer, "Children's Acquisition of Sex-Role Behavior in Lesbian Mother Families," *American Journal of Orthopsychiatry* 51 (March 1981); S. Golombok, "Children in Lesbian and Single Parent Households: Psychosexual and Psychiatric Appraisal," *Journal of Child Psychology and Applied Discipline* 24 (1983); E. F. Levy, "Lesbian Mothers' Coping Characteristics: An Exploration of Social, Psychological, and Family Coping Resources," unpublished doctoral dissertation (Madison: University of Wisconsin, 1983).
26. Kirkpatrick, Smith, and Roy, op. cit.
27. R. M. Berger, "Homosexuality: Gay Men," in A. Minahan, ed., *Encyclopedia of Social Work,* 18th ed. (Silver Spring, MD: National Association of Social Workers, 1987).
28. S. Susoeff, "Assessing Children's Best Interests When a Parent Is Gay or Lesbian: Toward a Rational Custody Standard," *UCLA Law Review* 32 (April 1985); M. Kirkpatrick and D. Hitchens, "Lesbian Mothers/Gay Fathers," in *Emerging Issues in Child Psychiatry and the Law* (New York: Brunner & Mazel, 1985).
29. N. J. Woodman, "Homosexuality: Lesbian Women," in A. Minahan, ed., *Encyclopedia of Social Work,* 18 Edition (Silver Spring, MD: National Association of Social Workers, 1987).
30. M. S. Weinberg and C. J. Williams, *Male Homosexuals: Their Problems and Adaptations* (New York: Oxford University Press, 1974).
31. R. M. Berger, "What Is a Homosexual? A Definitional Model," *Social Work* 28 (February 1983): 132–135.
32. Ibid.
33. Ibid.

34. E. Coleman, ed., *Integrated Identity for Gay Men and Lesbians: Psychotherapeutic Approaches for Emotional Well-Being* (New York: Harrington Park Press, 1988), p. 19.
35. J. Bradford and C. Ryan, *The National Lesbian Health Care Survey* (Washington, D.C.: National Lesbian and Gay Health Foundation, 1988): p. 4.
36. L. Icard and D. M. Traunstein, "Black Gay Alcoholic Men: Their Culture and Treatment," *Social Casework* 68, no. 5 (1987): 267–272.
37. S. C. Anderson and D. C. Henderson, "Working with Lesbian Alcoholics," *Social Work* 30 (June 1985): 518–525.
38. V. Brooks, *Minority Stress and Lesbian Women* (Lexington, MA: D.C. Heath, 1981).
39. J. B. Bradford, "Reactions of Gay Men to AIDS: A Survey of Self-Reported Change," unpublished doctoral dissertation (Virginia Commonwealth University, 1986).
40. R. Alcalay, "Health and Social Support Networks: A Case for Improving Communication," *Social Networks* 5 (1983): 71–88.
41. Bradford and Ryan, op. cit., pp. 3–5.
42. C. B. Germain and A. Gitterman, *The Life Model of Social Work Practice* (New York: Columbia University Press, 1980).
43. M. Coles and W. Rubenstein, "Rights of Gays and Lesbians," paper presented at the Biennial Conference at the University of Wisconsin, Madison, June 15–18, 1987.
44. Achtenberg, op. cit., p. 244.
45. T. Dougherty, "Economic Benefits of Marriage under Federal and Connecticut Law," National Gay and Lesbian Task Force Policy Institute, 2005, http://www.thetaskforce.org.
46. M. Hall, "Lesbian Families: Cultural and Clinical Issues," *Social Work* 23 (1978): 380–385.
47. Ibid., p. 380.
48. Ibid.
49. K. Lewes, *The Psychoanalytic Theory of Male Homosexuality* (New York: Simon & Schuster, 1988).
50. A. Rosenthal, "Heterosexism and Clinical Assessment," *Smith College Studies in Social Work* 52 (February 1982): 145–159.
51. A. P. Bell and M. S. Weinberg, *Homosexualities: A Study of Diversity among Men and Women* (New York: Simon & Schuster, 1978).
52. J. Krajeski, "Psychotherapy with Gay Men and Lesbians: A History of Controversy," in T. S. Stein and C. J. Cohen, eds., *Contemporary Perspectives on Psychotherapy with Lesbians and Gay Men* (New York: Plenum, 1986).
53. C. Golden, "Diversity and Variability in Women's Sexual Identities," Boston Lesbian Psychologies Collective, ed., in *Lesbian Psychologies: Explorations and Challenges* (Urbana: University of Illinois Press, 1986).
54. A. Hochschild, *The Second Shift* (New York: Viking Press, 1989).
55. S. Crawford, "Lesbian Families: Psychosocial Stress and the Family-Building Process," in *Lesbian Psychologies: Explorations and Challenges* (Urbana: University of Illinois Press, 1986).
56. R. M. Berger, "Realities of Gay and Lesbian Aging," *Social Work* 29 (January 1984): 57–62; see also M. Kehoe, "Lesbians over Sixty Speak for Themselves," *Journal of Homosexuality* 16 (March–April 1988): 1–78.
57. M. Adelman, ed., *Long Time Passing: Lives of Older Lesbians* (Boston: Alyson Publications, 1986).
58. Gay and Lesbian Medical Association (GLMA). *Healthy People 2010: A Companion Document for Lesbian, Gay, Bisexual and Transgender Health*. San Francisco, CA. Available at http://www.glma.org.

59. G. Smith, A. Bartlett, and M. King, "Treatments of Homosexuality in Britain since the 1950s—an Oral History: The Experience of Patients," *British Journal of Medicine* (2004); M. King, G. Smith, and A. Bartlett, "Treatments of Homosexuality in Britain since the 1950s—an Oral History: The Experience of Professionals," *British Journal of Medicine* (2004).
60. GLMA, op. cit..
61. Bradford and Ryan, op. cit.
62. Ibid.
63. Ibid.
64. GLMA, op. cit.
65. N. A. Humphreys and J. K. Quam, "Middle-Aged and Old Gay, Lesbian and Bisexual Adults," in G. A. Appleby and J. W. Anastas, eds., *Not Just a Passing Phase: Social Work with Gay, Lesbian and Bisexual People* (New York: Columbia University Press, 1998).
66. L. Daimant, ed., *Homosexual Issues in the Workplace* (Washington, D.C.: Taylor & Francis, 1993); C. Kitzinger, "Lesbians and Gay Men in the Workplace: Psychosocial Issues," in M. J. Davidson and J. Earnshaw, eds., *Vulnerable Workers: Psychosocial and Legal Issues* (New York: John Wiley & Sons, 1991), pp. 223–257.
67. K. J. Harowski, "The Worried Well: Maximizing Coping in the Face of AIDS," in Coleman, op. cit.
68. M. C. Quadland and W. D. Sattles, "AIDS, Sexuality, and Sexual Control," in Coleman, op. cit.
69. G. A. Appleby, "What Social Workers Can Do," in S. Alyson, ed., *You Can Do Something about AIDS* (Boston: The Stop AIDS Project, 1989).
70. M. P. Levine and R. Leonard, "Discrimination against Lesbians in the Work Force," *Signs: Journal of Women in Culture and Society* 9 (April 1984): 700–710.
71. J. Rabin, K. Keefe, and M. Burton, "Enhancing Services for Sexual-Minority Clients: A Community Mental Health Approach," *Social Work* 31 (April 1986): 292–298.
72. Lewes, op. cit.
73. W. Paul, "Social and Cultural Issues," in *Homosexuality: Social, Psychological, and Biological Issues* (Beverly Hills, CA: Sage, 1982).

chapter 18

Social Work Practice with Children and Youth

Prefatory Comment

Children and youth in the United States are thought of as cherished beneficiaries of America's past, symbols of the quality of the society, and conveyors of the nation's hopes for the future. Unlike many nations, the United States invests considerable resources in social, recreational, and educational programs to benefit its youngest members. Political and philosophical differences exist about how to best enhance the quality of life for children and youth, but there is little disagreement that their physical, psychological, and intellectual development is important. Social workers play key roles in each of these areas of human development.

Children were once exploited as a source of labor in the sweatshops of urban America and on family farms in rural areas. Just a century and a half ago, it was not uncommon for poor white families to abandon their children to the urban streets during hard economic times, for black slave children to be sold away from their parents for a profit, for children of Mexican migrant families to toil each day in the hot sun doing backbreaking farm labor, and so on. The condition of housing in which children lived was often crowded, unsanitary, and dangerous in urban tenements, Appalachian coal towns, and migrant camps, largely because wealthy owners were in complete control and their priority was to make a profit for themselves and their corporations. Children's education, too, was viewed as a luxury and was often available to them only before they were old enough to provide productive labor in factories or, in rural areas, at the times of the year when crops were dormant and their labor was not needed in the fields.

In the early 1900s, concerns about the damaging conditions experienced by children were elevated to a national issue, with social workers leading this public education effort. The public gradually became aware of the plight of children, and sentiment that this important resource should be protected and nourished began to evolve. Committees concerned about housing quality, child labor, basic child health issues, and the excessive placement of children in orphanages and other institutions contributed to President Theodore Roosevelt calling a White House Conference on the Care of Dependent Children in 1909. The subsequent formation of the U.S. Children's Bureau, which, under the direction of social worker Katherine Lenroot, initiated government oversight and advocacy in the interest of children, was a milestone in social welfare history.[1] As a result, child labor legislation was passed, mother's pensions (later public assistance) were provided, minimum housing quality was required, and public education mandated.

Current Demographics

Compared with conditions prior to the twentieth century, the quality of life for children and youth in the United States has improved considerably. Yet more is needed. Based on an analysis of U.S. Census data, Kominski, Jamieson, and Martinez identified seven conditions experienced by school-age children that are strong indicators of undesirable outcomes later in life. These at-risk factors include:

▶ At least one disability
▶ Retained in grade at least once
▶ Speaks English less than "very well"
▶ Does not live with both parents
▶ Either parent immigrated to the United States in past five years
▶ Family income below $10,000 annually
▶ Neither parent/guardian employed

Although 54 percent of the children and youth experienced none of these risk factors, 28 percent were affected by one factor, and 18 percent experienced more than one of these conditions.[2]

There are, of course, many other factors that increase risk for children and youth. The following pages present estimates regarding the number and/or percent of children who experience a variety of conditions that place them at greater risk for problems—both now and in the future. Given the Census Bureau estimate of more than 73.2 million children and youth in the United States, the variety of issues that might make them vulnerable to social problems is extensive. For social workers, awareness of these problems provides a background for recognizing their impact on individual clients being served and for advocating for change in public attitudes and social policies to reduce or prevent them from harming our children and youth in the future.

Personal Characteristics

People possess a number of personal characteristics and have had experiences that shape their personalities that, at times, make them particularly vulnerable to social problems. For example, one factor, the racial/ethnic mix, in the United States is changing with the percent of the Hispanic population (19.1 percent) increasing, the non-Hispanic white population (58.8 percent) decreasing, and the other groups (African American, 14.9 percent; Asian American, 3.1 percent; and the other non-Hispanic groups, 7.2 percent) remaining about the same as in the past.[3] Also, the percent of foreign-born children is getting larger (2.3 percent), and the number who have difficulty speaking English fluently (4.9 percent) is also increasing.[4] Like the other characteristics, possessing one or more of these factors does not assure a negative outcome. Human resilience can minimize the impact of a risk factor for any individual and thus affect that person's vulnerability.

Family Composition

The varying family structures in the United States are another factor that affects the opportunities and experiences of children and youth. For all children and youth, 69.7 percent live in a two-parent household, including one or two biological parents and/or an adoptive parent or stepparent. However, there is considerable racial and cultural variation in children living in these two-parent households, with Asian families (87.2 percent) the most stable, followed by white non-Hispanic (77.8), Hispanic (64.1), and black non-Hispanic families (37.7). What is the typical composition of these black non-Hispanic families? As compared with 23.0 percent of the overall population, 49.6 percent of the black non-Hispanic families are headed by a single mother, where the chances of growing up in poverty are 4.5 times greater than in other living arrangements. Also, compared with 2.2 percent of the total children, 5.5 percent of the black non-Hispanic children and youth live with a grandparent.[5] This phenomenon, sometimes known as *grandfamilies*, is expanding in all population groups as increasingly biological parents experiencing a substance abuse problem or other form of impairment are leaving their children in grandparents' custody. When grandfamily and other kinship-care arrangements are made, social workers are often involved in securing financial resources and legal sanction to assure the safety, stability, and general well-being of the children. Similarly, social workers are also involved in placements where no biological family is present—especially when foster care is being provided to more than 300,000 children.

Housing and Living Environment

One area of improving conditions for children relates to where they live. Today, only 5 percent of children live in inadequate housing (compared with 9 percent in 1978), and those living in crowded conditions (defined as more than one person per room) has held steady at 6 percent the last few years—also down from 9 percent in 1978. The one ominous sign related to housing is the increasing percentage of households in which children live where the *cost burden* of housing is excessive. In 2005, the housing cost burden for 34 percent of the families was 30 percent or more of their income, and for 14 percent of the families, the burden was more than one-half of their income.[6] In times of economic downturn, these families are at high risk of foreclosure and homelessness. Social workers are expected to assist with money management and help these families secure housing.

The leading cause of death for children is unintentional injuries—usually occurring at home. For children ages 1 to 4, fatal falls or being struck by an object occurred at a rate of 79 per 100,000 children and 53 per 100,000 for children ages 5 to 14. For every fatality, there were another 33 hospitalizations and 1,350 emergency room visits.[7] Social workers in hospitals and emergency rooms can expect to deal with these problems. Warm and safe housing is essential for meeting the very basic needs of people, and social workers are often involved in promoting and helping people secure appropriate housing.

Family Income and Employment

A child's well-being is improved if the family income is adequate to support good-quality housing, health care, food, clothing, and so on. The median income for all households in the United States in 2006 was $48,201. However, 36.5 million families were living in poverty (i.e., less than $21,000 for a family of four), thus many families have less than the expected quality of life standards. The disparity in income is best captured by the fact that the 20 percent of households with the lowest income possess only 3.4 percent of the total U.S. income, while the 20 percent of the households with the highest income hold 50.5 percent of the wealth—and that disparity is increasing.[8]

A variety of risk factors are associated with a family's income level, although race and single-parent households are factors that consistently have a strong association with the amount of income. Where Asian and white families have an average income somewhat above the national median of $48,201, Hispanic families fall $10,420 below the national norm, and black families average $16,232 below the median. Married-couple families, many having two employed members, average nearly $69,715 per year, yet families headed by a single male averaged $22,638 less, and for a single female–headed family, the average was $37,898 less than for married-couple families. Increasing income, however, comes at a cost. Two-parent families increase their income when both parents can be employed and, as a result, more than one-half of the mothers work full-time and another 18 percent work part-time. The trade-off for additional financial resources is the parents' available time and energy to devote to their children's growth and development.[9]

Poverty and Hunger

The single clearest predictor of social problems for children and youth is living in poverty. When reporting their study of the impact of poverty on children, Lewitt, Terman, and Behrman[10] conclude:

> Not only do poor children have access to fewer material goods than rich or middle-class children, but also they are more likely to experience poor health and to die during childhood. In school, they score lower on standardized tests and are more likely to be retained in grade and to drop out. Poor teens are more likely to have out-of-wedlock births and to experience violent crime. Finally, persistently poor children are more likely to end up as poor adults. (p. 8)

Kearnsey, Grundermann, and Gallicchio[11] estimate that without the income supports of various social programs, the child poverty level would double. The social action agenda of the National Association of Social Workers supports maintaining or increasing the level of support for children and their families through income maintenance programs.

Poverty and its associated problems do not fall equally on children and youth. In a wealthy country such as the United States, it is troubling that 17.4 percent of all children experience poverty. The poverty rate is high at 10.0 percent for white children and 12.2 percent for Asian children, but it is much greater at 23.4 percent for the black population and 26.9 percent for Hispanics.[12] Being Hispanic or black doubles a child's risk of living in poverty. In addition, as indicated above, living with a single mother is another high-risk factor. Although 6.4 percent of the children living with married parents experience an income below the poverty line, the chances of living in poverty increases almost sixfold (36.5 percent) when living with a single mother. Race, again, is a compounding factor, with the poverty rate for Asian single mothers at 24.1 percent, and for white single mothers with children in the home, it is 30.2 percent. Yet for Hispanic single mothers, the poverty rate is 42.5 percent, and it is 43.3 percent for black single mothers.[13]

Poverty-related factors such as inadequate health care and substandard housing typically have a long-term negative impact on the well-being of children. Hunger has an immediate impact on poor people because it represents a threat to one's very survival. The U.S. Department of Agriculture reports that more than 13 million families with children (affecting one in five children) experience *food insecurity* (i.e., not having enough food at all times for active healthy living), and more than 420,000 children face food insecurity and hunger (simply not enough food for all family members). Households with $70,000 or more income were found to spend 7 percent of their income on food, while low-income families devoted nearly 25 percent of their income to purchasing food.[14] When there is an inadequate food supply for a family, often children will be fed inadequate portions, and adults will skip meals (decreasing their functioning and risking their employment) or select inexpensive and unhealthy foods that are high in fat, calories, and sugar. The result is often more health problems, missed days of school or work, less income, inability to afford appropriate housing—and the cycle of poverty continues. How do we break that cycle?

Learning Stimulation and Educational Status

In many ways, hope for a nation's future depends on the education of its children and youth. In an increasingly high-tech universe, persons with limited education find it difficult to compete for jobs and lack the ability to earn the income necessary to support themselves and their families. From the basic learning provided through families, in child care facilities, and through formal education in elementary and secondary schools, the learning potential of children and youth is developed. With two-thirds of all mothers employed, the quality of day care arrangements for pre-kindergarten children is critical for children's safety and maximum development. For the 11.3 million children in this age group, 20 percent were cared for by a grandparent on a regular basis while the mother was working; another 23.8 percent participated in a day care center, nursery school, or Head Start program; and the remainder received day care from a relative, were placed in the care of nonrelatives, or had no regular arrangements. Paid arrangements place an especially heavy burden on poor families who averaged spending 29 percent of their monthly income on day care, as compared with their wealthier counterparts spending an average of 6 percent of their income on such services.[15]

In 2005, 9.4 percent (nearly 3.5 million) of those between the ages of 16 to 24 were not enrolled in a high school program and had not received a diploma. In short, they had dropped out of the educational system. The decision to drop out not only precludes gaining a high school diploma, but, unless the young person completes a general education diploma (GED), he or she is also ineligible for college enrollment. The highest dropout rates are among males (10.8 percent), Hispanic students (22.5 percent), those who are foreign born (24.4 percent), or children of foreign-born parents (16.0 percent).[16] Advanced education is considered to add substantially to the quality of one's life, yet the long-term impact on annual earning power is even more evident. In 2007, for those 18 and older with no high school diploma, the average weekly income was $428, and the unemployment rate was 7.1 percent. Weekly earnings increased to $604 if one completed high school, and the unemployment rate dropped to 4.4 percent. For those completing a bachelor's degree, weekly earnings increased to $987, and unemployment dropped to 2.2 percent. Finally, for the few who earned a professional degree (in most professions, a master's or doctorate), earnings increased to $1,427, and the unemployment rate shrunk to 1.3 percent.[17] In terms of annual wages in 2006, persons with an advanced degree averaged $82,320, compared with those with less than a high school degree earning $20,873.[18] It is evident that one goal for social workers should be to help all children remain in school whenever possible, as increased education is closely associated with both earning power and a decreasing likelihood of being unemployed. In the United States, education has been the primary factor that reduces the chances a family will experience poverty, and, with more education, the well-being of the family's children will be improved.

Health Status and Chronic Physical Conditions

Another critical factor in the successful growth and development of children and youth is their health, and, unfortunately, the health care system in the United States has failed many of the nation's young people. Lack of adequate health insurance usually means there will be little attention to preventing health problems or even for early treatment when illnesses can be more readily treated. Evidence of the long-term impact of not having adequate health care can be seen in the fact that more than twice as many poor people have less than "good" or "excellent" health, as compared with those above the poverty line. The high cost of health care places at risk the 11.7 percent of all children living in families that have no health insurance. Like other factors making children vulnerable, the interrelated conditions of race, income, and educational level of the parents are all associated with having or not having health insurance. More specifically, in 2006, 7.9 percent of white children were uninsured, as compared with 11.3 and 19.7 percent of black and Hispanic children, respectively. Additionally, 29.9 percent of children living near the poverty line were uninsured, as compared with the overall average of 11.7 percent. When a parent had a graduate or professional degree, only 5.8 percent of the children were uninsured, while that percentage increased to 9.0 for those with a college degree, 18.5 if a parent had only completed high school, and 38.0 if high school was not completed.[19]

Two broad indices of health issues experienced by children and youth provide a snapshot of the prevalence of these conditions. First, nearly 18 percent of all children aged 5 through 17 experienced at least one *chronic health problem* that limits their activities—with males experiencing these conditions at a much higher rate than females. Social workers often work with these children and youth because the conditions affect their social, psychological, physical, and educational functioning. Among the several chronic health conditions affecting children, the three top problems in 2007 were obesity (18 percent), asthma (9 percent), and attention deficit hyperactivity disorder (ADHD) at 6 percent.[20] Second, an estimated 20.8 percent of the children and youth ages 9 through 17 experience emotional difficulties—including 4.8 percent with *definite/severe difficulties* (i.e., affecting interaction at home, school, or with peers).[21]

Child maltreatment, too, can have devastating emotional and physical effects on children and youth. As the primary profession providing child welfare services, social workers often deal with the victims, as well as the perpetrators, of child abuse. In 2006 there were 905,000 substantiated reports of child maltreatment—resulting in 1,530 deaths, i.e., more than 2 deaths per 100,000 children. Girls experienced slightly higher rates than boys, and the rates of victimization were highest among the youngest and most vulnerable children. Children age 3 and under were twice as likely to be abused than youth ages 16 and 17. Further, among the substantiated cases of child maltreatment, 64.1 percent experienced neglect, 16.0 percent were physically abused, 8.8 percent were sexually abused, and 6.6 percent were emotionally or psychologically maltreated. The death rates were highest for both infants and youth ages 15 to 17. The infant deaths were typically unintended injuries (e.g., falls, being struck by an object, accidental poisoning), and the additional factors causing death among the older youth were motor vehicle accidents, homicide, and suicide.[22]

At-Risk Social Behaviors

In addition to the above risk factors, various social behaviors place children and youth at further risk for long-term problems. For example, among twelfth-graders, 15 percent regularly smoke cigarettes, nearly 30 percent engage in binge drinking, and 25 percent reporting using illicit or illegal drugs. Nearly one-half are also sexually active, and 5.4 percent of the girls in the 15- to 17-year age group become pregnant each year. Of the children born to unmarried parents (37 percent in 2005), nearly 7 percent had late or no prenatal care, and almost 8 percent were of low birthweight (i.e., below 5.5 pounds), thus increasing the chance of serious medical and developmental problems.[23] Violence is also a part of life for many 14 to 17-year-olds, with more than 5 percent committing a violent crime each year, 17 percent carrying a weapon to school, 9 percent becoming victims of dating violence, and another 1.5 percent being a victim of a serious crime.[24] These social behaviors also become associated with increased health problems, single parenthood, lack of success in school, lowered employability, and so on.

In its 2007 report, "America's Cradle to Prison Pipeline,"[25] the Children's Defense Fund provides disturbing statistics that summarize the negative experiences of children and youth today. Each day in the United States:

4	children are killed by abuse or neglect
5	children or teens commit suicide
8	children or teens are killed by firearms
33	children or teens die from accidents
77	babies die before their first birthdays
192	children are arrested for violent crimes
383	children are arrested for drug abuse
906	babies are born at low birthweight
1,153	babies are born to teen mothers
1,672	public school students are corporally punished
1,870	babies are born without health insurance
2,261	high school students drop out
2,383	children are confirmed as abused or neglected
2,411	babies are born into poverty
2,494	babies are born to mothers who are not high school graduates
4,017	babies are born to unmarried parents
4,302	children are arrested
17,132	public school children are suspended

People created an environment in their homes, in schools, in communities, and in the larger society that contributed to these conditions. Difficult and time consuming as it may be, people can also change those conditions.

The Ecosystems Model

It is likely that many of these children or their parents will be in contact with a social worker. With the social worker's attention focused on both the person and the person's environment, the social worker must gather and analyze large amounts of information about the situation both to provide services to those affected and to generate or support changes in social policies that will prevent or reduce these conditions. One way to organize an enormous amount of social, cultural, and physical and mental health data is to apply the five-level ecosystems model depicted in

Figure P5.1 (shown previously in Part 5). To demonstrate the applicability of this model, the case of "Joe" captures some of the background information, as well as specifics for this case, that a social worker might consider.

THE CASE SITUATION

Joe is a 17-year-old biracial male who, upon being discovered in his girlfriend's apartment, hid in a closet while armed and shot through the door when called out by the police. He wounded one of the police officers. When Joe fired first, the officers (including the wounded officer) retaliated in self-defense and fired twenty shots through the door, of which twelve bullets hit Joe. Joe's explanation was simply, "I wanted them to kill me. I shot at them so they would kill me." Is this normal behavior for adolescents? Is this a form of homicide, suicide, or both? What factors led to this tragic confrontation, which resulted in the adolescent being tried as an adult for assault to commit murder upon police officers? Joe could join nearly 2 million other troubled people in prison in the United States whose high-risk behavior began in childhood and adolescence. To assist the court and jury in understanding the reasons for this behavior, a social worker was appointed by the court to analyze these issues.

Individual-Level Considerations

The ecosystems model calls for an analysis at the *individual level,* focusing on the biological and psychological endowment of each person. In the case of children and adolescents who are beginning to show symptoms of the risk behaviors mentioned earlier in the chapter, it is especially important to investigate the biological, genetic, and psychosocial factors in the family history, such as addictions, behavioral problems, hospitalizations (health and mental health), juvenile/adult corrections history, and psychiatric histories, such as depression, anxiety disorders, schizophrenia, and developmental disabilities. A thorough assessment will find the social worker asking questions about pertinent family history and obtaining this information from each parent, their parents, and, if possible, even their parents, which, in effect, would be the children's great-grandparents. Such family histories can offer extremely important clues to understanding the current problem behavior of a child or adolescent.

> Joe was interviewed in jail in English, which is his only language. He is of Anglo and African American descent, six feet three inches, very slim, about 143 pounds, and has light, olive-complexioned skin. He was dressed in the traditional bright orange jail clothing with one hand only showing out of his uniform. His right hand had been amputated as the result of wounds he received during his violent confrontation with the police. He exhibited excellent verbal skills and vocabulary and was of above average intelligence with an IQ of 118, although he dropped out of school in the eleventh grade. He had fifteen prior contacts with police since age 11, most of these for minor offenses such as trespassing, running away, vandalism, curfew violations, and theft from a neighbor. His most serious offense previously was for stealing a car and reckless driving in this stolen vehicle while being pursued by the police.
>
> During the entire interview, Joe was attentive, socially comfortable, and friendly; made good eye contact; was cooperative; and answered all questions without hesitation, even elaborating in some of his responses. He was well-oriented to time, person, place, and

surroundings. No distortions in perceptions were noted, nor was there evidence of psychosis, hallucinations, delusions, depersonalization, or other perceptual disturbances. Joe's thought processes were clear, and there was no evidence of a thought disorder. His thought content was not paranoid or delusional. He was not homicidal or suicidal, and, prior to the instant offense, he had never made homicidal attempts against anyone. He had never made any suicide attempts, although a year ago when his grandmother died he had suicidal thoughts, but with no specific plan. Now, while in jail, he has had occasional suicidal ideation, but with the absence of a specific plan. No brain disorder symptoms were present. He has always had sleeping problems, going to bed very late and getting up very late in the morning, almost at noon. In jail he is required to get up early and go to bed early, but he still suffers from insomnia. He has a poor appetite, and while in jail he has lost thirty pounds. The weight loss and sleep disturbance could be related to depression and trauma, which then become an important area for further assessment.

Depression can also be caused by alcohol and drugs. In Joe's case, it is seen that he began using alcohol at age 12 with regular use by age 13, usually two to three 40-ounce bottles of beer nightly. He smoked marijuana "like cigarettes." In his case, the marijuana lifted his depressed mood caused by the alcohol.

Family-Level Considerations

At the *family level* in the ecosystems model, emphasis is placed on the nature of the specific family lifestyle, culture, organization, division of labor, sex role structure, and interactional dynamics. Each family *is* unique. For children and youth raised in one intact, nuclear family, the task of incorporating all these potential benefits is far less difficult than it would be for children who are raised in foster or group homes, with relatives, or in separate two-parent families. Consider the often complex issues faced by minors in the *reconstituted* family, which finds two newly wed parents, each with his or her own children from a prior marriage (each child with his or her own sibling rivalry issues), moving into "one happy home." Each parent has his or her way of raising children, and the children in turn might resist the authority of the new parent, who might have different ideas of the role of children in the family and how they should be disciplined. Because of their complex developmental stage, adolescents sometimes are found to rebel in these types of families. It becomes even more complicated in reconstituted families when the new parents each come from a different culture. However, the majority of these families find ways of surviving in spite of all the obstacles.

Joe's parents were never married, although they always lived in the same city. They lived together for the first four or five years in a stormy relationship. The mother's parents never approved of her "being with a black man." The mother, age 34, a part-time waitress of Anglo American descent, gave birth to Joe when she was 16 years of age. She still lives with her parents. Teenage motherhood can place a child at high risk for future psychosocial problems. Joe's father, age 35, is of African American descent and is a periodically employed auto mechanic. He reports that he is an alcoholic, as are his parents and three brothers and sisters. Joe's mother also admits to an occasional drinking problem and has used cocaine in the past. She reports that her only brother is dying of alcoholism. Addiction and depression genes run in families and can be inherited. Joe received a double genetic loading of addiction genes from both sides of the family, which certainly contributed to his alcoholism.

Joe did not have a stable childhood and really was never happy. He cried often as a child and was always angry as he got older. He was raised by at least three family groups: first by his mother and father; later by his mother and her parents; and thereafter by his mother, at times by his father when his mother could not tolerate him, and in later adolescent years by his maternal grandparents. After his maternal grandmother died, he lived with his maternal grandfather. Discipline was inconsistent and confusing for Joe as a child and later as an adolescent. For punishment, his mother would make him stand in a closet for hours as a "time-out"; his grandparents felt sorry for him and did not set any limits or form of discipline; and his father spanked him and on occasions hit him with his fists to counterbalance the grandparents' permissiveness.

Culture-Level Considerations

At the *cultural level* in the ecosystems model, the focus is on the values, belief systems, and societal norms of American culture, but care must be given not to ignore the cultural heritage of children and parents who were born and raised in other cultures. In most cases, children and youth possessing more than one culture are viewed as enriched, because they speak more than one language and have more than one culture to draw on as prescriptions for life and survival. In some states, however, this is viewed as anti-American, and efforts are made to discourage children and youth from using other languages in school or being taught in their own language as a transitional learning phase into English. In some states, these programs are called "English as a second language" programs. Social workers therefore need to understand local and state policies that enhance educational development, as well as those that place additional burdens on children and youth, because poor academic performance is the highest predictor related to crime and delinquency.

Culture also determines the way in which families raise and discipline their children. For example, American culture condones corporal punishment of children and youth by their parents. Some cultures outlaw this practice, yet some countries practice severe forms of corporal punishment that Americans would consider criminal. Social workers need to understand these differences and assess whether the practice is traumatic for the specific recipient of the punishment, as opposed to the rationale provided by the person administering the discipline.

Joe is multicultural, having absorbed both the positive and negative elements of African and Anglo American culture. Although his parents did not complete high school, they valued education and tried to persuade Joe to do his homework, even to the point of severely punishing him, which made him resent school, education, and authority even more. A "drinking culture" and an acceptance of firearms were valued by all three family units, and each family had firearms in the home. At times Joe would go target shooting with his mother or rabbit hunting with his father. Only the maternal grandparents attended church regularly—Joe's parents had different religions, and they fought about which religion Joe should incorporate into his moral value system. The problem was "solved" by Joe not being exposed to any religion. Corporal punishment is also determined by the cultural values of a society. Joe's three family units believed in corporal punishment, but only the father actually used it. Joe felt that both the father's corporal punishment and the mother's lengthy time-outs were equally stressing. Being raised in the U.S. culture that has embraced racism for centuries, it was especially painful for Joe as a child to hear his white grandparents' rejection of his father because he was black. Some of the heated arguments between his parents involved the "race card," with the mother calling the father "nigger" and the father calling the mother "dirty white trash."

Such conflict in his early years contributed to an identity crisis in Joe; his mother recalls him frequently crying at home until 9 or 10 years of age, wishing he were "white." As he entered adolescence, he rejected the "white" in him, which he perceived as weakness, and instead accepted the "black" in him, which brought him power and respect. He began to dress in black-gang-oriented clothing, with Raiders logos. He founded a gang called the HBRs (Half-Breed Rainbows) composed of biracial adolescent males (Japanese Anglos, Mexican Anglos, African American Anglos, Filipino Anglos, and American Indian Anglos). Apparently, these biracial youths, or "half-breeds" as Joe preferred that they be called, were experiencing the same stresses and identity conflicts as Joe; together, they were a surrogate family.

Environmental–Structural Considerations

Applying the ecosystems model at the *environmental–structural level*, it is evident that the quality of life has improved significantly for most children and youth in the nation. This, however, is directly related to affluence; that is, the higher the affluence, the better the child's environment. The structure of the environment is largely determined by policies, laws, rules, regulations, and allocation of resources by those in political power. Again, families with the most influence receive the best treatment for their surroundings. For example, when the Los Angeles earthquake struck in January 1992, the areas that received the quickest relief; police and fire services; street, freeway, and building repairs; and food and water were the affluent areas of Los Angeles. American-born children and youth of undocumented parents were denied assistance, even though the poorest families lived in the hardest hit areas. Social workers need to develop the critical and analytical skills to assess the presence of such cultural issues that cause children and youth harm, and they should attempt to minimize their impact.

Joe's three family units resided in either white lower middle class or the poor African American community. Through elementary school, when living with his mother or grandparents, he was only one of just a handful of biracial children in a 95 percent–plus white school. Almost on a daily basis, his mother reports that he would come home crying because the "white kids" called him "nigger." It was not much better for him in the elementary school when he stayed with his father, because then he was rejected by the African American children because he was not "all black." When he formed his gang and dressed in black, he intimidated white high school students and earned some "respect." In the poor environment where juvenile gang culture was almost everywhere, it was not difficult to establish his gang. Frequent police harassment of gangs and Joe for being black only added to his defiance toward authority. Joe was never referred for counseling or mental health services in the middle-class community he was residing in, and these services did not exist in the African American section of town.

Historical Considerations

At the *historical level*, when one considers historical issues affecting children and youth in the United States, it is clear that this country has come a long way from the days of exploiting children during the Industrial Revolution and even into the 1930s and 1940s. This practice is improved today, except for migrant farmworker children who do not attend school in order to earn income to help their underpaid parents support the family. Authorities, business owners, and schools seem to look the other way when this is happening. There are areas of progress, yet at the same time there are many examples of humanitarian violations and lack of compassion toward troubled youths.

> Joe received a sentence of twenty-five years to life in state prison for attempted murder of a police officer. Had he killed the officer, he would have automatically received the death penalty, because his state required this for the killing of a law enforcement official. Our penal code laws have evolved over a period of centuries for the protection of society and properly serve this function. Historically, Americans believe in deterrence and the value of corporal punishment in meeting this end. However, corporal punishment is a practice that is risky, with no scientific proof that it does or does not work. Time-outs, too, can also be harmful and psychologically torturing, as seen in Joe's case—again it depends on how it is perceived and felt by the recipient of the punishment.
>
> Our historical values encourage firearms, drinking, and male assertiveness and masculinity. These factors were also very much present in this case. The centuries-old presence of white and black racism also played a significant role in this case. Joe was literally caught in the middle of this powerful, toxic, painful issue from birth up until the present. Historically, our nation finds it very difficult to have, as a budget priority, the provision of quality mental health services in poor communities. The nation maintains a chronic indifference to the plight of the poor and prefers instead to spend billions of dollars on incarceration. In Joe's case, when he comes out of prison in twenty-five years, the government will have spent at least $1 million for his incarceration, and not one cent for rehabilitation or prevention.

The Social Worker's Psychosocial Impressions

The social worker diagnosed Joe as suffering from a conduct disorder, adolescent type, alcohol and cannabis dependence in full remission because of incarceration, and a recurring major depression, moderate type without psychotic features. Current stressors adding to his depression include incarceration and the loss of his hand. The initial depression, which might have had a biological origin, was present since childhood and could also have been caused by trauma (corporal punishment and time-outs in a closet).

Perhaps the stressor that exacerbated his depression was the painful loss of his grandmother, who he felt was really his mother. Following this loss, he was very depressed and talked with friends about being killed in a shoot-out with rival gangs (suicide by gang) or the police (suicide by cop). Persons who are suicidal are ambivalent about dying. Prior to being shot, he was attempting to avoid a confrontation with police by hiding in the closet, which unconsciously also represented his old familiar chamber for punishment. However, the confrontation escalated, and he forced the police to shoot him (suicide by cop). Psychoanalytically, he was expressing his rage at his own parents (police) for all the punishment they had administered to him. Now he was seeking the ultimate punishment from these parent figures: death! The social worker recommended treatment for him, but neither the jail nor prison had these mental health resources available, because the primary goal of such facilities is detention and punishment.

Although Joe clearly made decisions that negatively affected his life, he was also a victim of his genetic makeup, his family and environment, and the culture of U.S. society that tolerates racism and fails to actively prevent human problems.

Macro Considerations

Some children and youth become part of the solution to human problems. It is estimated that, in 2006, 30 percent of high school–age children were involved in some form of volunteer activities.[26] It is not uncommon, for example, for a child to befriend an elderly neighbor, to develop a special caring relationship with a person experiencing a handicapping condition, or to become an active volunteer providing services in hospitals, schools, churches, or synagogues and in other forms of human services organizations.

Youth also become involved in the macro side of human services. Although human services agencies do not uniformly engage young people in making policy and program decisions, those that do—and particularly those programs that provide services to youth—find that the engagement of representatives of their consumers can lead to programs that are more relevant to today's youth. Just as effective school principals and teachers actively involve students and student organizations in important decisions about their schools, so too should social workers and human services agencies.

One macro function that supports human services that is frequently performed by children and youth has been fund-raising to support an agency cause. Children selling cookies, candy, and magazines to support schools and human services agencies have become an accepted part of U.S. society. Similarly, people are asked to pledge contributions for agencies based on a child's distance in running, skating, swimming, or biking. Certainly, children and youth have a great deal to contribute to society, particularly to the human services. Social workers and other human services providers too often overlook this important resource that cannot only enhance the services and also help tomorrow's adults prepare for their role as citizens.

To fulfill their mission, social workers, too, must become involved in the macro side of practice, i.e., advocating for changes that improve the services already being provided, creating new and more effective ways of delivering services, affecting social policies that set the tone or provide resources for human services, and engaging in public education activities that help the people in the larger society address values and attitudes that shape our views of children and youth and thus prevent some of these conditions from developing in the first place. For example, we might make far better use of resources and reduce damage to children by shifting our approach to issues from primarily one of punishment to treatment, to one of early intervention. Setting aside the human cost for the moment, consider just the economic merits of different options to serving children and youth.[27]

▶ The average annual per-child cost of a mentoring program is $1,000.
▶ The cost of providing a year of employment training for unemployed youths is $2,492.

- The annual per-child cost of a high-quality after-school program is $2,700.
- The average cost of ensuring that a low-income family has affordable housing is $6,830.
- The average annual per-child cost of Head Start is $7,028.
- The annual per-child cost for a high-quality, comprehensive full-day, full-year early childhood education program is $13,000.
- The average annual per-prisoner cost is $22,650. States spend on average almost three times as much per prisoner as per public school pupil.

Indeed, it is important that social workers provide micro or direct services to children and families to help them overcome the conditions they experience. It is equally important, however, that they also address the broader issues in the environment that affect clients and client functioning.

Concluding Comment

Growing up in America as an infant, child, and adolescent can be stressful for many and deadly for a small number of young people. There is a certain amount of risk for all young people, but, as this chapter has identified, such risk factors intersect with race, poverty, single-parent households, and lower levels of education and multiply the difficulties for children and families. However, in spite of the many problems and barriers outlined in this chapter, the resilience of individuals, and the services that are available to assist them, make it possible for most to become productive citizens. Yet, we cannot be satisfied with less than providing every child the opportunity to use his or her potential to the fullest.

For the social worker to be effective in his or her intervention with young clients and their families, in-depth knowledge about the issues they face is necessary. As can be seen in the case of "Joe," the ecosystems model can guide the worker in organizing the direction of the case inquiry so that the information is organized in a form supportive of an accurate assessment of and helpful services to the client. Joe's case, a micro (or direct service) case, was presented to help the reader to understand the many bio-psychosocial issues that may appear in one case and to identify the dynamic interplay of these factors. Effective macro interventions are also needed to strengthen social and mental health services in poor communities and to call attention to the prejudice, discrimination, and racism directed at very vulnerable children and adolescents, such as Joe, in U.S. society.

Social workers can also play a vital role by involving young people in establishing and critiquing existing programs and policies, raising funds for social programs, and preparing for responsible citizenship. Perhaps social workers and others have done too little to engage youth in community activities, allowing those who are troubled, destructive, or harmful to others to become inaccurately viewed as representative of the young people in the United States today. Macro practice also provides the opportunity for social workers to fulfill their commitment to improve the environmental factors that contribute to clients' problematic conditions or prevent those problems from ever occurring.

KEY WORDS AND CONCEPTS

U.S. Children's Bureau
Child maltreatment
At-risk social behavior
Intersection of poverty and race
Intersection of income, poverty, and education
Resiliency

SUGGESSTED INFORMATION SOURCES

Annie E. Casey Foundation, *2007 Kids Count Data Book Online.* http://www.kidscount.org/datacenter/databook.jsp.

Children's Defense Fund. http://www.childrensdefense.org.

Hamilton, Stephen F., and Mary Agnes Hamilton, eds., *The Youth Development Handbook: Coming of Age in American Communities.* Thousand Oaks, CA: Sage Publications, 2004.

McWhirter, J. Jeffries, ed. *At-Risk Youth: A Comprehensive Response.* Belmont, CA: Brooks/Cole, 2004.

Quinn, William H. *Family Solutions for Youth at Risk: Applications to Juvenile Delinquency, Truancy, and Behavior Problems.* New York: Brunner-Routledge, 2004.

ENDNOTES

1. Robert H. Bremner, *From the Depths: The Discovery of Poverty in the United States* (New York: New York University Press, 1969), pp. 204–229.
2. Robert Kominski, Amie Jamieson, and Gladys Martinez, "At-Risk Conditions of U.S. School-Age Children," U.S. Census Bureau, http://www.census.gov/population/www/documentation/twps0052/twps0052.html.
3. U.S. Census Bureau, "Detailed Living Arrangements of Children by Race, Hispanic Origin, and Age: 2004," Table 1, http://www.census.gov/population/www/socdemo/children.html.
4. ChildStats, "Children of at least one foreign-born parent," http://www.childstats.gov/americaschildren07/famsoc4.asp.
5. U.S. Census Bureau, "Detailed Living Arrangements," op. cit.
6. ChildStats, "Housing Problems," http://www.childstats.gov/americaschildren/phenviro4.asp.
7. ChildStats, "Child Injury and Mortality," http://www.childstats.gov/americaschildren/phenviro6.asp.
8. U.S. Census Bureau, "Income and Earnings Summary Measures by Selected Characteristics: 2005–2006," Table 1, http://www.census.gov/prod/2007pubs/p60-233.pdf.
9. Ibid.
10. Eugene M. Lewitt, Donna L. Terman, and Richard E. Behrman, "Children and Poverty: Analysis and Recommendations," in Richard E. Behrman ed., *The Future of Children: Children and Poverty* (Los Altos, CA: Center for the Future of Children, 1997), p. 8.
11. John R. Kearnsey, Herman F. Grundmann, and Salvatore J. Gallicchio, "The Influence of Social Security Benefits and SSI Payments on the Poverty of Children," *Social Security Bulletin* 57 (Summer 1994): 27–38.

12. U.S. Census Bureau, "Historical Poverty Tables," Table 3 (2006), http://www.census.gov/hhes/www/poverty/histpov/hstpov3.html.
13. Ibid., Table 4, http://www.census.gov/hhes/www/poverty/histpov/hstpov4.html.
14. Children's Defense Fund, "Over 13 Million Children Face Food Insecurity," http://www.childrensdefense.org/site/DocServer/foodinsecurity2005.pdf?docID=482.
15. U.S. Census Bureau, "Who's Minding the Kids? Child Care Arrangements," http://www.census.gov/population/www/socdemo/childcare.html.
16. Child Trends DataBank, "Dropout Rates," Table 1, http://www.childtrendsdata-bank.org/tables/1_Table_1.htm.
17. U.S. Department of Labor, "Education Pays," http://www.bls.gov/emp/emptab7.htm.
18. U.S. Census Bureau, "One-third of Young Women Have Bachelor's Degrees." http://www.census.gov/Press-Release/www/releases/archives/education/011196.html.
19. CoverTheUninsured, "Facts and Research," http://covertheuninsured.org/factsheets/display.php?FactSheetID=103; see also Agency for Healthcare Research and Quality, "Medical Expenditure Panel Survey," Statistical Brief #141, http://www.meps.ahrq.gov/mepsweb/data_stats/Pub_ProdResults_Details.jsp?pt=Statistical%20Brief&opt=2&-id=776.
20. ChildStats, "Activity Limitation," http://childstats.ed.gov/americaschildren/health4.asp; see also Kathleen Doheny, WebMD, "Chronic Health Problems Soar in Kids," http://children.webmd.com/news/20070703/chronic-health-problems-soar-in-kids.
21. ChildStats, "Emotional and Behavioral Difficulties," http://www.childstats.gov/americaschildren/health3.asp.
22. Administration for Children and Families, *Child Maltreatment: 2006*, U.S. Department of Health and Human Services, http://www.acf.hhs.gov/programs/cb/pubs/cm06/figure3_1.htm; see also ChildStats, "Child Injury and Mortality," http://www.childstats.gov/americaschildren/phenviro6.asp.
23. ChildStats, "Births to Unmarried Women," http://www.childstats.gov/americaschildren/famsoc2.asp.
24. ChildStats, "Youth Victims of Serious Violent Crimes," http://www.childstats.gov/americaschildren/phenviro5.asp.
25. "America's Cradle to Prison Pipeline," Children's Defense Fund, http://www.childrensdefense.org/site/DocServer/CPP_report_2007.pdf?docID=5041.
26. Child Trends Databank, "Volunteering," http://childtrendsdatabank.org/indicators/20Volunteering.cfm. http://www.childtrendsdatabank.org/indicators/20Volunteering.cfmo.
27. "America's Cradle to Prison Pipeline," op. cit., p. 20.

chapter 19

Social Work Practice with Older Adults

Prefatory Comment

The most rapidly growing segment of the U.S. population is its older people. Estimated at 37.3 million people in 2006, the number of older Americans is expected to increase to more than 71.5 million by 2030 and to nearly 87 million in 2050. Even more dramatically, the population age 85 and over is expected to increase four-fold, from 5.3 million in 2006 to 21 million in 2050.[1] Although many older Americans are healthy, active, and productive, many others face declining physical and mental health, erosion of financial resources, and loss of friends and family. This high incidence of social problems experienced by older people leads to projections of an increased demand in future years for social workers especially prepared to work with this population group. Organized around the Ecosystems Model, this chapter addresses the special needs of older people and the competencies expected of social workers providing social programs for them, and it includes a case example involving an elderly person that demonstrates how micro- and macro-level practice can benefit older clients.

Many older people enjoy good health, positive interaction with friends and family, and have adequate income to help achieve a favorable quality of life. Yet, the phrase "old age isn't for the faint of heart" reveals the inevitable decline in physical and mental health, as well in social supports when older adults approach the later phases of the life cycle. We are buoyed by visions of successful athletes in the "Senior Olympics" and saddened by reports that the highest suicide rate in the United States is among males ages 65 and over. This period of life typically involves a series of transitions: from enjoying an active and healthy lifestyle to dealing with accumulating health problems that may be limiting or even life-threatening; from meaningful employment and adequate income to retirement and sharply reduced financial resources; and from being surrounded by an intimate group of family and friends to increasing loneliness created by a shrinking set of loved ones as illness and death take their toll. The roles for social workers in working with older people along this continuum from the healthy to the frail are many and varied—but all are important.

Population demographics indicate that social work practice with older people is likely to be the social work profession's most substantial growth industry. This population has been growing in both numbers and as a portion of the U.S. population for more than a century, and as the "baby boomers," sometimes referred to as "senior boomers," begin to reach age 65 in 2011, the demand for social work services will expand even more. Further, people now live substantially longer, and thus the population of older people will inevitably grow even more rapidly. For example, a person born in 1900 was expected to live an average of 49.2 years, and by 2004 that expected life span had increased by nearly 30 years—to 77.8 years.[2] The result of this growth in the number of older people will create an associated demand for a variety of health and human services.

Demographic Factors Affecting Human Services for Older Adults

In the last century, the older adult population increased more than eleven-fold, compared with only a three-fold increase for those under age 65—and that growth is continuing. The number of older adults is projected to reach 40.2 million by 2010, 71.5 million by 2030, and 86.7 million by mid-century. This 12.4 percent of the total U.S. population is projected to become 20.6 percent in 2050 and remain somewhat constant after that. Further, the oldest segment of this population that draws most heavily on social workers and human services is increasing even more dramatically. The 5.3 million people 85 years and older today is expected to reach 9.6 million in 2030 and then more than double to 21.0 million people, or 5 percent of the U.S. population, by 2050.[3] Indeed, the demand for new social programs and social workers prepared to address the needs of this increasingly frail population inevitably will increase. The NASW Workforce Study indicates that this growth in demand is occurring at the same time there will be "a substantial cohort of frontline social workers leaving the workforce" and calls for the profession "to focus on both recruitment and retention strategies to address this problem."[4]

Today the white population lives approximately five years longer than minority group members. However, whites will decline as a percentage of older people—from an estimated 81 percent in 2006 to a projected 61 percent by 2050. Among the minority racial groups, the older Hispanic population is expected to triple by 2050 (from 6 percent to 18 percent of the older population), and the black and Asian groups are also expected to show substantial growth.[5] The need for culturally relevant programs for seniors will increase dramatically during this period, and Spanish-speaking social workers or those with a facility with various Asian languages will no doubt be in increased demand.

For many, older adulthood may not be the "golden years" that people often think of when they plan for retirement. For some, retirement from the workforce is a difficult transition associated with loss of identity and lack of employment where one can make a contribution, as well as experiencing substantial decline in annual income. For others, retirement is a welcome reprieve from tedious work and rigid schedules that allow little time for travel, socializing with others, and gaining enjoyment from life. The three factors of social contact, income security, and health are central contributors to older people experiencing satisfaction in their later years.

Social Contact vs. Isolation

Social supports tend to diminish in peoples' later years. Changes in the amount and type of social support from family and friends can occur when their adult children and/or grandchildren move to a different geographic location, when they experience the death or incapacity of a spouse or partner, or when many of their peers have passed away. One older man in his 80s somewhat humorously made this last point saying, "I don't have an enemy in the world—I have outlived all of them."

Partially because of the longer life expectancy for women, the problems especially of the oldest-old are primarily the problems of women. In relation to social isolation, the life expectancy of five years more than men results in older women being more likely than men to live alone. In 2006, 38.6 percent of this age group of women lived alone compared with only 19 percent of the men. At age 75 and over, the differential becomes 48.8 percent of women compared with only 22.0 of percent of men living alone. The social isolation is partially reflected in the fact that older people report spending 55.1 percent of their leisure time watching television, compared with only 11.1 percent of their time socializing and communicating.[6] Part of the social isolation occurs because leisure activities require use of discretionary income, and older women, in particular, are often without the benefit of sufficient pension incomes to have resources for discretionary spending. Pensions have been tied to the employee's wages, and the history of today's older people was that pensions were based almost entirely on contributions from a husband's employment—with limited pension income guaranteed to the surviving spouse. Correcting the fallout from this pattern will require a significant shift in existing retirement, income maintenance, health care, and other social programs to more adequately address the needs of older women.

Financial Stability

The older population presents a mixed bag in regard to their financial well-being. Like other population groups, the U.S. economic structure is allowing the rich to get richer with the result that the poor get poorer. Based on the government's established poverty threshold for number of people in a household, 9.4 percent of the older people were living in poverty in 2006. Yet 28.6 percent of older people had more than four times that amount of income—and that percentage is increasing. The positive news is that—given that the poverty rate for older people was dramatically higher in 1959 (35 percent) and given the success in reducing poverty among older people through Social Security, Medicare, prescription assistance, senior housing, and other social programs—this indicates that if political forces can be activated to address a social problem, dramatic results can follow. Nevertheless, poverty among older adults has not been eliminated, and more than 3.4 million older people continue to live at or below the poverty line. Many older people experience economic vulnerability.[7]

Consistent with the income distribution pattern for all population groups, the poverty rate differences among older people in 2006 disproportionately favored the white population and men. White, non-Hispanic older people experienced a poverty rate of 7.0 percent, compared with 22.8 percent for the black population, 19.4 percent for Hispanics, and 12.0 percent for persons of Asian background. In terms of gender, men age 65 and over averaged a 6.6 percent poverty rate and, for women, a rate of 11.5 percent. At age 75 and over, the poverty rate for men improved to 6.2 percent and worsened for women to 12.9 percent.[8] Although it is not realistic to expect equal income distribution among the various population groups in a capitalistic society such as the United States, clearly there are factors of systematic bias in this culture that disadvantage certain population groups—and that condition is not improving over time.

Where do older people get their income? The importance of Social Security as an income source for many older people is evident in the fact that 37 percent of their total income is from that source, with a person's earnings generating 28 percent, pensions 18 percent, income from assets held by the older people 15 percent, and other income sources 3 percent. A comparison of the income sources for the lowest one-fifth of the older population and the highest one-fifth reveals why there may be relative disinterest among the powerful high-income population to resolve the solvency problems of Social Security and supporting an adequate income maintenance program for older people, as Social Security and public assistance contribute only 17.7 percent of the income for the most wealthy one-fifth of the older population—compared with 90.0 percent for those in the lowest one-fifth.[9]

Where do older people spend their income? Fully one-third (33.6 percent) of the expenditures of people 65 and over is devoted to housing, followed by expenditures for transportation (15.7 percent), health care (12.8 percent), and food (12.7 percent). These housing expenditures are largely for older people living in traditional community housing (93 percent) with the remainder living in community housing that also provides some services (2.4 percent) and 4.6 percent living in nursing homes. It is recommended that families not exceed spending 30 percent of their income on housing (i.e., *housing cost burden*), yet one-third of the older-person households exceed the housing cost burden guideline. Further, 8 percent of the traditional community housing is considered physically inadequate or crowded.[10] Typically social workers have given relatively little attention to housing issues and, perhaps, could improve older people's well-being by focusing more on improving people's housing and addressing housing costs.

Health Conditions

Often the emphasis on the health problems experienced by older people masks the fact that older people consider themselves to be healthy and vibrant participants in life. In 2006, 74 percent of the older adults rated their health as good to excellent, and only 26 percent believed their health was only fair or poor. Health statistics, like other indicators of well-being, reflect the toll of adverse social conditions on minority groups. Where there was a positive health assessment by 76.3 percent of the older white population, that was true for only 60.3 percent of the black and 62.9 percent of the Hispanic older Americans.[11] As opposed to prevailing perceptions about the clients and activities involved in gerontological social work, much of this practice should involve helping older people improve the quality of their lives through social and recreational activities, as well as preventing or adapting to declining health.

The positive attitude many older people report regarding their health, however, should not minimize the fact that many older people experience one or more chronic health conditions. Chronic physical and mental health problems, including sensory impairments, increasingly affect people as they get older and affect men and women at different rates. Table 19.1 reveals the incidence of a selected set of physically and socially limiting health conditions for persons age 65 and older.

Physical and mental health problems among older people are costly. Payments to physicians, hospitals, and for prescription drugs are major expenses for older people. The average cost for health care per year in 2004 for persons age 65 and over was $13,052. Low-income people typically do not have adequate, if any, health insurance and thus neglect prevention and early intervention with health problems, yet they pay a considerably larger share of their income for out-of-pocket medical

Table 19.1

Physical Problems Experienced by Older Men and Women: 2006

Physical Condition	Men	Women
Overweight	73.9%	64.6%
Hypertension	52.0	54.3
Trouble hearing	47.7	35.1
Arthritic symptoms	43.1	54.4
Heart disease	36.8	26.5
Obesity	29.9	31.1
No natural teeth	26.8	25.1
Cancer	23.6	19.3
Diabetes	19.1	17.3
Trouble seeing	16.1	18.5
Clinically relevant depression	11.0	16.8

Source: Federal Interagency Forum on Aging-Related Statistics, *Older Americans 2008: Key Indicators of Well-Being* (Washington, D.C.: U.S. Government Printing Office, March 2008), pp. 100, 101, 103, 110; see also http://agingstats.gov/agingstatsdotnet/Main_Site/Data/2008_Documents/OA_2008.pdf.

expenses. Where the higher income brackets average paying 8.1 percent of their medical expenses out-of-pocket, those in the poor or near-poor categories average 29.3 percent out-of-pocket.[12] The absence of an adequate national health care system in the United States excessively burdens the poor with the cost of medical care. These expenditures are not only a drain on the affected individuals, but, if they cannot pay for these services, it taxes the health care system and the U.S. economy as a whole.

Social workers employed in nursing homes, hospitals, and other health-related human service agencies must be knowledgeable about the limitations in social functioning associated with the more prevalent health conditions. The problems of older people is one of the most neglected areas in the fields of mental and physical health in the United States and demands more research and knowledge and skill development among social workers. Nevertheless, social workers in many settings can expect to work with older people experiencing health and mental health issues.

Ecosystems Model Analysis

The ecosystems model developed for this text provides a useful analytic scheme for the social worker committed to a disciplined structure for learning more about working with older people. By examining social work practice with older adults from the various perspectives defined in the model (i.e., historical, environmental–structural, cultural, family, and individual), an enhanced understanding of the complex needs of this population emerges.

Historical Factors

The health problems of older people, the quality of their lives, their ability and willingness to care for themselves, their capacity to cope with stress—all are shaped not only by individual histories, such as hereditary and early family life, but also by experiences throughout their lives. When working with older people, social workers might explore questions such as: What was your family life like? Have you received social services? Were there economic calamities, such as a recession or the loss of employment? To what extent was your employment rewarding? What health problems did you experience?

Certainly, the milieu of today's aged population is very different from that when they were young. Employment with a company usually anticipated ending with formal retirement and a pension. Today, many employers are downsizing by offering buy-out packages to older employees or replacing them with younger employees at lower wages, less seniority, and without pension funding. For some employers, pension fund reserves have failed to maintain a sufficient balance to meet the requirements for retired members, and they have declared bankruptcy—leaving the retired person without anticipated income. Many older people have returned to employment at minimum wage to make ends meet. For older people with limited education and having worked at hourly wage or other low-pay jobs in their younger years, poverty is often the reward of a lifetime of labor, since there are no pensions and no room for elderly workers in an increasingly technology-driven industrial society. Often starting a new career is difficult for persons in their 50s and virtually impossible for those in their 60s and 70s. The Great Depression and the subsequent cycles of recession and depression have left their economic and psychological scars. A lifetime of relatively low earning now results in almost complete dependence on Social Security for income for many older people.

Less quantifiable changes have also occurred. In the early twentieth century, the family was essential for survival. Grandparents, parents, and children assumed various roles in ensuring the integrity and well-being of the family. In rural areas, each person could contribute to the success of the family farm, where today sophisticated equipment, the demand for highly technical knowledge about agriculture and international markets, and the growth of corporate farming too often minimizes the role the older person can play in meeting the family's needs. In urban areas, the extended family is often employed in a variety of unrelated jobs, and families function primarily as independent family units with limited interaction.

Indeed, various forces on the family such as emphasis on the nuclear family, employers requiring greater mobility, and two parents working outside the home to make ends meet have changed the traditional interdependencies between older people and their children and grandchildren. The family today is radically different from the extended family unit of the past, and there is evidence of further forces for change. For example, single-parent families have become a significant phenomenon, and single mothers and their children experience America's highest poverty rates. Older parents often sacrifice some of their limited income to help improve their children's and grandchildren's quality of life. An increasing proportion of children are being cared for by a grandparent while the parent(s) work outside the home. A new and growing phenomenon is known as "*grandfamilies*," where grandparents gain custody of grandchildren when parents are unable to raise their children due to drug involvement or other incapacitating factors.

The future needs and demands for older adults will be different from those of today. It is clear that, if older people are to begin new employment patterns in their later years, they will need to be better educated. Their Social Security pensions should be substantial enough to enable them to sustain a decent standard of living, although with changing demographics in which there are fewer people in the high employment age groups and with the baby boomer generation reaching retirement age and drawing on Social Security benefits, the solvency of the Social Security system is unclear.

All in all, an understanding of the terrain in which today's older people have lived and are living is needed if the social worker is to perform the task of providing the information and insight needed to optimally serve current and future older clients. Just as important is developing the perspective to initiate or support public education and social legislation that will protect and enhance the quality of life for older people.

Environmental–Structural Factors

What perceptions do different groups of older people have of their status in society and how they are regarded by younger people? How are these perceptions formed, and what do they imply about the importance to society of older people? How do these perceptions square with the society's needs? How does U.S. society and its high value on youth prepare older individuals for retirement, for the change in income, and for the reduced status that may accompany it? How does the individual who has had employment as a central part of his or her identity find different values, friendships, and activities when no longer employed?

Prejudice against older people—*ageism*—is displayed in several ways: (1) in our obsession with youth; (2) in the emphasis by the media on extraordinary achievements of the aged, rather than on their ordinary, often satisfying lives; and (3) in the poor general understanding of the contributions older people can make to society. Anthropologists have documented that older people are regarded differently in different cultures. Views of the aged widely held in Western societies, including the notion that the old have little to contribute to society, are not shared by other societies. Bias against the old is not inevitable; rather, it is shaped by various, only partly understood forces.

One important element affecting the Western attitude toward older adults is the materialistic economic valuation of human worth—how much money a person makes, how big his or her house is, how valuable are his or her material possessions. In retirement, income drops markedly for most Americans, and one's income is no longer determined as much by one's capacity as an employee as by pension policies. Such changes in level and source of income may result in a loss of esteem among the elderly.

In addition to ageism and the potential loss of status as a result of reduced income from retirement, older people generally face a number of additional stresses during the later years of life. As stated by Butler and Lewis, "The elderly are confronted by multiple losses, which may occur simultaneously: death of a partner, older friends, colleagues, relatives; decline of physical health and coming to personal terms with death; loss of status, prestige, and participation in society; and for large numbers of the older population, additional burdens of marginal living standards."[13]

The process of aging, even in the absence of health problems or loss, can be acutely distressing. Confusion and uncertainty confront many older people as they attempt to deal with the variety of changes accompanying the aging process. Some of these changes occur slowly, such as physical appearance and social status, whereas others occur much more dramatically, such as catastrophic health problems or forced retirement. The process of aging should be visualized as a continuous stream of changes occurring within one's environment that more or less dictates how the changes will affect the person. The increasing unpredictability and loss of physical and mental control accompanying aging, plus the inevitability of death, contribute to making this life stage one of considerable difficulty.

The sensitivity of one's environment in responding to the multitude of physical, economic, and social needs accompanying old age symbolizes the value placed on the older person. Social workers must advocate for more effective policies, planning for the future, and enabling both society and older people to make optimum use of available resources.

Culture

The question of whether a unique culture of aging exists remains unclear in the social science literature. Seeking to identify comparability to other minorities, such as ethnic or racial subgroups, as well as other age groups (e.g., teenagers), some researchers conclude that treating older adults as a cultural subgroup is inappropriate because of their special role in our society. This can be noted in the following excerpt:

> The aged do not share a distinct and separated culture; membership in the group defined as "aged" is not exclusive and permanent, but awaits all members of our society who live long enough. As a result, age is a less distinguishable group characteristic than others such as sex, occupation, social class, and the like. True, many aged persons possess distinctive physical characteristics. But even here there is a broad spectrum, and these "stigmata" do not normally justify differential and discriminatory treatment by others.[14]

With the rapid increase in the number of individuals 65 years of age and older, the social and political visibility of older people has never been higher. A multitude of political, economic, and social organizations representing older adults have developed, forcing an increased focus on both social services and political action. The tremendous heterogeneity among today's older people (e.g., race, ethnicity, economic status, health, education level, and geographic location) makes it quite difficult to think of them as an age-segregated subculture. It makes more sense to think of older people as a group with many common concerns related to their physical, social, and economic status and that our social service delivery systems should become more cognizant of these needs in developing effective intervention modalities. The concept of a distinct subpopulation, however, does assist in the reorganization and development of social policy, planning, and service delivery.

Family Issues

With increased life expectancy, separate generations of children, parents, and grandparents will be able to share many experiences of adulthood such as work, parenting, and even retirement. The fact that contemporary parents, children, and grandchildren are likely to all be living at the same time, perhaps for decades, speaks directly to the opportunity to form deep bonds of rapport and empathy—if our social structures permit sufficient opportunity for interaction. In addition, with smaller nuclear families, there are fewer individuals within the family network, thus affording the opportunity for not only a more extensive *intergenerational network*, but a more intensive one as well. As a result, our society is currently confronted with a situation in which, for the first time in history, the average family has more parents than children. With a significant reduction in the average number of childbearing years due to trends toward late marriage, as well as a reduction in the number of years between the first- and last-born child, generation demarcations have become clearer. And with the extension of life, grandparents are now typically living independently of their children for twenty-five years or more. The implications of this are not totally clear, but elevating older people in the culture to serve as a familial stabilizing force due to their experience, wisdom, and economic resources is a distinct possibility.

Older adults are frequently portrayed as a frail and dependent group who create a drain on our national resources and are a strain on family caregiving. There is no doubt that the oldest-old, those 85 and above, are in greater need of medical assistance and long-term care. Meeting the physical and social needs of our rapidly growing oldest-old represents one of the major social welfare concerns of the future. However, there are a vast number of our older people who are healthy, independent, and willing to contribute to the enhancement of their family's well-being. In fact, available research indicates that the older generations in industrialized societies tend to provide more economic assistance than they receive.[15]

The ability of older adults to serve as a "safety valve" within the family network can express itself in a variety of ways. They sometimes serve as arbitrators between their children and grandchildren, specifically assisting grandchildren in understanding parental responsibilities, as well as providing economic backup during the usual family problems of home ownership, educational expenses for children and grandchildren, and unexpected financial crises. With the increasing number of separations, divorces, and single-parent households, grandparents are frequently called on to serve as stress buffers for their children, as well as serving as substitute parents for their grandchildren (i.e., in 2002 the U.S. Census Bureau estimated that 1.8 percent of all children lived with their grandparents).[16]

Clearly, the changing roles of older people in family life include an increasing degree of multigenerational networking. The opportunities for more extensive and intensive bonding within families could also provide the basis for the strengthened ability to meet older individual's needs in the final decades of the life cycle.

Individual Issues

Self-concept among older adults has shown some interesting changes throughout history. In preindustrial eras, older people generally enjoyed revered status. In the industrial and technology eras, however, the value placed on accumulated historical knowledge and experience has given way to innovation, creativity, and productivity. Older people have increasingly been perceived as outdated and a burden on society's overall economic development. Over time, more and more employers developed strategies to remove older individuals from the workforce with early retirement incentives or outright dismissal. As a consequence, the perception of growing old began to imply that the person was physically incapable, unproductive, and not retrainable. Many older people accepted these negative stereotypes, thus creating a diminished sense of self-worth and low motivation to continue to engage society in a meaningful manner.

These negative stereotypes are beginning to change. What it means to be 65 and older in today's society differs significantly from what it meant in earlier periods. The majority of those over 65 today are healthy, youthful in outlook, and willing to remain actively involved in the world of work, family, and community affairs. Clearly, older adults in contemporary society are redefining the concept of being old, particularly as it applies to societal expectations of age-appropriate behavior. Old age should be seen as a fluid concept, defined by the traits and abilities of each generation as it becomes older, not determined by past expectations and norms. Perhaps for the specific individual, being "old" is more related to "lifestyle" or "attitude" than chronological age.

Today, with better health and independence in the later stages of life, becoming 65 does not have to begin a period of withdrawal and decline. On the contrary, this period of the life cycle should represent the opportunity for renewal, with the development of new skills and goals for leading a productive and satisfying life. For example, many of today's older people seek part-time employment or volunteer work. And, contrary to stereotypes of older people, research reported in 2007 by the University of Chicago's National Social Life, Health and Aging Project concludes that "many men and women remain sexually active—participating in vaginal intercourse, oral sex, and masturbation—well into their 70s and 80s."[17] Indeed, older adults are capable of remaining meaningfully engaged in life. For social workers, helping older adults maintain their sense of self-worth, achieve overall good health, and engage in satisfying activities are important tasks for social workers and our human services agencies.

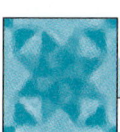

Intervention Strategies with Older People

The Ecosystems Model provides a framework for developing both macro and micro practice strategies for working with older clients. The inclusion of multiple factors regarding the internal as well as external influences on older clients provides a useful guide in structuring an effective intervention strategy. In addition, the profession of social work, with its values and interactional approach, is ideally suited to effectively serve our elderly population. With the variety of changes and needs confronting older clients (e.g., financial instability, demand for acute and long-term health care, inadequate housing, loss of a spouse and other family members, etc.), a profession such as social work, with its focus on making changes in the environment as well as within the individual, provides the necessary practice base for effectively developing intervention strategies.

The profession of social work has enjoyed a longer period of involvement with older adults than many other practice professions. However, social work, as is the case with the other professions, is frequently guilty of ageism. Butler has defined *ageism* as a "process of systematic stereotyping of and discrimination against people because they are old, just as racism and sexism accomplish this with skin color and gender. Old people are categorized as senile, rigid in thought and manner, old-fashioned in morality and skills."[18] The categorization of all older people by a simple set of stereotypes leads to their exclusion from the more advanced techniques of social, mental, and physical health interventions. The great diversity among older people in terms of health, income, educational, occupational, and familial status should immediately disprove any simplistic assumption about who they are and what we can do for them.

In general, the development of any intervention strategy for the elderly, whether macro or micro, should have as its basic objectives: (1) the promotion of independence to the maximum degree possible; (2) assistance in obtaining the necessary resources for the maintenance of a good quality of life; (3) facilitation of effective interaction between the elderly and others in their environment; and (4) influencing of the development of social policy enhancing the elderly's lives. As noted by Cantor, "Basic to the concept of social care is the notion that assistance is provided as means of augmenting individual competency and mastery of the environment, rather than increasing dependency."[19] With these premises in mind, it is useful to consider how these matters play out with a case in which a social worker develops micro and macro strategies to serve an older adult.

A CASE EXAMPLE OF SOCIAL WORK PRACTICE WITH AN OLDER ADULT

Judie Winter, a 74-year-old Caucasian woman, met with Elizabeth Summer, the social worker who had been assigned to her case by the county senior assistance program. Judie had been through a number of transitions resulting from the death of her husband, having limited resources, and now more serious financial troubles as health problems have begun to accumulate. When they met that morning, Elizabeth asked Judie to share her background as a way of beginning to discover how she might be helpful.

Judie began by indicating that she was the third of three children born to her parents in Van Nuys, California. She lived with her mother in Van Nuys for sixteen years and has good memories of this time in her life, although her parents divorced when she was young. In time, Judie overcame an initial strained relationship with her stepfather, Bill, and feels close to him today. In fact, Judie occasionally travels to Los Angeles from her nearby suburban community to visit Bill where he lives in a retirement center. Bill is now pushing "95 years young," as he often jokes during their visits. Bill's health is generally good, but his mental capacity has dropped off dramatically in the past six months following his wife's (Judie's mother's) death due to complications from a malignant neoplasm (cancer). Bill is becoming quite frail, but he refuses to respond whenever Judie brings up the subject of planning for his eventual death. Elizabeth recalled a chapter she had read on death, dying, and grief for her Human Behavior class when studying for her social work degree and wondered if the recent death of his spouse was taking a toll on Bill—and if talking with someone other than his stepdaughter about his grief and preparation for death would be beneficial.

Judie shared that she herself worried about how long she would be able to continue living independently in her apartment by herself. Judie angrily reported that she had been victimized recently when two young "punks," as she described them, assaulted her and took her handbag as she walked home from the bus stop just around the corner from where she lived. The assault put Judie in the hospital with a mild concussion and bruising to several ribs. "But enough about that stuff," she exhaled, "I was telling you my story!"

Elizabeth realized that Judie was not one to keep focus on the negative very long. Judie continued with her story and flashed back to an earlier time in her life. At 16, Judie had entered into a relationship with Thomas, an African American man whom she deeply cared for, and they soon had Jessica. This relationship caused many issues within the family and eventually resulted in isolation for Judie from her mother and stepfather because they did not respect or honor her choice to wed outside her race and culture. Judie found refuge with her biological father, who after the divorce from her mother remarried to an African American woman, Barbara. Judie's stepmother was a loving woman who offered support, guidance, and friendship to Judie—along with caring for her own three children with Judie's father. Elizabeth had previously learned that Judie eventually had two other children with Thomas, but she did not interrupt Judie's story. Judie recalled how sad she was being estranged from the Caucasian side of her family, but she found comfort in the interactions with her stepmother, Barbara, and the African American community that had taken her and her family into their extended family network.

When requested, Judie went on to share with Elizabeth information about her prior work experiences. She had spent a number of years working as a preschool teacher and childcare provider. She viewed this as supporting other mothers wanting to find work, knowing their children would be safe and properly nurtured in Judie's care. Judie was proud that she had spent most of her life successfully working with young children. She had eventually received her GED and then went on to complete additional training in early childhood education. With these credentials she opened her own childcare center, which she operated for almost thirty years. There was great satisfaction for Judie in this work, and also she was able to provide a second income for her own family. The family did well, but times were sometimes difficult and challenging both financially and socially, particularly after Judie's husband, Thomas, was fatally injured in a tragic motorcycle accident when returning from work late one evening. Unfortunately, they had just cancelled their health insurance because the cost was prohibitive when Judie become too old to handle the work with active preschool children. The medical and funeral bills were costly and exhausted much of the small retirement nest egg they had saved. This tragedy took a tremendous toll on the family financially and on Judie both physically and socially. Though they received a small death benefit and monthly check from Social Security, it was not enough to help her retain the family's home. After the children had all moved out on their own, Judie got a small apartment and maintained a minimal standard of living. However, with costly rent she was always struggling to meet her basic medical and nutritional needs.

Retrieving a small picture book from her purse, Judie shifted the conversation to her three children. Judie's three children had completed high school and began lives of their own. Her son, Thomas, Jr., went into the military, and the oldest daughter, Jessica, married and moved to Florida with her husband. The youngest, Karen, who had struggled to complete high school, "was always into the fast life," she explained. Judie had helped her from time to time, but Karen's persistent drug use and inability to hold a job made things difficult. Judie had allowed Karen and her daughter, Cloe, to come and live with her until

Karen's drug problems improved. They never did. Karen had stolen money for drugs from her mother and written checks forging Judie's name. Judie could not bring herself to turn in her own child to the authorities, but she did ask her to leave after Karen's refusal to get help. Tearfully, Judie stated that she had not heard from Karen for some time and was growing concerned about her and the welfare of Cloe. The last she had heard, Karen had been living with a man in the slums in South Central L.A., and Judie was concerned about Cloe's safety. Hearing all the issues, Elizabeth became concerned that the stress would eventually have a negative impact on Judie's physical and/or mental health.

Because family relationships were a part of the problem, as well as a potentially important source of social support for Judie, Elizabeth wanted to be sure she was keeping all the family connections straight. She sketched out a genogram (see Figure 19.1) and asked Judie to suggest any corrections. Some of the issues Elizabeth identified were concerned with family dynamics, but others specifically related to Judie's age and factors associated with growing older. Elizabeth knew her extra effort to get NASW's Social Work in Gerontology certificate after graduation would provide an additional perspective and experience for understanding and helping to deal with Judie's situation.

Some weeks later, Elizabeth had made significant progress in establishing a positive working relationship with Judie. About that time, Judie was contacted by child welfare services, who reported that her daughter, Karen, and her boyfriend had been arrested for drug possession and prostitution, and the state had taken Cloe into custody. Karen had suggested Judie as a caregiver for Cloe, rather than having her placed in long-term foster

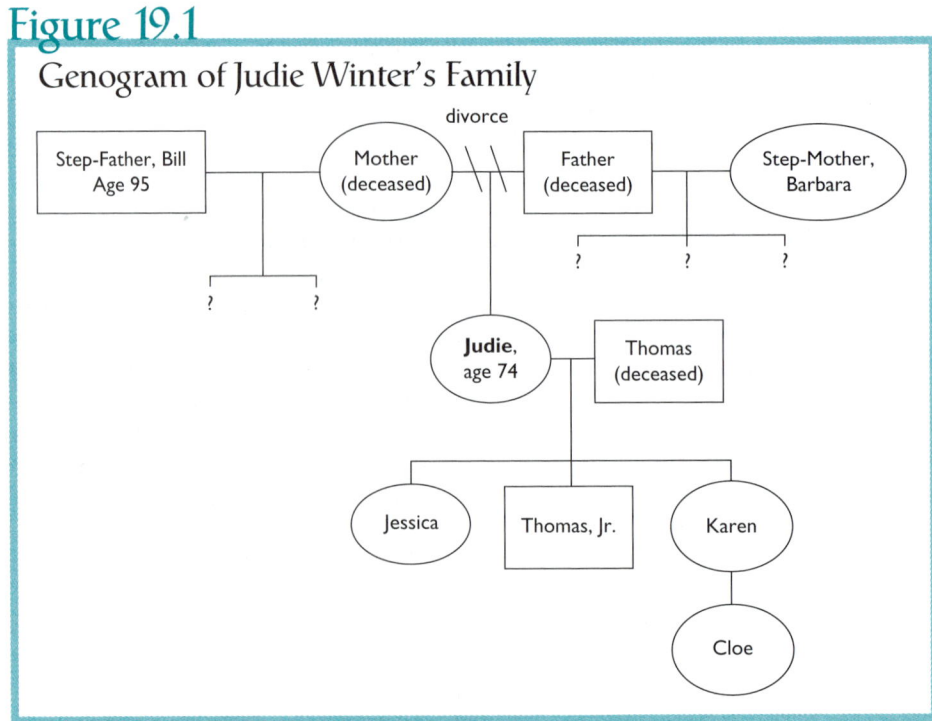

Figure 19.1

Genogram of Judie Winter's Family

care. The state also gives priority to placing children in a kinship placement before considering foster care or adoption, and a child welfare social worker contacted Judie. Because she had limited funds, was still recovering from the assault, and experienced hypertension, Judie wondered if she could provide her grandchild the quality of care she needed and asked Elizabeth to meet with her to discuss her options. Judie shared that she had a long-time family friend, Janice (78 years old), who had recently begun looking for a housemate so that she could remain in her home rather than moving into a nursing home. Should Judie and Cloe move in with Janice?

Elizabeth and Judie reviewed Judie's health concerns, the needs of her sometimes sickly grandchild, the issues Janice was experiencing that were indicating she might require nursing home care, and ways Judie could be of assistance to Janice. Another benefit for Judie would be that Janice's home would be closer to many of the city's health and human services and would reduce her transportation issues greatly. If Judie and Cloe should move in with Janice, and if Judie could find a part-time job, perhaps something like a "people greeter" with the local Wal-Mart, it just might work out. Judie believed she could handle these responsibilities and welcomed the opportunity for a mutually supportive living arrangement with her friend. Elizabeth worked with the child welfare caseworker for Cloe's placement, facilitated help with the move, and brokered connections with local agencies for services that might be needed by Judie and Janice.

As a result of Elizabeth's training, knowledge, and skillful advocacy, Janice remained in her home and would have a nurse's aide make regular home visits to the house each week. In addition, Judie was helped to make plans for Cloe to attend school, and Elizabeth worked on getting Judie enrolled for medical assistance. In time it became evident that Judie had other medical problems, and these were also a concern for Elizabeth. Judie admitted that she had occasional flare-ups with fibromyalgia, which causes exhaustion and pain throughout her body and requires that she take prescription medications and a preventative regimen of vitamins. Elizabeth helped her enroll in the Medicare, Part D, prescription assistance program. She also contacted Judie's other two children, but they were unable to help as they lived many miles away and had responsibilities for their own families.

Eventually, the state of California subsidized Cloe's care and provided Medicaid. Judie initially anticipated that Cloe would eventually return to live with her mother or with another family member. However, before long, Judie had grown extremely close to Cloe and realized she did not feel right sending her to live with anyone else. Besides, the three of them (Judie, Janice, and Cloe) had gotten a pretty good routine going, and Cloe was "a precious bundle of excitement and joy" for both Judie and Janice. Consequently, Elizabeth connected Judie with a social services foster care social worker and a guardian ad-litem. The court then approved the formal adoption of Cloe by her grandmother. Though Cloe had medical issues that involved hearing deficits and some language delay resulting from her mother's drug use during pregnancy, the courts granted Judie $304 a month and Medicaid until Cloe reached age 18. Now Judie and Cloe both have medical coverage, which helps tremendously with their financial situation, and if Judie dies before Cloe reaches 18, Cloe can receive a portion of Judie's Social Security with the legal adoption in place. Although she has now returned to school to study for her MSW degree, Elizabeth often thinks about the satisfying practice experience she had with Judie.

Trends in Gerontological Social Work

The Social Workers

More than three-fourths of the licensed social workers participating in the NASW Workforce Study indicated that they conduct some of their work with older adults, and one-fourth reported that older people make up more than 50 percent of the clients they serve. Twelve percent of the social workers in the NASW study identified aging as their primary practice area, and 93 percent of those believed that the opportunities in this field of practice will increase.[20] The basic competencies expected of all social workers make it possible to provide these needed services. However, social work is increasingly recognizing that services to older adults require sufficient specialized knowledge and skills to address this as a unique field of social work practice, gerontological social work. Social work practice with older adults presents the potential for a highly productive and satisfying career, and persons with the knowledge and skill to effectively work with this rapidly expanding segment of the population will find a substantial market for their talents.

Where do gerontological social workers work? The settings for practice when serving older adults are quite varied. They include both *institutional settings* where clients or patients are in residence, as well as *community settings* where clients reside elsewhere and make use of community services. Examination of these varied practice settings suggests the wide range of services in which a gerontological social worker might be involved. According to the Social Work Leadership Institute, the range of institutional settings includes acute care hospitals, assisted living facilities, non-medical residential care homes, congregate housing (with support services), dementia special care units, hospice or palliative care facilities, skilled nursing homes, and rehabilitation facilities. Non-residential, or community, services in which a social worker might be involved includes adult foster care or day care, work with an area agency on aging, providing services from a community health or mental health center, working with faith-based organizations, delivering services at a senior center or senior housing complex, assisting with income and housing needs from a public social service agency, and staffing a retirement community.[21] The opportunity to practice gerontological social work in one or many of these settings indicates the breadth of practice opportunities with this population group.

What do gerontological social workers do? The NASW Workforce Study revealed that the primary practice tasks were providing information and referral to services, screening and assessment of client conditions and needs, and case management.[22] More specifically the Social Work Leadership Institute identifies a wide range of interventions used by social workers when working with older people. These interventions include advocacy (for both the client and in relation to new social policies and improved services); care coordination; caregiver support services; client representation; leading client support groups; using a variety of individual, couples, family, and group therapies; caretaker training; and social work counseling.[23] In short, social workers working with older adults use most of the intervention strategies and approaches they would use with other client groups. Because these services are provided to clients in the later stages of their lives, social workers should be especially prepared to address end-of-life issues related to both the clients' preparation to "die with dignity" and to address deaths among their peer group. Thus grief therapy and other forms of assisting people address loss and face terminal illness should be part of the gerontological social worker's repertoire of services.

What do gerontological social workers need to know? What social workers do must always be underpinned by knowledge. In particular, a sampling of necessary competencies when working with older people includes a thorough knowledge of the structures in the society that have made older people a vulnerable population; mastery of the human behavior theories addressing the later life stages—including death and dying (subject matter that is often minimized in social work education); cultural competence regarding gender, racial, cultural, sexual orientation, and spiritual diversity within the older population; familiarity with social policies that are intended to meet specific needs of older adults (e.g., Social Security, Supplemental Security Income, Medicaid and Medicare, the Older Americans Act—especially the National Family Caregiver Program); and familiarity with the health care and social services frequently used by older people in one's community.[24]

Concluding Comment

Social workers have a key role to play in improving the quality of life for the expanding population of older adults, and career opportunities specializing in this practice area can be especially rewarding as the variety of practice opportunities with this population is substantial. Through generous support and effective leadership provided by the John A. Hartford Foundation and the Council on Social Work Education, many curricula of BSW and MSW social work education programs are infused with content to prepare new social workers with the knowledge and skill to work more effectively with older people and the issues they face. This includes such preparation as understanding the upper end of the aging process; learning about programs such as Medicare, hospice, and Social Security; addressing the quality of life issues for both the healthy and infirmed; being sensitive to cultural differences related to caregiving and grief; understanding the importance of maximizing a client's end-of-life-autonomy; and dealing with one's own attitudes toward death and dying.

At the macro level, social workers must advocate the development of policies and programs that will further enhance the quality of life for older people. The NASW Policy Statement regarding "Senior Health, Safety, and Vitality" enumerates a number of areas where social workers are committed to seeking change.[25] Among these changes are policies related to improving older people's social interaction, economic stability, housing, health and mental health care, and so on. As indicated in this chapter, improvement in these and other conditions for older people benefits the society as a whole. This country cannot afford to think of fragmented subpopulations as separate from each other but must conceive an intergenerational partnership providing the resources, time, and caring to ensure that those most in need receive the appropriate assistance.

KEY TERMS AND CONCEPTS

Older adults
Ageism
Oldest-old

Intergenerational caregiving
Gerontological social work
Healthy to frail continuum

SUGGESTED INFORMATION SOURCES

Berkman, Barbara, ed. *Handbook of Social Work in Health and Aging.* New York: Oxford University Press, 2006.

Greene, Roberta R. *Foundations of Social Work Practice in the Field of Aging: A Competency-Based Approach.* Washington, D.C.: NASW Press, 2007.

Kaye, Lenard W., ed. *Perspectives on Productive Aging: Social Work with the New Aged.* Washington, D.C.: NASW Press, 2005.

McInnis-Dittrich, Kathleen. *Social Work with Elders: A Biopsychosocial Approach to Assessment and Intervention.* Boston: Allyn & Bacon, 2005.

Richardson, Virginia E., and Barusch, Amanda S. *Gerontological Practice for the Twenty-First Century: A Social Work Perspective.* New York: Columbia University Press, 2005.

The Future of Social Work with Older Adults. *Families in Society* 86 (July–September, 2005). http://www.familiesinsociety.org/new/SpecialIssue/OlderAdults/spissue2.asp.

ENDNOTES

1. Federal Interagency Forum on Aging-Related Statistics, *Older Americans 2008: Key Indicators of Well-Being* (Washington, D.C.: U. S. Government Printing Office, March 2008), p. 74.
2. Ibid., p. 93.
3. Ibid., p. 74.
4. Tracy Whitaker, Tobi Weismiller, and Elizabeth Clark. *Assuring the Sufficiency of a Frontline Workforce: A National Study of Licensed Social Workers. Special Report: Social Work Services for Older Adults* (Washington, D.C.: National Association of Social Workers, 2005), p. 23.
5. Federal Interagency Forum, op. cit., p. 77.
6. Ibid., pp. 79, 93, 115.
7. Ibid., p. 83.
8. Ibid., p. 82.
9. Ibid., p. 85.
10. Ibid., pp. 89, 92, 130.
11. Ibid., p. 102.
12. Ibid., p. 123.
13. Robert N. Butler and Myrna I. Lewis, *Aging and Mental Health*, 2nd ed. (St. Louis, MO: C.V. Mosby, 1977), p. 34.
14. G. F. Streilb, "Are the Aged a Minority Group?" in B. L. Newgarten, ed., *Middle Age and Aging* (Chicago: University of Chicago Press, 1968), pp. 46–47.
15. Reuben Hill and Nelson Foote, *Family Development in Three Generations* (Cambridge, MA: Scheukman, 1970).

16. Child Trends, "Child Trends Data Bank," http://www.childtrendsdatabank.org.
17. Stacy T. Lindau, Edward Laumann, Philip Schumn, Colm A. O'Muircheartaigh, and Wendy Levinson, "A National Study of Sexuality and Health among Older Adults in the U.S.," *New England Journal of Medicine* (2007): 762–774.
18. Robert N. Butler, *Why Survive? Being Old in America* (New York: Harper and Row, 1975), p. 12.
19. M. H. Cantor, "Social Care: Family and Community Support Systems," *The Annals* 503 (May 1989): 100.
20. Whitaker, op. cit., pp. 7, 9.
21. Social Work Leadership Institute, "Glossary of Terms: Service Settings," New York Academy of Medicine, 2008, http://www.socialworkleadership.org/nsw/cap/glossary.php?q=S.
22. Whitaker, op. cit., p. 8.
23. Social Work Leadership Institute, "Glossary of Terms: Interventions," New York Academy of Medicine, 2008, http://www.socialworkleadership.org/nsw/cap/glossary.php?q=I.
24. CalSWEC Aging Initiative, "California Social Work Education Center (CalSWEC) Aging Initiative: Aging Competencies," 2006, http://calswec.berkeley.edu/CalSWEC/Aging_Competencies.html.
25. *Social Work Speaks: National Association of Social Workers Policy Statements 2003–2006* (Washington, D.C.: NASW Press), pp. 320–326.

chapter 20

Social Work Practice with People with Disabilities*

Prefatory Comment

Social work students trickled into the classroom on the first day of class to take the required course called "Social Work Practice with People with Disabilities." Among the last to arrive was the professor, Dr. Sue Gary, who used a joystick to guide her electric wheelchair deftly around the trash can and podium to settle in at the desk.

"I am Professor Gary," she said, "and, please, on this first day of class, I would like for you to tear out a sheet of notebook paper and write your name and today's date." She continued, "When you have done that, write 'First Exam,' at the top of your paper in block letters." After the groans subsided, she read out a short series of true/false questions. Below are the actual questions. See how you would do:

1. True or False: A person can have a disability and not be handicapped.
2. True or False: There are many more people with mental retardation than there are with mental illness.
3. True or False: People with disabilities demonstrate unusual courage and determination as they work within the limitations of their disabilities.
4. True or False: People with disabilities are appropriately described as a minority group.
5. True or False: The medical condition is the foremost factor in determining how well a person with a disability will carry out the activities and responsibilities of life.
6. True or False: The majority of people 65 to 74 years old have a disability.
7. True or False: The United States has never had a president with an obvious physical disability.

---

*This chapter was prepared by Dr. Celia Williamson, a social worker, Deputy Provost and Dean of Undergraduate Studies at the University of North Texas.

The phrase "people with disabilities" is now familiar to many in the United States. During the 1980s, the debate surrounding the Americans with Disabilities Act (ADA) and its final passage in 1990 helped to cultivate a growing awareness of disability. Since that time, social work literature has increased its focus on disability issues. Introductory and human behavior textbooks now address disability issues, and social work journals have increasingly engaged in discussions of this emerging area.

But why would this be considered a relatively new area for social work practice? Disability is certainly not new. Since the beginning of time, individuals and families have encountered illness and injury and, as a result, have had to adjust their lives. Social work, from its inception, has been involved in helping people to deal with a wide variety of life's problems, including those that come from disability. In fact, a close look at early social work history shows a clear involvement with people affected by disability. The settlement house movement grew up around immigrants who were drawn to cities during the industrial revolution and was vitally involved in issues surrounding occupational injuries, workers' compensation, and public health. Social workers have long played prominent roles in advocacy and service delivery for people with mental and physical disability.[1]

The phrase "people with disabilities" first began appearing in literature in the 1980s.[2] Its appearance is more than just a matter of semantics, more than simply a new term to address old problems. It represents a significant change in the understanding of how disability affects individuals and society—one that conceptualizes people with disabilities as a minority group, instead of as isolated individuals with specific disorders.

Before this change occurred, discussions about disability emphasized medical conditions. The "problem" was the disorder itself, and interventions were directed at the micro level, at helping individuals to correct, compensate, or cope with their own specific medical conditions. In the wake of the civil rights movement, however, people with disabilities began to gain an awareness of how the environment played a role in their disability. They began to address their situations in light of what they had learned from civil rights advocates and racial minority groups. They took a more "macro" look at the situation, and it changed the whole approach. Suddenly, solutions could be found by changing the environment as well as by changing the individual.

This is a clear application of the Morales-Sheafor ecosystems approach,[3] because it allows for a comprehensive examination of the problems and resources by directing attention to each of five different levels of systems, nested one inside the other. These include the individual level, the family level, the level of culture, the level of environmental and structural influences, and the historical level. Each of these levels affects the development and the resolution of human problems.

Consider this example: As you walk across town, you happen to pass a man without legs who is sitting in a wheelchair outside a restaurant. There are five steps up to the front door of the restaurant and no ramp. How would you describe this problem?

The medical model would focus on the fact that the man cannot walk. It would seek to fix his condition or find him prosthetic legs. The ecosystems model, on the other hand, might just as easily see the lack of a ramp as the problem. The environment could be adjusted so that the man could use his wheelchair to get into the restaurant, as could other wheelchair users and mothers with strollers. In fact, today this would be a legal problem, as well, because public access to restaurants is covered by the ADA.

When the ecosystems viewpoint is used, the problem no longer resides solely with the individual. The focus moves to a much broader issue: the right of all citizens to access the benefits of society and the obligation of society to remove barriers to that access. There is a distinct civil rights ring to it, eloquently voiced by 12-year-old Jade Calegory in his 1988 testimony before Congress in support of the ADA:

> I guess my teacher was right about history repeating itself. I learned in school that black people had problems with buses, too. They had to sit in the back of the bus, but some of us with disabilities cannot even get on the bus at all. Black people had to use separate drinking fountains, and those of us using wheelchairs cannot even reach some drinking fountains. We get thirsty, too. Black people had to go to separate theaters, schools, restaurants, and some of us have to, also. That is not because we want to but because we cannot get in.[4]

Defining Disability

Language is a powerful vehicle for the expression of our cultural understanding. The words we speak convey both overt and covert meanings and subtly affect the way we think. Thus, it is not surprising to see that the reconceptualization of disability from a medical condition to a civil rights issue is reflected in the words we use in discussing it.

In everyday discussions, the terms "impairment," "disability," and "handicap" are often used interchangeably, a reflection of the earlier medically based emphasis, where the impairment and the handicap were one and the same. A broader understanding of disability requires a careful delineation of these terms and an understanding of how they differ.[5]

The term *impairment* refers to loss or abnormality at the level of body system or organ. Examples might include a distortion in vision caused by a weakening of blood vessels in the retina or the loss of a limb by amputation. A medical diagnosis is often used in describing an individual's impairment, and the focus is not on the whole person but on the specific part of the anatomy that is affected.

A *disability* results when an impairment causes a restriction in the ability to carry out normal life activities. For example, the loss of a leg, the impairment, results in limitations to mobility. The weakening of the blood vessels in the retina results in an inability to read standard-size print. The focus here is on the *functional results* of the impairment for the individual. Because short-term medical problems have a more limited impact on individuals, the term disability is usually reserved for discussions related to functional limitations, which are long term or result from chronic conditions.

The term *handicap* takes an even broader perspective and looks at the barriers that are created by an interaction between the disability and the environment. If a restaurant does not have large-print menus and if the waiters have not been trained to assist patrons by reading the menu to them, individuals with visual disabilities might be handicapped in regard to eating out. The combination of poor vision and lack of accommodation results in a loss of public access for the individual and a loss of revenue for the restaurant.

It is very possible for a person to have a disability but not to be handicapped. In fact, this is the focus of the new approach—to remove barriers so that people with disabilities are not handicapped in regard to their life activities.

It should be noted that, in addition to clearly delineating the meaning of words, it is also important to understand the emotional impact words can carry. The word "handicap" is a good example of this. In the 1970s, "handicap" was the politically correct term. It was seen as a term that helped to normalize the experience of disability. After all, golfers were given a handicap to compensate for differences in ability levels so that all could compete from an equal starting point. When the historical roots of the word were discovered, however, it lost its political correctness. Historically, it referred to beggars, seeking handouts with "cap-in-hand." This was certainly not the image that people with disabilities wished to reinforce. Although the term handicap can still be appropriately used to denote the interplay between environment and disability, the term *barrier* is more often used today. In fact, "barrier" places the problem even more squarely in the environmental context.

Other changes in our language have also occurred in this process of reconceptualizing disability. One of the most important is the delineation of the principle of "people first language." The underlying concept is that the structure of verbal expression itself can reinforce either the predominance of the disability as the defining characteristic of an individual (retarded child) or relegate the disability to only one element among many that define that person (child with mental retardation). By putting the disability in the secondary position, the preeminence of personhood is emphasized: people with disabilities are always *people first*.

In choosing words that honor personhood, derogatory terms, such as imbecile or cripple or deformed, should be avoided altogether, as should the implication that people with disabilities are inevitably victims. For example, people are not "confined" to wheelchairs, they use them. In fact, wheelchairs are liberating devices. To refer to people with disabilities as afflicted, unfortunate, or stricken places them in a disempowered position. Even suggesting that they are unusually courageous because they live with a disability sets them apart. It broadens the impact of the disability from its specific functional implications and places an aura over the whole character and life circumstance of the individual. When people with disabilities are assumed to be essentially *un*able, the societal stigma turns out to be much more of a barrier to effective functioning than the specific limitations of the disability itself.[6]

Demographic Considerations

The 2000 U.S. Census indicates that 47.9 million people in the United States live with a disability or some other long-lasting condition.[7] Figure 20.1 shows the distribution of various types of disability based on the functional impact. The

Figure 20.1
Americans* with Disabilities or Long-Term Conditions

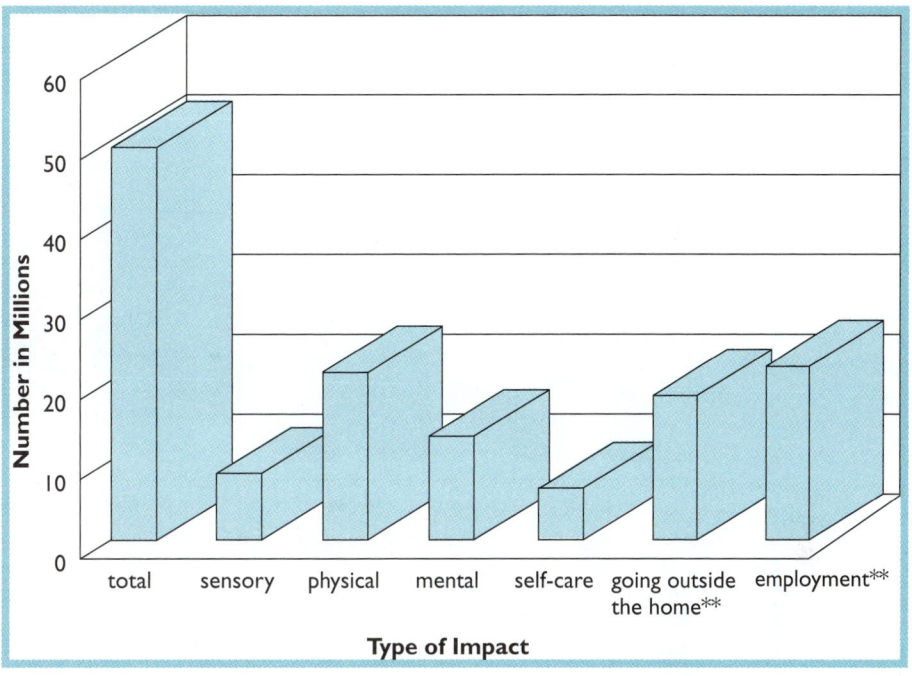

*Civilian noninstitutionalized population of the United States aged 5 and older

**Includes only individuals aged 16 and older

Source: J. Waldrop and S. M. Stern, *Disability Status: 2000*, U.S. Census Bureau (March 2003). Retrieved on September 6, 2005, from http://www.census.gov/prod/2003pubs/c2kbr-17.pdf.

numbers across these columns add up to considerably more than 48 million because many individuals experience more than one disability. This means that nearly one in six Americans has a disability or other long-lasting condition. Clearly, social workers will be involved with people with disabilities in every type of agency or service setting.

It should be noted that the incidence of disability is not evenly spread across the population. Figure 20.2 shows that older individuals are much more likely to experience disability than younger ones. It makes sense that the longer one lives, the more chances one has of encountering illness or injury. Lifelong choices about smoking, drug use, diet, and exercise have a cumulative effect, affecting function more in later years. Notice, though, that even in the highest age group, not all individuals experience disability. It is important not to assume that aging and disability are inevitably related. This figure also illustrates that males are somewhat more likely to be affected by disability in early and midlife. In maturity, females are more likely to be affected.

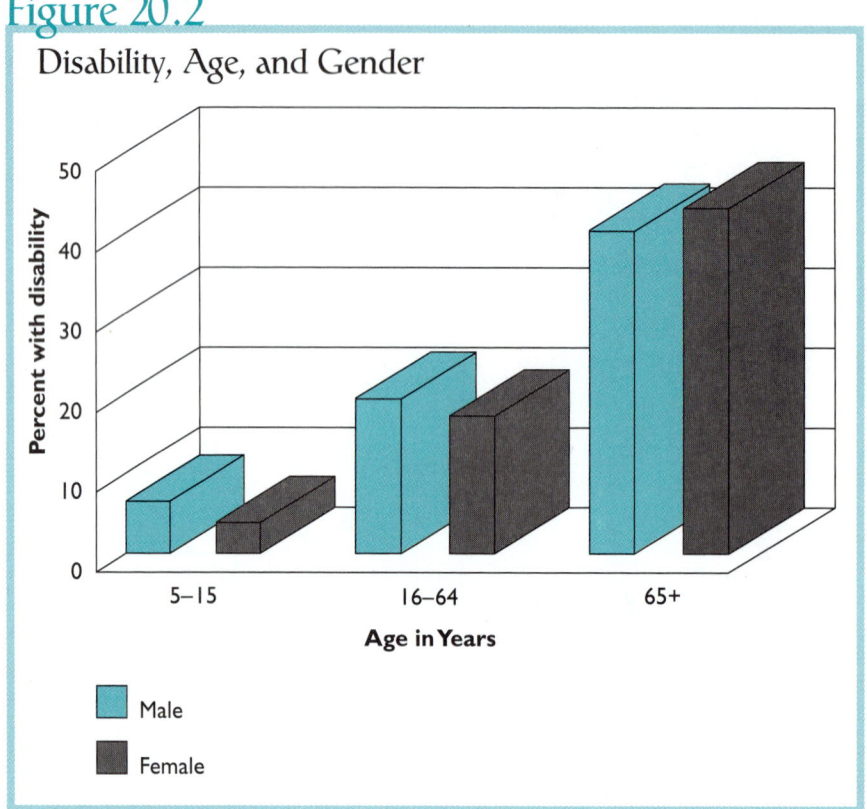

Figure 20.2
Disability, Age, and Gender

Note: This includes the civilian noninstitutionalized population.
Source: J. Waldrop and S. M. Stern, *Disability Status: 2000*, U.S. Census Bureau (March 2003). Retrieved on September 6, 2005, from http://www.census.gov/prod/2003pubs/c2kbr-17.pdf.

Figure 20.3 reveals some correspondence between race, ethnicity, and disability. This is a complex relationship that is not yet fully understood. Some disorders are hereditary and thus more likely to appear in genetically related populations. Health conditions that result in disability may be positively or negatively affected by dietary and other cultural practices. Beliefs about medical practices, access to culturally relevant health care, and economic disparities among various racial groups also affect the prevalence and persistence of disability. Even the likelihood of reporting disability may vary among different groups. Although the membership in a racial or ethnic group may be biologically based, the impacts may be sociologically grounded. Clearly, disability must be addressed within the cultural context of the individuals who feel its impact.

There is also a correlation between earnings and disability,[8] which is revealed in Figure 20.4. Lower income is associated with higher rates of disability. The data does not necessarily reveal a causal link, however. Individuals with

Figure 20.3
Americans* with Disabilities by Race and Ethnic Origin

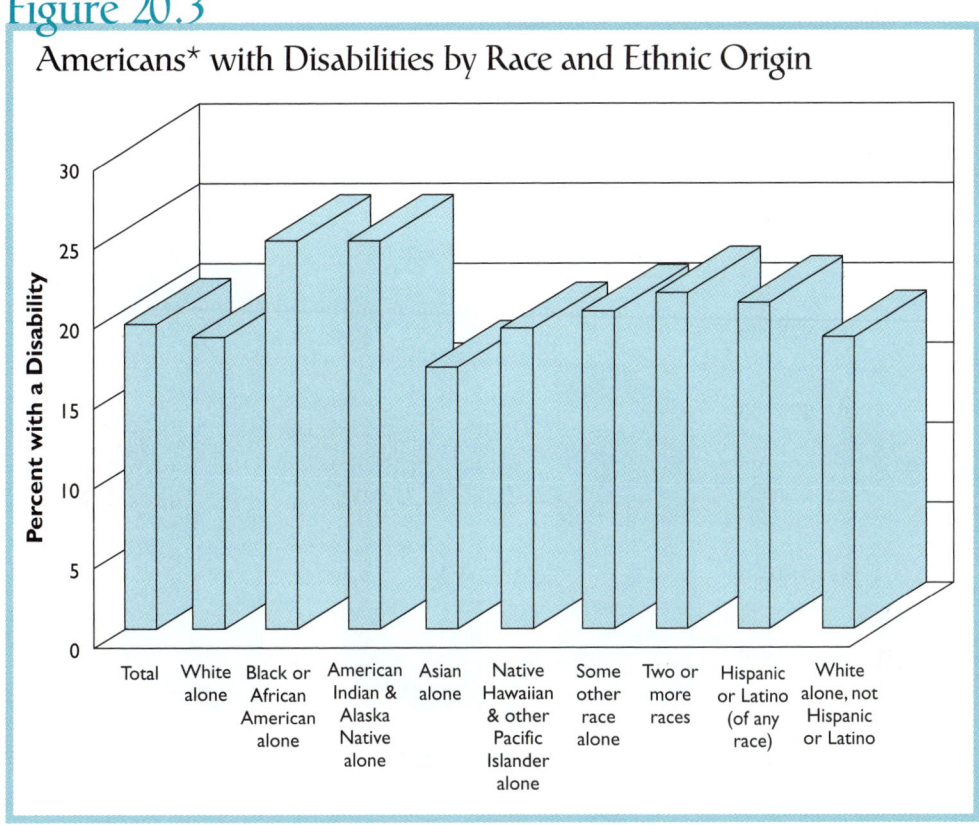

* Civilian noninstitutionalized population of the United States aged 5 and older

Source: J. Waldrop and S. M. Stern, *Disability Status: 2000*, U.S. Census Bureau (March 2003). Retrieved on September 6, 2005, from http://www.census.gov/prod/2003pubs/c2kbr-17.pdf.

lower earnings are less likely to have access to health care and may be more likely to be employed in high-risk jobs. This makes them more subject to incurring disability. On the other hand, a person with a disability is less likely to be employed (Figure 20.5). So, the interplay of income and disability is complex. This same reciprocal causality is evident in the relationship between education and disability (Figure 20.6). Mental retardation and other significant disabilities that affect individuals early in life may reduce access to higher education. At the same time, the jobs that are open to those with lower educational levels are more likely to involve physical labor and risk of injury, meaning those with lower educational levels may be more likely to become disabled later in life. In income, employment, and education, people with less severe disabilities reflect patterns more similar to the nondisabled population than those with severe disabilities.

Figure 20.4

Disability and Earnings

Note: This includes individuals in the United States who are 21-64 years old.
Source: U.S. Census Bureau, 1996 Survey of Income and Program Participation, August–November 1997, as reported by McNeil, 2001.

Two things seem very evident in looking at the statistics that reflect disability patterns in the United States. The first is that disability affects a large proportion of the population—nearly one in five individuals—making it an extremely important consideration for the social work profession. The second is that the medical model, which focuses on the physical impact of the disabling condition, can only partially explain the differences across populations. Biological explanations are insufficient. Factors in the social environment must also be taken into consideration. Even age, which seems so firmly rooted in the biological perspective, is subject to the impact of societal perceptions. Several researchers have suggested that older people are less likely to receive rehabilitation services than younger ones.[9]

Figure 20.5

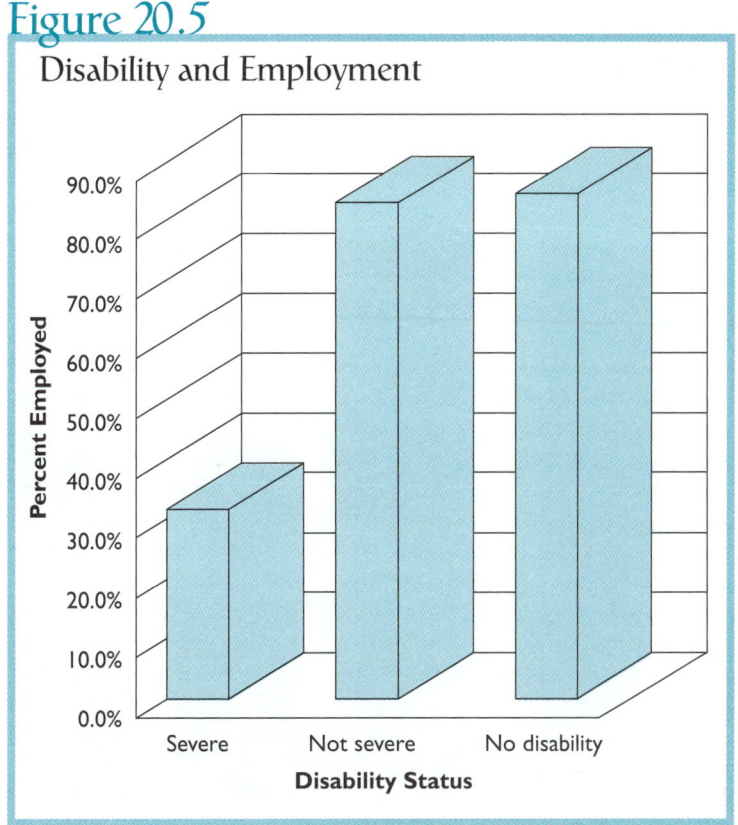

Note: This includes individuals in the United States who are 21–64 years old.
Source: U.S. Census Bureau, 1996 Survey of Income and Program Participation, August–November 1997, as reported by McNeil, 2001.

Ageism allows people to assume that dysfunction is simply part of getting older. So, for example, instead of treating urinary incontinence, we sigh and talk of getting older and just change the sheets. In fact, incontinence is often reversible. In such cases, it is not so much the medical condition but the attitude that is the problem.

Other Risks Associated with Disability

It is important to briefly mention some additional risks that are associated with disability. Some studies have suggested that children and adults with disabilities are more often the targets of physical and sexual abuse than people without disabilities, though other studies have failed to support this finding.[10] It is clear that injuries

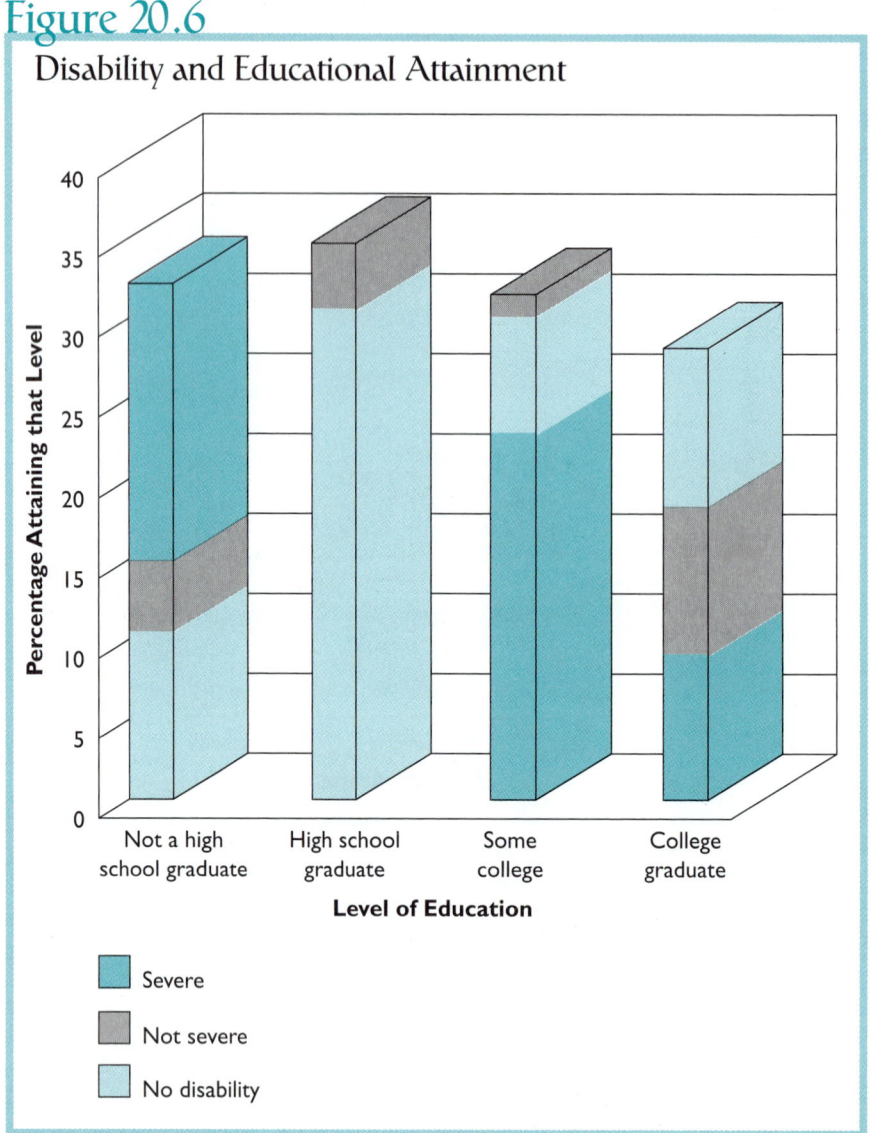

Figure 20.6 Disability and Educational Attainment

Note: Includes individuals in the United States who are 25 years old and over.

Source: U.S. Census Bureau, 1996 Survey of Income and Program Participation, August–November 1997, as reported by McNeil, 2001.

resulting from abuse, including child abuse, and other forms of family and societal violence can cause disability.

While chemical dependency is itself a disability, studies indicate increased rates of substance abuse and chemical dependency among people with other disabilities.

Again, reciprocal causality makes it difficult to fully interpret these figures. Although it is true that many traumatic head injuries occur as a result of intoxication, and as many as 62 percent of injuries resulting in mobility impairments are substance abuse related, there are also indications that substance abuse rates are higher among people with congenital disabilities,[11] indicating that disability may also precede chemical dependency.

Disability and each of these other variables—education, income, abuse, and addiction—are interrelated in a complicated fashion. No straight-line cause-and-effect pattern can be established. Instead, there is a circular interaction pattern, where each variable affects all other variables. This pattern of interaction requires an ecosystems approach because that model provides a framework in which to examine these complicated interrelationships.

Disability and the Minority Model

It is clear from the demographic information presented above that people with disabilities comprise a large subgroup of the American population, larger than any single racial or ethnic minority group. But is it really appropriate for people with disabilities to think of themselves as a minority? Stroman describes four essential criteria for a group to be accorded minority status.[12] A minority group:

1. is *identifiable,* either in terms of appearance or behavior;
2. experiences *less access to power* so that fewer resources, influence, and control are afforded to it;
3. experiences *discriminatory treatment,* often evidenced by segregation and stereotyping; and
4. *sees itself as a separate group.*

Many people with disabilities are readily identifiable in terms of appearance. A difference in physical appearance itself, such as the body posture of a person with cerebral palsy, or the visibility of the accommodations, such as braces or a white cane, announce the presence of a disability. Behaviors, such as the use of sign language or the onset of a seizure, also serve to identify the person as someone with a disability.

Some individuals may choose not to disclose or to hide their disability and thus avoid probing questions, stereotypes, and other issues of discrimination. During the 1930s, President Roosevelt was rarely photographed in his wheelchair or using his crutches. In the 1996 presidential campaign, Senator Robert Dole incorporated his disability into his public image, neither hiding nor emphasizing its presence. The very fact that one would have to choose whether to talk about a facet of themselves because of possible discrimination reinforces the group's separate identity.

If one considers income and education as indices of power,[13] then people with disabilities clearly fit the second criteria for minority group status. Figures 20.4 and 20.5 clearly illustrate that lower levels of income and education are highly associated with disability.

The discriminatory treatment of people with disabilities is also easy to establish. When diagnostic terms can be hurled as insults, as "retarded" and "spastic" often are, the presence of stereotyping becomes very apparent. Federal law recognizes that "individuals with disabilities continually encounter various forms of discrimination in such critical areas as employment, housing, public accommodations, education, transportation, communication, recreation, institutionalization, health services, voting and public services."[14] Attitude surveys of human service providers, employment rates, and research in basic patterns of social interaction suggest that American society harbors significant prejudice against people with disabilities.[15] Physical barriers result in de facto segregation. People with disabilities clearly meet the third criterion for designation as a minority group.

It is the fourth criterion that has most recently been met. Until the late 1960s, the medical model dominated the conceptualization of disability, and separate diagnostic groups often found themselves competing with each other for limited federal funds. People may have labeled themselves with a particular diagnosis and joined in advocacy activities to support services for that group, but they did not necessarily see themselves as objects of discrimination. "Object" is the correct term here—discrimination denies personhood.

The 1960s, however, focused public attention on civil rights, feminism, deinstitutionalization, and consumerism. It was in the context of these social movements that the conceptualization of disability began to change.[16] In 1972, in Berkeley, California, a group of students with disabilities banded together to demand access to classes on the University of California campus and to pool their resources for transportation and attendant care. They developed the first Center for Independent Living, building it on the principles of consumer sovereignty, self-reliance, and political and economic rights.

As people with disabilities began to recognize that they were being treated differently based on the stigma associated with being disabled, rather than merely in regard to differences in functional abilities, they began to see similarities that spanned across disability areas. This cross-disability awareness led to coalitions between groups that previously saw each other as competing for the same funds. This alliance of various disability-specific advocacy groups provided the political muscle that helped to bring about the passage of the ADA.

Thus, the minority perspective holds some distinct advantages for people with disabilities. It allows the cultivation of cross-disability alliances that results in increased political power. It provides a vehicle for identification with a group that looks at itself with pride, as self-reliant survivors, and it expands the pool of potential solutions, because environmental change as well as personal change is now an option.

Societal Responses to Disability

In addition to broader sociocultural influences, the way a society responds to disability is influenced by its perceptions about the causes of disability, the threats that it perceives to be related to the disability, and the amount and kinds of resources that are available to deal with the disability.[17]

The perceived causes of disabilities have shifted dramatically over the course of history. Early explanations often centered on spiritual dimensions. Mental and physical disorders alike were often viewed as punishment from the gods, and those with disabilities were often shunned or even tortured. In the latter half of the eighteenth century, when genetics was seen as the cause of mental deficiency, laws prohibiting marriage or providing for sterilization of people with mental or emotional disorders were passed in half of the states.[18] Later, the perception that disability was essentially a medical condition came to prominence, and medical interventions were the preferred course of action.

When society was seen as the cause, there was increased pressure for the society to provide solutions. Historically, services for people with disabilities have been afforded first to soldiers injured in war because societal responsibility was clear. Indeed the first federal-level public aid program in the United States established pensions for soldiers who were disabled during the War for Independence.[19]

Society also responds differently to specific impairments based on perceived cause. People with mental retardation or congenital disorders are not often seen as responsible for their disorder, and public willingness to provide services is relatively high. Visible volunteer efforts and fund raising keep these disabilities before the public eye and encourage increased private and public support. Mental illness or chemical dependency, which are still perceived by many as resulting from character flaws, receive less public attention and support, although the prevalence of either mental illness or chemical dependency far exceeds that of mental retardation.[20]

The potential threat of a disability can also greatly influence societal response. The polio scare of the late 1940s and early 1950s brought significant governmental and volunteer response. The March of Dimes was born out of the impetus to stop this public threat, and government as well as private research efforts helped to eradicate the virus. Once the vaccine was developed, the presence of a clear and decisive medical intervention helped to mobilize the community response to the disease. Here, a "guilt-free" cause, a substantial threat, and an effective technology combined to shape society's response in a positive way. It should be noted that the disease itself and the disability resulting from it are different. Society mobilized primarily against the disease, but the wave of public sentiment carried over into the provision of services for those who became disabled because of the virus.

The Acquired Immune Deficiency Syndrome (AIDS) epidemic reveals an interesting, though distressing, interplay between perceived cause and perceived threat and resources. It stands in contrast to the polio epidemic. Early on, those who were identified as "responsible for" the spread of the Human Immunodeficiency Virus (HIV) that causes AIDS were seen as the only ones threatened. The general public response was low. Later, when the extent of the threat was realized, efforts at prevention and intervention were intensified. Now, ironically, the potential threat is an economic one as well as a medical one, and the level of economic resources that might be required to provide services for individuals with AIDS makes the public somewhat uneasy about committing itself to a specific level of care. The fact that no clear medical response is yet available also complicates efforts to gain public and governmental support in combatting the disease.

Social Workers and People with Disabilities

Social workers will encounter people with disabilities in all aspects of their lives—as friends, colleagues, clients, and even in the mirror. All service settings should provide access to people with disabilities, and social workers should not assume that a client with a disability is seeking services in relation to the disability. Some service systems, however, are designed to address issues specific to disability. Social workers can find active roles within these systems of services.

Five major areas of legislation address disability issues specifically. These include workers' compensation, rehabilitation, Social Security, education, and civil rights. In addition, a distinct service system exists to serve veterans with disabilities. Each of these legislative areas addresses different issues and addresses them from a unique viewpoint that grew out of the historical context in which they were formulated. They do not always complement one another.

Workers' compensation laws were passed on a state-by-state basis during the early 1900s. This means that many different workers' compensation laws exist, and a disability incurred in California may be addressed very differently from one incurred in Mississippi. Most of these laws address disability from within the medical model, with specific impairments resulting in specific reparations. In some states, each part of the anatomy is assigned a percentage, so that, for example, the loss of the index finger on the dominant hand results in a particular percentage of disability for the individual.[21] Other states allocate a lump sum payment of a specified amount for each body part lost. Social workers, along with nurses and rehabilitation professionals, often fill roles in medical case management as a part of the workers' compensation service system.

On the heels of World War I, the federal government enacted the 1918 Soldier's Rehabilitation Act. It authorized vocational rehabilitation services for veterans whose disabilities were a result of military service. The first civilian rehabilitation services followed two years later, in 1920, under the Smith-Fess Act. This separation of veterans' and civilian services continues to this day. Although veterans are not excluded from the civilian system, veterans' services often provide for more extensive benefits. Social workers fill positions in Veterans' Administration hospitals and may work extensively with veterans with disabilities and their families in the process of adjustment to disability and in finding the resources to support employment and independent living.

The overriding purpose of the civilian act, which has since been designated as the Rehabilitation Act, is to help people with disabilities become employed. Each state provides vocational rehabilitation services under the auspices of this act. Vocational rehabilitation counselors purchase a range of services for people with disabilities in order to help them to secure employment. These may include medical services, vocational assessments, training or education, counseling services, adaptive equipment, supported employment, and job placement services. Social workers may contract to provide services directly to the consumers of the vocational rehabilitation program.

The act also has provisions for funding independent living centers, which are charged with promoting consumer control, self-help, and self-advocacy and with assisting communities to meet the needs of people with disabilities. Services provided by independent living centers include peer counseling and individual and community advocacy.

Typically the staff members of independent living centers are, themselves, individuals with disabilities. Social workers with disabilities can play a vital role in bringing both professional training and personal experience to bear in these service settings.

The Social Security Act provides important income and medical insurance supports for people with disabilities through the Supplemental Security Income (SSI) and the Social Security Disability Insurance (SSDI) programs. Special work incentive programs are available through SSI and SSDI to help individuals with disabilities make the transition from Social Security income supports to employment. Social workers are often employed by SSI/SSDI programs to assist people in accessing these services.

The Individuals with Disabilities Education Act mandates that all children with disabilities have access to a free, appropriate public education designed to meet their unique needs. These educational services are provided through the local school district, and school social workers often assist in the process of determining just what services are needed and then help families and schools to access those services. Efforts are made to keep children involved with their non-disabled peers, avoiding isolated, "special" settings.

Although there are provisions in other laws to help secure the civil rights of people with disabilities, the ADA is the seminal piece of legislation in this area. There are no services provided under this bill, but social workers need to be aware of its provisions in order to help people with disabilities to maintain their full rights as citizens of this country. Social workers can also take an active role in ensuring that the services they provide are available to all people, regardless of disability.

In addition to these government programs, social workers may provide disability-specific services in private for-profit and private not-for-profit service systems. Today many companies are taking a proactive stance toward work-related injuries, establishing their own disability management programs that are focused on making accommodations that allow workers to quickly return to work after an injury. Social workers find active roles in this arena, both through positions in disability management programs themselves and through involvement of employee assistance programs.

Social workers can also be found in private not-for-profit organizations that often contract with government agencies to provide services in relation to disability. Disability-specific organizations and foundations, such as United Cerebral Palsy or the Arthritis Foundation, employ social workers. In addition to direct services that may be provided by these organizations, social workers are involved in extensive public education and advocacy campaigns. It is clear that there are many roles that social workers can fill in providing services to people with disabilities, their families, and the communities in which they live.

The Ecosystems Model and People with Disabilities

The ecosystems framework[22] provides the opportunity for a broader conceptualization of disability, recognizing that the history of discrimination against people with disabilities, the structural impact of governmental policies, the cultural assumptions about what people with disabilities can and cannot do, and the impact of disability on the family, as well as the individual psychological and biological specifics of the disorder, all play a part in determining both problems and solutions. Figure 20.7 frames some of the issues specific to disability that must be considered within each level of the concentric spheres of the ecosystems model.

Social workers may focus the intervention at any one of these levels or at several levels at the same time. Wherever the intervention is focused, its success will be dependent on the social worker's understanding of the impact at all levels. This is clearly illustrated in the following case example.

THE INDIVIDUAL

Jerry Desoto is almost ready to be discharged from a rehabilitation hospital where he spent the past two months. He was injured three days after his eighteenth birthday, when he crashed his motorcycle, a birthday gift from his parents, into a telephone pole. He was intoxicated at the time of the crash. His spinal cord injury resulted in paralysis from the waist down.

Jerry had been a starter on the high school basketball team. School began three weeks ago. Jerry has been working with a tutor and will be able to return to school on a part-time basis. Between attending classes and continued tutoring, he should be able to finish his senior year with his class. His superb physical condition before the injury has greatly helped his recovery.

Jerry is counting the days until discharge. For him, it represents a milestone in his recovery, a move back into the "real world," and a chance to reestablish his friendships. For Jerry's social worker, Chris, the process of discharge began as soon as Jerry was admitted to the rehabilitation hospital.

At the micro level, the biopsychosocial factors that affect Jerry are many and varied. Jerry has lost all sensation and all voluntary use of all his muscles below the waist. His friends are aware that he can no longer walk and that he would need a specially equipped car in order to drive. Only his family and closest friends are aware that he has also had to learn new ways to control bowel and bladder elimination. He has learned to handle the catheter well but still has occasional difficulties with bowel control. That is one of his major concerns about returning to school. Jerry has also lost sexual function, though he has not yet allowed himself to admit it. He is having enough trouble adjusting to the fact that he will not be the school's top basketball player and is not ready to address the way his sexual function will affect his self-image.

Jerry had been looking forward to leaving home at the end of the year. This accident has placed him back in a more dependent mode, at least temporarily, and it irritates, even angers, him that he will have to look to his mother for assistance. He cannot even go to town without getting someone to take him. His mother is too eager to help. She wasn't really ready for her youngest to leave home, anyway.

THE FAMILY

Jerry's father is a line worker in an automobile assembly plant, and his mother teaches fifth grade. He has an older brother, Jake, who works in an autobody repair shop and has just moved out into an apartment. Even with good medical insurance coverage, the

Figure 20.7
Example of Ecosystems Model for People with Disabilities

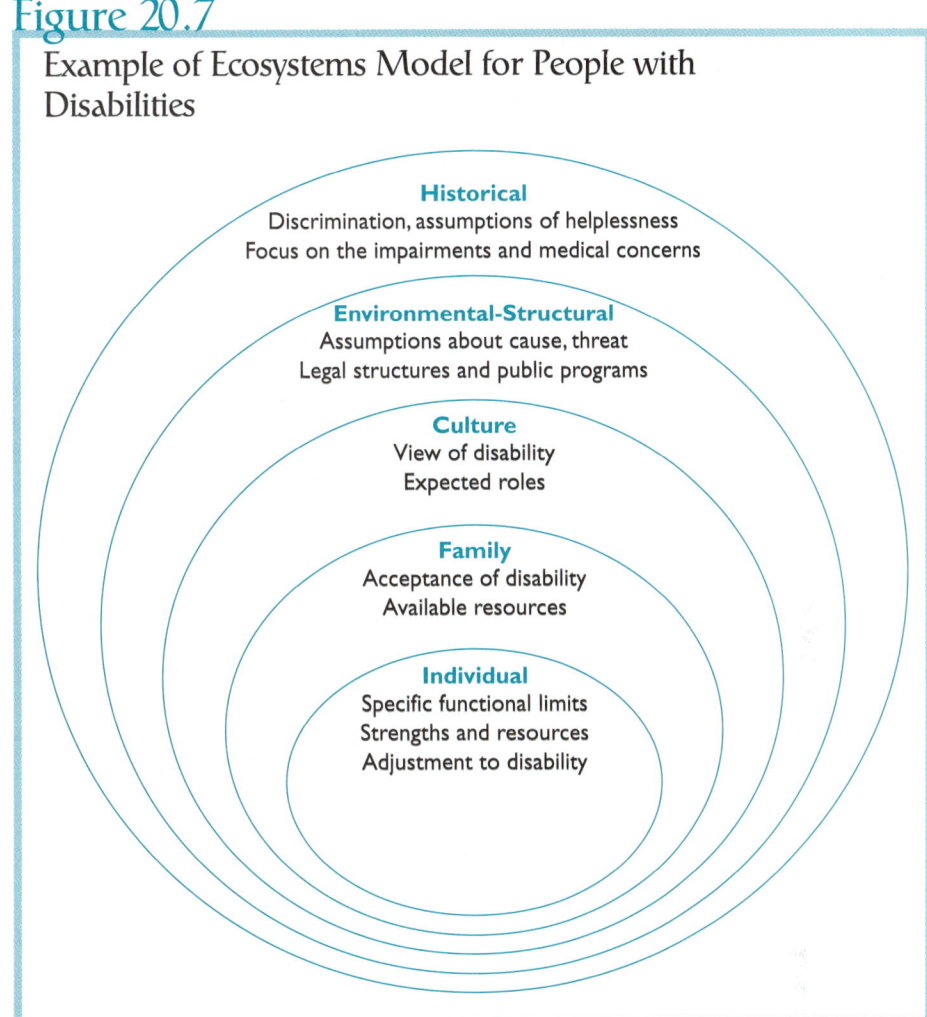

costs of this accident have been substantial, and Jerry's father takes every opportunity to work overtime. His mother has been primarily responsible for working with the hospital in regard to Jerry's rehabilitation.

Jerry is acutely aware of the additional financial burden that the accident has placed on the family. He blames himself because he had been drinking. His parents could not afford to give him a car, so they had compromised when his father found the used bike. Now they blame themselves for being stingy with his safety. In addition to medical expenses, there were renovation expenses. Jerry's home had to be modified so that he could live there. The strain over finances has caused some old issues in the marriage to resurface.

CULTURAL ISSUES

Jerry's buddies have been attentive, but Jerry is a bit wary of the town's response. It's not that he is afraid that they will not welcome him; it's just that he is afraid of their expectations. They raised money for renovations to his home by putting a change jar in the local hamburger joint. They want to see him happy, but he is often angry, depressed, and discouraged. The church youth group has asked him to speak about his "courageous recovery" and how his faith has helped him through. He hasn't been to church in two years.

Jerry's status in his community to this point has been built on American youth cultural issues such as his athletic abilities, his ability to drink and go out with his buddies, and his ability to charm the girls in his class. While there are accommodations that can help him to overcome the biological limitations of his condition, he must also come to terms with how his status as a person with a disability has affected the way people expect him to act. Society has proscribed certain "sick roles" that require that he play the part of an always optimistic, grateful recipient of the kindness of others. In his community, it would be selfish for him to expect accommodations to be made on his behalf, and it would be presumptive of him to think that any girl's parents would be willing to have their daughter date someone who is "damaged."

ENVIRONMENTAL–STRUCTURAL ISSUES

Jerry is fortunate that his injury occurred after the passages of the Individuals with Disabilities Education Act and the Americans with Disabilities Act. These important pieces of legislation provide a legal framework to ensure his access to education, transportation, and governmental and public services. His legal rights and the physical realities of his community environment do not always match, however, and there is pressure on him not to pursue the issue. "Surely," his old girlfriend's mother confides in a friend, "he does not expect the school to spend all that money putting in a lift so he can get into the weight room in the school basement when that means they will have to delay buying new band equipment another year. After all, it's so much money to spend on only one person."

HISTORICAL ISSUES

Historical patterns of discrimination have left a deep mark on the lives of people with disabilities, particularly in the area of employment and economic self-sufficiency. Even with the non-discrimination assurances in the ADA, Jerry will have to counterbalance years of Labor Day telethons and pity-based pleas with a strong message of his own competence if he is to persuade employers to truly consider his job application. The history of discrimination is ensconced not only in employer attitudes but in legislation, such as the Social Security Act, that defines disability as an inability to work, and in the very brick and mortar of our cities, in stairs and curbs without cuts. Changes are not realized with the stroke of a legislative pen. History is affected only by living life differently day to day, building tomorrow's history with today's actions.

MULTILEVEL INTERVENTIONS

Chris, Jerry's social worker, has begun to work with Jerry's mother, both to ensure that she knows how to assist Jerry and also to help her see how important it is for Jerry to take charge of his life, to make his own decisions. Chris was also able to involve Jerry's father in renovating the house. She arranged for a staff member from an independent living center to visit the home and work with the father to develop a common-sense and cost-effective plan for renovation that the family can afford. The independent living center also offered the services of a peer counselor to help Jerry learn how to negotiate his town in a wheelchair and do minor wheelchair repairs. The peer counselor can also talk to Jerry on a personal and practical level about using catheters and facing stereotypes, including Jerry's own stereotypes, about what life is like from a wheelchair.

At the time of discharge, several issues hang in the balance. Jerry has learned to handle the biological demands of his condition within the context of the hospital, but the community brings new challenges. He must also find a new place for himself socially, within his high school and community, and come to terms with the impact of his injury upon his sense of who he is. Despite the fact that this accident had been related to alcohol use, Jerry has been looking forward to drinking with his buddies once he gets out. He figures, if nothing else, he can still drink with the best of them. In addition, both Jerry and his mother have important lifecycle steps to accomplish, which his accident has complicated. Family finances may also require changes in his plans for college.

When Chris attended Jerry's high school graduation several months later, she could point to several specific interventions that helped to tip the balance in Jerry's favor. With Chris's encouragement, Jerry's mother turned her attention from its intense focus on Jerry to a broader look at the community's, and particularly the school's, accessibility issues. Mrs. Desoto enlisted the help of a sixth-grade student who had spina bifida and had used a wheelchair all his life. Together, they made a survey of all the local schools and delivered a list of needed accommodations to the school board. Mrs. Desoto was encouraged by this student's easy acceptance of his disability and his clear enjoyment of life.

Chris used a macro perspective to work with Mrs. Desoto to understand the provisions of the ADA and the best tactics to take in advocating change. The top priority was to make the high school weight room accessible. When Jerry began using the weight room, he was able to reduce his outpatient trips for physical therapy to once a month. It gave Jerry an opportunity to work out with his friends and reestablish the easy camaraderie he had with them in the context of sports. The coach asked him to help manage the basketball team.

Chris had also referred Jerry to vocational rehabilitation to assist him in finding employment. A combination of student loans, grants, and assistance from vocational rehabilitation will make it possible for Jerry to attend a community college next year and receive training specifically targeted to his vocational goals. His brother will move to an accessible unit in his apartment complex, and they will share expenses.

As is true in any situation, each level of analysis in the ecosystems framework affected Jerry's recovery and adaptation process, from individual factors of biology to the presence of federal laws that ensure the availability of accessible educational opportunities and housing options. For Chris, once again micro and macro practice dovetail. In her experience, it is often the energy and insight gained from personal experience that give direction and focus to larger advocacy efforts.

 ## Emerging Issues for Social Work Practice with People with Disabilities

Health care has been an important political issue for the nation as a whole and is a predominate concern for people with disabilities. Although many individuals with disabilities are quite healthy and one should be careful not to confuse illness with disability, portability of health insurance and coverage of pre-existing conditions has a particular impact on many people with disabilities. Often insurance packages only cover acute care, leaving the continuing costs associated with a chronic condition uncovered. Specific disorders, such as mental illness, may be poorly covered or not covered at all. In addition, because work is the primary vehicle in the United States for access to health insurance and many people with disabilities are unemployed, a large percentage of individuals with disabilities do not have health care coverage at all.[23]

Employment itself is a major concern. Employment rates for people with severe disabilities are the lowest of any minority group, making full participation in society more difficult. Work provides not only the financial means for participation, but it also accords adult status and establishes networks for building friendships and community connections. Not only is employment important for people with disabilities, it is vitally important for the economic health of the nation as well. When individuals with disabilities move from Social Security rolls to active roles in the workforce, the economy profits from their productivity and avoids the cost of the income support.

Unfortunately, disincentives exist within the Social Security legislation, often making it difficult for people with disabilities to move from SSI and SSDI rolls into the workforce. Insurance availability is one such issue. People who move from SSI or SSDI to a job will eventually lose access to Medicare or Medicaid, though current provisions allow for a transition period. Individuals must have an assurance of other sources of health care coverage before they can risk moving off Social Security rolls.

The Americans with Disabilities Act was signed into law in 1990, but people with disabilities continue to face issues of access and equality. Inaccessible work, education, and recreational environments continue to present barriers to full participation in society, and those who push for changes may be seen as "ungrateful" or "selfish" because they have moved outside of the expected "sick role" of passive acceptance. Other attitudinal barriers also persist. Old stereotypes of helplessness and incapacity continue to limit the opportunities open to people with disabilities and reduce their contributions to their communities and to the nation. Many people incur a disability later in life and may, themselves, hold some of these assumptions about incapacity. Discrimination, therefore, must be fought at all levels—from self-image to societal image.

Concluding Comment

while medical advances hold great promise for the treatment of many disabling conditions, the impact of disability on American society is likely to increase greatly over the next five to ten years. At this time, medicine has advanced further in the area of emergency services than it has in rehabilitative care. More people are surviving head injuries and other traumas, but often with multiple disabilities. In addition, the American population is becoming older—and age increases the risk of disability. Add to this the number of infants affected by fetal alcohol syndrome and the ingestion of other chemicals of abuse during pregnancy. Add, again, the number of individuals who may be affected by AIDS. It is clear that, in the near term, the number of people with disabilities in the United States is likely to increase substantially.

The need for services will also increase dramatically. Medical professionals will continue to address the biological issues, and vocational rehabilitation counselors will focus on issues of employment, but social workers will bring a unique focus that includes interventions at all system levels. Social workers must join hands with the disability rights movement in recognizing that disability issues should not focus exclusively on the medical problem or the individual's skills for a particular job. Disability issues are civil rights issues. Social workers must work to ensure that public policies and service programs are made more responsive. They must help individuals, families, and their communities to find room within their own cultural frameworks to value the lives and contributions of people with disabilities. In this way, social workers can truly work *with* people with disabilities, enhancing their lives and enriching society.

KEY WORDS AND CONCEPTS

ADA
People with disabilities
Medical model

Reciprocal causality
People first language
Impairment vs. disability

SUGGESTED INFORMATION SOURCES

Asch, A., and N. R. Mudrick. "Disability," in Richard L. Edwards, ed. *Encyclopedia of Social Work*, 19th ed. Washington, D.C.: NASW, 1995.

Ferguson, P., D. Ferguson, and S. Taylor, eds. *Interpreting Disability: A Qualitative Reader.* New York: Teachers College Press, 1992.

Nagler, M., ed. *Perspectives on Disability: Text and Readings*, 2nd ed. Palo Alto, CA: Health Markets Research, 1993.

ENDNOTES

1. N. Groce, *The U.S. Role in International Disability Activities: A History and a Look Towards the Future* (New York: Rehabilitation International, 1992).
2. J. Blaska, "The Power of Language: Speak and Write Using 'Person First,'" in M. Nagler, ed., *Perspectives on Disability,* 2nd ed. (Palo Alto, CA: Health Markets Research, 1993), pp. 25–32.
3. A. Morales, "Social Work Practice with Special Populations," in A. Morales and B. Sheafor, *Social Work: A Profession of Many Faces,* 7th ed. (Boston: Allyn & Bacon, 1995), pp. 287–293.
4. U.S. Congress, Senate Committee on Labor and Human Resources, Subcommittee on the Handicapped, *Americans with Disabilities Act of 1988: Joint Hearing Before the Subcommittee on the Handicapped of the Committee on Labor and Human Resources, United States Senate, and the Subcommittee on Select Education of the Committee on Education and Labor, House of Representatives,* 100th Congress, 2nd session on S.2345, September 27, 1988 (Washington, D.C.: USGPO, 1989).
5. World Health Organization, *International Classification of Impairments, Disabilities and Handicaps* (Geneva: World Health Organization, 1980).
6. Blaska, op. cit., pp. 25–32.
7. J. Waldrop and S. M. Stern, *Disability Status: 2000*, U.S. Census Bureau, Census 2000 Brief, #C2KBR-17 (Washington, D.C.: U.S. Department of Commerce, Economics and Statistics Administration, March 2003), retrieved September 5, 2005, from http://www.census.gov/prod/2003pubs/c2kbr-17.pdf.
8. J. McNeil, *Americans with Disabilities: Household Economic Studies*, U. S. Census Bureau, Publication # P70-73 (Washington, D.C.: U.S. Department of Commerce, Economics and Statistics Administration, February 2001), http://www.census.gov/hhes/www/disability/disabstat2k.html.
9. G. Becker and S. Kaufman, "Old Age, Rehabilitation and Research: A Review of the Issues," *Gerontologist* 28 (August 1988): 459–468; B. Holland and D. Falvo, "Forgotten: Elderly Persons with Disability—A Consequence of Policy," *Journal of Rehabilitation* 56 (April, May, June 1990): 32–35.
10. J. Garbarino, "The Abuse and Neglect of Special Children: An Introduction to the Issues," in J. Garbarino, P. Brookhouser, K. Authier, eds., *Special Children—Special Risks: The Maltreatment of Children with Disabilities* (New York: Aldine DeGruyter, 1987), pp. 3–14.
11. D. Corthell and J. Brown, "Introduction," in *Substance Abuse as a Coexisting Disability*, Eighteenth Institute on Rehabilitation Issues (Menomonie, WI: Research and Training Center, Stout Vocational Rehabilitation Institute, 1991), pp. 1–25.
12. D. Stroman, *The Awakening Minorities: The Physically Handicapped* (Lanham, MD: University Press of America, 1982), pp. 6–8.
13. Ibid., p. 7.
14. Americans with Disabilities Act of 1990 (Preamble) 42 U.S.C.A. Section 12101 *et seq.* (Washington, D.C.: West, 1993).
15. U.S. Congress, House of Representatives, Committee on Small Business, *Americans with Disabilities Act of 1989,* 101st Congress, Serial No. 101–45, February 22, 1990 (Washington, D.C.: USGPO, 1990).
16. G. DeJong, *The Movement for Independent Living: Origins, Ideology, and Implications for Disability Research* (East Lansing: University Centers for International Rehabilitation, Michigan State University, 1979).

17. S. Rubin and R. Roessler, "Historical Roots of Modern Rehabilitation Practices," in *Foundations of the Vocational Rehabilitation Process*, 4th ed. (Austin, TX: Proed, 1995), pp. 1–40.
18. Ibid., pp. 15–16.
19. President's Committee on Employment of the Handicapped, "Disabled Americans: A History," *Performance* 27 (November–December 1976): 8.
20. M. LaPlante, "How Many Americans Have a Disability?"*Disability Abstracts #5 (Washington, D.C.: National Institute of Disability, Rehabilitation and Research, 1992)*, p. 2.
21. Rubin and Roessler, op. cit., pp. 23–24.
22. Morales, op. cit., pp. 287–293.
23. A. Asch and N. Mudrick, "Disability," *Encyclopedia of Social Work*, 19th ed. (Washington, D.C.: NASW, 1995), pp. 752–761.

chapter 21

Social Work Practice with Muslims in the United States*

Prefatory Comment

The attack on Pearl Harbor on December 7, 1941, shocked and angered the United States and thrust Americans into a more than three-year war with Japan. Domestically, *all* Japanese immigrants and U.S.-born Japanese Americans were perceived as dangerous enemies and were placed in relocation centers for the duration of the war. They lost their land, property, and possessions. Sixty years later, nineteen Muslim al-Qaeda terrorists crashed three civilian airliners into the Pentagon and New York World Trade Center towers, killing approximately 3,200 American citizens. This launched the United States into a war in Afghanistan in search of Osama bin Laden, who was believed to have masterminded the attacks on the United States, and into a more prolonged war in Iraq. Foreign-born Muslims were spared the extreme public backlash visited upon Japanese, but, nevertheless, American Muslims were and still are being subjected to prejudice, discrimination, and stereotyping.

In adhering to the proactive spirit of this text in guiding students and practitioners into uncharted waters requiring the profession's attention, this chapter is concerned with the treatment of Muslims in the United States during the years following the 9/11 attacks. To be effective in serving Muslim clients and effecting unwarranted negative attitudes about the estimated four million to six million Muslims in the United States, social workers must be accurately informed about the Muslim religion and Muslim people. This chapter introduces this basic information.

Muslims have existed in American society since the founding of the United States.[1] In the past few decades, the size of the Muslim population has grown dramatically.[2] At least three factors underlie this growth: high levels of immigration, comparatively high birth rates among Muslim women, and Americans converting to Islam. Ascertaining the exact size and composition of the Muslim population in the United States is problematic, however, as U.S. law prohibits the Census Bureau from

---

*This chapter was prepared by Dr. David Hodge, assistant professor, Arizona State University, West.

inquiring about respondents' religion. Although estimates vary, a number of observers believe that Muslims may now be the second largest spiritual tradition in the nation.[3]

As the Islamic community continues to grow, social workers will increasingly be called upon to provide services to this discrete cultural group. Islam, however, represents a distinct worldview that differs substantially from the dominant secular worldview that informs American society. Consequently, widespread concern exists among Muslims that helping professionals trained in secular educational settings will have little knowledge or understanding of Islamic values.[4] Indeed, although this textbook represents a step in the right direction, research indicates that most social work students receive no educational content on religious diversity during their education.[5]

It is important to note that social workers are ethically mandated to develop and exhibit spiritual competency.[6] *Spiritual competency* can be understood as a more specific, faith-based form of cultural competency.[7] Accordingly, spiritual competency can be thought of as the process of developing (1) an empathic understanding of the client's spiritual worldview; (2) intervention strategies that are appropriate, relevant, and sensitive to the client's worldview; and (3) knowledge of one's own biases that might affect the proper implementation of steps one and two.[8] It is helpful to think of spiritual competency as a lifelong endeavor in which no one ever achieves complete competency. All of us are in process.

The ecosystems model cited in the introduction to Part Five of this text is particularly useful in developing spiritual competency with Muslims. This method represents a holistic approach in which four external systems to the individual—family, culture, environmental-structural factors, and history—are viewed as salient aspects in the client's life. Flowing from the European Enlightenment's emphasis upon the rational, autonomous person, the secular culture tends to accent the role of the individual *apart from* environmental systems. Conversely, Islamic culture tends to view the individual as a person who is *part of* environmental systems.[9] In other words, the ecosystems model offers the advantage of understanding reality in a manner that is congruent with how Muslims tend to view the world. As the following section implies, Islam is not as much an individualistic belief system as it is a way of life that unifies the metaphysical and material systems.[10]

A Preliminary Understanding of Islam

Islam is commonly understood to mean submission, specifically submission to Allah, the supreme and only God. Individuals who practice this submission are called *Muslims*. Both terms, Islam and Muslim, appear repeatedly in the Quran, making Islam the only world religion to have a built-in name from its inauguration.[11] The Quran was revealed to the honored founder of Islam, the Prophet Muhammad

(570/580AD–632), the "Messenger of God." The Quran is held to be God's revelation to humankind. While the Quran states that Allah communicated with other prophets, recognized by Jews and Christians, the Quran is God's final, immutable revelation.

Out of gratitude for Allah's goodness and compassion, Muslims seek to follow the straight path of God's precepts, the *shari'a*. The common Western demarcation between the personal, which may incorporate the spiritual, and the public, which is secular, is foreign to Islam. The shari'a governs all aspects of one's life. In other words, Islam offers adherents a holistic way of life in which the personal and the public are integrated. The primary basis for the shari'a is the Quran. The shari'a is also informed by the *hadith,* the recorded collections of the sayings of the Prophet.[12]

Significantly, Muslims date their history from the creation of the Islamic community, or *ummah,* rather than from their founder's birth or death or the inception of the Quran.[13] Two significant expressions of Islam characterize the worldwide Islamic community. Approximately 90 percent of Muslims are *Sunnis*. The remaining 10 percent are *Shiites,* who form the overwhelming majority in Iran.[14] Renard suggests a helpful comparison can be made between Protestantism and Sunni Islam, and Roman Catholicism and Shiite Islam.[15] In Sunni Islam and traditional Protestantism, there is an emphasis upon a direct relationship between the believer and God, unmediated by external authority structures. Similar to Roman Catholicism, Shiites have a hierarchical authority structure of legal scholars, based upon the consensus of the Shiite community, who hold an added responsibility for interpreting the Word of God for the faithful.

Since the time of the Prophet Muhammad, the Islamic community has grown to approximately a billion people.[16] Islam is frequently associated with the predominantly Islamic Arab nations of the Middle East where the faith originated. Yet, among the global Islamic community, Arab Muslims are a minority.[17] The largest populations of Muslims are found in South and Southeast Asia.[18] Indeed, the Islamic community encompasses the globe.

Local culture, political concerns, issues of interpretation, and other factors all function to shape the expression of Islam among self-identified Muslims. While there is extensive agreement that the shari'a should govern all facets of one's conduct, the practices that exemplify a "true Muslim" are contested throughout the Islamic world.[19] In reality, the Islamic community comprises many smaller Muslim communities, each with its own distinct characteristics.

Consequently, readers should bear in mind that no particular set of beliefs and values are representative of all Muslims. Many individuals who self-identify as Muslims are likely to disavow a number of the perspectives presented in this chapter. Rather than offering the final word on Islam, this chapter is better viewed as providing readers with an initial, tentative understanding of Islam. Although much diversity exists within Islamic discourse, it is important to acknowledge that a number of commonalities also exist that serve to demarcate Muslims from other populations. Perhaps the most significant of these distinguishing commonalities are the "five pillars" upon which the Islamic faith rests.[20]

The Five Pillars of Islam

The five pillars of faith are widely affirmed by Muslims as central facets of Islam. These practices can be thought of as the heart of a wider set of beliefs and practices.[21] While the wider framework of beliefs and practices is often influenced by local cultural factors, the five pillars are viewed by Muslims around the world as providing a basic outline for the expression of Islamic spirituality.[22]

The first and most fundamental tenet of the Islamic faith is the Declaration of Faith.[23] The declaration is the method by which individuals enter into the worldwide Islamic community. Individuals simply profess, "There is no god but God, and Muhammad is His Messenger." The declaration testifies to the absolute, singular theism of Islam and the primary role of Muhammad as his last prophet.[24] Thus, it serves to remind Muslims that they are part of a worldwide community of believers under the care of a compassionate, merciful God, who is personally involved with his creation.

The second pillar of faith is the performance of ritual prayers. Prayer is preceded by symbolic physical cleansing and is understood to be a holistic practice that encompasses body, mind, and emotions. Different positions are adopted, including standing straight, bending over at the waist, and kneeling with the head to the floor. The prayers are performed five times throughout the day, with the individual facing Mecca, the holy city of Islam, in Saudi Arabia, where God first entered into a covenant with the Islamic people. The offerings of prayers at dawn, midday, midafternoon, sunset, and an hour after sunset reinforce the concept that daily life and faith are continuously intertwined.[25] Similarly, for many Muslims, the uniformity of practice embodied in the ritual observance symbolizes the equality of humankind before God.[26]

The third pillar is charity, or alms giving. Each year a percentage, typically 2.5 percent of accumulated wealth, is given to address economic inequalities and promote the general welfare of the Islamic community.[27] Individuals who are poor are exempt from giving. The act of giving helps to ameliorate materialistic desires and reminds the giver that the source of all wealth is God rather than oneself.[28] Put differently, giving fosters a sense of thanksgiving to God for his goodness and a sense of community identity and responsibility.[29]

The fourth pillar is the yearly fast held during the month of Ramadan. Because Ramadan is based on the lunar calendar instead of on the solar calendar, Ramadan occurs roughly ten days earlier each year. Able-bodied adults abstain from eating, drinking, smoking, and sexual activity from sunrise to sunset to foster spiritual renewal.[30] In addition to facilitating a closer relationship to God, the Ramadan fast also encourages Muslims to empathize with those less fortunate than themselves.[31]

The final pillar of faith is the pilgrimage to Mecca. At least once during their lifetime, individuals are expected to make the pilgrimage unless financial or physical impediments exist.[32] During the pilgrimage, individuals often experience a oneness with God and recognize the equality of all people before God, as Malcolm X's experience illustrates.[33] The pilgrimage was instrumental in changing Malcolm X's hatred of whites into an affirmation of the equality of all races.[34]

In many cases, the degree to which individual Muslims practice the five pillars may be a good indication of the salience of faith in their lives. Conversely, it is also important to note that Muslims may say extra prayers later in the day or trust in God's benevolent understanding when faced with circumstances that make compliance difficult (e.g., an employer refusing to allow time for prayer during work hours, restrictive school policies, child care responsibilities, etc.).[35] For Muslims in the United States, this may be a particularly important consideration, as the cultural context in the United States often differs radically from that experienced in one's culture of origin.

The Demographics of Muslims in the United States

Obtaining data that accurately reflect the status of Muslims in the United States is difficult due to the methodological limitations associated with surveying relatively small, faith-based communities that may not be evenly dispersed across the nation. For instance, perhaps the most representative survey to date, the American Muslim Poll based upon a national sample of 1,781 self-identified Muslims in 2001, may have underweighted the views of African Americans, nominal Muslims, and perhaps Anglo converts. With these limitations in mind, the American Muslim Poll indicates that close to two-thirds (64 percent) of Muslims in the United States were born outside of the country.[36]

In 1965, the United States immigration policy was changed so that the needs of the labor market replaced racial/ethnic criteria.[37] The implementation of a more equitable immigration policy allowed highly skilled Muslims from around the world to join previous generations of European immigrants in seeking a better life for themselves and their families in America. This has led to the development of a richly diverse community. Currently, the Islamic community in the United States is composed of individuals from at least eighty nations.[38] In many ways, American Muslims are a microcosm of the global Islamic community, with significant numbers arriving in recent decades. Among those born outside the United States, 36 percent arrived between 1980 and 1989, and 24 percent arrived between 1990 and 2001.[39]

Estimates of the number of Muslims in the United States range from one million[40] to eleven million,[41] with most authorities suggesting a population of four million to six million.[42] Approximately 80 percent of American Muslims are Sunnis.[43] Although most major cities have Muslim populations, large concentrations are located in Boston, Chicago, the Detroit–Toledo corridor, Houston, Los Angeles, and New York City.[44] Shiites, who constitute the remaining 20 percent, form significant communities in Chicago, Detroit, Los Angeles, New York City, and Washington, D.C.[45] While almost every state has a Muslim population of some size, particularly heavy concentrations exist in California and New York.[46]

Reflecting global demographics, the American Islamic community is composed of significant populations from Asia and the Middle East and North Africa, as well as African Americans.[47] Data on ethnicity from the American Muslim Poll are reported in Table 21.1. As stated above, this survey may underestimate the number of African American Muslims since the survey methodology specified that 20 percent of the

Table 21.1

Demographics of Muslims in the United States (N = 1,781)

Ethnicity		Age Group	
South Asian	32%	18–29 years	23%
Pakistani	17%	30–49 years	51%
Indian	7%	50–64 years	20%
Bangladesh	4%	65 + years	7%
Afghan	4%	**Education**	
Arab	26%	< High school	6%
African American	20%	High school graduate	12%
African	7%	Some college	24%
Other	14%	College graduate	58%
Unsure	1%	**Income***	
Gender		<$15,000	10%
Male	59%	$15,000–$24,999	10%
Female	41%	$25,000–$34,999	13%
Marital Status		$35,000–$49,999	17%
Married	69%	$50,000–$74,999	22%
Single, never divorced	19%	$75,000 or more	28%
Divorced, separated, widowed	11%		

*17 percent of respondents declined to report their income.
Source: American Muslim Poll (Washington, D.C.: Project MAPS, 2001).

respondents were African Americans. Estimates of the number of African Americans in the Islamic community tend to be higher, typically in the 30 to 40 percent range.[48]

The vast majority of African American Muslims, who are largely converts to Islam, are Sunnis.[49] Although the Nation of Islam, headed by the charismatic Louis Farrakhan, is often portrayed in the media as representative of African American Muslims, it speaks for only a small portion of African American Muslims. The Nation of Islam, which has an estimated membership of 10,000[50] to 50,000,[51] is widely considered by other Muslims to be outside the bounds of mainstream Islam.

As the demographic data in Table 21.1 suggest, Muslims in the United States tend to be highly educated and financially secure.[52] More than 40 percent work in managerial, medical, or professional/technical occupations, and half earn more than $50,000 annually.[53] Foreign-born Muslims, in particular, tend to be members of the middle to upper-middle class.[54]

Concurrently, it is important to recall that many Muslims are disadvantaged. There tends to be a significant cultural, occupational, and economic gap between foreign-born and African American Muslims. In addition, some immigrants are quite poor, such as those individuals who were forced to immigrate because of political unrest in their country of origin. Roughly a quarter of regular mosque participants live in households with incomes below $20,000, less than half the median household income.[55]

As one might expect, given the diversity that exists among American Muslims, some degree of tension exists within the Islamic community.[56] These tensions are frequently mitigated, however, by the community's need to face the dominant secular culture with a united front. As they struggle to preserve their faith, Muslims often focus on points of shared interest that are particularly important to the Islamic community at large, such as the family.

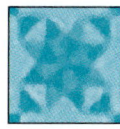

Muslim Families

Family plays a central role in Islamic culture. The word *family* can be used in a more expansive sense than is typical in Western secular culture. Within secular culture, the image that the term family tends to bring to mind is that of the "nuclear family," two adults and possibly one or more children. Within Islamic culture, the term family is often associated with what the secular culture would refer to as the extended family or kin network. In its broadest usage, family can even refer to the local, national, or global Islamic community.[57]

Marriage is perceived, not just as the joining of two individuals, but also as a union of two extended kin networks. The concept of lifelong singleness is foreign to Islam, and divorce, while permitted, is strongly discouraged. Marriage is viewed as a means of spiritual and personal fulfillment that fosters the social good.[58] In contrast with the secular culture's emphasis on appearance, qualities such as education, spirituality, and quality of character are emphasized in mate selection in Islamic culture. As is the case with many other important decisions in life, many Muslims seek the wisdom of the wider kin networks for advice on appropriate marriage partners.[59] In some cases, this trust may be exemplified by marriages that are arranged by the kin networks. The family also bears responsibility for ensuring that the marriage succeeds and that all parties are content.

The American *egalitarian marriage model* held up as an ideal in secular culture generally holds little appeal to Muslims, who value mutual respect rather than secular notions of equality.[60] Husbands and wives are traditionally held to be of equal worth but also to have complementary roles.[61] Men are responsible for the material provision and leadership of the family, while women have the primary responsibility for maintaining the home and raising the children. Men generally oversee and have the final word on decisions in the public sphere, while women make the decisions about child-rearing and household concerns.

Affirmation of a *complementary marriage model* does not necessarily mean that women are precluded from working outside the home or that men do not participate in housework.[62] In actuality, women commonly work outside the home, and men frequently assist with housework. As a mark of mutual respect, spouses often consult with each other when faced with important decisions.[63]

Women's employment outside the home is typically held in tension with providing a nurturing environment for the family, particularly young children. Children are considered a blessing from God, and large families are generally encouraged. A secure mother–child attachment is held to be critical to children's well-being and, by extension, the future health of the Islamic community. Mothers generally prefer to spend as much time as possible with their children, which also allows them the opportunity to enculturate Islamic values and preserve their heritage.[64]

Parents often play a role in the lives of their children that is analogous to the role played by peer groups in the lives of children in the secular culture.[65] Girls participate with their mothers in various activities, and boys often accompany their fathers. Children typically bond closely with their parents, siblings, and other family members. Youth are considered to be men and women upon reaching puberty, at which point they often begin practicing the five pillars of faith. Furthermore, little concern is expressed that post-puberty youth differentiate from the family unit, as interconnectedness among family members is valued.[66] Youth are encouraged to care for other family members, and it is common for parents to role model this value by having elders stay with the family rather than placing them in an institutional setting.[67] Elders are respected for their wisdom and experience and often function as mediators for other members of the kin network when family problems arise.

Families are typically marked by a strong sense of cohesion and interdependency. Group counseling may be seen as a violation of family privacy and consequently is not widely accepted among Muslims.[68] Family and individual counseling is usually advised. Utilizing spiritual ecomaps,[69] which highlight an existential relationship with environmental resources, and spiritual genograms,[70] which focus on family relationships over time, can be useful in identifying personal and environmental assets.

For social workers socialized to view secular norms as "universal," Muslim families can seem to be enmeshed in a maladjusted, unhealthy manner.[71] As an expression of spiritual competency, it is important for social workers to work within the family's value system to find solutions to problems. Practitioners must refrain from imposing, either explicitly or implicitly, secular values that popular culture may affirm as "normal" and "universal." Social workers must ensure that they respect complementary marriages, cohesive family units, and other Islamic values that Muslims may hold.

Common Cultural Values in Islamic Discourse

Muslims commonly affirm a number of values, including community, God's sovereignty, modesty, virtue, and nutrition. Rather than understanding these values as a series of separate entities, they should be viewed as interrelated constructs reflecting the unified, holistic Islamic cosmology.

Community

Community is a significant Islamic value.[72] Flowing from the belief that all people are equal under God, Muslims tend to see themselves a part of an extended, faith-based family—the Islamic community. As occurs with a family, members care for and are responsible to the community, and the community is responsible for and cares for its members in a reciprocal relationship.

Because Muslims see themselves as part of a larger community, individual aspirations are held in tension with the preferences of others. Muslims tend to emphasize benevolence, care for others, cooperation between individuals, empathy, equality and justice between people, the importance of social support, and positive human relatedness.[73] As part of being in a community, individual preference is often circumscribed so as not to harm other members of the community. Consequently, in contrast to the explicit, overt communication valued in the secular culture, Muslims often prefer implicit forms of communication that are highly sensitive to others' needs and concerns.[74] Similarly, secular individualistic values such as personal success, self-actualization, self-reliance, and personal autonomy hold somewhat less attraction for Muslims, who tend to find meaning in group success, community development, interdependence, and consensus.[75]

Much like the extended family, the community protects and empowers the individual.[76] For instance, African American women report finding a safe social space from the inequalities they experience in the larger culture, and this empowers them to redefine themselves in a positive manner.[77] Similarly, immigrant Muslim women report that the Islamic community provides a haven of safety that is instrumental in helping them cope with the stresses of adapting to a new societal context.[78]

Because individual identity is intertwined with the community's identity, every individual has a responsibility to protect the community.[79] In school settings, for instance, Muslim students may feel responsible to defend siblings, family, and faith when these dimensions of community are attacked.[80] Similarly, as an expression of their desire to protect the well-being of the community, elders often mentor other community members.

God's Sovereignty

Muslims believe that God brought the Islamic community into being. God is understood to be omnipotent and personal—at the center of the Muslim's existence.[81] Nothing happens to the Muslim apart from God's will. While this belief is sometimes thought to engender fatalism, more properly it prepares Muslims to face hardship and fosters perseverance during trials. Further, because life is a transitory journey on the road to eternal life, Muslims can face the future with optimism. The eternal perspective can foster a sense of existential meaning that facilitates coping during difficult situations.[82]

In keeping with the centrality of God in the Muslim's life, cognitive interventions based upon the shari'a may be particularly effective. While traditional psychotherapy and group counseling may not be widely accepted among Muslims,[83] cognitive therapy, in which unproductive beliefs are identified and replaced with God's precepts, has been demonstrated to be at least as effective as traditional forms of therapy with anxiety disorders,[84] bereavement,[85] and depression,[86] while concurrently ameliorating problems at a faster rate.

In addition to God, the Muslim cosmology includes belief in Satan, angels, and supernatural beings referred to as *jins*. Possession by a jin is a legitimate possibility in the Muslim cosmology and, accordingly, should not automatically be taken as an indication of psychosis.[87] As noted in the DSM, it is important to take cultural norms and values into account when conducting an assessment.[88]

Modesty

Another cultural value that is widely affirmed is modesty, particularly around members of the opposite sex.[89] While there is wide agreement in the Islamic community that modesty is an important value, much debate has occurred regarding how this value should be operationalized in American society. For men, the issue is not as keenly felt since Islamic standards regarding what is considered modest clothing for men overlap with secular views. The issue is more significant for women. Views on what constitutes modest apparel for women range from what secular culture deems modest to clothing that covers everything except the hands and face. Thus, many Muslim women wear a headcovering of some type, such as a scarf, a practice referred to as veiling or *hijab*. Because the practice of veiling has no mainstream cultural counterpart, women who choose to veil often face ridicule and discrimination.[90]

Related to modesty are Islamic views on social relationships between the sexes. Many Muslims feel that men and women should not mix socially with members of the opposite gender.[91] Some Muslims feel that, outside of interactions that occur within the family, the sexes should be separated after kindergarten.[92] Others believe that interaction between the sexes is permissible in a group context. When working with youth, in particular, social workers should be careful to respect Islamic norms about mixing with members of the opposite gender. In cases where it is necessary to meet with someone of the opposite gender, holding the meeting in an open, public forum may be acceptable.[93]

Secular dating patterns are widely seen as problematic, especially for youth. Dating can be a contentious issue in Muslim households, particularly when parents and youth hold different views of what constitutes proper Islamic behavior.[94] While social workers may be tempted to side with a youth's desire for greater freedom, it is advisable to explore solutions that are congruent with the family's value system.

Virtue

Modesty can be seen as one dimension of virtue. In classic Islamic thought, virtue provides the foundation for human happiness.[95] Islam affirms a set of moral and ethical norms that have much in common with other theistic faiths. Behavior that is injurious to others—whether mentally, physically, or morally—is forbidden. The equality of all individuals before God is upheld, along with the need to treat others with respect and honesty.[96]

Muslims also affirm the sanctity of human life, generally from conception to natural death. Thus, euthanasia, suicide, and abortion, except in instances when the mother's life is at stake, are not permitted.[97] Homosexuality, which is understood to be socially constructed, is not sanctioned.[98] Sexual activity is reserved for marriage and is viewed as a gift from God.[99]

Nutrition

As part of a holistic cosmology, Muslims generally follow a dietary code to promote physical and spiritual well-being. Many Muslims only eat meat that is considered *halal*, a term used to describe beef, poultry, and sheep that have been lawfully slaughtered according to Islamic specifications.[100] Some Muslims adopt a vegetarian diet to avoid meat that is not halal.[101] Others may accept kosher-prepared meals, which, although not the same as halal food, may be similar enough to be acceptable to some Muslims.[102] Still others will eat items from a standard Western menu as long as the food does not contain pork. The dietary code also prohibits mind-altering substances, such as alcohol.

As an aid to developing spiritual competency with Muslims, Table 21.2 delineates a number of values that are commonly affirmed in Islamic discourse and secular discourse. As emphasized above, social workers should not assume that Muslims

Table 21.2

Value Differences in Secular and Islamic Discourses*

Secular Discourse	Islamic Discourse
Individualism	Community
Separateness	Connectedness
Self-determination	Consensus
Independence	Interdependence
Self-actualization	Community actualization
Personal achievement and success	Group achievement and success
Self-reliance	Community reliance
Respect for individual rights	Respect for community rights
Self-expression	Self-control
Sensitivity to individual oppression	Sensitivity to group oppression
Identity rooted in sexuality and work	Identity rooted in culture and God
Egalitarian gender roles	Complementary gender roles
Pro-choice	Pro-life
Sexuality expressed based on individual choice	Sexuality expressed in marriage
Explicit communication that clearly expresses individual opinion	Implicit communication that safeguards others' opinions
Spirituality and morality individually constructed	Spirituality and morality derived from the *shari'a*
Material orientation	Spiritual/eternal orientation

*Table adapted from D. R. Hodge, "Social Work and the House of Islam: Orienting Practitioners to the Beliefs and Values of Muslims in the United States," *Social Work* 50 (2005): 162–173.

or secularists will affirm all the delineated values. Many secularists, for example, hold pro-life views, and many self-identified Muslims exhibit explicit communication styles that clearly express their opinions. In addition, many of the values listed in Table 21.2 are held in tension with one another. Muslims retain a sense of individualism, for example, while conceiving of themselves as a community. In short, Table 21.2 should not be viewed as a rigid typology but rather should be seen as a visual means of creating awareness regarding possible value differences that may exist between adherents of an Islamic worldview and a secular worldview.

Structural Factors in the Social Environment

Social work theory on oppression states that a difference in worldviews in conjunction with a power differential between the worldviews tends to foster bias toward the worldview without access to power.[103] In other words, the dominant culture tends to oppress the subordinate culture in areas where a conflict in worldviews or value systems occurs. As Gilligan's[104] work illustrates, females and males affirm different value systems; consequently, females tend to encounter discrimination in settings where males have more power.

Diaphobia and Religious Stereotypes

Just as the term sexism was developed to describe gender-based bias, the term *diaphobia* has been used to describe animosity that is directed toward a divine worldview in which a transcendent God serves as the ultimate point of reference.[105] As adherents of a subordinate, theistically based culture in the dominant secular culture, Muslims often encounter bias. Diaphobia is manifested in the formation of spiritual prejudices and religious stereotypes among secularists. The beliefs, values, and practices of Islamic culture are not evaluated on their own terms. Rather they are evaluated according to the criteria established by the secular culture. Secular culture functions as the final arbitrator of right and wrong. Values falling outside of the secular value system are implicitly characterized as morally deficient. In short, diaphobic tendencies manifest themselves most prominently in areas where Islamic values differ from those affirmed by the secular culture.[106]

Muslims consider prejudice and stereotyping to be one of the most important issues facing the Islamic community in the United States.[107] Spiritual prejudices and religious stereotypes are disseminated throughout American society via the media, educational sector, and other culture-shaping institutions. Research has documented that secular actors, such as the *New York Times,* exhibit bias toward Muslims.[108] Observers have delineated how the rich diversity of Islamic culture is frequently transformed in media depictions of Muslims into denigrating images connoting ignorance, oppression, fanaticism, and violence.[109] Muslims are acutely aware of how they are characterized. More than two-thirds (68 percent) think that the media is unfair in its portrayal of Muslims and Islam, and almost eight in ten (77 percent) think that Hollywood portrays Muslims and Islam unfairly.[110]

Similar tendencies have been documented in the social work literature. Research has explored how people of faith, including Muslims, are portrayed in social work textbooks.[111] The small amount of material devoted to faith groups tends to reflect the worldview of the dominant secular culture rather than the perspective of Muslims and other people of faith. In other words, Muslims are not depicted as they would tend to characterize themselves, a practice that leaves social workers unequipped to work in a spiritually sensitive manner. Rather, texts tend to depict Muslims as they are seen through the lens of the dominant secular culture, a practice that sets social workers up to reinforce the diaphobic stereotypes and prejudices that exist in the larger secular culture.

For instance, one social work textbook reports that the Muslim world abounds with "horror tales of crimes against humanity," and that the "moral agenda" of Middle Eastern countries "is the complete enslavement of women."[112] Such portrayals do not represent the self-descriptions of most Muslims. The Muslim world, of course, is not completely devoid of human atrocities, but then neither is the secular world free of "crimes against humanity." As Gellner[113] has observed, the secular worldview flowing from the European Enlightenment directly fostered the French Revolution, communism, and, indirectly, National Socialism. These movements have resulted in the deaths of tens of millions of human beings and inflicted untold suffering upon millions of others. It is noteworthy that human atrocities of this magnitude are essentially without parallel in the Muslim world.

Research that has examined the relationship between Islam and human rights has found that governments rooted in Islam do not foster the abuse of human rights.[114] An examination of 23 predominantly Muslim countries with a control group of non-Muslim nations found that both upheld the same level of human rights. Highlighting examples of human depravity in Muslim nations while simultaneously downplaying or even ignoring instances of human depravity flowing from a secular worldview does little to foster understanding between people.

As implied above, similar dynamics occur when discussing women. The issue of veiling in particular is a flashpoint in secular discourse. In some Western nations, secularists have even worked to abrogate Muslims' rights by attempting to ban girls from wearing the hijab in public schools.[115] For many in the secular culture, hijab has come to symbolize the oppression of women that is believed to occur in Islamic culture.[116]

Muslim women, however, frequently view the situation quite differently. From the perspective of many Muslim women, it is secular culture that oppresses women.[117] Secular culture is viewed as fostering lack of respect for women by, for example, reducing women to sexual objects; engendering high levels of debilitating eating disorders; promoting a hedonistic, narcissistic climate in which men walk away from their commitments to their wives and children; producing popular music that glamorizes the humiliation of women; and creating a milieu in which rape, sexual assault, and physical violence against women are everyday occurrences. Such degradation of women is comparatively rare in Islamic communities, where, it is held, women are treated with respect.[118]

Counter to secular assumptions, many women view the practice of hijab as liberating.[119] Veiling is seen as emancipation from a secular culture that celebrates immodesty. Donning hijab communicates that the woman is to be elevated above the level of a sexual object and that she is to be treated with respect based upon her abilities. It is also important to note that veiling occurs for many other mutually compatible reasons. For example, as an expression of their spirituality, many women veil to express their obedience to God. Many Muslims veil for the sense of safety and peace that the practice engenders. The practice may also symbolize pride in Islam.

Social workers must guard against reducing complex, multifaceted issues to simplistic caricatures. Portraying secular values as liberating and Islamic values as oppressive does little to foster understanding. To work effectively with Muslims, it is important to be able to see the world through an Islamic lens. Spiritually competent practice occurs at the point where social workers have developed an empathetic understanding of how Muslims view the world.

The biased characterizations in the secular culture have fostered a sense of mistrust and dislocation among Muslims in the United States. These portrayals also help create an atmosphere in which discrimination against Muslims is legitimated in schools, workplaces, and other public forums.[120] Employers, for instance, may fire Muslims for praying during lunch hour. Public school teachers may attempt to abrogate Muslims' constitutional rights by banning students from wearing the hijab or discriminating against papers that deal with Islamic topics.

Due to fear that they will be misunderstood or discriminated against, Muslims may be reluctant to seek assistance from social workers and other human services professionals.[121] Social workers can address this concern by showing interest in Islam[122] and becoming familiar with Islamic values.[123] Emphasizing traditional empathetic qualities, such as care, genuineness, respect, support, and warmth, can also help overcome initial concerns.[124] Similarly, meeting practical needs, such as advocating on behalf of oppressed Muslims, can also help build bridges.[125]

Civil Rights

To advocate for Muslim concerns, social workers must be aware of the environmental resources that exist. Social workers should take the time to familiarize themselves with relevant statutes, organizations, and institutions so that the appropriate resources can be brought to bear in a given context. The free exercise clause of the U.S. Constitution protects individuals' right to freely express their faith in public settings. The web sites of the U.S. Equal Employment Opportunity Commission (EEOC) and the Department of Education contain information on, respectively, employees' and students' free exercise rights. Particularly useful is the updated version[126] of former President Clinton's[127] memorandum on the free exercise rights of students in public schools.

School social workers, in particular, should also be aware of the Equal Access Act (P.L. 98-377) and Protection of Pupil Rights Amendment (PPRA) (20 U.S.C. §1232h). The Equal Access Act ensures that students of faith have the same right to school facilities as secular students. Schools cannot, for example, allow an environmental club to meet in an empty classroom and refuse to provide a classroom for Muslim students to perform daily prayers.[128] The PPRA provides federal protection for parents' and students' rights whenever federal funding is involved. Under PPRA, parents have the right to inspect instructional material that addresses a number of controversial areas, including content on sexuality, to ensure that it conforms to their values. To prevent the imposition of secular values, schools must make parents aware that such material is being presented and obtain written consent from parents before exposing children to any of the material.

Muslim Organizations

Social workers should also be aware of the institutions that Muslims have developed to cope with living in a secular culture. Perhaps the most prominent is the *masjid*, or *mosque*. More than 1,200 mosques exist in the United States, and almost 90 percent were founded since 1970.[129] The services offered by mosques in the United States have evolved substantially to meet the unique needs of the Islamic community. In traditional Muslim countries, mosques tend to be places where Muslims have the option of gathering for prayer, particularly Friday midday prayers. In North America, to provide a greater degree of social support to the Islamic community, mosques have tended to expand the range of services they offer. In addition to traditional prayer services, mosques often function as centers for an increasingly diverse array of services, including education for children and adults, counseling services, prison programs, daycare, and youth activities.[130]

The Muslim Student Association (MSA) is the largest student organization serving the Islamic community in the United States. According to Altaf Husain (personal communication), president of the MSA, there are currently more than 500 chapters in the United States. They offer a number of religious and cultural services, including, perhaps most importantly, social support to the hundreds of thousands of Muslims enrolled in American college campuses.[131]

As an outgrowth of the MSA, former students founded the Islamic Society of North America (ISNA), perhaps the most prominent Muslim organization in the United States.[132] The ISNA attempts to foster a degree of commitment and community among American Muslims, both through its own actions and by facilitating a large number of locally based organizations throughout the country.[133] ISNA activities are diverse and address most dimensions of Muslim life in America. Services include the provision of instructional materials, journals, workshops, library facilities, housing assistance, a charity fund, women's services, and a marriage bureau that operates a computerized database for matching single individuals with potential partners. Although ISNA attempts to serve all segments of the Muslim population, it tends to be perceived as an organization tailored primarily to meet the needs of immigrants.[134] The Muslim American Society performs many of the same functions for African American Muslims, and numerous additional Muslim organizations have been founded in recent years, with varying degrees of support among the general Muslim population.

Recently emigrated Muslims may be unaware of the range of programs available, since many of the services that have evolved are unique to the American Islamic community. Social workers who are familiar with the array of services in a given area can often function as brokers, linking Muslims to extant programs. The resources and social support such programs provide are often crucial in helping Muslims deal with the stress associated with religious stereotypes, racism, gender inequality, and immigration.[135]

Similarly, many Muslims may be unaware of the legislative statutes that protect their religious liberties in the United States. The history of their own people in their nation of origin may incline Muslims to believe that the justice system in this nation is also partial and prejudiced. While the court system in the United States is far from perfect, perpetrators of violence and discrimination against Muslims are regularly convicted.

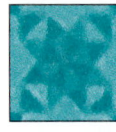

Historical Factors

While historical influences are critical to any population, they may be especially salient with Muslims who have recently immigrated to the United States. As noted previously, Muslims in the United States originate from at least 80 different nations.[136] Traumatic events, such as war, famine, and persecution in individuals' culture of origin, can shape how individuals interact with governments, the extent to which they trust "the system," and even their willingness to trust social workers. Similarly, African American Muslims are shaped by a history of racism that often affects their ability to trust European American institutions.

Social workers who regularly work with Muslims from a particular ethnic or national background should consider learning more about that cultural group and the historical influences that shape its interpretation of Islam. For instance, social workers who regularly work with African American Muslims might review Solomon's article on African Americans.[137] Even though the article does not specifically address Muslims, readers are likely to find many of the historical and cultural insights useful in work with African American Muslims. The ramifications of events from previous eras echo down through time, influencing present attitudes and practices.

In tandem with culturally specific influences, it is also important to develop an awareness of historical developments that have shaped the collective Islamic identity. In attempting to work out the implications of an Islamic worldview, Muslims have provided numerous scientific, literary, and artistic contributions to the world. Social workers are unlikely to be familiar with many of these developments since the dominant secular culture tends to highlight advancements that flow from the European Enlightenment. Consequently, social workers might consider familiarizing themselves with some of the major Islamic innovations in these fields.

September 11th

Another historical influence that all Muslims in the United States share is the legacy of the terrorist attacks on American facilities, the most prominent being the September 11, 2001, attacks on the Pentagon and the World Trade Center towers. The effects on the Islamic community and the general population have been complex. The fact that the terrorists were Arab and self-identified as Muslims played into lingering stereotypes and prejudices with the result that innocent law-abiding Muslims were often victimized in the immediate aftermath of the attacks.[138] In a series of high-profile appearances, President Bush stressed that Islam is a religion of peace, emphasized that Muslims should be treated with respect, and defended the right of Muslim women to wear the hijab in public settings without fear.[139]

Subsequently, public perceptions of Muslims became significantly more favorable. In fact, the general public's view of Muslims was more favorable six months after September 11 than it was before the terrorists' attack.[140]

These developments seem generally congruent with the experience of Muslims in the United States in the months after the attack. When asked to give their opinion on Americans' attitudes toward Muslims since September 11, approximately three-quarters (74 percent) stated that, in their personal experience, Americans had been respectful and tolerant of Muslims.[141]

Concurrently, it is important to note that September 11 fostered an increase in anti-Muslim discrimination. Incidents of alleged discrimination filed by Muslims with the Equal Employment Opportunity Commission (EEOC) from September 11, 2001, to May 7, 2002, more than doubled compared with the number filed one year previously (497 vs. 193).[142] Muslim organizations that track reports of bias reported a threefold increase, including incidents of murder, with reports of discrimination being particularly prominent at airports and ports of entry.[143] Just over half of Muslims (52 percent) know of at least one incident of anti-Muslim discrimination in their community since September 11.[144]

While incidents of discrimination may have declined in the months following September 11,[145] a more long-term concern may be The Uniting and Strengthening America by Proudly Appropriating Tools Required to Intercept and Obstruct Terrorism Act of 2001 (H.R. 3162), better known by its acronym, the USA Patriot Act. The USA Patriot Act was passed by Congress in the aftermath of September 11 with little debate. Criticized by members of both the political right and left, the legislation expands government powers, critics argue, at the expense of civil liberties, while the erosion of civil liberties diminishes everyone's freedom, and many Muslims are concerned that they will be unduly targeted.

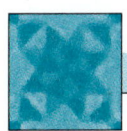

Implications for Micro and Macro Practice

The ecosystems approach helps social workers look beyond the level of the individual to complex environmental realities that shape Muslims' existence in the United States. More specifically, it is important to remember the following: the Muslim client is part of an extended family that is informed by Islamic values, which exists in a social environment animated by both detrimental and beneficial structural factors, which in turn is influenced by culturally specific historical events such as September 11. As noted previously, Figure 21.1 encapsulates some of the issues that should be examined at each level of the ecosystems model when working with Muslims.

In assessing problems and designing solutions, social workers should consider each of the concentric spheres of the ecosystems approach. Interventions can be aimed at any single level or combination of levels. Clients, however, are much more likely to own and apply suggested interventions if social workers have considered the multiple facets of existence that are represented by the ecosystems model. As the following example illustrates, developing intervention strategies that are appropriate, relevant, and sensitive to the client's worldview typically requires consideration of each level of the ecosystem model.

Figure 21.1
Example of Ecosystems Model for Muslims in the United States

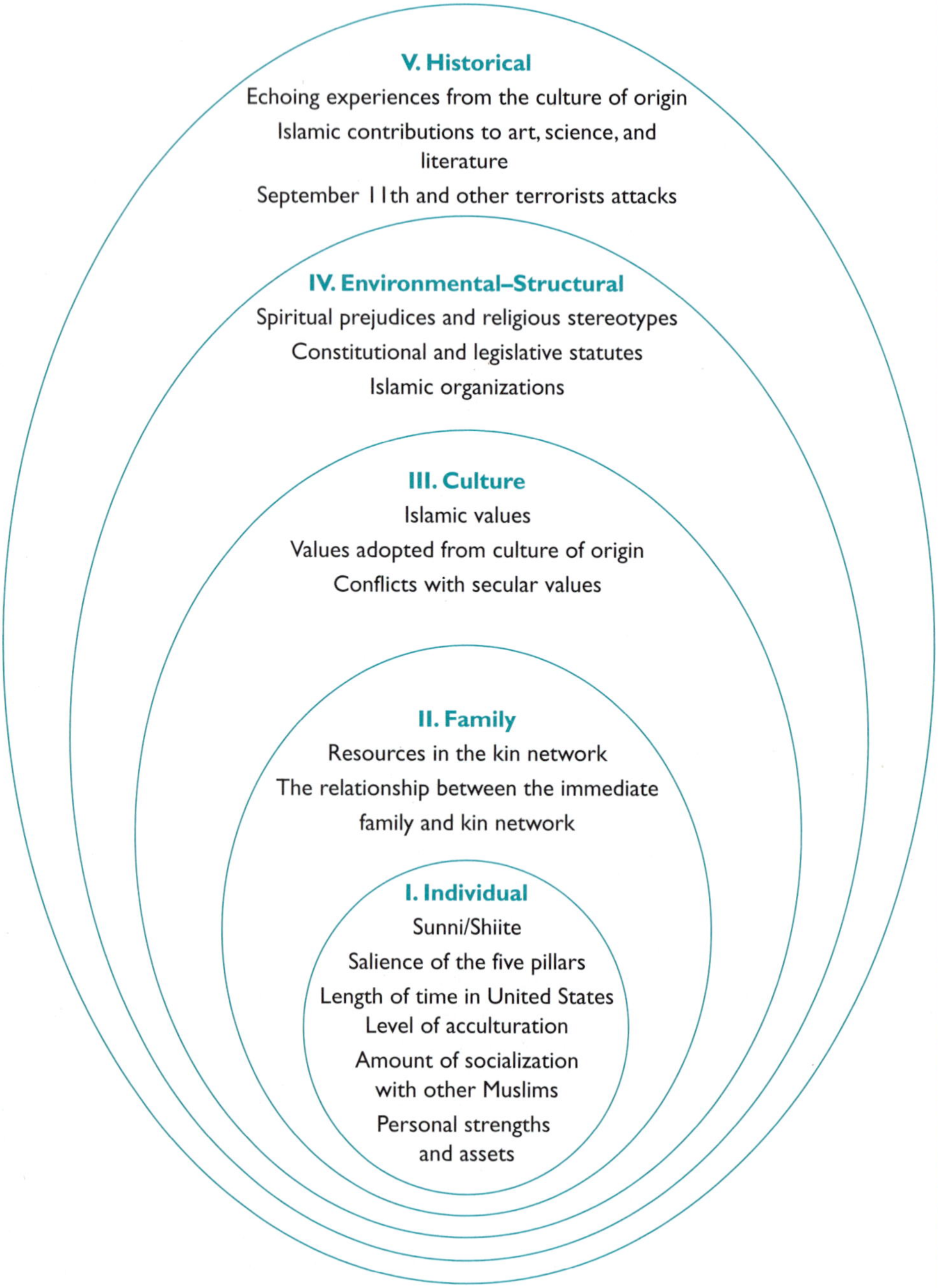

V. Historical
Echoing experiences from the culture of origin
Islamic contributions to art, science, and literature
September 11th and other terrorists attacks

IV. Environmental–Structural
Spiritual prejudices and religious stereotypes
Constitutional and legislative statutes
Islamic organizations

III. Culture
Islamic values
Values adopted from culture of origin
Conflicts with secular values

II. Family
Resources in the kin network
The relationship between the immediate family and kin network

I. Individual
Sunni/Shiite
Salience of the five pillars
Length of time in United States
Level of acculturation
Amount of socialization with other Muslims
Personal strengths and assets

THE INDIVIDUAL

Mustafa, a 12-year-old boy, was in danger of being expelled from public school for fighting. A Sunni Muslim, Mustafa was born in Detroit, to where his parents had emigrated from Turkey. In previous years, Mustafa had attended a private Islamic school. When Mustafa's father was transferred to California, the family decided to enroll Mustafa in a public school since there were no Islamic schools in the local vicinity. Bright and articulate, and in previous years an excellent student, Mustafa's grades had dropped considerably since he started attending public school a few months ago.

Although Kerry, the school social worker, initially found Mustafa to be somewhat uncommunicative, Mustafa became increasingly open as Kerry wondered about the difficulty Mustafa must have encountered switching from an Islamic school to a public school. Mustafa slowly began sharing some of the problems he was facing as a student of faith in a secular environment. He often found himself going hungry on days the cafeteria served food that contained pork. On Earth Day, one of his teachers had led the class in a meditation session in which students were to visualize themselves as part of Mother Nature, a practice that made Mustafa extremely uncomfortable due to its spiritual overtones. Another teacher had given a writing assignment in which students could write about any subject and then rejected Mustafa's paper, which argued for the sanctity of life from an Islamic perspective, on the grounds that it was "too religious." Although he got along with most students, some ridiculed his faith, called him a "terrorist," and disparaged his mother, who wears a veil, when she came to pick him up at school. Mustafa felt that he had to defend his faith and family, with his fists if necessary.

THE FAMILY

Kerry arranged a meeting between Mustafa and his main system of social support, his immediate family. His family was surprised at the situation. Mustafa had not shared the problems he encountered at school because he felt that he had to stand up for the Islamic community on his own. His parents resolved to support Mustafa and communicated to him that they would handle the situations together, as a team. His mother and sisters volunteered to come to school and give a classroom presentation on hijab, explaining the reasons why Muslim women choose to veil. His father offered to share some of his experiences at his place of employment along with strategies he had developed to address the religious stereotypes and prejudices he encountered at work.

CULTURAL ISSUES

Upon meeting Mustafa's family, Kerry built trust by addressing the husband first and then, later in the conversation, asking his permission to speak to his wife and daughters. Kerry also wore modest attire and used more indirect forms of communication (e.g., "In my professional judgment…" rather than "I feel…"). Adopting a slightly more directive approach, Kerry explored a number of concrete options that might meet the family's goals. Sensitivity was shown to nonverbal forms of communication, as Kerry worked toward coming to a consensus regarding how to tackle the situation. Trust was enhanced by Kerry's demonstrated willingness to advocate with school officials on the family's behalf in a number of areas.

To address the dietary issues concerning pork, Kerry contacted the food services personnel. They arranged for school menus to be sent to Mustafa's mother a week in advance. With prior notice, she was able to prepare a lunch for Mustafa to take to school when the menu consisted of food that was not halal.

ENVIRONMENTAL–STRUCTURAL ISSUES

After contacting the U.S. Department of Education and obtaining constitutional guidelines on the free exercise of religion, Kerry set up a meeting with school officials. In the ensuing discussion, Kerry emphasized two points that directly addressed Mustafa's situation. First, the establishment clause of the U.S. Constitution stipulates that schools must maintain neutrality between competing spiritual belief systems. The classroom implementation of New Age forms of visualization and meditation are prohibited. Second, Kerry noted that the free exercise clause protects students' right to express their religious beliefs. Teachers cannot discriminate against a student's paper just because it presents a religious perspective.

Kerry also phoned a number of mosques in the wider vicinity to ascertain if any offered youth programs or knew of any Islamic organizations that sponsored youth programs. After locating a couple of programs, Kerry sent a letter to Mustafa's father, drawing his attention to the options.

HISTORICAL ISSUES

The historical, media-propagated associations between Islam and terrorism represented a difficult issue to address. Kerry decided to use the school's interest in environmentalism in an attempt to weaken the link between Islam and terrorism. Kerry worked with school officials to highlight that Ted Kaczynski, the Unabomber, self-identified as an environmentalist and was in a significant following in the environmental movement. Yet, because environmentalists generally affirm a value system that resonates with the dominant secular worldview, the media carefully distinguished between the majority of self-identified environmentalists, who advocate for the environment peacefully, and those self-described environmentalists who use terrorist tactics in the name of environmentalism. Consequently, few people associate environmentalism with terrorism.

Kerry pointed out that the media adopt a different agenda with Muslims since their spiritual value system fails to resonate with the secular values held by most members of the media. Even though the overwhelming majority of Muslims condemn the use of violence in the name of Islam, the media often fail to distinguish between peaceful Muslims and those who commit acts of violence. Yet, just as it is inappropriate to judge all environmentalists by those who commit violence, so too it is inappropriate to judge all Muslims by those who commit violence. We must deconstruct the ethnocentric discourse propagated by the dominant culture, Kerry argued, and welcome the enriching perspectives Muslims bring to our school, society, and nation.

From one perspective, Kerry's interventions met with mixed results. Having access to the school menus resolved the dietary issues. The presentation by Mustafa's mother and sisters on veiling, in conjunction with Kerry's coupling of Islam and environmentalism, helped foster a more tolerant environment at the school. Conversely, while the school eventually implemented a policy to end the imposition of New Age religious practices on the student population, some teachers still exhibited reluctance to accept spiritually themed papers, and Mustafa often felt that he received lower grades when his work presented an Islamic perspective. Although this discrimination was grounds for a lawsuit, Mustafa's parents declined to press the issue in court.

From the perspective of Mustafa's parents, however, Kerry's combination of micro- and macro-level interventions was a success. Mustafa's grades had improved to their former level. While Mustafa's peers at school still didn't always accept or agree with his Islamic views, they were more respectful, and, consequently, fights were a thing of the past. As is the case in other situations, consideration of each level of the ecosystems model is vital for effective, spiritually competent work with Muslims.

Concluding Comment

Muslims in the United States face an uncertain future. International events over which individual Muslims have little control, such as the U.S. military attack and occupation of Iraq, have the potential to dramatically affect the well-being of innocent, law-abiding Muslims. In addition to living with this unpredictability, Muslims must continually deal with the oppression that people of faith encounter in the dominant secular culture.

As a minority population in a hostile cultural environment, Muslims are often in need of advocacy on their behalf. Individual initiatives, legislative efforts, and international actions are needed to ensure that the rights of Muslims and other people of faith are protected. Social workers, due to their unique skill sets, are often ideally situated to provide this advocacy.

Unfortunately, in at least some instances, the social work profession itself has adopted the stance of dominant culture, propagating diaphobic stereotypes that foster misunderstanding and bias toward Muslims. Social workers, however, are called to deconstruct the assumptions of the dominant culture that affect their ability to provide services. Personal biases must be identified and addressed.

As an ethically based profession, the NASW Code of Ethics provides clear guidelines regarding the stance that social workers must adopt toward Muslims and other people of faith. More specifically, social workers should educate themselves about the oppression religious people encounter, avoid derogatory religious language, and refrain from facilitating any form of religious discrimination while actively working to prevent and eliminate religious discrimination. As the NASW Code of Ethics states, social workers are to foster respect for cultural and social diversity within the United States and globally, seeking to ensure justice for *all* people.

KEY WORDS AND CONCEPTS

Muslim
Islam
Hijab
Mosque

Diaphobia
The Five Pillars
Spiritual competency

SUGGESTED INFORMATION SOURCES

Aswad, B. C., and B. Bilge, eds. *Family and Gender Among American Muslims.* Philadelphia: Temple University Press, 1996.

Carolan, M. T., G. Bagherinia, R. Juhari, J. Himelright, and M. Mouton-Sanders. "Contemporary Muslim Families: Research and Practice," *Contemporary Family Therapy* 22, no. 1 (2000).

Crabtree, S. A., F. Husain, and B. Spalek. *Islam and Social Work: Debating Values, Transforming Practice*. London: British Association of Social Workers, 2008.

Esposito, J. L., ed. *The Oxford Encyclopedia of the Modern Islamic World*. New York: Oxford University Press, 1995.

Hodge, D. R. "Social Work and the House of Islam: Orienting Practitioners to the Beliefs and Values of Muslims in the United States," *Social Work* 50 (2005): 162–173.

Mahmoud, V. "African American Muslim Families," in M. McGoldrick, J. Giordano, and J. K. Pearce, eds., *Ethnicity and Family Therapy*, 2nd ed. New York: Guilford Press, 1996, pp. 122–128.

Smith, J. I. *Islam in America*. New York: Columbia University Press, 1999.

ENDNOTES

1. Yvonne Yazbeck Haddad and Jane I. Smith, "United States of America," in John L. Esposito, ed., *The Oxford Encyclopedia of the Modern Islamic World*, vol. 4 (New York: Oxford University Press, 1995), pp. 277–284.
2. J. Gordon Melton, *The Encyclopedia of American Religions*, 6th ed. (London: Gale Research, 1999).
3. Yvonne Yazbeck Haddad, "Make Room for the Muslims?" in Walter H. Conser Jr. and Summer B. Twiss, eds., *Religious Diversity and American Religious History* (Athens: The University of Georgia Press, 1997), pp. 218–261; P. Scott Richards and Allen E. Bergin, *A Spiritual Strategy* (Washington, D.C.: American Psychological Association, 1997).
4. Belkeis Y. Altareb, "Islamic Spirituality in America: A Middle Path to Unity," *Counseling and Values* 41, no. 1 (1996): 29–38; Manijeh Daneshpour, "Muslim Families and Family Therapy," *Journal of Marital and Family Therapy* 24, no. 3 (1998): 355–390; Anahid Kulwicki, "Health Issues Among Arab Muslim Families," in Barbara C. Aswad and Barbara Bilge, eds., *Family and Gender Among American Muslims* (Philadelphia: Temple University Press, 1996), pp. 187–207; Eugene W. Kelly, Amany Aridi, and Laleh Bakhtiar, "Muslims in the United States: An Exploratory Study of Universal and Mental Health Values," *Counseling and Values* 40, no. 3 (1996): 206–218; Vanessa Mahmoud, "African American Muslim Families," in Monica McGoldrick, Joe Giordano, and John K. Pearce, eds., *Ethnicity and Family Therapy*, 2nd ed. (New York: Guilford Press, 1996), pp. 122–128.
5. Edward R. Canda and Leola Dyrud Furman, *Spiritual Diversity in Social Work Practice* (New York: The Free Press, 1999).
6. NASW Code of Ethics, 1999, http://www.socialworkers.org/pubs/code/default.asp (accessed November 24, 2008).
7. David P. Boyle and Alyson Springer, "Toward a Cultural Competence Measure for Social Work with Specific Populations," *Journal of Ethic and Cultural Diversity in Social Work* 9, no. 3/4 (2001): 53–71.
8. Derald Wing Sue, Patricia Arredondo, and Roderick J. McDavis, "Multicultural Counseling Competencies and Standards: A Call to the Profession," *Journal of Counseling and Development* 70, no. 4 (1992): 477–486.
9. Daneshpour, op. cit.
10. Marsha T. Carolan, et al., "Contemporary Muslim Families: Research and Practice," *Contemporary Family Therapy* 22, no. 1 (2000): 67–79.
11. Dale F. Eickelman, *The Middle East and Central Asia*, 3rd ed. (Upper Saddle River, NJ: Prentice Hall, 1998).

12. David Waines, *An Introduction to Islam* (Cambridge: Cambridge University Press, 1995).
13. John L. Esposito, *Islam* (New York: Oxford University Press, 1988).
14. Eickelman, op. cit.
15. John Renard, *Responses to 101 Questions on Islam* (Mahwah, NJ: Paulist Press, 1998).
16. Waines, op. cit.; Syed Arshad Husain, "Religion and Mental Health from the Muslim Perspective," in Harold G. Koenig, ed., *Handbook of Religion and Mental Health* (New York: Academic Press, 1998), pp. 279–291.
17. Paul Lawrence and Cathy Rozmus, "Culturally Sensitive Care of the Muslim Patient," *Journal of Transcultural Nursing* 12, no. 3 (2001): pp. 228–233.
18. Eickelman, op. cit.
19. Ibid.
20. Mahmoud M. Ayoub, "United States of America," in John L. Esposito, ed., *The Oxford Encyclopedia of the Modern Islamic World*, vol. 3 (New York: Oxford University Press, 1995), pp. 333–334.
21. Esposito, *Islam*, op. cit.
22. Ayoub, op. cit.
23. Gamal Abou El Azayem and Zari Hedayat-Diba, "The Psychological Aspects of Islam: Basic Principles of Islam and Their Psychological Corollary," *The International Journal for the Psychology of Religion* 4, no. 1 (1994): 41–50.
24. Esposito, *Islam*, op. cit.
25. Gamal Abou El Azayem, op. cit.
26. Eickelman, op. cit.
27. Husain, op. cit.
28. Renard, op. cit.
29. Esposito, *Islam*, op. cit.
30. Eickelman, op. cit.
31. Altareb, op. cit.
32. Esposito, *Islam*, op. cit.
33. Altareb, op. cit.
34. Akbar S. Ahmed, "Popular Religion in Europe and the Americas," in John L. Esposito, ed., *The Oxford Encyclopedia of the Modern Islamic World*, vol. 3 (New York: Oxford University Press, 1995), pp. 354–358.
35. Elise Goldwasser, "Economic Security and Muslim Identity: A Study of the Immigrant Community in Durham, North Carolina," in Yvonne Haddad and John L. Esposito, eds., *Muslims on the Americanization Path?* (Atlanta: Scholars Press, 1998), pp. 379–397; Jane I. Smith, *Islam in America* (New York: Columbia University Press, 1999).
36. American Muslim Poll (Washington, D.C.: Project MAPS: Muslims in the American Public Square, 2001).
37. Haddad and Smith, "United States of America," op. cit.
38. American Muslim Poll, op. cit.
39. Ibid., op. cit.
40. Barry A. Kosmin and Seymour P. Lachman, *One Nation Under God* (New York: Harmony Books, 1993).
41. Haddad, "Make Room for the Muslims?", op. cit.
42. Richards and Bergin, op. cit.; Eickelman, op. cit.; Akbar S. Ahmed, op. cit.; Smith, op. cit.; Frederick Mathewson Denny, "Islam in the Americas," in John L. Esposito, ed., *The Oxford Encyclopedia of the Modern Islamic World*, vol. 2 (New York: Oxford University Press, 1995), pp. 296–300.

43. Smith, op. cit.
44. Haddad and Smith, "United States of America," op. cit.; Smith, op. cit.; Denny, op. cit.; Carol L. Stone, "Estimate of Muslims Living in America," in Yvonne Yazbeck Haddad, ed., *The Muslims of America* (New York: Oxford University Press, 1991), pp. 25–36.
45. Haddad and Smith, "United States of America," op. cit.; Raymond Brady Williams, "South Asian Religions in the United States," in John R. Hinnells, ed., *A New Handbook of Living Religions* (New York: Penguin Books, 1997), pp. 796–818.
46. Kosmin and Lachman, op. cit.
47. American Muslim Poll, op. cit.; Denny, op. cit.
48. Haddad and Smith, "United States of America," op. cit.; Richards and Bergin, op. cit.; Smith, op. cit.; Kosmin and Lachman, op. cit.
49. Melton, op. cit.; Smith, op. cit.
50. Melton, op. cit.
51. Jonah Blank, "The Muslim Mainstream," *U.S. News and World Report* 20, 7 (1998): 22–25.
52. American Muslim Poll, op. cit.; Kosmin and Seymour P. Lachman, op. cit.; Denny, op. cit.
53. American Muslim Poll, op. cit.
54. Denny, op. cit.
55. Ihsan Bagby, Paul M. Perl, and Bryan T. Froehle, *The Mosque in America: A National Portrait* (Washington, D.C.: Council on American–Islamic Relations, 2001).
56. Haddad and Smith, "United States of America," op. cit.; Denny, op. cit.
57. Elizabeth Warnock Fernea, "Family," in John L. Esposito, ed., *The Oxford Encyclopedia of the Modern Islamic World,* vol. 1 (New York: Oxford University Press, 1995), pp. 458–461.
58. Dena Saadat Hassouuneh-Phillips, "'Marriage is Half of Faith and the Rest is Fear of Allah,'" *Violence Against Women* 7, no. 8 (August 2001): 927–946.
59. Smith, op. cit.
60. Carolan, et al., op. cit.
61. Altareb, op. cit.
62. Carolan, et al., op. cit.
63. Kulwicki, op. cit.
64. Smith, op. cit.
65. Yvonne Y. Haddad and Jane I. Smith, "Islamic Values Among American Muslims," in Barbara C. Aswad and Barbara Bilge, eds., *Family and Gender Among American Muslims* (Philadelphia: Temple University Press, 1996), pp. 19–40.
66. Daneshpour, op. cit.
67. Kulwicki, op. cit.
68. Munir A. Shaikh, *Teaching About Islam and Muslims in the Public School Classroom,* 3rd ed. (Fountain Valley, CA: Council on Islamic Education, 1995).
69. David R. Hodge, "Spiritual Ecomaps: A New Diagrammatic Tool for Assessing Marital and Family Spirituality," *Journal of Marital and Family Therapy* 26, no. 1 (2000): 229–240.
70. David R. Hodge, "Spiritual Genograms: A Generational Approach to Assessing Spirituality," *Families in Society* 82, no. 1 (2001): 35–48.
71. Daneshpour, op. cit.
72. Alphonso W. Haynes, et al., "Islamic Social Transformation: Considerations for the Social Worker," *International Social Work* 40 (1997): 265–275.
73. Kelly, op. cit.
74. Daneshpour, op. cit.

75. Kelly, op. cit.
76. Mumtaz F. Jafari, "Counseling Values and Objectives: A Comparison of Western and Islamic Perspectives," *The American Journal of Islamic Social Sciences* 10, no. 3 (1993): 326–339.
77. Michelle D. Byng, "Mediating Discrimination: Resisting Oppression Among African American Muslim Women," *Social Problems* 45, no. 4 (1998): 473–487.
78. Fariyal Ross-Sheriff, "Immigrant Muslim Women in the United States: Adaptation to American Society," *Journal of Social Work Research* 2, no. 2 (2001): 283–294.
79. Haynes, et al., op. cit.
80. Mahmoud, op. cit.
81. Altareb, op. cit.
82. Rafic Banawi and Rex Stockton, "Islamic Values Relevant to Group Work, with Practical Applications for the Group Leader," *The Journal for Specialists in Group Work* 18, no. 3 (1993): 151–160.
83. Ibid.
84. M. Z. Azhar, S. L. Varma, and A. S. Dharap, "Religious Psychotherapy in Anxiety Disorder Patients," *Acta Psychiatrica Scandinavica* 90 (1994): 1–2.
85. M. Z. Azhar and S. L. Varma, "Religious Psychotherapy as Management of Bereavement," *Acta Psychiatrica Scandinavica* 91 (1995): 233–235.
86. M. Z. Azhar and S. L. Varma, "Religious Psychotherapy in Depressive Patients," *Psychotherapy and Psychosomatics* 63 (1995): 165–168.
87. Husain, op. cit.
88. *Diagnostic and Statistical Manual of Mental Disorders*, 4th ed. (Washington, D.C.: American Psychiatric Association, 1994).
89. Haddad and Smith, "Islamic Values Among American Muslims," op. cit.
90. Carolan, et al., op. cit.
91. Mahmoud, op. cit.
92. Cyril Simmons, Christine Simmons, and Mohammed Habib Allah, "English, Israeli-Arab and Saudi Arabian Adolescent Values," *Educational Studies* 20, no. 1 (1994): 69–86.
93. Richard B. Carter and Amelia E. El Hindi, "Counseling Muslim Children in School Settings," *Professional School Counseling* 2, no. 3 (1999): 183–188.
94. Ibid.
95. Majed A. Ashy, "Health and Illness from an Islamic Perspective," *Journal of Religion and Health* 38, no. 3 (1999): 241–257.
96. Haddad and Smith, "Islamic Values Among American Muslims," op. cit.; Julia Mitchell Corbett, *Religion in America,* 2nd ed. (Englewood Cliffs, NJ: Prentice Hall, 1994).
97. Haddad and Smith, "Islamic Values Among American Muslims," op. cit.
98. J. Mark Halstead and Katarzyna Lewicka, "Should Homosexuality Be Taught as an Acceptable Alternative Lifestyle? A Muslim Perspective," *Cambridge Journal of Education* 28, no. 1 (1998): 49–64.
99. Husain, op. cit.
100. Smith, op. cit.
101. Charles Kemp, "Islamic Cultures: Health-Care Beliefs and Practices," *American Journal of Health Behavior* 20, no. 3 (1996): 83–89.
102. Kulwicki, op. cit.
103. Tim Hamilton and Satish Sharma, "The Violence and Oppression of Power Relations," *Peace Review* 9, no. 4 (1997): 555–561; Kathryn G. Wambach and Dorothy Van Soest, "Oppression," in Richard L. Edwards, ed., *1997 Supplement*, 19th ed. (Washington, D.C.: NASW Press, 1997), pp. 243–252.

104. Carol Gilligan, *In a Different Voice: Psychological Theory and Women's Development* (Cambridge, MA: Harvard University Press, 1993).
105. David R. Hodge, "Conceptualizing Spirituality in Social Work: How the Metaphysical Beliefs of Social Workers May Foster Bias Towards Theistic Consumers," *Social Thought* 21, no. 1 (2002): 39–61.
106. Bobby S. Sayyid, *A Fundamental Fear* (New York: St. Martin's Press, 1997).
107. American Muslim Poll, op. cit.
108. Amal Omar Madani, "Depiction of Arabs and Muslims in the United States News Media," Dissertation, California School of Professional Psychology—Los Angeles, 2000, p. 9-B; Nadege Soubiale and Nicolas Roussiau, "Social Representation of Islam and Changes in the Stereotypes of Muslims," *Psicologia, Teoria e Pesquisa: Brasilia* 14, no. 3 (September–December 1998): 191–202.
109. Greg Noakes, "Muslims and the American Press," in Yvonne Haddad and John L. Esposito, eds., *Muslims on the Americanization Path?* (Atlanta: Scholars Press, 1998), pp. 361–378; Ronald Stockton, "Ethnic Archetypes and the Arab Image," in Ernest McCarus, ed., *The Development of Arab-American Identity* (Ann Arbor: The University of Michigan Press, 1994), pp. 119–153.
110. American Muslim Poll, op. cit.
111. David R. Hodge, Lisa M. Baughman, and Julie A. Cummings, "Moving Toward Spiritual Competency: Deconstructing Religious Stereotypes and Spiritual Prejudices in Social Work Literature," Paper presented at the [Forty-Eighth Annual Program Meeting] Council on Social Work Education, February 24–27, Nashville, TN, 2002.
112. Katherine Van Wormer, *Social Welfare* (Chicago: Nelson-Hall Publishers, 1997).
113. Ernest Gellner, *Postmodernism, Reason and Religion* (New York: Routledge, 1992).
114. Daniel Price, "Islam and Human Rights: A Case of Deceptive First Appearances," *Journal for the Scientific Study of Religion* 41, no. 2 (2002): 213–225.
115. Sayyid, op. cit.; Esmail Shakeri, "Muslim Women in Canada: Their Role and Status as Revealed in the Hijab Controversy," in Yvonne Haddad and John L. Esposito, eds., *Muslims on the Americanization Path?* (Atlanta: Scholars Press, 1998), pp. 159–178.
116. Shakeri, op. cit.
117. Carolan, et al., op. cit.; Debra Reece, "Covering and Communication: The Symbolism of Dress Among Muslim Women," *The Howard Journal of Communication* 7, no. 35 (1996): 35–52.
118. Renard, op. cit.; Louise Cainkar, "Immigrant Palestinian Women Evaluate Their Lives," in Barbara C. Aswad and Barbara Bilge, eds., *Family and Gender Among American Muslims* (Philadelphia: Temple University Press, 1996), pp. 41–58.
119. Carolan, et al., op. cit.; Reece, op. cit.
120. Council on American-Islamic Relations Research Center, *The Status of Muslim Civil Rights in the United States 2002: Stereotypes and Civil Liberties* (Washington, D.C.: Council on American-Islamic Relations, 2002).
121. Altareb, op. cit.; Daneshpour, op. cit.; Kelly, op. cit.; Mahmoud, op. cit.; Zari Hedayat-Diba, "Psychotherapy with Muslims," in P. Scott Richards and Allen E. Bergin, eds., *Handbook of Psychotherapy and Religious Diversity* (Washington, D.C.: American Psychological Association, 2000), pp. 289–314.
122. Vanessa Mahmoud, "African American Muslim Families," in Monica McGoldrick, Joe Giordano, and John K. Pearce, eds., *Ethnicity and Family Therapy*, 2nd Edition (New York: Guilford Press, 1996) pp. 122–128.
123. Kelly, op. cit.

124. Sarah Shafi, "A Study of Muslim Asian Women's Experiences of Counseling and the Necessity for a Racially Similar Counselor," *Counseling Psychology Quarterly* 11, no. 3 (1998): 301–314.
125. Alean Al-Krenawi, "Group Work with Bedouin Widows of the Negev in a Medical Clinic," *Affilia* 11, no. 3 (1996): 303–318.
126. Richard W. Riley, "Religious Expression in Public Schools," 1998. http://www.ed.gov/Speeches/08–1995/religion.html (accessed July 11, 2001).
127. William J. Clinton, "Memorandum for the U.S. Secretary of Education and the U.S. Attorney General," 1995, http://w3.trib.com/FACT/1st.pres.rel.html (accessed December 11, 1999).
128. Riley, op. cit.
129. Bagby, Perl, and Froehle, op. cit.
130. Smith, op. cit.; Bagby, Perl, and Froehle, op. cit.; Corbett, op. cit.
131. Haddad and Smith, op. cit.
132. Denny, op. cit.; Bagby, Perl, and Froehle, op. cit.
133. Smith, op. cit.; Gutbi Mahdi Ahmed, "Muslim Organizations in the United States," in Yvonne Yazbeck Haddad, ed., *The Muslims of America* (New York: Oxford University Press, 1991), pp. 11–24.
134. Smith, op. cit.
135. Byng, op. cit.; Ross-Sheriff, op. cit.
136. American Muslim Poll, op. cit.
137. Barbara Bryant Solomon, "Social Work Practice with African Americans," in Armando T. Morales and Bradford W. Sheafor, *Social Work: A Profession of Many Faces*, 9th ed. (Needham, MA: Allyn & Bacon, 2001), pp. 519–539.
138. RNS News Service, "Report: Anti-Muslim Violence May Be Declining," Religion News Service, October 26, 2001, http://pewforum.org/news/index.php3?NewsID-827, accessed May 23, 2002).
139. Shelvia Dancy, "Bush Visits Mosque, Warns Against Anti-Muslim Violence," Religion News Service, September 17, 2001, http://pewforum.org/news/index.php3?NewsID=730 (accessed May 23, 2002).
140. Luis Lugo, "Muslim-Americans Gaining Respect," *The Atlanta Journal-Constitution*, March 25, 2002, http://accessatlanta.com/ajc/opinion/0303/0325muslims.html (accessed May 23, 2002).
141. American Muslim Poll, op. cit.
142. U.S. Equal Employment Opportunity Commission, "EEOC Provides Answers About Workplace Rights of Muslims, Arabs, South Asians and Sikhs," U.S. Equal Employment Opportunity Commission, May 15, 2002, http://www.eeoc.gov/press/5-15-02.html (accessed July 23, 2002).
143. Council on American-Islamic Relations Research Center, op. cit.
144. American Muslim Poll, op. cit.
145. RNS News Service, op. cit.

chapter 22

Social Work Practice with Asian Americans*

Prefatory Comment

One of the fastest growing segments of the U.S. population is the people of Asian background. The 2000 Census counted almost 10.7 million people of Asian descent (3.8 percent of the total population) and projects this will grow to 14.2 million people (4.6 percent) by 2010 and almost 18 million (5.4 percent) by 2020.[1] This population is difficult to describe because it is made up of people from many different Asian countries, such as Korea, India, Japan, China, Laos, Vietnam, Cambodia, the Philippines, Guam, and others, and thus culturally competent social work practice with this population requires knowledge of and skill in working with many cultures.

The term *Asian American* may be seen as a geographical and political designation that covers a wide and diverse group of people whose country and culture of origin are from the continent of Asia and islands of the Pacific. The proper designation for this group is *Asian American/Pacific Islander*.

From a geographical perspective, there are thirty-eight Asian nations, which can be grouped into the five following entities: (1) China and India dominate the Asian population and land mass; (2) Japan is an island group; (3) Korea is positioned between China and Japan; (4) the Southeast Asian satellite primary countries are Vietnam, Thailand, Cambodia, Laos, and Malaysia; and (5) the island nations of Indonesia and Philippines, which are closer to Asia than the island regions of Micronesia, Melanesia, and Polynesia.

The Asian population in the United States is projected to grow from 10.7 million people in 2000 to 33.4 million in 2050, increasing to 8 percent of the total U.S. population.[2] Driving the Asian population growth is Asian immigration. An estimated 63 percent of Asian Americans are foreign born; most speak English, with only 37 percent unable to speak English fluently or very well.[3]

---

*This chapter was prepared by Dr. Doman Lum, professor emeritus, California State University, Sacramento.

Six countries of national origin made up nearly 90 percent of the U.S. Asian population, according to the 2000 U.S. Census. These countries were China (2.7 million people), the Philippines (2.4 million), India (1.9 million), Vietnam (1.2 million), Korea (1.2 million), and Japan (1.1 million). No more than about 200,000 Asian Americans were from any of the other Asian countries.[4] The regional distribution of Asians is approximately 2.1 million (18.8 percent) in the Northeast, 1.2 million (10.7 percent) in the Midwest, 1.9 million (17.0 percent) in the South, and 6.0 million, or 53.6 percent, in the West.[5]

Selected Characteristics of the Asian American Population

Gender

Recently attention has been devoted to Asian American women due to a lack of information about their gender status and condition.[6] There is a high rate of interracial marriage among Asian American women, with Japanese American women outmarrying the most in the continental United States and Chinese Americans in Hawaii. Domestic violence against Asian battered women is often hidden due to family and marriage images portrayed to the Asian community. Asian women spousal abuse reveals factors such as extreme isolation; immigration dependency; reinforced powerlessness from society; traditional views of family and community, which place family before oneself; and a lack of economic and cultural resources to leave a violent situation.[7]

Socioeconomic Issues

Education is an important priority for every population group, and Asian Americans are better educated than any other racial or cultural group in the United States. The 2000 Census indicates that, although the percent of Asian people who do not complete high school is about the same as the national average (19.6 percent), 44.0 percent complete a bachelor's degree or higher as compared with 24.4 percent for the total population.[8] These trends are due to the value placed on educational achievement by students' parents and the hard work ethic and willingness of Asian American students to make economic and social sacrifices to achieve academic success. Higher education is the gateway to professional jobs in such fields as science, medicine, engineering, law, business, and social work.

Linked to success in higher education and the value placed on industriousness in many of the Asian/Pacific Island cultures is a relatively high average income. In 2007, as compared with the total U.S. population with a median family income of $61,794, the median income for Asian households was $75,686.[9] It was estimated that 6.1 million Asians (66.4 percent of the age 16 and older civilian population) were employed in 2003, and only 4.0 percent of those who wanted jobs were unemployed. The significantly higher median income and solid employment record should not obscure the fact that more than one out of ten Asian people were living in poverty.[10] Poverty was more common among recent immigrants from Southeast

Asian countries who tend to lack education, are limited in speaking English, and have few marketable job skills. Thus Asian refugees tend to end up in dead-end jobs, such as restaurant and garment factory workers, and often lack occupational mobility due to low levels of educational preparation.[11] Social work, therefore, has a role to play in addressing the socioeconomic issues of a substantial part of the Asian American population.

Housing and Health Status

In 2005, it was estimated that only 53.2 percent of the Asian American and 45.5 percent of the Native Hawaiian and Pacific Island populations own their own homes, as compared with the national average of 66.2 percent. In these cultures, priority is typically given to securing education and employment over home ownership. The lower level of ownership results in Asian Americans paying high rents (particularly on the West Coast), loss of the opportunity for tax write-offs on mortgages, and the necessity of living in crowded conditions. Statistics from the Asian Pacific American Community Development Data Center rate 14 percent of the Asian American homes as overcrowded, as compared with 3 percent of the housing units in the United States.[12]

Regarding health status, Asians have lower rates of infant mortality (4.8 deaths before age 1 per 1,000 live births) in 2002, compared with a total population indicator of 7.0 for all races. In addition, the age-adjusted death rate, too, is substantially lower: the national average is 853.3 per 100,000, while for Asian Americans it is only 299.5. However, there is an above-average incidence of tuberculosis (45.4 compared with a total population indicator of 9.4 per 100,000) due to the high number of Asian immigrants living in cramped quarters in metropolitan areas with poor air quality. The most recent life expectancy data indicates that Asians as a group were above average; they were expected to live an average of 80 years versus 77.3 years for the general population.[13] Thus social workers are especially needed to address the need for quality housing and assisting families as they support the older Asian people.

Health and Mental Health Risk Factors

Among the health and mental health problems of Asian Americans are depression, somatic complaints, anxiety disorders, adjustment disorders, and suicide.[14] Lee reports: "Work-related stress among the Asian American working class and underclass has exacerbated domestic tensions. Adjustment difficulties and challenges to traditional relations have troubled many marriages. Indeed, domestic violence afflicts all classes of Asian American families."[15] Hate crimes due to racism have compounded the environmental stress experienced by the Asian American community. Posttraumatic stress disorder is common among Southeast Asian refugees (particularly Vietnamese, Cambodian, Hmong, and Mien), who fled their homelands and experienced atrocities (e.g., rape, murder, and robbery) in the process of leaving their countries, in refugee camps, and upon entering the United States.

 Ethnic Group Stressors

Loo has documented sustained racism against Asian Americans in the United States during recent decades.[16] She declares: "In the 1980s, Asian Americans became scapegoats for America's economic woes. Americans of Asian ancestry wore the mantle of foreignness, falsely blamed for the economic recession of the U.S. automobile industry. The 1982 race-hate murder of Vincent Chin in Detroit and rising incidents of anti-Asian violence in the 1980s were cases in point."[17] Later Loo observes: "The focus on suspected illegality of Asian donations to the Democratic Party campaign funds ha[s] reactivated racial stereotypes of the Chinese. Racist cartoons of President Clinton, Hillary Clinton, and Al Gore with slant eyes and clothed in Mandarin coats, appeared in the *National Review*. The cartoon was a startling throwback to anti-Asian cartoons of the 1800s."[18] Minority group racism against Asian Americans remains a national reality. Among older Americans, there are traces of racism against Japanese Americans, who were scapegoats during World War II. In many parts of the country where there are few Asian Americans, an individual experiences being an isolated and lonely minority person surrounded by invisible barriers of exclusion.

Intergenerational Asian American group stressors include the "parachute kid" phenomena of teenage children from the upper-middle class and wealthy Asians from Hong Kong, Taiwan, and other Asian areas who are dropped off in large metropolitan areas populated by Asian Americans, housed in exclusive-area homes, and left to attend American high schools on their own. Parents visit periodically from abroad or ask relatives in the United States to look after them. An alternative is to ask a sister or a brother in the United States to be a surrogate parent and to raise a teenage nephew or niece so that an Asian-born child can graduate from an American high school and enter an American university. Family development and raising a child are sacrificed for an American education. Parental responsibilities are abdicated by parents in their own country for a relative to assume teenage rearing in the United States.

Asian husband "astronauts" are depicted as businessmen who must travel abroad between their homes and family in the United States and various parts of Asia to maintain their business contacts and enterprises in, say, Hong Kong. Being left alone for months, Asian American families are stressed by the absence of the father, by the role of the mother as interim head of the household, and by the acting out of the children. Such families must constantly adjust and readjust to the husband and father who is coming and going.

The frail, elderly, single male in Chinatown who never married due to miscegenation laws lives alone in a small and dingy room. Early state laws prohibited the marriage of white women and nonwhite men. At the same time, immigration laws excluded admitting Chinese into the United States during the first half of the twentieth century. With no family to care for him and little government assistance, this elderly person struggles from day to day on small means, is isolated, and dies alone and forgotten.

Asian youth gangs in large cities with overseas-born members who are marginal students or school dropouts have been responsible for intimidating Asian businesses, such as restaurants and grocery stores, for protection money or have committed home invasion robberies, which target Asian families who keep large sums of money, jewelry, and other valuables in their homes. Some Asian families avoid putting assets in the bank for safe keeping and have them available at home for ready access. Brutal force (beatings or murder) is used to obtain "easy money."

Asian American gays and lesbians have experienced stress in coming out to their families. The homosexual lifestyle is against Asian cultural mores and the importance of perpetuating the next generation of the family and is still a source of shame for many traditional Asian Americans. Sexuality is a private matter. Social support networks are needed to work with gay and lesbian persons, their families, and the attitude of the Asian American community.

Service Systems

Service Delivery

Service delivery involves the detailed arrangements of programs, staffing, facilities, funding, and administrative management that take into account the unique features of the Asian community. Five principles are related to service delivery: (1) location and pragmatic services, (2) staffing, (3) community outreach programs, (4) agency setting, and (5) service linkage.[19] The following discussion explains the meaning of these service delivery areas.

It is important for the *location* of services to be within walking distance of the designated Asian American target group that the agency wishes to serve as a provider. Many Asian service centers are located in areas heavily populated by Asian Americans and are housed in storefronts, churches, ethnic associations, and agencies. Chinatown, Japantown or Little Tokyo, Koreatown, Little Saigon, and other designated areas reach Asian clients who live in the area, depend on public transportation, and are without private cars. Asian clients tend to avoid services labeled mental health center (mental illness is a social stigma) and are drawn toward services that have a pragmatic value (child and family education). An agency should select a location and a name that reflect these principles.

Bilingual and bicultural *staffing* should reflect the Asian American client population. In Asian American agencies, there are ethnic and linguistic skilled workers who are Chinese, Filipino, Japanese, Korean, Vietnamese, Hmong, and related groups and who have access to bilingual workers matching other clients. At the same time, a non-minority social worker who is both bilingual and bicultural can be an integral and effective part of the staff, if he or she is able to speak the language and is familiar with the culture.

Community outreach programs afford an agency staff exposure and credibility to the key institutions in the Asian American community. It is crucial to conduct educational workshops and set up information booths at ethnic festivals, language schools, ethnic churches, family associations, and related community groups. Planting the seeds of knowledge and service provision reap referrals and follow-up opportunities with community leaders.

The *agency setting* should reflect art and cultural items that communicate a message of sensitivity to the Asian community. A friendly bilingual receptionist, a welcome and relaxed atmosphere, and a plan to respond to walk-in clients create a conducive environment that sends a positive message to client and community.

Service linkage establishes a working relationship between existing agencies in the Asian community and institutions in the wider social service network. It is important to establish professional ties to key workers in grass-root ethnic organizations, churches, and service professional groups so that Asian clients are able to move easily through the service systems.

Role of the Social Worker

The role of the social worker in the service delivery system to Asian Americans involves the development of culturally specific services to meet the needs of specific Asian American client groups. There has been a debate between culture-common (etic) and culture-specific (emic) service delivery that can be framed around Asian American service agencies.[20] That is, should there be culturally common services that meet the needs of all clients, or should there be culturally specific services to address the particular needs of Asian American people? Or, in a narrower perspective, should there be culturally common services for all Asian Americans, or should there be single-ethnic agencies to meet the unique problems of a specific Asian American group? The social worker could advocate for a service agency to meet all types of Asian Americans, because it is cost effective and integrates the diversity of the Asian American community. At the same time, the worker might see the need for a service agency that addresses a particular group (e.g., Chinese, Japanese, Korean, or Vietnamese) due to the heavy community demands and ethnic leader support.

Sue, Mak, and Sue point out that the diversity in the Asian American community is becoming even more heterogeneous. There are Asians who have resided in the United States for many generations and those who immigrated here recently and cannot speak English, and their socioeconomic status is quite diverse, from those considered affluent to those far below the poverty line. They conclude: "Coupling these factors with the varying ethnicities (e.g., Asian Indian, Cambodian, Chinese, Filipino, Hmong, Japanese, Korean, Laotian, Samoan, Thai, Tongan, Vietnamese) it does not take much to conclude that any single theory of Asian American identity development would be an oversimplification and inadequate."[21] Discussion around focusing services on all Asian American groups housed under one roof or fostering single Asian group services is an interesting point of communication among social workers who are concerned with service delivery arrangements.

Service Gaps and Needs

Asian American communities in large metropolitan areas, such as Los Angeles, New York City, San Francisco, Seattle, and Sacramento, have nurtured clusters of Asian American social service networks that meet a variety of needs in their locales.

Service delivery cooperation and coordination among Asian American service providers are crucial as funding diminishes or shifts toward specialized needs or new immigrant influx, and federal or state programs come on line to meet other needs.

Iglehart and Becerra offer a number of interesting agency linkage principles that are applicable to Asian American service delivery. They point out that ethnic agencies often receive funding for specialized services to ethnic groups from mainstream social services on the county or state levels. This means that Asian American agencies must conduct program evaluations to justify their existence and be accountable to government entities. Moreover, they must be cost effective and target funding wisely. In an interorganizational relationship, they observe that the ethnic agency has access to a particular ethnic population because of its presence in the ethnic community and its relationship with specific target populations.[22] In other words, Asian American agencies must cultivate good lines of communication, cooperation, and collaboration with the local Asian community, in general, and with particular groups if they want to continue serving them. Moreover, changing federal funding requirements develop partnerships between mainstream agencies and ethnic agencies, demand reduction in service duplication, and define special populations in need. Asian American agencies should cultivate working relationships with county, state, and federal officials who have special knowledge about service program trends affecting Asian American populations. There is a nucleus of important Asian Americans in the House of Representatives and the U.S. Senate who are willing to brief Asian service providers about legislative program development and funding that is anticipated or available. These are some of the ways that social workers in the Asian American community can proceed to close gaps and meet needs.

Micro Practice Perspectives

The Problem-Solving Approach

Chin reports that Asians who seek assistance expect a generalist helper or advice giver, an authority figure who takes a directive approach and provides concrete social services.[23] Lee asserts: "*A problem-focused, goal-oriented, and symptom-relieving approach* is highly recommended in the beginning phases of treatment. Rather than defining goals in abstract, emotional terms, goals may be best stated in terms of external resolution or symptom reduction."[24] Lee recommends the following treatment strategies with Asian American families:

1. Form a social and cultural connection with the family during the first session.
2. Acknowledge the family's sense of shame.
3. Establish expertise, power, credibility, and authority.
4. Define the problem.
5. Apply a family psycho-educational approach.
6. Build alliance with members with power.
7. Employ reframing techniques.

8. Assume multiple helping roles.
9. Restructure the social support system.
10. Integrate Eastern–Western health approaches.
11. Mobilize the family's cultural strength.
12. Employ the concept of empowerment as a treatment goal.
13. Understand the family's communication style.
14. Acknowledge countertransference and racial stereotypes.[25]*

The problem-solving, task-centered intervention is familiar to social work practitioners. Uba observes that Asian Americans expect the worker to give advice, recommend courses of action, and tell them how to resolve their problems. In a way, the social worker is asked to behave like a physician: to conduct an examination, make a diagnosis, and write out a prescription. This intervention strategy emphasizes a clear, detailed plan and straightforward solutions to concrete and immediate problems.

Problem solving is a rational, step-by-step procedure that requires cognitive mental comprehension and behavioral action. It involves six steps:

1. *Problem identification.* It is important for the Asian client to acknowledge and define the problem he or she is facing. It may be done in an indirect way ("I have a friend who has this problem...") or the worker may have to piece together the problem and define the problem cluster or the interrelated set of problems for the client who may be too ashamed to articulate the problem directly.

2. *Problem analysis.* Analyzing a problem involves uncovering its history, placing the events and persons in chronological order, and assessing the needs of the person involved. It is important to find out what has happened in the past four to six weeks (acute crisis) and within the past six months to one year (important past history). Socioenvironmental stressors affecting the Asian client are an integral part of problem analysis.

3. *Solution alternatives.* Based on the identified problem, problem solving moves to examining a range of alternative solutions. The worker should ask the Asian client about possible solutions to the problem, several of which may be realistic and possible. The worker and the client should work on feasible solutions together, although the worker may have to generate some alternatives to initiate discussion. A potential solution is clear, realistic, specific, and attainable in a short period.

4. *Solution prioritization.* Each viable solution should be reviewed to find the most effective and realistic way to solve the problem. It is important to engage the client in a discussion of the pros and cons of each potential solution so that the client may ultimately "own" the solution for him- or herself.

5. *Solution implementation.* After the client selects a solution, the next step is to implement the solution by constructing a number of task assignments that lead the

---

*The reader is encouraged to read Chapter 1, "Overview: The Assessment and Treatment of Asian American Families," in Evelyn Lee, ed., *Working with Asian Americans: A Guide for Clinicians* (New York: Guilford Publications, 1998).

client from the present situation to the changes needed. A task is a constructive action taken in response to a problem.

6. *Problem-solving evaluation.* It is important to observe and monitor behavioral and situational changes that have occurred in the process of implementing a problem solution. Keeping a diary or journal and logging who was involved, where and when the changes occurred, and what actually happened provide an opportunity for the worker and client to review progress at the next session.[26]

Ecosystems Model Framework

With the problem-solving, task-centered approach as a micro practice intervention for Asian Americans in mind, we turn to the ecosystems model framework, which involves gathering information and exploring and weighing dynamics in problem-solving processing. There are five dimensions of ecosystems problem solving: historical factors, environmental–structural factors, culture, the family, and the individual. Figure 22.1 illustrates the various levels.

Historical Factors

Asian Americans may incorporate a *psychohistorical reaction response.* That is, the history of oppression affecting this group may cause a psychological survival response from an Asian American client. Uba summarizes research on Asian American personality patterns regarding abasement, affiliation, anxiety, assertiveness, autonomy, conformity, expressiveness, extroversion, formality, locus of control, self-concept, and sex roles, with allowances for intraethnic variation in personality. The social worker should take a brief ethnic history of the client.[27]

During the mid-1800s and early 1900s, Asians of many nationalities came to the United States to pursue economic opportunities, to escape political oppression, and to migrate permanently to the West. Many Chinese and Japanese entered as laborers who expected to return to their homeland and retire in comfort after making their fortune in this country. As the Chinese succeeded in agricultural and mining endeavors, growing anti-Chinese sentiment spread among white gold miners and farmers, riots, hangings, and evictions of Chinese spread throughout the West Coast. The Chinese were barred from entering the country through the Chinese Exclusion Act of 1882, denied American citizenship and the right to intermarriage, and contained in Chinatowns of major American cities. Similarly, the Japanese suffered limited immigration in the 1907 Gentlemen's Agreement and were denied ownership of land in the 1913 Alien Land Bill. The Immigration Act of 1924 closed the door to Asian immigrants and favored those from European countries. At the early stages of World War II, President Roosevelt issued Executive Order 9066 on February 12, 1942, removing Japanese Americans along the West Coast from their homes and businesses to rural internment camps for the duration of the war. This had a major psychohistorical impact on all Japanese Americans,

Figure 22.1
Ecosystems Model for Analysis of Factors Impacting Asian Americans

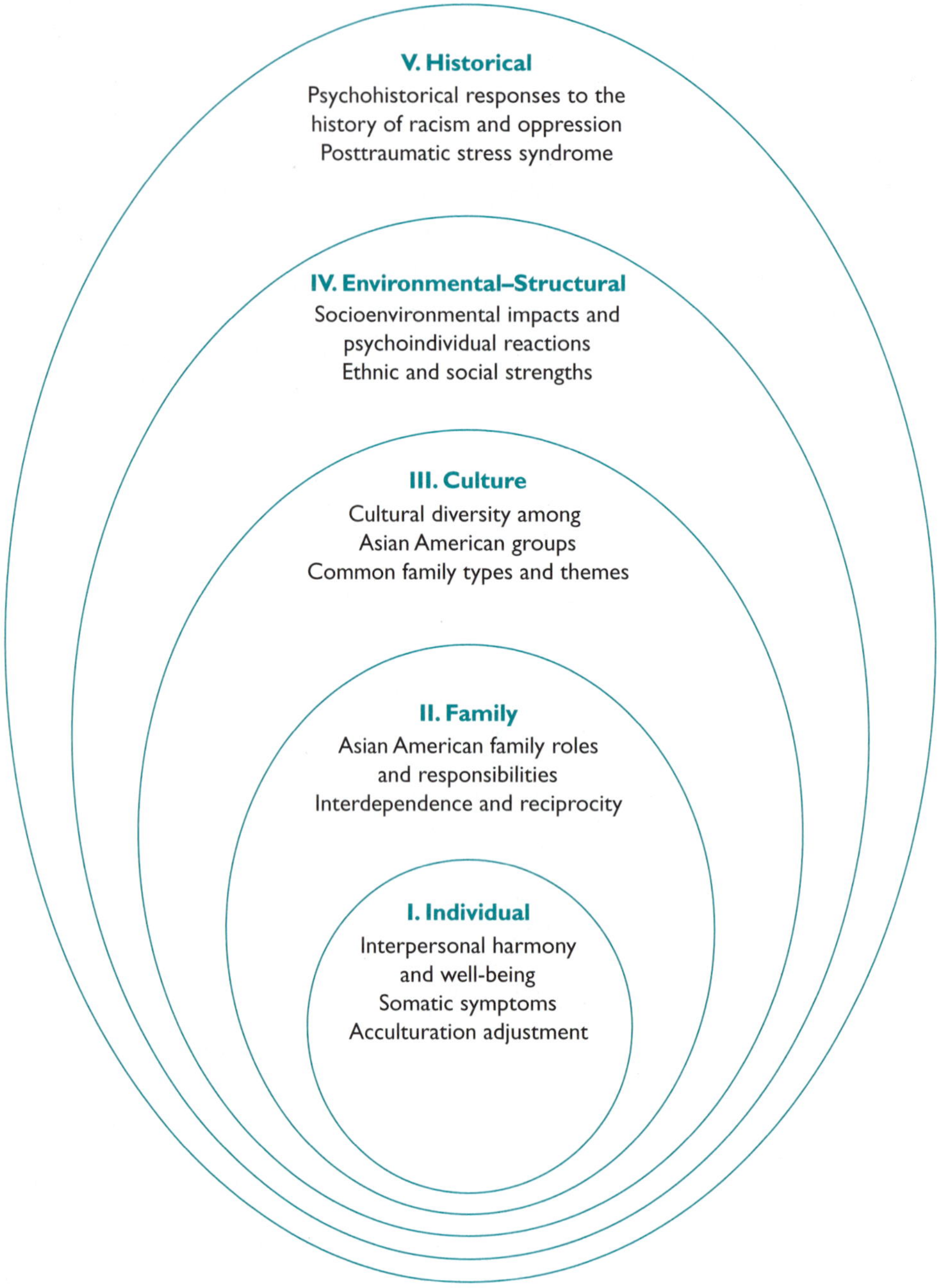

V. Historical
Psychohistorical responses to the history of racism and oppression
Posttraumatic stress syndrome

IV. Environmental–Structural
Socioenvironmental impacts and psychoindividual reactions
Ethnic and social strengths

III. Culture
Cultural diversity among Asian American groups
Common family types and themes

II. Family
Asian American family roles and responsibilities
Interdependence and reciprocity

I. Individual
Interpersonal harmony and well-being
Somatic symptoms
Acculturation adjustment

which is still felt today. However, since China was an ally during the war, war refugees from China were allowed into the United States for relief purposes.

The 1965 Immigration Act opened the United States to all countries. Asian immigrants from Hong Kong, Korea, the Philippines, and later from Southeast Asia after the Vietnam War (Vietnamese, Hmong, Mien, Laotians, and Cambodians) streamed into the United States.

Ho reports that the Filipino immigration population in the 1960s consisted of young professional males and females, many of whom experienced difficulties with obtaining U.S. professional licensure for foreign graduates. Moreover, many elderly Filipinos who came as unskilled laborers in the early 1920s are alone and isolated, with health care problems and living in cheap substandard housing. Korean immigration since 1965 has mushroomed due to political problems and the influx of Koreans who have been educated in the United States. The Korean American community is represented in the major West and East Coast metropolitan areas with small businesses (e.g., dry cleaning shops, convenience stores) and Christian churches. Pacific Islanders, particularly residents of American Samoa and Guam, have arrived in the United States because of their U.S. citizenship. Pacific Islanders from Tonga, Fiji, and Hawaii have been influenced by the Church of Jesus Christ of Latter-Day Saints, who believe that these regional groups are part of the lost tribe of Israel. Vietnamese, Cambodians, Hmong, and Mien entered this country as a result of the Vietnam War. Many Southeast Asian refugees have suffered posttraumatic stress in their flight from their homelands through holding camps in Thailand to their entrance into the United States. The first wave of refugees, mainly from Vietnam, consisted of highly educated and professional Vietnamese who integrated into this country, while succeeding waves were unskilled and minimally educated and became welfare dependent. Second-generation American-born Vietnamese have graduated from American universities and adjusted and acculturated in their communities.[28]

Part of taking an ethnic history incorporating psychohistorical factors is becoming aware of *acculturative stress* (e.g., loss of family members, role reversal, language handicaps) and related mental health needs. The social worker should look for the following signs of posttraumatic stress, even among Asian immigrants who have been in this country for several years but who may have residual elements. The chief symptoms are the following:

1. Recurrent or intrusive recollections of past traumas
2. Recurrent dreams and nightmares
3. Sad feelings, as if the traumatic events are recurring
4. Social numbness and withdrawal
5. Restricted affect
6. Hyperalertness; hyperactive startled reaction
7. Sleep disorders
8. Guilt
9. Memory impairment
10. Avoidance of activities that might trigger recollection of events
11. Reactivation of symptoms caused by exposure to events similar to the original trauma

Environmental–Structural Factors

Lum holds that there are external socioenvironmental impacts that cause a psycho-individual reaction of the client. Among these are basic survival needs (language barrier, reasonable housing, adequate employment, transportation, school for children), which trigger such psycho-individual reactions as culture shock (stressful adjustment to unfamiliar culture) and cultural conflict (e.g., loss of face, self-hatred, negative identity, and marginality).[29]

The task is to assess the environmental and social strengths of the client and the environment and to mobilize these potentials. Positive coping skills (e.g., the ability to restore cognitive commonsense problem solving in the client), cultural strengths (e.g., the mobilization of the extended family and ethnic community agencies, such as family associations and the local church), and other positive assessment areas are ways that the social worker can move rapidly to utilize environmental–structural support systems for the Asian American client.

Tran and Wright conducted a study of social support and well-being among Vietnamese refugees, underscoring the need for environmental and structural supports. According to their findings, a contented Vietnamese refugee seems to have stronger social supports, is not afraid to interact with Americans, has a relatively high family income, and is married. "To be happy in America," state Tran and Wright, "a Vietnamese person also needs good English communication ability, a high level of formal education, and a relatively long time of living in this country, and that person also needs to be in the younger age cohort."[30] The social worker should strive toward opening such environmental–structural doors as family and community groups, job training and employment opportunities, English as a second language classes, high school and technical school or college education, and a stable residence in a community.

Culture

Culture is the sum total of life patterns passed on from generation to generation within a group of people and includes institutions, language, religious ideals, habits of thinking, artistic expressions, and patterns of social and interpersonal relationships.[31] Asian/Pacific Islander cultures are varied and different from each other. On the Asian continent, the history of China as the Middle Kingdom and the dominant culture of Asia has influenced Japanese, Korean, and Southeast Asian cultural expressions (e.g., art, food, religion, and language), although each group has evolved its own variations. While it is important to acknowledge the uniqueness and difference of each Asian/Pacific Island group, there are common cultural themes that cut across the spectrum of Asian Americans.

Asian American parents who were born in an Asian country and their first-generation, American-born children have gone or are going through culture shock and bicultural conflict. Coming from an Asian country to the United States poses particular challenges to acculturate from a culture of origin to the dominant American society. Asian American families are in the process of integrating a meaningful life by selecting values and traditions from both societies. Often social workers help Asian American families resolve cultural tension and conflict and achieve bicultural integration.

Social workers must also learn *cultural boundaries* and protocols when working with Asian Americans. Cultural boundaries are lines of demarcations that separate an Asian American individual and/or family unit from the larger society. There may be personal matters that are kept within the family. Mental health problems, socioeconomic issues, and related family areas are withheld from the public. Cultural protocols are exercised in terms of formality, proper subject areas for discussion, and respect. To go beyond these spheres and to reveal personal problems affecting family well-being may require more time and patience on the part of the social worker, who must gain the trust and confidence of the Asian American person or family.

Asian Americans often operate in a *cultural duality*. They appear assertive, competent, and influential in their business dealings or on the job in the workplace, but they may exercise restraint, respect, and deference to their parents and elderly in the home situation. This is a cultural-integration example of how Asian Americans survive and cope with two related cultures that may require differing sets of expectations.

Maintenance of culture is important for many Asian Americans, who hold that the use of cultural beliefs, customs, celebrations, and rituals are a source of strength, renewal, and identity. Cultural values and practices are a means to cope with present and future life problems.

The Family

The family is the central value of the Asian American. Traditional Asian American families have specific roles and relationships. The family is patriarchal, with father as the leader of the family, mother as the nurturing caretaker, and sons with more value and status than daughters. The child is expected to obey parents and elders, while the parents are responsible to raise, educate, and support their children. The family's reverence for their ancestors is important for traditional families. Family members are interrelated with each other. The emphasis is on interdependence (caring for one's family and integration into the extended family). The family fosters positive life events and avoids negative shame. Modesty and reciprocity are important family characteristics to the extent of understating and minimizing individual achievement. Children, particularly sons, are expected to bring honor to the family. The son carries on the family name. Family strengths include valuing respect, interacting with the extended family, and offering support for each other.

Lee identifies five types of Asian American families as follows:

Type 1: The Traditional Family All family members are born and raised in Asian countries and have limited contact with the mainstream of American society. Family members hold traditional values, speak their native language, and belong to family associations and other social clubs of people with similar cultural orientations.

Type 2: The Cultural Conflict Family The family consists of parents and grandparents with traditional beliefs and values and children with more Western acculturated perspectives, which are in conflict with each other. Issues are related to independence versus interdependence, obedience versus freedom, respect versus self-assertiveness. Arguments occur over dating, marriage, educational goals, and career choice. There is role reversal when the children speak better English and can broker problems for parents who have minimal English skills.

Type 3: The Bicultural Family Bicultural families consist of acculturated parents who are born in Asia or in America and are acculturated to the industrial Western society. Parents are usually well-educated and hold professional jobs, are bilingual, and have an egalitarian family structure in which problems are resolved through negotiation between family members. These families live in integrated middle-class neighborhoods and visit and care for grandparents on weekends.

Type 4: The Americanized Family Parents and children are born and raised in the United States, have a reduced understanding and practice of Asian culture, speak primarily English, and operate as individuals in an egalitarian relationship. Friends of the family may include Asians and non-Asians, and the mentality and attitude are more Americanized than Asian.

Type 5: The Interracial Family An Asian American has intermarried with another Asian American (e.g., Chinese with Japanese or Korean with Vietnamese) or has chosen a spouse outside the Asian American groups. There is a wide variety of family responses, including acceptance, resignation, indifference, and rejection, depending on the traditional and nontraditional spectrum of cultural values. Children of interracial families must shape their ethnic identity, ethnic group affiliation, and socialization.[32]

Cultural family types may be a useful vehicle for understanding the common dynamics of varying Asian American families, which transcend viewing separate but differing groups.

Yee, Huang, and Lew have also identified a number of common Asian American family concepts and themes, such as the following:

1. Strong family and social ties that buffer families from the consequences of life crises
2. Family problem-solving skills, culturally shaped emotional responses and communication patterns
3. Healthy identities with life and social skills to deal with life-span development challenges
4. Interdependence, reciprocity, and collectivism in family patterns
5. Cultural traditions that offer a prescription for living and a code of behavior
6. A sense of autonomy and competence within close family relationships
7. The importance of repaying parents for their sacrifices through high educational achievement and occupational aspirations
8. A system of hierarchical roles based on age, birth position, and gender
9. Marriage as the continuation of the husband's family line

10. Reciprocity between generations based on emotional, financial, and child-care support exchanges
11. Caring for elderly relatives as the family's responsibility[33]

The Individual

The biopsychosocial dimensions of the Asian American client involve an examination of biological, psychological, and social aspects. From a biological health perspective, the Asian American concept of *interpersonal harmony* advocates minimizing conflict and maximizing getting along with each other. Health and healthy relationships in balance are interrelated to each other. Thinking "good thoughts" is more important than dwelling on sickness, mental illness, or death. The latter is a self-fulfilling prophecy for misfortune, whereas the former leads to good fortune. Somatic symptoms or the psychophysiological interaction between mind and body are important to uncover if an Asian American client has internalized stress and manifests physical problems. Often Asian Americans are taught to suppress negative feelings and reactions, rather than openly ventilate them. Mental health problems tend to be expressed as psychosomatic complaints (e.g., headaches, backaches, digestive troubles, and peptic ulcers). This goes back to maintaining harmony and cultivating a pleasant disposition. Physical problems are culturally acceptable expressions, but mental health problems are taboo areas that evoke a social stigma for the family in the eyes of the local Asian community. If there are biological health problems, the social worker should work with the client's physician to clear up somatic symptoms.

From a psychological perspective, it is important to assess the relation between the person's mental state and his or her behavioral interaction with significant others in the cultural community and the society as a whole. The level of motivation for change, as well as the resistance or unwillingness to cooperate or participate in the process of growth, are crucial to uncover from a psychological assessment. Stressing positive change and acknowledging feelings of anger and disgrace change the psychological atmosphere. Prolonged silence may be part of the psychological mix. Asian Americans may remain silent as a sign of respect to the authority of the worker or as a culturally distinct way of relating and responding in an indirect manner. Significant others investigate the relationship of self and others, particularly family, peers, and other persons who are meaningfully related. The social worker needs to know the following:

1. Does the Asian client come from a nuclear, single-parent, blended, or extended family?
2. Are the parents foreign-born or American-born?
3. Does the family have a clear sense of parental authority and interdependence, a sense of democratic autonomy, or a mix of both?
4. Are the parents recent immigrants or refugees who are acculturating well or poorly to a new environment?
5. Are there differing value systems between the parents from their country of origin and their Americanized children?
6. Does the mother function as a go-between for an authoritative distant father and their children?

The answers to these questions may affect the psychological state of the Asian American client.

The social assessment of the Asian individual focuses on how the person interacts with group and community living. Lum identifies four aspects of social assessment:[34] (1) immigration history or the family's transition from the culture of origin to American society; (2) acculturation or the adjustment, change, and maintenance of culture in the family; (3) school adjustment or the academic and social experiences of children in their primary institution; and (4) employment or the primary work setting critical for adult self-esteem and respect in the ethnic community.

MICRO CASE EXAMPLE

Annie, a 15-year-old teenager from Hong Kong, was sent to relatives in Monterey Park, California, by her parents who have an import–export business and travel throughout Asia and the United States. Annie is the oldest of four siblings and has misgivings about leaving her friends in school behind. Her parents want her to graduate from an American high school and establish citizenship and residency so that she can be admitted to a University of California school. Her relatives in California consist of an uncle and his wife, who are in their early thirties, without children, and married for five years.

Annie has had difficulties for several months adjusting to her new environment (living situation, school, peer relations) after arriving and entering school. She has cut classes, been in arguments with her uncle and his wife, and has made friends with some overseas-born Asians at school. She is a parachute kid (literally dropped into an American community from an Asian country of origin) who is separated from her primary nuclear family and is going through her teenage identity crisis with her surrogate parents, an uncle and aunt.

After repeated attempts by Uncle Chuck and Auntie Phyllis to resolve Annie's problems, they turn to the Asian American/Pacific Islander Counseling Center in Los Angeles for help. The social worker, David Lee of Chinese descent and Cantonese–English speaking, is assigned the case and has worked at the Asian Youth Center.

After becoming acquainted with the background and home situation of Annie and her uncle and aunt, the social worker obtains the following ecosystems dimensional information.

HISTORICAL FACTORS

Annie is reacting to her particular psychohistorical situation. It is common among upper-middle-class and wealthy families in Hong Kong and other Asian countries to send their children abroad for schooling. While Annie's friends remain in Hong Kong, the social worker finds out from Annie and her relatives that teenage children have been sent to various large American cities, Canada, and England where there are relatives and friends of families. At the same time, Annie reveals that many of the American-born Asians have made fun of her since she is a FOB (fresh off the boat) or foreign-born Asian. This type of intragroup racism has isolated Annie from her school peer group and has caused her to gravitate toward some Asians who are marginal students. She also feels rejected by her parents and has flashbacks of being sent away by her parents, who have no time for her because of their business and social commitments.

ENVIRONMENTAL–STRUCTURAL FACTORS

Annie's present environment involves an uncle and an auntie who are trying to help her make a transitional adjustment to a new environment (Monterey Park, a predominately Asian American affluent suburb near east Los Angeles); a new school, which is academically demanding, with few friends; and a new set of surrogate parents, who have tried to be flexible but firm with her. Her immediate reactions have been mixed: cutting classes and hanging out with other Asian high schoolers who are not interested in learning; testing her limits with her uncle and auntie, who previously allowed her freedom and space but have misgivings about how to deal with Annie; and expressing her unhappiness about being away from her family and friends in Hong Kong, whom she dearly misses.

Yet Annie has some ethnic and social strengths. In Hong Kong she was a happy, serious, and bright student in her grade school. She was friendly and able to garner a variety of neighborhood and school mates. Yet in Monterey Park the opposite is true, because many of the Asian students are American born, speak English without an accent, and are Americanized in their behavior.

CULTURE

Annie is the product of a traditional Asian family who is a part of the Hong Kong business and social circles. Her parents could be termed "Asian jet setters"; they travel to nearby countries on business, pleasure, and shopping trips and leave their children in the care of nannies and relatives. Annie's Asian peers in California are either bicultural Asians who came from Hong Kong, Taiwan, and Malaysia many years ago or are American-born and Americanized to the point of speaking English without a trace of an Asian foreign accent and/or being unable to speak a Chinese dialect. Often these students are student body government leaders and model minorities, who academically compete well with their white counterparts and have Asian and non-Asian friends. Annie is painfully aware of the contrast and how she does not fit in with Asian American teenagers in terms of dress, makeup, language, conversational topics, and circle of friends.

FAMILY FACTORS

Annie's parents in Hong Kong have a role responsibility to be fulfilled on behalf of their daughter. Her father and mother need to come for a visit and to be aware of Annie's feelings and situation. Annie's mother could ease the transition by staying with her for an indefinite period until an adjustment has been made. A sense of interdependence and reciprocity should be established between parents and daughter. That is, Annie will try to make an adjustment to her new situation, and Annie's father and mother will each take turns staying with her in Monterey Park until everyone involved feels that there is progress in this transition. Otherwise, the family should agree that Annie may be happier and can thrive if she returns to her home, school, and friends in Hong Kong.

INDIVIDUAL FACTORS

Annie is painfully aware that she is unhappy, lonely, and somewhat depressed and that her sense of interpersonal harmony and well-being has been impaired by this move to California. Rather than dealing with her stress, she internalizes her feelings and keeps her personal thoughts to herself. At times the stress has been exhibited with such somatic symptoms as periodic outbreaks of acne, stomachaches, and headaches. When she is anxious or worried, Annie catches herself picking her lips, a nervous gesture. There are hole marks and raw patches in her lower lip as a result. Annie is an example of the acculturation adjustment for a growing number of teenage Asians from various countries of Asia who have been called parachute kids. As they parachute to various parts of the United States, their landing is at times rough and unwelcomed. They must fend for themselves alone or with the help of relatives and friends of their families of origin who are forced to become surrogate parents. One wonders whether the family disruption and resulting instability and crisis are worth the effort of fulfilling the American dream, without the necessary parental support that is necessary for growing up from childhood through adolescence to young adulthood.

As you review the ecological problem-solving approach, the ecological systems model, and the unique case study of Annie, brainstorm the various intervention strategies that you would employ as the social worker in this situation.

Macro Practice Perspectives

Macro practice with Asian Americans involves large regional and institutional change that results in social justice, new institutional structures, and the distribution of wealth and resources to meet the problems of this particular target group. Social policy, planning, and administration are macro intervention tools to affect social change in problem areas.

Of all the various Asian American groups in need, Asian refugees and immigrants have the greatest acculturation adjustment and socioeconomic survival needs. High-risk refugees face problems of underemployment, breakdowns in the family network, and changing family roles. Moreover, with the implementation of welfare reform (the 1996 Personal Responsibility and Work Opportunity Reconciliation Act), legal immigrants have partially lost medical and food stamp benefits. The previous Clinton administration proposed a $1.3 billion five-year restoration program that was to benefit 132,000 people, particularly Latino and Asian immigrants. The Balanced Budget Act of 1997 restored Supplemental Security Income for disabled persons and Medicaid benefits to 420,000 legal immigrants who were in the country before welfare legislation was enacted on August 22, 1996. The Agricultural Research Act of 1998 provided food stamps for 225,000 legal immigrant children, senior citizens, and the disabled who came to the United States before the new welfare law.[35] Asian American refugees and immigrants in the welfare system need to be trained in such jobs as gardeners, restaurant cooks, bakers, child-care workers, and other hands-on positions. These Asians are hard working and dependable if they are given the opportunities of employment.

On the local level, social policy, planning, and administration are tools to organize the indigenous Asian American community to meet the specific needs of Asian elderly, unemployed, new arrivals, and other target groups in need. Rather than waiting for federal and state assistance, it is more effective to identify Asian American leaders who have the social awareness and financial knowledge and skills to plan and implement local projects that benefit the Asian American community. An example of this was accomplished in Northern California.

In twenty-five years as an Asian American faculty member of California State University, Sacramento Division of Social Work, the author has witnessed a remarkable alliance among Asian American social work students, working professionals, and county officials. During the early 1970s, a nucleus of graduate Asian American social work students and faculty developed a National Institute of Mental Health (NIMH) training grant that offered field stipends and placed students in various Asian American field settings among the Japanese and Filipino elderly, downtown refugees and immigrants, and Asian residents of low-income public housing. As a result of these field placements and Asian American social work courses, Master of Social Work (MSW) Asian American graduates founded a variety of Asian American social service centers, as follows:

Health for All June Otow of Japanese descent researched the needs of Asian and other ethnic groups for adult day health care and started a downtown center that included nursing services, rehabilitation, and day-care programs for the disabled and a health screening program for preschool children.

Asian Liaison Worker Hach Yasumura of Japanese descent became the Asian liaison worker for Sacramento County Department of Social Services upon his graduation. His task was to establish a planning and program exchange network among the various Asian groups and grass-roots agencies in the county and to coordinate existing and future services to the local Asian community.

Asian Resource Center May Lee of Chinese descent began a job training and employment service for Asian Americans and focused on the growing Asian immigrant and refugee populations who need English as a second language training, job testing and training, and employment placement in the greater Sacramento area. Periodic job fairs for adults and career planning workshops for Asian high school youth have resulted in strengthening the economic stability of the Asian American community.

Asian/Pacific Counseling Center Harriet Taniguchi of Japanese descent was instrumental in founding, with a group of Asian mental health and health care professionals, an Asian multilingual counseling program with staff representing major Asian ethnic groups. Funding came from the United Way, the minority mental health advisory board that oversees Sacramento County mental health funding, and various short-term state and federal grants, which have been shaped to meet the medical problems of Asians.

Southeast Asian Assistance Center Ninh Van Nguyen, a social work graduate and ordained Presbyterian minister of Vietnamese descent, started the Southeast Asian Assistance Center, which focused exclusively on the employment and family needs of Vietnamese, Hmong, Cambodian, Mien, and Thai refugees. The emphasis is on responding to the practical, everyday living needs of these populations.

Asian American Nursing Home Under the leadership of the Asian Community Center, led particularly by Japanese and Chinese prominent professionals in Sacramento, funds were raised through community campaign drives, large-scale bingo, and federal grants for the construction and operation of a ninety-bed Asian nursing home that serves Asian food and promotes Asian family care involvement for bed-ridden elderly clients. A former social work graduate student, Calvin Hara of Japanese descent, recently became the administrator of the nursing home. Graduate Asian American social work students participated in a county-wide research assessment project to pinpoint the needs of the Asian elderly.

The Sacramento model for Asian American community planning brings together social work students who conduct research, participate in Asian field placements, and later assume agency roles in the Asian social service community; Asian American social work faculty, who foster an interest in academic and research projects that benefit the local Asian needs; and Asian community leaders, who are responsive to the changing social trends of the Asian groups in need. There is a unique town and gown arrangement that has borne the fruit of Asian American social service agencies that are affecting the lives and well-being of Asian clients today. On the drawing boards for the Sacramento Vietnamese community are two research proposals for a Vietnamese elderly adult day health care center, written by Vanessa Nguyen, and a Vietnamese senior center patterned after the On Lok program in San Francisco, by Lena Chon.

Asian American social workers in heavily populated Asian metropolitan areas of the United States may wish to adopt this cooperative macro practice model, which involves social work students, faculty, and community leaders in a creative partnership.

Emerging Issues

Asian Americans are an almost 11 million member minority group in the United States. There are heavy populations in the western United States in Los Angeles–Long Beach, San Francisco, Honolulu, and Seattle; on the East Coast, there are moderate populations in New York City, Boston, and Washington, D.C.; and they are modestly represented in the American heartland (Chicago and Houston). As indicated in this chapter, Asian Americans have been the subject of racism and racial stereotypes and acts of racial violence and hate crimes, and they continue to cope with this stress.

At the beginning of the twenty-first century, Asian Americans are still aware of their weak influence on the political scene in the United States. With few Asian American politicians on the state and national levels, there is no political or legislative force to advocate for the rights of this group. There have been no cabinet-level appointments of Asian Americans at the presidential level in the history of the United States. Asian Americans were the focus of investigation in the 1997 Senate and House investigation on presidential campaign reform and abuse as a result of the 1996 Clinton versus Dole election. The selection of a Chinese American, Bill Lee, as the civil rights head of the Department of Justice in 1998 was heavily contested by the Republican Congress and sent a message about conservative politics and Asian Americans. Chinese dissenters who were expelled from the People's Republic of China and came to the United States for political refuge were ignored in 1998 and 1999 by the Clinton administration and U.S. State Department officials for fear that their counsel may offend U.S. and China relations.

Asian Americans need to organize themselves in an effective way on a par with the Japanese American Citizenship League, which has chapters in major cities where there is a Japanese American constituency and is a lobbying force at the national level in Washington, D.C. As the population of Asian Americans exceeds the 11 million mark, Asian Americans will be heard as a formative political, financial, technological, and scientific force to shape and influence the American political, medical, and engineering scene. An Asian American governor, Gary Locke, was elected in the state of Washington in 1998, which is a major breakthrough. However, this offers a small glimmer of hope in a realm of dominant forces that intentionally exclude the presence of Asian Americans as full partners in promise of the American dream.

Concluding Comment

Asian Americans/Pacific Islanders are diverse groups of ethnic persons who were born in or whose parents came from the continent of Asia and the Pacific areas. Lee offers a sensible appraisal of Asian Americans in the United States when he reports that, with the dawn of the twenty-first century, Asian Americans undoubtedly will play an increasingly important and complex role in American society. With the growth and expansion of Asia's economy, some Asian Americans are intermediaries between the two continents, whereas others are continuing the fight for freedom and democracy in their homelands. Lee observes:

> Some are achieving high office as governors of states or managers in corporations, whereas others are barely surviving on poverty wages or hiding from the Immigration and Naturalization Service. All are grappling with the age-old issues of place and identity that inhabit the boundaries between disparate cultures. Coming to understand the forces and conditions that have created such diversity requires far-reaching and diligent efforts. The task will continue to challenge scholars in the years ahead.[36]

The paradoxes of economic influence versus political underrepresentation, political dissent versus democratic exile, and places of leadership versus illegal immigration fuel the fires of trying to figure out the place of Asian Americans in the United States. With such a disparity of diversity among Asians and such nonrecognition by the dominant political forces of America, it will be interesting to see how Asian Americans steer their course in human history.

In the year 2005, Asian Americans/Pacific Islanders are still aware of their weak influence on the political scene in the United States. However, as their population nears 11 million, this group will be heard as a formative political and financial force in shaping and influencing the American political scene. At the same time, hard work, education, the drive for achievement, thriftiness, and helping each other have been ethnic-group qualities that have caused this group to cope with racism, prejudice, and discrimination in spite of societal barriers.

KEY WORDS AND CONCEPTS

Acculturative stress
Asian American/Pacific Islander
Chinese Exclusion Act of 1882
Cultural boundaries

Cultural duality
Family types
Interpersonal harmony
Psychohistorical responses

SUGGESTED INFORMATION SOURCES

Fong, Rowena. "Cultural Competence with Asian Americans," in Doman Lum, ed., *Culturally Competent Practice: A Framework for Understanding Diverse Groups and Justice Issues.* Belmont, CA: Thomson Brooks/Cole, 2007.

Lee, Evelyn, and Matthew R. Mock. "Asian Families: An Overview," in Monica McGoldrick, Joe Giordano, and Nydia Garcia-Preto, eds., *Ethnicity & Family Therapy.* New York: Guilford Press, 2005.

Morelli, Paula T. "Tanemura. Social Work Practice with Asian Americans," in Doman Lum, ed., *Cultural Competence, Practice Stages, and Client Systems: A Case Study Approach.* Belmont, CA: Thomson Brooks/Cole, 2005.

Wong, Janlee. "Asian Pacific Islanders," in Krishna L. Guadalupe and Doman Lum, ed., *Multidimensional Contextual Practice: Diversity and Transcendence.* Belmont, CA: Thomson Brooks/Cole, 2005

ENDNOTES

1. U.S. Bureau of Census, "U.S. Interim Projections by Age, Sex, Race, and Hispanic Origin, 2004, http://www.census.gov/ipc/www/usinterimproj.
2. Ibid.
3. C. Russell, *Radical and Ethnic Diversity: Asians, Blacks, Hispanic, Native Americans, and Whites* (Ithaca, NY: New Strategist Publications, 1998), p. 7.
4. U.S. Census Bureau, Census 2000. "U.S. Asian Population, Census 2000." Information Please Database: 2005, Pearson Education, Inc., http://www.infoplease.com/ipa/A0778584.html.
5. Russell, op. cit., p. 65.
6. R. Homma-True, "Asian American Women," in E. Lee, ed., *Working with Asian Americans: A Guide for Clinicians* (New York: Guilford Press, 1997), pp. 420–427; M. P. P. Root, "Women," in L. C. Lee and N. W. S. Zane, eds, *Handbook of Asian American Psychology* (Thousand Oaks, CA: Sage Publications, 1998), pp. 221–231.
7. R. Masaki and L. Wong, "Domestic Violence in the Asian Community," in E. Lee, ed., *Working with Asian Americans: A Guide for Clinicians* (New York: Guilford Press, 1997), pp. 439–451.
8. "College Degree Nearly Doubles Annual Earnings, Census Bureau Reports," *U.S. Census Bureau News,* http://www.census.gov/Press-Release/www/releases/archives/education/004214.html.
9. J. H. Lee, "Asian Median Income," *Theme,* 11/10/08, http://www.thememagazine.com/blog/asian median-income/.
10. U.S. Census Bureau, *Statistical Abstract of the United States: 2004–2005* (Washington, D.C.: U.S. Census Bureau), pp. 40, 452.
11. F. T. L. Leong, "Career Development and Vocational Behaviors," in L. C. Lee and N. W. S. Zane, eds., *Handbook of Asian American Psychology* (Thousand Oaks, CA: Sage Publications, 1998), pp. 359–398.
12. Freddie Mac and the National Coalition for Asian Pacific American Community Development, "Asian American Housing and Homeownership Trends," http://ncvaonline.org/archive/prj_GSE_APIHousing_Briefing_Chicago_080505.pdf.
13. *Health, United States, 2004.* National Centers for Health Statistics, Tables 19 and 28, http://www.cdc.gov/nchs/data/hus/hus04trend.pdf#002.

14. E. Lee, "Overview: The Assessment and Treatment of Asian American Families," in E. Lee, ed., *Working with Asian Americans: A Guide for Clinicians* (New York: Guilford Press, 1997), pp. 3–36.
15. L. C. Lee, "An Overview," in L. C. Lee and N. W. S. Zane, eds., *Handbook of Asian American Psychology* (Thousand Oaks, CA: Sage Publications, 1998), p. 16.
16. C. M. Loo, *Chinese America: Mental Health and Quality of Life in the Inner City* (Thousand Oaks, CA: Sage Publications, 1998).
17. Ibid., xxii.
18. Ibid., xxviii.
19. D. Lum, *Social Work Practice & People of Color: A Process Stage Approach*, 5th ed. (Belmont, CA: Thomson, Brooks/Cole, 2004).
20. D. Lum and C. Guzzetta, "Should Programs and Service Delivery Systems Be Culture-Specific in Their Design?" in D. de Anda, ed., *Controversial Issues in Multiculturalism* (Boston: Allyn & Bacon, 1997), pp. 54–70.
21. D. Sue, W. S. Mak, and D. W. Sue, "Ethnic Identity," in L. C. Lee and N. W. S. Zane, eds., *Handbook of Asian American Psychology* (Thousand Oaks, CA: Sage Publications, 1998), p. 312.
22. A. P. Iglehart and R. M. Becerra, *Social Services and the Ethnic Community* (Boston: Allyn & Bacon, 1995).
23. J. L. Chin, "Toward a Psychology of Difference: Psychotherapy for a Culturally Diverse Population," in J. L. Chin, V. De La Cancela, and Y. M. Jenkins, eds., *Diversity in Psychotherapy: The Politics of Race, Ethnicity, and Gender* (Westport, CT: Praeger, 1993), pp. 69–91.
24. E. Lee, op. cit., pp. 26–27.
25. Ibid., pp. 28–33.
26. L. Uba, *Asian Americans: Personality Patterns, Identity, and Mental Health* (New York: Guilford Press, 1994).
27. Ibid., pp. 61–87.
28. M. K. Ho, "Social Work Practice with Asian Americans," in A. Morales and B. W. Sheafor, eds., *Social Work: A Profession of Many Faces*, 8th ed. (Boston: Allyn & Bacon, 1998), pp. 465–483.
29. Lum, op. cit., Chapter 8.
30. T. V. Tran and R. Wright, Jr., "Social Support and Subjective Well-Being among Vietnamese Refugees," *Social Service Review* 60 (1986): 449–459.
31. J. L. Hodge, D. K. Struckmann, and L. D. Trost, *Cultural Bases of Racism and Group Oppression* (Berkeley, CA: Two Riders Press, 1975).
32. E. Lee, op. cit., pp. 11–13.
33. B. W. K. Yee, L. N. Huang, and A. Lew, "Families: Life-Span Socialization in a Cultural Context," in L. C. Lee and N. W. S. Zane, eds., *Handbook of Asian American Psychology* (Thousand Oaks, CA: Sage Publications, 1998), pp. 83–135.
34. Lum, op. cit., Chapter 8.
35. M. Janofsky, "Some Legal Immigrant Benefits May Return," *Sacramento Bee*, January 25, 1999, A4.
36. L. C. Lee, op. cit., pp. 18, 19.

chapter 23

Social Work Practice with Indigenous Peoples and Tribal Communities*

Prefatory Comment

The concept of *cultural competency* is central to social work but often difficult for new students to fully comprehend. Perhaps this difficulty is not surprising because, for a long period of time, the United States embraced a "melting pot" philosophy, assuming that, as generations passed, people would throw off their old cultures and meld into a similar set of beliefs and cultural practices. Of course, the descendants of each immigrant group thought the resulting culture would be much like theirs and chafed at the vestiges of other cultures, particularly those racially and ethnically different, that persisted in their difference.

Perhaps more than any other group, the Indigenous population (variously called Native Peoples, American Indians, Alaska Natives, First Nation Peoples, and Native Americans) resisted assimilation. After all, they did not experience a voluntary or involuntary transition to a new land—others invaded their land. Although there were hundreds of tribes, each with some unique elements of culture, their preservation of cultural uniqueness was substantial enough that the new social worker must carefully consider practice modifications that are specifically responsive to the needs of America's 4.5 million Indigenous people. Indeed, social workers can expect to work with members of the Indigenous population group, as it is the most vulnerable to social problems of all racial or ethnic groups addressed in this section of *Social Work: A Profession of Many Faces*.

In this chapter, some specific adaptations are identified through the lens of the Ecosystems Model and illustrative case examples. The chapter does not intend to be inclusive of all of the variations in Native culture or to address all of the social issues they experience. Rather, it is anticipated that readers will increase their *cultural competency* to this part of the U.S. population, avoid initial assumptions

---

*This chapter was prepared by Roe Bubar, associate professor of social work, ethnic studies, and women's studies, Colorado State University, and Dana Klar, assistant professor of social work, Lindenwood University, St. Charles, Missouri.

> that might harm relationships with Native clients, and provide a base for continued learning.

Indigenous peoples today are located in rural areas (i.e., homelands, reservations, pueblos, Rancherias, villages, colonies), urban and suburban communities, and in geographically isolated areas throughout the United States. The movement of Indigenous peoples among these locations is common, and sense of place, as well as connection to tribal homelands, remains important in the twenty-first century. *Indigenous peoples* define themselves tribally, and tribalism affects the social, cultural, and political aspects of daily life. Therefore many Native peoples define themselves in terms of their tribal affiliation first and then as Native or Native American. There continues to be reclamation of all things Indigenous, and recognition of enculturation is emerging in the social science literature as one potential protective factor for Native youth. Given the high out-of-marriage rates in the Indigenous population, many Native people today identify as "mixed bloods" and claim descendency, which presents individual complications for enrollment and thus identity challenges. Some tribes have responded to the needs of their members and descendents by adjusting enrollment criteria.

In some tribal communities, economic development has enabled tribes to reduce unemployment and improve conditions in their homeland areas, whereas other tribes less strategically located or less resource rich continue to struggle with some of the highest levels of poverty and unemployment in the country. Indian nations, tribal communities, and Indigenous peoples remain the most diverse group within the United States today.

The power to name and label oneself is both cultural and political. Even though Indigenous peoples refer to themselves as "Indian," the term "Indian" is not a preferred label for non-Natives to use. However the term "Indian" remains embedded in many legal and political terms defined within policies and legislation and thus provides a particular legal meaning and status. Use of the term *Indigenous* is the most inclusive yet may not be preferred by many tribal communities and peoples since it is not tribally specific, although it is more inclusive globally. The term Native American will not be used in this chapter since it is not as inclusive and does not specifically include Alaska Natives or Native Hawaiians and First Nations, a term most often used in reference to the Indigenous peoples in Canada. The terms Native and Indigenous are used interchangeably in this chapter to refer to this population group.

Native people today are located in communities often set apart from the American mainstream. In addition, Native issues and concerns are highly invisible in the U.S. mainstream, whether we consider the news, Internet, or other media sources. Many have come to refer to Indigenous peoples as the "invisible" minority, partially because 65 percent of the population lives off reservation and remains somewhat "hidden" in urban or rural areas. Most Americans study about Native peoples as though they were the people of the past with little emphasis on contemporary issues or contemporary tribal communities. This tendency, coupled with the fact that Natives make up just over 1.5 percent of the U.S. population, also contributes to the "invisibility" of Native peoples and Indigenous issues.

Current Demographics

In 2007 the U.S. Census indicated that Indigenous peoples comprise 4.5 million people. The Native population is younger than the population as a whole, with a median age of 31, compared with 36.4 years for the U.S. total,[1] and Indigenous peoples have one of the highest out-of-marriage rates. More people are identified as Cherokee than any other tribal affiliation, yet the Navajo Nation, the second largest tribe, maintains the largest land base of any Indian nation. Their reservation extends into three states: New Mexico, Arizona, and Utah.[2]

Currently there are 562 federally recognized tribes, 230 of which are located within the state of Alaska. There are 322 federally recognized Indian reservations, and most are located in the West.[3] Federally recognized tribes are eligible for services that are provided by the Bureau of Indian Affairs (BIA). In addition, there are a number of state-recognized tribes, which means they are recognized and have a certain status within the state in which they reside but are not necessarily recognized by the federal government. Federal recognition is a process in which tribes either apply to meet set criteria within the BIA's administrative process or lobby Congress for recognition via legislation. Today there are many tribes that remain unrecognized by either state or federal governments.

Key Social Issues

Sovereignty

Tribal communities represent sovereign Indian nations, and their sovereign status predates both the U.S. Constitution and the arrival of colonist or settler populations in this country. *Sovereignty* includes the concept of self-governance and thus internal control over land, resources, and membership. Therefore, there are federal, state, and also tribal governmental structures within the United States. The U.S. Constitution is the organic authority for federal and state existence but not for tribes. As a result, Native people are not considered minorities but instead are viewed as Indigenous. Because of their nationhood status, tribes have a unique relationship with the U.S. government. Many people believe that Indigenous peoples receive money or entitlements from the government for being "Indian," which is not accurate. Instead, the federal government's relationship with Indian nations is described as a *trust relationship:* one in which the federal government is obligated or has a duty to uphold treaty promises. Indigenous nations were compelled to grant to the United States large tracts of aboriginally held lands and reserved unto themselves smaller pieces of land in exchange for promises that the United States is obligated to fulfill as a party to treaty agreements. The United States is thus obligated via laws, treaties, and pledges to protect the sovereign status of tribes in this country, to protect tribal resources, and to provide education and health care to federally recognized tribes and tribal members. Native peoples place a high value and emphasis on the sovereign status of Native nations, and sovereignty is considered a critical concept for social workers to understand and respect when interacting with tribal communities and Indigenous peoples, whether working with urban or reservation-based communities.

Socioeconomic and Persistent Poverty Issues

On virtually every social indicator, the U.S. Native population falls substantially behind the dominant population—the white, non-Hispanic segment of the population. Consider the comparison of the two population groups in Table 23.1, compiled from data released by the U.S. Census Bureau in 2007. It is apparent that the Indigenous people in the United States are exceptionally vulnerable to social problems.

Poverty is apparent in most reservation communities, as well as the experience of many urban Native people. Housing is a serious challenge in reservation communities with 40 percent of available housing considered inadequate, and one in five homes is found without plumbing.[4] In urban areas, the average household income reported for

Table 23.1

Social Indicator Comparison of U. S. White, not Hispanic Population with American Indian Alaska Native (AIAN) Population in 2004

Social Indicator	White, not Hispanic	AIAN, not Hispanic
Median age	40.1 years	32.7 years
Married (age 15 and older)	57.3 %	42.2 %
Birth to unmarried woman in past year	20.5 %	50.2 %
Household headed by female, no husband present	8.9 %	20.9 %
Education level		
Less than high school	11.4 %	21.6 %
High school graduate	88.6 %	78.4 %
College graduate	29.7 %	15.1 %
Median household income	$48,784	$30,815
Poverty rate		
All ages	8.8 %	25.1 %
Under age 18	11.0 %	31.6 %
65 and older	7.2 %	19.7 %
Owner of own home	73.9 %	56.8 %
Median value of home	$153,396	$92,753

Source: U.S. Census Bureau, *The American Community—American Indians and Alaska Natives: 2004* (Washington, D.C.: U.S. Department of Commerce, 2007).

the 2000 Census was $15,312, compared with the average urban non-Native household income of $22,736.[5] Creating economic solutions to poverty and unemployment is key to addressing social challenges within Indigenous homeland and urban areas.

Over the past 25 years, there has been a push for Indigenous economic development. One common method to encourage such development is nation-owned business enterprises. These enterprises are extremely diverse and include the use of tribally owned natural resources seen in timber enterprises or in tribally created recreational offerings, best known for gaming operations. Casinos, in particular, are often thought of as "the solution" for Indigenous poverty given the economic development challenges in most tribal areas. However, while gaming has been successful for strategically located tribes, many tribes have yet to experience much profit. For the small number of tribes where gaming operations have been successful, profits have been used to subsidize schools, recreation, health care, and provide more social services for tribal members.

Gaming as an economic enterprise is limited in its capacity to enrich many tribal communities. Most reservations were established on "undesirable" land, in rural and extremely isolated locations. The successful casinos are located on or near major interstates, thus able to draw from large metropolitan areas, or have access to the traveling public. There are only a dozen or so large, successful tribally owned and operated gaming operations. It is important to consider that tribal members remain divided over economic development opportunities such as casinos, tourism, and development of natural resources. While some Native people see such development as positive sources of income, others view it as devastating compromises to cultural and spiritual integrity.[6]

Sovereignty and nation-building are critical components of Indigenous economic development. It is important to understand that for economic development in Indian country to be successful it must take account of sovereign nation status, historical realities, and tribally specific and culturally appropriate methodology. Cornell and Kalt recognize that economic success is tied to a *nation-building approach,* one that puts genuine decision-making power in Indigenous hands, backs up that power with capable institutions of self-governance, matches those institutions to Indigenous political culture, has a strategic orientation toward long-term outcomes, and is guided by public-spirited leadership.[7]

Unfortunately, Indigenous economic development is subjected to continued threat of discrimination and oppression as witnessed with the fraud perpetuated on six separate gaming Native nations, and the general public, by Jack Abramoff and Michael Scanlon, former political lobbyists. These six nations together contributed more than $82 million for lobbying efforts to occur on their behalf. Unbeknownst to the tribes, Abramoff and Scanlon devised a scheme together where they pocketed $40 million of that money, in effect providing to the nations much less than the original bargain. These six nations were not found to be participants in the actual fraud, yet they experienced national embarrassment in their association with Abramoff.[8] This crime amplified the reality that Native nations remain a target of negative stereotypes that can lead to attempts to take advantage of the less sophisticated consumer. Until more tribal members complete higher education and gain experience in mainstream politics and the global economy, the potential for such crime perpetuation exists.

Education

The history of Indian education in the United States is often contextualized in a *historical trauma* framework. Forced removal of children to distant boarding schools created serious harm for individual children, families, and tribal communities and is often considered one of the most genocidal policies ever passed in the history of the country. Starting in the late 1800s and continuing into the early 1970s, forced Indian education removed Native children as young as 4 to live in boarding school settings located far away, as well as more local institutions. Boarding schools were often run and administered by a myriad of Christian missionaries, and children were typically kept in boarding school settings until the age of majority, when many returned to their tribal communities. Separated from family and tribal communities, children were forced to assimilate into white mainstream Christian culture—where use of Native language, spirituality, clothing, or culture was forbidden—was enforced, and compliance was obtained with physical punishment and, in extreme cases, torture.[9] There are some Natives who consider their boarding school experiences to be more positive and were thankful that, in times of great economic struggle, boarding school offered both food and shelter. However, the majority of Indigenous peoples in the United States, Canada, and Australia consider the policy to be a genocidal example of Indigenous historical trauma and liken their experiences to those who lived through the holocaust. The Canadian government has made a formal apology and reached a settlement to compensate First Nations peoples for the trauma that was caused from their country's boarding school policies. In Australia, aboriginal children taken from their homeland areas and placed in institutionalized school settings are referred to as the "stolen generation."*

In the United States today, Indian boarding schools still exist but are voluntary in attendance. The 1975 Indian Self-Determination and Education Assistance Act, the Tribally Controlled Schools Act of 1988, and the 1978 Educational Amendments Act have each affected Indian education issues, thus providing for more local control, as well as restructuring BIA and tribally operated schools to obtain direct funding.[10] Indian education continues to face serious challenges in tribal communities, and students are not afforded the same access to educational resources available to other American students. Today the National Indian School Board Association is responsible for addressing local school board training, and the trend has been to empower Native communities around education. Public schools are also eligible to obtain funding for Native student special needs under the Johnson-O'Malley Act of 1934. Bilingual and Native language immersion programs have started up in more recent years. For example, in the Kamehameha schools, a new online program allows Native Hawaiian adults to study alongside other family members in an effort to reclaim their culture and language. Other new trends include making classrooms more culturally relevant by including elders and tribal members in the classroom, providing more Native-appropriate curriculum, and incorporating Native language in the curriculum.

---

*The movie *Rabbit-Proof Fence* tells the true story of one aboriginal family's experiences when the government forcefully took three children from their homeland area, their subsequent escape from the Moore River Native Settlement, and their 1,500-mile trek back home on foot to Jigalong.

Health and Mental Health Issues

Today access to adequate health care and services for health-related problems are some of the greatest challenges facing contemporary tribal communities. Prior to colonization, Native peoples addressed and administered their own health needs. Different tribal members specifically addressed health challenges, specializing in some combination of plant medicines and healing ceremonies.[11] Health needs and *health disparities* continue to be two of the most critical issues facing Indigenous peoples and tribal communities today. Life expectancy rates have hit an all-time high in the United States, with overall life expectancy at 78.1 years of age in 2006 (80.7 years of age for women and 75.4 years of age for men). Native people today have the lowest life expectancy of any ethnic population within the United States, where Native men have a life expectancy of 69.4 years and Native women have a life expectancy of 77.6 years.[12] Cancer, heart disease, accidents, and diabetes are the four leading causes of death for Indigenous peoples in the United States.

Provision of health care by the federal government is considered a treaty right for federally recognized tribes.[13] Of increasing concern are the health disparities experienced by Indigenous peoples and the underfunding of treaty-promised health care for Natives in both urban and tribal community settings. In *A Quiet Crisis: Federal Funding and Unmet Funding Needs in Indian Country,* the U.S. Commission on Civil Rights chronicles the large deficit in spending for Native programs historically and describes the present state of health disparities for Native peoples. Most Native people living in tribal communities do not have access to the same programs, services, and resources experienced by other Americans, even though the federal government is obligated to provide such services. In many tribal communities, there are limited health facilities with inadequate medical equipment to provide health care services, and the average age of the facilities is thirty-two years. The majority of the Indigenous population lives in urban areas yet has less access to health care and health care facilities than others. Natives access health care less than any other ethnic group. For comparative purposes, the doctor visit rate for Anglo Americans is 239, Asian Americans 233, African Americans 211, and Natives only 54.

The Indian Health Service (IHS) is a federally funded government agency responsible for the delivery of health care in urban and tribal community settings. IHS serves approximately 60 percent of the eligible 2.5 million people. Funding isn't statutorily determined, which makes IHS funding vulnerable to annual discretionary appropriations, and it doesn't accrue annual increases to keep pace with inflation like Medicare and Medicaid funding. Over the past 30 years, a pattern of chronic underfunding has occurred, and this arguably contributes significantly to the disparate health status of Natives making them 20 to 25 years behind other Americans in health status. Consider the cost of health care in 2003: $5,775 was spent for the average American person, $5,915 for Medicare recipients, $5,214 for veterans, $3,803 per federal prisoner, and $1,914 per Native in the IHS system.[15]

Alcohol and drug use represents a serious challenge in the untreated mental health needs of Native peoples. Mental health services are severely limited and largely provided by the behavioral health program within Indian Health Service

(IHS). Suicide remains a critical concern for Native youth. Mental health problems persist in populations where poverty exists, and Natives are no exception. Many tribal communities have developed outpatient tribally run alcohol programs. Mental health services are even more seriously limited with regard to tribal children living in tribal communities.

HIV/AIDS has significantly affected many communities of color, including tribal communities. With limited health care and an overall lack of prevention programs, HIV/AIDS and other sexually transmitted diseases and infections have presented serious health concerns to Native communities. In recent years, funding has been available to provide some outreach, prevention, and educational materials developed to specifically address HIV/AIDS in urban and reservation tribal communities. Health programming that includes Native-specific images and HIV/AIDS walks and events can be found in a variety of settings. The National Native American AIDS Prevention Center (NNAAPC) works with a number of agency and tribal partners to address HIV/AIDS prevention for Native peoples.

Family

Family within an Indigenous worldview is inclusive of extended family members. Much importance is placed on family, tribe, and thus community. In a Native worldview, great emphasis is placed on the idea and importance of "other" versus the emphasis on "self" experienced in the non-Native worldview. Since family is held up as important, family is defined broadly and, in a general sense, many Native people define family via clan, blood, societies, marriage, and adoption (both formal and informal). Familial roles and the concept of family differ significantly from definitions of family and familial roles within the non-Native context. For example, the roles of aunts, uncles, and cousins, as well as the concept of adoption, can vary greatly within the various Indigenous communities. Extended family networks have been a source of resilience in tribal communities. Native families traditionally practiced kinship care and continue to do so today, evidencing strong family networks. Many grandparents are taking care of grandchildren to support single-parent family needs and rescue their grandchildren from serious challenges faced by their adult children.

Spirituality

Indigenous spirituality is diverse and, like other religions, provides an explanation of how the world came to be, the forces around them, death, and other great mysteries of life. Some scholars claim it may be more appropriate to refer to Native religion as the "sacred and the ceremony" since many tribes did not have an actual word for religion. Lack of true understanding of Native spiritual life has led to cultural misunderstandings and cultural appropriation of Native spirituality. Native spirituality is interwoven with Native cultural life and involves complex relationships with the natural world and the homeland environment.

Many urban and tribal human services programs include traditional practices and healing as a part of the services that are offered. Western-type mental health resources are often limited in tribal community settings and traditional healing offers Native people an indigenous approach to health, healing, and spiritual practices.

Indigenous spiritual belief systems are an area of fascination for many non-Natives. Previous federal policies outlawed many Native spiritual practices, some of which have been characterized as cultural genocide. As a result, many tribes do not allow non-Natives or non-members to participate in their ceremonies and cultural practices. In mainstream film and media, Native people are often stereotyped by their spiritual beliefs or practices. Given this fascination by non-Natives and past federal policies, it is important for social workers to approach Indigenous spiritual beliefs and traditional cultural practices with respect and refrain from prying into areas that people have not brought up or are reluctant to openly discuss.

Indigenous Women

Indigenous women have a history of egalitarian relationships and being viewed with respect within their tribal communities. Historically, in many tribal practices, Native women had decision-making ability over land, children, leadership, marital status, and resources.[16] Even in tribes that practiced strict sex roles, women were viewed in interdependent relationships with men and were accorded the respect that accompanied their roles within the tribal community. Many Indigenous women define their identities in terms of their relationship to the land and to family/tribe/community. Gender is mediated by tribal identity, in some instances motherhood, and family relationships within the urban or tribal community setting. *Heteropatriarchy,* the intersection of oppressions such that heterosexuality and patriarchy are presented as the natural order was a practice brought to the New World by colonists, and today tribal communities have struggled with sexism, homophobia, and gendered policies that have placed Native women, as well as members of the Native lesbian, gay, bisexual, and transgender (LGBT) community, in more marginalized situations. Various genders and gender identities were well established and accepted in many tribal communities before contact with settler populations.

Native women experience the highest rates of sexual assault, domestic violence, and stalking of any women within the United States. Native women are 2.5 times more likely to be sexually assaulted and 2 times more likely to be stalked than other women.[17] In a 2006 study, Native providers from around the country identified race/ethnicity as the major risk factor for sexual assault and other forms of violence. Native women discussed the idea that non-Natives are not knowledgeable and thus unconcerned about the violence and safety issues affecting tribal communities.[18] Native women stand out today as activists and program administrators developing sustainable initiatives to address violence against both women and children, as well as creating prevention programming for Native men.

Children and Adolescents

Native children have always been central to Indigenous life and community. Parenting practices may vary in tribal communities, but in general children are viewed as important within the family and thus tribal milieu. Many Native children today still have access to a cultural life and traditional teaching practices. Child maltreatment is a critical social issue since health care dollars and prevention programming resources are not as available as they are for other American children. Safety concerns are critical in many tribal communities, and unintentional injuries are the number one cause of death for tribal children.[19] Child maltreatment also poses serious health and safety risks, and Native children are overrepresented in child abuse cases, foster care placement, and fatality cases.[20] In response, a number of tribes have developed children's advocacy center programs and three national organizations—the Native American Children's Alliance, the Tribal Law and Policy Institute, and the National Indian Child Welfare Association (NICWA)— that provide training, resources, technical assistance, and public policy analysis regarding child abuse and neglect, particularly for NICWA as it applies to the Indian Child Welfare Act.

Violence and Criminal Justice

Indigenous peoples have historically had justice systems in place, and many modern alternative justice programs have features of Indigenous justice incorporated within them. In 1999 the American Indians and Crime Report made the front page of newspapers across the country announcing that Native Americans experience the highest violent crime rates of any people within the United States and that the crimes perpetrated upon them is committed primarily by non-Natives.[21] Crime and mistreatment of Native people is largely uncovered in mainstream media. Native people are statistically over-represented in the criminal justice system. Tribal sovereignty yields authority to create judicial programming in tribal communities, but chronic underfunding of judicial services and case law has crippled progress in rehabilitation and crime prevention. For some criminal acts on tribal lands, federal, state, and tribal law could apply, and convictions of most felony crimes committed on reservations will result in incarceration within the federal penal system. Criminal jurisdiction is a complex issue for tribal lands and people.

In tribal communities, there are infrequent incarcerations and historically little use of a penal system. And while there are some jails present in tribal communities, many communities do not have a system of secure confinement or jail facilities even for the most serious of crimes. Traditionally there were ways of punishing or providing a consequence to tribal members who violated social and moral codes of behavior. These traditional practices are part of *customary law* since they were traditional in a number of tribal communities. These customary practices include public shaming and ridicule, whippings, banishment from the community, termination of membership rights, restitution whether by financial payments or providing labor, and community service.[22] Mediation, family conferencing, and peacemaker courts, which reflect traditional Indigenous justices, are contemporary methods in a number of tribal communities. The Navajo Nation, for example, has a number of peacemaker courts in place, and mediation is used in many First Nations communities in Canada.

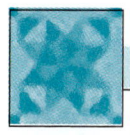

The Ecosystems Framework

Historical Challenges and Federal Indian Policy

Prior to contact (with the white population in the United States), the Indigenous peoples had a sophisticated culture, well-developed societies, and complex governmental systems in place. Successful in living off the land and maintaining healthy lifestyles, tribes were in a strong position when settlers came to the Americas. Recognizing the status of tribes, Spain, England, France, the Dutch, and later the American colonies entered into treaty negotiations with tribal nations. Settlers brought new diseases to America, and Native people died in large numbers from the introduction of those diseases. Once weakened by disease and reduced in numbers, tribes were vulnerable to colonist populations. Federal Indian policy began with treaty negotiations and changed over the course of the formation of the United States. These policies encouraged further oppression, removal, and diminishment of tribal nations. This process of colonization by settler groups is considered to be ongoing since the impact of many federal policies is still experienced today. The continued negative impact of federal policies is conceptualized as a form of structural racism. Given this treatment, there is a historic distrust and disconnection particularly with outside agencies, some state governments, and non-Natives.

In young adulthood, when young people become aware of the "American ideals" of justice and freedom that this country was founded upon, it presents a contradiction for many young Natives considering how very different that experience has been for Native people in the eighteenth, nineteenth, twentieth, and even twenty-first centuries. This revelation can be difficult for Indigenous youth, and many experience being torn between loyalty to country and loyalty to ancestors and tribal traditions. This disillusionment and anger at times is turned inward and can manifest as depression, or it may be turned outward and experienced as acting out.[23] One movement in the United States has been to reclaim all that is Indigenous, and cultural revitalization attempts are being introduced in both urban and reservation communities to embrace culture that was lost or taken away.

These experiences and other specific impacts of policy, particularly removal, assimilation efforts, and termination, were experienced in great intensity—especially for the direct descendants of war or for others who are the survivors of the forced boarding school era—and have culminated in what is referred to as *historical trauma*. There is a growing body of work and important interventions being developed to help address historical trauma for the Native population.[24]

Deloria and Lytle identify six primary "eras" of tribal–federal relations that many historians, legal theorists, and academicians turn to today to categorize the historical experience of Indigenous peoples in America. These six periods of time have vacillated between time periods with particularly harsh policies to fairly positive time periods for the treatment of Native peoples. We refer to these six distinct periods as 1) Discovery, Conquest, and Treaty-making; 2) Removal and Relocation; 3) Allotment and Assimilation; 4) Reorganization; 5) Termination; and 6) Self-determination.[25]

Discovery, Conquest, and Treaty-making (1532–1828) was a period that posed particularly difficult concessions and compromises by Native nations. Even though treaties are old and have been broken, they are still considered supreme law, are thus enforceable today, and represent the foundation of tribal sovereignty. The *Removal and Relocation* period (1828–1887) posed significant continued harm to Native nations as the new government rejected the notion that settlers and Native nations could live peacefully as neighbors. Nations were forced to migrate westward, and on many forced marches, such as the Cherokee Nation's "Trail of Tears," many lives were lost. *Allotment and Assimilation* (1887–1928) was the period of federal policy aimed at forcing Native nations to assimilate through private property ownership (by means of individually allotting reservation lands) and through forced boarding school attendance. During this period, the Native land base that had been provided through treaty was reduced from over more than 138 million acres to only 48 million acres. *Reorganization* (1928–1945) was a period of revitalization for Native nations. The Indian Reorganization Act called for an official end to the devastating allotment policy and provided opportunities for economic development and self-governance. During the *Termination* era (1945–1961), the federal government passed a policy to terminate the status of more than 100 tribes. Many of those tribes remain ineligible for BIA services and are still not federally recognized today. Termination policies were implemented by the government in an attempt to relinquish their responsibilities for Native nations to the states. Tribal sovereignty took severe blows during this phase as some nations lost their recognized status, while many others were brought under state civil and criminal jurisdiction.

Self-determination (1961–present) characterizes the current era of federal–tribal relations, recognizing the shift in emphasis in Congress that resulted from the socially oriented Great Society Programs of the 1960s. Finally, Indian nations are being given the opportunity to design, manage, and control their own federally funded programs. Tribal nations are more fully asserting their sovereignty now than in any period since the initial treaties were signed. While Native nations recognize the freedoms and opportunities of this positive phase, most are cautious in their optimism as they have an abundance of historical information that disallows a prolonged sense of security with the status of federal–tribal relations.

Environmental-Structural Factors

Many American citizens have changed their attitudes regarding both the historic wrongs and current treatment of Native people. However, injustices embedded in past and current policies are what were referred to earlier in this chapter as *institutional or structural racism*. State governments continually assault tribal sovereignty and pressure federal agencies and Congress to side with states' rights on many issues, thereby further diminishing tribal sovereignty. So while individual attitudes may have changed over time, there continues to be an ongoing impact that posits Natives in a seriously marginalized position resulting from the racialization of Natives carried out in ongoing policies and procedures. For example, there continues to be significant underfunding of health care, education, and justice systems in tribal communities, which contributes to lower educational attainment by Native youth, shorter life expectancy rates, serious safety risks for women and children, and the mounting untreated mental health challenges. Lack of federal funding has also affected the sustainability of tribal programs. The U.S. Commission on Civil Rights has characterized this level of underfunding as a human rights concern.[26]

Native communities continue to be isolated, with less access to resources and less access to the typical structures of society, including education, health, and welfare. Thus resources available to other Americans are not as plentiful or available to Native peoples. Even in the areas where Native communities are empowered and taking control of their economy or programs, progress remains slow, and tribal members are still subjected to acts of racism and marginalization within the states where their tribal communities are located.

The continued reference to Natives and tribes as imagery for fierce-looking team mascots and stereotypical advertising is a form of continued discrimination, and many Native people experience this as an unacceptable form of American racism. Americans take for granted, for example, the name "Washington Redskins," and are largely unaware of its potential for harm to Native people. The negative impact and potential for encouraging lower self-esteem for Native youth and their identity development is of concern when *Native imagery* is presented more as an "object" fixed in time or labeled with racialized terminology. In the twenty-first century, it is hard to imagine any other ethnic or racial group in America being labeled in such a way that is then embraced by the majority of Americans.

The trend is to be more inclusive of tribes and Native people's voices in social welfare policy initiatives, research, case management, and program planning. Universities and research centers are increasingly engaging in "community-based and participatory" research initiatives that allow for full engagement of the community. In this form of research, tribes are included as partners, and Natives are involved in each phase of a project. Many Native people believe this approach will lead to less *appropriated knowledge* (knowledge that has been acquired under the pretense of helping the Native community but that ultimately does not provide any benefits), and therefore the much needed benefits of the projects will return to the tribal community.

Cultural Considerations

There is tremendous diversity in Indigenous populations within the United States, and it is critical for social workers to consider and ask their clients about individual tribal customs and practices. Indigenous cultural considerations are complex and often shift depending on the context and nuance of the social or family situation, and some tribal practices are simply very different than the practices of other tribes. There are, however, some cultural values that are found in many different tribal communities. These include a sense of generosity, spirituality, emphasis on "other" versus the individual, and sense of time and place.

In a Native worldview, time is not viewed rigidly. Rather, emphasis is on personal relations, and considerable value is placed on taking the time for family and other necessary social interactions. Also, sense of place and connection to homeland areas resonates for many Natives, even those with relocated populations. Generosity, too, can be seen in formal and informal gifting, sharing knowledge, time, and helping to care for others. Finally, spirituality is considered central to health and happiness, and living in balance is a cultural value embraced in most tribal communities. In an Indigenous worldview, spirituality is connected with all other aspects of life, and this is how health and harmony is achieved. Many Indigenous people integrate Native belief systems with Christian practices. Thus, use of Western medicine may be fully embraced or mediated with the use of traditional healing methods and medicine people.

Family, Group, and Community Practice Considerations

Intervention techniques when working with Indigenous people should be client-centered, group focused, and concerned with the well-being of the whole. Thus the Ecosystems Model must be adapted to reflect the culture by addressing family, group, clan or tribe, and community simultaneously.

Family When there is a social issue to address, the family must define the problem and be active participants in identifying the solution. Great resistance will be encountered if a social worker (particularly one who is not of the tribal community) attempts to define the family's needs. It is important to note that many Native people are carefully trained in family relationships and traditions, and that person's social place is largely determined by family connections. For these reasons, family involvement in social work intervention is critically important as fulfillment of family obligations, and a comfort level with current family interactions is crucial for Native peoples' mental health. Important decisions generally require the approval of significant family members (spouses or elders). In particular, extended family approval and involvement is important when traditional spiritual help is being considered. One example of implementing culturally competent programming can be seen in a variety of treatment programs that incorporate tribal elders as consultants or advisors. There is great diversity in tribal responses and programming as it relates to the familiar roles and tribal customs and practices.

Native identity is also rooted in tribal membership. Native people often refer to themselves as members of the Native community, regardless of their geographic location. Many identify first with their nation or tribe, second with a clan or society to which they belong, and lastly as a Native or Native American. Social cooperation is often valued over independent decision making.

Group Group involvement in decision making is compatible with Native culture. For example, one of the authors previously worked with an American Indian graduate studies program at a major university in a metropolitan area. The Native students in the program were honored with full scholarships for their two years of study and were provided numerous professional development opportunities. The students often experienced these years in closely knit groups (primarily composed of Native students) who became their "community" away from home.

As with any group, the student needs were dynamic, and the programmatic responses were the same. A repeated theme was a student request for an organizing force that called together "elders" to assist and support "younger" students. Initially, without a second year and thus more experienced MSW student cohort in place, the program instituted a "host family" system wherein Native students were matched with affiliated mainstream families who lived in the area and could serve as a resource to the students (e.g., provide a warm meal, a homelike setting, information about the university community, and advice on how the students may meet their shopping and recreational needs). Over time, feedback indicated that this programming, dependent of course upon the families involved, could at times feel paternalistic, and it was suggested that the graduate program instead provide a "mentor program," wherein a second-year student would be randomly assigned to mentor a first-year student. Through this program, similar assistance would be provided to the new student, yet this programming would only involve the Native community. This mentoring program survived many years, yet it also encountered difficulties as it became clear that some students were in conflict with their assigned mentors or mentees, thus there existed inequities in the assistance the program was meant to provide. It is important to note there are historic and modern intertribal tensions and differences that may emerge.

Students were consulted and suggested a programmatic change to more informal mentoring, programmatic offerings of advice and referral, and a voluntary "secret pal" program was instituted. This final method of group interaction and support has proven successful. This example of dynamic group work illustrates a number of points that are important in working with the Native population:

1. The Native group members wanted opportunities for group participation and demonstrated responsibility toward others.
2. The community and its needs were dynamic and sought a dynamic environment in which to flourish.
3. Fluidity of style was important, though the group purpose remained the same.
4. It was important that the group felt empowered to voice modifications needed to address their concerns.
5. The movement over the years in the methodology was from an externally imposed framework to one of self-government (following the maturity of the program).
6. This group participation provided a culturally effective framework for addressing the cultural adjustment issues experienced by the students encountering the most drastic cultural and environmental changes.
7. Many of these groupings or pairings remained close long after departure from the program, indicating the sense of community this group work created. It allowed for a much stronger bond than typical student programming.

Community Working with Native communities is critically important in the development of programs, developing collaborative relationships, or gaining support for existing programs. Tribal communities are unique, and, while some issues and common challenges persist across tribal communities, it remains important to understand what accounts for the differences, as well as successful interventions, across tribal communities. Community readiness serves as one potential model for developing specific community interventions that take into account culturally distinct tribal communities and tribally specific approaches.[27]

It is significant that most Native programs base health- and healing-related interventions on their respective tribal culture, which, again, can be quite unique. The *Community Readiness Model* (see Figure 23.1) integrates culture and tribally specific solutions in the analysis. This nine-stage model recognizes as a key issue the community's readiness to define and develop an intervention or program. The model is based on the theory of an individual's readiness for treatment applied on the community level. Just as people progress through readiness stages for a particular treatment intervention, communities also go through stages of readiness for program development. This concept of readiness provides an effective framework with which to view a social, economic, or policy-related issue. Developed initially to increase the potential for interventions to be effective in the area of alcohol and drug abuse, it is now implemented in urban and rural tribal communities to address challenges ranging from health and

Figure 23.1

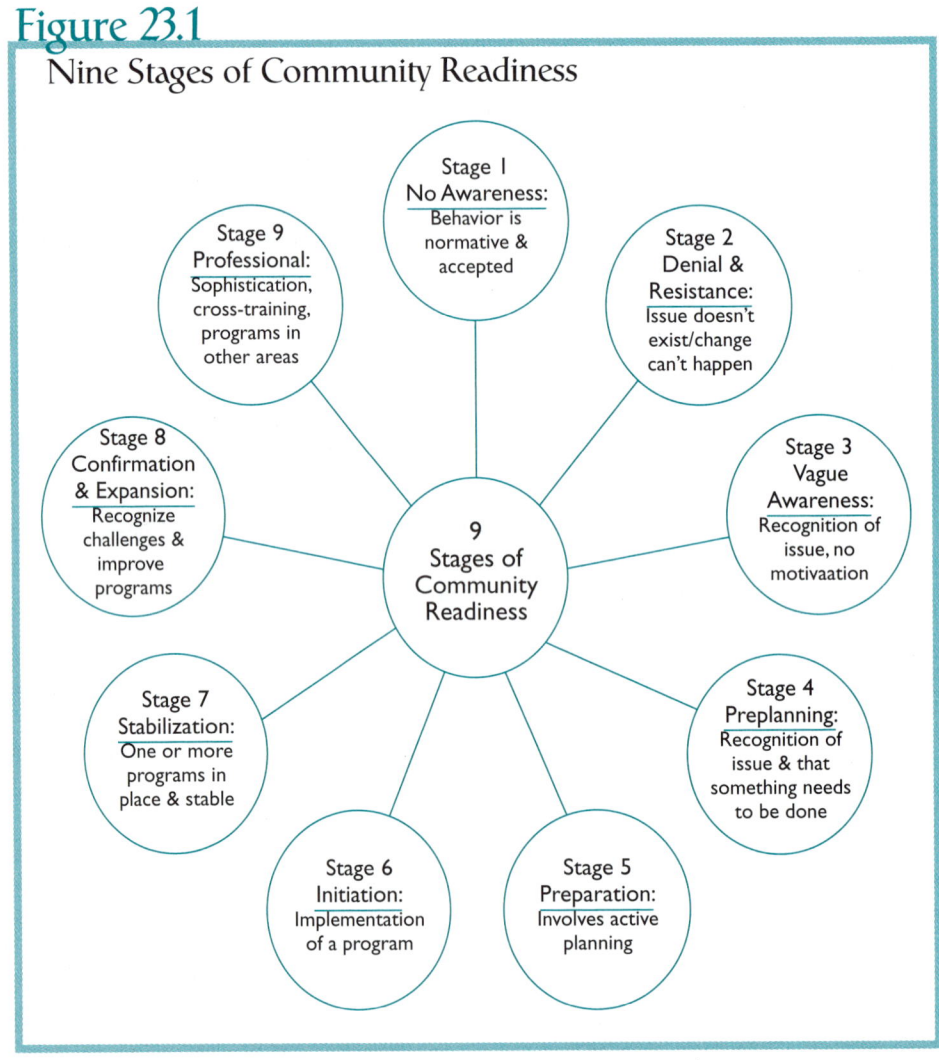

Nine Stages of Community Readiness

nutritional issues such as sexually transmitted diseases and infections to heart disease and diet, environmental issues such as water and air quality, HIV/AIDS intervention, child sexual abuse, sexual assault, and cultural competence. The model identifies specific characteristics related to different levels of problem awareness and readiness for change. To increase the potential for success, interventions introduced in a tribal community must be consistent with the history and awareness of the problem, along with the level of readiness for change present among tribal members.

The Community Readiness Model identifies nine stages of readiness. Stages of readiness are assessed by evaluating the community on six dimensions: A) Existing Efforts (programs, activities, policies, etc.), B) Community Knowledge of Efforts, C) Leadership (includes appointed leaders and influential community members), D) Community Climate, E) Community Knowledge about the Problem, and F) Resources (people, money, time, space, etc.). In recent years, a number of tribal communities have used the Community Readiness Model to assess existing programs or to determine if their community is ready to implement a particular program, including a Children's Advocacy Center and instituting a multidisciplinary approach to the investigation and intervention in child sexual and severe physical abuse cases. Once the tribal community has determined its level of readiness, it is time to develop strategies for moving the community from its current level to the next level of readiness to address a problem.

The selected interventions suggested here are by no means comprehensive but offer a very brief example of the types of interventions that are used with each readiness stage. For communities in the first stage, effective strategies are generally aimed at raising awareness that a problem exists. For example, interventions at the stages of "No Awareness" and "Denial" should focus on one-on-one and/or small group activities. Home visits can be utilized to discuss the issue and obtain individual buy-in for addressing the issue, and small activity groups, talking circles, and one-on-one phone calls are used in a variety of tribal communities effectively. At the "Vague Awareness" stage, communities can utilize small group events, pot lucks or potlatches, and newspaper editorials or articles. Although use of national or regional data may make little impression on tribal community members, local survey data may have impact, i.e., results of school surveys, phone surveys, focus groups, and so on. Communities at the "Initiation" stage might implement training for professionals and paraprofessionals, conduct consumer interviews to gain information about improving services, identify service gaps, and utilize computer searches to identify potential funding sources that match community needs.[28] In the context of child maltreatment, community readiness could be used to incorporate strategies that address intergenerational trauma and colonization that empowers and moves the community in a meaningful way to address child maltreatment in tribal communities.

This model suggests that effective community efforts must be based on a working knowledge of the historical factors in the community, a system-wide assessment, involvement of multiple systems, and utilization of resources and strengths within the community. Efforts must also be culturally relevant and accepted as long term in nature. The Community Readiness Model takes these factors into account and provides a tool that communities can use to focus and direct community efforts toward a desired result, maximizing their resources and minimizing discouraging failures.

Community readiness cannot be determined by the readiness of policymakers and providers it must relate to the readiness of the community to deal with the issue. There remain significant challenges to building effective program responses in both urban and reservation-based tribal communities. In the case of child maltreatment, for example, the importance of developing culturally competent approaches and providing education on the legacy of colonization, violence, alcohol and drug use, and historical trauma introduced via federal law and policy is fundamental in understanding contemporary challenges present in tribal communities today.

Individual Practice Considerations

The Ecosystems Model concludes with examination of factors affecting services provided to individuals. As identified in this chapter, the social issues experienced by Indigenous people often require the skills of professional social workers—whether the social worker is Native or not. This assistance includes tangible services such as assistance with obtaining financial aid, housing, clothing, legal advice, and so on. However, like other population groups, Native people require assistance from social workers in almost every field of practice, including mental and physical health, corrections, child welfare, alcohol and substance abuse, and youth services. The competencies learned in BSW and MSW social work education programs provide the fundamental skills for working with this population. However, application of these competencies is insufficient (and potentially harmful) without accompanying cultural competence and attention to social justice challenges. For example, the wishes and plans of individuals must be balanced along with the needs of family and community members. This emphasis on the group can lead to strong mutual support networks, particularly for those dwelling near or in tribal community settings. It is important to know that, when working with a Native individual, as in most communalistic cultures, almost all matters are of concern to the family, the extended family (in some instances clan), and on occasion, the entire community.

In short, when working with Indigenous people, the well-being of the whole (however that is defined by the individual in this situation) is paramount. Another key consideration is the long-term welfare of the group. Inherent in many tribal cultures is some form of recognition of the *seven generations* ideology. This is the understanding that we must consider what impact our every act is going to have upon our descendants seven generations from now.

Social Work With Native People: Case Examples

Applying the Indian Child Welfare Act

The Indian Child Welfare Act (ICWA) of 1978 represents one of the most sweeping statutes in the field of federal Indian law involving more litigation than any other federal legislation related to Native peoples. The ICWA was passed in an attempt to remedy a long history of child welfare abuses that occurred throughout the United

States, where Native children were taken from their communities and placed or adopted into non-Native families. The disparity of placement rates is shocking, and many families and tribal communities were severely affected by the permanent placement of their children, largely because social workers and other professionals were not trained in culturally competent ways to properly access the home environment. The ICWA remains an important piece of legislation protecting Native children, families, and upholding the sovereignty of tribes to make decisions for the welfare of their children.

Social workers and other professionals should receive ongoing training on the specifics of the ICWA and be prepared to comply with the act when cases involving Native children arise. When placement issues involve temporary placement, adoption, and pre-adoption settings for Native children who are eligible for tribal enrollment in a federally recognized tribe and have a Native parent who is also enrolled, these children are covered by the ICWA, and compliance with the Act is mandatory for social workers and others.[29] In these instances, preferences for placement are to first place children within their extended family, then with other members of the Native child's tribe, and finally with other Native families. Further, children should be placed in the least restrictive placement and within reasonable proximity of their own home.[30]

Working in an Urban Community

Urban Native populations are substantial in New York City, Los Angeles, Minneapolis, Oklahoma City, and Seattle, and the services afforded them are much more established. Yet, in other large metropolitan areas, Native populations are much less visible even though significant numbers of Indigenous people reside in these areas. The fact that the socioeconomic status of urban Natives is much lower than mainstream communities, combined with scarcity of resources for the urban population, creates a critical need for urban programming in a number of cities.

In this case example, we journey to one such metropolitan area. The greater metropolitan area of St. Louis is located in both Missouri and Illinois and includes nearly 3 million people. St. Louis was one of the original Native relocation cities in the relocation policy implemented in the 1950s and '60s. From the early 1970s through the 1990s, St. Louis housed an active Urban Indian Community Center, and then the center closed. In the years since, the Native community has struggled with the lack of services and the lack of a core community gathering place that the center had once provided. Thus, a community revitalization effort has been under way with the goal of once again creating a central place for community gatherings, a place to share cultural ideas and traditions, and a place to provide resources (or at least referrals) for the health, education, mental health, and welfare services for the Native community.

The community process for coming together did not involve the use of the Community Readiness Model, although in retrospect it seems the community moved through the readiness stages 1 through 3 (no awareness to vague awareness) and is working to move through stage 4 (preparation) and beyond. In 2005 and continuing into 2006, the Native Studies Program mentioned in the group work case (above) hosted many monthly community gatherings aimed at defining what revitalization could mean for this community. Initial efforts at engaging the various parts of the community found different stages of readiness, and certainly different definitions of need and five separate Native groups were identified within the community, each with different interests and needs. Some of the groups expressed a definite need for a community center, while others felt a community center would only bring harm and build a sense of distrust in the community, as there were too many varied interest groups with varied definitions of Native identity. A center might further divide the community around identity challenges.

After several months of successful community monthly gatherings with representatives of the groups (totaling about thirty to sixty people), the Native group hosting the meetings made significant attempts to move beyond the questioning and defining need stages and into more healing efforts. These efforts were met with significant failure (only eight were present for the Restorative Justice gathering and only six for the "Wiping of the Tears" ceremony). In considering the Community Readiness Model, it is clear that the St. Louis urban community was not ready for the healing type of initiatives that were implemented since the Native community itself was perhaps at a lower stage of readiness. It is interesting to note the community voiced with clarity its need to "just be together" and "learn once again to trust and enjoy each other's company" before moving into more formal planning and programming efforts. Later in the same year, the community was successful in promoting a holiday gathering involving more than one hundred people. Since that time, the community has taken a step back and decided to establish a coalition of the five different groups to determine the best steps moving forward, utilizing a Community Readiness Model so strategies that are implemented are culturally representative of the entire group given the tremendous differences that are often present in urban situations and position the community to move at a pace that reflects its level of readiness.

Concluding Comment

This chapter sought to provide a comprehensive introduction to the historical and contemporary complexities for working with Indigenous populations within urban, suburban, and reservation settings. Although the Native population is relatively small, it is important for social workers to become familiar with this group, as it is especially vulnerable to social problems and has preserved unique aspects of culture that must be addressed when providing human services. For example, the federal and many state governments have special relationships with Native tribes and nations that do not apply to other population groups, and social workers serving Indigenous peoples must practice within these differing legal requirements. As another example, when serving an individual, the social worker should recognize that a Native worldview will typically reflect a balance between emphasis on the individual and consideration of the interests of family, tribe, or community. These and other factors must be a part of the social worker's cultural competence if services are to be effective when working with Indigenous people.

KEY WORDS AND CONCEPTS

Sovereignty
Resiliency
Trust responsibility
Heteropatriachy
Community readiness

Indian Child Welfare Act
Institutional or structural racism
Self-determination
Colonization and historical trauma
Cultural competency

SUGGESTED INFORMATION SOURCES

Brave Heart-Jordan, M., and L. DeBruyn. "So She May Walk in Balance: Integrating the Impact of Historical Trauma in the Treatment of American Indian Women." In J. Adelman and G. Enguidanos, eds. *Racism in the Lives of Women: Testimony, Theory, and Guides to Antiracist Practice.* New York: Haworth Press, 1995, pp. 345–368.

Bubar, R., and I. Vernon. *Contemporary Native American Issues: Social Life and Issues.* Philadelphia: Chelsea House Publishers, 2004.

DeBruyn, L., M. Chino, P. Serna, and F. Fullerton-Gleason. "Child Maltreatment in American Indian and Alaska Native Communities: Integrating Culture, History, and Public Health for Intervention and Prevention." *Child Maltreatment* 6 (2001): 89–102.

Deloria, V. *God is Red: A Native View of Religion.* Golden, CO: Fulcrum Publishing, 2003.

Duran, E., B. Duran, and M. Y. H. Brave Heart. "Native Americans and the Trauma of History." In R. Thorton, ed. *Studying Native America: Problems and Prospects.* Wisconsin: University of Wisconsin Press, 1998, 60–76.

Evans-Campbell, T., T. Lindhorst, B. Huang, and K. Walters. "Interpersonal Violence in the Lives of Urban American Indian and Alaska Native Women: Implications for Health, Mental Health, and Help-Seeking." *American Journal of Public Health* 96(8) (2006): 1416–1422.

Harvard Project on American Indian Economic Development, Eric Henson, Jonathan B. Taylor, Catherine Curtis, Stephen Cornell, Kenneth W. Grant, Miriam Jorgensen, Joseph P. Kalt, and Andrew J. Lee. *The State of the Native Nations: Conditions Under U.S. Policies of Self-Determination.* New York: Oxford University Press, 2007.

Jaimes, A. *The State of Native America: Genocide, Colonization and Resistance.* Boston: South End Press, 1992.

LaDuke, W. *Reclaiming the Sacred: The Power of Naming and Claiming.* Cambridge, MA: South End Press, 2005.

Pilkington, D. *Rabbit-Proof Fence: The True Story of One of the Greatest Escapes of All Time.* New York: Hyperion Books, 1996.

Roscoe, W. *Changing Ones: Third and Fourth Genders in Native North America.* New York: St. Martin's Press, 2000.

Trask, H. K. *From a Native Daughter: Colonialism and Sovereignty in Hawaii.* Honolulu: University of Hawaii Press, 1999.

U.S. Commission on Civil Rights. *A Quiet Crisis: Federal Funding and Unmet Needs in Indian Country.* Washington, DC: U.S. Commission on Civil Rights, July 2003.

U.S. Department of Justice, Office of Justice Programs, Bureau of Justice Statistics, *American Indians and Crime,* Lawrence Greenfeld and Steven Smith, statisticians, (Washington, D.C.: U.S. Government Printing, February 1999), 4.

Vernon, I., and R. Bubar. "Child Sexual Abuse and HIV/AIDS in Indian Country." *Wicazo Sa Review* 16 (2001): 47–63.

Walters, K. L., J. M. Simone, and T. Evans-Campell. "Substance Use Among American Indians and Alaska Natives Incorporating Culture in an Indigenist Stress-Coping Paradigm." *Public Health Reports* 117(suppl. 1) (2002): S104–117.

Weaver, H. *Explorations in Cultural Competence: Journeys to the Four Directions*. Belmont, CA: Thomson Brooks Cole Publishers, 2005.

Wiebe, R., and Y. Johnson. *Stolen Life: Journey of a Cree Woman*. Toronto: Alfred A. Knoph Publishers, 1998.

Wilkins, D. E. *American Indian Politics and the American Political System*, 2nd ed. Lanham, MD: Rowman & Littlefield Publishers, 2006.

ENDNOTES

1. U.S. Census Bureau, "National Population Estimates—Characteristics," Table 3, 2007, http://www.census.gov/popest/national/asrh/NC-EST2007-srh.html, and http://www.census.gov/Press-Release/www.releases/archives/population/010048.htm.
2. U.S. Census Bureau, *The American Community—American Indians and Alaska Natives: 2004* (Washington, D.C.: U.S. Department of Commerce, 2007), p. 2; U.S. Census Bureau, *The American Indian and Alaska Native Population: 2000. Census 2000 Brief* (Washington, D.C.: U.S. Department of Commerce, 2002).
3. David H. Getches, Charles F. Wilkinson, and Robert A. Williams, Jr., *Cases and Materials on Federal Indian Law*, 5th ed. (St Paul, MN: Thomson/West, 2005).
4. U.S. Commission on Civil Rights, *A Quiet Crisis: Federal Funding and Unmet Needs in Indian Country*. (Washington, D.C.: U.S. Commission on Civil Rights, July 2003).
5. Eric Henson, Jonathan B. Taylor, Catherine Curtis, Stephen Cornell, Kenneth W. Grant, Miriam Jorgensen, Joseph P. Kalt, and Andrew J. Lee, *The State of the Native Nations: Conditions under U.S. Policies of Self-Determination* (New York: Oxford University Press, 2007).
6. Hilary N. Weaver, *Explorations in Cultural Competence: Journeys to the Four Directions* (Belmont, CA: Thomson Brooks Cole, 2005).
7. Stephen Cornell and Joseph P. Kalt, "Two Approaches to Economic Development on American Indian Reservations: One Works, the Other Doesn't," *Joint Occasional Papers on Native Affairs* (2005), retrieved from www.jopna.net.
8. Jeffrey Ian Ross, "Gambling, Native Americans and Lobbyist Jack Abramhoff," *The Examiner* (June 29, 2006).
9. J. Noriega, "American Indian Education in the United States: Indoctrination for Subordination to Colonialism," in M. Annette Jaimes, ed., *The State of Native American: Genocide, Colonization and Resistance* (Boston: South End Press, 1992), 380.
10. Getches, et al., op. cit.
11. Irene Vernon and Roe Bubar, "Child Sexual Abuse and HIV/AIDS in Indian Country," *Wicazo Sa Review* 16 (2001): 47–63.
12. U.S. Commission on Civil Rights, *A Quiet Crisis*, op. cit.
13. Office of Statistics and Programming, National Center for Injury Prevention and Control, CDC, "10 Leading Causes of Death: American Indian and Alaska Natives, Both Sexes, 1999–2000."
14. U.S. Commission on Civil Rights, *Broken Promises: Evaluating the Native American Health Care System* (Washington: U.S. Commission on Civil Rights, September 2004).
15. U.S. Commission on Civil Rights, *A Quiet Crisis*, op. cit.

16. T. Perdue, *Sifters: Native American Women's Lives* (New York: Oxford University Press, 2001), 4, 31.
17. P. Tjaden and N. Thoennes, "Full Report of the Prevalence, Incidence, and Consequences of Violence Against Women: Findings from the National Violence Against Women Survey," National Institute of Justice and Centers for Disease Control, 2000.
18. Roe Bubar and W. Bartlemay, "Native Women Left Behind: Sexual Assault in Tribal Communities," results from a National Pilot Study (Kyle, SD: Cangleska, 2006).
19. Office of Statistics and Programming, op. cit.
20. T. Morton, "The Increasing Colorization of America's Child Welfare System: The Overrepresentation of African American Children," *Policies and Practices of Public Human Services* 57 (1999); K. A. Earle and A. Cross, *Child Abuse and Neglect among American Indian and Alaska Native Children: An Analysis of Existing Data* (Seattle, WA: Casey Family Programs, 2001).
21. L. Greenfield and S. Smith, *American Indians and Crime* (Washington, D.C.: U.S. Department of Justice, Office of Justice Programs, Bureau of Justice Statistics, 2004).
22. A. Melton Pecos, "Indigenous Justice Systems and Tribal Society," *Judicature* 79, reprinted online by Tribal Court Clearinghouse, 1999.
23. M. Y. H. Brave Heart-Jordan, "Wakiksuyapi: Carrying the historical trauma of the Lakota," *Tulane Studies in Social Welfare* (2001): 21–22, 245–266.
24. Swinomish Tribal Mental Health Project, "A Gathering of Wisdoms, Tribal Mental Health: A Cultural Perspective" (LaConner, WA: Swinomish Tribal Community, 1991).
25. V. Deloria, Jr., and C. M. Lytle, "American Indians in Historical Perspective," in Vine Deloria, Jr., and Clifford M. Lytle, *American Indians, American Justice* (Austin: University of Texas Press, 1983), 1–24.
26. U.S. Commission on Civil Rights, *A Quiet Crisis*, op. cit.
27. Ruth W. Edwards, Pamela Jumper-Thurman, B. A. Plested, Eugene R. Oetting, and Lewis Swanson, "Community Readiness: Research to Practice," *Journal of Community Psychology* 28(3) (2000): 291–307.
28. Roe Bubar and Pamela Jumper-Thurman, "Violence Against Native Women" [Special issue], *Social Justice: A Journal of Crime, Conflict and World Order* (2004): 31, 70–86.
29. Indian Child Welfare Act (ICWA) of 1978, P.L. 95-608
30. Ibid.

chapter 24

Social Work Practice with Mexican Americans*

Prefatory Comment

In recent years, the Mexican American population passed African Americans as the largest ethnic minority group in the United States. Further, Mexican Americans are a young population with a high fertility rate, making them a significant population group that social workers must be prepared to serve. Understanding the culture, language, values, and traditions is a central part of the cultural competence each social worker should attempt to acquire.

This chapter maintains that, contrary to popular beliefs, Mexican Americans have clearly identifiable mental health needs and do avail themselves of direct services when they are provided at minimum cost, in their primary language (Spanish), and near their homes. Also, practice suggestions are provided that have implications for macro social work in the barrio such as mobilizing various indigenous social support systems including churches, neighbors, and the extended family. The intervention strategy of advocacy to reduce institutional barriers to services for Mexican Americans is also discussed. A police brutality case serves to highlight the micro and macro skills required in these delicate cases that are common in the Latino community.

Meeting the ever-increasing social service needs of disadvantaged groups, which are often isolated by class and cultural differences, is a continuing challenge to social work. If the social work profession hopes to be more viable among disadvantaged groups, especially among the Mexican American population, human services institutions must modify their service delivery systems. Moreover, social workers must understand the dynamics of both individual and institutional racism, which have discouraged or prevented Mexican Americans from availing themselves of existing services. At times those services have appeared impersonal and even nonsupportive.

Despite the recent attention focused on the special needs of Mexican Americans, any explanation of their situation is complicated by the difficulty of defining this pop-

---

*This chapter was prepared by Dr. Armando T. Morales (deceased) and Dr. Ramon Salcido, professor of social work, University of Southern California.

ulation as to size and demographic characteristics. More has to be learned about the variations within this group and its immigration pattern.

Demographic Profile

In the 2002 Census update, U.S. Hispanics reported that their ethnic origin was either Mexican, Puerto Rican, Cuban, Central or South American, or of some other *Latino* origin. The terms *Latino* and *Hispanic* are used interchangeably by the Census Bureau and in this chapter. More than one in eight persons in the United States is of Hispanic origin. In 2002, 13.3 percent of the U.S. population, representing 37.4 million people, were of Hispanic background. In this group, Mexicans were 66.9 percent; Puerto Ricans, 8.6 percent; Central and South Americans, 14.3 percent; Cubans, 3.7 percent; and "other Hispanics," 6.5 percent. *Latinos* of Mexican background were likely to live in the West and South, 54.6 percent and 33.3 percent, respectively.[1]

According to the 2002 Census, Hispanics are a very young group: 34.4 percent of Hispanics were younger than 18 years of age, compared with 22.8 percent of non-Hispanic whites. A smaller number of Hispanics were 18 to 64 (60.5 percent) compared with non-Hispanic whites (62.9 percent). In the 45 to 64 age category, Hispanics represented 14.3 percent compared with 25.7 percent of non-Hispanic whites. Mexicans had the highest proportion younger than 18 years of age (37.1 percent); those of Cuban origin had the lowest proportion at 19.6 percent.[2]

Fifteen million Hispanics (40.2 percent) in the United States were foreign born in 2002. Of this population, 52.1 percent entered the United States between 1990 and 2002, another 25.6 percent came to the United States in the 1980s, and 22.3 percent entered the United States before 1980. More *Latinos* live in family households with five or more people (26.5 percent) than those of non-*Latino* whites (10.8 percent). Mexican families were most likely to have five or more people (30.8 percent) compared with Central and South Americans (22.3 percent), Puerto Ricans (16.8 percent), other Hispanics (19.6 percent), and Cubans (10.6 percent).[3]

With regard to educational attainment, more than two in five *Latinos* age 25 and older have not graduated from high school. Among Hispanics 25 years of age and older, persons of Mexican descent had a lower percentage of high school graduates (50.6 percent) than Cubans (70.8 percent), Puerto Ricans (66.8 percent), Central and South Americans (70.8 percent), and other Hispanics (74.0 percent). Non-Hispanic whites had a much higher graduation rate at 88.7 percent.[4]

Looking at economic characteristics of Hispanics, in March 2002, 8.1 percent of Hispanics in the civilian labor force age 16 and older were unemployed, compared withto only 5.1 percent of non-Hispanic whites. Regarding full-time, year-round workers, 26.3 percent of Hispanics and 53.8 percent of non-Hispanic whites earned $35,000 or more. Of all *Latino* groups, those of Mexican descent had the lowest proportion of those earning $35,000 or more (23.6 percent). The percent of non-Hispanic whites earning $50,000 or more was 31.8 percent compared with 12.4 percent of all Hispanics and only 10.6 percent of Mexicans.

Latinos (21.4 percent) are far more likely than non-Hispanic whites (7.8 percent) to live below the poverty level. Puerto Ricans were the most impoverished group among the Hispanics (26.1 percent), closely followed by Mexicans at 22.8 percent. An important issue affecting the future of continued poverty for *Latinos* is the fact that those younger than 18 years of age were about three times more likely than non-Hispanic white children to be living in poverty (28.0 percent compared with 9.5 percent, respectively). Whereas *Latino* children represented 17.7 percent of all children in the United States, they constituted 30.4 percent of all children in poverty.[5]

Census data indicate that the percentage of persons speaking Spanish at home in the ten-year period from 1990 to 2000 increased consistently both at the national and state levels. It increased nationally from 7.5 percent to 10.7 percent, with the top three states in 2000 being New Mexico, 28.7 percent; Texas, 27.0 percent; and California, 25.0 percent.[6] Cities reveal an even more dramatic statistic regarding persons age 5 and older who speak a language other than English. The leading four cities were Santa Ana, California, 88.8 percent; Miami, Florida, 80.0 percent; El Paso, Texas, 77.3 percent; and Los Angeles, California, 61.1 percent.[7] These reports did not indicate if those persons speaking Spanish were of Mexican descent, but it can be assumed that Santa Ana, El Paso, and Los Angeles had large numbers of persons of Mexican descent.

Ecosystems Model

The five-level ecosystems model detailed in the introduction to Part Five has been adopted as an assessment tool to analyze the Mexican American experience. The five levels of analysis include historical, environmental–structural, cultural, family, and individual factors affecting Mexican Americans. The emphasis will be on mental health and psychosocial issues, as social work practice focuses on the interaction between the person and the environment. The term *person* may refer to an individual, a community, or even a larger social structure of society. Social work intervention might be directed at the person, the environment, or both. In each case, the social worker seeks to enhance and restore the social functioning of people and/or to change social conditions that impede the mutually beneficial interaction between people and their environment. This will be seen later in a police brutality case highlighting micro and macro intervention.

The ecosystems orientation involves the application of ecology and general systems theory to professional tasks. It permits social workers to look at psychosocial phenomena, account for complex variables, assess the dynamic interplay of these variables, draw conceptual boundaries around the unit of attention or the specific case, and then generate ideas for intervention. At this point methodology enters in, because in any particular case—meaning a particular individual, couple, family, group, institutional unit, or geographical area—any number of practice interventions might be needed. The ecosystems model can promote social workers' understanding of (1) the psychosocial problems experienced by Mexican Americans; (2) the crippling effects of institutional racism; and (3) the oppressive environments in which these people struggle to survive. For the purposes of this chapter, the five levels of analysis will be further subdivided as follows:

1. Historical
    a. History of treating mental illness (international)
    b. Mexico's approach to treating mental illness
2. Environmental–structural
    a. Mental health treatment for Mexican Americans in the United States
    b. The ethnosystem as an adjunctive helping service
3. Cultural
    a. *Barrio* service systems as adjunctive and alternative helping systems
4. The family
    a. Extended family, surrogate family, and support networks
5. The individual
    a. Assessment and treatment of a police brutality victim

Normally, for a deeper and more comprehensive understanding of a client's situation, the ecosystems five levels of assessment should be tied to and relevant to the specific case being assessed, as was shown in the case example in the box in Part Five's opener. With the exception of the *individual level,* this was not done in this chapter to allow for greater generalization to other Mexican Americans.

Historical Factors

History of Treating Mental Illness   Societies throughout the world have developed various approaches for treating persons suffering from psychological problems. Three basic explanations and corresponding intervention strategies pertaining to psychological problems can be traced back to the earliest times: (1) the attempt to explain diseases of the mind in physical terms, that is, the organic approach ("It's in your blood/chemistry"); (2) the attempt to deal with inexplicable events through spiritual or magical approaches ("The devil or spirits made you do it"); and (3) the attempt to find a psychological explanation for psychological problems ("It's all in your mind"). Hippocrates (460–377 B.C.), the father of medicine, pioneered the organic approach, believing that black bile caused depression. Several centuries later, Cicero (106–43 B.C.), the Roman statesman and attorney, objected to the black bile theory, maintaining that depression was the result of psychological difficulties. He proclaimed that people were responsible for their emotional and psychological difficulties—in a psychological sense, they could do something about them. Cicero laid down the theoretical foundations for psychotherapy. The magical or spiritual approach found people treating the afflicted person through appeasement, confession, incantations, magical rituals, or exorcism.[8]

The effectiveness of any treatment approach often depends on the suggestibility of the person on whom the approach is worked, the suggestive power of the influencing practitioner, and the sympathetic connection (relationship) between the practitioner and the person seeking assistance. If a person strongly believes, for example, his or her headache, stomachache, or depression has as its basis a physical or chemical factor and that only a medical person can help, a physician or psychiatrist who prescribes medication may have the greatest likelihood of relieving that person's symptom. If, on the other hand, the person believes he or she is suffering certain symptoms because he or she has sinned and that only a minister or priest can help, the church's representatives may indeed have the greatest impact. And if the person believes his or her symptom has a psychogenic basis and can only be alleviated by talking to someone who can be "objective" in understanding the symptom or problem, the psychiatrist or social worker may offer the best help.

Mexico's Historical Approach to Treating Mental Illness   Mexican society, like other societies, also developed approaches to help people with psychological problems. The ancestors of Mexican Americans, the Aztecs, numbering 20 million persons in Central Mexico in the fifteenth century, created a wealthy, powerful, and progressive empire. Their culture was highly developed, and in that intellectual atmosphere flourished highly advanced forms of psychiatry and psychotherapy. Translations of Aztec literature reveal that Aztec therapy was provided by competent personnel in institutions of high repute. They had an amazing grasp of psychology and developed concepts about ego formation similar to those advanced by Freud almost 500 years later. Those concepts appear in an Aztec document about dream interpretation. The Aztec psychiatrists knew how to recognize persons who were manic, schizoid, hysterical, depressive, and psychopathic—major mental disorder classifications not unlike the ones used today. Aztec patients were treated by a variety of methods, including an early form of brain surgery, hypnosis, "talking out" bad things in one's mind, and specific herbal potions for specific disorders.[9]

With the colonization of Mexico by Spain in the early sixteenth century came Spanish medicine based on European concepts. Spanish colonial physicians still held primitive ideas about the causes of disease, believing it was a punishment for sins caused by devils who had taken possession of the patient's body and spirit. Because military might was associated with racial superiority, Spanish medicine was also believed by Spaniards to be superior to that of the Aztecs. Had Spanish oppression not occurred, Aztec psychiatry might have made a very significant contribution to the mental health practices of the Western world. In spite of this overt conflict and clash over psychiatric approaches, however, the first hospital for the mentally ill founded in North America was in Mexico City in 1567.[10] The first hospital for the mentally ill in the United States was founded 185 years later, in 1752, in Philadelphia, Pennsylvania.[11] The United States established two additional hospitals for the mentally ill during this period, one in Williamsburg, Virginia, in 1773 and the Bloomingdale Asylum in New York in 1821. In a comparable period, Mexico also established a hospital in Yucatán in 1625, the Manicomio de lä Canoa in Mexico City in 1687, the Hospital Civil in Guadalajara in 1739, a hospital in Belém in 1794, and the Divino Salvado in Mexico City in 1796.

Other mental health milestones found Mexico establishing its first department of psychiatry in 1860 in Jalisco; the United States began its first program in 1906. Mexico began the systematic training of physicians in psychiatry in 1910; the United States initiated its training program in 1937. Mexico launched its community mental health movement in 1951 by establishing mental health programs in health centers; the United States initiated community programs in 1964 with the passage of the Federal Community Mental Health Act.[12] Today in Mexico the major mental health trends and various theoretical orientations are similar to those in other Western countries. No single therapy orientation prevails, and, as in the United States, psychiatrists are by and large in control of mental health programs, with psychologists, social workers, and psychiatric nurses having lesser roles. From the standpoint of mental health resources, the United States, being a much wealthier country, far overshadows Mexico in terms of mental health resources and manpower. The United States, for example, has 12.4 psychiatrists per 100,000, versus less than 1 psychiatrist per 100,000 in Mexico.[13]

Environmental–Structural Factors

Mental Health Treatment for Mexican Americans In the United States, persons of Mexican descent have found it very difficult to obtain mental health services. The nation's first community mental health program specifically for persons of Mexican descent was established in East Los Angeles in 1967. The staffing pattern included four psychiatrists, four psychiatric social workers, three nurses, a clinical psychologist, a rehabilitation counselor, a community services coordinator, a community worker, and six secretaries. All but one of the staff were bilingual. In applying one measure of utilization (the percentage of Spanish surname population in the area, 76 percent), the program was successful in that 90 percent of the clients seen had a Spanish surname. Clearly here there was maximum utilization of services by Hispanics. The program offered traditional mental health services provided in the clients' primary language and at a fee ranging from 50 cents to $15.[14] There are a few other rare examples of overutilization of mental health services by Hispanics,[15] but overall the utilization rate by this population rarely exceeds 50 percent. In other words, Hispanic receipt of services is usually one-half or less of their representation in the population.[16]

There are a number of reasons proposed to explain this underutilization. The literature is now making it increasingly clear that the major factors involved are structural in nature and pertain to the availability, accessibility, and acceptability of services to the very heterogeneous bilingual, bicultural characteristics of Hispanics.[17] When Hispanics finally do receive services, they are often of inferior quality, with diagnoses often based on assessment procedures developed for the middle-class Anglo population, which has no validity or applicability to these people. Furthermore, Hispanics are more likely to receive somatic and medication treatment and less individual or group therapy. These experiences can and do result in premature treatment termination.[18] Another important factor accounting for premature termination or resistance to treatment is whether the

Hispanic is a *voluntary client* seeking help for a problem *he* or *she* defines, or an *involuntary client* being referred for treatment regarding a problem of concern to the referring agency.[19] Racist and political policies and economic decisions (raising fees) by mental health agencies to deny services to "undocumented" or poor persons are other growing contributing factors related to the underutilization of services by Hispanics.

The Ethnosystem: An Adjunctive Helping System Assuming that social work abandons its constricted methods framework and adopts the ecosystems perspective, then this question must be asked: What other knowledge is needed to understand the psychosocial problems of Mexican Americans that is specific to their ethnic background? Solomon's framework provides one option for integrating Mexican American concerns into a practice framework.[20] She utilizes the ethnosystem and empowerment concepts as major integrative concepts. The *ethnosystem* is defined as a society comprising groups that vary in modes of communication, in degree of control over material resources, and in the structure of their internal relationships or social organization.[21] Moreover, these groups must be in a more or less stable pattern of relationships that have characteristics transcending any single group's field of integration—for example, the ethnosystem's political, educational, or economic subsystems. Solomon defines *empowerment* as a process whereby persons who belong to a stigmatized social category throughout their lives can be assisted to develop and increase skills in the exercise of interpersonal influence and the performance of valued social roles.[22]

Ethnosystems are the natural networks, the primary patterns of interaction, survival, and adjustment indigenous to societies. As used here, the concept of *natural networks* has its origins in several disciplines: social work, sociology, social psychology, and anthropology, as well as in the mental health "community support—significant others" literature.[23] Social workers need to be aware that these natural networks and primary systems exist apart from the usual modes of secondary interactions that Mexican Americans have developed for survival within Anglo-urbanized systems, including those with the social establishment. There is a basic similarity between the ethnosystem with secondary interaction for coping with the Anglo society and the concept of two environments, the immediate or nurturing environment and the wider environment. When, as Norton notes, the larger societal system rejects the minority group's immediate environment or ethnosystem, there is incongruence between the two (Solomon refers to this as negative valuation of a stigmatized collective), and power blocks are directed toward the minority individuals, groups, and communities.[24]

Cultural Factors: *Barrio* Service Systems

Mexican Americans have been immigrating to *barrios* (Mexican neighborhoods) in U.S. urban areas in large and small waves. The *barrio* is a microcosm of the dominant society as well as an ethnosystem. Although the communities interrelate with external institutional structures such as law enforcement, schools, and the public welfare system, *barrios* also have indigenous service systems that provide mutual aid and psychological support in time of need. Indigenous support systems include churches, neighbors, friends, family, and alternate services.[25]

Many Mexican Americans, especially the elderly and immigrant groups, have strong religious ties and attend church on a regular basis. The church, whether Roman Catholic or Protestant, is an important spiritual support for many Mexican Americans and, in addition, is a vehicle for disseminating information about *barrio* activities and services, reaching individuals who would be largely inaccessible to public agencies. There is trust in the church. For example, the parish priest or minister often knows of potential adoptive parents who would provide an excellent home for an unwed mother's child.

Concerned neighbors and friends also provide aid and act as a resource. Perceived as confidential sources of advice, these significant persons act as referral agents. Lee's study on the use of the services of a model neighborhood health center by Mexican Americans observed that some groups sought primary groups such as friends and neighbors as their major source of information about health care services.[26]

Family Factors

The family unit clearly plays an important role in providing economic, social, and psychological supports. Families also serve as adoptive parents for family members who are no longer able to care for their children. Especially in the case of older children, grandparents may care for and eventually adopt them. Other relatives, or the child's godparents or *compadres,* may also accept the responsibility of raising the child or children. Infants, of course, may also be adopted in the same manner. However, no matter how effective this network may be, it is the welfare agency, rather than the network itself, that has access at all times to the greatest amount of provision and greatest number of providers in the greatest geographical area; it is the agency that has legal responsibility for bringing services to the community.

As a result of the Chicano movement in the 1960s and 1970s, alternate service systems are being developed within the *barrio* to deal with the special needs of the Mexican American community. Although there are variations in the services offered in each *barrio,* common patterns in both structure and function are observable. Self-help groups, social action organizations, and specialized service agencies staffed exclusively by bicultural and bilingual personnel are considered the most essential aspects of the alternate service system.

Siporin writes that the ecological perspective is an "effort to improve the functioning and competence of the welfare service system of natural self-help mutual aid networks, and to improve the social functioning and coping competence of individuals and their collectivities."[27] This approach calls for the practitioner to broaden his or her view of the client. Intervention involves assessment of the total social, physical, and psychological needs of the client and his or her network system. Intervention also calls for advocacy in the amelioration of identified problems related to barriers created by social welfare systems. Intervention strategies are initiated in anticipation of resolving psychosocial problems. An example of a macrolevel strategy is networking.

Extended Family, Surrogate Family, and Support Networks Collins and Pancoast refer to *networks* as consisting of both people and relationships.[28] The social network is relatively invisible, though it is a real structure in which an individual, nuclear family, or group is embedded. The term *support systems,* as used here, parallels Caplan's conceptualization. He states, "Support systems may be of a continuing nature, intermittent or short-term in the event of an acute need or crisis."[29] Both enduring and short-term supports are likely to consist of three elements:[30]

1. The significant others help the individual mobilize his psychological resources and master his emotional burdens.
2. They share his tasks.
3. They provide him with extra supplies of money, materials, tools, skills, and cognitive guidance to improve the handling of his situation.

Individuals usually belong to several networks at the same time. Networks can be based on kinship, friendship, employment, recreation, education, politics, ethnicity, religion, or whatever interests or elements individuals find in common.

The content of exchanges can also be varied.[31] Although the informal network is important, it cannot provide for all needs. Formal resources (social services agencies, medical services, and other service providers) are likely to be utilized. Social network intervention, therefore, is an approach to service delivery that involves significant individuals in the amelioration of identified psychosocial problems.

Social network intervention takes into consideration both formal and informal systems. Also of significance to Mexican Americans is that this approach incorporates the sociocultural components of the family. The utilization of support systems can be conceptualized into two main divisions: (1) to engage existing networks and enhance their functioning and (2) to create new networks or "attach" a formerly isolated person or family to a network.[32]

The approach considers both psychological and environmental stresses and incorporates them into the total reality of a family. It focuses on rallying the life-sustaining forces of the individual and family. This viable system of self-help continues to function after the professional helper has been disengaged.

In social network intervention, the goal is to deal with the entire structure by rendering the network visible and viable and by attempting to restore its function. The social network for Mexican American families may include extended kin, *compadres* (co-parents), friends, *curanderos* (folk healers), and other concerned individuals. These subsystems are identified because of their potential to provide emotional strength, support, and other types of assistance to the family. Social network intervention, therefore, emphasizes engagement of the family's network of support systems.

Individual Factors

At the individual level of the ecosystems assessment model, attention is given by the social worker to the biopsychological endowment of the person, which includes personality strengths, level of psychosocial development, mental status, attitudes, values, cultural beliefs, lifestyle, educational attainment, and coping strengths when faced with physical and psychological stresses and problems. In turn, these factors are analyzed, not only within the ecosystems framework, but also in relationship to growth and development life-cycle theories such as those developed by Freud, Erikson, and Bowlby, to name a few.

Armed with the knowledge gained from the ecosystems assessment tool, the social worker is in a better position to plan his or her intervention. The central task for the social worker is to help clients resolve existing or potential problems in psychosocial functioning. This process may involve helping the client resolve problems within themselves or with other people such as a spouse, parent, children, friends, or coworkers. This focus is called direct service, or micro-level social work practice. Intervening on behalf of clients with larger social structures such as neighborhoods, organizations, or the community—in effect all those social work activities that fall outside of the domain of *micro* social work practice—is referred to as indirect service, or macro-level social work practice. In working with poor people, especially documented or undocumented Mexican immigrants who are often at the mercy of various social, economic, and political forces in society, both levels of intervention, micro and macro, are necessary for optimal helping effectiveness. What follows is a detailed case concerning *micro* intervention by a social worker with a documented Mexican immigrant adult male who was assaulted by the police. Following the *micro* intervention, a discussion will focus on what interventions were made at the *macro* level.

Micro Social Work Practice with Mexican Americans

CASE EXAMPLE

Mr. Sanchez, a Spanish-speaking, married, 35-year-old male of Mexican descent and father of three children, was referred for treatment to the barrio community mental health center by his attorney. He came to the center with his wife. He refused to tell the intake worker what his personal problems were that brought him to the center. He was unemployed and did not have money to pay for his treatment. The case was assigned to one of the licensed clinical social workers, Mr. Rubio.

The agency had a policy that, in special circumstances when a potential client did not wish to discuss the reason for seeking services, the social worker assigned to the case would discuss this matter with the client. The agency, in addition to having a sliding scale for payment, had a special fund raised through community donations to sponsor clients who did not have the means to pay for services. Mr. Sanchez primarily spoke Spanish, hence a Spanish-speaking worker was assigned to him. In those instances when a bilingual social worker is not available, a trained translator, rather than an interpreter, would be used. An interpreter "interprets" (provides his or her interpretation of what is being discussed), but a translator provides a literal word-for-word translation of the communication. To avoid emotional involvement in the translation, it is preferable not to use a family member or friend of the client.

Mr. Sanchez sat down and sighed, looking at Mr. Rubio with one eye as he had a fresh, medical eyepatch bandage over the other.

"Are you in pain?" asked Mr. Rubio.

"Not very much now, but I was in more pain a month ago when this happened," replied Mr. Sanchez.

"Please tell me what happened to you. Take your time, and if there is something I ask that you don't want to answer or find it too difficult to answer, please tell me," instructed Mr. Rubio.

Rather than going through a rigid interview format in this initial meeting, in order to obtain a social, family, educational, financial, employment, and health and mental health history, Mr. Rubio decided to begin "where the client is," that is, with what appeared to be an emotional and physical state of discomfort indicated by the sigh and possibly pain related to an eye injury. By permitting Mr. Sanchez to tell his story at his own pace and allowing him to determine what questions he would answer, the worker was, in effect, "empowering" the client to participate in the interview by having control of the content of the discussion. His wife was quiet and did not say anything. She had a worried, concerned look.

Mr. Sanchez stated that three weeks previously on a Sunday afternoon, he had been playing basketball at the park with a group of friends. The losers of the game purchased the beer. Mr. Sanchez smiled when he said he had been on the winning team and didn't have to pay for the beer. He drank three small cans of beer and was driving home with his brother-in-law seated in the passenger's side of the car. He passed a police car, which was going to make a right turn at an intersection. He continued traveling toward his home and noticed the police vehicle in his rearview mirror. Mr. Sanchez then turned right into his neighborhood street and parked his car in his driveway. Then he and his brother-in-law entered Mr. Sanchez's home where their wives were preparing dinner.

Mr. Sanchez entered his bedroom to change out of his gym clothes, which were wet with perspiration. As he was changing his clothes with his back to the bedroom door, the door opened swiftly, and he thought it was his children. He yelled out to close the door as he was changing. He then felt a powerful blow to his eye and did not remember anything after that. Mr. Sanchez bowed his head in silence, shaking his head "no" in a slow manner. Mr. Rubio joined him in this moment of silence, as if he were resting between rounds in a fight for his life. Mr. Sanchez looked at his wife as if he wanted her to continue with the story. Trying to hold back tears, Mrs. Sanchez stated, "It was the police. They hit him with a billy club on his right eye. After they hit him, there was complete silence. I was able to peer through the door, which was open about three inches, and my husband was lying on the floor, completely unconscious. I saw a lot of blood coming from the area around his eye, and I became very frightened and began screaming. I thought they had killed him." At this point, Mrs. Sanchez became very emotional and sobbed deeply. Mr. Rubio attempted to provide support to Mr. and Mrs. Sanchez by stating, "Few things in life cause so much pain and hardship." Both nodded in agreement. Mrs. Sanchez then continued, "I tried to push the door open, but the officers slammed it shut. My children started becoming hysterical and began crying, too. My sister and brother-in-law took my children with them, as they didn't want them to continue seeing their father in his unconscious state. After three or four minutes, the police officers picked up my husband, who was staggering and bleeding even more from his eye, and placed him in the police vehicle. One of the officers stated that they were taking my husband to jail for resisting arrest, assaulting police officers, and drunk driving. I asked the officers where they were taking him, and one officer yelled back, "To the station." I asked, "Which station?" and the officer smiled and said, "Just the station."

At this point in the interview, Mr. Rubio could have stated something like "You must have felt helpless," or "You probably thought you would never again see your husband." But these comments would have elicited even more affect or surfaced fears that might still have been unconscious, thereby changing the focus and purpose of the interview away from Mr. Sanchez. By coming to the interview and participating, Mrs. Sanchez was in a supportive role to her husband, and Mr. Rubio's intent was to help her in that role.

Mr. Rubio stated, "It must have been very difficult for you. You have been very helpful to your husband."

Mrs. Sanchez nodded "yes," as Mr. Sanchez tenderly hugged her. There was a brief silence as both looked at Mr. Rubio to continue the interview. Mr. Rubio then asked, "What was the extent of your eye injury?"

"The doctor said my eye was totally destroyed, and it's dying. I can't see anything out of it. In two weeks he'll remove it and then give me a brown leather patch because I can't afford to buy a glass eye." His remaining eye became red and teary as he stared at Mr. Rubio, searching for a solution to his problem.

Resisting the impulse to have a ready, quick answer such as "Everything will turn out all right, you'll see," instead Mr. Rubio went with the feelings Mr. Sanchez's tragic story had invoked in him. Mr. Rubio stated, "I feel stunned and speechless. No one can really know what it is to lose your sight in one eye, other than a person who has experienced it. It must be both physically and psychologically painful."

Mr. Sanchez nodded in agreement but added: "It is painful, especially at night. I can't sleep well because of the pain. I think I can stand it, and I'll eventually adjust to having only one eye. Maybe that is why God gave us two, in case we lose one." He smiled and then remarked, "But what I find most painful is that I cannot work and support my family and pay the rent. I don't know what I'm going to do. I don't feel like a man anymore."

Now Mr. Rubio had three major interrelated issues to consider in this first interview: (1) to increasingly focus on posttraumatic stress disorder (PTSD) questions to "rule out" PTSD; (2) to shift the focus of questions to determine the existence of and the gravity of depression Mr. Sanchez was experiencing or to rule out major depression; and (3) to focus on the issue of perceived loss of self and role as a man, husband, father, and only breadwinner in the family. This is especially catastrophic for those Hispanic males who have internalized a traditional cultural role wherein each family member has a clear, prescribed role. Losing the capacity to fulfill that role expectation for some traditional Latinos is like losing the meaning and purpose in life. For some wives, a comparable loss would be never being able to have a child. Cultural expectations are not set in concrete; hence, people can be helped to modify their position and adapt to a new situation. Mr. Rubio decided to deal with the "I don't feel like a man anymore" response, which, if not addressed, would have resulted in increasing depression, perhaps even leading to suicide since Mr. Sanchez was in a very high-risk age level and profile for Latino male suicide (75 percent of Latinos who commit suicide in the United States are married and between 20 to 35 years of age). In Mr. Rubio's clinical judgment, this currently was the most powerful stressor Mr. Sanchez was experiencing. Mr. Rubio had to help Mr. Sanchez view the situation in a less stressful way (cognitive restructuring, reframing).

"You certainly feel like a different person, and in some ways you are. I agree with you that eventually you will learn to adapt to using only one eye. You are in a psychological and economic crisis, which, in fact, will be only temporary. Once your eye pain lessens, you will be able to resume some type of work and once again support your family." His wife was nodding in agreement and smiling. "I never thought of it that way. I guess you are correct," stated Mr. Sanchez. "But what am I going to do for money now? We need food, and I have to pay the rent."

"I can go to work, and you can stay home and take care of the children and send them off to school," commented Mrs. Sanchez enthusiastically. "No, no. That is not right. A man's wife should never have to work. That is an insult," responded Mr. Sanchez, shaking his head from side to side. Mr. Rubio did not comment, creating an atmosphere for dialogue between a man and his wife during a period of crisis. "Why should we have to lose our home and return to Mexico to live with and depend on relatives when we can survive here if I go to work temporarily?" Mrs. Sanchez asked. "I know I can find work as a domestic or in a sewing factory. Besides, the children would really enjoy spending more time with you. They worry about you all of the time."

"They worry about me?" responded Mr. Sanchez in a surprised tone. "They really should not! I will be fine!" Mr. Sanchez responded in a firm, confident tone. This gave Mr. Rubio an opportunity to uncover Mr. Sanchez's inner strength and competitive spirit within a Latino cultural context.

"You are a proud man, good father, and husband. You are loved by your wife and children. You are a real macho, a man who provides for and protects his family in the most positive ways. A 'crisis' in Chinese philosophy means 'an opportunity to change.' This crisis has presented you an opportunity to become even more of a man, by providing your children and wife emotional support rather than primarily economic help as the sole breadwinner. You are being challenged to temporarily change in order to continue to help your family."

Mr. Sanchez sat up straighter and smiled again as his wife was nodding affirmatively and holding her husband's hand. "We can do it," she said. "I guess we can," replied Mr. Sanchez in a soft tone.

"And I will be here to continue to help you," added Mr. Rubio. "We're just about out of time. Do you want me to schedule an appointment for you three days from now?"

"Is this therapy? Is this all that is going to happen?" inquired Mr. Sanchez.

"This was our first visit, and in this hour we covered many important things," stated Mr. Rubio. "This is just the beginning of therapy, to get information in order to know what to do. Normally, we see people once a week to help them with their concerns. In your case, I want to see you in three days to see how this trauma has affected you. Do you think you feel well enough now so that I can see you in a few days?" Mr. Rubio asked. "Yes, that would be fine," replied Mr. Sanchez.

Mr. Rubio was attempting to assess whether Mr. Sanchez felt sufficiently emotionally and physically capable to return in a few days. It was a subtle way of empowering him to be involved in making important decisions about his welfare. Had he been in significant physical pain, he would have been referred to the center's staff psychiatrist for a medical opinion and treatment referral. Psychologically, Mr. Sanchez seemed intact, possessed good ego strength, and did not appear suicidal. Had Mr. Sanchez replied, "I don't even know where I'll be tomorrow, or if I'll even be alive" or verbal comments to that effect indicating possible suicidal ideation, Mr. Rubio would have extended the interview to assess his suicidality and, if indicated, treated it by evaluating the need for medication and/or hospitalization with the center's psychiatrist.

Mr. Sanchez returned for his appointment. He appeared less depressed, and his depression was "reactive" in nature; that is, it was in response to his two major losses—loss of an eye and loss of employment. In addition, Mr. Rubio confirmed his clinical opinion that Mr. Sanchez qualified for a diagnosis of PTSD, and he was placed on the appropriate antianxiety medication by the center psychiatrist. Subsequent treatment sessions involved conjoint sessions with Mr. Sanchez and his wife, who was now working, to help them adapt to their changing roles in the family and evaluation sessions with the three children. They had all observed their bleeding father taken away in the police car. One of the children was found to also be suffering from PTSD, and the other two children had adjustment disorder symptoms. The children were treated by another social worker. After ten visits, Mr. Sanchez's symptoms diminished significantly with the exception of being very fearful of uniformed police and "black and white" police vehicles. After three months of treatment, Mrs. Sanchez phoned to state that her husband had been convicted of misdemeanor drunk driving and had been sentenced to ninety days of jail. She added that her husband wanted her to communicate his appreciation for the help extended to him and his family and that he felt stronger and confident that he could handle this new crisis. Mrs. Sanchez stated that Mr. Sanchez's mother was coming up from Mexico to take care of the children to give her the opportunity to keep working.

Macro Social Work Practice with Mexican Americans

Mr. Rubio knew quite well that excessive force from police was not an uncommon experience in the barrio, occurring on the average of three to four times per day, and usually the victims were African Americans or Latinos. Mr. Rubio was also aware of volunteer "alternative community resources" in the barrio such as the "Police Misconduct Lawyer Referral Service." This service has a board of directors composed of community people, attorneys, and social workers and has a panel of private attorneys for representation in those cases where the conduct of the police was improper and caused injury or damages. Prior to his assault, Mr. Sanchez was working as a plumber's assistant earning $9 an hour. He did not have medical or unemployment insurance, as he was working for a relative who was a licensed, freelance plumber. Mr. Sanchez was also going to night school to learn English and to learn more about plumbing to prepare for his plumbing certificate. Mr. Rubio referred Mr. Sanchez to the police misconduct referral service.

This service was codirected by Cindy Torres, a licensed master's level social worker, and Roland Goya, an attorney. Both volunteered a few evenings per week to the program. They were assisted by a few social work and law students who handled most of the incoming calls and initial in-person interviews. Based on the legal merits of the cases, some were referred to the panel of volunteer attorneys who did "pro bono" (free service) work for the barrio. A panel of licensed and prelicense clinical MSWs belonging to "Trabajadores de La Raza" a Latino social work organization, likewise provided free clinical services for victims of police misconduct who could not afford to pay a modest fee for services.

In addition to clinical and administrative skills, Cindy Torres also had macro community organization skills and was attempting to mobilize several key community players, both elected and appointed leaders, and grass-roots barrio residents, to help reduce police malpractice and improve barrio–police relations. Law enforcement representatives were also invited to meetings, including the Chief of Police. Rather than emphasizing the negative by simply organizing groups to protest and be critical of the police, hence alienating them even further, Ms. Torres appealed instead to the positive forces, both in the police department and the barrio, who wanted to work on the problem of barrio–police conflict.

Ms. Torres prepared for the first meeting and had a good response from various members of the community, including the Chief of Police, who was going to send his Deputy Chief and local Precinct Captain as his representatives to the first meeting. At the meeting, which was the first of several meetings, Ms. Torres used a "force-field analysis" procedure developed for use with community groups in problem identification and problem solving. The basic concept in force-field analysis is to identify forces that are potential supports for, or barriers to, the achievement of a specific goal.[33] A group must already have a clear idea of the problem and have a desired goal. Barrio residents wanted the police to stop beating them and to treat them with more respect. The police wanted more respect and cooperation from the community in reducing crime.

Figure 24.1 illustrates the force-field chart written on the blackboard by Ms. Torres during the meeting as she obtained the input from the thirty-two participants.

As can be seen in Figure 24.1, after the major goal had been established and the competing forces (driving vs. restraining forces) list was created to show the status

Figure 24.1

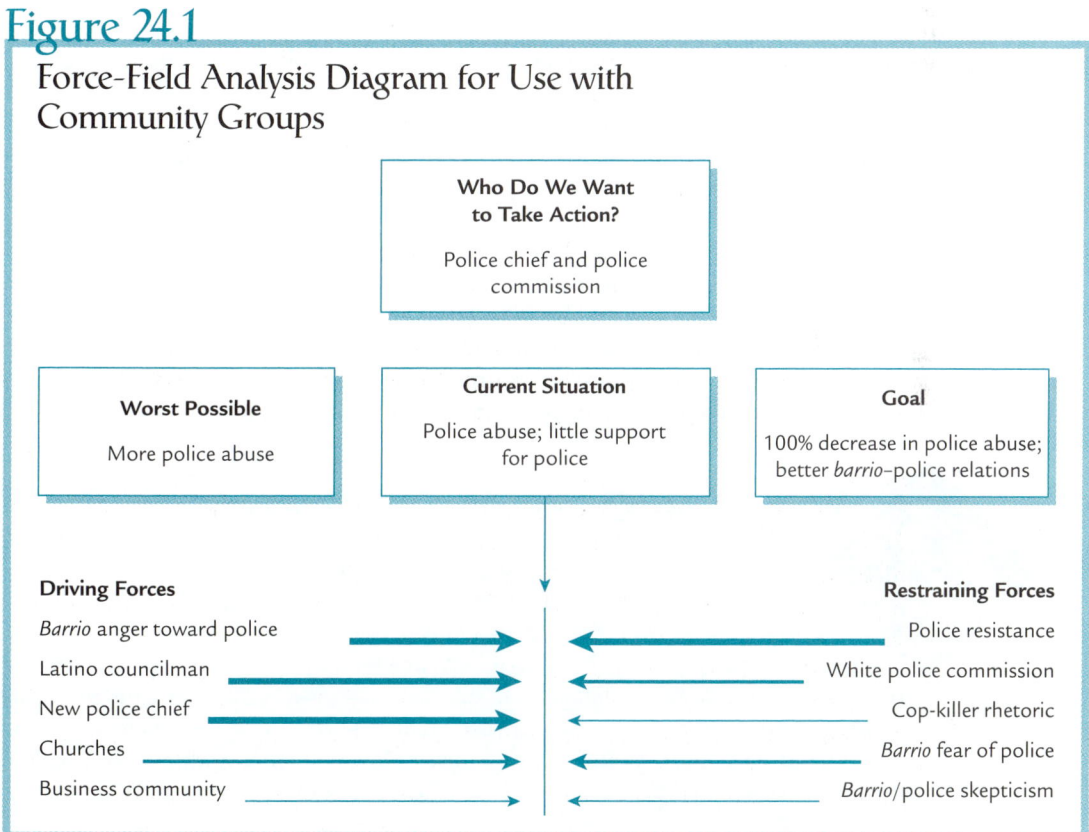

Force-Field Analysis Diagram for Use with Community Groups

quo, Ms. Torres guided the group in determining how powerful each force was and then drew an arrow (thin, medium, or thick depending on the estimated power of the force) in the direction of the force (toward or away from the goal). For example, the thicker the arrow, the stronger the driving or restraining force. This would indicate that more effort would be required to improve the situation in the identified problem area, especially when a thick arrow indicating a driving force encountered a thick arrow representing a restraining force. Such was the case in barrio anger toward the police (driving forces) being met with police resistance to change (restraining forces).

Thereafter, Ms. Torres helped the group establish small committees to mobilize the driving forces to work on the problem and other small committees to reduce the impact of the restraining forces. Applying her knowledge of group dynamics, she asked the group to establish mixed, balanced committees reflecting persons with law enforcement, barrio, political leader, church, "militant," and business community perspectives. Through such group composition, the committees were able to work out their differences in the small groups and develop cohesion before they approached other groups and bodies of resistance, such as the police commission.

The large group continued to meet on a monthly basis over a period of fifteen months, with the small committees meeting more regularly. An unexpected outcome was that the group, in working toward its goals, also planned and conducted a Barrio–Police Relations Conference a year later, which featured as speakers the District Attorney, the Latino Councilman, the Chief of Police, and a police brutality victim. The latter was Mr. Sanchez.

Following Mr. Sanchez's three months in jail for his drunk-driving conviction, his attorney filed a civil suit on his behalf against the police department and the city for pain, injury, permanent blindness in one eye, and suffering. The jury ruled that the police did not have a right to enter his home without a bench warrant because Mr. Sanchez had not committed a felony offense, only a misdemeanor drunk-driving violation. Mr. Sanchez was awarded $250,000. He donated $5,000 to the Police Misconduct Referral Service and $5,000 to the barrio mental health center, where he had been treated by Mr. Rubio. He told Mr. Rubio that he would prefer to have his eye back rather than the money he had received. Mr. Sanchez planned to return to Guadalajara, Mexico, because he found Southern California to be too violent.

Concluding Comment

Mexican Americans are one of this country's most diverse ethnic groups. Because they were an indigenous population, in their own land, prior to the Anglo-American conquest of Mexico in 1848, they, like Native Americans, are one of the oldest minorities. On the other hand, continuing immigration from Mexico also makes them one of the newest and largest immigrant groups. They are a very heterogeneous Hispanic group, responding to all categories of any language and cultural scale. Mexican Americans primarily reside in urban areas in the Southwest, generally occupy a low socioeconomic status, and have large families, a high unemployment rate, and low educational attainments—all symptoms of working class exploitation, sexism, and racism.

Mexican Americans have a small elderly population (4 percent), almost one-third the proportion of elderly whites, and a very large youth population. Because their age profile is the opposite of that of whites, their human services needs are different from those of whites, who are currently preoccupied with the needs of the elderly. As is the case with African Americans, Hispanics are increasingly being caught up in the juvenile justice system, a field of practice in which social work has not expressed much interest.

Mexican Americans *do* have mental health needs, and many do avail themselves of direct services when they are provided at modest cost, in their primary language, and near their homes. A rich psychiatric history, originating almost 700 years ago with the Aztecs, provides Mexican Americans with a foundation to build on, as both consumers and providers of mental health services. However, the current regressive trend in the United States, with its accompanying stresses, is creating new racism and poverty casualties among the poor and minorities. As needs for services increase, there is a corresponding increased effort to "economize" by "phasing out" or denying services to the poor. Mexican Americans are particularly affected by these trends, especially new Mexican immigrants and the "undocumented."

Practice suggestions were offered that may have implications for macro social work in the *barrio*. The *barrio* as an ethnosystem is composed of indigenous social support systems such as churches, neighbors, friends, alternative services (self-help groups), and the family. Applying the concept of social network intervention to Mexican Americans signifies the inclusion of extended family members, *compadres* (co-parents), friends, coworkers, and other concerned persons in their support systems. These subsystems have the potential to provide emotional strength, support, and other types of assistance to the family.

This chapter highlighted micro and macro social work practice intervention in a police brutality case. Police brutality has been an NASW practice priority since April 1992. These tragic incidents committed by a few irresponsible law enforcement officials under the "color of law" (in uniform, on official duty) number some 10,000 to 15,000 episodes per year. Police brutality affects 60,000 to 90,000 persons—mostly poor and racial/ethnic minorities—when emotionally affected family members are included. This is definitely a human rights and quality-of-life issue for the profession. The values and ethics of the profession demand social work practice involvement and inclusion in the curriculum of schools of social work.

KEY WORDS AND CONCEPTS

Mexican Americans
Curanderos
Chicano
Mexicans
Aztec psychiatry

Barrio
Compadres
Barrio service system
Positive *machismo*

SUGGESTED INFORMATION SOURCES

Burnette, Denise. "Custodial Grandparents in Latino Families: Patterns of Service Use and Predictors of Unmet Needs." *Social Work* (January 1999): 22–34.

Casas, J. M., and M. J. T. Vasquez. "Counseling the Hispanic Client: A Guiding Framework for a Diverse Population," in P. Pedersen, J. Draguns, W. Lonner, and J. Trimble, eds., *Counseling Across Cultures*, 4th ed. Honolulu: University of Hawaii Press, 1996, pp. 146–176.

Ruiz, Pedro. "Challenges in Providing Psychiatric Services to Hispanic Americans." *Psychline* 2(4) (1998), pp. 6–10.

Skolnick, Jerome H., and James J. Fyfe. *Above the Law: Police and the Excessive Use of Force* (New York: The Free Press, 1993).

Vargas, Luis A., and Joan D. Koss-Chioino, eds. *Working with Culture: Psychotherapeutic Interventions with Ethnic Minority Children and Adolescent.* San Francisco: Jossey-Bass Publishers, 1992.

Vega, William A., Bohdan Kolody, Sergio Aguilar-Gaxiola, and Ralph Catalano. "Gaps in Service Utilization by Mexican Americans with Mental Health Problems." *American Journal of Psychiatry* 156 (June 1999): 928–934.

Vega, William A., Bohdan Kolody, Sergio Aguilar-Gaxiola, Ethel Alderete, Ralph Catalano, Jorge Caraveo-Anduaga. "Lifetime Prevalence of DSM III-R Psychiatric Disorders among Urban and Rural Mexican Americans in California." *Archives of General Psychiatry* 55 (September 1998): 771–781.

ENDNOTES

1. Roberto R. Ramirez and G. Patricia de la Cruz, *The Hispanic Population in the United States: March 2002*, Current Population Reports, P20–545, (U.S. Census Bureau, Washington, D.C., 2002), pp. 1–2.
2. Ibid., p. 3.
3. Ibid., p. 4.
4. Ibid., p. 5.
5. Ibid., p. 6.
6. Sylvia A. Marotta and Jorge G. Garcia, "*Latinos* in the United States in 2000," *Hispanic Journal of Behavioral Sciences* 25(1) (February 2003): pp. 21–22.
7. U.S. Census Bureau, American Community Survey Office, August 10, 2004, pp. 1–3.
8. Franz G. Alexander and Sheldon V. Selesnick, *The History of Psychiatry* (New York: Harper & Row, 1966), pp. 7–14.
9. Guido Belsasso, "The History of Psychiatry in Mexico," *Hospital and Community Psychiatry* 20 (November 1969): 342–344.
10. Ibid.
11. Alexander and Selesnick, op. cit., p. 120.
12. Belsasso, op. cit.
13. Ramon Parres, "Mexico," *World Studies in Psychiatry* 2(3) (Medical Communications, Inc., 1979).
14. Marvin Karno and Armando Morales, "A Community Mental Health Service for Mexican Americans in a Metropolis," *Comprehensive Psychiatry* 12 (March 1971): 116–121.

15. Armando Morales, "Institutional Racism in Mental Health and Criminal Justice," *Social Casework* 59(7) (1978): pp. 394, 395.
16. Special Populations Sub-Task Task Panel on Mental Health of Hispanic Americans, *Report to the President's Commission on Mental Health* (Washington, D.C.: U.S. Government Printing Office, 1978), p. 3.
17. Ibid.
18. Joe Yamamoto, Quinston James, and Norman Palley, "Cultural Problems in Psychiatric Therapy," *Archives of General Psychiatry* 19 (1968): 45–49.
19. Armando Morales, "Social Work with Third-World People," *Social Work* 26 (January 1981): 49.
20. Barbara Bryant Solomon, *Black Empowerment: Social Work in Oppressed Communities* (New York: Columbia University Press, 1976), p. 6.
21. Dolores G. Norton, *The Dual Perspective: Inclusion of Ethnic Minority Content on the Social Work Curriculum* (New York: Council of Social Work Education, 1978).
22. Solomon, op. cit.
23. Ramon Valle, "Ethnic Minority Curriculum in Mental Health: Latino/Hispano Perspective," paper presented at Mental Health Curriculum Development Conference sponsored by Howard University School of Social Work, November 16–18, 1979, Chicago.
24. Norton, op. cit.
25. Valle, op. cit., p. 7.
26. E. P. Tsiaiah Lee, "The Pattern of Medical Care Use: Mexican American Patients at a Model Neighborhood Health Center in Los Angeles" (Doctoral thesis, University of California at Los Angeles, 1975).
27. Max Siporin, *Introduction to Social Work Practice* (New York: Macmillan, 1975).
28. Alice H. Collins and Diane L. Pancoast, *Natural Helping Networks: A Strategy for Intervention* (Washington, D.C.: National Association of Social Workers, 1976).
29. Gerald Caplan, *Support Systems and Community Mental Health* (New York: Behavioral Publications, 1974).
30. Ibid.
31. Collins and Pancoast, op. cit.
32. Carol Swenson, "Social Networks, Mutual Aid, and the Life Model of Practice," in Carel B. Germain, ed., *Social Work Practice: People and Environment and Ecological Perspective* (New York: Columbia University Press, 1979), pp. 213–238.
33. Mark A. Mattaini, *More Than a Thousand Words: Graphics for Clinical Practice* (Washington, D.C.: National Association of Social Workers, 1993), pp. 135–137.

chapter 25

Social Work Practice with African Americans*

> **Prefatory Comment**
>
> Central to social work are its core values of service, social justice, dignity, and worth of the person; the importance of human relationships; integrity; and competence. Through such values, the profession carries out its primary goal to help people in need address social issues and to challenge social injustice wherever it may be found. This chapter brings a strengths-based and empowerment perspective to this African American chapter. The authors acknowledge past challenges and successes but also recognize that considerable work remains to be done toward ensuring a brighter, more stable future for many African Americans. Recognizing that many of the age-old obstacles and barriers to success for some African Americans continue to persist, the chapter acknowledges the strengths and resiliency of a people who have always held strong to faith and hope and a steadfast endurance for achieving social, economic, and political justice.

It is essential that services be client focused and that practitioners aggressively seek to dismantle barriers that may prevent clients from receiving assistance. In implementing such admirable professional goals, it is important that social work practice skills and competencies are relevant to the populations being served and are culturally sensitive to those persons most apt to seek the programs and services social workers deliver. Understanding the dynamic interrelations among individual, family, culture, and environment, as well as the various historical factors that have influenced each population group, helps to establish the foundation for holistic change rather than depending on "band-aid" approaches that too often militate against people feeling empowered to problem-solve.

A national study of licensed social workers conducted by the National Association of Social Workers' Center for Workforce Studies concluded that social workers are not as diverse as the populations they serve in terms of race, ethnicity,

---

*This chapter was prepared by Malcolm E. Scott, assistant professor at Colorado State University, and Erma Borskey, assistant professor and field director at Southern University (Baton Rouge).

and gender. African Americans comprise 13 percent of the U.S. population and only 7 percent of licensed social workers, while the non-Hispanic, white population represents 68 percent of the population and 86 percent of licensed social workers. More notable is that, among licensed social workers reporting on the clients they serve with regard to race, nearly all social workers report serving non-Hispanic, white clients, and most reported they also serve some African American and Hispanic clients (85 percent and 77 percent, respectively). According to the NASW study, fewer licensed social workers reported working with ethnic groups such as Asian or Native American clients.[1] Although regional difference in the distribution of the several racial/ethnic population groups will affect the makeup of their clientele, it is clear that throughout most of the United States social workers must be sensitive to African American culture if they are to be prepared to serve this substantial part of their clients effectively.

For social workers and other professionals to provide comprehensive and culturally sensitive practice, it is vital that they study the various groups to understand their demographic characteristics and cultural uniqueness. A recent study found that 30 percent of faculty perceived that their social work students were ill-prepared to work with racial and ethnic groups different than their own.[2] One of the groups most vulnerable to social problems in America is clearly the African American population. Lagging well behind whites and other minority groups in social, economic, and health indicators, the African American community deserves and requires the most competent and comprehensive services social workers can offer. Efforts to revive a sense of community, build a sound infrastructure among the African American people, and secure needed community resources require social work practitioners who are professionally and culturally competent.

Issues once thought to be isolated incidences relegated to culturally and morally deficient inner-city minority neighborhoods—such as male youth violence, teenage pregnancy, illicit drug use, and broken marriages—can no longer be rationalized as "their" community's problems. As middle-class urban and suburban communities frantically search for solutions to recent school shootings, high incidence of divorce, and increased drug use, it becomes "our" challenge and "our" problem. Thus, all practitioners must be prepared to provide services to counter a number of different issues. Attaining the competence to provide this wide range of services is a sizable undertaking for social work, but it is one that most other professions are unprepared and ill-equipped to take on.

African Americans in the United States have been and continue to be a people contributing greatly to the building of this great nation. Often their historical sacrifices and contributions have been minimized, but recently more attention is being given to the significant role of African Americans in the United States. From civil rights leaders such as Frederic Douglass, Malcolm X, Martin Luther King, Jr., and Fannie Lou Hamer, America has been challenged time and time again to raise the level of its commitment to the poor and oppressed—and particularly to the African American community. Even though progress has been made in many areas regarding African Americans in this country, much remains undone. In spite of a sizeable

African American middle-class in a proportion never before seen in the United States, the struggle for social, economic, and political justice continues. Just as the efforts to end slavery faced great opposition, so did ending "Jim Crow" laws in the then–legally segregated South. Today the systematic economic and social isolation of many African Americans in communities across the United States provides great opportunity for the socially conscious social worker to become engaged in advocating for further improvements. Therefore, this chapter on social work with African Americans addresses a number of historical conditions and contemporary social issues of significant relevance, and it utilizes this book's Ecosystems Model to address the significant implications from the individual, family, culture, environmental–structural, and historical perspectives.

Current Population Demographics

Developing a community of physically, mentally, and emotionally healthy people is no small task. However, African Americans in general have shown remarkable perseverance in the face of legalized discrimination and remain a resilient and strong people. Often this strength has been overlooked by outside onlookers seeking to further invalidate the worth and dignity of the African American individual, family, and culture. However, there is great cause to resist such disempowering perspectives for a more strengths-based and empowering one. In size, African Americans, once the largest minority group in America, have slipped into second place recently as the number of Hispanic Americans has grown. The U.S. Census Bureau estimates that in 2006 there were 39 million African Americans living in the United States and nearly 45 million Hispanics. However, African Americans continue to be a significant group in the United States, representing just over 13 percent of the total U.S. population, which is roughly about the same proportion as was in the United States in 1900.[3]

As a historical reference point, "The Great Migration," as it was called, marked a time during which many African Americans moved northward in search of opportunity for employment and improved living conditions and life chances. In addition, this massive northward migration was fueled by hopes of escaping the racial violence and the "Jim Crow" South that sought to marginalize and disenfranchise their aspirations for better social, economic, and political opportunities. This migratory trend would reverse itself during the 1970s and 1980s with more African Americans moving south to the Sun Belt to escape the "urban predicament" (joblessness, rampant drug use, and violence) that plagued many urban inner-city communities of color. The Sun Belt is a region of the United States generally considered to stretch across the South and Southwest (the geographic southern United States, which includes such states as Alabama,

Arizona, California, Florida, Georgia, Louisiana, Mississippi, Nevada, New Mexico, South Carolina, and Texas).[4] It is arguable whether these migratory trends helped to significantly advance the economic, social, and political opportunities for many blacks toward fully integrating into communities in northern states. A review of selected key social issues and indicators of community and individual well-being provides evidence of current conditions experienced by African Americans in the United States.

Selected Social Issues

African Americans, like many other minority groups, tend to be represented disproportionately on the key problem indicators of social well-being, such as poverty, family challenges, women and men's issues, lack of education and training, and health issues. Though this list is not intended to be exhaustive, it serves as the basis for highlighting several key indicators of African American's overall wellness, both as individuals and as a minority group. It is important to note, however, that, for many African Americans who have successfully transitioned into the mainstream, these are much less representative indicators of well-being.

Persistent Poverty Issues

Perhaps the most comprehensive indicator of social problems is poverty, as it is strongly correlated with other issues such as nutrition, health, housing, and education. Identifying the percent of a population group below the poverty-threshold is one way to determine who among the population fall below this established marker accounting for family size and composition and thus is experiencing poverty. For the total U.S. population, the poverty rate in 2006 was estimated at 12.3 percent (see Table 25.1). However, individual African Americans experienced a poverty rate nearly twice as high as the national average, estimated at 24.3 percent. Only the Native population (American Indian and Alaska Native), which represents 1.5 percent of the population, experienced a higher rate of poverty, estimated at 26.6 percent. Comparatively, non-Hispanic whites in the U.S. experience an estimated poverty rate of 8.2 percent, which is three times lower than black and Native peoples.

Another example of the pervasive poverty issue among African Americans is evidenced in family life (see Table 25.1). Black families in the United States had an estimated poverty rate of 23.1 percent compared with 6.1 percent for white families. Further, African American female-headed family households with no husband present experienced a poverty rate of 39.2 percent, compared with 22.5 percent for whites in this same category. In fact, during times of economic growth and prosperity in the United States, such as was experienced in the mid-1990s, the African American child poverty rate was nearly 40 percent. In 2006, African Americans under age 18 experienced a slightly improved poverty rate of 33.0 percent, but still much higher than their white counterparts. For older Americans, too, these disproportionate

Table 25.1

Percent of Individuals below Poverty Level by Race, Age, and Family Relationship, 2006

	Non-Hispanic White Population	African American Population
Total Population	8.2%	24.3%
Population under age 18	10.0	33.0
Population 65 and older	7.0	22.7
Family household (all families)	6.1	23.1
Female-headed household (no husband present)	22.5	39.2

Source: U.S. Census Bureau, *Income, Poverty, and Health Insurance Coverage in the United States: 2006* (Washington, D.C: Department of Commerce, 2007), pp. 46–47.

trends in rate of poverty persist. For older African Americans and whites age 65 and older, the estimated poverty rates were 22.7 and 7.0 percent, respectively.

The inability of many African Americans to secure full-time employment and the resulting high rate of holding only part-time, low-wage service jobs, plus pervasive joblessness, are just a few of the factors that have helped to create the current socioeconomic disparity between African Americans and their Caucasian counterparts. These conditions have had a profound impact, affecting not just the individual but also having a negative influence on the black family as an institution.

Family Challenges

The African American family has perhaps been the most studied institution in the black community, and the dynamics of the African American family have often been compared to a traditional white family model. Two perspectives have been the primary focus of the debate around the challenges facing the African American family. One perspective is that the difficulties of the black family are a result of a dysfunctional family structure and cultural deficiencies. The other perspective is that these difficulties stem from structural and institutional bias resulting from long-standing racial and cultural patterns in the United States, as well as shifts in the economic structure affecting opportunities for African Americans in local communities.

One of the most controversial historical accounts of the African American family came out of the Moynihan Report.[5] In his account, Moynihan attributed much of the economic, social, and educational challenges facing the African American family to the prevalence of female-headed households. The backlash that followed was a number of publications providing a different perspective highlighting the strengths and root causes of the black family's troubles. Primary among the causes of these troubles is the fact that African American families have fewer financial resources and opportunities. The median household income in 2005 was $46,326 for all families. The average African American family's income is only 61 percent of the income of white households. The African American household income was approximately $30,858, compared with $50,784 for white families.[6] This disparity is important because it clearly shows that African American families have significantly fewer financial resources to invest in building and creating greater opportunity for themselves and their children. It follows, then, that the child poverty rate among African Americans, for example, was 33 percent in 2006 compared with only 10 percent for white children.[7] In other words, African American children start out with much less with regard to their families' resources than their white counterparts and are much more likely to remain in poverty.

Only limited research as been conducted regarding the psychological impact poverty has on human aspiration and self-defeating self-perceptions. Nevertheless, what is well documented is the negative impact of poverty on health status, educational opportunity, and financial capital (financial capital refers to money available for reinvestment in the creation of more wealth). The correlation between these social indicators of well-being and educational achievement and attainment is important to understanding the overall challenges African Americans confront in their lives.

Education

There is no greater factor an individual can be allied with than improving the educational opportunities and success of children and adults in order to minimize the ill effects of poverty, family challenges, health issues, and other social concerns. Obtaining equal educational opportunities has been a historical focal point of the African American community because of the association between education, economic opportunity, and overall well-being. One major result of the Civil Rights Movement of the 1950s and 1960s was increasing the accessibility of quality education for all Americans. One highly applauded Supreme Court decision that affected the African American community was *Brown v. Board of Education* in 1959, which declared it unconstitutional for "separate but equal" schools to receive federal funding. Before this Supreme Court decision, African Americans were typically educated separately, which for years resulted in their lagging behind in such educational indicators of success as college enrollment and completion rates.

Now, more than fifty years after the *Brown v. Board of Education* decision, many inner-city urban and rural community public schools continue to struggle to keep pace with suburban and private school students' achievement. A comparison of educational attainment among white and black people documents the achievement differences. In 2006 approximately 17.8 percent of African Americans age 25 and over had less than a high school diploma, compared with only 9.4 percent for non-Hispanic whites. Similarly, for those competing for jobs with only a high school diploma or less, the rates were 54.0 percent for blacks compared with 41.6 percent for whites. If jobs required a college degree, the Census Bureau estimates that 13.0 percent of African Americans would be eligible, and only 5.6 percent would qualify if a graduate degree was required. For white men and women, the estimated percentage completing a bachelor's degree was 20.8 percent, and graduate degrees were attained by 11.1 percent. Examination of gender differences revealed similar trends of disproportional degree attainment, i.e., black males to non-Hispanic white males, and black females to non-Hispanic white females (see Table 25.2).

Although there has been notable educational improvement within the African American community, concerns remain. One concern is the standardized test score gap among school-age African American and white children. In 2002, the College Board reported that the average SAT scores for white youths was 1060 compared with 857 for African American youth, which represents the lowest SAT scores of all ethnic and racial groups in the United States. Concern also remains regarding the relatively low graduate school achievement rates, particularly for African American males. Further, although graduate enrollment and completion increased dramatically for African American women, the overall educational indicators have improved only slightly for the African American population.[8]

The two primary predictors of academic achievement and success relate to parental education level and parents' income. The disparity in educational readiness in the African American community can be attributed to lower educational levels of parents and lack of educational exposure experienced by many African American children. Thus, the resulting phenomenon for the African American community is fewer black males and females entering the educational pipeline at key transition points, which decreases the applicant pool available for entry as freshmen and again

Table 25.2

Percentage Comparison of Educational Attainment by White and Black People Age 25 and Older, 2006

	Less Than High School	High School Graduate	Some College	Bachelor's Degree	Graduate Degree
Both Sexes					
Non-Hispanic White	9.4%	32.2%	26.5%	20.8%	11.1%
Black	17.8	36.2	27.5	13.0	5.6
Males					
Non-Hispanic White	9.8	32.0	25.0	20.9	12.3
Black	18.1	38.3	25.5	12.9	5.4
Females					
Non-Hispanic White	9.0	32.4	28.0	20.6	10.0
Black	17.4	34.5	29.1	13.3	5.7

Source: U.S. Census Bureau, *Current Population Survey, 2007: Annual Social and Economic Supplement.* Internet release date: January 10, 2008, http://www.census.gov/population/www/socdemo/education/cps2007.html.

at the graduate and professional education and job training levels. This is not to say that other key factors, such as school funding, adequately prepared teachers, and involvement with the criminal justice system do not affect educational opportunity and achievement. Indeed, the issues of educational opportunity and success are complex and multifaceted, but these factors are telling of the challenges African American men and women face in their communities.

The link between education and eventual earning power is clear. The U.S. Census Bureau reported in 2006 that the average annual earnings for a person with a high school diploma or less was $31,071, compared with those with a college degree or higher at $56,788.[9] Until African Americans are more able to meet the educational requirements for higher paying jobs, and thereby increasing the financial resources for gaining more wealth, they will continue to be vulnerable to the far-reaching effects of poverty and oppression in the United States.

Women's and Men's Issues

For the population of African American men and women in the United States, several issues of importance surface when considering overall well-being related to the sexes. Just as challenges arise between different racial and ethnic groups, similarly significant within group differences among male and female African Americans can be identified. For example, African American males have significantly more involvement with the criminal justice system, are more likely to be the victims of homicide, and continue to be plagued by high rates of new cases of HIV/AIDS infection. These factors have created a significant gender imbalance between African American males and females, as there are twice as many African American females as there are males available for marriage, thereby contributing to the lower marriage rate among black females. Additionally, African American females have the fastest growing rate of HIV/AIDS infection among newly reported cases. As a result, there is a high proportion of single female-headed households that also have a high rate of poverty.

Incarceration and African Americans Social justice, a core value of social work, requires that social work professionals confront discrimination, oppression, and institutional inequalities. The American criminal justice system has a sordid history of inequality and differential treatment of African American defendants and prisoners. Indeed, the African American male population has significant challenges. These challenges are often attributed to personal difficulties in attitude, aptitude, and socialization into the mainstream. However, it is important to point out that these challenges are particularly heightened in poor inner-city urban enclaves and are not indicative of most middle-class African American communities. Still, the disproportionate rate of incarceration of black males is cause for great concern. Arguably, incarceration rates of young black males age 20 to 34 is one of, if not the most, pressing issue facing black men, particularly those in urban inner-city communities with pervasive joblessness, violence, and drug use and distribution.

In nearly every state, the incarceration rate of blacks has skyrocketed since the 1960s. Human Rights Watch published *Punishment and Prejudice: Racial Disparities in the War on Drugs,* where it reported that racial disparities in incarceration increased in two consecutive decades, the 1980s and 1990s.[10] The report concluded that blacks were incarcerated at a rate some 8.2 times that of their white counterparts. The report further concluded that, in eleven states, African American men were more than 12 to 26 times more likely than their white counterparts to be incarcerated.

According to the Department of Justice, Office of Justice Programs, the prison population in the United States increased some 2.8 percent from June 2006 to June 2007. Much of the growth in the prison population is attributed to a rise in prison admissions, which was up 17.2 percent. Black men, the report concluded, comprised 37 percent of all inmates held in custody in the nation's prisons and jails as of June 2006. Nearly 4.8 percent of all black males in the general population, compared with 1.9 percent of Hispanic males and 0.7 percent of white males, were in prison.[11]

A 2008 report of the Justice Department estimates that 12 percent of African American men ages 20 to 34 are in jail or prison, compared with 1.6 percent of white men of the same age group. This is the highest rate on record, but it captures the rising trend of incarceration of recent years. Allen J. Beck (chief prison demographer for the Bureau of Justice Statistics), in an interview with the *New York Times,* said of the 12 percent of incarcerated black males and about the racial disparity in U.S. prisons and jails, "it is a very dramatic number, very significant."[12]

Though African American males are disproportionately represented among incarcerated individuals in the prison system, African American females' incarceration rates are also on the rise and equally disproportionate to their white female counterparts. According to the Bureau of Justice Statistics (2008), growth in the number of female prisoners under the jurisdiction of state and federal authorities was nearly twice that of male prisoners from mid-year 2005 to 2006. It is estimated that the female prison population increased 4.6 percent, and the male prison population increased 2.7 percent. In addition, the female prison population has increased on average 3.3 percent per year since year 2000, while the male prisoners only increased at the rate of 2.0 percent annually during this same time period. Though the female incarceration rate is growing much faster than their male counterparts, African American females represent nearly three-fourths of females in state and local prisons, according to reported data.[13] What is remarkable is that, like their African American male counterparts, black females are going to prison at rates significantly disproportionate to that of females of other races.

These incarceration rates are not without controversy regarding the ownership and responsibility of the individual. The often troublesome interplay among poverty, education, crime and incarceration, and disease are realities within many urban and rural communities across America. However, communities of color, and particularly African American communities, suffer disproportionately the ill effects of poor resources, limited access, and minimal opportunities afforded to many others.

Health Issues

There continues to be much public debate over the rising cost of medical care and the lack of adequate health insurance, if insured at all, of many Americans. In particular, there is concern for those among the poorest of the population who must purchase health insurance independent of their employment. According to the Centers for Disease Control's (CDC) National Center for Health Statistics, the U.S. mortality rate dropped sharply in 2006. However, there still exists a significant difference in life expectancy between blacks and whites. It is estimated that African American males can expect to live, on average, six fewer years than their white male counterparts. Life expectancy at birth was 70 years for African American males and 76 years for white males in 2006. For African American females, compared with white females, the numbers are only slightly improved (76 years and 81 years, respectively). While it is a longtime fact that African Americans experience more health problems and tend to, on average, die sooner than their white counterparts, the disparities become more real when looking at causes of death.[14]

Leading causes of death among African American males and females, compared with white males and females, differs slightly. Nationally, the leading causes of death for all races in the United States include heart disease, cancer, stroke, chronic respiratory diseases, unintentional injuries, diabetes, influenza and pneumonia, Alzheimer's, kidney disease, and septicemia. However, when considering race and gender, African American males are more likely to die from homicide (fifth-leading cause) and HIV/AIDS (seventh-leading cause of death). For no other ethnic and gender grouping is homicide and HIV/AIDS among the top ten leading causes of death. What is remarkable is, when factoring in gender and age for women of color ages 25 to 34 years of age, HIV infection was the leading cause of death, the third-leading cause of death for black women ages 35 to 44 years, and the fourth-leading cause of death for black women ages 45 to 54 years.[15]

Moreover, the major disparities among and between groups can be categorized by a range of factors. According to the Centers for Disease Control, these major disparities in health and health care can be attributed to socioeconomic status, race, ethnicity, and insurance status. Because such significant racial and ethnic disparities exist, improving health among the general population of Americans, and African Americans in particular, will require a multifaceted approach addressing many socioeconomic and cultural differences and insurance issues.

The Ecological Systems Model and African Americans: A Social Worker's Perspective

For social workers working with African Americans, the analysis of statistical data provides a perspective beyond that of individual conditions and choices as the sole causal factors of social problems. At the heart of social work is the person-in-environment perspective, which requires consideration of external factors and how these factors shape and influence individual and group behavior and worldviews. Indeed, just as women (who make up 50.9 percent of the U.S. population) experience discrimination and sexism, it is also conceivable that other minority populations (experiencing ageism, classism, racism, heterosexism, and ableism) are likely to be victimized by systemic issues and structural factors that marginalize and place them into subordinate positions within U.S. culture. With so much of America's national history being shaped and constructed using a patriarchal and racially laden social, economic, and political hierarchy, it is important to deconstruct these deeply embedded social, economic, and political structures, so that meaningful progress toward justice and equality can be made. The following section of this chapter considers the ecological systems model that has been a theme in the vulnerable populations' section of this text. However, the process has been inverted, and it begins with the broader (macro) context of historical factors, which reflects and considers how societal conditions mold human action, and it considers social environment and human behavior versus human behavior and the social environment. This inversion emphasizes the importance of the larger societal context in effectively addressing systemic and persistent social phenomena, as it relates to select groups and their overall social functioning.

Historical Perspective

African American history is a rich and diverse account of countless struggles, achievements, adversities, and triumphs. Often the view has been confined to the Western Shores, forgetting the established ancient civilizations on the African continent by African people. This history is rich with political leadership, empirical rulers, and scholars who mastered mathematics, sciences, and the arts. Africans were, and continue to be, a noble and strong people. Despite a popular perception that the first Africans arrived in the Americas as slaves, there is evidence that Africans were in North American long before they were forced over on slave ships. In fact, the first African Americans arriving in the colonies were not slaves at all but indentured servants like many others who came to the Americas during the time.[16]

The exploitation of Africans as free labor was seen by many European Americans as a necessity in order to grow capitalism and build a stable Western infrastructure. Thus, an estimated 15 million Africans were transported, unwillingly, to the new territory as nothing more than property in the minds of their captors. This pattern continued until African Americans and their offspring became lifelong servants to Anglo settlers. It is important to understand that the initial rationale for the enslavement of Africans was an economic practicality but also had significant and strong underlying supremacist ideology, which was supported by academic and Christian theologians alike. Such ideologies made slavery a legalized institution in the United States and subjugated Africans to the will and whims of whites. In addition, this legal casting of blacks into subordinate roles fed a superiority–inferiority construct that continues in the hearts and minds of some blacks and whites still today. Indeed, African Americans strongly believe that they suffer continuously from discrimination economically, socially, and politically in the United States. Many report discriminatory experiences in the workplace, using public transportation, while shopping, and when interacting with law enforcement officers. However, their white counterparts do not share this same perspective regarding their treatment. Many whites believe that many of the problems that plague the African American community are due to personal and cultural values, reliance on public assistance, and lack of motivation.[17]

The Africans' slow progress to full citizenship in America did not come easy. There are numerous historical examples of the overt and covert obstacles to their full participation as equal citizens. In addition, the struggle for social, economic, and political justice for African American people required tremendous collective efforts in grassroots community organizing, nonviolent protests, and civil disobedience. These collective engagements of many blacks and whites resulted in many milestones and legal successes. The Emancipation Proclamation of (1863) was the start of a long and intense struggle for equality. Subsequent legal and legislative actions such as *Brown v. Board of Education* (1954), the Civil Rights Act of 1964, the Voting Rights Act of 1965, and the Fair Housing Act of 1968 all serve as testaments to their persistence and the reluctance of American society to extend equal rights to all its citizens regardless of race, religion, or gender.

For many social workers, overcoming these challenges and their psychological, social, and economic impacts remains a primary focus of their practice with African American clients. However, still more efforts are required to engage in macro-level social and community change efforts toward a more just and equitable society. To establish and make more equal the social, economic, and political participation of African American people, the larger society was compelled to grapple with covert and overt efforts to oppress, marginalize, and disenfranchise African Americans. The "Jim Crow" laws in Southern states and the "restrictive covenants" in the North would not endure the persistent clarion call for lasting peace, equality, and justice to be realized for American society. For the social work practitioner today, proper attention must be given to these historical realities, as efforts to challenge persistent poverty, social and economic injustice, and health issues are waged. As these historical realities have greatly affected environmental–structural factors, it is equally important for the social worker to understand the societal constructs and deeply embedded "isms" that serve as barriers to access and opportunities.

Environmental–Structural Factors

To achieve comprehensive assessment regarding individual and group challenges, and to develop effective intervention strategies to subvert the current trajectory, social workers must consider environmental–structural factors and conditions. Thus, the elements of political, economic, and social structures and forces within the social environment must also be considered. For social workers working with African Americans, understanding structural forces that enhance or hinder social functioning becomes essential to lasting positive outcomes for the individual and the collective (family, group, and community). Therefore, when addressing systemic issues such as poverty and disease, there is value in considering how access to economic resources, or the lack thereof, influences the nature and quality of care received.

Consider for a moment the data presented earlier in this chapter on African Americans' experiences in the educational, welfare, and correctional systems as examples. These systems by nature are intended to strengthen society and provide protection and security. However, when viewed in context and with consideration to historical realities, important linkages that expose patterns of social and economic injustice can be uncovered. Take for example the poor or failing inner-city schools that potentially restrict access to higher education for some children who would otherwise be college bound. Further, these restrictions then potentially limit an individual's skill set and therefore his or her future economic potential. We have discussed how poverty or lack of economic resources can have a profound impact on an individual's and, for that matter, a community's health, educational, social, and political participation. For the social worker who is practicing at any level (micro, mezzo, or macro) with African Americans, the considerations of historical and environmental–structural factors are essential lenses through which to view individual and group functioning.

Cultural Factors

In recent years, much discussion and debate has occurred regarding the influence of culture. In fact, for the professional social worker, there is an ethical responsibility to be culturally competent and aware. This responsibility should not be taken lightly, as it is yet another essential part of effective service delivery.

Culture is the combination of values, norms, language, religion, beliefs, customs, and lifestyles that help to shape the larger society. However, the interplay between various cultures has not always been mutually beneficial. The tendency for the majority or dominant culture to force subordinate cultures to conform to the mainstream is well-documented. While true cultural pluralism is perhaps in the distant future, acculturation and assimilation have been hallmarks of the American establishment. For the African American, cultural issues of interdependence, cooperative economics, and unity run counter to the American idea of independence, self-reliance, and rugged individualism. Indeed the concept of family within the African American culture includes an extended family conception that is foreign in the eyes of one outside this culture. For many African Americans, the extended family network is a combination of kin and non-kin relationships that have sustained and strengthened the black experience in the United States. In the opinion of some, extended family has been essential to the very survival and thriving of the African American family.

Social work practitioners should seek cultural awareness and competencies as they are a required element of professional practice. Moreover they should seek competency in this area as it reaffirms one's commitment to learning from and effectively working with clients who express different views and ways of functioning within the larger societal structure. In so doing, social work practitioners open themselves up to the contributions of multiple ways of knowing and functioning within society and how these influence individual and family functioning.

Family Factors

There is no grater socializing institution in American society than the family. Within family, individuals are provided the tools and skills they need to function in the larger society. Without family fulfilling this primary function, individuals run the risk of potentially lacking essential social skills and tools they need to survive and even thrive. The family role is to pass on to the next generation the cultural artifacts, language, customs, values, strengths, and coping patterns required for participation in the broader society. However, much of the good within family, as well as that which is not so good, can potentially be transferred from one generation to the next.

For example, the transfer of family wealth, or lack thereof, can be an essential component of moving up or down on the socioeconomic ladder. Health conditions, mental, physical, and emotional capacity are also passed on to offspring. For the social worker, understanding the interplay of these factors and how they weigh heavily on life chances is important in assessing and selecting the most effective interventions. In addition, understanding the role of religion within the African American family and culture can potentially be a resource of tremendous strength and support. Overlooking this fact can leave untapped an important family and community support network that is far reaching in emotional and economic influence for African Americans.

Individual Factors

For many social workers, primary attention is often given to family and individual capacities. Many of the explanations for poor social functioning and limited economic capacity have often been based in individual maladies. For the professional social worker, these explanations alone are insufficient and require a more holistic perspective. However, the role of the individual and his or her bio-psychosocial endowment has merit and must be considered. The biological, psychological, and social capacity and capability of the individual and parental nurturing experiences are essential components in the establishment and maintenance of social functioning. Social work practitioners inevitably help individuals use their cognitive, verbal, and problem-solving skills to enhance or restore their capacity for social functioning. In working with African Americans, or any racial/ethnic group, there is a range of emotional maturity and temperament, personality strengths and limitations, and varying social skills and intelligence levels to be considered during the process of service delivery.

There is no substitute for a comprehensive assessment that identifies the capacity for the individual to take on and complete assigned tasks. However, it is the role of the social worker to ensure that these tasks are appropriate to the abilities and capacities of the client given his or her strengths and weaknesses. In addition, attention must be given to the aforementioned factors of family, culture, environment, and historical context, in order to intervene at all levels of service delivery. For the social worker, understanding that there are multiple issues of causality surrounding any given individual challenge or social problem is important. Particularly for the African American, one must confront an ideology of great historical force that continues to attempt to subtract from their human and intellectual value, their beauty, and their capability at every turn, but individually and collectively there must be a sufficient measure and level of resistance.

Social Work Practice with African Americans: A Case Example

THE CASE OF KAREN

Karen, a petite 11-year-old African American girl, has been assigned to the Foothills Residential Treatment Facility for emotionally disturbed adolescents. She has been diagnosed with Oppositional Defiant Disorder and often is the catalyst of much tension with the facility's direct-care staff. While at the facility, Karen's family came to visit. Because there were no such facilities in their local community, the family had to travel nearly 100 miles to visit her at the institution. On this sunny morning, Karen's mother, grandparents, siblings, cousin, and aunt were all excited to be making the trip to visit her.

During the initial greetings, some staff members who observed the family's interactions seemed confused. When the family greeted Karen with hugs and kisses, they all referred to her as Carolyn. She referred to her mom by her first name, Lisa, and her dad she called Frank. However, she referred to her grandparents as Mom and Dad. Karen's biological mother and father and her grandparents lived in close proximity, within the same public housing community in the inner city. Karen's biological parents were teenagers when she was born, and the grandparents played a prominent role in rearing Karen, while offering guidance and supporting Karen's mom. Karen's maternal aunts seemed more like siblings to her, as they all grew up together in her grandparents' home. Thus, Karen often referred to her aunts and cousins as her sisters (play sisters). Karen's visit with her family was an excellent one. As the facility employed a level-system, Karen's good behavior had earned her visitation privileges. In addition, continued progress toward her treatment goals would result in her eventual discharge.

During the initial assessment when Karen arrived at the treatment facility, Christine, the newly assigned social worker to her treatment team, discovered that the home environment was one where trust did not extend further than the immediacy of the housing complex. Indeed, it was territorial in some respects. All persons in the immediate area looked out for one another. The village did raise the children. Even while teaching the survival skills required to counter inner-city violence and perceived threats to one's physical safety and well-being, there was still much stress in the home.

As Christine discovered during her interviews, Karen's behavior seemed to get her in trouble at school and resulted in her suspension and eventual expulsion. Karen's peer-group interactions seemed to seldom go well. She often had physical confrontations with peers, and she failed to respond appropriately to teachers and other authority figures in the school setting. The school system saw her as aggressive and not conforming to rules and other social expectations. Christine also discovered in reviewing the case file that Karen had been to three different schools in the past eleven months because of her behavior. Now Karen was on her fourth expulsion in two years. A school social worker at her last school concluded that a recommendation to an adolescent treatment facility might be the best option in helping Karen deal with what was clear to her to be emotional disturbance and behavior problems.

While writing her case notes in preparation for the treatment team staffing, Christine took some time to review previous case notes on Karen's time at the facility. She recognized that, while in treatment, Karen presented as a normal 11-year-old except when she became "angry." During episodes of anger, her behavior was characterized by temper tantrums, defiance, hostility, and refusal to comply with commands by direct-care staff. However, she responded well to an African American licensed practical nurse (LPN) who was regularly assigned to Karen's unit, and Christine, who also happened to be African American, had good rapport with Karen. However, Karen did have difficulty responding to the psychologist and the director of recreation therapy, both white males.

The treatment team staff meeting that followed Karen's visit with her family, led by the clinical psychologist, included the clinical social worker, an educational specialist, nurses, the occupational therapist, a recreational therapist, a nutritionist, and several psychiatric aides. Christine was one of five social workers at the facility but was the only African American on Karen's treatment team.

After concluding with the usual greetings and pleasantries, the clinical director immediately weighed in on Karen's case. He explained that Karen's problems seemed to be related, in large part, to identity and role confusion and poor self-control, primarily because her family never referred to her by her name but rather called her Carolyn. He further replied that she never referred to her mother as Mom but rather called her grandmother Mom and referred to her mother by her first name, as if she were a sibling or other relative. However, Christine explained that nicknames are common in the black culture. She recalled an example of a close friend, another African American clinical social worker, whose name also was Karen and her family and friends referred to her as Carolyn. This social worker and her family were "well adjusted." The clinical director placed little value on Christine's example and gave no credence to this explanation, and Christine received no support from the other clinical staff, including her fellow social workers. Christine was not surprised by her colleagues' reactions, but she did have concerns about Karen's treatment and intervention plan if cultural issues were being overlooked.

Christine is confronted with several concerns. These concerns cover a range of issues with regard to her responsibility to the client, her coworkers, and the service agency. First, the NASW Code of Ethics clearly articulates that social workers have as a primary ethical responsibility to promote the well-being of clients. Christine had no doubt that the clinical staff at Foothills has Karen's well-being as a primary concern. However, in addition to their responsibility to clients' well-being, the code also recognizes social workers' ethical responsibility to understand culture and its function in human behavior and society, to have a knowledge base of their clients' cultures and be able to demonstrate competence in the provision of services, and to seek to understand the nature of social diversity and oppression with respect to race, ethnicity, and national origin. Second, the Code of Ethics recognizes social workers' responsibilities to colleagues. In addition to treating colleagues with respect, social workers should contribute in interdisciplinary collaborations and contribute to decisions that affect the well-being of clients by drawing on the perspectives, values, and experiences of the social work profession. Further, the code states that, when a team decision raises ethical concerns, the social worker should attempt to resolve the disagreement through appropriate channels. Third, regarding responsibility in practice settings, social workers have a duty to secure appropriate education and engage in continuing education and staff development activities.

Christine had a lot on her mind. How could she fulfill all of these responsibilities? What would happen to Karen if she remained silent on the issues? What would her colleagues think if she took a stand for Karen's right to have her treatment team and subsequent treatment plan grounded in culturally relevant data? As an African American herself, would she be accused of "playing the race card" by taking a hard position on the issue? Having only been at the agency six months, Christine really thought hard about these issues. Nevertheless, Christine knew she had a duty to provide competent and effective social work services to assist her colleagues in their awareness of culturally relevant issues.

Christine recalled reading an article titled *Voices of African American Families: Perspectives on Residential Treatment*. Perhaps she could share this article with the members of her team. The families participating in the study had concerns about the accuracy of clinical assessment and diagnosis of their children, concerns about staff prejudices negatively affecting their care, and concern that cultural incongruity between African American children and staff seemed to hamper effective intervention. One participant reported that a staff member said she felt really good about connecting her child to his emotions and teaching him to cry. Clearly she did not have any experience in the inner-city projects because "we all know you don't do much crying in the housing projects because people will whip your butt." On another occasion, the article highlighted that staff members labeled one particular male as potentially dangerous; "they" didn't want him to wear an Afro, wear braids, or hang around other black children, because, in the eyes of the other children, he and the other black children looked like a gang when they walked together. As a result, the staff separated the child from the other [black] children.[18] Christine really felt this article might be helpful for staff to review.

As Christine was Karen's primary caseworker, she had some autonomy regarding the development of the case plan and how it would be implemented. Though she respected and valued the input of her colleagues, she also felt they neglected to consider some key cultural issues that might assist in better understanding Karen and her family dynamics. Christine recalled on a separate occasion that she saw something published from the Jordan Institute of Families that discussed the multifaceted challenge of figuring out reasons for child neglect. The study found that the challenge becomes more complex when the cultural background of the family and the social worker are thrown into the mix.[19]

Christine was getting excited about all the knowledge she was able to recall with great ease. She wondered if Karen and her family were assessed and judged within the context of their culture and how their culture (African American) would be described or conceptualized? In another study, it was noted that, within the African American culture, like most groups, some differentiation exists between it and that of mainstream culture. In "Karen's Case," Karen and her family were assessed and judged within the context of the non–African American clinical staffs' experiences and realities. Hence, the "yardstick" for measurement was the dominant white, Euro American culture. Christine also understood that in the greater part of current research on African American families is a tendency to compare African American families with European American families, implying that the latter provides the norms for measurement. Such a yardstick relegates the culture of the African American as either insignificant or nonexistent. Moreover, it obviates the idea of strengths-based social work practice and the empowerment approach.[20]

Christine also believed that, if more attention was given to the cultural realities, some of her colleagues would recognize that a number of differences are well established within the African American family unit and in the practice literature. Five such examples really began to resonate with her as she continued to think on this issue and how she would approach and ground her work with Karen and her family. These included (1) extended family kinship networks, (2) egalitarian and adaptable family roles, (3) strong religious orientation, (4) strong education and work ethic, and (5) flexible and strong coping skills.[21]

In Karen's family, the kinship network included three generations. The network consisted of the individual family member's support system and the support system for the family group as a whole. Karen's network did not all share the same household but lived in close proximity and often shared resources, exchanged roles, and shared caregiving responsibilities. Christine felt this was a good thing. In fact, this idea of the extended family kinship network is embraced by the National Association of Black Social Workers in its Code of Ethics: "I adopt the concept of a Black extended family and embrace all Black people as my brothers and sisters, making no distinction between their destiny and my own."[22]

Christine was really on a roll, and as she was nearing the completion of her work, she found one more article that might help to further ground her justifications for a culturally sensitive case plan and intervention. Leslie Hollingsworth, in the article titled "Symbolic Interaction, African American Families, and Transracial Adoption Controversy," used symbolic interactionism as a framework for conceptualizing African American families as a unique and distinct group based on their common heritage and experience. She presented assumptions about the features of the African American community as a social world and about how areas pertaining to African American values and traditions can clarify attitudes and behavior of African American people.[23] Christine believed this conception would promote the belief in collective identity, which lends itself to a groups' ability to fulfill human needs, particularly the need for belonging and the development of a personal identity, esteem, and self-actualization.

As Christine thought about the next regularly scheduled staff meeting, she felt very prepared to introduce the ideas and research articles she had collected. She disagreed with the clinical director and had some ideas about how to approach the situation so that she did not challenge his assertions directly but would clearly state that she did not agree that Karen had an identity problem. Christine believed Karen merely lacked the skills to appropriately cope with her stress. In addition, Christine saw the family as a tremendous resource of love and support, which was evidenced by them all traveling more than 100 miles to see their beloved "Carolyn" at the Foothills treatment center. Surely this extension of love and affection was a benefit and not a deficit, which could be incorporated into the treatment plan. On her way into the meeting, Christine gathered her thoughts, inhaled deeply, and entered the team meeting with confidence in the work she had done.

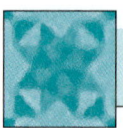

Competent Social Work Practice with African American Clients

Though case material can often address many issues in the educational setting, still, there are challenges. Case examples serve a specific purpose, but readers should understand the limitations of time and space. Like Dick Wolf's *CSI: Miami*, there is much that has to happen but only 60 minutes in which to get it done. Inevitably, in the practice of social work, at the point of intersection between clients and the workers who serve them are a host of emotions, conflicts, and struggles, as well as successes and achievements. Likewise, working with African Americans and their communities requires energy, competence, and professionalism. African American culture, like other groups, is dynamic and ever-changing. Indeed, as Nancy Hill described African American culture, it is a "moving target being created and recreated" over and over again.[24]

For the modern-day social worker, cultural competency is necessary to the helping relationship because approaches to service provision that fail to recognize the significance and value of culturally sensitive practice are inadequate. If social workers are to follow the well-established social work practice principle of "beginning where the client is," they must adapt their practice to the relevant personal and cultural characteristics of each client. Yet they must also consider information about characteristics that may be more prevalent in each special population.

Indeed, some cultural realities may hold true for many African Americans. The distrust of whites is one example. Stemming from more than a hundred years of slavery, broken promises, and institutional racism, it is not difficult to find cause or justification for this "healthy cultural paranoia."[25] Social workers who are not of African American background should be aware of this possible distrust of them and their work when they begin the process of attempting to establish a professional relationship.

Other realities that may affect helping relationships exist because social workers of majority background often are socialized to the images of African Americans that characterize the dominant society's misperceptions of this population. Even in the helping professions, African Americans continue to be stigmatized as being less intellectual, less motivated, more prone to violence, and less apt to be open to change. Such overgeneralizations about African Americans and their culture help to perpetuate the distrust and tensions many feel on both sides. It is imperative that social workers seriously address the validity of these societal stereotypes and examine their own belief systems to minimize the influence of such generalizations in their practice.

In social work practice, it is difficult to attribute cultural incompetence solely to white workers. In fact, such one-way stereotyping would be a fallacy. All social work professionals must guard against cultural incompetence, even when working with persons of similar ethnic origin. As Ryan proposes in his book, *Blaming the Victim*, we are likely to cast blame on those in need of help if we are not careful.[26] Deeply rooted in each of us are cultural biases and prejudices that cause us to act and react in certain ways to diversity and value differences. These values and biases shape our perceptions of the world, i.e., our socialized worldviews. Such perceptions potentially limit our ability to think objectively regarding situations that call into question these values.

Emerging Considerations for Work with African Americans

Traditional approaches and models of thinking about groups of people often assume that homogeneity exists among group members. This assumption postulates that members share most characteristics regarding their ecosystem, i.e., family form, socioeconomic status, values, and so on. However, it is important to note that group members often exhibit variations within groups that can be as extensive as those between groups.[27]

With this understanding, there are several considerations that could serve practitioners in becoming more culturally competent for work with African Americans. Traditional theories often fall short in giving sufficient consideration to such factors as geographical locale, socioeconomic status, sociopolitical issues, and countless other environmental and institutional influences that could make work with this population more successful. Topics social workers might consider studying in more depth as they add to their cultural competence are[28]

- African American history, culture, values, and traditions
- Help-seeking behaviors of African Americans
- Theories of black identity development
- Alternative perspectives on intelligences
- Oppression Theory
- Ecological Systems Theory
- Ethnicity, biculturalism, and bicultural socialization
- Levels of acculturation and its impact on the helping process
- Theories of ethnicity, culture, and social class
- African American family functioning and family forms
- Racial identity development across the life span
- African American male development
- Community building and community renewal
- Strengths-based perspectives
- The digital divide
- People- and place-based strategies
- Economic perspectives on community

Concluding Comment

This chapter sought to address some of the emerging practice implications for work with African Americans. Understanding these implications is important to every social worker if he or she is to engage in culturally competent practice that, for many social workers, equates to competent practice. Failing to become a culturally sensitive and competent practitioner could result in the continuation and persistence of poor access to services for the most vulnerable populations and further widening of the socioeconomic gap between the "haves" and the "have-nots." Truly, the cultural, racial, and ethnic differences that are so often used to divide us pale in comparison to the vast similarities that, if tapped, can unlock the rich human potential that too often lies mostly dormant. Frantz Fannon, a black West Indian revolutionary psychiatrist who had much to say in his theories on oppression, died in 1925 at the age of 36. However, during his short life, Fannon made great contributions to our understanding of the challenge and necessity to expand our knowledge and appreciation of human diversity. In his writing, he characterized our challenge this way,

"The human condition, plans for mankind, and collaboration between men in those tasks which increase the sum total of humanity are new problems, which demand true invention."[29]

Therefore, in making the world a better place for African American people, and all people, in spite of religious, economic, and cultural differences, we must move ever closer to a more inclusive, mutually beneficial coexistence and celebration of differences. Doman Lum helpfully proposes that we engage in a continuous process of enlightenment and discovery regarding the constantly changing nature of multicultural individual, family, and community dynamics.[30]

The profession of social work today and throughout history has been motivated and resolute in seeking multilevel systems change, both domestically and abroad, which increases the social well-being of the society's most challenged members. In keeping with this tradition, practitioners must seek new and inventive ways to overcome obstacles and barriers to better serving clients and creating those societal conditions that make social functioning better for all people.

KEY WORDS AND CONCEPTS

Adaptive-vital culture
African Americans
Black culture
Black family structure
Black identity development

Blacks in the criminal justice system
Blaming the Victim
Matriarchal
Oppression Theory
Unemployment/underemployment

SUGGESTED INFORMATION SOURCES

Carlton-LaNey, Iris B. *African American Leadership: An Empowerment Tradition in Social Welfare History.* Washington, D.C.: NASW Press, 2001.

Cohen, Neil. *Child Welfare: A Multicultural Focus.* Boston: Allyn & Bacon, 2000.

Devore, Wynetta, and Elffridge G. Schlesinger. *Ethnic-Sensitive Social Work Practice*, 5th ed. Boston: Allyn & Bacon, 1999.

Jones, Lee, ed. *Retaining African Americans in Higher Education: Challenging Paradigms for Retaining Students, Faculty & Administrators.* Sterling, VA: Stylus Publishing, 2001.

Lum, Doman. *Culturally Competent Practice: A Framework for Understanding Diverse Groups and Justice Issues*, 2nd ed. Pacific Grove, CA: Brooks/Cole, 2003.

Logan, Sadye L. M. *The Black Family: Strengths, Self-help, and Positive Change.* Boulder, CO: Westview Press, 2001.

Majors, R. *Cool Pose: The Dilemmas of Black Manhood in America.* New York: Lexington Books, 1992.

Parham, T. A., J. L. White, and A. Ajamu. *The Psychology of Blacks.* Upper Saddle River, NJ: Prentice Hall, 2000.

Raider, Melvyn, and Mary Beth Pauline-Morand. *Social Work Practice with Low Income, Urban, African-American Families.* Lewiston, NY: Edwin Mellen Press, 1998.

ENDNOTES

1. National Association of Social Workers, *Assuring the Sufficiency of a Frontline Workforce: A National Study of Licensed Social Workers* (NASW, Center for Workforce Studies, Washington, D.C.: NASW March 2006).
2. Rich Furman, Chance Lewis, and Jeffrey Shears, "Faculty Attitudes Regarding Students' Preparedness for Culturally Sensitive Social Work Practice," *International Education Journal* 5(3) (2004).
3. U.S. Census Bureau, "National Population Estimates—Characteristics," Table 3, 2007, http://www.census.gov/popest/national/asrh/NC-EST2007-srh.html.
4. U.S. Department of Commerce, Economics and Statistics Administration, Bureau of the Census, http://www.census.gov/geo/www/mapGallery/images/black.jpg.
5. Daniel Moynihan, *The Negro Family* (Washington, D.C.: Office of Planning and Research, U.S. Department of Labor, 1965).
6. Carmen DeNavas-Walt, Bernadette D. Proctor, and Cheryl Hill Lee, *Income, Poverty and Health Insurance Coverage in the United States: 2005* (Washington, D.C.: U.S. Census Bureau, 2006).
7. U.S. Census Bureau, *Income, Poverty, and Health Insurance Coverage in the United States: 2006* (Washington, D.C.: Department of Commerce, 2007), pp. 46–47.
8. U. S. Census Bureau, "Educational Attainment by Race, Hispanic Origin, and Sex: 1960–1999," Current Population Reports P20-528 (Washington D.C.: U.S. Department of Commerce, 2000).
9. U.S. Bureau of Census News. "One-Third of Young Women Have Bachelor's Degrees," U.S. Department of Commerce, News Release January 10, 2008, http://www.census.gov/Press-Release/www/releases/archives/education/011196.html.
10. Human Rights Watch, *United States: Stark Race Disparities in Drug Incarceration*, http://www.hrw.org/en/search/apachesolr_search/race+disparities; "Punishment and Prejudice: Racial Disparities in the War on Drugs," http://www.hrw.org/reports/2000/usa/Rcedrg00-01.htm.
11. U.S. Department of Justice, Bureau of Justice Statistics, Office of Justice Programs, "Prison and Jail Inmates at Midyear 2006" (2007), http://www.ojp.usdoj.gov/bjs/pub/press/pjim06pr.htm.
12. Fox Butterfield, "Prison Rates Among Blacks Reach a Peak, Report Finds" *New York Times*, April 7, 2003, http://query.nytimes.com/gst/fullpage.html?res=9D01E7DE1338F934A35757C0A9659C8B63&scp=1&sq=Prison%20Rates%20Among%20Blacks&st=cse.
13. William J. Sabol, Todd D. Minton, and Page M. Harrison, *Prison and Jail Inmates at Midyear 2006* (Washington, D.C.: U. S. Department of Justice, Office of Justice Programs, 2007), p. 5.
14. Centers for Disease Control, National Center for Health Statistics, Office of Communication, "Deaths: Preliminary Data for 2006" (June 2008), http://www.cdc.gov/nchs/data/nvsr/nvsr56/nvsr56_16.pdf.
15. Centers for Disease Control, "HIV/AIDS among Women" (CDC HIV/AIDS Fact Sheet, August 2008).
16. Ivan Van Sertima, *African Presence in Early America* (New Brunswick, NJ: Transaction Publishers, 1992).
17. Rudolph Alexander, *Racism, African Americans, and Social Justice* (Lanham, MD: Rowman & Littlefield Publishers, 2005).

18. Jean M. Kruzich, et al., "Voices of African American Families: Perspectives on Residential Treatment," *Social Work* 47(4) (2002): 461.
19. "Neglect and Cultural Sensitivity," *Children's Services Practice Notes, North Carolina Division of Social Services and the Family and Children's Resource Program*, 2(1) (Winter 1997).
20. Connie Kane, "African American Family Dynamics as Perceived by Family Members," *Journal of Black Studies* 30(5) (May 2000): 691.
21. Ibid.
22. National Association of Social Workers, *Code of Ethics* (Washington, D.C.: NASW Press, 1996).
23. Leslie Hollingsworth, "Symbolic Interactionism, African American Families, and Transracial Adoption Controversy," *Social Work* 44 (September 1999): 443.
24. Nancy Hill, et al., "Sociocultural Contexts of African American Families," in Vonnie C. McLoyd, et al., ed., *African American Family Life: Ecological and Cultural Diversity* (New York: Guildford Press, 2007), 21.
25. Freddy Paniagua, *Assessing and Treating Culturally Diverse Clients: A Practical Guide* (Thousands Oaks, CA: Sage Publications, 2005).
26. William Ryan, *Blaming the Victim* (New York: Pantheon Books, 1971).
27. Lawrence Shulman, *The Skills of Helping Individuals, Families and Groups*, 3rd ed. (Itasca, IL: Peacock Publishers, 1992), p. 35.
28. Joe M. Schriver, *Human Behavior and the Social Environment: Shifting Paradigms in Essential Knowledge for Social Work Practice*, 3rd ed. (Boston: Allyn & Bacon, 2001); Ruth G. McRoy, "Cultural Competence with African Americans" in Doman Lum, *Culturally Competent Practice: A Framework for Understanding Diverse Groups and Justice Issues*, 2nd ed. (Pacific Grove, CA: Brooks/Cole, 2003).
29. Cited in Neil Badmington, *Posthumanism* (New York: Palgrave, 2000, p. 4).
30. Doman Lum, *Culturally Competent Practice: A Framework for Understanding Diverse Groups and Justice Issues*, 2nd ed. (Pacific Grove, CA: Brooks/Cole, 2003).

chapter 26

Social Work Practice with Puerto Ricans*

> **Prefatory Comment**
>
> The Puerto Rican population on the mainland is the nation's second largest Hispanic group, having nearly 4 million persons living on the mainland, yet they maintain deep roots on the island of Puerto Rico, and families travel frequently between the two locations. They are perhaps the most heterogeneous of all Hispanic subgroups and one of the poorest. Puerto Ricans come in many forms, structures, and colors, reflecting extended families whose appearances range from black skin, dark hair, and dark eyes to blond hair, blue eyes, and white, freckled skin.
>
> Among Hispanic groups, tragically, Puerto Ricans remain among the poorest and, as a community, struggle with a myriad of issues that include extreme multigenerational poverty, high alcoholism and drug addiction rates, undereducation, poor housing, limited job skills, and lack of access to adequate health care. Puerto Ricans in the United States are truly the only "colonized" population group. While they do not face the problems associated with illegal immigration, they remain marginalized and trapped in cycles of poverty and social dysfunction.

Understanding the diversity of the Hispanic family requires a fundamental understanding of the different Hispanic subgroups in the United States. The total Hispanic population in 2004 was 40.4 million—a 14 percent population increase since 2000.[1] Each group has a particular history with the United States that has shaped the manner in which the family and its supportive institutions have emerged. Only one group, Mexican Americans/Chicanos, originates in the area that is now the continental United States, but the bulk of the Hispanic population, like Puerto Ricans, Cubans, Dominicans, and Central and South Americans, immigrated into this country. Hispanics are not a homogenous population group and have different countries of origin. This fact becomes one of the most important differentiators

---
*This chapter was prepared by Dr. Gloria Bonilla-Santiago, professor of public policy administration, Rutgers University, New Jersey.

between Hispanic population subgroups. The diversity in birth places influences many of the attitudes and experiences of Hispanics on the mainland. Puerto Ricans are U.S. citizens and move freely between the island of Puerto Rico and the mainland. The adaptation of the Puerto Rican population in both urban and rural settings stems from the socioeconomic and historical relations between their home country and the United States. Migration, in their case, continues to be based primarily on labor needs and, to varying degrees, a continued relationship with home regions.

Current Demographics

Population

Mainland Puerto Ricans are the second largest Hispanic subgroup in the United States. There are approximately 3.8 million Puerto Ricans living in the United States, and more than 3 million living in the Commonwealth of Puerto Rico. They constitute 10 percent of the U.S. Latino population and are relatively youthful, highly urbanized, and primarily concentrated in a few states in the Northeast, although their numbers are increasing in Midwestern, Western, and Southeastern states. The states with the largest Puerto Rican populations in 2000 were New York, Florida, New Jersey, Pennsylvania, and Massachusetts. During the past 30 years, there has also been significant population growth in Connecticut, Illinois, California, Ohio, Texas, and other areas in the Midwest, thus expanding the national presence of Puerto Ricans.[2]

Puerto Ricans became citizens of the United States with the passage of the Jones Act in 1917. They began a northward migration in the late 1940s and 1950s as part of "Operation Bootstrap," a plan to establish a yearly migration of thousands of Puerto Ricans to the agricultural farmland of the Northeast corridor. As a result of this plan, an Economic Development Administration that brought industrial incentives designed to develop and diversify the economy was created in Puerto Rico. That plan is responsible for what today is a relatively stable, growing middle class of Puerto Ricans on the island and a growing underclass of Puerto Ricans on the island and mainland who are experiencing the most serious socioeconomic problems of any minority group, including Native Americans. Of important significance are the socioeconomic changes on the island of Puerto Rico, resulting from the discontinuation of tax incentives essential to job creation and the changing federal policy contributing to the growing erosion of education, health, and welfare systems on the island. The resulting socioeconomic outlook for Puerto Rican families is concerning and challenging, and it translates into a community that is increasingly economically polarized. Puerto Ricans continue to have the highest poverty rate in comparison with other Hispanic subgroups. Growing poverty on the island coupled with circular migration patterns makes Puerto Rico a major exporter of poverty to the mainland.[3] For example, as of 2000, 26 percent of Puerto Rican families lived below the poverty level. A significant number of these families were headed by single women. Forty-four percent of the single female–headed households on the mainland are poor and 91 percent on the island.[4] Zavala-Martinez attributes this to four social and historical processes that have a direct impact on the reality of Puerto Rican women: (1) the political and economic relationship between Puerto Rico and the United States shaped by "colonialism"; (2) the development of capitalism in Puerto Rico and the economic transformation from an agricultural to an industrial society; (3) the role and social status of women in Puerto Rico and in the class society; and (4) the emerging forms of consciousness and struggle among Puerto Ricans, given the political relationship with the United States.[5]

Education

Although Puerto Ricans have made gains in educational attainment over the past ten years, nationally only 67 percent of Puerto Ricans and 57 percent of Hispanics over the age of 25 hold at least a high school degree, as compared with 89 percent of non-Hispanic whites. Only 14 percent of Puerto Ricans under age 25 have earned a bachelor's degree or higher.[6] A number of risk factors contribute to this disproportional educational outlook. The majority of Hispanic and Puerto Rican students attend underperforming schools that do not prepare them for postsecondary education. A survey conducted by the Pew Hispanic Center documents that only one in four Latino students were qualified for the postsecondary world.[7] Other risk factors include parents without a high school degree, low family income, multigenerational history of school dropout, lack of achievement in the early grades that leads to grade retention, high mobility rates among families, teen pregnancy, and lack of aspirations. Those students who enter postsecondary education tend to begin their studies in a community college, thus reducing their chances for completing a four-year degree. These numbers grow slimmer when looking at master's and doctoral degrees. Cabrera and La Nasa argue that students who have been historically underrepresented at the postsecondary level—those who are poor, of color, and first generation—are less likely to prepare for, apply for, enroll in, and persist through postsecondary education.[8] The long-term effect of the undereducation of Puerto Ricans and other Hispanics is a factor in the persisting low socioeconomic conditions of these communities.

Characteristics of Poverty

During the mid-1980s when most families experienced economic recovery, Puerto Rican families continued to experience extremely high poverty rates. The 1990s began with the Puerto Rican poverty rate at the same level at which it peaked in the 1980s. The pattern of poverty and despair remained constant in the early 2000s. Child poverty is one of the most pressing challenges Puerto Ricans face and is an important factor in the development of intervention strategies and policy initiatives. Puerto Rican children represent the poorest population group in the United States.[9] In 2001, more than 33 percent of Puerto Rican children lived in poverty, as compared with 28 percent of Latinos and 9.5 percent of non-Latino white children. In addition, more than half (58.4 percent) of the child population in Puerto Rico lives below the poverty level.[10] Children in families with high poverty rates are less likely to report being in good health than children in higher income households. Poverty also has a negative impact on child nutrition, what neighborhood a family can afford to live in, and the quality of schools. These conditions can give rise to cyclical patterns as poor families have greater difficulties rising out of poverty.

A disproportionate number of Puerto Rican families remain trapped in the welfare system, without options or hopes for adequate long-term employment. Factors such as low educational attainment, inadequate job skills, language barriers, lack of access to transportation, and poor employment opportunities in their communities contribute to this overreliance on the welfare system. As a result of the "work first" nature of the welfare system, many welfare recipients do not receive the training they need to obtain jobs that pay a livable wage. Even when a family is able to leave the system, it often remains underemployed and poor.

Housing and healthy neighborhoods are also factors that contribute to the development and growth of families and their communities. Home ownerships and greater access to financial resources are critical requirements for a healthier lifestyle and for better family outcomes. Puerto Ricans and Hispanics face low rates of homeownership and tend to live in substandard housing. Though overall homeownership rates have increased on a national level to 68 percent, the Latino homeownership rate is still 20 points below that, at 48 percent, and nearly 30 points below the non-Hispanic white homeownership rate of 75 percent. Low wages and lack of a good credit history hinder their access to decent housing. As a result, many Puerto Rican families are forced to live in overcrowded and substandard homes and pay a higher percentage of their income for rental housing. Other factors such as discrimination, predatory lending practices, language barriers, and lack of trust in financial institutions make it difficult for Latinos to achieve the dream of homeownership.[11]

Among some factors associated with Puerto Rican poverty are low educational attainment, concentration in low-wage work, growth in single-mother families, immigration, and discrimination, but these factors only partially explain the persistence of high poverty rates among Puerto Ricans. According to research, six principal factors underlie and help to explain the persistent poverty of Puerto Ricans. These include industrial and economic changes, changes in skill requirements, gaps in educational attainment between Puerto Ricans and non-Hispanic whites growth in women-maintained households, unstable participation in the labor force, and geographical location and concentration.

Industrial Economic Changes Industrial and economic changes in the economy during the 1960s and 1970s greatly affected the Puerto Rican community. Specifically, U.S. cities lost thousands of low-skilled, well-paid manufacturing jobs when the shift from a manufacturing to a service economy began. The "deindustrialization" of cities, especially in the Northeast where Puerto Ricans were heavily concentrated at that time, eliminated jobs filled by Puerto Ricans with limited levels of education.

Changes in Skill Requirements The demands of the growing service sector economy increased the labor market demand for higher literacy and numeric skills, displacing low-skilled segments of the population. Since 1979, almost nine out of every ten new jobs created have been in industries like business and health services that require high levels of education and for which many Puerto Ricans are not qualified.

Gaps in Educational Attainment between Puerto Ricans and Non-Hispanics Over the past two decades, Puerto Ricans have made gains in their educational attainment, as measured by median years of school completed. However, examination of high school dropout rates and high school and college completion data shows that there are still wide educational disparities between Puerto Ricans and non-Hispanic whites that put Puerto Ricans at a disadvantage when competing for jobs.

Growth in Women-Maintained Households The proportion of Puerto Rican, female-headed households increased during the 1980s but has been decreasing since 1989. Such families experience higher rates of family and child poverty than do two-parent families; Puerto Rican single mothers tend to have limited work experience and to rely heavily on public assistance.

Unstable Participation in the Labor Force The labor force status of Puerto Ricans has changed dramatically since the major migration of Puerto Ricans to the United States during the early 1950s. Upon their arrival, Puerto Ricans, including women, were more likely to be working or looking for work than their non-Hispanic white counterparts. For economic reasons highlighted in this chapter, forty years later, both Puerto Rican men and women lag behind non-Hispanic white people in labor force participation, and they experience higher unemployment rates than whites, other Hispanics, and, in some cases, African Americans.

Geographical Location and Concentration Recent research has begun to examine the labor market experiences of mainland Puerto Ricans based in the area of the country in which they reside—primarily the Northeast and Midwest, areas that have been especially affected by economic changes and that offer Puerto Rican workers poor employment opportunities.

Health and Mental Health Risk Factors

The 1980s saw significant growth in the mental health literature addressing cultural, socioeconomic, clinical, and developmental issues of Puerto Ricans in the United States.[12] In addition, there was more cross-cultural therapy and counseling literature concerning Puerto Ricans.[13] However, a gap seemed to exist between the valuable information being published and the application of that knowledge. The "pathologization" of Puerto Ricans and other minority groups in the United States continues to be a problem of significant proportion, as are the blaming, judgmental, and moralistic attitudes of many service providers. Furthermore, some authors still offer heavily stereotyped descriptions of Puerto Ricans, presenting a static rather than an evolutionary, dynamic, transactional view of the culture.[14]

Cultural awareness in therapy must include awareness of class differences, an awareness often absent in family therapy literature and practice. Socially disempowered families or individuals cannot be assessed separately from the position they occupy in the power structure of the society in which they live. Behaviors labeled as "mental illness" or "dysfunction" may actually be survival strategies in response to poverty, racism, sexism, or other types of oppression. In such instances, the victims end up being blamed.

Even when therapist and client share the same ethnic background, if issues related to poverty and migration are not considered, therapy is not likely to be successful. Values and belief systems usually differ significantly across classes, and ideology is usually linked to one's position in the social hierarchy. Having a common national origin or language does not mean that significant class differences will disappear inside the therapy room; in fact, they may be exacerbated.[15]

The scarcity of bilingual professionals available to offer mental health services to Puerto Ricans increases the difficulties in therapy. Although recruitment of Puerto Ricans by U.S. agencies is becoming common, it seldom includes basic orientation and training sessions about the characteristics and socioeconomic environment of the population these professionals are to serve. It is often incorrectly assumed that a common national origin will automatically increase the quality of services.

In mental health clinics, newly arrived clinicians from middle-class backgrounds often feel overwhelmed, frustrated, and impotent when they face the types of problems that migrant Puerto Rican clients present. Clients may far outnumber available bilingual practitioners; thus, clinicians may be assigned large case loads with no backup support system provided by the clinic. During their years of study, these practitioners may have never dealt with mental health issues related to poverty and migration.[16]

It is imperative that orientation and training be provided to practitioners and that they engage in clinical practice with Puerto Ricans. Comas-Diaz states that cross-cultural mental health training is not only useful where racial and ethnic differences exist between patient and clinician, but is also needed when the clinician and the patient are racially and ethnically similar but have different socioeconomic backgrounds or different value systems.[17] This is seen in the following cases.[18]

CASE ONE

The G family comprised both parents Pedro (49 years old) and Teresa (41), plus seven children. Carmen, the oldest, was 23, and Papo, the youngest, was 10. Pedro, Jr., Jaime, Fernando, Margarita, and Flor ranged in ages from 14 to 21 years. An eighth child had died five years previously at age 4. The circumstances of her death are described below.

The request for mental health and medical services was initiated by the father, who for six years had been the "identified patient." He attended the first therapy session with his older daughter, Carmen. He arrived tearful, head hung low, and depressed. Carmen did most of the talking during the initial stage. She reported that her father's symptoms included depression, crying spells, social withdrawal, insomnia, irritability, lack of appetite, excessive cigarette smoking (two packs a day), and continuous coffee drinking.

To get Pedro to talk, I asked him questions about the history of his present emotional state. Highlights of his report are as follows:

Six years previously, he had suffered an accident while working in Puerto Rico. The accident occurred while Pedro was driving a trailer. The fellow worker who was with him died instantly. Pedro spent three months hospitalized with head and back injuries, the first three weeks of which he was unconscious.

Upon discharge he went back to work, still experiencing visual and memory problems in addition to back pain. A year later he had a second accident while driving. The company laid him off with a total compensation of less than $2,000. (He had worked for the company for more than twenty years.) Pedro requested help from the Legal Services Corporation (a U.S. federal agency with offices in Puerto Rico), but in his opinion the services offered were not adequate and an appeal of the company's decision never reached the court.

Pedro began experiencing mood swings from severe depression to rage. This created crisis situations for the entire family, who, according to their report, had a fairly normal life up until then. During this time Pedro underwent eye surgery for lesions caused by the accidents.

Shortly after his layoff, his 4-year-old daughter was hospitalized with a high fever of unknown origin. She died of a generalized infection caused by an infected intravenous tube administered at the public hospital. His daughter's death increased Pedro's depression, sense of despair, and feeling of powerlessness. Moreover, his wife Teresa also experienced severe depression as a result of their child's death.

Three years ago the family started to break up. The oldest daughter, Carmen, moved to the East Coast of the United States, followed gradually by her older siblings. Two years later Pedro's wife, Teresa, left him and also migrated to the United States with the two younger children. According to Pedro, she could no longer deal with his mood swings and outbursts of anger. Pedro reported that he often became very irritable, could not tolerate noise, and screamed and threw things when he got very upset. He stated that he had never become physically violent with his family.

Pedro remained in Puerto Rico, living alone in the family's house. Shortly after Teresa left, Carmen was contacted by an uncle who requested that she visit her father because his depression was getting worse and he was becoming physically ill. Carmen complied. She went to see her father and decided to bring him back to the United States with her.

When I started working with the Gs, Pedro and Teresa did not speak to each other and lived in separate apartments. Pedro was living with Carmen and her husband. Margarita, who had already been "adopted" by her older sister, also lived with them. Teresa lived with Papo and Flor in an apartment next to one of the older sons.

Jaime and his wife, who was pregnant, were estranged from the rest of the family. Carmen explained that she thought they avoided the family because her brother's wife, although Puerto Rican, did not speak Spanish and didn't feel comfortable with the family because of the language barrier. (This was a vague response, but I respected their apparent wish to maintain areas of privacy at that point.)

Fernando lived with friends and was also in conflict with his parents. Pedro explained that Fernando had a tendency to get himself in trouble (for example, borrowing more money than he could possibly repay) and then rush to his father requesting help. These requests, Pedro said, made him feel even worse because it made it more obvious that he could no longer "support or even help his family economically."

Pedro had "given up." The changes in the family structure from how they lived and functioned in Puerto Rico to their circumstances in the United States were too much for him to handle. Having lost his role as the family provider, he declared himself "terminally disabled" and allowed Carmen to "mother" him by taking care of all his needs except for personal hygiene. His depression continued, and the crying spells occurred more frequently. However, his outbursts of anger, which appeared to have been the only expression of power he had left, disappeared. Carmen even became his "voice" as a result of the language barrier.

The living arrangements gave Teresa a "break" from dealing with Pedro's depression as well as space to let her own depression be expressed. Teresa described herself as being "sick of her nerves" since her daughter died. The younger children, all of whom described Pedro as having been a "very strict father," found themselves liberated from his "law and order," as well as from his anger, while still maintaining physical closeness to both parents.

The family was experiencing turmoil when they started therapy: the sudden separation and lack of communication of the parents after more than twenty years of marriage; the migration of all family members to the United States, with the consequent difficulties of adaptation to a new land (the parents did not speak English); the organization of the family in the United States; the older daughter as the focus of support for the entire family system; the humiliation of having to request welfare support from local agencies (expressed by both parents in tears in one of the sessions); and the two teenage daughters having to work as waitresses for the first time due to economic difficulties.

The family's expressed goal in therapy was to get the parents back together: "If father could get his nerves cured!" I interpreted their request for therapy as a sign of readiness to assume control of their lives again. They needed me to facilitate the process by "legitimizing" their emotional reactions to the tragedies they had experienced and by helping them obtain financial aid from the disability, welfare, and rent-subsidy programs. Pedro was ill with a kidney infection; as a result of his accident, he still had visual problems and severe back pains. Teresa had never worked outside the home. In addition, their lack of skills in English reduced their job opportunities. Nonetheless, Pedro wanted to be recognized as the family provider, even at the cost of being declared "officially disabled."

Part of the work during therapy was to reframe their sense of shame at having to ask for help from Puerto Rican immigrants already established in the community while they reestablished themselves as a new immigrant family. A series of family rituals, such as collective dinners and presenting the history of their family through photographs and role playing, were incorporated into the treatment process.

In addition, throughout the process I shared with them my interpretations of their situation and development stages while requesting their feedback. I made it clear that therapy required teamwork and that their input and expertise about themselves were of utmost importance. I have found emphasizing teamwork to be very effective for empowering families: they are the experts, and I am the facilitator.

Family therapy lasted five months, at the end of which Pedro and Teresa were back together, had been granted the diverse financial aids for which they had applied, and had a support system in the community to help them deal with ongoing challenges.

CASE TWO

In the late 1970s, at age 16, Javier migrated to the United States from a slum in metropolitan San Juan. He had dropped out of school prior to completing the seventh grade because he felt he "wasn't learning anything, and it was a waste of time." He learned auto mechanics while helping a friend who had a garage. His father had left home when Javier was 10 years old, and they seldom saw each other. His mother had migrated to the United States the previous year with two younger children. Javier joined them with the intention of getting a job quickly as a mechanic and moving into his own apartment. He acquired basic English language skills within several months.

After a year of searching unsuccessfully for a job, he started to drink and get into fights. In one fight, he mortally stabbed another Puerto Rican. While in prison, he was diagnosed as "schizophrenic" by the consulting psychiatrist, apparently due to his continuous expression of anger, and was transferred to a psychiatric prison. After four years, during which he was medicated with antipsychotic drugs, he was released on probation. He returned to his mother's apartment and resumed his search for a job. Four months later he got a job at a gas station working for minimum wage. He lasted three weeks at this job. Someone informed the owner that Javier had been in a psychiatric prison, and he was fired. Once again, he turned to drinking to work out his frustrations.

Javier was 23 when I first saw him in therapy. He was seeking to be declared "disabled" so that he could get financial assistance. He was willing, he said, to "act crazy if that was necessary—he was already carrying the label anyway." Therapy lasted six months and consisted of several components: individual work with Javier on rebuilding self-esteem; and family work, which meant including his mother in some of the sessions in an effort to establish additional support and to plan strategies that could help Javier deal with the stigma of "madness." Together, they decided that moving to another community would help them in obtaining a fresh start.

During therapy, we contacted various agencies until we located one that was willing to train and certify Javier as an auto mechanic. With the certification in hand, Javier started his own business of fixing cars in front of his apartment (not uncommon in Puerto Rican barrios). He soon earned a solid reputation; staff from the clinic and other related agencies began going to him with their cars.

Discussion of Cases

These two cases are typical of the low-income migrant Puerto Rican situation in the United States. In both cases, disability was regarded as the solution to economic difficulties that the identified patients were facing.

Understanding these phenomena requires knowledge of the impact of socioeconomic conditions on people's lives. Without such knowledge, it is difficult, if not impossible, to understand how illness, either physical or mental, may become an asset. Low-income and poor families confront the therapist with issues of economic survival, compared with the more existential or other clinical issues commonly addressed in graduate training programs.

The loss of jobs or absence of jobs poses a severe problem for male and female heads of households. Moreover, a significant number of employed Puerto Rican migrants continue to work at low-paying jobs. The fact that women receive even lower salaries than do men complicates the economic survival of the Puerto Rican family.

Clinicians need to be aware of these environmental circumstances and be sensitive to the particular situations of the family. Making generalizations about the unwillingness of a people to work helps no one. The quality of the clinician's interaction with the clients is essential to how the family reality is constructed, interpreted, and dealt with. It is important when working with families who are disempowered within societal structures that an ecosystemic assessment be conducted for the family.

General Data on Health Care and Puerto Ricans

The data concerning Puerto Ricans' national health status provide several overall findings. In general, the major national killers—heart disease, stroke, and cancer—are also the major causes of death among Puerto Ricans. Rates may be distorted, however, by the population's relative youthfulness. Among Puerto Rican families, the leading cause of death is heart disease; the second leading cause of death is AIDS; and the third leading cause is violence, including accidents, suicides, and homicides. Health status is significantly affected by lifestyle and behaviors. For example, improper diet, smoking, and excessive alcohol consumption are known to increase the risks for developing significant health problems such as diabetes, cardiovascular disease, and cancer.

Data from the National Health Interview Survey suggest that the overall rate of smoking among Puerto Ricans is 54 percent higher than that of other groups, largely because of the low incidence of smoking among females in other racial and cultural groups. Prevalence of smoking also was highest for both Puerto Rican men and women (35 percent) compared with any other Hispanic subgroup.[19]

Puerto Rican families are under considerable stress as they adapt to a different culture and way of life, as they cope with low income and poor housing, and as they experience exploitation and mistreatment from both individuals and institutions. For some people, such stressors increase the risk for somatic and functional illness, depression, organic disease, and interpersonal tensions.[20] Indeed, Puerto Ricans have been identified as a high-risk group for mental health problems, particularly depression, anxiety, and substance abuse.[21] Health professionals and social work providers working with Puerto Rican populations need to be aware that many Puerto Ricans believe in the interaction between mental health and physical health—that the physical affects the mental and vice versa.[22] Thus, it is important to understand mental health issues prevalent among Puerto Ricans in order to better address their specific needs and to design relevant preventive modalities.

Migration and subsequent culture shock are thought to engender anxiety and depression.[23] People in transition often experience feelings of irritability, anxiety, helplessness, and despair. They must mourn the loss of family, friends, language, and culturally determined values and attitudes. Some Puerto Ricans respond to migration with a "hangover depression" that may include suicide attempts.[24] Puerto Rican women are particularly vulnerable to depression. Severe psychiatric disorders are sometimes diagnosed incorrectly when practitioners are not aware of prevalent cultural beliefs and practices. This is further exacerbated by the use of psychological tests that have not been standardized for bilingual populations.

In general, babies born with low birth weights are at highest risk for neonatal illness and death. Teenage mothers tend to have less prenatal care and to bear a larger percentage of low-birth-weight babies than do mothers in their 20s. Puerto Ricans bear children at about the same rate as African Americans, and their incidence of low-birth-weight infants (9 to 10 percent) falls between that of non-Hispanic whites and African Americans.[25] Puerto Rican women also tend to have the lowest levels of early prenatal care (55 percent) and the highest levels of delayed or no prenatal care (17 percent).[26]

Beliefs and Practices That Influence Puerto Ricans' Health

Factors such as economic status, level of education, and length of time in this country (recent arrivals, first or second generation, etc.) may influence individuals' health behavior more than cultural factors. Thus, among Puerto Ricans in the United States, there is not one predictable "Puerto Rican response." For example, the traditional Puerto Rican diet is high in fiber, relying heavily on beans and grains, rather than on meats, for protection. However, Puerto Rican diets reflect many current dietary recommendations and also play a key role in some illnesses.

Healthy practices can be encouraged through use of traditional cultural sayings. The "health beliefs model" postulates that, in order for people to make changes in their lifestyle, they must believe that they are susceptible to a disease, that the disease is serious, and that prevention can be helpful. Some commonly known Puerto Rican sayings suggest that events in one's life result from luck, fate, or other powers beyond an individual's control: *Que sera* (What will be will be); *Que sea lo que Dios quiera* (It's in God's hands); *Esta enfermedad es una prueba de Dios* (This illness is a test of God); and *De algo se tiene que morir uno* (You have to die of something). Indeed, persons with acute or chronic illness may regard themselves, and often are regarded by others, as innocent victims of malevolent forces. In such cases, family and friends expect support throughout the healing process. Similarly, when receiving traditional health services, Puerto Ricans may become passive, expecting the provider to "take charge" of them—a stance that doesn't fit with the active participation required to prevent or heal much disease.

Balance and harmony also are considered important to health. A person's sense of *bienestar* (well-being) is thought to depend on balance in emotional, physical, and social arenas. Imbalance may produce disease or illness. For example, some Puerto Ricans attribute physical illness to *los nervios* (nerves), believing that illness results from having experienced a strong emotional state. Thus, they try to prevent illness by avoiding intense rage, sadness, and other emotions.

In the absence of adequate access to health care, some Puerto Rican families seek the services of folk healers instead of, or simultaneously with, mainstream health care. However, Puerto Ricans' reliance on folk medicine is minimal—fewer than 4 percent of any group consult a folk healer over a twelve-month period.[27] Belief in folk healers assumes that one can have contact with God and the supernatural without intervention of the traditional church; indeed, the traditional church and folk healing coexist. The following briefly describes the folk healing systems used by Puerto Ricans: *Santeria* combines the African Yoruban deities with Catholic saints; *Santeros/santeras* are both priests/priestesses and healers.

Among Puerto Ricans, a belief in *espiritismo* holds that the world is populated with spirits, including religious figures, who intervene in the lives of individuals. These *espiritistas* can communicate with the spirits and have the power of healing. These persons may know about different types of home remedies, herbs, and so on and have skills in treating certain physical conditions (such as joint deviation) or have other special powers.

The extent of Puerto Ricans' reliance on folk healers is a subject of some controversy in research. Perhaps because the belief systems and practice are so interesting, many people have studied and reported on them. Their prevalence in the literature, however, does not reflect its very modest use among Puerto Ricans.

In other Hispanic groups, one observer found the use of folk healers to be common though ancillary to a health care system among Mexicans in southern California. Apparently, they used them when they were pressured by family or friends, when they disagreed with a physician's diagnosis, or when they were disappointed with the quality of care provided by a physician.[28]

Folk healers and some home remedies cause no harm and may well be helpful, but such remedies or practices may be harmful when they are used as substitutes for needed medical care. In such instances, social workers and other social service providers must carefully consider what approach to take so that clients are not "driven underground." It usually does not help to ask people if they use folk healers or folk medicine. People don't think of what they do in those terms. It does help to ask routinely, "Which prescription medications, over-the-counter medicines, or herbs are you taking now?" If you want to know something specific, ask a specific question. For example, pediatric health providers in certain areas routinely ask, "What do you do when your child has *empacho* (lack of appetite, stomachache, diarrhea, and vomiting)?"

Respecting and affirming your patients' efforts to stay or become healthy will enhance your ability to influence them through positive education. Opportunities abound to educate through one-to-one interaction, culturally sensitive program posters, pamphlets, and other displays in your waiting room, and so on.

Ecosystems Perspective

The practice of social work focuses on the interaction between the person and the environment. The goal of social work practice is to enhance and restore the psychosocial functioning of persons or to change oppressive or destructive social conditions that negatively affect the mutually beneficial interaction between persons and their environment. In assessing Puerto Ricans' needs for services, the social worker should seek to understand the clients' feelings and attitudes about those oppressive and destructive factors and to ascertain their negative impacts.

The ecosystems model of practice developed by Morales and Sheafor[29] is adopted for analysis of psychological factors affecting Puerto Ricans. The ecosystem consists of five interconnected levels: (1) historical, (2) environmental–structural, (3) cultural, (4) family, and (5) individual. An analysis of each level as it affects the lives and social conditions of Puerto Ricans follows.

Historical Influences

Puerto Ricans, the second-largest Hispanic group in the United States, have been migrating to the mainland United States since the turn of the twentieth century. In 1917, the Jones Act granted all Puerto Ricans born on the island U.S. citizenship. This is a striking difference from all other Latino immigrants to the country, as

Puerto Ricans can move freely between their country of origin without the legal restrictions and entanglements of U.S. immigration law.

Migration to the continental United States became a viable alternative to living in the deteriorating economic and social situation on the island. Economic changes on the island, brought about by foreign control of land for sugar and coffee plantations and tobacco, created high unemployment and a steady stream of immigrants to the United States that has continued to the present. One of the first casualties of this economic change was the incremental decline of family patterns based on subsistence. High unemployment coupled with gradual industrialization caused both increased unemployment and dependence on outside commodities. This imbalance created surplus labor at a time when jobs in New York City and elsewhere on the mainland needed to be filled. Puerto Ricans began migrating to the United States and, in particular, to New York City.

The decades before 1945 are considered the period of the "Great Migration" and pioneer migration. Many of the people emigrating from Puerto Rico were contract laborers who came to work in industry and agriculture. These individuals were the basis for many of the Puerto Rican communities that currently exist outside of New York City. By 1940, there were a total of almost 70,000 Puerto Ricans in the United States; more than 87 percent, or almost 61,000, were living in New York City.

By 1960, a total of 887,662 Puerto Ricans had migrated to the mainland; 69 percent of these people, or about 612,000, resided in New York City. Like other Hispanic immigrants, Puerto Ricans did not travel together in family groups at the beginning of the migration. Usually, young men immigrated to find work and then began sending for spouses and families. But the social conditions in the United States, especially in New York where new communities were established, set parameters that changed family patterns and continued the adaptation of Puerto Ricans to the city.

Poverty became a significant factor in the lives of families in both Puerto Rico and the United States. It is impossible to discuss the Puerto Rican family in the United States without discussing the extreme conditions that have pervaded the Puerto Rican community here. From a historical perspective, Puerto Ricans have never recovered from the early colonial period when U.S. capital interest took over the ownership of the majority of land on the island and created a labor force that was dependent on cash crops. Puerto Rico had one of the highest infant mortality rates in the world and one of the lowest rates of average income per worker during the early years of U.S. jurisdiction over the island. Consider, for example, that in 1899 Puerto Ricans maintained ownership of 93 percent of all farms, but by 1930 foreign (U.S.) interest controlled 60 percent of sugar cultivation, 80 percent of tobacco lands, 60 percent of all banks, and 100 percent of maritime lines that controlled commodities entering and leaving the island.[30]

Although migration between Puerto Rico and mainland United States has been described as a primary reason for the poor socioeconomic status of Puerto Ricans in the United States, migration as a contributor to Puerto Rican poverty is difficult to confirm because Puerto Rican migration data are not regularly, or scientifically, collected. Moreover, little research exists on the demographic characteristics of migrants and the effects of migration on the socioeconomic status of mainland Puerto Ricans. The limited research that has been done has examined the number of Puerto Ricans migrating and the reasons behind their migration.

Significant Puerto Rican migration to the United States continued into the late 1940s and the early 1950s. As economic opportunities on the mainland increased during the post–World War II economic boom, low airfares between New York and Puerto Rico were introduced, thereby facilitating migration between Puerto Rico, where there was a surplus of low-skilled labor, and the mainland. According to the Bureau of Applied Research on the Puerto Rican Population in New York City, Puerto Rican migrants in the early 1950s included both men and women of all ages. The data showed that about four in ten were men between the ages of 15 and 45; the Bureau noted that Puerto Rican migration, compared with foreign immigration, was characterized by family, as opposed to individual, movement.

At the end of the 1960s and into the early 1970s, what has become known as "revolving door" migration began. This is a back-and-forth stream of people moving between the United States and the island. It is no longer focused in New York, although a majority of Puerto Ricans continue to migrate and settle in the Northeast.

Since those early dates of migration to the mainland, the economies of both the United States and Puerto Rico have undergone serious changes. Instead of leaving the island because of economic opportunities in the United States, many Puerto Ricans are now leaving the island because of the lack of economic opportunity in Puerto Rico. Therefore, in addition to the promise of jobs, a wider range of employment options, and higher salaries on the U.S. mainland, the lack of economic opportunity in Puerto Rico also influences migration. Shifts and trends in the mainland economy also have consequences for the Puerto Rican economy, causing some islanders to migrate when they cannot find employment.[31] Migration to and from Puerto Rico between 1982 and 1988 showed that more than 151,000 more Puerto Ricans left the island than moved to it.

Environmental–Structural Factors

Puerto Ricans have had a history of being victims of exploitation and racism in the United States. Unlike mainstream culture, which is predominantly Western European, the ancestral roots of the Puerto Ricans are Indian (indigenous to Puerto Rico), African, and Spanish. In the past, a number of publicly accepted practices excluded people of color, and in particular Puerto Ricans, from many institutions and positions of influence. Jobs were advertised in separate categories (male or female, white or "colored"), allowing organizations to exclude people who were viewed as undesirable. Puerto Ricans were largely confined to low-paying jobs and perceived as being inferior in intellect, training, and motivation to white men, women, and African Americans in the workplace.

When affirmative action legislation started to take hold, it did little to address the underlying assumptions and stereotypes that plagued nontraditional managers and created the barriers to advancement that persist today in views about Puerto Ricans. When the law forced them to hire and promote nontraditional employees, some responded with "malicious compliance" by deliberately appointing nontraditional candidates who were weak or ill suited to the jobs available so that they would have little chance of succeeding.

Barriers to Advancement for Puerto Ricans The most significant barriers today are the policies and practices that systematically restrict the opportunities and rewards available to Puerto Ricans and other Hispanics. This is a fundamental finding in Bonilla-Santiago's study,[32] wherein managers agreed that prejudice is still a serious problem and the number one employment barrier.

Prejudice is defined here as the tendency to view people who are different from some reference group in terms of sex, ethnic background, or racial characteristics, such as skin color, as being deficient. For example, prejudice is the assumption (without evidence) that nontraditional individuals are less competent or less suitable than white males.

Ethnic and sex differences are sometimes used, consciously or not, to define "inferior" groups in a caste system. For example, Puerto Ricans were labeled as "unassertive people"—they "sit back" in meetings while others hurl and debate ideas. Some whites consider Puerto Ricans and Latinos "too polite" (and, consequently, as lacking in conviction), perhaps because of their concern for showing respect or maintaining cooperative teamwork.[33] There is also a trust barrier. Puerto Ricans and Latinos are perceived as dishonest and corrupt by individuals from the dominant culture. The prevailing stereotypes of African Americans are that they are lazy, uneducated, and incompetent. Women are often assumed to be indecisive and unable to be analytical. A survey by the University of Chicago's National Opinion Research Center, along with other research findings, shows that these stereotypes are still prevalent. This survey revealed that whites believe that people of other ethnic backgrounds are less intelligent, less hard working, less likely to be self-supporting, more violence prone, and less patriotic than whites.[34]

Restrictions against Puerto Ricans consist of additional discrimination in housing, employment, educational opportunities, and access to social services. Such structural, social, and psychological barriers are prevalent in the Puerto Rican culture today.

Puerto Rican Culture

Social workers need to focus on understanding the cultural values, belief systems, and societal norms of U.S. culture as Puerto Rican culture. In an attempt to understand the Puerto Rican client and to work effectively with this population, the following describes several important cultural values operating among Puerto Ricans: importance of the family; familism versus individualism; and the values of *respeto* and *personalismo,* styles of communicating that will continually affect your interaction with the client. To the extent that you can appreciate and respond to the client's values and language needs, you will be more effective. A further look at these cultural values follows:

1. Importance of the Family: Traditionally, Puerto Ricans include many relatives as "family" not only parents and siblings but grandparents, aunts, uncles, cousins, close family friends (who are often considered honorary uncles or aunts), and *padrinos* (godparents). All may be involved in an individual's health. During illness, people frequently consult other family members and often ask them to come along on medical visits.

2. Familism versus Individualism: Familism emphasizes interdependence, affiliation over confrontation, and cooperation over competitions.[35] Within familism, important decisions are made by the family, not by the individual alone. Thus, family members expect to be involved in treatment plans that require a shift in lifestyle, for example, a change in diet, if the family network is involved in providing and preparing food. Migration and geographic mobility may put stress on Puerto Ricans' values of familism. For example, a young family that has recently moved into your area may have left behind its extended family support system. Similarly, teenagers who are quickly adopting the manners of their peers in the U.S. culture may be in marked conflict with their parents who maintain traditional values and customs.

3. *Respeto* Requires Deference: The way Puerto Ricans show respect to one another, establish rapport, express caring, treat each other as males and females, and communicate nonverbally to one another is different from that of the dominant culture. *Respeto* dictates appropriate deferential behavior toward others on the basis of age, sex, social position, economic status, and position of authority. Elders expect to receive respect from younger individuals, adults from children, men from women, teachers from students, employers from employees, and so on. Social work providers, by virtue of their treating functions, education, and training, are seen as authority figures and as such are awarded *respeto*.

Respeto Establishes Rapport: *Respeto* further implies that relationships are based on a common humanity, wherein one is required to establish—not simply assume—rapport, decency, and respect.[36]

As in the general population, positive interactions between social workers and the Puerto Rican client require providing information about the examination, diagnosis, and treatment; listening to the client's concerns and taking individual needs into consideration in planning treatment; and treating the client in a respectful manner. For example, Puerto Rican clients can be shown *respeto,* even by providers with limited Spanish, by always using the formal "*usted*" (Sir) for "you" until the patient explicitly offers the use of the informal "*tu*" (you). Address Puerto Ricans formally as *Señor* (Mr.) or *Don* (Sir), *Señora* (Mrs.) or *Doña* (Madam), and greet clients in Spanish with *buenos dias* (good morning) or *buenas tardes* (good afternoon).

4. *Personalismo*—Warm, Friendly, Personal Relationships: Younger social workers, even though they will be awarded *respeto* as authority figures, are expected to be especially formal in their interactions with older Puerto Rican clients. Formality as a sign of respect, however, should not be confused with distance. Puerto Ricans tend to stress the importance of *personalismo*—personal rather than impersonal or institutional relationships. Thus, many Puerto Ricans expect social work providers to be warm, friendly, and personal and to take an active role in the client's life. For example, a social worker might greet a client, "*Buenos dias, Señora* Santiago. How are you today? How is your family feeling after the accident?" or "How are the children doing at school?" Such a greeting acknowledges *personalismo,* conveying to the client that the provider is interested in her as a human being. *Personalismo*

also stipulates that the client's relationship is with the individual provider, not with the institution. When asked where they receive medical care, Puerto Ricans often respond with the name of the provider: "I am seeing Doctor (nurse)" rather than with the name of the institution.

5. Communication Styles Guided by *Respeto* and *Personalismo:* Verbal communication among Puerto Ricans tends to be structured, guided by the cultural values of *respeto* and *personalismo*. When interacting with social work providers, many Puerto Rican clients tend to avoid confrontation and conflict by not disagreeing, not expressing doubts about the treatment, and, often, by not asking questions. Many would rather not admit that they are confused about their instructions or treatment.

Communication Style Includes Nonverbal Communication and Expressiveness: Many Puerto Ricans communicate intense emotion and may appear quite animated in conversations—behavior that is sometimes misperceived by non-Puerto Ricans as being "out of control."

Physical Touching: Puerto Ricans tend to physically touch others. Many expect the provider to shake hands when greeting; males often hug family members and friends to express their affection, and they may express their gratitude to providers and other health care personnel by kissing or giving gifts.

Expression of Pain: Similarly, Puerto Ricans may express pain more openly than is expected among other cultural groups. For example, some Puerto Rican patients moan when in pain.

Eye Contact: Traditionally, Puerto Ricans have been taught to avoid eye contact with authority figures (such as health or mental health providers) as a sign of *respeto;* such behavior should not be misinterpreted as being uninterested in the communication. Conversely, the provider is expected to look directly at the client, even when communicating through an interpreter.

Closeness versus Distance: When interacting with others, Puerto Ricans typically prefer being closer to each other in space. Overall, Puerto Ricans tend to be highly attuned to others' nonverbal messages. Non-Spanish-speaking providers must be particularly sensitive to this tendency when establishing relationships with patients who speak only Spanish.

6. *Fatalismo* (Fatalism): Fatalism and Puerto Rican values need to be examined in the context of Catholicism and colonialism. The notion of a "colonialist personality" is found throughout a good part of the literature. A few may see life's events as inevitable ("*Lo que Dios manda*"—What God wills). They feel themselves at the mercy of supernatural forces and are resigned to their fate. This fatalistic attitude of some Puerto Ricans has partly contributed to their unwillingness to seek outside professional help.

Family Structure

The Puerto Rican family is not monolithic. The traditional Puerto Rican family is no longer the norm. Although the family continues to be central in Puerto Rican lives, it has taken on a variety of forms to meet changing personal and social conditions.

The high unemployment of the 1980s and the change in the American economy from one based on manufacturing to one based on information and services has had staggering consequences on the Puerto Rican family. In fact, the Puerto Rican family is changing as the world around them changes. Family size, geographical distribution, and other characteristics in U.S. society have had obvious effects on the Puerto Rican family. Still, the Puerto Rican family tends to be family-oriented with strong kin networks, and fertility rates are about 50 percent higher than in the rest of the U.S. population. These relatively high rates result from a combination of traditional Catholic beliefs and relatively low family income and individual educational attainment. Because of profound psychological stressors caused by poverty and white racism, Puerto Rican families are also more likely to divorce or separate than Anglos.

Puerto Rican families come in many forms, structures, and colors. Extended families may have members whose appearances range from black skin, dark hair, and dark eyes to blonde hair, blue eyes, and freckled white skin. Within one family, all or some may speak Spanish, all or some may speak English, all may be bilingual, or in some families members may speak three or more languages. They also vary in social class. Many are poor and uneducated, and others are middle class in income and education; however, Puerto Ricans are the poorest of any Hispanic subgroup. Puerto Ricans tend to be mostly urban. They usually cluster together in communities where they can preserve their language, customs, and tastes. Generally, there are three types of Puerto Rican families: recently arrived families, return migration families, and second-generation descendant families.

Intervention Strategies

Social workers who provide direct service, or microlevel social work intervention, and indirect service, or macrolevel societal intervention, with Puerto Ricans need to have firsthand knowledge of how this unique ethnic minority group has traditionally responded to mental health and social services.

Puerto Rican families, for the most part, retain values, attitudes, and behaviors that can be used constructively in the context of mental health services. Such strengths include the affective bonds among extended family members, the value placed on the community in providing diverse types of support to its members, and *personalismo* as a commonly shared character trait. The willingness of the Puerto Rican family to be warm and sharing in relationships allows the social worker to approach and intervene. Open discussion among family members can resolve many problems, some of which may be related to conflicts caused by the closed bonds of the extended system. Knowledge of the family's specific cultural, socioeconomic, and religious background, together with sound intuitive skills, help clinicians use the strengths of Puerto Rican families.

Concluding Comment

When working with Puerto Rican families, social workers need to possess personal qualities that reflect genuineness, empathy, nonpossessive warmth, and the capacity to respond flexibly to a range of possible solutions. It is important that an acceptance of and openness to differences among people be respected. Willingness to learn to work with clients that are ethnically different is also important.

The social workers' articulation and clarification of their personal values, stereotypes, and biases about their ethnicity and social class, as well as those of others, and ways they may accommodate or conflict with the needs of the Puerto Rican client are essential in any process of intervention. Understanding the culture (history, traditions, values, family systems, and artistic expressions) of Puerto Rican clients is very important. It is important that the impact of ethnicity on therapists' and clients' behavior, attitudes, and values is understood.

When helping Puerto Rican families, the social worker must always consider cross-cultural issues and account for multiple components beyond those that pertain specifically to "culture." Issues related to socioeconomic class are particularly important to consider, as affluent Puerto Ricans have, for example, far more resources than impoverished Puerto Ricans, whose poverty becomes an additional psychosocial stressor. Social workers must always be clear about their professional practice role and intervention methods, being careful not to promote conformity and dependence in their clients. A cross-cultural micro and macro practice will achieve the best results.

KEY WORDS AND CONCEPTS

Puerto Ricans
Colonialism
Espiritismo
Mainland Puerto Ricans
Fatalismo
Personalismo

Respeto
Jones Act
Island Puerto Ricans
Independence
Puerto Rican culture

SUGGESTED INFORMATION SOURCES

Bonilla-Santiago, G. *Breaking Ground and Barriers: Hispanic Women Developing Effective Leadership.* San Diego, CA: Marin Publications, 1993.

Comas-Diaz, L., and E. H. Griffith, eds. *Clinical Guidelines in Cross-Cultural Mental Health.* New York: John Wiley & Sons, 1988.

Facundo, America. "Sensitive Mental Health Services for Low-Income Puerto Rican Families," in Marta Sotomayor, ed. *Empowering Hispanic Families: A Critical Issue for the '90s.* Milwaukee: Family Service America, 1991.

Garcia-Coll, C. C., and M. L. Mattei, eds. *The Psychosocial Development of Puerto Rican Women.* New York: Praeger, 1989.

Mizio, Emelicia. "The Impact of Macro Systems on Puerto Rican Families," in Armando T. Morales and Bradford W. Sheafor. *Social Work: A Profession of Many Faces*, 6th ed. Boston: Allyn & Bacon, 1992.

Zavala-Martinez, Iris. "En La Lucha: The Economic and Socioemotional Struggles of Puerto Rican Women," in Lenora Fulani, ed. *The Politics of Race and Gender in Therapy.* New York: Haworth Press, 1987.

ENDNOTES

1. *Hispanic Trends 2005,* Pew Research Center (Washington, D.C., 2005), http://www.pewhispanic.org.
2. "Puerto Ricans in the United States," Wikipedia (November 2008), http://en.wikipedia.org/wiki/Puerto_Ricans_in_the_United_States.
3. Ibid.
4. Ibid.
5. Iris Zavala-Martinez, "En La Lucha: The Economic and Socioemotional Struggles of Puerto Rican Women," in Lenora Fulani, ed., *The Politics of Race and Gender in Therapy* (New York: Haworth Press, 1987).
6. *Latino Youth Finishing College: The Role of Selective Pathways,* Pew Hispanic Center (June 2004), http://www.pewhispanic.org.
7. Ibid.
8. A. F. Cabrera and S. M. La Nasa, "Understanding the College Choice of Disadvantaged Students," *New Directions for Institutional Research* (San Francisco: Jossey-Bass, 2000).
9. "Hispanic Poverty Fact Sheet," National Council of La Raza, Census Information Center, November 2000, http://www.nclr.org.
10. "Latinos in the United States," op. cit.
11. "Barriers to Homeownership for Latino Families," Washington, D.C.: Democratic Caucus, U.S. House of Representatives (June 2005), http://democrats.assembly.ca.gov/members/a23/pdf/HousingSummary.pdf.
12. C. C. Garcia-Coll and M. L. Mattei, eds., *The Psychosocial Development of Puerto Rican Women* (New York: Praeger, 1989); L. Comas-Diaz and E. Griffith, eds., *Clinical Guidelines in Cross-Cultural Mental Health* (New York: John Wiley, 1988); C. Falicov, ed., *Cultural Perspectives in Family Therapy* (Rockville, MD: Aspen Press, 1983); M. McGoldrick, J. K. Pearce, and J. Giordano, eds., *Ethnicity and Family Therapy* (New York: Guilford Press, 1982); I. Canino and G. Canino, "Impact of Stress on the Puerto Rican Family," *American Journal of Orthopsychiatry* 50 (1980).
13. P. B. Pedersen, "Ten Frequent Assumptions of Cultural Bias in Counseling," *Journal of Multicultural Counseling and Development* 15 (1987); I. Ibrahhim and P. M. Arrendondo, "Ethical Standards for Cross-Cultural Counseling: Counselor Preparation, Practice, Assessment and Research," *Journal of Counseling and Development* 64 (1986); C. Falikov, ed., *Cultural Perspectives in Family Therapy* (Rockville, MD: Aspen Press, 1983); D. Sue, *Counseling the Culturally Different* (New York: John Wiley, 1981).
14. J. M. Dillard, *Multicultural Counseling: Toward Ethnic and Cultural Relevance in Human Encounters* (Chicago: Nelsen-Hall, 1983).
15. America Facundo, "Sensitive Mental Health Services for Low-Income Puerto Rican Families," in Marta Sotomayor, ed., *Empowering Hispanic Families: A Critical Issue for the '90s* (Milwaukee: Family Service America, 1991), p. 124.

16. G. Bernal and I. Flores-Ortiz, "Latino Families in Therapy: Engagement and Evaluation," *Journal of Marital and Family Therapy* 8 (1982): 357–365.
17. Comas-Diaz and Griffith, op. cit.
18. These cases are reprinted from America Facundo, op. cit., pp. 126–130. © 1991, Family Service America. Used with permission.
19. S. Haynes, B. Cohen, C. Harvey, and M. McMillan, "Cigarette Smoking Patterns Among Mexicans and Puerto Ricans" (paper presented at the 113th Annual Meeting of the American Public Health Association, Washington, D.C., November 19, 1985).
20. W. A. Vega and M. R. Miranda, "Stress and Hispanic Mental Health: Relating Research to Service Delivery" (Rockville, MD: U.S. Department of Health and Human Services, National Institute of Mental Health, Public Health Service, 1985).
21. Comas-Diaz and Griffith, op. cit.
22. A. Padilla and R. Ruiz, *Latino Mental Health: A Review of the Literature* (Rockville, MD: National Institute of Mental Health, 1973).
23. A. C. Garza-Guerrero, "Culture Shock: Its Mourning and Vicissitudes of Identity," *Journal of the American Psychoanalytic Association* 22 (1974): 408–429.
24. E. Trauatman, "Suicidal Attempts of Puerto Rican Immigrants," *Psychiatric Quarterly* 35 (1961): 544–554.
25. S. J. Ventura, "Births of Hispanic Parentage, 1983 and 1984," National Center for Health Statistics, Monthly Vital Statistics Report, 36(4) Supplement (PHS), 1-19 (Public Health Service, National Center Statistics, 1987).
26. Ibid.
27. N. Garcia-Preto, "Puerto Rican Families," in M. McGoldrick, J. K. Pierce, and J. Giordano, eds., *Ethnicity and Family Therapy* (New York: Guilford Press, 1982), pp. 164–186.
28. S. E. Keefe, "Acculturation and the Extended Family," in A. Padilla, ed., *Acculturation* (Boulder, CO: Westview Press, 1980).
29. Armando Morales and Bradford W. Sheafor, *Social Work: A Profession of Many Faces*, 10th ed. (Boston: Allyn & Bacon, 2004), pp. 230–235.
30. J. Jennings and Monte Rivera, *Puerto Rican Politics in Urban America* (Westport, CT: Greenwood Press, 1984).
31. I. Perez-Johnson, "Industrial Change and Puerto Rican Migration to the United States, 1982–1988" (paper presented at conference on Puerto Rican Poverty and Migration, New School for Social Research, New York, May 1, 1992).
32. G. Bonilla-Santiago, *Breaking Ground and Barriers: Hispanic Women Developing Effective Leadership* (San Diego, CA: Marin Publications, 1993).
33. Ibid.
34. T. W. Smith, "Ethnic Images," National Opinion Research Center, GSS Topical Report No. 19 (Chicago: University of Chicago, December 1990).
35. Falicov, op. cit.
36. R. Maduro, "Curanderismo and Latino Views of Disease and Curing," *Western Journal of Medicine* 139 (1983): 868–874.

part six

Social Workers in Action

Part Six is the culminating section of this book. It is a complex case originally prepared by the late Armando Morales. The case displays experienced social workers using the advanced knowledge and skill obtained through their MSW education when responding to a tragedy in a community. In Chapter 5, "Entry to the Social Work Profession," social work was described as an "applied profession," that is, a discipline in which knowledge is applied to helping people address social issues. The primary goal of this chapter is to demonstrate how much of the information about social work included in the previous sections of the book is applied by social workers as they carry out their many and varied practice activities.

In the overall structure of *Social Work: A Profession of Many Faces*, the beginning and ending chapters might be viewed as bookends, that is, case materials that introduce and then summarize the way social work practice plays out. In Chapter 1, "A Child Welfare Case: The Social Worker in Action," Demetria, the social worker, was a beginning-level professional—a new BSW graduate on her first independent case—addressing a report of suspected child neglect. Through the early chapters of the book, the work of Demetria was used to illustrate the application of some of the concepts and theories in each chapter. The final chapter, Chapter 27, "Social Workers in Action: School Homicide and the Death Penalty," examines a high school homicide incident, a tragedy that too often occurs across the nation, showing how advanced-level social workers responded to this crisis, which resulted in the death penalty for the female adolescent offender. The social workers in this case not only use in-depth knowledge and skill in assessing the case situation and counseling with the client, but they also engage in many activities that address organizational, community, and social policy matters. Also, under the leadership of a social work faculty member, BSW students developed a concept paper concerning the controversial issue of capital punishment and hopefully begin the process of the state considering legislation around this topic.

chapter 27

Social Workers in Action: School Homicide and the Death Penalty*

Prefatory Comment

In this chapter, "Social Workers in Action: School Homicide and the Death Penalty," one can observe experienced professional social workers addressing one of the United States' most perplexing issues, violence and homicide among youths. The case demonstrates the complexities of advanced-level social work practice. All people are threatened and terrorized by the rising tide of random violence occurring at shopping malls, fast-food restaurants, schools, and other public places. Evidence about violence and who is predisposed to violence can be gained by drawing conclusions based on quantitative research, a deductive process, and/or through an inductive process drawing conclusions from a qualitative, in-depth analysis of one case and then generalizing to other cases. The inductive approach was adopted for this chapter. The case is based on a composite of several cases, re-created to convey important concepts, underlying theories of violent and homicidal behavior, and the multiple micro and macro roles performed by advanced social work practitioners in addressing this problem. We obverse both the clinical and administrative work of Bob Pla, an advanced generalist social worker, and additionally experience the work of BSW students who, under the supervision of a social work professor, developed a position paper concerning capital punishment and the execution of women.

Bob Pla, MSW, was making his usual morning drive to work on a sunny, yet windy, day. Bob was singing along with his favorite "Oldies but Goodies" radio station. He was happy and felt very fortunate to be living in Olas,† California, a moderately sized, predominantly middle-class beach community of nearly 200,000 people. It had a small minority population of mostly working-class people, which included 5 percent African Americans, 7 percent Asian Americans, and 12 percent Latinos. Bob thought it was a good place to raise a family because of the community's outstanding schools and low crime rate, ranked fourth in the nation as to the lowest ratio of crime per population. Although there were a few gangs in the community,

---
*This chapter was originally prepared by Armando Morales.
†In Spanish, *olas* means ocean waves.

Bob knew from prior street gang group work in violent, crime-ridden Los Angeles that they were not the violent type. They were more like "wanabes" (want-to-be), trying to impress their peers in school. Bob smiled as he reflected that Olas was a relatively safe, crime-free community.

Actually, there had been four to five homicides each year in Olas, but Bob had blocked them out of his mind. Bob was seduced by the media into believing that violence and homicide were predominantly a poor "black and brown inner-city" phenomenon. Olas did have several, mostly minority-group, gangs, and, even though they had engaged in tagging and committed some burglaries and minor and serious assaults, they had not committed any homicides.

Bob also reminded himself, from experience providing forensic court testimony in violent crimes cases in Los Angeles, that nationally, out of the homicides committed over the past thirty years where the relationship between the victim and offender could be identified, 29 percent involved a family member killing another family member or a boyfriend or girlfriend, and nearly 50 percent were killings by friends or other acquaintances. These are called *criminal homicides,* where the primary intent is to kill another human being. The majority of public media attention, however, focuses on the other 21 percent of homicides, *felony homicides,* when the killing of another person is committed by strangers,[1] usually during the commission of a felony crime such as a robbery, burglary, or "carjacking." "We're in greater danger from being killed by someone we know well rather than by a complete stranger," concluded Bob.

Bob continued on his way, and he began to collect his thoughts in preparation for the things he needed to do as soon as he arrived at work. He now had been executive director of the Olas Family Services Center for nearly four years. He enjoyed his job and believed he had a very competent staff, composed of ten MSW-licensed clinical social workers, four BSW-level social workers, a quarter-time psychiatrist, and five administrative and clerical staff. The music on his radio was suddenly interrupted. Danny Jones, the popular Olas DJ, stated:

> Sorry folks. We have to take a time out. I just received a bulletin. There was a possible homicide at Olas High School. Details are not yet confirmed, but police report that a 12-year-old girl was shot several times by an unknown assailant in what appears to be a gang "drive-by" shooting. Three ambulances are on the scene, but so far only one person is confirmed injured. Hundreds of students entering the campus on their way to their first class witnessed the tragic event. Many are hysterical.

Bob resisted the impulse to drive to the school to see if he could help. He wondered if some of his staff had had the same thought and had already gone to the school. Using his cellular telephone, he called his office from his car and asked his secretary to notify all staff to remain at the office for a staff meeting. The agency had to coordinate an appropriate response to this crisis at Olas High School. Danny Jones again interrupted the music on the radio and said:

> I have just been handed some current information concerning that shooting at Olas High. The 12-year-old white female victim died at the scene. She has been identified, but this information will remain confidential until her parents have been notified.

Bob turned off his radio. He was shocked and saddened and did not wish to hear any more music. When he arrived at the Olas Family Services Agency, he quickly went into the conference room where most of the staff were congregating. They appeared to be upset and angry and wanted to go immediately to the school to help. Two staff members were arguing with each other. One member stated that Olas was a fine, safe community until Mexican immigrants and L.A. African Americans moved into town. The other staff member, a Hispanic female social worker, argued that, had it not been for the racism in Olas, there would not be any problems in the community. Two social workers demanded that Bob cancel the staff meeting so that they all could go to the school to help the distraught students.

Others were numb with shock and did not say anything. Mrs. Scott, a social worker, asked for permission to take time off and go to the school to look after her two children who were students there. She was the only staff person with children at Olas High, and her request was granted as she now was functioning as a parent and not as a representative of the agency. Bob also knew that her anxiety and emotional state of mind would interfere with her attempts to help others at the school. Several thoughts ran through Bob's mind. His professional staff was in chaos given the current high school crisis. Anxiety, guilt, anger, and feelings of helplessness were quite prevalent. He wondered how his staff could go out and help others given their current states of mind. He had to assume leadership for the staff and develop an overall strategy to address the problem and its various manifestations.

Planning Social Work Interventions

Bob Pla knew that the school would be immediately shut down and the children sent home. Thus there was time to receive input from his staff and develop an intervention plan. Bob taped several large sheets of butcher paper to the walls of the conference room. On one he wrote at the top, "IMMEDIATE STAFF AND AGENCY PRACTICE TASKS." On the next, "DIRECT PRACTICE TASKS FOR FAMILIES AND THE SCHOOL." And on another, "INDIRECT AND PREVENTION PRACTICE TASKS." When the staff arrived for the meeting, he gave each a colored marker and invited them to list actions that they thought the agency would need to take to address this tragedy. The resulting lists included the following:

Immediate Staff and Agency Practice Tasks

1. Review online information and brief the staff about crisis theory and crisis intervention with specific emphasis on "best practices" for counseling children and families in an emergency situation.
2. Encourage sharing and venting of feelings among agency staff prior to contacting the school.
3. Develop a strategy for dividing the workload and providing assistance at the school.

4. Obtain agency board authorization to work with the school and for overtime and weekend work, if needed, to deal with the crisis.
5. Make plans for staff coverage to deal with the emotional upset created by this incident for any current clients of the agency.
6. Contact the school principal and counseling staff to make plans to bring the agency's mental health services to the school.
7. Contact and coordinate resources with other mental health agencies and professionals willing to provide mental health services to the school, especially to those students most affected by the school homicide.

Direct Practice Tasks for Families and the School

1. Provide clinical assistance for the deceased victim's family.
2. Provide clinical and mental health consultation to students and their families as needed.
3. Provide clinical and mental health consultation to school faculty and administrators as indicated.
4. Provide clinical and mental health consultation to paramedics and law enforcement personnel as needed.
5. Offer services if requested by the perpetrator(s) and their families.

Indirect and Prevention Practice Tasks

1. Meet with the media to encourage calm, brief reporting to avoid provoking fear, anger, anxiety, and hysteria in the community by dramatic, sensationalistic reporting.
2. Provide consultation to the mayor and Board of Supervisors and urge them to call for calm in the community and discourage minority-group scapegoating and vigilantism.
3. Provide consultation to the informal leaders of the minority communities, appealing to "cool heads" during this crisis period.
4. Spearhead the creation of a multidisciplinary, multiethnic task force to investigate the causes of the school violence and develop recommendations for the prevention of such incidents.

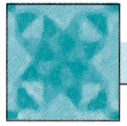

Mobilizing the Agency and Staff for Action

The first set of tasks had to be dealt with immediately. Recognizing the importance of evidence-based practice, Bob asked his most senior supervisor, Melissa Valentine, to drop everything else and conduct an online search for information about the emotional impact of such trauma on children, families, and communities, as well as searching for "best practices" research on intervention approaches. Ms. Valentine was to brief the staff at another staff meeting to be held that afternoon. Bob asked each social worker to assess his or her existing caseload and to identify any clients who might have been victims of violence or homicide for whom this event may cause a relapse and bring a list of those clients to the meeting. Also at this meeting, a plan would be made with the staff regarding their assignments for the next few days. In addition, Bob had his secretary phone the president of the agency's board who gave Bob cart blanche permission for staff overtime, weekend pay, and whatever extra resources would be needed to help the community address this tragedy. Bob then personally called the school principal, who was familiar with the agency's work because the school often referred students with behavioral problems to Olas Family Services Center. The principal appreciated the agency's offer to provide assistance because his two school counselors were trained in psychometrics and career counseling, rather than in treating emotional crises. Finally, working through representatives of the local unit of the National Association of Social Workers, Bob sent an e-mail to all members asking those who had experience in providing counseling in such crisis situations to contact the center if they were willing to provide services, if needed.

At the afternoon staff meeting, before Bob began planning to address the initial tasks, he gave the staff the opportunity to vent their feelings. The staff responses to the tragedy were not predictable but perhaps not different from conversations occurring in homes and businesses all over Olas. Some minority staff believed they had worked very hard to advance themselves and their families to get out of the *barrio* and *ghetto*, and now their safety was being threatened. They wanted to see more and better schools built in the poor minority communities so that these children would not have to travel into the affluent areas. Some staff members strongly objected, stating that this thinking was racist and would take them back to segregated schools such as they had prior to the 1950s. Mrs. Smith, one of the senior social workers, wanted to see metal detectors installed in all schools and police stationed on campuses. Others argued against this, pointing out that the perpetrator of the homicide was in a vehicle and not on campus when the incident occurred. Miss Garcia asserted that the availability of guns was the main "culprit." Many agreed, but Mr. Karls, an NRA member and hunter, strongly disagreed, stating that "people, not guns, kill people!"

Bob was surprised by the varied responses and the divisiveness among his staff. He had been under the impression that he had a cohesive staff. "Social workers are no different from the general public," he reflected, "and represent the many faces not only of social work, but of the society at large." He decided to try to unify them around a common goal and assumed control of the meeting by stating:

> I can see that we have several conflicting viewpoints. It seems clear there is not a single answer or cause of this problem. The causes are many as are the solutions, but we have to agree on a common strategy and intervention plan as social workers. We have to keep our focus on doing our best for our clients—the students, their families, and the general community, which includes the minority communities. So far we do not have a lot of facts concerning this homicide, other than that "someone" fired a weapon from a vehicle into a crowd of students on campus, resulting in the death of a white, 12-year-old female student. Things are still rather sketchy, and we really do not know whether the perpetrator was a minority-group person or even whether the crime was gang related. These incidents are not uncommon in the inner cities of Los Angeles, New York, Chicago, or Detroit, but in the past the general public in Olas has not been alarmed because many have thought: "At least it doesn't happen here." But it did happen here, in our "nice" community, and this time the victim was a white girl from an affluent family. We feel rage

and guilt, and we project blame onto many people and factors. But we also carry a lot of fear because, on some level, we do not feel safe—it's just like living in the poor, minority community. We feel powerless, just like the poor.

As professionals, we need to go to our strength and look at the total situation. We need to bring our micro and macro skills to the tasks that must be accomplished in order to reduce the anger, guilt, anxiety, frustration, and fear in our clients. Our clients are the students, their families, the high school faculty and administrators, the minority communities, the police, and the general community. We are all in a crisis. We must be challenged by that crisis and respond with the best that social workers have to offer. We must work together and not lose sight of that goal. This campus homicide was a "wake-up call" for all of us. Let's pull together and get on with our obligation to serve the needs of our community.

There was initial silence in the group. Then Mrs. Smith remarked that she felt proud to be a social worker and that they all had a professional role to play. Another social worker responded that this was like a natural disaster and that usually people respond accordingly and pitch in to help. Yet another social worker commented, "I feel overwhelmed. What are we supposed to do?"

Bob took this opportunity to review the items on the three sheets of butcher paper and asked Ms. Valentine to report to the group on what she had learned from her search for evidence regarding issues and emotions to expect and best practices to use when working with persons affected by tragedy. Knowing that people do their best in activities suited to their skills, he asked the staff to volunteer for activities within these three areas of work to be done. The staff began to show some enthusiasm and believed they could accomplish their goals now that the tasks were outlined.

Preparing to Serve the Families and School

Bob asked the group to reflect on the information Ms. Valentine gathered regarding helping people in crises. He summarized for them that a crisis can occur at any point in a person's life and that some people react to a greater degree than others to the emotional hazards inherent in certain events. A *crisis* is an emotional state, the reaction of an individual, family, or community to a hazardous situation. A hazardous event calls for a solution new to the individual, group, family, or community in relation to that life experience.[2] There are three broad types of crisis situations that may enrich or endanger people's functioning: (1) those that are "biologically tinged," such as adolescence or menopause, and therefore may be anticipated by all people as part of the life cycle; (2) those that are "environmentally tinged," such as a change of job or retirement, and hence are somewhat less inevitable but are usually anticipated; and (3) those that are "adventitious," such as disasters, floods, and fire, which are attributable to chance and cannot be anticipated.[3]

Floods, fires, and earthquakes are *natural disasters*. Wars, mass killings, and public homicides such as the Olas High student killing are *man-made disasters*. Victims of the latter often have more difficulty getting over their symptoms because they were intentionally caused by another human being, who, if not apprehended, could strike again. People feel especially vulnerable. Bob had learned that during the crisis period an individual is in a state of acute anxiety. Feelings of helplessness and hopelessness are evident.

In this situation, ego patterns are more likely to be open to influence and change. Because defenses are lowered during this temporary period of disequilibrium, the client is usually more accessible to therapeutic influence than prior to the crisis or following establishment of a new equilibrium with its accompanying defense patterns.[4] During this period of upset, there are emotional symptoms such as tension, anxiety, shame, guilt, and even hostility. Past conflicts that may or may not have been satisfactorily resolved may be reactivated because the stresses of a crisis may be viewed as a threat, either to "instinctual" needs or to one's sense of integrity; as a loss of either a person or something else causing a feeling of acute deprivation; or as a challenge.[5]

Each of these states is usually accompanied by a typical emotional effect. If the crisis situation is primarily experienced as a threat, it will be accompanied by a great deal of anxiety. If the crisis is experienced primarily as a loss, it will involve depression and mourning. If viewed as a challenge, it will be accompanied by some anxiety or drive for problem solving. In many respects, a crisis presents a new opportunity for change that might result in a higher level of psychosocial functioning.

Crisis intervention strategies should also take into consideration the biopsychosocial development stages of the persons being helped. For example, Olas High included grades seven through twelve, hence, these youths ranged in age from 12 to 18 years. The deceased victim, Tammy Rowan, was 12; therefore, it would be anticipated that those students most affected would be her peers, particularly those who might have witnessed the shooting. Twelve-year-olds are usually growing out of the latter developmental stages of latency and the security of childhood experienced in the family and grammar school. They are now entering a period of greater independence coupled with increased anxieties spurred on by physical development and hormonal changes. In addition, they are in the less secure social and physical environment of a high school that has significantly more students than the previous elementary school. The random killing of a peer can seriously traumatize seventh graders who are already psychologically vulnerable.

Mobilizing Related Mental Health Disciplines

Recognizing that the Olas Family Service Center staff was not the only agency with a staff qualified to provide grief counseling, Bob contacted the local NASW chapter, the Olas Community Mental Health Center, the Olas Psychological Association, and the Olas Psychiatric Association. As an agency executive, he knew the leaders of these professional bodies, who agreed that Bob should coordinate the helping effort of these professional groups. Their first meeting was held that evening at the Olas Community Mental Health Center, which was closest to the school.

The response was overwhelming as twenty mental health professionals attended the meeting, calling themselves the "Olas High Crisis Team." The majority of assistance would be provided at the school beginning the next morning the school would be open. They agreed the highest priority would go to those students who actually witnessed the killing, irrespective of age or grade level. Second in priority would be all of the seventh graders, followed by eighth and ninth graders. A crisis team member would visit each classroom for one period. With the tenth, eleventh, and twelfth grade students, the approach would involve inviting them, via the public address system, to meet with the crisis team in the auditorium after school. Still another identified high-risk group would be those students who were too frightened or "stressed out" to attend school. With this latter group, it is possible that the traumatic event might reactivate pre-existing, unresolved conflicts or have a severe reaction on a fragile, vulnerable individual. A special outreach effort would have to be made on their behalf. It was agreed the Olas Family Services Center staff would take responsibility for this group.

It was also recognized that consultation services should also be available for administrators and teachers, either individually or in groups, and the school social workers from other schools in Olas assumed this responsibility. Similar offers were made to law enforcement agencies and paramedics involved in handling the case. Another targeted group would be other families who did not have students at Olas High. Evening and weekend meetings would be provided for them by volunteers from the professional associations.

To minimize the traumatic effects of the school homicide on all affected parties described above and to reduce any long-term psychiatric consequences related to the event such as posttraumatic stress disorder (PTSD) and adjustment disorder symptoms, the Olas High Crisis Team developed the following psychosocial intervention model. The goal of the model was to help people return to their previous level of functioning:

1. The team makes assessments of symptom responses, being particularly sensitive to *physical* changes such as eating, sleeping, headaches, and other somatic symptoms, and *psychological* changes such as anger, irritability, anxiety, frustration, poor concentration, preoccupation, depression, and increased family dependence or withdrawal.
2. The crisis team attempts to diffuse and neutralize some of these feelings through group and individual counseling. Calm listening, venting, and assisting the consultees to "problem solve," make decisions, and refocus has been found to be helpful in these crisis situations.
3. The crisis team will teach persons to use their inner strengths and to develop techniques for managing stress.
4. The crisis team is prepared to make referrals in those cases that are found to require more intensive, in-depth treatment. They will develop a list of licensed clinical social workers and psychologists in private practice who will be able to see clients on a reduced fee or no-fee (pro bono) basis. In fact, the parents and siblings of Tammy Rowan were already seeing a social worker in private practice.

Addressing Community Needs: Indirect and Prevention Tasks

The Chief Executive Officers (CEOs) representing the various mental health disciplines decided to meet with representatives of the media. The CEOs, however, felt that it was important to also involve the Chief of Police and the County Sheriff in order to present a united front. A press conference was called the third day after the homicide, and by this time rumors were rampant. Some media were reporting that L.A. gangs were fighting for the "turf" around Olas High in order to sell drugs. Others were saying that the killing was an "initiation rite" by "Crips" (African American gang members). Other media reports were that local Olas minority gangs were attempting to establish a reputation so that big city gangs would respect them. These media reports, all unfounded but fed by the typical bravado of non-gang and gang-member adolescents, caused the white community to begin patrolling their neighborhoods in the evening hours. There were also rumors that some of these residents were armed and were planning to go into the minority communities to "teach them a lesson" to stay on their side of town.

The Chief of Police opened the meeting stating that they had the license number of the vehicle involved and were very close to apprehending the suspects, who were local adolescents. He did not know if they were gang members but asked the media not to print speculative stories because this might cause retaliation and conflict between gangs. Representatives of the press replied that they had a First Amendment right of freedom of speech to report the news (including speculation) as they saw fit.

Bob Pla joined in the discussion, identifying himself as representing the Olas High School Crisis Team, and commented that the speculative reporting was causing a significant amount of unnecessary fear and anxiety in the community and that even small children were reluctant to attend school. Some parents were also prohibiting their children from going to school. Mr. Pla pleaded for more restrained reporting to keep the incident in perspective. He reminded the news reporters that this was the first homicide at a school in Olas since the founding of the town in 1888. One of the reporters asked Reverend Hudson, who was 87 years of age and born in Olas, if Mr. Pla's statement was true, and the reverend confirmed Bob's statement.

Bob Pla also pointed out that, even if the killing had been gang-related, Olas gangs had not committed one homicide in the past ten years. "There is your story," replied Bob. "We have a fine community that really is very safe. The killing of Tammy Rowan was an aberration—an extremely rare occurrence! The odds of this happening in Olas are forty-million-to-one." Some members of the press thought that people really did not want to hear about statistics; rather, they feared that their community was "going down the tubes," and many were talking about moving out of Olas. Sensing that what the media really wanted was a "story," the law enforcement representatives again called for restrained, factual reporting, promising that, if they would pursue a policy of discretion in reporting, the media in Olas would be the first to know who the suspects were once they were apprehended. Representatives of the media were responsive to this suggestion and agreed to cooperate.

Representing the crisis team, Bob contacted the mayor and the chair of the Board of Supervisors to apprise them of the importance of their exercising their influence as elected officials of the community to call for calm, rational thinking and to ask the public to wait for actual facts from the ongoing investigation to avoid prejudging or jumping to conclusions. Both elected representatives thought it was a helpful suggestion. The mayor, however, decided to reach the public through a prepared five-minute television announcement, to be aired several times a day. The Board of Supervisors chair decided to call a press conference and to have his staff prepare a brief statement for the local newspapers.

Mr. Pla asked his minority-community liaison staff member to contact the informal leaders in the African American, Latino, and Asian American communities to assess their current thoughts regarding the school homicide. The Asian Americans, especially those of Japanese descent, believed that Americans were too violent as a people and very trigger-happy, calling the United States a land of "sick shooters." In Japan, the contact person noted, in one year, handguns claimed forty-six lives, compared with the United States, where handgun homicides numbered 8,092.[6] The Asian community representatives concluded that their group did not want any involvement in the current crisis and just wanted to be left alone to manage their own community, which they felt was the safest in Olas.

Reacting to the vigilante threats emanating from the Olas white community, the African American and Latino communities promised retaliation if any minorities were attacked. Latinos were particularly worried about a resurgence of anti-immigrant sentiment among whites and an escalation of U.S. Immigration and Naturalization Services "raids" into their *barrio*. These two minority communities also threatened violent retaliation if armed white vigilantes invaded their communities. Bob hoped that all of this posturing was simply rhetoric to frighten off the white community. Nevertheless, he presented this information to law enforcement intelligence officials, urging them to be especially alert to armed or unarmed whites entering the minority communities. He also asked law enforcement to be particularly careful in making any arrests in the minority communities during this tense climate, because even a routine arrest could trigger a riot, as had been the experience in other communities that rioted in the 1960s and 1970s.

The Case Continues

A week later, as promised, law enforcement representatives and the district attorney contacted the Olas media for a special press conference. The suspects had been identified. At the press conference, the district attorney announced that he had in custody an 18-year-old female adolescent, Rita Gomez, who admitted to police that she had been in the moving vehicle and had fired the shots that struck Tammy Rowan. Police did not believe the incident was gang-related, because Ms. Gomez was not a gang member. She was a resident of Olas, living in *Barrio Town*, the poor, Latino section of Olas. She did not know the victim. After waiving her rights to an attorney, she confessed to the police that she had fired the semiautomatic weapon at the students merely to "scare them." She was not intending to injure anyone.

The co-defendant, who was driving the vehicle, was 33-year-old Michael Webster, a native of Olas and an unemployed high school dropout and laborer. He was residing with his parents in the white, affluent section of Olas at the time of the murder. He had a long history of substance abuse and heroin and cocaine addiction, both as a juvenile and as an adult. He had just completed a five-year prison sentence for selling drugs and was on parole. According to Ms. Gomez, he left the state the same day of the shooting. A warrant for his arrest was issued. First-degree murder charges with "special circumstances" were filed against Ms. Gomez; if convicted, Ms. Gomez could receive the death penalty.

After the announcement by the media of the primary suspect being in custody and confessing that she had fired the weapon that had killed Tammy Rowan, the community appeared quite relieved and more secure. The crisis team consultation groups continued for a few more weeks, with most of the groups disbanding by the eighth week. Several of the students who actually witnessed the slaying continued in individual treatment, as many of their PTSD symptoms were still in the acute stage. A few needed medication to calm symptoms such as insomnia and nightmares, as the memories of violence were interfering with their school functioning.

Daily television and newspaper interviews of Olas residents kept asking the same question: "Why did Rita Gomez kill Tammy Rowan?" Even the police did not understand the motive. Rita Gomez was relatively unknown in Olas. She did not attend high school, and there were rumors saying that she had dropped out of school in the seventh grade. The court appointed an attorney on her behalf, Eddie Falls, a new resident of Olas, who, like Bob Pla, had left Los Angeles to enjoy a healthier and safer environment for his family. Mr. Falls wanted to change Ms. Gomez' plea to "not guilty," but Ms. Gomez insisted on pleading "guilty" because she wanted to "get it over as soon as possible."

Mr. Falls attempted to plea bargain with the district attorney to have the charge reduced to manslaughter or even second-degree homicide with a guilty plea, but to no avail. The community was angry and wanted "the book thrown at her." "Nothing less than first-degree murder and the death penalty," argued the district attorney representing the people of California. Attorney Falls finally was able to persuade Ms. Gomez to enter a "not guilty" plea, hoping to have the jury reduce the charge to second-degree murder or manslaughter to avoid the death penalty. The determining factor for Ms. Gomez was that she wanted to avoid being executed because she wanted to be able to see her two children, aged 2 and 4, grow up.

The Case Goes to Trial

During the following weeks, a jury was impaneled. It was composed of six middle-class non-Hispanic white women and six non-Hispanic white men. All were from the Olas community. After a relatively short trial, the jury went into deliberation. In one day, they returned a unanimous "guilty" verdict of first-degree homicide with "special circumstances." In Ms. Gomez's case, the jury found the following two special circumstances to be true:

- The murder was especially heinous, atrocious, or cruel, manifesting exceptional depravity. As utilized in this section, the phrase *especially heinous, atrocious, or cruel manifesting exceptional depravity* means a conscienceless or pitiless crime, which is unnecessarily torturous to the victim.
- The victim was intentionally killed because of his or her race, color, religion, nationality, or country of origin.

The jury determined that eight 9-millimeter bullets struck and killed an innocent, unsuspecting 12-year-old child in the upper chest, heart, neck, and head, and that this was a heinous and atrocious violent act manifesting exceptional depravity on the part of the perpetrator. Also, because the victim was a white Anglo-American and the perpetrator a person of a different nationality (Mexican descent), the jury concluded that the homicide had a racial and nationality motive.

Following the guilty verdict with special circumstances, the jury now had to deliberate the death penalty phase of the case to decide whether there were any mitigating factors (for or against) that might justify life imprisonment without the possibility of parole rather than execution by the state. Eddie Falls, Rita's attorney, asked Bob Pla if he would be willing to participate in the death penalty phase of the Gomez case by evaluating Ms. Gomez, writing a report with accompanying recommendations, and thereafter testifying in court.

Bob's evaluation would have to address two central questions before the jury and the court: (1) Are there any mitigating factors in the case justifying life imprisonment without the possibility of parole rather than execution? And (2) of what value is Ms. Gomez's life to society that she should not be executed? Initially Bob felt overwhelmed by the proposed assignment, stating that he had not been trained to play God. The attorney stated that he had read about Bob's testimony concerning homicide cases in Los Angeles in which he had evaluated defendants prior to sentencing in a legal newspaper. Bob admitted he had done this and had established himself as an expert witness when testifying in assault, suicide, riot, gang violence, police brutality, and homicide cases—but never in a death penalty case. The attorney argued that, because of these experiences, he would be in the most advantageous position to "educate" the judge and jury about what factors would lead a teenaged girl to commit such a heinous crime. "If competent people like you take a pass on these things, how can Olas learn from this experience? How can we prevent this from happening again?" demanded the attorney.

Bob decided to do it. "You've just convinced me. You are correct! How else are we going to learn? And you used the magic word—*prevention!* There might be dozens or even hundreds of persons like Rita Gomez out there. As social workers, we are trained to look at the interface of the person and the environment and the transactions occurring between the person and the environment. What are the biopsychosocial factors relevant to this case? What went wrong?" Bob agreed to take the case contingent on receiving authorization from his agency board.

He was later granted permission by the board because they saw this as an opportunity for the agency to make a contribution to the community in reducing tension and learning more about factors that contribute to violence. The board felt honored that one of its employees was being asked to participate in a very high-profile case that was in the news daily. Bob felt proud that, as a representative of the social work profession, he was being asked to use his micro and macro knowledge and skills in the comprehensive assessment of a case extremely important to the welfare of the community and to the 18-year-old Hispanic female whose life was at stake.

In preparing for the trial, the attorney submitted a written request to Superior Court Judge William Banks who was presiding in the Rita Gomez case, asking him to appoint Bob Pla, MSW, as an expert defense witness. The judge approved and signed the order, defining Bob Pla's role as an expert in violence and homicide. Bob was given a copy of the order, which permitted him to visit Ms. Gomez in the Olas County Jail. The attorney also gave Bob several boxes of case materials that included the police investigation reports, the medical autopsy report, Rita's school, Rita's information, her health and employment records, a record of the defendant's prior contacts with law enforcement, her psychiatric and psychological evaluations, numerous witness accounts, videotapes showing a four-hour taped confession with an accompanying typed copy of the confession, and selected court transcripts of the murder trial including testimony by various forensic, medical, and law enforcement experts.

A "strategy conference" was held with the defense team led by Eddie Falls, his assistant attorney, and the chief investigator. At this conference, Mr. Falls set forth his theories related to causation, which would form the foundation of mitigating factors that, if accepted by the jury, would warrant life imprisonment without the possibility of parole rather than death. The attorney believed that the strongest mitigating factor was that Ms. Gomez was a drug addict and, while under the influence of drugs, her judgment had been impaired, leading to the killing of Tammy Rowan. Bob agreed to this approach, stating that he would look carefully into the drug problem as well as the possibility of other mitigating factors presently unknown. The attorney believed that any additional mitigating factors could "score points" with the jury.

Bob's next task was to interview Rita Gomez. Visiting someone in jail is a sobering experience, even for Bob Pla, who has worked with jail and prison populations for many years. The suspicious, skeptical looks from jail personnel that one receives even after presenting the appropriate authorization and identification is something one never gets used to. This discomfort was further exacerbated by having to go through a metal detector and having one's briefcase searched for hidden weapons or contraband such as drugs. "Don't personalize it," Bob thought to himself. "It's just a part of their job for security reasons." Then the female sheriff's deputy cautioned Bob that he was entering the women's jail at his own risk and that the sheriff had a policy of not recognizing or responding to demands if he were to be taken hostage by the inmates. "Thanks a bunch," responded Bob in a somewhat sarcastic tone. "I'm only doing my job," responded the deputy in a defensive manner.

Bob was sitting in the empty attorney's room, which was filled with about thirty stalls. "I guess attorneys do not work on Sundays like social workers," mumbled Bob. After waiting about thirty minutes, Bob was pleasantly surprised when Rita Gomez was led into the interview room by a deputy. She did not look mean or hard and actually was quite cooperative, friendly, and soft-spoken. She was an attractive, slim, 18-year-old Mexican American Catholic female, born and raised in Olas. Bob already had a psychosocial framework in mind as to the information he was seeking that related to her early childhood, family, marital, educational, and social history and health, drug, and delinquency history.

Bob explained to Rita that this would be the first of three interviews and that, with her permission, he was also planning on interviewing her parents, grandparents, aunts and uncles, husband, and children. After Bob explained the reasons why it was important to interview all these family members, Rita approved of this plan. She warned Bob that he was going to hear a lot of bad things about her and that she had worn out the welcome mat with her immediate family as well as with other close relatives. "What did you do?" asked Bob. Rita rolled her eyes, smiled, and stated, "What didn't I do?" She went on to say that she was a "junkie" and had stolen from the family to support her habit and had lied to everybody, including her husband, to get money for drugs. "I even was turning tricks for money to buy drugs," she confessed. She became emotional and began to cry, stating that, most of all, she missed her children. "And that poor little girl who I killed. I can imagine the pain her mother is in. I didn't mean to shoot her. I've never physically hurt nobody. I'm an alcoholic and an addict but not a violent person," she cried. She seemed very remorseful, and Bob recalled that, in the videotapes, she was crying nonstop for nearly four hours.

"Why do you think you killed her?" inquired Bob. "I didn't know her and was not planning on hurting anyone," replied Rita. "Mike (Michael Webster, second suspect, at large) and me were slamming several times that morning (injecting heroin and cocaine), and then Mike said 'Let's go cruising in my car.' We got in his car and then he showed me a gun. It was real heavy. I don't know what kind it was. I've never held a gun in my life. Then Mike said 'Let's go by the school and scare the squares. I'll drive by, and you just wave the gun at them and watch them run and drop.' Mike was laughing, and I thought it was funny, too. We drove by the school once, and I waved the gun out of the window, and some of the students saw us and started running, yelling 'drive-by, drive-by!' That was a real trip. Then we went around the block a second time, and I waved the gun again, and we were laughing real hard. Then Mike said 'Pull the trigger, pull the trigger!' I did, and the gun went off a lot of times, like a machine gun. I was so loaded that I could hardly aim the gun. I aimed above their heads and didn't think I hit anyone. Then we sped away. We were still laughing. Then later we heard on the radio that someone had been shot at the school. I got real scared. Mike dropped me off at home and then took off. I haven't seen him since. A few days later I was arrested at home after someone at school ID'd me."

The Psychosocial Evaluation

Bob Pla followed through with his plan of interviewing Rita's family members, spouse, children, and significant relatives who could provide an insight into Rita's personality and behavior. There was one area of common agreement; during periods of complete abstention from drugs and alcohol, she was a sensitive, responsible, loving, and caring daughter, mother, and wife. But when using drugs and alcohol, she became a completely different person, doing anything short of violence to get money or things of value to use to purchase drugs. Sometimes she would exchange sex for drugs. In addition to the interviews described above, Bob relied on various reports and documents to arrive at his conclusions and recommendations. He then prepared a report for the attorney (see Box 27.1), who in turn would present it to the judge and prosecutor for their consideration.

chapter 27 ◆ Social Workers in Action: School Homicide and the Death Penalty   543

Box 27.1

Rita's Psychosocial Evaluation

Olas Family Services Agency
2301 N. Pacific Coast Highway
Olas, California 92133

December 1, 2008

Eddie Falls
Attorney at Law
321 South Oak Street
Olas, California 92134

Re: Rita Gomez, Case #C-93187

Dear Mr. Falls,

On November 7, Superior Court Judge William Banks signed an order appointing me as a violence, homicide, and psychosocial evaluation expert for the Defense in the case of Rita Gomez, case #C-93187. The information in this report should assist the jury in resolving the issue of the appropriateness of life without the possibility of parole *versus* execution by the state.

By way of professional credentials, I received my master's degree in social work from the University of Southern California and thereafter had twenty years of professional experience in probation, parole, community mental health, and, simultaneously, as an adjunct faculty member at UCLA. For the past four years, I have been directing the Olas Family Services Agency, where I supervise a staff of fifteen and where I continue to treat clients. I have given numerous presentations at professional conferences concerning the assessment and treatment of suicidal and homicidal patients and homicide perpetrators. Additionally, I have had more than twenty years' experience in working with juvenile and adult male and female criminal offenders, including many who abused drugs and alcohol.

PSYCHOSOCIAL EVALUATION

What follows is my psychosocial evaluation of Ms. Gomez, which is based on three interviews with her in the Olas County Jail, totaling five hours, and fourteen hours of interviews with her parents, maternal grandparents, four aunts and uncles, and her husband and two children. In addition, I analyzed numerous reports and documents related to her medical, psychological, psychiatric, and juvenile history and her law enforcement investigation, including a lengthy videotaped confession. This psychosocial evaluation has two major functions:

1. To provide the court with a comprehensive analysis to understand what factors contributed to making a Hispanic adolescent female (18.2 years of age at the time of the offense) commit such a violent crime, and
2. To assess whether this young woman has any value to society as a human being that might warrant a life sentence rather than execution by the state as the result of her conviction for first-degree murder with special circumstances.

This social work–oriented psychosocial evaluation will focus not only on the individual but also on the interface of Ms. Gomez with her total environment, which includes her family, relatives, and other groups in the community.

(Continued)

Box 27.1 (Continued)

PART ONE: DATA AND DIAGNOSIS

1. IDENTIFYING DATA

Rita Gomez is a slim, attractive, dark-haired, 18-year-old, bilingual, bicultural Hispanic female of Mexican descent born at the Olas County General Hospital. She is the mother of two male children, aged 2 and 4. She married the father of her children, Pedro Gomez, age 22, when she was 14 years of age. He works six days a week at a gas station during the days and as a parking lot attendant during the evenings. The marital relationship has always been conflictual due to his wanting to know her whereabouts during his long working hours. Having one child by age 16, let alone *two* children by that age, and being minimally educated and unemployed places a young adolescent female at even higher risk for additional problems.

2. PERTINENT GENETIC-BIOLOGICAL FAMILY HISTORY

There is a strong genetic factor for alcoholism that is seen to run in families. Children of alcoholics become alcoholic four times more often than children of nonalcoholics. Ms. Gomez is an alcoholic in remission, as well as a drug addict, also in remission. She continues to be addicted to the nicotine in cigarettes and has been a chronic smoker of one to two packs per day since she was 12 years old.

Rita Gomez comes from a traditional, male-dominated, hard-working, religious, Catholic Mexican family, originally from Puebla, Mexico. Her great-grandfather on her maternal grandfather's side was a ranch-hand and died at age 80 due to cirrhosis of the liver. He was an alcoholic. His wife had died two years previously due to heart disease. She had been a chronic smoker. Ms. Gomez's great-grandmother on her maternal grandmother's side was also a nicotine addict who smoked three to four packs of cigarettes per day. She died of lung cancer at age 70, and her husband, a general construction worker, was an alcoholic and died of cirrhosis of the liver at age 40. Ms. Gomez' biological father is also an alcoholic, as is his mother. Both of her parents are chronic smokers.

Ms. Gomez's maternal grandparents, ages 60 and 62, report good health, with the exception of the grandmother who suffers occasional anxiety attacks related to stresses brought on by her granddaughter's murder case. The grandparents, as well as Ms. Gomez's mother, are employed at the local Sears department store, where the mother is head of the shoe department and the grandparents are in the janitorial department. Combining their modest incomes, they purchased and reside in their home located just inside the lower-middle-class area of Olas. They moved here because the area had better schools. This area, which is near *Barrio Town,* is 90 percent non-Hispanic white.

With the exception of Ms. Gomez, no member of the family dating back to the great-grandparents has received psychiatric treatment, been hospitalized for mental illness, or been arrested for any violent or criminal acts. Ms. Gomez's maternal grandparents had eight children, currently ranging in age from 23 to 42, with her mother being the second oldest of these children. In turn, her mother had four children, with Ms. Gomez being the second oldest child. Her older brother graduated from college and is a high school teacher in a neighboring community. The other two siblings are attending high school. Ms. Gomez's children reportedly are in good health. According to her mother, Ms. Gomez was drug-free during her pregnancies, with only occasional light alcohol consumption.

3. EARLY CHILDHOOD DEVELOPMENTAL FACTORS

Ms. Gomez was a seven-pound, four-ounce natural-birth baby who was bottle-fed by family members because the mother had to work to support the family. She always had a healthy appetite but was always thin. She was quite active as an infant and began walking rather early,

chapter 27 ◆ Social Workers in Action: School Homicide and the Death Penalty

at 10 months of age. Ms. Gomez slept well, had a calm demeanor, and did not present behavioral problems as a child. She was a very affectionate, trusting child and bonded well with her mother and other family members residing in the home, especially her maternal grandmother. Her first and primary language was Spanish, but this did not handicap her in kindergarten or first and second grade at Olas Tree Elementary School located in *Barrio Town,* which had 85 percent Latino students. As they improved their economic circumstances, the family moved to a more affluent area, where they currently reside. She transferred to Cherry Lane Elementary, which had only 3 percent Latino students, and the rest were non-Hispanic white students.

At this school, Ms. Gomez began to experience stress, as students mimicked and made fun of her Spanish accent and her very slim appearance, calling her "toothpick," "ostrich legs," and "dirty Mexican." Quite often she would cry at home because she did not want to go to school. She developed various somatic complaints and on occasion would vomit, causing her mother to keep her home from school, thinking her ill. The mother often complained to school officials but "nothing was done about it," and the insults continued. In spite of frequent absences and the prejudice and scapegoating she was suffering, Ms. Gomez still was able to maintain above-average grades, such as a few As, a few Bs, and the rest Cs. She began to resent school because it had become a very negative experience. She felt not only rejected but also that she did not fit in. Her academic performance suffered and was reflected in poorer grades in the fourth, fifth, and sixth grades. Rejection during these important, formative years can lead to a child's low self-esteem at a critical time in his or her life, when an important psychosocial developmental task is learning to become industrious in an atmosphere of validation by the school and peers.

4. FAMILY EMOTIONAL ENVIRONMENT

A warm, secure, loving home environment is extremely important for a child to develop healthy emotions, emotional security, confidence, and self-esteem. According to the parents and grandparents, this happened for Ms. Gomez during her first seven years of life in spite of the negative experiences she was having in school. The loving validation provided by her warm, very traditional Hispanic family helped her feel that, at least somewhere in her life, she was valued. This was reflected in her being a loving child who reached out to and established close relationships with her siblings, immediate relatives, and playmates. This emotional foundation and empathic capacity still exist, according to all of her relatives, except when she is under the influence of drugs and alcohol, when she becomes a totally different person who is emotionally distant and cold and exploits people for her own benefit.

During these initial developmental years, her hard-working father was a light-to-moderate drinker of alcohol. However, as she approached 7 years of age, his drinking escalated because he had been laid off from several low-skilled jobs. His arguments with her mother evolved into physical battering in the presence of Ms. Gomez, which caused her a significant amount of anxiety. Sometimes she was afraid of leaving her mother at home and would not go to school.

5. CHILDHOOD PSYCHOLOGICAL TRAUMA

It is very traumatic for children to observe their parents in violent confrontation, especially when it occurs frequently. On one occasion, when Ms. Gomez was 9 years old, she attempted to protect her mother from her father's abuse by stepping in between them, but this was met with physical retaliation against her. Thereafter, these physical beatings also began to include Ms. Gomez. The beatings lasted until her father left home when Rita was almost 12 years old. Ms. Gomez cannot recall these beatings even though she had scars on her arms that her

(Continued)

Box 27.1 (Continued)

mother stated had been caused by them. This "blocking out" of painful trauma is not uncommon for post-traumatic stress disorder (PTSD) victims, especially children. Ms. Gomez did recall one painful episode when she was 10 years old and "glue-sniffing" with friends in a neighbor's garage. She was raped by two 15-year-old boys. Fearing that she would be blamed for this incident, she did not tell anyone. Such a traumatic event could also cause PTSD.

In my assessment of Ms. Gomez, she clearly had several symptoms that met the criteria for a PTSD diagnosis. These symptoms of acute anxiety, hypervigilance, fear, and depression were never treated. In such situations, some people, especially when they are poor and do not have the resources to obtain professional treatment, have been known to "treat" themselves. In my judgment, this motivated Ms. Gomez to engage in self-medication with chemical substances such as paint, gasoline, "glue-sniffing," marijuana, PCP, heroin, cocaine, and alcohol. These substances help numb the person from psychological pain and, while in the intoxicated state, help suppress painful memories, at least temporarily. A psychological and physical dependence upon this "solution" reinforces its repetition.

6. SEARCHING FOR A SUBSTITUTE FAMILY

When children are rejected by the school and their families as they approach early adolescence (which is a developmental period of elevated need to be part of a social group), they begin to gravitate to and are attracted to other youths having similar experiences and needs. These are the needs that give growth to gang involvement. As Ms. Gomez was approaching age 13, she began to absorb some of the nonviolent aspects of adolescent female gang culture. She avoided school even more to be with her new friends. Michael Webster, the "at-large" co-suspect in this case, introduced her to heroin at age 13 when he was 28 years of age.

Rita quickly developed a psychological and physical dependence on this drug and identified with a new group of friends that she called "street junkies." In her frequent association with this group, she began to incorporate the subculture and lifestyle of the lower-class female street addict. To support her drug habit, she stole from her family and friends, lied, and manipulated people in her pursuit of drugs. She was nicknamed "Bandit" by her group, and she had this name tattooed on her left arm when she was 14. Female street addicts rarely, if ever, are violent. Instead, they prey on potential victims whom they might be able to exploit for drugs, particularly recently paroled ex-convicts who are potential sources for drugs with their "gate money" (prison release money).

Ms. Gomez has no formal criminal history other than the current homicide offense. Her record indicates only one petty theft arrest as a juvenile when she stole cosmetic items from Thrifty Drug Store. She did not have to appear in court because no petition was filed. She simply was counseled and released by the police.

7. PSYCHOSOCIAL ANALYSIS AND DIAGNOSIS

In analyzing the above six predisposition factors, any one of these factors could place a child, adolescent, or adult at a high risk for emotional, behavioral, criminal, or substance abuse and dependence problems. In the case of Ms. Gomez, her primary strength was the foundation of her relatively normal early childhood up until the age of 7. The six factors were: (1) beginning motherhood before the age of 16, being unemployed, having only a seventh-grade education, and being in a conflicted marriage; (2) having inherited four generations of a biological vulnerability to alcohol addiction, which also made her biologically vulnerable to other addictions such as to drugs and nicotine; (3) language and cultural difficulties in elementary school, further complicated by discriminatory rejection by non-Hispanic white students; (4) being raised in an unstable family after age 5, which progressively deteriorated due to her father's alcoholism and physical abuse of her mother; (5) the traumatization from Ms. Gomez's rape at age 10 by two 15-year-old males while all were glue-sniffing, compounded by beatings by her father until age 12; and (6) her increased involvement with a "surrogate family" (the street addict subculture), which met her needs for companionship, affection, and drugs.

Throughout her young life, from ages 5 to 18, the dynamics of these six interacting, predisposing factors negatively affected her psychosocial development and functioning, thereby contributing to her offense, which occurred while she was under the influence of heroin, cocaine, and alcohol. In this intoxicated state, her judgment was impaired and, being with an older, more experienced ex-convict and drug addict—who often enjoyed respect and status among the younger, less experienced "junkies"—she was more vulnerable and prone to influence.

Being the victim of sexual and physical assaults as a child severely traumatized this adolescent. To this day, these emotional scars remain untreated. These symptoms demanded calming and, through self-medication beginning at the tender age of 10 when most little girls are still playing with dolls, she began to ingest mood-altering chemicals (sniffing paint, gasoline, and glue). Four generations of a dormant, chemical genetic vulnerability toward addiction surfaced. In a relatively brief time after graduating to heroin and cocaine use, she became an addict and joined the street addict culture.

Ms. Gomez's career as a female street drug addict did not follow the usual pattern of most female drug addicts, that is, continued use with the possibility of death due to AIDS resulting from prostitution or using infected needles, suicide evolving from major depression, or "burning out" as an aging addict and then becoming an alcoholic. A few are able to leave drugs and assume a normal life. In the case of Ms. Gomez, however, she did not have the maturity nor the physical and emotional strength to alter her eight-year street drug addict pattern, which culminated in the death of a 12-year-old child, and which now may result in her own death.

SUMMARY DIAGNOSIS
Following my interviews with Ms. Gomez, it is my diagnostic impression that she definitely is depressed. After her arrest, Ms. Gomez was suicidal but did not make any attempts. A year ago when her husband was threatening to leave her and take her children, she made a suicide attempt by slashing her wrists with a broken bottle. It was a serious attempt while intoxicated and required emergency room treatment and seventy-two hours of hospitalization. She did not receive treatment following release due to lack of insurance and financial resources. Such attempts are not uncommon among very depressed female adolescents. Her depression, in part, is also *reactive,* that is, it is an emotional reaction to being separated from her children, husband, family, and friends. Her depression may also be a long-term *dysthymic* (chronic low to moderate) depression arising from untreated PTSD symptoms since age 10. In addition to four generations of genetic factors predisposing toward alcoholism in the family history, there might also be an underlying *endogenous* (biological) depression having a genetic origin. With regard to the latter, a careful, extensive psychiatric evaluation should be made of the defendant and selected family members. Based on the *Diagnostic and Statistical Manual of Mental Disorders,* 4th edition, text revised (DSM IV-TR), the following is my diagnostic impression of the defendant:

(Continued)

Box 27.1 (Continued)

DSM IV-TR, 312.82. Adolescent Conduct Disorder (stealing, lying, running away), severe, present since age 12 to date arrested in present offense.
DSM IV-TR, 309.81. Post Traumatic Stress Disorder, chronic type, present since age 10.
DSM IV-TR, 303.90. Alcohol Dependence, in full remission since arrested in present offense.
DSM IV-TR, 304.80. Polysubstance Dependence, in full remission since arrested in present offense.

PART TWO: THE DEFENDANT'S VALUE TO SOCIETY

In complying with the social work profession's ethical responsibility to promote the general welfare of society and to respond to this nation's great need for new and current knowledge to advance its understanding of violence and homicide, it becomes imperative that Ms. Gomez be permitted to live in order to assist social and psychiatric scientists toward that end. This tragic case presents a unique opportunity to advance our current state of knowledge concerning the nature versus nurture debate and the relationship between American and Mexican culture. The Gomez case represents five generations of genetic vulnerability to addiction in one family, from the great-grandparents to and including Ms. Gomez's two children. Where this genetic vulnerability to alcohol and drug addiction coexists with too-easy access to firearms in the context of a violent Anglo-American culture, many young women with similar characteristics are being transformed into agents of violence and homicide. Ms. Gomez may simply be a female "pioneer" in this regard.

Due to Ms. Gomez's intelligence and verbal skills, from this case we can also learn about the specific points of the process of early adolescent decision making that lead a troubled youngster to choose a gang or a street addict group or to become a "loner," a criminal offender, homeless person, a runaway youth, or some other alternative. All this information is valuable to society in the identification of genuine high-risk youths and their families in order to prevent these excessively violent crimes, by either young females or young males. There is sufficient research information that documents the severe emotional impact upon immediate family members when there is a suicide in the family. This impact places each family member at very high risk for suicide, because, in periods of major depression, they tend to identify with the "solution" adopted by the dead family member.

In those cases in which a family member was a victim of a homicide, similar emotional vulnerabilities occur. Furthermore, it is a fact that *any* child who has lost a parent "by any means before the age of 13" has a higher risk for affective disorders and suicide than does a child who has not experienced such a loss. In the defendant's case, the execution of Ms. Gomez by the state would place both of her children at a very high risk for possible homicidal and/or suicidal behavior in later years, because they would have to live with the emotions and the label of having been given birth by a mother who was so "evil" she had to be executed by the state. The defendant is a classic case of a victim of childhood sexual and physical abuse who later becomes a perpetrator of violence. Her execution would perpetuate this cycle of violence in her children.

Ms. Gomez would become the first woman and mother with minor children to be executed in the United States. Granting her a life sentence without the possibility of parole will spare her children this overwhelming, high-risk burden. When sober, Ms. Gomez can be an affectionate, nurturing mother, and she can continue her mothering responsibilities with her children through weekly and even once-a-month, weekend prison visits available to mothers with minor children.

> She is quite remorseful and accepts full responsibility for all her actions in the homicide. All her statements to me have been corroborated by her family and other secondary sources. Her attitude was very positive, and this was evident in reading unsolicited letters shown to me by her relatives. Over the last few months, she has written letters to several of her younger cousins, nieces, and nephews, advising them to do well in school and listen to their parents. Her misfortune can be of a continuing educational benefit to other youths. Her death would end that important communication link.
>
> Respectfully Submitted,
>
> Bob Pla, MSW, LCSW
> Executive Director

The Report Is Challenged by the People

After the psychosocial report was read by the judge and the district attorney (DA), the DA challenged Mr. Pla's credentials as an "expert" witness. The challenge contested the usefulness of Bob's MSW degree, stating that a social worker's training did not qualify him to be an expert on violent and homicidal behavior. The defendant's attorney, Eddie Falls, granted that Mr. Pla's graduate training and education did not in itself qualify him as a violence expert but that, following graduation, one of Mr. Pla's specialty areas had become the assessment and treatment of violent offenders as well as murderers who had been released on parole. The judge ruled that he was satisfied that there was sufficient evidence to show that Mr. Pla had earned expert witness status in previous trials.

The DA then challenged Mr. Pla's "psychosocial evaluation" report and diagnosis, stating that only a licensed physician, psychiatrist, or psychologist was qualified to render a diagnosis, *not* a social worker. Attorney Falls produced a current copy of Mr. Pla's LCSW, his professional license, and cited the California laws authorizing licensed clinical social workers not only to diagnose a patient or client but also to provide that person psychotherapy of a nonmedical nature. The judge ruled that Mr. Pla is permitted to diagnose patients and that the report would be admissible evidence for the jury.

Recognizing that the report's description of a four-generation genetic vulnerability for alcoholism in the defendant's family could be construed as a favorable mitigating factor and a foundation for a life sentence rather than the death penalty, the DA attempted to strike out the content related to family history. He argued that the family history was based on "hearsay," there were no medical records to prove the existence of alcoholism, and that there was insufficient evidence of genetic links pertaining to alcoholism. The judge ruled that the scientific knowledge on this point was inadequate and the mitigating factor of genetic inheritance of alcoholism could not be heard by the jury. Further, the DA challenged the report's description of the rape experience at age 10 because Ms. Gomez had not reported the incident to anyone, including the police. The judge supported the district attorney in this request to keep the jury from hearing this information.

The DA mounted his strongest challenge to Part Two of Mr. Pla's report, the assertion that the execution of Ms. Gomez would place both of her children at high risk for subsequent suicidal or homicidal behavior in later years and thus her life should be spared. During the hearing, Mr. Pla quoted from research that concluded that the death of a parent increased suicide risk twenty-fold for a child 13 years of age and under and that violent and homicidal behavior in family members placed youth at high risk for modeling that violent behavior. The judge calculated that, since the suicide rate was on the average 12 per 100,000, according to Mr. Pla's figures, increasing the rate twenty-fold would result in a figure of "only" 240 per 100,000. The judge concluded that the fact that 99,760 persons would *not* commit suicide following the death of a parent was statistically a stronger argument.

The judge further inquired of Mr. Pla whether there was any research to indicate that the execution of a mother resulted in suicide or homicidal behavior on the part of her children. Mr. Pla replied that, although there were many women on "death row" in the nation, there had not been any specific research to address that question. Bob restated the documented argument, however, that the death of the parent for *any* reason—including execution by the state—placed a child 13 years of age and under at very high risk for suicide. The judge ruled that the jury would not be permitted to hear the argument that Ms. Gomez's execution would place her children at risk for either suicide or homicidal behavior. The DA also argued that the taxpayers and voters of California wanted to see the prompt execution of criminals committing heinous crimes, especially the killing of a child, rather than the expense of keeping that person alive and in prison.

The judge did rule that the arguments presented by Mr. Pla of Ms. Gomez's value to her own children if kept alive for mothering–nurturing purposes and her potential value to young, extended family members and other youths that she might be able to affect in a positive way by reflecting on her tragic story were accepted by the judge over the opposition of the DA.

The Death Penalty Trial for Rita Gomez

Bob Pla testified for two days before the jury under a barrage of challenging, often cynical questions advanced by the DA. Mr. Falls made a valiant effort in his *direct* (initial testimony) examination of Mr. Pla, which was followed by a lengthy *cross* (challenging the initial testimony) examination by the DA. The factual premise of each of Mr. Pla's statements in his report (minus all of the sections withheld from the jury as the result of the pretrial hearing) was challenged by the DA as to its source, research validity, and conclusions. Bob Pla was well prepared and defended each position with confidence and a presence of authority, hoping to impress the jury. Attorney Falls fought to retrieve any "points" scored by the DA during his *redirect* (further clarification of initial testimony provided during the direct examination) examination of Mr. Pla. Finally, following two days of the direct, cross, and redirect testimony of Mr. Pla, the defense rested its case. The attorneys were given two days to prepare their closing arguments for the jury.

The prosecution was first to present its closing argument on behalf of the people of the state of California, followed by the closing argument of the defense. The district attorney provided a tough law-and-order argument, calling for the death penalty, which was followed by the closing statement of the defense. Attorney Falls pleaded to the jury that, because Ms. Gomez was an adolescent and a mother with no prior criminal convictions and whose judgment was gravely impaired because she was under the influence of alcohol and drugs at the time of the commission of the crime, these mitigating factors should warrant a sentence of life imprisonment without the possibility of parole, rather than execution.

The prosecution then was permitted to rebut the defense's closing arguments. The district attorney argued that, in California, an 18-year-old is legally an adult, not an adolescent, and the fact that she is a mother had matured her far beyond her age. He granted that Ms. Gomez was an alcoholic and a heroin and cocaine addict but that there was no factual evidence to prove that she was intoxicated at the specific moment that she fired the gun at the victim. The DA further advised the jury that, even though there were no criminal convictions in her history, by her own statements she had admitted stealing items from home to sell in order to purchase her drugs.

The all-white jury that had already convicted Ms. Gomez of first-degree murder deliberated the death penalty phase of the trial for two days. The court then reconvened when the jury had reached a verdict. The courtroom was filled to capacity, and media cameras were running. The judge asked the jury whether it had reached a decision. The jury foreman stood up and replied, "Yes we have, your honor." The foreman then read the verdict, which was written on a piece of paper, in a businesslike voice, stating:

> Based upon the court instructions given to us, we the jury can find no mitigating factors or circumstances which would warrant life imprisonment without the possibility of parole for the defendant. We are unanimous in our opinion that her criminal actions involved the taking of a child's life and warrants the death penalty.

After the first sentence had been read, the victim's family and supporters were crying and cheering, drowning out the second sentence. Ms. Gomez held her head down, crying, and loudly stated to the victim's family, "I'm sorry! I'm sorry!" Her attorney, who also had tears in his eyes, attempted to comfort his client.

A Social Worker's Work Is Never Finished

It had been a little over a week since Bob Pla had testified in the Rita Gomez case. It was the noon hour, and Bob was driving to the local "In & Out Burger" for his favorite double-burger and fries. His radio was again tuned in to Danny Jones and his

"Oldies but Goodies" program. He pulled up to the speaker and placed his order and was waiting in the long line of cars. Danny Jones cut in stating:

> Well folks. The verdict that you've all been waiting for has just come in. It looks like one of our Olas residents is going to fry! I guess what goes around comes around. It's too bad that we'll be losing a second beautiful young lady. Catch you later....

Bob was immobilized until the car in back of him honked its horn, waking him out of his preoccupied trance. He pulled up and paid for his order and received his lunch. By habit he reached for the hot fries, but they seemed tasteless. "Maybe they forgot to put salt on them," he thought. For some reason, he had lost his appetite. He could not believe the verdict. Danny Jones's words "what goes around comes around," kept interfering with his thoughts about the case. "That's it! That is what all of this is about. What goes around comes around. Rita was abused, and, in turn, she abused!" Bob reasoned. She was subjected to physical punishment, and she had easy access to weapons; she killed, and now the state is going to kill her. "As social workers out to improve the human condition," Bob reflected, "we need to stop physical punishment, reduce easy access to firearms, and end capital punishment."

Bob recalled that, in the original micro and macro psychosocial intervention strategy he had developed, all tasks had been addressed and completed except for the last task, prevention. This final task involved the creation of a multidisciplinary and multiethnic task force to investigate the causes of youth violence and develop recommendations for the prevention of such incidents. After making at least two dozen phone calls to social workers and other professionals, school representatives, and minority community people to work on this project, he found very little interest. Most believed that the case was closed and that everyone should move beyond it and "heal."

Others felt that Olas was still a safe community and the Gomez case was just an aberration and would never happen again. "I guess communities are just like people," thought Bob. "As soon as the crisis is over, everything cools off, and denial once again darkens our path so we don't have to admit how dangerous it really is." Some minorities advised Bob, "Let sleeping dogs lie, man. Don't wake up the white monster (racism in Olas). Don't you remember how they wanted to come into our neighborhoods and shoot us?" Bob was becoming a little discouraged and had to remind himself that, just because he had been so intimately involved in practically all aspects of the case and understood clearly its wide-ranging implications to Olas and other communities, others did not seem to share his concerns. He also knew, however, that one can always find others who share one's concerns.

Bob decided to begin "at home," that is, with other social workers—after all, social workers are concerned with both the person and the environment. He asked to be placed on the agenda for the following month's Olas NASW meeting. At the meeting, he explained his concerns regarding the growing youth violence problem, not only in Olas but also throughout the nation, stating that the Gomez case was *not* an abnormality; rather, there were literally hundreds of persons in Olas with similar predispositional factors and dynamics, just waiting to explode. Many of the social workers agreed. Early childhood experiences of physical and sexual abuse were not uncommon in many families. "They should outlaw corporal punishment of children by parents as they did in the schools," exclaimed one of the social workers, with others quickly joining in and nodding agreement. "Corporal punishment starting with children is just at the beginning of a continuum of punishment," commented Ms. O'Leary, "that ends with the ultimate punishment—death!" "Maybe we need to get rid of the death penalty, too," remarked still another social worker.

Bob was sensing a certain enthusiasm in the group, often generated when people got together to discuss a particular issue. No longer were they feeling isolated or powerless. The group wanted to develop strategies related to violence prevention, agreeing that what was most needed was a response to the massive social welfare needs of the many people with very few resources. NASW, through its national committees, commissions, and local chapters, was already working on these issues. The group did not see any reason to involve itself in that area nor in the discussion of capital punishment since NASW already had a national policy statement favoring its abolition.

"Even though NASW has officially taken a position against the death penalty," interrupted group member Rocco Vincent, "do we really know much about the women being sentenced to death and for what crimes?" Rocco Vincent, a professor of social work at Cal State University at Olas, was teaching in the BSW program. "I would like to raise this issue with my students and see if I can interest a few of them to take this on as their term paper topic," added Professor Vincent.

Professor Vincent presented this information to his upper division social policy course the following week. "I assume that many of you have been following the newspapers concerning the Rita Gomez case. And you probably know that Ms. Gomez received the death penalty as punishment for her involvement in the high school homicide," he reminded the class. He then led a discussion of the class attitudes for and against the death penalty as it concerned women. The class seemed to mirror society's attitudes, as nearly 70 percent of the students favored the death penalty. When Professor Vincent inquired about their attitudes concerning the state execution of women, however, the percent favoring this outcome dramatically dropped to about 20 percent.

"I notice that about 90 percent of the class is composed of women," Professor Vincent pointed out, "and I wonder if there might be an element of sexism or gender bias in your attitudes as you seem to favor the death penalty significantly more for men than women." This caught the class by surprise and some began to become defensive regarding the accusation of sexism. Some students began to argue that it was a "fact" that men were just naturally more violent than women. "Yes, indeed, there can be biological factors contributing to violence and aggression and even murder. Can you think of anything else?" the professor asked, challenging the group. One of the male students stated that culture could also be a contributing factor as males, beginning as early as childhood, were acculturated to be more aggressive and violent than females. The class nodded in agreement. "But let us get back to why women end up on death row and what crimes they committed that would lead to this bleak outcome," Professor Vincent said, trying to refocus the discussion. "Everyone knows why some women end up on death row. It's because they killed their mate who had been subjecting them to spousal abuse over a period of years and the women just got tired of it," pointed out one of the students receiving support from other female students. "But aren't we just guessing and playing with 'facts' that we grab out of the thin air? As social work students, should you not be able to prepare yourself with documented data as it concerns human behavior?" asked Professor Vincent. The class was quiet as many nodded in agreement with this assessment.

"I have been meeting regularly with the crisis mental health committee since the high school homicide tragedy. Following the death penalty sentence for Rita Gomez, the committee became interested in the issue of the death penalty, specifically which women receive this harsh sentence, and for what crimes. Are there any students who would be willing to research this issue for the class and the crisis committee in lieu of the required term paper?" Three students volunteered for this assignment, and a month later the three were ready to present their concept paper, which Professor Vincent reproduced for the class (see Box 27.2). The students reported they were surprised by the volume of information available and were able to identify through Internet resources.

Box 27.2

Capital Punishment for Women in the United States

Submitted by: Sangyong Woo, Maria Lopez, and April Love

The death penalty dates as far back as the eighteenth century B.C., under the rule of the king of Babylon. In the United States, legal capital punishment has been used in such varied situations as the Salem Witch Trials and the execution of Timothy McVeigh in the Oklahoma City Federal Courthouse bombing. Today only twelve states and the District of Columbia do not allow capital punishment. Throughout our history, racism has been a significant factor influencing decisions about who will be put to death. For example, although not "legal" executions, as many as 2,954 African Americans were executed by lynch mobs between 1889 and 1932, and in modern times a review of who was put to death in the thirty-eight states with capital punishment found disparities in relation to the race of the victim. It was determined that, under similar circumstances, a minority defendant was more likely to receive a death sentence if the victim was white than if the victim was of minority background.[1]

Internationally, there appears to be a strong connection between conservative, oppressive governments and their use of the death penalty in attempting to intimidate or control the masses. In April 1999, the United Nations Commission on Human Rights voted overwhelming support for a moratorium on the death penalty. The resolution was introduced by the European Union with the only nations opposing the resolution being China, Rwanda, Sudan, and the United States. The international human rights community considers the United States among the worst violators of human rights because of its stated commitment to capital punishment as a deterrent to crime. The international human rights community has identified the following issues warranting U.S. reform:[2]

▶ The execution of juvenile offenders (under 18 when capital crime committed)
▶ The execution of those with mental retardation or severe mental illness
▶ The execution of foreign nationals not informed of their rights under the Vienna Convention on Consular Relations (VCCR)
▶ The application of the death penalty is associated with racial and economic bias
▶ The length of time the condemned spend in extreme isolation and deprivation between sentencing and execution

chapter 27 ◆ Social Workers in Action: School Homicide and the Death Penalty

Finding itself increasingly isolated as a nation, especially after the erosion of European support in the pre-emptive Iraq War, the United States has started to make some positive changes in three of the five death penalty policies listed above. First, in 2002 the U.S. Supreme Court issued a ruling ending the execution of mentally retarded prisoners, stating that it was a violation of the Eighth Amendment of the U.S. Constitution, i.e., cruel and unusual punishment.

Second, even though the United States signed Article 36 of the Vienna Convention on Consular Relations in 1969, for nearly forty years the United States has ignored the requirement to inform foreign nationals of their right to have their consulate notified in the event of their detention or death sentence. Complying with Article 36 would require the foreign nationals to be returned to their non–death penalty countries under a life without parole sentence. In 2004 Mexico brought a suit against the United States in the International Court of Justice concerning the U.S. failure to inform 54 Mexicans on death row of their right to talk to their consular officials prior to sentencing. The International Court of Justice ruled in favor of Mexico and ordered the United States to have a judicial review of these capital convictions.[3] In 2005, President Bush, bowing to international law, issued a Presidential Order that the Mexican nationals on death row in several states who were not notified of their right to contact Mexican officials about their death sentence would be granted a new hearing to determine if they were harmed by this error.[4]

Third, a landmark five-to-four Supreme Court decision was issued in 2005, when the court ruled that the Constitution forbids the execution of homicide perpetrators on death row who were under 18 years of age when they committed a capital crime.[5] The United States is the only nation in the world following the practice of executing juveniles. The continuing execution of poor minorities, mostly African Americans and *Latinos,* and housing death row inmates for 30 to 40 years continues to keep the United States lagging behind the rest of the world as it concerns capital punishment reform.

Reacting to mounting international human rights criticism, the U.S. policy response is that it believes it reserves the right within U.S. Constitutional constraints to impose capital punishment on any person duly convicted under existing laws permitting the imposition of capital punishment. As of January 1, 2005, there were 3,455 inmates on death row, including 110 persons ages 60 to 89 and older,[6] in addition to 50 women.[7] There appears to be an ambivalent and less punitive attitude at all levels of the criminal justice system toward the execution of women. For example, women make up more than one-half of the U.S. population, but represent only 10 percent of all homicide arrests in the United States—and they are only 2 percent of persons receiving the death penalty following conviction. Today women account for 1.4 percent of persons currently on death row, and 1.1 percent of persons actually executed in modern times.[8]

Whereas nearly 90 percent of males on death row were convicted of a capital offense involving a *felony homicide* (the killing of one or more persons during the commission of a felony offense), for women it is significantly less: 40 percent. The majority of women, twenty-eight out of fifty (56 percent) are on death row for having killed a loved one. More specifically, fifteen killed a spouse or boyfriend, and in most of these cases a "hit man" was hired in an effort to acquire insurance benefits or other economic gain. Eleven mothers committed *filicide* (killing of their children between 2 years and 14 years of age), two women were convicted of *familicide* (killing their spouse and children), one woman was convicted for having killed a police officer, and another was on death row for intentionally killing six pedestrians with her vehicle.[9]

Race and ethnicity continue to be a factor in capital punishment when it relates to women. Although non-Hispanic white women are 67.7 percent of the female population, they are only 52 percent of the women on death row. This compares to 30 percent of African American women

(Continued)

Box 27.2 (Continued)

(12.9 percent of the U.S. female population). The Hispanic and American Indian females on death row are in the approximate percentages as in the U.S. population—14 percent Hispanic and 2 percent American Indian. In analyzing felony homicide convictions that placed women on death row, nine inmates were non-Hispanic white, and nine were African American, followed by one Hispanic and one American Indian. Twelve non-Hispanic white women, two African American women, and one Hispanic woman are on death row for having killed their spouse or boyfriend. Five Hispanic mothers, four non-Hispanic white mothers, and two African American mothers committed filicide. One African American and one non-Hispanic white woman committed familicide.[10] In sum, minority women, who number nearly one-half of the women on death row, are greatly over-represented, as they make up only about one-third of the total female population.

Although 50 women are languishing on death row in the United States, only ten were executed between 1984 and 2002. Among the ten women who were executed, three in particular drew national and/or global media and public attention. One was a non-Hispanic white woman, Christina Riggs, a licensed registered nurse who committed filicide in 1997 by medicating and smothering her 5-year-old son and 2-year-old daughter. She was suffering from major depression and PTSD resulting from her clinical work with victims of the Oklahoma City bombing. Ms. Riggs actively sought the death penalty, indicating that she wanted to join her deceased children and therefore "used" the criminal justice system as a vehicle to achieve her ultimate wish, i.e., "suicide by capital punishment."[11] Karla Faye Tucker, an attractive, 39-year-old, non-Hispanic white woman, was executed for her double murder felony crime, committed at the age of 24 with her boyfriend. The case received world attention due to protests (ultimately unsuccessful) based on the belief that (1) a woman should not be executed, and (2) that Karla Fay Tucker had transformed herself into a born-again Christian; hence, she was a different person than the one who committed the heinous crime.[12] The American ambivalence and interest concerning the execution of women was also evident in the execution of Aileen Wuornos, a non-Hispanic white female, who was the only female serial killer (confessing to the murders of six men) on women's death row. This public interest resulted in a movie called *Monster* about her life and death, starring Charlize Theron, who was awarded an Oscar for best actress in 2003.[13]

There are indications that capital punishment reform is beginning to surface in the United States as seen in recent major policy actions taken by state governors, the president of the United States, and the U.S. Supreme Court. For example, then Republican Governor of Illinois, George Ryan, who was previously a supporter of the death penalty, commuted the death sentences of all 156 inmates on death row. In defending his actions, Ryan stated: "Because the Illinois death penalty system is arbitrary and capricious and therefore immoral, I no longer shall tinker with the machinery of death." He had halted executions three years previously after discovering that thirteen death row inmates had been wrongfully convicted.[14] As identified above, the other death penalty reforms in the United States include (1) the prohibition of executing the "mentally retarded" or those with severe mental illness (U.S. Supreme Court); (2) the prohibition of executing those who committed a capital crime when they were younger than 18 years of age (U.S. Supreme Court); and (3) the suspension of the death penalty for foreign nationals. In light of these reforms, it is now timely to seek strategies to end capital punishment altogether—for both women and men—in the State of California and the United States.

RECOMMENDATIONS:

1. Because the United States is the only nation in the world that, with very rare exceptions, still executes women, it is recommended that this human rights violation be terminated.
2. It is recommended that the local NASW chapter of Olas adopt our recommendations and forward them to the main body of the 150,000 member NASW for adoption and distribution to the local chapters in the thirty-eight death penalty states.
3. It is further recommended that the local NASW chapters, in turn, contact their elected state officials for adoption and recommendation to the state governor for a prohibition of the death penalty for women and a commutation (changing the death sentence to life without parole) of the death penalty of women currently on death row.

ENDNOTES

1. M. Robinson, "International Perspectives on Death Penalty: A Costly Isolation for the U.S.," (Washington, D.C.: Death Penalty Information Center), p. 18, online at http://www.deathpenaltyinfo.org. The states and districts without the death penalty include Alaska, Hawaii, Iowa, Maine, Massachusetts, Michigan, Minnesota, North Dakota, Rhode Island, Vermont, West Virginia, Wisconsin, and the District of Columbia.
2. Ibid., p. 7.
3. "U.S. Violated Rights of Mexicans on Death Row," Human Rights Watch, March 31, 2004, online at http://hrw.org.
4. D. G. Savage, "Bush Orders Hearings for Mexicans on Death Row," *Los Angeles Times* (March 9, 2005), p. A21.
5. D. G. Savage, "Supreme Court Bans Execution of Juveniles," *Los Angeles Times* (March 2, 2005), p. A1.
6. "Growing Elderly Population on Death Row," Death Penalty Information Center, p. 2, online at http://www.deathpenaltyinfo.org.
7. "Facts about the Death Penalty," Death Penalty Information Center, February 23, 2005, online at http://www.deathpenaltyinfo.org.
8. V. L. Streib, "Death Penalty for Female Offenders, January 1, 1973, through September 30, 2004," pp. 1–21, online at http://www.law.onu.edu/faculty/streib.
9. Ibid., p. 3.
10. Ibid., p. 6.
11. "Christina Marie Riggs," http://www.clarkprosecutor.org/html/death/US/riggs629.htm.
12. "A Memorial to Karla Faye Tucker Brown," http://www.geocities.com/RainForest/canopy/2525/karlamain.html.
13. "Aileen Wuornos," http://www.ccadp.org/aileenwuornos.htm.
14. "News—Illinois Governor Ryan Commutes ALL Death Sentences," http://www.ccadp.org/news-ryan2003.htm.

Not only did the class have an excellent and well-informed discussion about capital punishment for women, but the three students earned "A" grades for their term paper. Professor Vincent then arranged for the students to present this material at the next NASW meeting and sent it to all local NASW members as an e-mail attachment to the meeting announcement. Jerry Russell, an Olas representative to the California House of Representatives and NASW member, attended the meeting and participated in the discussion. With the students' permission, Mr. Russell agreed to share this paper with other legislators and, if there was sufficient support, possibly draft a bill for consideration by the California State Assembly.

Concluding Comment

The profession of social work is indeed a profession of many faces as seen in this high school homicide case. The "social workers in action" in the Olas tragedy possessed a repertoire of micro- and macro-level intervention skills based on a foundation of biological, psychological, social, and community social work–related knowledge obtained through professional education, on-the-job training, and subsequent experience. Whereas psychiatrists rely primarily on the strengths of their biological training in medicating and treating individuals, and psychologists rely heavily on their psychological testing instruments in assessing their patients, social workers are trained to have the potential for macro- as well as micro-level intervention.

In the high school homicide case, Bob Pla, MSW, was an advanced professional practitioner involved in various direct service (micro) tasks, such as assessment and treatment of individuals, couples, families, and nonfamily groups. His in-depth, comprehensive assessment skills were evident in the Gomez case, where he uncovered a generational alcoholism genetic link and identified other predispositional factors related to Ms. Gomez becoming a homicide perpetrator. Additionally, he was the chief administrator of a social work family services agency and was part of a team identifying and organizing resources in the community to deal with the Olas crisis.

Bob Pla also undertook various indirect service (macro) tasks utilizing prevention theories to help create conditions that would result in a safer community. During a period of heightened community tension and anger, he deployed staff members into the minority communities to help them vent their frustrations in response to being scapegoated by the dominant white community. Simultaneously, he worked with law enforcement and community groups in the majority community to discourage any vigilante-type retaliation.

Another indirect service prevention task to create a safer community directly evolving from the Rita Gomez case concerned the increasingly easy access to guns by youths and the dependence on corporal and capital punishment to "solve" problems of violence in the United States. The nation's obsession with firearms and its long-term continued commitment to corporal and capital punishment with its powerful "modeling" impact for the country were prevention issues and tasks that Bob and his colleagues could have undertaken, but there were simply not enough hours in a day—even for social workers—to tackle all three issues. Therefore, with BSW student resources provided by Professor Rocco Vincent, the timely issue of abolishing the capital punishment of women, encouraged by new death penalty reforms, became the focus of attention. In their review of the literature, the students uncovered unique, interesting information resulting in a concept paper with accompanying recommendations concerning the execution of women in the United States. Utilizing

> the social action vehicle of the local NASW chapter, a plan that could potentially result in a social policy change in California was developed.
>
> We know that one social worker *can* make a difference, as was seen in the Gomez case, and further that a committee of social workers, with the assistance of social work students, can make even *more* of a difference.

KEY WORDS AND CONCEPTS

Homicide
Criminal homicide
Felony homicide
Pro bono

Dysthymia
DSM IV-TR
Capital punishment

SUGGESTED INFORMATION SOURCES

Meyer, Cheryl L., and Michelle Oberman. *Mothers Who Kill Their Children.* New York: New York University Press, 2001.

Morales, Armando. "Homicide," in Richard L. Edwards, ed., *Encyclopedia of Social Work,* 19th ed. Washington, D.C.: NASW Press, 1995, pp. 1347–1358.

O'Shea, Kathleen A. *Women and the Death Penalty in the United States, 1900–1998.* Westport, Conn.: Praeger Publishers, 1999.

Scheck, Barry, Peter Neufeld, and Jim Dwyer. *Actual Innocence.* New York: Doubleday: 2000.

ENDNOTES

1. Homicides of children 4 and younger number about 2.5 per 100,000 in the United States. Mothers are the most frequent perpetrators, followed by fathers, mother's boyfriends, and caretakers. See "Children's Safety Network," in *A Data Book of Child and Adolescent Injury* (Washington, D.C.: National Center for Education in Maternal and Child Health, 1991).
2. Lola G. Selby, "Social Work and Crisis Theory," *Social Work Papers* 10 (1963): 3.
3. See John Cummings and Elaine Cummings, *Ego and Milieu* (New York: Atherton Press, 1962), as cited in Howard J. Parad, "Crisis Intervention," in Robert Morris, ed., *Encyclopedia of Social Work* 1(16) (New York: National Association of Social Workers, 1971), pp. 196–202.
4. See Gerald Caplan, *Principles of Preventive Psychiatry* (New York: Basic Books, 1964); Erich Lindemann, "The Meaning of Crisis in Individuals and Family Living," *Teachers College Record* 57 (February 1963), as cited in Parad, op. cit., pp. 198–199.
5. Lydia Rapoport, "Crisis-Oriented Short-Term Casework," *Social Service Review* 41 (March 1967): 35.
6. "They Think We're a Land of Sick Shooters," *U.S. News and World Report* (June 7, 1993): p. 9. Also, L. A. Fingerhut and J. C. Kleinman, "International and Interstate Comparison of Homicide Among Young Males," *Journal of the American Medical Association* 263(24) (June 27, 1990).

Photo Credits

frontispiece	EyeWire/Photodisc/Getty Images
p. 4	Ed Kashi/Corbis
p. 14	Robert Harbison
p. 30	Jim Pickerell/The Image Works
p. 52	AP Wide World Photos
p. 74	Bruce Flynn/Stock Boston
p. 94	Dana White/PhotoEdit
p. 114	Abraham Menashe/Veer, Inc.
p. 132	Anton Vengo/SuperStock
p. 148	Robert Harbison
p. 162	Marilyn Humphries/The Image Works
p. 174	Jeff Greenberg/PhotoEdit
p. 186	Neville Elder/Sygma/Corbis
p. 202	AP Wide World Photos
p. 218	Brooks Kraft/Sygma/Corbis
p. 234	AP Photo/Ajit Solanki
p. 254	Michael Newman/PhotoEdit
p. 288	AP Wide World Photos
p. 322	Will Hart
p. 340	A. Ramey/PhotoEdit
p. 360	James Pickerell/The Image Works
p. 384	Tony Savino/The Image Works
p. 412	Jean Claude Lejeune/Stock Boston
p. 436	Esbin-Anderson/The Image Works
p. 460	Tony Freeman/PhotoEdit
p. 480	Najlah Feanny/Corbis SABA
p. 504	Richard Lord/PhotoEdit
p. 528	Image Source/Jupiter Images

Name Index

Abbott, Edith, 41
Abbott, Grace, 62
Abramoff, Jack, 441
Addams, Jane, 62
Alcalay, R., 301
Alexander, Paul, 127
Anastas, Jeane W., 289n
Appleby, George A., 289n
Armstrong, M. I., 119

Balinsky, Rosalie, 41
Barretta-Herman, Angeline, 242
Barth, Michael, 48
Barton, Clara, 56
Beck, Allen J., 489
Bell, A. P., 298
Berger, R. M., 300
Bethune, Mary McLeod, 62
Bilmes, Linda, 215
bin Laden, Osama, 188, 194, 196, 385
Blumenfeld, W. J., 295
Bonilla-Santiago, Gloria, 505n, 519
Borskey, Erma, 481n
Bradford, J., 301
Bretell, C. B., 221
Brill, Naomi I., 137
Bubar, Roe, 437n
Bullis, Ronald K., 168, 169
Bush, George H. W., 66
Bush, George W., 26, 199, 215, 401
Butler, Robert N., 348

Cabot, Richard, 62
Canda, Edward, 163, 165
Cannon, Ida, 62
Cantor, M. H., 352
Caplan, Gerald, 469
Carballo-Dieguez, A., 293
Carter, Jimmy, 20
Cassidy, Gerald, 212
Chin, J. L., 419
Chin, Vincent, 416
Chon, Lena, 432
Cicero, 464
Clancy, Joanne E., 203n
Clinton, Bill, 21, 23, 266, 398, 416
Clinton, Hillary, 416
Cochran, S. D., 293
Cohen, Nathan, 64
Collins, Alice H., 469
Cornell, Stephen, 441

Day, Kristin, 212
Deloria, V., 447
Derezotes, David S., 169, 170
Devine, Edward T., 61
Dix, Dorothea, 19, 56, 57
Dole, Robert, 212, 371
Douglass, Frederic, 482

Epsing-Anderson, G., 240, 241, 243

Fannon, Frantz, 500
Farrakhan, Louis, 390
Flexner, Abraham, 63, 65
Fred, Sheryl, 248
Frey, W., 222
Frost, Robert, 220
Furman, Leola, 165

Gallicchio, Salvatore J., 326
Gallup, George, 164
Garner, B., 295
Gellner, Ernest, 397
Germain, C. B., 302
Ghavam, Hamid Reza, 247
Gilligan, Carol, 396
Gitterman, A., 302
Gordon, William E., 66
Gore, Al, 416
Graff, Dorothy L., 167
Greenwood, Ernest, 65
Grossman, S. F., 198
Grundermann, Herman F., 326

Hadi, Kani, 181
Hall, M., 304
Hamer, Fannie Lou, 482
Hammersmith, S. K., 298
Hara, Calvin, 432
Hardwick, W., 221
Harper, Ernest, 64
Haynes, George, 62
Hill, Nancy, 499
Hippocrates, 464
Ho, M. K., 423
Hodge, David, 385n
Hokenstad, M. C., 142
Horejsi, Charles R., 177
Howe, Samuel Gridley, 56
Huang, L. N., 426

Jamieson, Amie, 324
Jenkins, Lowell E., 42
Johnson, Lyndon, 20, 66, 262
Jorve, Beth K., 108

Kahle, Lynn R., 137
Kalt, Joseph P., 441
Kearnsey, John R., 326
Kelley, Patricia, 127
Kennedy, John F., 20
King, Martin Luther Jr., 482
Klar, Dana, 437n
Kominski, Robert, 324
Koresh, David, 188
Kravetz, Diane, 255n

Lathrop, Julia, 62
Lee, Bill, 432
Lee, E, 419
Lee, E. P. Tsiaiah, 468
Lee, L. C., 433
Lee, May, 431
Lee, Porter, 61
Lenroot, Katherine, 62, 323
Levine, Joanne, 137
Lew, A., 426
Lewis, Myrna I., 348
Lewitt, Eugene M., 326
Lindsay, Michael, 164
Locke, Gary, 433
Loewenberg, Frank, 165
Lowell, Josephine Shaw, 56
Lubove, Roy, 62
Lum, Doman, 413n, 424, 428, 501
Lytle, C. M., 447

Mak, W. S., 418
Malcolm X, 388, 482
Mankiller, Wilma, 263
Martinez, Gladys, 324
Maslow, Abraham, 15
Mays, V. M., 293
McVeigh, Timothy, 1889
Meyers, J. C., 119
Moore, Wilbert, 53
Morales, Armando, 195, 362, 461n, 516, 526
Moynihan, Daniel, 485

Newby, J. H., 293
Nguyen, Ninh Van, 431
Nguyen, Vanessa, 432
Nornes, Sonia, 34n
Norton, Dolores G., 467

O'Connor, Sandra Day, 263
Otow, June, 431

561

Pancoast, Diane L., 469
Paul, W., 295
Pavalko, Ronald, 54
Pierce, Franklin, 19
Pires, S. A., 119
Powell, Colin, 199
Pruger, Robert, 123
Puig, Maria Elena, 219n

Quadland, M. C., 314

Reagan, Ronald, 20, 21, 66
Renard, John, 387
Reno, Janet, 188
Richmond, Mary, 40, 61, 63, 64
Ride, Sally, 263
Riggs, Christina, 556
Rivera-Sanchez, Ilia, 68
Rokeach, Milton, 134
Roosevelt, Franklin D., 19, 371, 423
Roosevelt, Theodore, 323
Ryan, C., 301
Ryan, George, 556
Ryan, William, 499

Salcido, Ramon, 461n
Samudra, Imam, 194
Sanders, Marion K., 67, 68
Sattles, W. D., 314
Scanlon, Michael, 441
Schatz, Mona S., 42
Scott, Malcolm E., 481n
Serrano, John, 178
Shalala, Donna, 212
Shank, Barbara W., 108
Sheafor, Bradford W., 34n, 42,
    128, 177, 182, 203n, 362, 516
Singer, A., 221
Smith, R. W., 295
Smolak, Alex, 167
Solomon, Barbara Bryant, 400, 467
Spergel, I., 198
Stiglitz, Joseph, 215
Stroul, B. A., 119
Sue, D., 418
Sue, D. W., 418

Taniguchi, Harriet, 431
Teare, Robert J., 128, 182

Tran, T. V., 424
Truth, Sojourner, 56
Tubman, Harriet, 56
Tucker, Karla Faye, 556

Uba, L., 420

Wallace, Marquis
    Earl, 127
Weinberg, M. S., 298
Weinrich, J. D., 295
Weiss, Idit, 243
Wilensky, Harold, 55
Williams, Mark, 167
Williamson, Celia, 361n
Wilson, Joe, 211
Wolf, Dick, 498
Wright, R. Jr., 424
Wuornos, Aileen, 556

Yasumura, Hach, 431
Yee, B. W. K., 426

Zavala-Martinez, Iris, 506
Zilboorg, Gregory, 165

Subject Index

AA (Associate of Arts) degree, 80
Abortion, 265
Abuse
  of children, 329
  disabilities and, 369–370
  of women, 260, 414
Academy of Certified Baccalaureate Social Workers (ACBSW), 77
Academy of Certified Social Workers (ACSW), 77, 90
Accreditation
  CSWE Standards for, 88–89
  process of, 76–77
  of social workers with advanced degrees, 89n
Acculturative stress, 227, 423–424
ACSW. *See* Academy of Certified Social Workers (ACSW)
Action orientation of
  case workers, 5
  social work, 33
ADA. *See* Americans with Disabilities Act (ADA)
Adaptive-vital culture, of African Americans, 493
Addiction. *See* Substance use and abuse
Adolescents. *See* Children and youth; Lesbian, gays, bisexuals and transgenders (LGBT)
Adoption
  adoption services, as field of social work practice, 100
  same-sex couples and, 266
Adultification, 226
Advanced degrees, 89n. *See also* Advanced professional; specific degrees
Advanced generalist level, 42–43
Advanced professional, 90–91
Advocacy, skill in, 154
Affirmative action legislation, Puerto Ricans and, 518
Affirmative asylum application, 228
Afghanistan
  Afghanistan War, 204, 214
  gangs in, 194
African Americans, 19, 483–484
  criminal justice system and, 488–489
  culturally competent practice with, 498–499
  demographics of, 483–484

diversity and resilience of, 491–492, 493
ecosystems model and, 490–494
education and, 486–488
family structure of, 267–268, 493–494
in history and social work, 62
poverty of, 483–486
social issues of, 490–494
youth gangs, 198
Aged, views of, 349
Ageism, 348, 352
  mental health professionals, elderly, and, 355–357
Agencies. *See also* specific agencies and organizations
  advantages of, 125–126
  carrying out programs of, 152
  interprofessional cooperation in, 124
  oversight resources of, 156
  procedures and decision-making structures of, 154
  responsibility to, 123
  services offered by, 125
  social worker contributions to, 123–124
  support for programs from, 155
Agency-based practice, issues affecting, 119–126
Agency setting, 418
Age structure, changing, 238–239
Aging, as field of social work practice, 96–97. *See also* Older adults
AIDS. *See* HIV/AIDS
Alaskan Natives. *See* Indigenous peoples
Alcohol abuse. *See also* Substance use and abuse
  among lesbians, gays, and bisexuals, 301, 312
  as field of social work practice, 97–98
Alienation, immigrants and, 226
Aliens, 223. *See also* Immigrants/immigration
al-Qaeda, gang terrorism and, 187–188, 193, 195, 196
American Association of Schools of Social Work (AASSW), 61, 64, 85–86
American Association of Social Workers, 38, 63

American Indians. *See* Indigenous peoples
Americanized family, of Asian Americans/Pacific Islanders, 426
American Muslim Poll, 389, 390
American Red Cross, 56, 68
Americans with Disabilities Act (ADA), 362, 372, 378, 380
Anti-Chinese Act (1882), 220
Anxiety, immigrants and, 226
Arab world, gangs in, 196
Asian American social service centers, 431
Asian Americans/Pacific Islanders
  culture of, 424–425
  demographics of, 414–415
  disparity of diversity in, 433
  economic influence *versus* political underrepresentation of, 433
  ecosystems model for, 421–430
  education and, 414
  emerging issues, 432–433
  ethnic group stressors and, 416–417
  family types of, 425–427
  gender issues and, 414
  health status and risk factors of, 415–416
  housing of, 415
  income of, 414–415
  macro practice for, 430–432
  micro practice for, 419–421, 428
  service systems for, 417–419
  socioeconomic issues of, 414–415
  socioenvironmental impacts on, 424
  women in families of, 269–270
  youth gangs of, 417
Assessment
  of instructional activities, 155
  intake, 155
  skill in using technique of, 152, 153
Assimilation, of Indigenous peoples, 20, 437, 448
Association of Social Work Boards, licensing defined by, 78
Association of Training Schools for Professional Social Workers, 64
"Astronauts," Asian husbands as, 416

563

Subject Index

Asylees, 224. *See also* Immigrants/immigration
At-risk factors for protective services, identifying, 156
At-risk social behavior, of children and youth, 329–330
Aztec psychiatry, 465

Baby boomers, aging of, 342
Baccalaureate-level degrees. *See* BSW (baccalaureate-level) degrees
Baltimore, Strike II programs in, 179
Barbell economies, 222
Barrio, 464, 474–476
Barrio service systems, 467–468
"Basic Eight," primary division of social work practice as, 88
Basic social work professional, 84–87
Battered women
 macro practice with, 279–280
 micro practice with, 276–279
Behrman, Richard E., 326
Bias, 397. *See also* Prejudice
Bicultural family, of Asian Americans/Pacific Islanders, 426
Biculturality, 297
Bilingualism
 of practioners in mental health care, 510
 and staffing for Asian American service delivery, 417
Biracial family, case example, 333–336
Bisexuals. *See* Lesbian, gays, bisexuals and transgenders (LGBT)
"Blocked-out" subculture theory, of delinquency, 195
Bombings, domestic terrorist, 189
Border and Transportation Security, by Homeland Security Department, 180
Boston School of Social Work, 62
Boston Youth Program, 179
Branch Davidians, 188
Brown v. Board of Education, 486, 492
BSW (baccalaureate-level) degrees, 44, 45, 48. *See also* Education
 disciplines related to, 80–81, 84
 levels of social work practice and, 84–91
 professional niche of, 84–87
 reemergence of social work for, 67

Budgets. *See* Funding
Bureaucratic model, 122–124
Bureau of Indian Affairs (BIA), 439, 442, 448
Business (for profit) sector, 118–119
Business systems, operation of, 156

California. *See also* Los Angeles
 Serrano v. Priest case in, 178
Canada, indigenous peoples of, 438
Cancer, among lesbians, gays, and bisexuals, 312–313
Capital punishment. *See* Death penalty
Careers, 75–92
 for community college graduates, 80
 degree of bureaucracy, 121
 entry to social work profession, 75–92
 in human service practice, 79–84
 patterns of, 44–45
 for professional social worker, 84–87
 in related helping professions, 81
Caregiving, intergenerational, 349–350
Caring, 36
Case advocacy, 151–152
Case planning and maintenance, competency in, 151–152
Casework, 41. *See also* specific topic
Casinos, on reservations, 441
Casualties, of U.S. Middle East wars, 203–216
Certification, 76, 77–78
Chain immigration, 222
Change, expertise in guiding process of, 151
Changing society, 36–37
Charity organization societies, 19, 61
Charity Organization Society (Buffalo, NY), 61
Charity Organization Society (New York City), 61, 88
Chicago
 gangs in, 198
 "Little Village Project" in, 198
 settlement houses in, 61, 62
Chicano movement of 1960s and 1970s, 468. *See also* Mexican Americans
Child abuse, 329
Childbearing
 age at, 265
 out-of-wedlock, 259
Child maltreatment, 329

Children and youth, 323–337
 African American, 486, 487, 493, 495, 497
 at-risk social behavior of, 329–330
 biracial, 333–336
 culture-level considerations, 333–334
 decline in percentage of, 238
 demographics, 324–330
 ecosystems model for, 330–336
 education status of, 327–328
 environmental-structural considerations, 334
 family demographics for, 256–259
 family income, employment and, 326
 family-level considerations, 332–333
 family structure of, 325
 foster care for, 99–100
 in gay, lesbian, and bisexual families, 266, 299, 309–310
 health status/chronic physical conditions of, 328–329
 historical issues affecting, 334–335
 housing for, 325–326
 Indigenous, 445–446
 individual-level considerations, 331–332
 macro practice with, 333–336
 micro practice with (ecosystems model format), 333–336
 in Muslim families, 391–392
 "non-gang," 190, 191
 "parachute kid" phenomena, 416
 personal characteristics of, 324–325
 poverty among, 26, 326–327
 protective services for, 98, 99
 Puerto Rican, 507–508
 of soldiers, 212–213
 trafficking of, 228
 unaccompanied minors, 224–225
 unmarried parents and, 100
Child welfare
 case study, 5–11
 as field of social work practice, 98–100
Child Welfare League of America, 120
Chinese Exclusion Act (1882), 421
Chinese immigrants, 220. *See also* Immigrants/immigration
Chronic physical conditions, of children, 328–329
Cities. *See* specific cities
City gangs, 194

Subject Index 565

Civil rights, 21
  erosion of protections, 180–181
  of Muslims, 398–399
Civil Rights Movement, results of, 492
Civil War, social workers in, 56
Class action social work
  lesbians, gays, bisexuals and, 302
  prevention and, 177–181
Classification system, for social work entry points and educational requirements, 44
Classroom sessions, planning, 155
Clients. *See also* specific client populations
  confidentiality of relationship with, 140
  delivery of services to, 115, 116
  developing ability to help themselves, 125, 139
  efforts for, 138–140
  engaging in examining problems, 153
  gathering and analyzing information from, 151
  knowledge of background factors, 152
  responsibility to agency and, 133–134
  values of, 133, 137, 138
Client transitions, facilitating, 153
Cluster of practice activity, 150
Code of ethics. *See also* National Association of Social Workers (NASW) Code of Ethics
  by IFSW, 244
  sensitivity to religion/spirituality of clients and, 166, 170
  for social work, 63
Cognitive interventions, based on shari'a, 393
College
  African Americans in, 487
  Puerto Ricans and other Hispanics in, 509
Colonialism
  Mexicans and, 465–466
  Puerto Ricans and, 516–518
Colonial period, social welfare in, 17–20
Columbine massacre, 189
Combat
  survivor trauma and, 209–210
  women in, 213
Communication styles, of Puerto Ricans, 521
Community
  Indigenous concept of, 451–454
  in Islam, 392–393

Community-agency-based gang homicide prevention model, 179–180
Community-based gang crime prevention programs, 179–180
Community college graduates, careers for, 80
Community data collection and analysis, 155
Community development, as field of social work practice, 101–102
Community organization, 41, 101
Community outreach programs, 418
Community planning, as field of social work practice, 101
Community Youth Gang Services Corporation (Los Angeles), 180
Compadres (Mexican), 468, 469
Competencies
  frequently utilized, 151–153
  low-utilization, 157
  occasionally needed by social workers, 154–157
  for social work practice, 124–125, 149–159
  universal, 150–151
Complementary marriage model, 391–392
Conduct, standards of, 141–142
Confidentiality, of client relationship, 140
Conflict gangs, 195
Conflict resolution, with clients, 151
Conflict situations, dealing with, 156
Conservatism, 20
Constitution (U.S.), detention of terrorist suspects and, 181
Consultation, 127–128, 151
Consumer service model, of occupational social work, 109
Consumers' League, 56
Continuing care, for older people, 351–355
Contra-culture, of gangs, 195
Conversion therapy, 301
Cooperation, interprofessional, 124
Corporal punishment, against children and youth, 330, 333
Corporate social reponsibility model, of occupational social work, 109
Corporatist welfare state, 240
Corrections/criminal justice, as field of social work practice, 102–103
Costs, of war, 214–215

Council on Social Work Education (CSWE), 44, 45, 64, 65, 76, 86–87, 243, 357
Counseling, with clients, 151
Couples, lesbian, gay, and bisexual, 307–310, 315
Court-based gang crime prevention programs, 179–180
Crime prevention, urban violence and, 179–180
Criminal gangs, 195
Criminal homicides, 530. *See also* Homicide
Criminal justice system
  African American experience in, 488–489
  school homicide trial and, 555, 556
  social work practice in, 102–103
Crisis intervention skill, 153. *See also* School homicide case
Crisis recovery work, 248
Crisis theory, in school homicide case, 535–536
CSWE. *See* Council on Social Work Education (CSWE)
CSWE-NASW Ad Hoc Committee on Manpower Issues, 86
Cult/occult gang, 195, 196
Cultural awareness, in mental health care, 509–513
Cultural boundaries, 425
Cultural competency
  comprehension of, 437
  religion and spirituality in, 168
  in serving returning troops, 213–214
  spiritual competency and, 386
Cultural conflict family, of Asian Americans/Pacific Islanders, 426
Cultural duality, 425
Cultural factors (ecosystems model)
  for African Americans, 493
  for Asian Americans/Pacific Islanders, 424–425
  for children and youth, 330–336
  for Indigenous peoples, 449–450
  for lesbians, gays, and bisexuals, 296–297
  for Mexican Americans, 463–470
  for Muslims, 392–396, 403–404
  older adults', 349
  for people with disabilities, 378
  Puerto Rican, 516–522
  women's, 263–264
Cultural patterns, understanding of, 150
Cultures. *See* specific group

Curing, 36
Curriculum
  content of, 88–89
  development of, 155
Curriculum Policy Statement (CSWE), 86, 88

Data collection, 150–151, 155
Death, causes of
  infant/child/youth, 329
  in Native American culture, 453
  soldiers' experiences with, 209–211
Death penalty
  moratorium, 554, 556
  phase, of school homicide trial, 540
  reforms in, 556
  U.S. and, 554–556
  women and, 554–556
Debt, from war, 214–215
Decision making
  by policy makers, 157
  skill in facilitating, 153
Defense of Marriage Act (DOMA), 266, 316
Defense spending, 23
Defensive application, 228
Degrees, of social workers, 44–45. *See also* specific degrees
Delivery services, 115, 116
  for Asian Americans/Pacific Islanders, 417–419
  fragmentation of, 84
  knowledge development of, 152
Demand, for social work, 237–239
Demographic profiles. *See* specific populations
Departments of government. *See* specific departments
Depression
  among women, 271–272
  dysthymic, 547
  endogenous, 547
  immigrants and, 226
  reactive, 547
Detection, in secondary prevention, 177–178
Detention, of suspected terrorists, 181
Developmental disabilities, as field of social work, 103
Developmental Disabilities Assistance and Bill of Rights Act (Public Law 95-602), 103–104
Diaphobia, toward Muslims, 396–398
Diplomate in Clinical Social Work (DCSW), 77, 90
Direct practice, 149, 151–152

Disabilities (physical and mental). *See also* People with disabilities
  defined, 363–364
  demograhics of, 364–369
  as field of social work, 103–104
Disasters
  disaster relief, 248
  natural and man-made, 534
Discrimination. *See also* Oppression
  Indigenous peoples and, 449
  against lesbians, gays, and bisexuals, 264, 266–267, 295
  against Muslims, 400
  against people with disabilities, 371
  against Puerto Ricans, 518–519
Disease, 259–260. *See also* Health
Dispute resolution, 154
Diversity
  of African Americans, 493
  appreciation for, 33
Division of labor, in bureaucracy, 121
Divorce
  increase in female-headed households and, 257, 258
  poverty of women and, 259
Doctorates in social work, 89n, 90–91. *See also* DSW (Doctor of Social Work) degree; Ph.D. (Doctor of Philosophy) degree
Domestic gang terrorism, 189–195, 198, 529
Domestic social programs, U.S. expenditures for national defense and, 215
"Don't ask, don't tell" military policy, 316
Downward assimilation, 221
Driving force, in force-field analysis, 475–476
Drug abuse. *See also* Substance use and abuse
  as field of social work practice, 97–98
DSW (Doctor of Social Work) degree, 44, 89n, 90–91
Dual focus, on person and environment, 39
Dysthymic depression, 547

Early childhood education, 327–328
Earnings, disability and, 366–367, 368
Eating disorders, 272
Ecological theory, 251

Economy
  global wealth disparities and, 235–236
  technology, society, and, 17
Ecosystems model
  ability to apply, 153
  for African Americans, 490–494
  for Asian Americans/Pacific Islanders, 421–430
  for children and youth, 330–336
  for disabled people, 376–379
  for Indigenous peoples, 447–454
  for lesbians, gays, and bisexuals, 294–302
  for Mexican Americans, 463–470
  for Muslims, 386, 392–396
  for older people, 346–351
  for Puerto Ricans, 516–522
  for women, 260–273
Education. *See also* specific degrees
  African Americans and, 486–488
  Asian Americans and, 414
  for basic social work professional, 84–87
  careers for community college graduates and, 80
  disability and, 367, 370
  emergence of social work, 242–245
  gender differences in, 256
  Indigenous peoples and, 442
  levels of social work practice and, 84–91
  Mexican American, 462
  professional, 63–64
  Puerto Rican, 507, 509
  in related disciplines, 80–81, 84
  social work, 44–45, 63–65
  of specialized professional, 87–89
  spending on, 22
  status of children and youth, 327–328
  undergraduate *vs.* graduate, 66–67
Education, Department of, free exercise rights information, 398
Educational Amendments Act (1978), 442
Educational prevention models, 179
Efficiency, effectiveness and, 120–122
Egalitarian marriage model, 391
Elderly. *See* Ageism; Aging; Older adults
Emotional assistance, for families of soldiers, 206
Empathy, for battered women, 277
Employee service model, of occupational social work, 108–109

Employment
  of Asian American/Pacific Islander women, 269–270
  disability and, 367, 369
  earnings and training requirements for related professions, 82–83
  gender differences in, 257
  of Hispanic women, 269
  Indigenous peoples and, 448
  in international social work, 246–247
  of Muslim women, 391–392
  of older people, 343
  people with disabilities and, 380
  primary sector for NASW members, 115, 116–117
  Puerto Ricans and, 518–519
  in related professions, 81, 84
  in social work, 76–79, 115–130
  women's, 261, 262
Employment relations, social work in, 63
Empowerment
  battered women example, 277–279
  of women, 274, 276–279
End-of-life issues, 356
Endogenous depression, 547
Engagement, of client, 152
English as a second language programs, 333
Environmental impact, on person, 38–39, 41
Environmental-structural factors (ecosystems model)
  African American, 492–493
  for Asian Americans/Pacific Islanders, 424, 429
  for children and youth, 331
  for Indigenous peoples, 448
  lesbians, gays, bisexuals and, 295–296
  for Mexican Americans, 464, 466–467
  for Muslims, 396–400, 404
  older people's, 348–349
  for people with disabilities, 378
  Puerto Rican, 518–519
  women's, 264–265
Equal Access Act, 398
Equal Employment Opportunity Commission (EEOC), 398
Equal partner, social work as, 125
Equal Rights Amendment (ERA), 263–264
Espiritismo, 515
Esteem needs, 16

Ethical code. *See* Code of ethics; National Association of Social Workers (NASW) Code of Ethics
Ethical responsibilities in practice settings, in NASW *Code of Ethics*, 141–142
Ethics, 134–135. *See also* National Association of Social Workers (NASW) Code of Ethics
  of social workers globally, 244–245
  values illustration in social work practice, 133–146
Ethnic group stressors, Asian Americans/Pacific Islanders and, 416–417
Ethnicity
  among elderly, 342
  composition of households by, 484
  disability and, 366
  education and, 328
  groups served by practitioners, 482
  lesbians, gays, bisexuals and, 292–294
  mental health care for elderly and, 349
  of minorities in gang identification, 190
  poverty and, 327
Ethnic patterns, 150
Ethnic-sensitive perspective, 176
Ethnocentrism, 247
Ethnosystem, Mexican Americans and, 467
Evaluation
  of instructional activities, 155
  of staff, 153
  of worker performance, 156
Executions. *See* Death penalty
"Experimental Draft of a Code of Ethics for Social Case Workers" (1923), 63
Extermination, of Native Americans, 20
Extreme functional impairment, of children, 329

Faith-based programs, 116–117
Familicide, 555, 556
Families
  African American, 485–486
  Asian American/Pacific Islander, 425–427
  biracial (case example), 333–336
  children in, 325
  child welfare and, 99
  in colonial period, 17–20
  foster care and, 99–100

gangs and, 195, 197
income and employment status of, 326
of Indigenous peoples, 444, 450
knowledge of functioning of, 152
of lesbians, gays, and bisexuals, 266–267, 297–298
of Mexican Americans, 468–469
micro practice with, 274–275
Muslim, 391–392
needs met by, 23
older people and, 346–347
Puerto Rican, 506–507, 508, 519, 521–522
responsibility for members of, 23
as welfare recipients, 21
women in, 264–271
Familism, among Puerto Ricans, 520
Familismo, 268
Family behavior patterns, 151
Family factors (ecosystems model), 450. *See also* Families
  for African Americans, 493–494
  for Asian Americans/Pacific Islanders, 425–427, 430
  for children and youth, 332–333
  for lesbians, gays, and bisexuals, 266–267, 297–298
  for Mexican Americans, 468–469
  for Muslims, 403
  for people with disabilities, 377–378
  for Puerto Ricans, 521–522
  women's, 264–271
Family interventions, with Indigenous peoples, 454–456
Family life education, 105
Family services, as field of social work practice, 104–105
Family Services Association of America, 120
Family treatment, competence in, 152
Family types, of Asian Americans/Pacific Islanders, 426
Fatalism, Puerto Ricans and, 521
Federal Community Mental Health Act, 466
Federal expenditures, 22
Felony homicides, 530, 554
Female-headed households
  African American, 485, 488
  increase in, 258, 259
  Puerto Rican, 506–507, 509
Female soldiers, 213
Feminist perspective, 176
Fertility rates, decrease in, 237

Fields of social work practice, 95–111
  adoption services, 100
  aging, 96–97
  alcohol and substance abuse, 97–98
  child welfare, 98–100
  community/neighborhood work, 101–102
  corrections/criminal justice, 102–103
  disabilities (physical and mental), 103–104
  family services, 104–105
  foster care, 99–100
  income maintenance and, 105–106
  medical and health care, 106–107
  mental health and illness, 107–108
  occupational or industrial social work, 108–109
  protective services, 99
  residential care for children, 100
  schools, 109–110
  of specialists, 43
  status of social work in, 125
  unmarried parents, 100
  youth services, 110
Filicide, 556
Finances, of soldiers, reservists, and National Guard personnel, 207
Financing. See Funding
First Nation Peoples. See Indigenous peoples
Five pillars, of Islam, 388–389
Folk medicine, Puerto Rican, 515–516
Food insecurity, 327
Food Stamps, 25, 106
Force-field analysis, 475–476
For-profit organizations, 118–119
For-profit sector, employment in, 118–119
Foster care, as field of social work practice, 99–100
French Enlightenment, 18
Freudian psychology, 40
Frustration, with clients, 140
Functional results, of impairment, 363
Funding
  in agencies, 126
  of faith-based programs, 116–117
  of private agencies, 117
  of public agencies, 120
  for social change activities, 66
  for social programs, 21–26
  of social provisions, 25
Fund-raising, for human services organizations, 156

Gang Behavior Career Continuum, 190–194
Gangs. See also Gang violence and homicide
  deaths in Los Angeles from, 199
  ethnicity and minorities in, 190
  gang banging, 179–180
  gang-prevention model, 179
  gang terrorism defined, 190
  member characteristics, 190, 194
  prevalence of, 179–180
  theories of, 194–195
  types of, 195–197
Gang violence and homicide
  area and demographic characteristics related to risk of, 179–180
  prevention of, 175–184
  psychosocial prevention models, 179–181
Gay Liberation Movement, 294
Gays. See Lesbian, gays, bisexuals and transgenders (LGBT)
Gender
  Asian Americans/Pacific Islanders and, 414
  Muslims and, 394
  of population, 238
Gender inequality
  in education, 256
  in employment, 258, 265
  social work practice and, 272, 273
Gender-role analysis, 274
Gender system, 261, 263
Generalist social work practice, 41–43, 176
Gentlemen's Agreement (1907), 421
German immigrants, 221. See also Immigrants/immigration
Gerontological social work, 345, 355–357. See also Older adults
Global demand, for social work, 237–239
Global social concerns, 237–238
  social issues as, 245
  social work approach as, 242–245
Global social work, 242–245
God
  belief in, 164
  sovereignty of, in Islam, 393–394
Governance, of social agencies, 121
Government (U.S.)
  allocations to health, education, and social welfare, 22–24
  employment in sector of, 115, 116
  international social positions through, 246–247

  international social work employment through, 246–247
  policies toward Indians, 447–448
Graduate education, 66–67, 87–89. See also specific degrees
Grandparents (or "grandfamilies")
  children living with, 325
  family issues of, 350
Great Depression, social welfare in, 20–21
"Great Migration," of Puerto Ricans, 517
Great Society, 20, 66
Grief, immigrants/refugees and, 225
Group differences, respect and appreciation for, 139
Group living facilities, as field of social work practice, 97
Group practice, 41, 127
  competencies in, 154
  and family interventions, in micro practice with Indigenous peoples, 450–451
  staff role in, 154
  structures and function of, 154
  for women, 274–275
Group therapy, 154
Guerrilla warfare, in Afghanistan and Iraq, 214
Guilt
  immigrants/refugees and, 225–226
  in returning combat soldiers, 210

Hadith, 387
Handicap, defined, 363–364
"Hard-core" level, of gang career continuum, 193
Hawaiians. See Indigenous peoples; Native Hawaiians
Health care
  federal programs for, 22–23
  for Indigenous peoples, 443–444, 453
  lesbians, gays, bisexuals and disparities in, 311–315
  for older people, 344–346, 351–355
  people with disabilities and, 380
  poverty and, 327
  Puerto Rican, 513–514
  social support and, 301–302
  status of children and youth, 329
  for women, 259–260
Health professions, violence prevention by, 177–181
Helping professions
  related, 81
  social work as, 31–49

Helping relationships
  natural, 31
  professional, 31–32, 150
  for providing clients with social provisions, 157
Heteropatriarchy, 445
Heterosexism, lesbians, gays, bisexuals and, 264, 295
Hierarchy
  in bureaucracy, 121
  of human needs (Maslow), 15
Hijab, 394
  bans on, 397
  reasons for wearing, 397–398
Hispanics. *See* Latinos; specific groups
Historical factors (ecosytems model)
  for African Americans, 491–492
  for Asian Americans/Pacific Islanders, 421–424, 428–429
  for children and youth, 334–335
  focus of, 252
  for Indigenous peoples, 447–448
  for lesbians, gays, bisexuals, 294–295
  for Mexican Americans, 464–466
  for Muslims, 400–401, 404–405
  older people's, 346–347
  for people with disabilities, 378
  for Puerto Ricans, 516–518
Historical perspective, on social work, 55–67
Historical trauma, 447
HIV/AIDS
  lesbians, gays, bisexuals and, 311, 313–315
  societal response to, 373–374
  in women, 260
Hollis-Taylor Report, 41, 64
Homeland Security Act (2002), 227
Homeland Security Department, as prevention effort, 180–181
Homeownership, Puerto Rican and Hispanic, 508
Homicide. *See also* Gang violence and homicide
  criminal *vs.* felony, 530
  familicide as, 555, 556
  filicide, 555, 556
  gang violence and, 179–180
  Los Angeles county-wide gang-related, 199
  in schools (*See* School homicide case)
Homohatred, 295, 296
Homophobia, 295
Homosexuality. *See* Lesbian, gays, bisexuals and transgenders (LGBT)

Horizontal affiliations, of human service organizations, 119–120
Hospital-based gang homicide prevention model, 180
Hospitals, social work practice in, 106
Households, composition by race/ethnicity, 485
Housing
  for Asian Americans/Pacific Islanders, 415
  for children, 325–326
  improvements for older people, 351
  poverty and, 326
  for Puerto Ricans, 508
Housing cost burden, 344
Hull House (Chicago), 62
Human development, 81, 152
Human dignity, 244
Human diversity. *See* Diversity
Human needs, identifying, 15–16. *See also* Needs
Human rights, 244, 397
Human Rights Campaign (HRC), 302
Human Rights Revolution, 20
Human Rights Watch, 488
Human service practice, career options for, 79–84
Human service programs
  fragmentation of delivery services in, 84
  horizontal affiliations of, 119–120
  knowledge of, 152
  in states, 56
  successes and failures of, 26–27
  vertical affiliations of, 119–120
  worldwide approaches to, 239–242
Human services system, social worker as guide to, 95–111
Hunger, of children, 326–327

Identity development
  African American, 498
  oppression theory, 499, 500
  sexual orientation and, 300–301
Identity issues, of gang members, 194
IFSW. *See* International Federation of Social Workers (IFSW)
Illegal aliens, 181, 223, 228. *See also* Immigrants/immigration
Immigrants/immigration, 219–231
  areas of concern for social workers, 225–226
  illegal immigrant case example, 229–231
  immigration gateways, 221–222
  Mexicans as, 219, 221, 468, 477
  Muslim, 389
  social work with, 222–225

Immigration Act of 1921, 220
Immigration and Naturalization Act (1965), 221
Impairment
  physical, of children, 324, 329
  vs. disability, 363
Impersonality, in bureaucracy, 121
Incarceration, of African American males, 488–489
Income
  of Asian Americans/Pacific Islanders, 415–416
  family, children and, 326
  of older adults, 343–344
Income maintenance, as field of social work practice, 106
Independent social worker, 89–90, 115
Indian Child Welfare Act (ICWA), 454–455
Indian Health Service (IHS), 443
Indians, use of term, 438. *See also* Indigenous peoples
Indian Self-Determination and Education Assistance Act (1975), 442
Indigenous peoples, 437–456
  case examples with, 454–456
  children and adolescents of, 445–446
  community concept of, 451–452
  cultural considerations in interventions with, 450–451
  culture of, 449–450
  demographics of, 439
  ecosystems model for, 447–454
  education of, 442
  families of, 444, 450
  government policies toward, 447–448
  health and mental health status of, 443–444
  intervention strategies for, 450–452
  as "invisible minority," 438
  macro practice with, 450–454
  micro practice with, 447–454
  relationship strategies with, 454–456
  self-governance initiatives of, 439–440, 448
  social group work and family interventions for, 450
  socioeconomic issues for, 440–441
  sovereignty of, 439–440
  spirituality and, 444–445, 450
  use of term "indigenous," 438
  violence and criminal justice with, 446
  women of, 270–271, 445

Indigenous workers, 80
Individual
  importance in society, 136, 138
  meeting needs by, 25
  in Western culture, 136–138
Individual behavior patterns, 151
Individual differences, respect and appreciation for, 139
Individual factors (ecosystems model)
  for African Americans, 494
  for Asian Americans/Pacific Islanders, 427–430, 429–430
  for children and youth, 331–332
  focus of, 251
  gangs and, 195–197, 196
  for Indigenous peoples, 447–454
  lesbians, gays, bisexuals and, 299–302
  for Mexican Americans, 470
  for Muslims, 403
  for older people, 350–351
  for people with disabilities, 379–380
  for women, 271–273
Individualism, *vs.* familism, 520
Individuals with Disabilities Education Act, 375, 378
Individual treatment, competence in, 152
Indochinese Refugee Act (1977), 221
Industrialization
  human services and, 239–240
  social welfare and, 18
Industrial social work, 108–109
Infants. *See also* Children and youth
  causes of death, 329–330
Information, for public, 157
Information gathering, about clients, 151
Initial generalist level, 42
Injury, wartime, 204–206
Institutional racism, 442, 448
Instruction, by social workers, 155–156
Instrumental values, 134
Intake assessment, 155
Interagency coordination, 152
Interagency networks, 120
Interdependence, in familism, 520
Interdisciplinary collaboration, 153
Interdisciplinary practice, 84
Intergenerational caregiving, 357
International Association of Schools of Social Work (IASSW), 243
International Conference on Social Work (1928), 243
International Development Corporation Agency, 246

International Federation of Social Workers (IFSW), 243
  code of ethics, 244
  issues in policy statements from, 244
International professional organizations, 243–244
International social work, 242–245
  employment in, 246–247
  preparation for, 246–247
International terrorist gangs, 188, 196
Interpersonal harmony, 427
Interpersonal helping, competencies for, 150–151
Interpreter *vs.* translator, 470
Interracial
  family, of Asian Americans/Pacific Islanders, 426
  marriage, among Asian American women, 414
Intervention, 151–152
Intervention strategies. *See* Macro practice; Micro practice; specific group
Introspection, by social worker, 151
Involuntary client, in mental health treatment, 467
Iraq War, 203, 214
Islam. *See also* Muslims
  background information, 386–389
  community in, 387, 388, 392–393
  five pillars of, 388
  God's sovereignty in, 393–394
  human rights and, 397
  modesty in, 394
  nutrition in, 395
  value differences in secular and Islamic discourses, 396
  virtue in, 394
Islamic Society of North America (ISNA), 399

Jewish Welfare Federation, 101, 117
Jihad, 193, 197
"Jim Crow" laws, 492
Jins, in Islam, 393
Johnson-O'Malley Act (1934), 442
Jones Act (1917), Puerto Rican citizenship and, 506, 516
Justice system. *See* Criminal justice system
Juvenile offenders, death penalty and, 555

Kearnsey, John R., 326
Kinship networks, of Asian Americans/Pacific Islanders, 269–270
Ku Klux Klan, 196

Labor force. *See also* Employment
  Puerto Ricans in, 508–509
  women in, 261, 262–263, 263–264
Labor relations, social work in, 62
Labor unions, as mutual aid setting, 117
Language skills, for international social work, 247
Latinos. *See also* specific groups
  families of, 268–269
  in gangs, 199
  population in 2004, 506
  poverty of, 462–463
  subgroups of, 506
  use of term, 463
Law and legal processes. *See also* Criminal justice system
  class action social work and, 178
  for protective services, 156
Learning. *See* Education
Learning activities, executing, 155–156
Legal rights
  for lesbians, gays, bisexuals, 295, 302–304
  of women, 261–263, 263–264
Legislation, on disability issues, 374–375
Lesbian, gays, bisexuals and transgenders (LGBT), 289–290, 316–317
  as adolescents, 310
  Asian Americans/Pacific Islanders, 417
  cancer among, 312–313
  coming-out process and, 304–307
  couples, 307–309
  culture of, 266, 296–297
  defining, 264, 292
  demographics, 290–294
  ecosystems model, 294–302
  families of, 266–267, 297–298
  health disparities and, 311
  issues and trends, 311–315
  legal rights for, 302–304
  macro practice with, 302–304
  mental health and, 311–312
  micro practice with, 304–311
  older, 310–311
  as parents, 309–310
  PFLAG organization, 183
  population characteristics, 292–294
  psychological distress factors for, 272–273
  social workers as, 315

Subject Index

substance use and abuse by, 312
violence against, 313
LGBTQ, defined, 292
Liberalism, 21
Liberal welfare state, 241
Licensing, by state, 77, 78
Life expectancy, by gender, 238
Lifestyle, homosexuality and, 291
"Literacy test," 220
Littleton, Colorado, "Trench Coat Mafia" in, 189
"Little Village Project, The" (Chicago), 198
Long-term health care, as field of social work practice, 96
Los Angeles
  gang prevention model in, 180
  gangs in, 195, 199
Low-rent Public Housing, 25

Machismo, 269
Macro practice
  for Asian Americans/Pacific Islanders, 430–432
  with battered women, 279–280
  with children and youth, 336–337
  with domestic terrorist gangs, 198
  with Indigenous peoples, 450–454
  with lesbians, gays, and bisexual clients, 302–304
  with Mexican Americans, 474–476
  with Muslims, 401–405
  in school homicide case, 536
  with women, 275–276
Males. *See* Men
Managed care, 119
Mandated programs, 21
Manifest destiny, 19
Manmade disasters, 534
Marianismo, 269
Marketing, for human services organizations, 157
Market system, 18
Marriage
  age at, 265
  complementary model of, 391
  depression and, 272
  egalitarian model of, 391
  interracial, among Asian American women, 414
  lesbians, gays, bisexuals and, 308
  military service members and, 212
  Muslim, 391
  same-sex, 266–267
Masjid. *See* Mosque
Maslow's hierarchy of human needs, 15
Massachusetts Board of Charities, 56, 61

Massachusetts General Hospital social work program, 62
Master of Social Work. *See* MSW (Master of Social Work) degree
Media, in school homicide case, 536–537, 539
Mediation, 154
Medicaid, 380
Medical care, as field of social work practice, 106–197
Medical model, 363
Medical social work, 62
Medicare, 97, 116, 380
Medicine, traditional Native American, 443
Men
  African American in criminal justice system, 488–489
  life expectancy of, 238
Mental disabilities, as field of social work, 103–104
Mental health, 62
  of Asian Americans/Pacific Islanders, 415–416
  as field of social work practice, 106–108
  of Indigenous peoples, 443–444
  of lesbians, gays, and bisexuals, 311–312
  of Mexican Americans, 466–467
  of older people, 344–346
  Puerto Ricans and, 509–513
Mental health services
  mobilizing in school homicide case, 532–534
  for older people, 356
Mental health treatment
  for combat troops, 205
  of Mexican Americans, 466–467
Mental hygiene, 62
Mental Hygiene Movement, 19
Mentally ill, government responsibility for, 19
Mexican Americans, 19, 461
  barrio service systems of, 467–468
  demographic profile of, 462–463
  ecosystems model for, 463–470
  education and, 462
  families of, 268
  macro practice with, 474–476
  mental health treatment of, 466–467
  micro practice with, 470–474
  police brutality and, 470–476
  social work practitioners and, 474–476

Micro practice
  with Asian Americans/Pacific Islanders, 419–421, 428–430
  with battered women, 276–279
  with children and youth (ecosystems model format), 330–336
  with Indigenous peoples, 447–454
  with lesbians, gays, and bisexuals, 304–311
  with Mexican Americans, 470–474
  with Muslims, 401–405
  with older people, 346–351
  in school homicide case, 536
  with women, 274–275
Middle East
  social work with U.S. casualties of war in, 203–216
  terrorism in, 188
Migration of Puerto Ricans, 516, 518
Military
  federal expenditures and, 23
  people of color in, 213
  reintegration of, 207–211
  social work treatment for, 203–216
Minorities. *See also* Ethnicity; specific groups
  contacting in school homicide case, 538
  death penalty and, 555
Minority model, of people with disabilities, 371–372
Mission, of social work, 36–37
"Mixed bloods," 438
"Moderate-core" level, of gang career continuum, 191, 192
Mosque, 391, 399
Moynihan Report, 485
MSMs (men who engage in same-sex behavior), 291
MSW (Master of Social Work) degree, 44, 48, 67, 76, 88. *See also* Education
Multidisciplinary practice, by private social worker, 127–129
Multilevel interventions
  African American example, 500
  people with disabilities (case example), 379
Multimethod social work practice, 41
Murrah Federal Building bombing, 189
Muslims
  civil rights of, 398–399
  cultural values of, 392–396

Muslims (*Continued*)
  demographics of (U.S.), 389–391
  diaphobia toward, 396–398
  dietary code of, 395
  ecosystems model of, 386, 392–396
  families of, 391–392
  intervention strategies (micro and macro practice), 401–405
  modesty and, 394
  NASW *Code of Ethics* and, 405
  organizations of, 399–400
  religious beliefs of, 386–389
  September 11 attacks and, 400–401
  stereotyping of, 396–398
  as terrorists, 385
  in U.S. population, 385
  virtue and, 394
Muslim Student Association (MSA), 399
Mutual aid, 18, 56, 116

NASW. *See* National Association of Social Workers (NASW)
National Association of Black Social Workers (NABSW), 498
National Association of Schools of Social Administration (NASSA), 64, 86
National Association of Social Workers (NASW), 38, 44, 65, 244. *See also* National Association of Social Workers (NASW) Code of Ethics
  BSW degrees and, 44
  Committee on Inquiry, 79
  definition of social work, 38
  Diplomate in Clinical Social Work from, 77, 90–91
  membership requirements of, 65
  National Conference on Charities and Correction, 62, 63
  National Conference on Social Welfare (1923), 63
  private practice monitoring and, 126
  professional certification by, 77–78
  professional classification system of, 44
  Qualified Clinical Social Worker credentials, 77, 90
  "Senior Health, Safety, and Vitality" Social Policy Statement, 355, 356
  social work values from, 138–140
National Association of Social Workers (NASW) Code of Ethics, 66, 77, 79, 134, 140, 289, 405
  areas of practice addressed by, 141–142
  guidance for ethical dilemmas in, 142–145

  illustrations of values and ethics in social work practice, 142–145
  knowledge and application of, 151
National Council of Negro Women, 62
National debt, 22
National defense spending, 214–215
National Freedman's Relief Association, 56
National Gay and Lesbian Task Force (NGLTF), 303
National Social Workers Exchange, 63
National Urban League, 62
Nation of Islam, 390
Native Americans. *See* Indigenous peoples
Native Hawaiians, 438, 442. *See also* Indigenous peoples
Native Peoples. *See* Indigenous peoples
Natural disasters, 534
Natural helping, 31
Natural networks, Mexican Americans and, 468
Navajo Nation, 446. *See also* Indigenous peoples
Needs
  of battered women, 277
  social welfare responses to, 136, 239–242
  values and, 136
Needs assessment research, 157
Negotiation skills, 154
Neighborhood development, as field of social work practice, 101–102
Neo-Nazis, 196, 199
Networks
  defined, 469
  interagency, 120
New Deal, African Americans during, 62
New York City
  Charity Organization of, 61, 88
  settlement houses in, 61
  social workers during 9/11 attacks and, 68
New York School of Philanthropy, 61, 62, 88
9/11. *See* September 11, 2001 terrorist attacks
Nineteenth Amendment, 261
"Non-gang" level, of gang career continuum, 190–191
Nonprofessional service providers, in human service practice, 80
Nonprofit, use of term, 117
Nonprofit sector settings, 116–117
Nonsectarian programs, 117
Nurses, in Civil War, 56, 57
Nursing homes, as field of social work practice, 97

Occult gangs, 195, 196
Occupational social work, 108–109
Occupation of social work, recognition as profession, 53, 56
Office of Refugee Settlement (U.S. government), 246
Oklahoma City, Murrah Federal Building bombing in, 189
Old Age Survivors, Disability, and Health Insurance (OASDHI), 106
Older adults, 341–357. *See also* Aging
  aging process and, 346–347
  Asian American, 416
  culture of, 349
  demographic factors affecting services for, 342–346
  demographics of, 342–346
  disabilities and, 366
  economic conditions of, 351
  ecosystems model, 346–351
  end-of-life issues for, 357
  families issues, 347, 349–350
  financial stability of, 343–344
  health care for, 351, 356
  health indicators of, 344–346
  housing for, 351
  income sources of, 343–344
  increase in, 238
  individual issues of, 350–351
  intergenerational caregiving and, 357
  intervention of strategies for, 351–355
  lesbian, gay, and bisexual, 310–311
  life span of, 351
  macro practice with, 351–355
  mental health of, 344–346, 356
  micro practice with, 346–351
  in Muslim families, 392
  physical problems of, 344–346
  social contact *vs.* isolation, 343
  stresses for older women, 272
  women as majority of, 259, 342
"Operation Bootstrap," 506
Oppression. *See also* Bias; Prejudice
  of Asian Americans/Pacific Islanders, 421–424
  of homosexual population, 264, 291, 295, 296, 305–307
Oppression theory, 499, 500
Oral presentations, 153
Organic approach, to mental illness, 464–466
Organizational maintenance, 156
Organizational structure, 156
Origins quota, 220

Subject Index

Pacific Islanders. *See* Asian Americans/Pacific Islanders
Paperflow, creating and managing, 157
Parachute kid phenomena, among Asian Americans, 416
Paramount Plan (Los Angeles), 179
Parentification, 226
Parents. *See also* Families; Single parents
   Asian American, 425
   gays, lesbians, and bisexuals as, 299, 309–310
   Muslim, 392
   unmarried, 100, 257–258, 258
Parents, Families, and Friends of Lesbians and Gays (PFLAG), 183
Parolees, 224. *See also* Immigrants/immigration
Passing, by gays and lesbians, 298
Patriarchy, 261
Patriot Act. *See* USA Patriot Act
Peace Corps, 247
Peer Dynamics program (Nebraska), 179
Pentagon, social workers during 9/11 attacks and, 68
People with disabilities, 361, 362
   barriers to, 380
   demographic considerations, 364–369
   disability-associated risks and, 369–371
   disability classifications for, 363–364
   earnings and, 368
   ecosystems model with, 376–379
   employment and, 380
   health care and, 380
   legislation for, 374–375
   minority model and, 371–372
   Social Security issues, 375, 380
   social work practice with, 361–363
   societal responses to, 372–376
Personal feelings and needs, separating from 1, 139–140
Personalismo, of Puerto Ricans, 520–521, 522
Personal Responsibility and Work Opportunity Reconciliation Act (PRWORA) (1996), 223
Personal services, 25
Person-environment mission, 39
Personnel, matching with job assignments, 156
Ph.D. (Doctor of Philosophy) degree, 44, 89n, 91
Physical abuse, 260. *See also* Child abuse

Physical disabilities. *See also* Disabilities (physical and mental)
   as field of social work, 103–104
Physicians' offices, social work practice in, 106
Physiological survival needs, 15
PL 95-602, 103, 104
Planning, 151–153
Police brutality, against Mexican Americans, 470–474, 474–476
Policy Coordination and Sustainable Development, UN Department of, 245
Policy development, research and, 157
Political action, settlement house movement and, 62
Political climate, welfare responsibility and, 15
Population
   characteristics of U.S., 96–97
   global changes in, 236–239
   worldwide estimate, 236
Populations-at-risk, 43
Postindustrial societies, social welfare systems in, 240–241
Posttraumatic stress disorder (PTSD), 205, 415
Poverty
   of African Americans, 484–485, 488
   among Southeast Asian immigrants, 415
   in children, 326
   Clinton and, 23
   in families, 23
   feminization of, 259
   as global concern, 235–248
   by group, 26
   increased rates of, 26
   of Indigenous peoples, 440–441
   of Latinos, 462–463
   by location, 26
   of Mexican Americans, 463
   of older women, 259
   of Puerto Ricans, 463, 507–509, 516–518
   rates of, 26–27
Poverty level, 26n
Practice contexts and perspectives, 43
Practice methods, 40–43
   generalist, 41–43
   multimethod, 41
   specialist, 43
   traditional, 40–41
"Pre-gang level" of gang career continuum, 191, 192
Preindustrial societies, human services in, 239–240

Prejudice. *See also* Oppression
   against Muslims, 396–398
   against Puerto Ricans, 518–519
Prevention. *See also* Gang violence and homicide
   balancing problem solving with, 182–183
   class action social work and, 178
   by Homeland Security Department, 180–181
   at national and international levels, 180–181
   of social problems, 23–24
   social work in, 177–181
   theories and practices, 178
Primary discipline, social work as, 125
Primary job function, competencies for, 150–151
Primary prevention, 177
Prisons, social work in, 62
Private nonprofit agency, 116–117
Private practice
   advantages of, 128–129
   concerns of, 128
   issues in, 126
   organization of, 127–128
   services delivered in, 116
   types of social workers in, 127–129
   use of term, 118
Privatization, 118
Problem analysis, 420
Problem areas, for specialists, 43
Problem identification, 420
Problem prevention, 177–181
Problem solving
   for Asian Americans/Pacific Islanders, 419–421
   balancing with problem prevention, 182–183
   with clients, 152
   skill in facilitating, 153
   social worker's role in, 175–177
Problem-solving evaluation, 421
Pro bono services, in *barrio*, 474
Professional associations, 55. *See also* specific associations
Professional authority, 53, 126
Professional autonomy, 53
Professional certification. *See* Certification
Professional conduct, 244–245
Professional development, guiding, 153
Professional education. *See also* Education
   in social work, 242
   of social workers, 43–48, 44–45
Professional ethical responsibilities, in NASW *Code of Ethics*, 141–142

Professional growth, staff development for, 126
Professional helping, 31
Professional knowledge, using and extending, 151
Professional model, 66–67, 122–124
Professional monopoly, 53
Professional organizations, international, 243–244
Professional relationships, separation of personal feelings and needs from, 139–140
Professional responsibility, 53
Professional standards, 79
Professions
  attributes of, 44–45, 53–55
  social work as, 12–13, 55–67, 75–92, 45–48
  sociology of, 241–242
Program assessment research, 157
Program development, 155
Program support, 155
Protection of Pupil Rights Amendment (PPRA), 398
Protective services, 156
  as field of social work practice, 98, 99
Psychohistorical responses, 421, 422
Psychological abuse, of women, 260
Psychological explanation, for mental illness, 464
Psychological problems
  from life-threatening experiences, 205
  mental illness and, 464
Psychology, of giving and receiving help, 150–151
Psychosocial analysis
  competency in, 152
  of factors impacting gangs, 197–199
Psychosocial evaluation report (school homicide case), 542–549
Psychosocial gang violence and homicide prevention models, 180
Psychosocial intervention (in school homicide case), 536
PTSD. See Post traumatic stress disorder (PTSD)
Public, informing, 157
Public agencies
  funding of, 116
  vertical relationships of, 119–120
Public health clinics, 107
Public housing, 25
Public social work, 55–67

Puerto Ricans
  culture of, 519–521
  demographics, 506–509
  ecosystems model, 516–522
  education and, 507, 509
  family characteristics, 268, 506–509, 519–521
  health beliefs and practices influencing, 514–516
  industrial/economic changes and, 508
  intervention strategies for, 522
  island and mainland, 506
  labor force status of, 509
  mental health care and, 509–513
  population of, 506–507
  poverty of, 507–509
Puerto Rico, socioeconomic changes on, 506–507
Purchase-of-service agreements, 118
Puritan ethic, 18

Qualifications, professional, 66–67
Qualified Clinical Social Worker (QCSW), 77, 90
Quran, 196, 197, 386–387

Race
  African Americans and, 485
  among elderly, 342–343
  composition of households by, 485
  disability and, 367
  education and, 327–328
  lesbians, gays, bisexuals and, 292–294
  males going to prison by, 489
  mental health care for elderly and, 357
  of minorities in gang identification, 190
  poverty and, 327
Racism
  African American women and, 267
  against Asian Americans/Pacific Islanders, 416
  black and white, 333–334
  Mexican American mental health treatment and, 467
  poverty and, 27
Reciprocal causality, 371
Reconstituted families, 332
Referrals, to appropriate resources, 155
Reforms, in 19th century, 19
Refugee Relief Act (1953), 221
Refugees, 221, 223–224. See also Immigrants/immigration
Rehabilitation legislation, 381
Relationship strategies, with Indigenous peoples, 454–456

Religion. See also Spirituality
  in cultural competence, 168
  homosexuality and, 294–295
  NASW Code of Ethics and sensitivity to, 166
  in professional practice, 168–172
  social work education and, 166–168
  spirituality and, 163
Religious groups, agencies under, 101
Relocation, of Indigenous peoples, 447
Remediation, of social problems, 23
Research
  policy development and, 157
  social, 61
Reservations (Native American), 448
Residential care, for children, 98, 100
Residential institution, in states, 61–62
Resiliency, of African Americans, 485–486
Resources
  for clients in danger, 156
  for social provisions (local), 157
  teaching clients to use effectively, 157
Respeto, by Puerto Ricans, 520
Responsibilities to colleagues, in NASW Code of Ethics, 140
Restraining force, in force-field analysis, 475–476
"Restrictive covenants," 492
Retaliation, domestic terrorism as, 189
Retreatist gangs, 195, 196
"Revolving door" migration, by Puerto Ricans, 518
Risk assessment, 153
Rules
  agency, 122–124
  in bureaucracy, 122
Rural areas, colonial social welfare in, 17–18

Sacramento model, for Asian American community, 430–432
Safety needs, 15
Safety net approach, 24
Salaries, of social workers, 47–48
Santeria, 515
Santeros/santeras, 515
SCAN Team, 180
School-based intervention strategy, in school homicide case, 531–532
School-based violence prevention programs, 179–180
School districts, wealthy vs. poorer, 178

School homicide case, 529–559
    crisis theory applied in, 531
    media interactions and, 536–537, 539
    mental health disciplines mobilization for, 535–536
    post-verdict activity, 550–551
    psychosocial evaluation and, 542–549
    public challenges to psychosocial evaluation, 549–550
    trial aspects in, 539
Schools. *See also* School homicide case
    as field of social work practice, 109–110
    gang activities in, 189
Secondary deviance, 299
Secondary discipline, social work as, 125
Secondary prevention, 177. *See also* Prevention
Sectarian (faith-based) programs, 116–117
Sectors. *See* Settings
Self, in facilitating change, 150
Self-actualization needs, 15
Self-awareness, as social work competency, 150
Self-determination
    battered women and, 277
    of Indigenous peoples, 448
Self-evaluation, by social worker, 151
Seminars, planning, 155
"Senior boomers," 342
September 11, 2001 terrorist attacks, 15
    "Arab-looking" males after, 189
    social work and, 67–68
    U.S. Muslims and, 400–401
Serrano v. *Priest*, 178
Service linkage, 418
Service planning and monitoring, 152
Services. *See also* Delivery services
    connection tasks, 154–155
    protective, 156
    purchase-of-service agreements for, 118
    settings for delivery of, 115–119
Service systems, for Asian Americans/Pacific Islanders, 417–419
Settings
    government sector, 116
    of social work practice, 115–130
    voluntary (nonprofit) sector, 116–117
Settlement Houses, 19, 61–62
Seven generations ideology, 454

Sexism
    lesbians and, 264
    poverty and, 27
Sexual abuse, of women, 260
Sexual identity, 291–292
Sexuality, 308–309
Sexual orientation, 291, 292, 300–301
Sexual preference, 291
Shari'a, 387, 392–393
Shiites, 387
Significant functional impairment, of children, 328–329
Single-female-headed households
    African American, 484–485, 488
    children, poverty and, 325
    increase in, 258
    Puerto Rican, 506, 508, 509
Single parents. *See also* Unmarried parents
    African American, 488
    Puerto Rican, 506, 508, 509
Skill building, in recovery of injured soldiers, 208–209
Skills, transmitting, 139
Skinheads, 196
"Skipped generation" families, 268
Slavery, African Americans in, 491
Social, use of term, 16
Social action, 25–26
Social assessment, of Asian Americans, 428
Social betterment, as social work theme, 32
Social casework, 40–41
Social change, 37
    commitment to, 138
    federal support for, 66
    as social program goal, 24
Social control, as social program goal, 24
Social democratic welfare state, 241
Social development, in preindustrial societies, 239–240
Social Diagnosis (Richmond, 1917), 40, 56, 61, 64
Social functioning, enhancing, 32–33
Social integration, as social program goal, 24
Social invisibility, of lesbians, gays, bisexuals, 295
Social issues, global views of, 245
Socialization, as social program goal, 24
Social justice, 138–139, 245
Social mobility, African Americans and, 494
Social movements, in 1970s and 1980s, 66–67
Social networks, 469
Social policy analysis, 157

Social programs
    critical assessment of, 155
    designing and implementing, 155
    for Native Americans, 20 (*See also* Indigenous peoples)
    professionals to execute, 28
    purpose and goals for, 23–24
Social provisions
    clients access to, 157
    tangible resources as, 25
Social research, 61
Social science disciplines, baccalaureate degree in, 80–81
Social Security
    as income source, 344
    people with disabilities and, 375, 380
    Trust Fund, 357
Social Security Disability Insurance (SSDI), 375
Social stressors, for lesbians, gays, bisexuals, 301–302
Social supports, for lesbians, gays, bisexuals, 301–302
Social systems theory, generalist practice approach and, 41–43
Social utilities approach, 24–25
Social values, 136–138, 137n
Social welfare
    conservatives and, 21
    defined, 16
    in early 2000s, 21–26
    evolution of, 17–21
    government responsibility for, 19
    in Great Depression, 20–21
    from Great Depression to present, 20–26
    historical timetable of, 57–60
    Puritan ethic and, 18
    as responses to human need, 239–242
    responsibility for, 16
Social work, 2, 75–92
    accreditation for, 76–77
    advanced professional in, 90–91
    "Basic Eight" divisions of, 88
    basic professional in, 84–87
    centrality of, 124–125
    certification for, 77–78
    defining, 37–40
    dual focus of, 39
    education for, 76–77
    emergence as profession, 12, 63–65
    as helping profession, 31–49
    historical perspective on, 55–67
    independent professional in, 89–90
    levels of practice, 84–91
    mission of, 36–37
    paid positions in, 56
    preparation and employment issues, 76–79

Social work (*Continued*)
  as profession, 55–67
  on September 22, 2001, 68
  specialist practice approach, 43
  standard of, 79
  state regulation of, 78
  themes of, 32–36
  in U.S. society, 12–13
  values and ethics in, 133–146
Social workers. *See also* Education
  activism among, 66
  for Asian Americans/Pacific Islanders, 417–418, 418
  career patterns of, 44–45
  characteristics of, 45–48
  child welfare case, 5–11
  ethics of, 141–142
  lesbian, gay, or bisexual, 315
  qualifications of, 76–79
  religion/spirituality and professional practice, 165
  values of, 138–140
  versatility of, 33–36
Social work intervention, focal point of, 40
Social work practice, 133–134. *See also* Macro practice; Micro practice
  addressed by NASW *Code of Ethics*, 141–142
  with African American clients, 498–500
  approaches to, 40–43
  competencies for, 149–159
  fields of, 95–111, 110–111
  generalist approach, 41–43
  multimethod approach, 41
  with people with disabilities, 361–363
  with Puerto Rican clients, 522
  qualifications for, 44–45
  settings for, 115–130
  values and ethics in, 142–145
Social work professional, and NASW *Code of Ethics*, 141–142
Society
  importance of individual in, 136, 138
  NASW *Code of Ethics* responsibilities to, 141–142
  responses to disabilities by, 372–376
  responsibilities to, 141–142
  responsibility for meeting human needs, 16–17
  social work in, 12–13
  urbanization, industrialization and, 18
Socioeconomics
  American Indians, Alaska Natives and, 440–441
  Asian Americans/Pacific Islanders and, 414–415
  Puerto Ricans and, 506–507
Sociology of professions, 241–242
"Soft-core" level, of gang career continuum, 191, 192
Soldiers
  ages of, 212
  experiences with death by, 209–211
  reintegration of, 207–211
  social work with, 204–206
  social work with families of, 206
  transition to civilians, 208–209
  as volunteers, 212
Soldier's Rehabilitation Act (1918), 374
Sole owners, private practice social workers as, 127
Solution alternatives, 420
Solution implementation, 421
Solution prioritization, 420–421
Southeast Asian immigrants, 221. *See also* Immigrants/immigration
Sovereignty, of Indigenous peoples, 439–440
Special Immigrant Juvenile Status, 228
Specialist practice approaches, 43
Specialized groups, chronology of development of, 63–64
Specialized social work professional, 87–89
Special populations, 251. *See also* specific populations
Special Relief Department (U.S. Sanitary Commission), 56
Spending
  federal, 23
  on national defense, 214–215
Spiritual competency, 386
Spirituality, 163–172
  in cultural competence, 168
  historical context of, in human services, 164–166
  Indigenous peoples and, 444–445, 450
  NASW Code of Ethics and sensitivity to, 166
  in professional practice, 168–172
  social work education and, 166–168
  spiritual challenge case example, 170–171
Spiritual/magical approaches, to mental illness, 464
Spousal abuse, against Asian women, 414
SSI. *See* Supplemental Security Income (SSI)
Staff
  bilingual and bicultural, 417
  competency in staff information exchange, 152–153
  development of, in agencies, 126
  mobilization in crisis, 535–536
  supervision, 153
Staff deployment, 156
Standardized tests, 487
Standards, 63, 140
Standards for Accreditation (CSWE), 88–89
State boards of charities, 61
States, licensing or regulation by, 78
State terrorism, 188
Stereotypes
  of Indigenous peoples, 449
  of lesbians, gays, bisexuals, 298
  of older people, 348, 351
  of people with disabilities, 380
Stonewall rebellion, 264, 294
Straight, defined, 291
Street gangs, 189, 190–194
Street junkies, 546
Strengths perspective, 176
Stress, acculturative, 423–424
Strike II program (Baltimore), 179, 180
Structural factors, environmental, 197–199
Structural racism, 442, 448
Subculture, gay and lesbian, 296, 297, 298
Substance use and abuse
  disabilities and, 370–371
  as field of social work practice, 97–98
  by lesbians, gays, bisexuals, 312
Suburban areas, and gangs, 199
Suicide
  by capital punishment, 556
  by Latino males, 472
Sunnis, 387
"Super-hard-core" level, of gang career continuum, 193–194
Supervision
  bureaucratic, 122
  of staff, 153
Supplemental Security Income (SSI), 25, 106, 357, 376–379
Supporting Child Adult Network. *See* SCAN Team
Supportive practice, private social work as, 127
Support systems
  defined, 469
  elements of, 469
Surrogate family, gang as, 195
Suspected Child Abuse and Neglect (SCAN) Team. *See* SCAN Team
Systems advocacy, in macro practice with battered women, 279–280
Systems perspective, 176
Systems theory, ability to apply, 153

Taliban, 196
Talking circles, 453
TANF (Temporary Assistance for Needy Families), 25, 106
Tangible services, providing, 157
Task analysis, 151
Taxes, in private agency budgets, 117
Teaching, by social workers, 155–156
Technology, 16–17
Temporary Assistance to Needy Families. *See* TANF (Temporary Assistance for Needy Families)
Temporary Inter-Association Council of Social Work Membership Organizations (TIAC), 65
Terman, Donna L., 326
Terminal values, 134
Termination, 153
Termination policy, Indigenous peoples and, 448
Terrorism. *See also* Gangs; September 11, 2001 terrorist attacks
  in Afghanistan and Iraq, 214
  defined, 188
  domestic and international gang terrorism, 188–190
  prevention of, 180
  by region, 195
  of September 11, 2001, 15
  social workers during, 67–68
  by state, 188
Terrorist gang, defined, 190
Tertiary prevention, 178. *See also* Prevention
Therapy, group, 154
Time, in Indigenous worldview, 449–450
Time limitations, on safety net programs, 24
Toynbee Hall (London), 61
Trabajadores de La Raza, 474
Traditional family, of Asian Americans/Pacific Islanders, 426
Traditional native medicine, 443
Traditional practice methods, 40–41
Trafficking, of children, 228
Training. *See also* Education
  emergence of social work, 241–242
  by social workers, 155–156
Transgender people, 290n. *See also* Lesbian, gays, bisexuals and transgenders (LGBT)
Transition services, 153
Translator *vs.* interpreter, 470
Trauma, from combat, 209–211
Treatment
  for female military personnel, 213
  of veterans, 211–212

Treatment modalities, individual and/or family, 152
Trench Coat Mafia, 189, 196, 199
Tribal communities, 438, 446. *See also* Indigenous peoples
Tribal-federal relations, 447–458
Tribally Controlled Schools Act (1988), 442
Triple oppression, women of color and, 264
Trust relationship, between U.S. government and Indian nations, 439
Tsunami disaster, o578
Turf-territorial conflict gang, 195
T-Visa program, 228

Ummah, 387
Unaccompanied minors, 224–225. *See also* Immigrants/immigration
Undergraduate education, 44, 66–67, 85, 86
Undocumented immigrants, 223. *See also* Immigrants/immigration
Unemployment insurance, 106
United Nations
  death penalty moratorium of Commission on Human Rights, 554
  Development Program, 245
  High Commission for Refugees, 245
  social work and, 243, 246
United Nations Children's Fund (UNICEF), 245
United States
  Children's Bureau, 62, 323
  death penalty and, 554–556
  gang violence in, 197–198
  Homeland Security Department, 180–181
  International Development Corporation Agency (USAID) foreign aid programs, 247
  social values in, 136–138
United States Sanitary Commission, 56
United Way, 101, 117
Universal social work competencies, 150–151
Unmarried parents
  birth rate among, 258
  children living with, 258
  services to, 100
Urban communities, Indigenous peoples and, 455–456
Urbanization, social welfare and, 18
U.S. Commission on Civil Rights, 443
USA Patriot Act, 401

Value conflict, 135
Values, 134–135
  illustrations in social work practice, 142–145
  Indigenous peoples, 449–450
  nature of, 134–135
  social, 136–138
  of social workers, 138–140, 244–245
  values clarification, 135
Values suspension, 136
Value system, 135
Vertical affiliations, of human service organizations, 119–120
Veterans
  skill building for, 208–209
  social work with, 204–206
  social work with families of, 206
Victimization
  of children, 329
  of lesbians, gays, bisexuals, 313
  of women, 272–273
Vienna Convention on Consular Relations (1969), 554, 555
Vietnam War, 204
Violence
  African Americans and, 488–489
  against children, 329
  against lesbians, gays, bisexuals, 296, 313
  against Mexican Americans, 470–474
  prevention of, 175–184
  U.S. gangs and, 197–199
  against women, 260, 272–273
Violent crimes, gang-related, 180
Virtue, Muslims and, 394
Voluntary client, in mental health treatment, 467
Voluntary (nonprofit) sector settings, 116–117
Voluntary organizations, 19, 21, 119–120
Voluntary social services, for meeting family needs, 21
Volunteer, in human service practice, 79–80
Vulnerable populations. *See also* specific vulnerable group
  defined, 250
  ecosystems model for, 251–253

Waco, Texas, Branch Davidian attack, 188
"Wannabe" level, of gang career continuum, 191, 192
War casualties
  social work and prevention of, 214–215
  of U.S. Middle East wars, 203–216
War on Poverty, 20, 26

Wealth, distribution among elderly, 343–344
Welfare, use of term, 16
Welfare reform, 21
Welfare states, typology of, 240–241
Welfare system
  barriers in, 468–469
  Puerto Rican families in, 508
Westward movement, 19
White racism, 199
White suburban gangs, 199
Women, 255–281
  battered, 276–280
  black female-headed households, 484–485, 488
  of color, 264, 267–271, 272
  death penalty and, 554–556
  demographics, 256–259
  depression and, 272
  eating disorders and, 272
  ecosystems model for, 260–273
  emerging issues and trends, 280–281
  in families, 264–271
  as head of family, 258
  health risk factors for, 259–260
  intervention strategies for, 273–280
  in labor force, 257, 262–263, 263–264
  legal rights of, 261–263
  lesbian (See Lesbian, gays, bisexuals and transgenders (LGBT))
  life expectancy of, 238
  macro practice with, 275–276
  micro practice with, 274–275
  Muslim, 397–398
  poverty and, 259
  Puerto-Rican female-headed households, 506, 508, 509
  as social workers, 45
  as soldiers, 213
Worker evaluation, conducting, 153
Workers' compensation, 374
Worker's Compensation Insurance, 106
"Working Definition of Social Work Practice" (1958), 38, 65
Workshops, planning, 155
World Health Organization, 245
World War I, social work by, 63
World War II, 20, 204
Written presentations, 153

Youth. *See also* Children and youth
  violence and, prevention of, 175–184
  youth gangs, 197
  youth services, as field of social work practice, 110